Lecture Notes in Computer Science 11980

More information about this series at http://www.springer.com/series/7410

Sokratis Katsikas · Frédéric Cuppens ·
Nora Cuppens · Costas Lambrinoudakis ·
Christos Kalloniatis · John Mylopoulos ·
Annie Antón · Stefanos Gritzalis ·
Frank Pallas · Jörg Pohle ·
Angela Sasse · Weizhi Meng ·
Steven Furnell · Joaquin Garcia-Alfaro (Eds.)

Computer Security

ESORICS 2019 International Workshops,
CyberICPS, SECPRE, SPOSE, and ADIoT
Luxembourg City, Luxembourg, September 26–27, 2019
Revised Selected Papers

Editors
Sokratis Katsikas
Open University of Cyprus
Latsia, Cyprus

and

Norwegian University of Science
and Technology
Gjøvik, Norway

Nora Cuppens
IMT Atlantique
Brest, France

Christos Kalloniatis
University of the Aegean
Mytilene, Greece

Annie Antón
Georgia Institute of Technology
Atlanta, GA, USA

Frank Pallas
Technical University of Berlin
Berlin, Germany

Angela Sasse
Ruhr University Bochum
Bochum, Germany

Steven Furnell
University of Plymouth
Plymouth, UK

Frédéric Cuppens
IMT Atlantique
Brest, France

Costas Lambrinoudakis
University of Piraeus
Piraeus, Greece

John Mylopoulos
University of Toronto
Toronto, ON, Canada

Stefanos Gritzalis
University of Piraeus
Piraeus, Greece

Jörg Pohle
Alexander von Humboldt Institute
for Internet and Society
Berlin, Germany

Weizhi Meng
Technical University of Denmark
Kongens Lyngby, Denmark

Joaquin Garcia-Alfaro
Télécom SudParis
Evry, France

ISSN 0302-9743 ISSN 1611-3349 (electronic)
Lecture Notes in Computer Science
ISBN 978-3-030-42047-5 ISBN 978-3-030-42048-2 (eBook)
https://doi.org/10.1007/978-3-030-42048-2

LNCS Sublibrary: SL4 – Security and Cryptology

This Springer imprint is published by the registered company Springer Nature Switzerland AG
The registered company address is: Gewerbestrasse 11, 6330 Cham, Switzerland

CyberICPS 2019 Preface

This book contains revised versions of the papers presented at the 5th Workshop on Security of Industrial Control Systems and Cyber-Physical Systems (CyberICPS 2019). The workshop was co-located with the 24th European Symposium on Research in Computer Security (ESORICS 2019) and was held in Luxembourg during September 26–27, 2019.

Cyber-physical systems (CPS) are physical and engineered systems that interact with the physical environment, whose operations are monitored, coordinated, controlled, and integrated by information and communication technologies. These systems exist everywhere around us, and range in size, complexity, and criticality, from embedded systems used in smart vehicles, to SCADA systems in smart grids, to control systems in water distribution systems, to smart transportation systems, to plant control systems, engineering workstations, substation equipment, programmable logic controllers (PLCs), and other Industrial Control Systems (ICS). These systems also include the emerging trend of Industrial Internet of Things (IIoT) that will be the central part of the fourth industrial revolution. As ICS and CPS proliferate, and increasingly interact with us and affect our lives, their security becomes of paramount importance. CyberICPS 2019 brought together researchers, engineers, and governmental actors with an interest in the security of ICS and CPS in the context of their increasing exposure to cyber-space, by offering a forum for discussion on all issues related to their cyber security.

CyberICPS 2019 attracted 13 high-quality submissions, each of which was assigned to 3 referees for review; the review process resulted in 5 full and 2 short papers being accepted to be presented and included in the proceedings. These cover topics related to threats, vulnerabilities, and risks that cyber-physical systems and industrial control systems face; cyber attacks that may be launched against such systems; and ways of detecting and responding to such attacks.

We would like to express our thanks to all those who assisted us in organizing the events and putting together the programs. We are very grateful to the members of the Program Committee for their timely and rigorous reviews. Thanks are also due to the Organizing Committee for the events. Last, but by no means least, we would like to thank all the authors who submitted their work to the workshop and contributed to an interesting set of proceedings.

December 2019

Sokratis Katsikas
Frédéric Cuppens
Nora Cuppens
Costas Lambrinoudakis

CyberICPS 2019 Organization

General Chairs

Nora Cuppens	IMT Atlantique, France
Costas Lambrinoudakis	University of Piraeus, Greece

Program Chairs

Sokratis Katsikas	Norwegian University of Science and Technology, Norway and Open University of Cyprus, Cyprus
Frédéric Cuppens	IMT Atlantique, France

Publicity Chair

Anis Bkakria	IMT Atlantique, France

Program Committee

Marios Anagnostopoulos	Norwegian University of Science and Technology, Norway
Youssef Laarouchi	EDF R&D, France
Chris Mitchell	Royal Holloway, University of London, UK
Vasileios Gkioulos	Norwegian University of Science and Technology, Norway
Stefano Zanero	Politecnico di Milano, Italy
Samiha Ayed	IMT Atlantique, France
Mauro Conti	University of Padua, Italy
Joaquin Garcia-Alfaro	Télécom SudParis, France
Pankaj Pandey	Center for Cyber and Information Security (CCIS), Norwegian University of Science and Technology, Norway
Houbing Song	Embry-Riddle Aeronautical University, USA
Georgios Spathoulas	University of Thessaly, Greece
Andrea Saracino	CNR, Italy
Weizhi Meng	University of Denmark, Denmark
Sjouke Mauw	University of Luxembourg, Luxembourg
Cristina Alcaraz	University of Malaga, Spain
Khan Ferdous Wahid	Airbus Group Innovations, Germany
David Espes	University of Brest, France
Dieter Gollmann	Hamburg University of Technology, Germany
Masahiro Mambo	Kanazawa University, Japan

SECPRE 2019 Preface

This volume contains revised versions of the papers presented at the Third International Workshop on SECurity and Privacy Requirements Engineering (SECPRE 2019) which was co-located with the 24th European Symposium on Research in Computer Security (ESORICS 2019) held in Luxembourg during September 26–27, 2019.

For many years, software engineers have focused on the development of new software, thus considering security and privacy mainly during the development stage as an ad-hoc process rather than an integrated one initiated during the system design stage. However, the data protection regulations, the complexity of modern environments (such as IoT, IoE, Cloud Computing, Big Data, Cyber-Physical Systems, etc.) and the increased level of users awareness in IT have forced software engineers to identify security and privacy as fundamental design aspects leading to the implementation of more trusted software systems and services. Researchers have addressed the necessity and importance of implementing design methods for security and privacy requirements elicitation, modeling, and implementation in the last decades in various innovative research domains. Today Security by Design (SbD) and Privacy by Design (PbD) are established research areas that focus on these directions. The new GDPR regulation sets even stricter requirements for organizations regarding its applicability. SbD and PbD play a very critical and important role in assisting stakeholders in understanding their needs, complying with the new legal, organizational, and technical requirements, and finally selecting the appropriate measures for fulfilling these requirements. SECPRE aimed to provide researchers and professionals with the opportunity to present novel and cutting-edge research on these topics.

SECPRE 2019 attracted 14 high-quality submissions, each of which was assigned to 3 referees for review; the review process resulted in 9 papers being selected for presentation and inclusion in these proceedings. The topics covered include: security and privacy requirements, assurance and evaluation, security requirements elicitation and modeling, and GDPR compliance.

We would like to express our thanks to all those who assisted us in organizing the events and putting together the programs. We are very grateful to the members of the Program Committee for their timely and rigorous reviews. Thanks are also due to the Organizing Committee of the events. Last, but by no means least, we would like to thank all the authors who submitted their work to the workshop and contributed to an interesting set of proceedings.

December 2019

John Mylopoulos
Christos Kalloniatis
Annie Anton
Stefanos Gritzalis

SECPRE 2019 Organization

General Chairs

Annie Antón	Georgia Institute of Technology, USA
Stefanos Gritzalis	University of Piraeus, Greece

Program Chairs

John Mylopoulos	University of Toronto, Canada
Christos Kalloniatis	University of the Aegean, Greece

Program Committee

Frédéric Cuppens	IMT Atlantique, France
Sabrina De Capitani di Vimercati	Università degli Studi di Milano, Italy
Vasiliki Diamantopoulou	University of the Aegean, Greece
Eric Dubois	Luxembourg Institute of Science and Technology, Luxembourg
Carmen Fernandez-Gago	University of Malaga, Spain
Eduardo Fernandez-Medina	University of Castilla-La Mancha, Spain
Mohamad Gharib	University of Florence, Italy
Maritta Heisel	University of Duisburg-Essen, Germany
Jan Juerjens	University of Koblenz-Landau, Germany
Costas Lambrinoudakis	University of Piraeus, Greece
Tong Li	Beijing University of Technology, China
Javier Lopez	University of Malaga, Spain
Fabio Martinelli	CNR, Italy
Aaron Massey	University of Maryland, USA
Haralambos Mouratidis	University of Brighton, UK
Liliana Pasquale	University College Dublin, Ireland
Michalis Pavlidis	University of Brighton, UK
William Robinson	Georgia State University, USA
David Garcia Rosado	University of Castilla-La Mancha, Spain
Mattia Salnitri	University of Trento, Italy
Pierangela Samarati	Università degli Studi di Milano, Italy
Jessica Staddon	North Carolina State University, USA
Nicola Zannone	Eindhoven University of Technology, The Netherlands
Jianying Zhou	Singapore University of Technology and Design, Singapore

SPOSE 2019 Preface

Over the past decades, a multitude of security and privacy enhancing technologies have been developed and brought to considerable maturity. However, the design and engineering of such technologies often ignores the organizational context that respective technologies are to be applied in. A large and hierarchical organization, for example, calls for significantly different security and privacy practices and respective technologies than a small and agile startup. Similarly, whenever employees behavior plays a significant role for the ultimate level of security and privacy provided, their individual interests and incentives as well as typical behavioral patterns must be taken into account and materialized in concrete technical solutions and practices. Even though research on security- and privacy-related technologies increasingly takes into account questions of practical applicability in realistic scenarios, respective approaches are typically still rooted in the technical domain alone, motivated by technical givens and constraints from the practice.

On the other hand, a substantial body of organization-related security and privacy research already exists, incorporating aspects like decision-making and governance structures, individual interests and incentives of employees, organizational roles and procedures, organizational as well as national culture, or business models and organizational goals. Nonetheless, these research activities are only rarely translated into concrete technical mechanisms, frameworks, and systems.

This disconnection between rather technical and rather organization-related security and privacy research leaves substantial room for improving the fit between concrete technologies on the one hand and organizational practices on the other hand. Achieving a better fit between these two sides through security and privacy technologies that soundly incorporate organizational and behavioral theories and practices promises substantial benefits for organizations and data subjects, engineers, policy makers, and society as a whole.

The aim of the First Workshop on Security, Privacy, Organizations, and Systems Engineering (SPOSE 2019) therefore was to discuss, exchange, and develop ideas and questions regarding the design and engineering of technical security and privacy mechanisms with particular reference to organizational contexts. We invited researchers and practitioners working in security- and privacy-related systems engineering as well as in the field of organizational science to submit their contributions. Besides regular and short papers, we also invited practical demonstrations, intermediate reports, and mini-tutorials on respective technologies currently under development to stimulate forward-looking discussions.

The papers included on the following pages demonstrate the possible spectrum for fruitful research at the intersection of security, privacy, organizational science, and systems engineering. Yang Liu and Andrew Simpson present an empirical study on privacy attitudes, utility preferences, and respective trade-offs of mobile device users across cultural boundaries. In their demo-paper, Hugh Lester and Martin Miller provide insights into the practical application of discrete event simulation for fostering organizational change in the domain of jail operations, which may (and, in fact, actually did during the workshop) serve as an inspirational mind-opener for thinking about structurally similar challenges in the context of information security. Jan Zibuschka, in turn, presents a first analysis of existing automation potentials for the execution of privacy impact assessments as demanded for several use-cases by the EU General Data Protection Regulation. Finally, Sebastian Pape and Jelena Stankovic present revealing results from an empirical study on the role of security aspects in companies' selection of cloud providers.

Altogether, these papers, complemented by an open-minded, keen-to-debate, and constructively thinking audience as well as a stunning keynote on "A User-Centric Approach to Secure the Internet Ecosystem" given by Katharina Krombholz from the Saarbrücken-based CISPA Helmholtz Center for Information Security, made the first iteration of the workshop a raving success that definitely calls for many recurrences in the years to come. We would like to thank everybody who contributed to this success – authors, presenters, participants, reviewers, and, of course, the organizing team of ESORICS 2019 - and are looking forward to the next iteration of SPOSE.

December 2019

Frank Pallas
Jörg Pohle
Angela Sasse

SPOSE 2019 Organization

Organizers

Frank Pallas	TU Berlin, Germany
Jörg Pohle	Humboldt Institute for Internet and Society, Germany
Angela Sasse	Ruhr-University Bochum, Germany

Program Committee

Jatinder Singh	Cambridge University, UK
Seda Gürses	KU Leuven, Belgium
Ronald Leenes	Tilburg University, The Netherlands
Burkhard Schäfer	Edinburgh University, UK
Heleen Janssen	Cambridge University, UK
Daniel Le Métayer	Inria, France
Marit Hansen	ULD Schleswig-Holstein, Germany
Melanie Volkamer	KIT, Germany
Ingolf Becker	UCL, UK
Max-R. Ulbricht	TU Berlin, Germany

Additional Reviewers

Peter Mayer	KIT, Germany
Alireza Zarei	KIT, Germany

ADIoT 2019 Preface

This volume contains the papers that were selected for presentation and publication at the Second International Workshop on Attacks and Defenses for Internet-of-Things (ADIoT 2019), which was held in Luxembourg on September 26, 2019. Internet of Things (IoT) technology is widely adopted by the vast majority of businesses and is impacting every aspect of the world. However, the nature of the Internet, communication, embedded OS, and backend recourses make IoT objects vulnerable to cyber attacks. In addition, most standard security solutions designed for enterprise systems are not applicable to IoT devices. As a result, we are facing a big IoT security and protection challenge, and it is urgent to analyze IoT-specific cyber attacks to design novel and efficient security mechanisms. This workshop focused on IoT attacks and defenses, and sought original submissions that discussed either practical or theoretical solutions to identify IoT vulnerabilities and IoT security mechanisms.

This year, 5 full papers out of 16 submissions were selected with an acceptance rate of 31.3%. We also accepted two short papers, and all papers were reviewed by at least three members of the Program Committee. We would like to extend our thanks to the Program Committee members as well as the additional reviewers who contributed their precious time and expertise to provide professional reviews and feedback to authors in a timely manner. We would also like to express our thanks to all the authors who submitted papers to ADIoT 2019.

December 2019

Weizhi Meng
Steven Furnell

ADIoT 2019 Organization

General Chairs

Anthony T. S. Ho	University of Surrey, UK
Shouhuai Xu	University of Texas at San Antonio, USA

Program Chairs

Weizhi Meng	Technical University of Denmark, Denmark
Steven Furnell	University of Plymouth, UK
Qian Chen	University of Texas at San Antonio, USA

Program Committee

Alessandro Bruni	IT University of Copenhagen, Denmark
Kai Chen	Chinese Academy of Sciences, China
Sebastien Faye	Luxembourg Institute of Science and Technology, Luxembourg
Jinguang Han	Queen's University Belfast, UK
Georgios Kambourakis	University of the Aegean, Greece
Sokratis Katsikas	Norwegian University of Science and Technology, Norway
Wenjia Li	New York Institute of Technology, USA
Rongxing Lu	University of New Brunswick, Canada
Xiaobo Ma	Xi'an Jiaotong University, China
Javier Parra-Arnau	Universitat Rovira i Virgili, Spain
Kewei Sha	University of Houston–Clear Lake, USA
Jun Shao	Zhejiang Gongshang University, China
Hao Wang	Shandong Normal University, China
Ding Wang	Peking University, China
Lam Kwok Yan	Nanyang Technological University, Singapore
Guomin Yang	University of Wollongong, Australia
Kehuan Zhang	The Chinese University of Hong Kong, Hong Kong
Peng Zhou	Shanghai University, China

Additional Reviewers

Yue Zhao
Mitra Sananda
Florian Gondesen
Yuxuan Chen
Marios Anagnostopoulos
Zhixiu Guo

Steering Committee

Steven Furnell	University of Plymouth, UK
Anthony T. S. Ho	University of Surrey, UK
Sokratis Katsikas	Norwegian University of Science and Technology, Norway
Weizhi Meng (Chair)	Technical University of Denmark, Denmark
Shouhuai Xu	University of Texas at San Antonio, USA

Contents

CyberICPS Workshop

SECPRE Workshop

ADIoT Workshop

CyberICPS Workshop

Anomaly Detection for Industrial Control Systems Using Sequence-to-Sequence Neural Networks

Jonguk Kim(✉), Jeong-Han Yun, and Hyoung Chun Kim

The Affiliated Institute of ETRI, Daejeon, Republic of Korea
{jongukim,dolgam,khche}@nsr.re.kr

Abstract. This study proposes an anomaly detection method for operational data of industrial control systems (ICSs). Sequence-to-sequence neural networks were applied to train and predict ICS operational data and interpret their time-series characteristic. The proposed method requires only a normal dataset to understand ICS's *normal* state and detect outliers. This method was evaluated with SWaT (secure water treatment) dataset, and 29 out of 36 attacks were detected. The reported method also detects the attack points, and 25 out of 53 points were detected. This study provides a detailed analysis of false positives and false negatives of the experimental results.

Keywords: Anomaly detection · Deep learning · Operational data · Industrial control system

1 Introduction

Since Stuxnet struck a nuclear facility in 2010, threats towards industrial control systems (ICSs) have increased. Unfortunately, as most of ICS attackers are state-sponsored and use zero-day vulnerabilities, signature-based detection (maintaining the blacklist and updating it) is inappropriate.

The most common and safe approaches that do not harm the availability of ICSs monitor the network traffic of these systems. ICSs present more periodic behavior than information technology systems. Several studies [5,13,20] applied the statistical characteristics of traffic for ICS-specific security mechanisms. Although this approach is suitable for ICS traffic characteristics, it presents limitations in detecting attacks at the ICS operation level.

Other researches focused on the detection of anomalies with physical properties [14]. By using the specification or control logic, the monitoring system rarely emits false alarms [3,15]. However, it is relatively expensive to obtain and specify the specification or control logic. An ICS recognizes the environment with sensors, makes decisions for its purpose, and delivers the right action with actuators. To detect anomalies at the ICS operation level, its *normal* state must be defined and the control logic that decides actuators' behaviors must be

S. Katsikas et al. (Eds.): ESORICS 2019 Workshops, LNCS 11980, pp. 3–18, 2020.
https://doi.org/10.1007/978-3-030-42048-2_1

understood. However, understanding the entire set of the control logic is complicated. In fact, the volume of the control logic is enormous, and acquiring it from vendors is not allowed in most cases.

Herein, the aim is to monitor the ICS operational data. A feasible alternative is the *data-driven* approach. Machine-learning-based approaches have been highly studied and especially deep-learning-based anomaly detection methods which have been reported recently using fully-connected networks (FCN) [18], convolutional neural networks (CNN) [10], recurrent neural networks (RNN) [7], and generative adversarial networks (GAN) [12].

We propose a deep learning-based anomaly detection method using a sequence-to-sequence model (seq2seq) [19]. Seq2seq is designed initially for natural language translation. It encodes the words of a given sentence with RNN into a latent vector, then decodes from it to a set of words in the target language. Seq2seq's encoding-decoding approach presents a significant advantage as it can understand the context of the entire sentence, while vanilla RNN gives the output immediately for every input. Seq2seq is expected to be an effective method for learning the context or semantics of time-series operational data, and obtain a better prediction based on the given data.

To date, no abnormal samples have been reported to train machine learning models robustly. Therefore, the reported model is trained with the only normal dataset (training dataset), and it is considered that the training data are clean. In the detection phase, the developed model investigates unseen data with trained neural networks. Using the model after the learning phase, the detection method proceeds in three steps: Step 1, the model predicts the future values of the sensors and actuators, Step 2, the difference between the prediction and actual data is determined, and Step 3, alerts are sent for significant differences.

The rest of this paper is organized as follows. Section 2 introduces the anomaly detection method using the seq2seq neural network. Section 3 presents the experimental results after applying the proposed method to the secure water treatment (SWaT) dataset [6]. Section 4 analyzes the experimental results in detail and Sect. 5 concludes this study.

2 Proposed Method

2.1 SWaT Dataset

Several studies have recently been reported on dataset generation for ICS research [4,6,11,17]. The most frequently used dataset is the SWaT dataset [6] by Singapore University of Technology and Design (SUTD), which has operational data and attack labels. Herein, the method is developed and evaluated with the SWaT dataset.

The SWaT dataset was collected from a testbed water treatment system. Fifty-one tags (25 sensors and 26 actuators) are sampled every second. Some are digital, and others are analog. Tag names define their roles. For example, MV denotes motorized valve, P for pump, FIT for flow meter, and LIT for level transmitter.

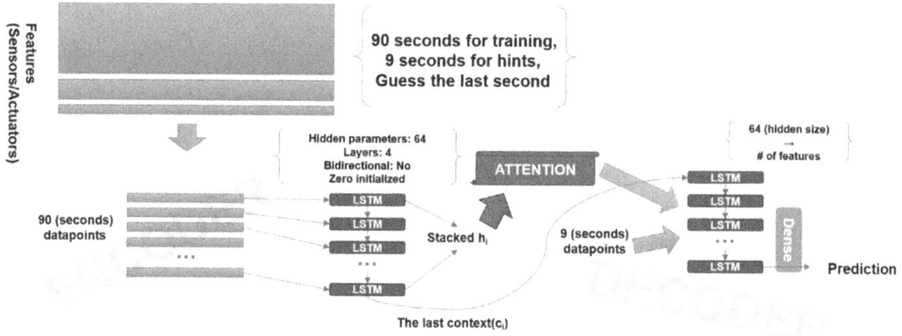

Fig. 1. Proposed learning model using seq2seq with attention

SWaT consists of six processes. Water flows from process 1 to the process 6. The numbers following the tag names indicate the process ID and the gadget ID. For example, MV-101 is the first motorized valve in process 1.

In the SWaT dataset, normal and attack datasets are separated. The normal part has 480,800 samples, and the attack part includes 41 attacks during 449,919 samples.

2.2 Data Preprocessing

Multiple machine learning schemes normalize the input into a Gaussian distribution with an average of 0 and a standard deviation of 1. However, to ensure that the distributions of most tags in the normal part of the SWaT dataset were not distorted nor had multiple peaks, min-max normalization was chosen. Long-short term memory (LSTM) [8], which is a RNN cell used in the developed model, has a sigmoid function inside that gives a (0, 1) output. The minimum and maximum for normalization were chosen as 0 and 1.

The operational data were time-series. The model used sliding windows of length 100 s to understand the temporal context, and each window slides 1 by 1 s.

2.3 Sequence-to-Sequence Neural Networks

There are various ways to build a neural network for learning time-series data. We chose the sequence-to-sequence network with attention [2] for training and evaluation. Since RNN is proper for learning a series of data, we expected that RNN is able to encode the current window of data and to anticipate the next values. Figure 1 shows the data flow of the proposed model. The shape of inputs for the encoder is (# of sequences, batch, # of tags). The encoder obtains the first 90 s of the window. The encoder's output is two-fold: (1) the last cell state of the last layer and (2) all hidden states of the last layer. The first one has the context of the given sequences. The second one helps the decoder predict future

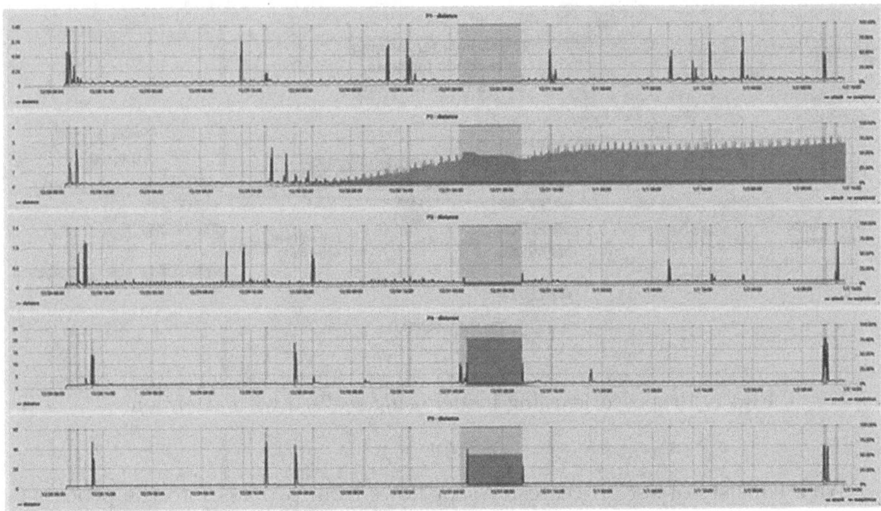

Fig. 2. Prediction errors for processes 1, 2, 3, 4, and 5 of SWaT (red: attack, purple: prediction error, and blue: anomaly score) (Color figure online)

operational data with the attention mechanism. The decoder part is optional. The reason why we added a decoder with attention is that it gives us more accurate results. The decoder predicts the last second with a 9-second hint. The values of 9th second of the hint is almost the same with those of the last record of the window (we wanted to expect), which helps the model give almost-zero prediction error. The shape of the decoder's final output is (batch, # of tags).

An independent model was applied for each process of SWaT. The model n learns the process n. Figure 2 shows the prediction error of each process. At the early stage of this study, a holistic model[1] was tested for six processes. The result was not accurate because each process shows a different prediction error pattern, especially the process 2, as observed in Fig. 2.

2.4 Measuring Prediction Error

The mean absolute error (MAE) is a typical measuring method. However, p-norm can also be used, with $p > 2$. The greater the value of p, the greater the value of the vector. ∞-norm returns the maximum value of the vector. Herein, a 4-norm was chosen, while Kaspersky chose a 6-norm [18] for SWaT dataset.

The prediction error (distance) D can be extracted as follows:

$$D = \sqrt[4]{\sum_{i=1}^{n} d_i^4} \text{ where } d_i = I_i - O_i \quad (1)$$

[1] [18] used this approach: one model for the whole processes.

where n is the number of tags, I_i is the i-th tag values in the dataset, and O_i is the i-th output of the model.

2.5 Anomaly Decision Using Prediction Errors

The proposed method considers that the system is under attack if the model has never seen the current state. The developed model was trained to perform a precise prediction. When the model detects a never-seen window, it cannot perform an accurate prediction, which leads to more notable 4-norm value.

Multiple approaches can be used to determine anomalies such as cumulative sum (CUSUM) and anomaly likelihood [1]. The custom rating method was applied by considering the prediction errors – due to the following factors:

1. A learning model often presents periodic noises, but it is hard to remove noises because of the limited learning data.
2. From a specific time, the distances of process 2, especially AIT-201 in SWaT, are increasing and never recovered (this issue is discussed in Sect. 4.2).

A similar (but not significant) phenomenon occurred in process 5. It is assumed that an insufficient amount of training data and unexpected dynamics can cause growing prediction errors.

A sliding window for rating was also applied. First, the top-k outliers were removed. As aforementioned, the developed model presents noise (the impulse of prediction error). The sum of remains except the outliers represents the distance of the window. Fortunately, attacks last at least 2 min (the shortest attack is attack 34). For a large summation on a specific window, a high rate can be attributed to that particular region.

Second, N summations were collected to compare the current sum with near-by ones. Two hyper-parameters were defined: H and L. L is the 20th percentile, and H is the 90th percentile. H is not the 80th because top-k values (outliers) were already removed to reduce noises. The ratio $\frac{H}{L}$ and divided by R, which is another hyper-parameter. Here, $R = 20$.

In short, if the 90th percentile is 20 times greater than the 20th percentile, it is certain that an attack happens. The rate for suspicious region S is derived as follows:

$$S = min(\frac{H}{LR}, 1.0) \tag{2}$$

Finally, if S is greater than 0.3 (30%), it is regarded as an attack. All numbers mentioned above (90 for H, 20 for L, 20 for R, and 0.3 for threshold) are hyper-parameters which are dataset-dependent.

Equation 2 determines high rates at the start and end of the attack because it measures the change. We use both sides: start and end. Depending on the attack the high rate can be obtained at the start or at the end. Figure 3 shows D and S of attack 41.

As D grows slowly at the start and shrink quickly at the end, S is low at the start but high at the end.

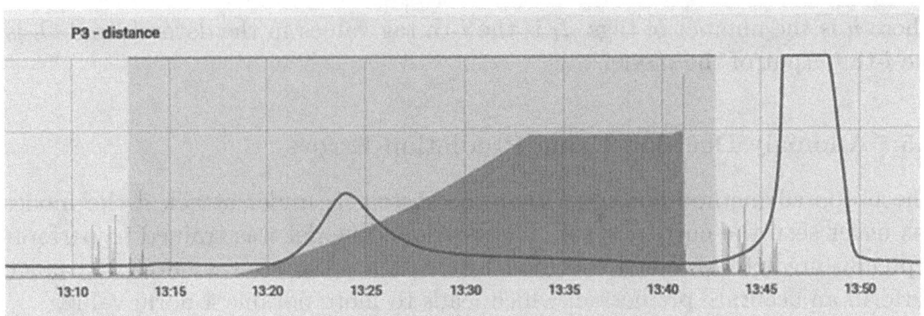

Fig. 3. Asymmetric ratings at the start and end of attack 41 (red: attack, purple: prediction error, and blue: anomaly score) (Color figure online)

Table 1. Training time for 150 epochs

	Process 1	Process 2	Process 3	Process 4	Process 5	Process 6
Trial 1	1 h 48 m	2 h 00 m	1 h 53 m	1 h 54 m	2 h 23 m	2 h 27 m
Trial 2	1 h 50 m	1 h 59 m	1 h 59 m	2 h 01 m	2 h 01 m	2 h 12 m

3 Experiment

All source codes, pre-processed datasets, trained network parameters, and results are available at https://github.com/jukworks/swat-seq2seq.

3.1 Training

Occasionally, a neural network goes bad local minima during training process. A general approach to solve this issue is to train the neural network multiple times independently and choose the best result among the multiple training results. As a neural network is trained with a stochastic gradient descent and mostly initialized with random numbers, different results are obtained every run. Two independent training sessions were run for each model (each process) and the network presenting the lowest training loss was chosen.

The model was optimized with Adam [9], amsgrad [16], and without weight decay. Each model trained 150 epochs with a 4,096 batch size. Early stopping was not applied.

The hardware consisted of Intel Xeon CPU E5-2960 v4 2.60 GHz, 6 NVIDIA Tesla V100, and 512 GB RAM. Table 1 shows that the training time was approximately 2 h on average. Six models have a different size of input and output, but their internal LSTM architectures were entirely the same. Therefore, the number of trainable parameters is similar, which leads to similar training time.

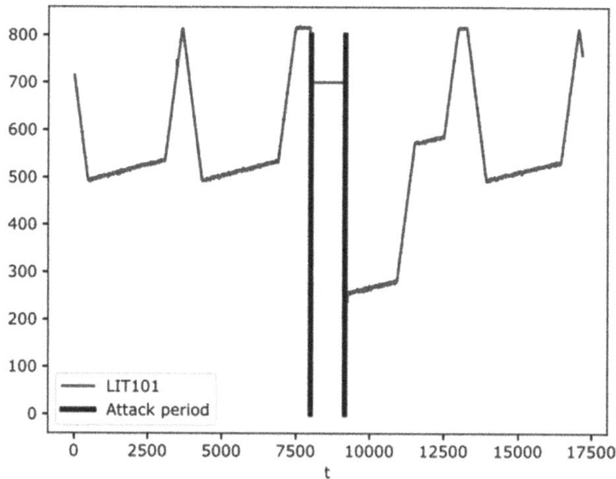

Fig. 4. LIT-101 was not stable after attack 30 happens (from [10])

3.2 Anomaly Detection

The results are compared with Kaspersky's research [18] because this is the only study providing the list of found attack points.

If an alert is received within 15 min after the attack range of SWaT, it is considered as a detection. 15 min is chosen as attacks attacks on cyber-physical systems tend to have a long impact. The shortest attack in SWaT, attack 29, lasts 2 min[2]. Figure 4 shows LIT-101 on attack 30 [10]. The two black vertical lines represent the start and end of the attack. After the end of the attack, LIT-101 was unstable. As the reported model learns the normal-labeled data only, it may perceive the stabilizing region as an anomaly.

Tables 2 and 3 compare the detection results with those of [18]. Attacks 5, 9, 12, 15, and 18 have no physical impact. These attacks were ignored as they cannot be detected with operational data. The first column shows the attack numbers. The second column presents the answer to attack points labeled in the SWaT dataset. The third column represents the detection of the attack: *Yes* means 100% sure, *not sure* means 30%–100% means sure, and *No* means less than 30% sure. As mentioned in Sect. 2.5, 30% represents the heuristic threshold. The fourth and fifth column represents the attack points determined by the model and [18], respectively. Bold text indicates correct answers. The parentheses indicate the second-longest distance. *N/A* indicates that the model failed to detect.

[18] reported 25 attacks and 11 attack points (nine with the first predictions and 2 with the second predictions). Herein, the model found 29 attacks and 25 attack points (22 with the first predictions and 3 with the second predictions). 21 attacks were detected by both the developed model and that in [18]. Four

[2] The longest attack in SWaT is attack 28, which lasted 9.5 h.

Table 2. Anomaly detection results compared with those of [18] (attacks 1 to 30)

Attack #	Answer (by SWaT)	Detection (our work)	Attack point (our work)	Attack point ([18])
1	MV-101	Yes	**MV-101**	N/A
2	P-102	Yes	MV-101 (**P-102**)	MV-301 (**P-102**)
3	LIT-101	Not sure (65%)	MV-101 (**LIT-101**)	N/A
4	MV-504	No	N/A	N/A
6	AIT-202	Yes	**AIT-202**	**AIT-202** (P-203)
7	LIT-301	Yes	**LIT-301**	**LIT-301** (PIT-502)
8	DPIT-301	Yes	**DPIT-301**	**DPIT-301** (MV-302)
10	FIT-401	Yes	**FIT-401**	**FIT-401** (PIT-502)
11	FIT-401	Yes	**FIT-401** (FIT-504)	MV-304 (MV-302)
13	MV-304	No	MV-304	N/A
14	MV-303	No	N/A	N/A
16	LIT-301	Yes	**LIT-301**	MV-301 (MV-303)
17	MV-303	Yes	MV-301 (**MV-303**)	N/A
19	AIT-504	No (15%)	AIT-504	**AIT-504** (P-501)
20	AIT-504	Yes	**AIT-504**	N/A
21	MV-101, LIT-101	Not sure (35%)	**LIT-101**	UV-401 (P-501)
22	UV-401, AIT-502, P-501	Yes	FIT-401, FIT-504	DPIT-301 (MV-302)
23	P-602, DPIT-301, MV-302	Yes	**DPIT-301**	P-302, P-203
24	P-203, P-205	No	N/A	LIT-401
25	LIT-401, P-401	No (20%)	LIT-401	P-602, MV-303
26	P-101, LIT-301	Yes (25% at P3)	P-102, LIT-301	LIT-401 (AIT-402)
27	P-302, LIT-401	Yes	**LIT-401**	N/A
28	P-302	Yes	FIT-401, AIT-504	MV-201, LIT-101
29	P-201, P-203, P-205	No	N/A	LIT-401, AIT-503
30	LIT-101, P-101, MV-201	Yes	**LIT-101**	LIT-301 (FIT-301)

attacks were detected only by the model in [18]: attacks 19, 24, 25, and 29. Eight attacks were detected only by the developed model: attacks 1, 3, 17, 20, 27, 32, 33, and 41, which also detected attacks 21 and 31 with 35% and 50% rates, respectively. The SWaT dataset indicates that the attack points of attack 35 is process 1, but it was detected by the developed model for process 3 (20% rate at the model for process 1). Both methods failed to detect three attacks: attacks 4, 13, and 14.

Table 3. Anomaly detection results compared with those of [18] (attacks 31 to 41)

Attack #	Answer (by SWaT)	Detection (our work)	Attack point (our work)	Attack point ([18])
31	LIT-401	Not sure (50%)	**LIT-101**	P-602, MV-303
32	LIT-301	Yes	**LIT-301**	N/A
33	LIT-101	Yes	**LIT-101**	N/A
34	P-101	Yes	**P-101**	MV-201 (P-203)
35	P-101, P-102	Not sure (20% at P1, 45% at P3)	P-101	MV-201, MV-303
36	LIT-101	Yes	**LIT-101**	**LIT-101**, AIT-503
37	P-501, FIT-502	Yes	FIT-401, FIT-504	FIT-504 (FIT-503)
38	AIT-402, AIT-502	Yes (15% at P5)	MV-101, **AIT-402**, AIT-502	**AIT-502**, **AIT-402**
39	FIT-401, AIT-502	Yes	**FIT-401**	**FIT-401**, P-201
40	FIT-401	Yes	**FIT-401**, FIT-504	UV-401 (**FIT-401**)
41	LIT-301	Yes	**LIT-301**	N/A

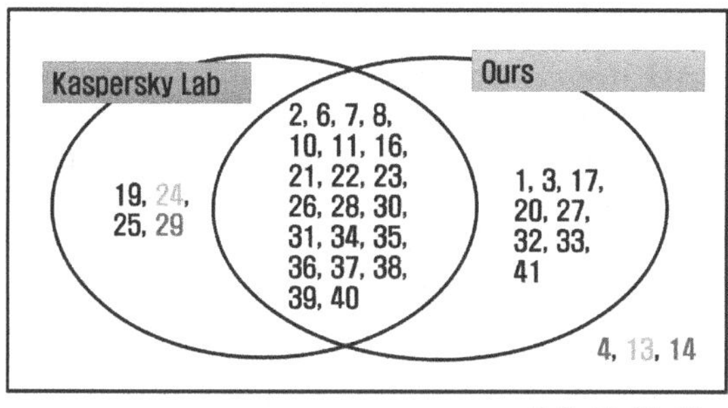

Fig. 5. List of detected attacks and comparison with [18]. Red (4, 14, 29) represents attacks that are impossible to detect. Yellow (24) represents attacks that are difficult to detect. (Color figure online)

The model was not used with process 6 as it has only two tags. The SWaT dataset presents only one attack[3] and has an impact on process 6.

[3] Attack 23 also has an impact on process 3. The developed model for process 3 detected this attack.

4 Analysis of Experimental Results

Three pairs of attacks, (10, 11), (19, 20), and (27, 28) were indistinguishable for the developed model because they occur almost continuously[4] and have the same attack point.

4.1 Analysis on False Negative (Undetected Attacks)

The model failed to detect attacks 4, 13, 14, 19, 24, 25, and 29.

Impossible-to-Find Attacks. It appears that attacks 4, 14, and 29 were impossible to detect (in red in Fig. 5). The developed model, the model in [18], and the model in [10] all failed to detect attacks 4, 13, and 14.

Attack 4. This attack opens MV-504 that does not exist in the dataset. The description [6] in SWaT's *list of attacks* indicates that this attack has no impact.

Attack 14. According to SUTD, the attack 14 failed because tank 301 was already full [6].

Attack 29. SUTD said that P-201, P-203, and P-205 did not start because of mechanical interlocks. In the dataset, nothing was changed around 2015/12/31 at 3:32:00 PM.

Difficult-to-find Attacks. According to [6], attacks 13 and 24 have a small impact (represented in yellow in Fig. 5). The developed model did not detect these attacks. The model also failed to detect attacks 19 and 25.

Attack 13. This attack attempted to close MV-304 but MV-304 was closed later than when this attack occurred. In the SWaT dataset, MV-304 did not change.

Attack 19. This attack attempted to set value of AIT-504 to 16 µs/cm. AIT-504 is below 15 µs/cm in the normal state. In Fig. 6, the attack appeared to be detected, but the high rate was derived from attack 20 which set a value of AIT-504 to 255 µs/cm. The distances provided by the developed model are too short to detect for attack 19. The rate S was of approximately 20% for attack 19.

Attack 24. This attack attempted to turn off P-203 and P-205 (both are pumps are used for injecting chemicals). However, there was only a small impact due to the closure of P-101.

Attack 25. This attack attempted to set the value of LIT-401 to 1,000 and open P-402 while P-402 was still operating. LIT-401 presented notable distances but the rate was of approximately 20% (Fig. 7). According to [18], attack 25 was detected but wrong attack points were determined.

[4] Their intervals are 0, 42, and 1 s respectively, while the developed model uses a 100-second sliding windows.

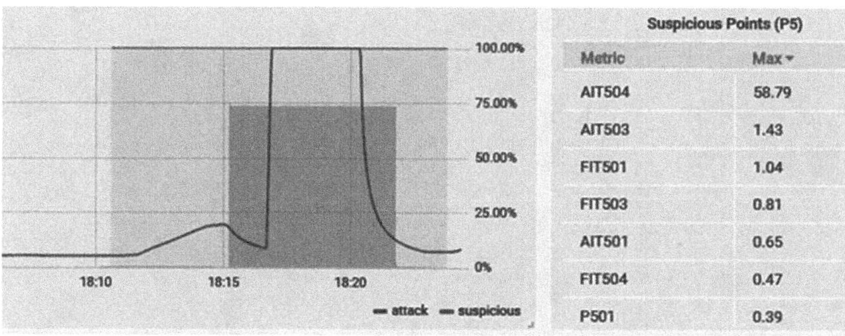

Fig. 6. Attack 19 in process 5 (red: attack, purple: prediction error, and blue: anomaly score) (Color figure online)

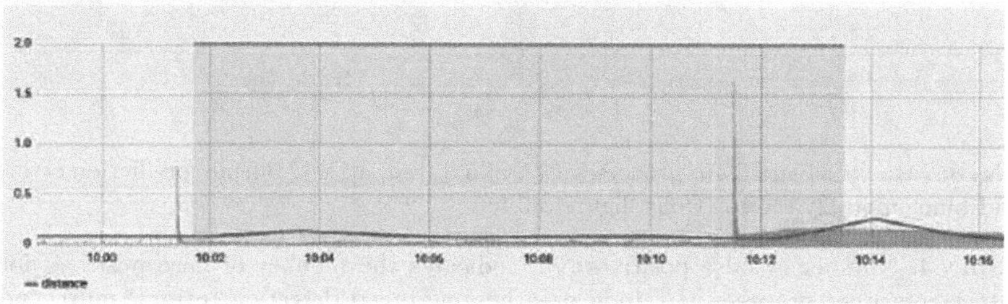

Fig. 7. Attack 25 in process 4 (red: attack, purple: prediction error, and blue: anomaly score) (Color figure online)

Managed-to-find Attack. The developed model managed to detect attack 35 with a rate of 45%.

Attack 35. According to [6], attack 35 occurred at process 1, but herein, the attack was detected at process 3. Before the attack, P-101 was open, and P-202 was close. The attack opened P-101 and kept P-102 close. Figure 8 shows the attacks 34 and 35. Processes 1, 2, and 3 presented remarkable distances. The distance of process 2 appears to be large, but the scale is small. There are two high peaks of rate in process 1, but they come from the attack 34.

Attack 34 closed P-101 (2 $\rightarrow$ 1) and opened P-102 (1 $\rightarrow$ 2). Later, P-101 was opened (1 $\rightarrow$ 2) at 17:14:59 and P-102 was closed (2 $\rightarrow$ 1). Attack 35 was different from attack 34 as it kept P-102 closed. In the training (normal) dataset, P-102 was closed (of value 1) at all time, which is why the developed model always indicated 1. Because P-102 is a backup pump for P-101, the developed model must understand their connection. However, the model could not learn the connection as the training dataset did not give enough information.

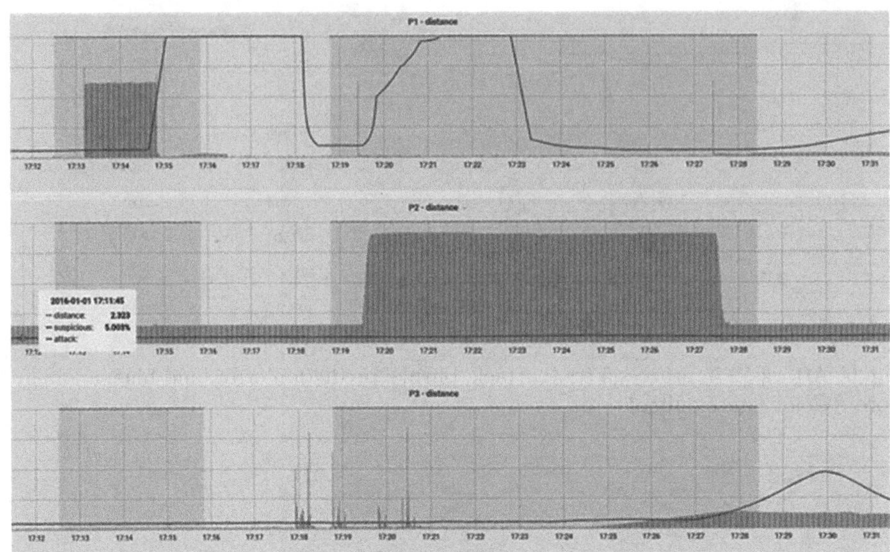

Fig. 8. Attacks 34 and 35 in processes 1, 2, and 3 (red: attack, purple: prediction error, and blue: anomaly score) (Color figure online)

Table 4. Number of false positives. OP indicates the number of false positives for attacks on other processes, LT indicates the long-tailed detection (over 15 min), and TFP indicates the true false positives.

Process	False positives (all duplicates)	OP	LT	TFP
1	7(11)	4	2	1
2	5(8)	0	0	5
3	0	–	–	–
4	1(1)	1	0	0
5	0	–	–	–

4.2 Analysis on False Positives (False Alarms)

This subsection analyzes false positives. The evaluation script is also available at https://github.com/jukworks/swat-seq2seq/tree/master/evaluation.

Sixty seven false positives were obtained from all models, and many of them were timely overlapped. After removing the duplicates, twenty false positives were found. The number of false positives is presented in Table 4. Processes 3 and 5 present no false positives.

The decision method described in Sect. 2.5 reacted twice at the start and end of the attack. The second column represents the number of false positives after removing the duplicates. The third column, OP, represents the number of positives caused by the attacks on the other processes. The fourth column, LT, represents the number of long-tailed positives. 15 min after the end of the attack as a true-positive, but sometimes the tail was too long and the attack lasted over 15 min. The long-tail positives were not counted as true-positives. In summary, there was one true false positive (TFP, the fifth column) in process 1 and five in process 2.

False Positives in Process 1. There were eleven false positives in process 1. In Table 5, (2, 3), (4, 5), (7, 8), and (10, 11) are pairs of start-end having the same related attacks. Therefore there were seven independent false positives. One of them was true false positive. Four of them were simultaneous detection for attacks targeting other processes. Two of them were long-tail detection.

Table 5. The analysis of false positives in process 1. OP means the number of false positives for attacks on other processes; LT for long-tailed detection (over 15 min); TFP for true false positives.

No.	Time	Related attacks	Tags	Type of false positive
1	2015-12-28 12:19:05 PM - 2015-12-28 12:20:46 PM	7	P-101	OP
2	2015-12-29 02:32:36 PM - 2015-12-29 02:36:34 PM	17	MV-101	OP
3	2015-12-29 02:39:42 PM - 2015-12-29 02:43:39 PM	17	MV-101	OP
4	2015-12-30 01:51:41 PM - 2015-12-30 01:55:36 PM	–	MV-101	**TFP**
5	2015-12-30 02:06:12 PM - 2015-12-30 02:09:55 PM	–	MV-101	**TFP**
6	2015-12-30 06:20:01 PM - 2015-12-30 06:21:07 PM	26	–	LT
7	2016-01-01 10:58:18 AM - 2016-01-01 11:02:11 AM	32	MV-101	OP
8	2016-01-01 11:10:06 AM - 2016-01-01 11:13:38	32	MV-101	OP
9	2016-01-01 03:02:23 PM - 2016-01-01 03:04:04 PM	33	–	LT
10	2016-01-02 11:32:16 AM - 2016-01-02 11:36:10	38	P-101	OP
11	2016-01-02 11:47:29 AM - 2016-01-02 11:51:04 AM	38	P-101	OP

False Positives in Process 2. The developed model for process 2 created eight false positives. In Table 6, pairs (1, 2), (4, 5), and (6, 7) have the same related attacks. Therefore, there were five independent false positives, and four of them were true.

Most false positives occurred at P-201, P-205, and MV-201. P-201 is the NaCl injection jump; P-205 is the NaOCl injection pump. In the training dataset, P-201 never changed. We guess that the model regarded any change of P-201 as an attack. AIT-201, a sensor for NaCl, caused a false positive (No. 8 in Table 6) because P-201 had changed the level of NaCl.

After the last false positive, the prediction errors of AIT-201 and AIT-203 went high. AIT-201 and AIT-203 are sensors for NaCl and NaOCl, respectively. We guess that the unexpected behaviors of P-201 and P-205 led to new but *normal* dataset.

Table 6. Analysis of false positives of process 2. OP indicates the number of false positives for attacks on other processes, and TFP indicates true false positives.

No.	Time	Related attacks	Tags	Type of false positive
1	2015-12-29 07:18:41 PM - 2015-12-29 07:22:14 PM	–	P-201, P-205	**TFP**
2	2015-12-29 07:29:56 PM - 2015-12-29 07:33:38 PM	–	P-201, P-205	**TFP**
3	2015-12-29 09:23:58 PM - 2015-12-29 09:26:36 PM	–	MV-201, P-201	**TFP**
4	2015-12-29 09:44:08 PM - 2015-12-29 09:47:43 PM	–	MV-201, P-201	**TFP**
5	2015-12-29 09:52:23 PM - 2015-12-29 09:54:07 PM	–	MV-201, P-201	**TFP**
6	2015-12-29 11:12:18 PM - 2015-12-29 11:12:58 PM	16	P-201, P-205	OP
7	2015-12-29 11:19:43 PM - 2015-12-29 11:20:37 PM	16	P-201, P-205	OP
8	2015-12-30 01:12:39 AM - 2015-12-30 01:14:50 AM	–	P-201, AIT-201	**TFP**

False Positives in Process 4. In Table 7, there was one false positive in process 4, which came from attack 37 hitting process 5.

Table 7. Analysis of false positives of process 4. OP indicates the number of false positives for attacks on other processes

No.	Time	Related attacks	Tags	Type of false positive
1	2016-01-02 11:19:16 AM - 2016-01-02 11:23:15 AM	37	–	OP

5 Conclusion

It is difficult to get internal specification and control logic of ICSs. If routine ICS operational data is the only information available, a data-driven approach is a proper way to develop security products.

We proposed an anomaly detection method for industrial control systems using sequence-to-sequence neural networks with attention. Due to the difficulty of defining the abnormal state, the model learns the normal dataset in an unsupervised way. In the detection phase, the model predicts future values based on the previously observed ones. The difference between the model's prediction and the measured value is the key criterion to detect anomalies.

The alarm decision depends on the threshold, and heuristic hyper-parameters were necessary for this experiment. Our proposed method is not dedicated to the dataset. It can be generalized to train any ICS datasets and extract the decision grounds because the specification of operational data and control logic inside was not required. It is also able to detect anomalies with only the dataset from normal operations.

References

1. Ahmad, S., Lavin, A., Purdy, S., Agha, Z.: Unsupervised real-time anomaly detection for streaming data. Neurocomputing **262**, 134–147 (2017)
2. Bahdanau, D., Cho, K., Bengio, Y.: Neural machine translation by jointly learning to align and translate. In: 3rd International Conference on Learning Representations, ICLR 2015, San Diego, CA, USA, 7–9 May 2015 (2015). Conference Track Proceedings
3. Chen, Y., Poskitt, C.M., Sun, J.: Learning from mutants: using code mutation to learn and monitor invariants of a cyber-physical system. In: 2018 IEEE Symposium on Security and Privacy (SP), pp. 648–660. IEEE (2018)
4. Choi, S., Yun, J.-H., Kim, S.-K.: A comparison of ICS datasets for security research based on attack paths. In: Luiijf, E., Žutautaitė, I., Hämmerli, B.M. (eds.) CRITIS 2018. LNCS, vol. 11260, pp. 154–166. Springer, Cham (2019). https://doi.org/10.1007/978-3-030-05849-4_12
5. Formby, D., Srinivasan, P., Leonard, A., Rogers, J., Beyah, R.A.: Who's in control of your control system? device fingerprinting for cyber-physical systems. In: Network and Distributed Systems Security (NDSS) (2016)

6. Goh, J., Adepu, S., Junejo, K.N., Mathur, A.: A dataset to support research in the design of secure water treatment systems. In: Havarneanu, G., Setola, R., Nassopoulos, H., Wolthusen, S. (eds.) CRITIS 2016. LNCS, vol. 10242, pp. 88–99. Springer, Cham (2017). https://doi.org/10.1007/978-3-319-71368-7_8
7. Goh, J., Adepu, S., Tan, M., Lee, Z.S.: Anomaly detection in cyber physical systems using recurrent neural networks. In: 2017 IEEE 18th International Symposium on High Assurance Systems Engineering (HASE), pp. 140–145. IEEE (2017)
8. Hochreiter, S., Schmidhuber, J.: Long short-term memory. Neural Comput. **9**(8), 1735–1780 (1997)
9. Kingma, D.P., Ba, J.: Adam: A method for stochastic optimization. In: 3rd International Conference on Learning Representations, ICLR 2015, San Diego, CA, USA, 7–9 May 2015 (2015). http://arxiv.org/abs/1412.6980. Conference Track Proceedings
10. Kravchik, M., Shabtai, A.: Detecting cyber attacks in industrial control systems using convolutional neural networks. In: Proceedings of the 2018 Workshop on Cyber-Physical Systems Security and Privacy CPS-SPC 2018, pp. 72–83 (2018)
11. Lemay, A., Fernandez, J.M.: Providing SCADA network data sets for intrusion detection research. In: Proceedings of the 9th USENIX Conference on Cyber Security Experimentation and Test, CSET 2016, Berkeley, CA, USA, p. 6 (2016)
12. Li, D., Chen, D., Shi, L., Jin, B., Goh, J., Ng, S.: MAD-GAN: multivariate anomaly detection for time series data with generative adversarial networks. CoRR abs/1901.04997 (2019)
13. Lin, C.Y., Nadjm-Tehrani, S., Asplund, M.: Timing-based anomaly detection in scada networks. In: D'Agostino, G., Scala, A. (eds.) CRITIS 2017. LNCS, vol. 10707, pp. 48–59. Springer, Cham (2018). https://doi.org/10.1007/978-3-319-99843-5_5
14. Mitchell, R., Chen, I.R.: A survey of intrusion detection techniques for cyber-physical systems. ACM Comput. Surv. (CSUR) **46**(4), 55 (2014)
15. Mitchell, R., Chen, R.: Behavior-rule based intrusion detection systems for safety critical smart grid applications. IEEE Trans. Smart Grid **4**(3), 1254–1263 (2013)
16. Reddi, S.J., Kale, S., Kumar, S.: On the convergence of adam and beyond. In: 6th International Conference on Learning Representations, ICLR 2018, Vancouver, BC, Canada, April 30–May 3 2018 (2018). Conference Track Proceedings
17. Rodofile, N.R., Schmidt, T., Sherry, S.T., Djamaludin, C., Radke, K., Foo, E.: Process control cyber-attacks and labelled datasets on S7Comm critical infrastructure. In: Pieprzyk, J., Suriadi, S. (eds.) ACISP 2017. LNCS, vol. 10343, pp. 452–459. Springer, Cham (2017). https://doi.org/10.1007/978-3-319-59870-3_30
18. Shalyga, D., Filonov, P., Lavrentyev, A.: Anomaly detection for water treatment system based on neural network with automatic architecture optimization. In: DISE1 Workshop, International Conference on Machine Learning (ICML) (2018)
19. Sutskever, I., Vinyals, O., Le, Q.V.: Sequence to sequence learning with neural networks. In: Ghahramani, Z., Welling, M., Cortes, C., Lawrence, N.D., Weinberger, K.Q. (eds.) Advances in Neural Information Processing Systems, vol. 27, pp. 3104–3112 (2014)
20. Yun, J.-H., Hwang, Y., Lee, W., Ahn, H.-K., Kim, S.-K.: Statistical similarity of critical infrastructure network traffic based on nearest neighbor distances. In: Bailey, M., Holz, T., Stamatogiannakis, M., Ioannidis, S. (eds.) RAID 2018. LNCS, vol. 11050, pp. 577–599. Springer, Cham (2018). https://doi.org/10.1007/978-3-030-00470-5_27

Reflective Attenuation of Cyber-Physical Attacks

Mariana Segovia[1(✉)], Ana Rosa Cavalli[1(✉)], Nora Cuppens[2(✉)], Jose Rubio-Hernan[1(✉)], and Joaquin Garcia-Alfaro[1(✉)]

[1] Institut Polytechnique de Paris, CNRS SAMOVAR, Telecom SudParis, Palaiseau, France
{segovia,ana.cavalli,rubio_h,garcia_a}@telecom-sudparis.eu

[2] IMT Atlantique, Cesson Sévigné, France
nora.cuppens@imt-atlantique.fr

Abstract. Cyber-physical systems (CPS) integrate computation and networking resources to control a physical process. The adoption of new communication capabilities comes at the cost of introducing new security threats that need to be handled properly. Threats must be addressed at cyber and physical domains at the same time in order to detect and automatically mitigate the threats. In this paper, we elaborate an approach to attenuate cyber-physical attacks driven by reflective programmable networking actions, in order to take control of adversarial actions against cyber-physical systems. The approach builds upon the concept of *programmable reflection* and *programmable networking*. We validate the approach using experimental work.

Keywords: Cyber-physical security · Critical infrastructures · Attack detection · Adversary model · Attack mitigation · Networked control systems

1 Introduction

Cyber-physical systems (CPS) are modern control systems used to manage and control critical infrastructures [7]. Physical properties of such infrastructures are modeled via control-theoretic tools, e.g., *control-loops* and *feedback controllers* [16]. Feedback controllers have to be able to manage the behavior of the CPS, by confirming that the commands are executed correctly and the information coming from the physical states is consistent with the predicted behavior [26]. Feedback controllers are also used to compute corrective actions, e.g., by minimizing the deviation between a reference signal and the system output measurements.

A CPS is composed of three main layers: (1) the *physical layer*, which involves the physical process (monitored and controlled by physical sensors and physical actuators); (2) the *control layer*, which is in charge of regulating the operation of the physical process via control commands; and (3) the *cyber layer*, which

S. Katsikas et al. (Eds.): ESORICS 2019 Workshops, LNCS 11980, pp. 19–34, 2020.
https://doi.org/10.1007/978-3-030-42048-2_2

is responsible for monitoring operation and supervision tasks. These three layers are interconnected using a communication network. In other words, the CPS can be modeled as a networked-control system [21]. The interconnection between information and operational systems leads to new security threats [20,21]. Traditional *cyber attacks* are well know and countermeasures have been studied. However, launching a *cyber-physical attack* requires a different knowledge from the one used in traditional cyber security and different protection techniques are also required.

A cyber-physical attack causes tangible damage to physical components, for instance, adding disturbances to a physical process via exploitation of vulnerabilities in computing and networking resources of the systems (i.e., the components at the cyber layer). However, to achieve just a cyber attack, the adversary may be able to inject any input in the system but this does not necessarily mean to be able to influence the processes in the physical world. The processes and their dynamics have to be properly understood to cause a real damage [12].

A physical process has automatic safety measures and operational constraints, e.g., to disable a physical process when certain dangerous conditions are met. For instance, to properly react when a physical component fails. For this reason, an adversary who aims at damaging the physical process needs to understand how the dynamics of the physical plant works. This means that compromising and disrupting a device or communication channel used to sense or control a physical system is a necessary requirement to perform cyber-physical attacks. However, the damage can be limited if the adversary succeeds at affecting the cyber layer, but remains unable to manipulating the control system (i.e., fails at perturbing the physical process). To achieve the desired impact and achieve a cyber-physical attack, the adversary needs to assess how the attack will perform at the control level. Therefore, to achieve a cyber-physical attack, the first step is to hack the cyber layer, to obtain a remote access within the target system. Then, the second step is to learn about the physical process and how the control layer works in order to manipulate the physical layer and cause a damage to physical components. Adversaries need to know how the physical process is controlled, failure conditions of the equipment, process behavior and signal processing [20,21].

In this paper, we propose a technique to attenuate cyber physical attacks that uses programmable reflection and programmable networks to sanitize the malicious actions introduced by some cyber-physical injection attack such as false data injection, bias injection, replay attack, command injection and cover attack [27]. The adversary uses the network to manipulate the process through the modification of specific payloads. Then, the proposed technique uses the network to neutralize the attack effects. This concept relies on the use of programmable reflection, which is a meta programming technique that has the potential to allow a programmable system manipulate itself at runtime and the use of programmable networks to sanitize the traffic.

The main contributions of the paper are summarized as follows: (1) we propose a technique to handle cyber-physical injection attacks; (2) we revisit the use of programmable networking in [23], to achieve as well reflective attenuation of CPS attacks; and (3) we provide experimental work to validate the approach.

Paper organization—Section 2 provides the related work. Section 3 provides preliminaries and assumptions. Section 4 presents our attenuation approach. Section 5 reports the experimental work. Section 6 concludes the paper.

2 Related Work

We survey next some related work, structured in terms of *attack tolerance*, *programmable networking* and *programmable reflection*.

2.1 Attack Tolerance

A defense in depth strategy proposes to defend a system against any particular attack using several independent methods [13]. Many proposed security solutions for CPS focus in detection and attack prevention. However, preventing every single possible attack is hard to achieve and although the efforts, attacks on the systems can happen and be successful.

Attack tolerance is the capability of a system to continue functioning properly with minimal degradation of performance, despite the presence of attacks. The main techniques proposed in the literature to achieve this are [1]: indirection, voting, redundancy, diversity, dynamic reconfiguration, distributed trust, recovery and moving target defense mechanisms.

- *Indirection* separates components using an additional layer that works as a protection barrier. For instance, proxies, wrappers, virtualization and sandboxes are used in this technique.
- *Voting* can resolve differences in redundant responses, to reach consensus w.r.t. the responses of perceived non-faulty components. The process involves comparing the redundant responses and reaching an agreement on the results to find the appropriate response. It masks the attacks, thus tolerating them and providing integrity of the data.
- *Redundancy* uses extra reserved resources allocated to a system that are beyond its need in normal working conditions. If the system finds that the output values of a primary component are not correct, then the responsibility is transferred to one of the redundant components.
- *Diversity* means that a component should be implemented in multiple different ways in order to ensure independent failures with non-overlapping patterns. To achieve this, replicas shall hold diversity in terms of hardware and software. For instance, to generate software diversity it is possible to generate diverse functionality from the same source code or automatically change the configuration of a system from time to time to confuse the adversary [9].
- A *dynamic reconfiguration* takes place after the detection of an attack. In traditional systems, reconfiguration is mostly reactive and generally performed manually by the administrator. Thus, it involves some downtime. Survivable systems need an adaptive reconfiguration to be proactive, instead.

- *Distributed trust* relies on control-sharing strategies, e.g., dividing control into shares, such that the system needs to reach a given threshold prior granting control. Below the threshold, information gets concealed to the eyes of the adversary.
- *Recovery* involves detecting the attack and modifying the system to a state that ensures the correct provision of the functions.
- *Moving target defense* enables to deploy diverse mechanisms that change over time to increase the complexity, the attack surface or the cost for an attacker in order to limit the exposure of vulnerabilities and increase system resiliency.

Our proposal combines dynamic reconfiguration and recovery approaches, via control theory and programmable networked reflection techniques. It allows a CPS to reconfigure itself and neutralize the adversary actions via dynamic traffic sanitization.

2.2 Programmable Networking

Programmable networking facilitates network management. It enables efficient network configuration that can be used for neutralizing attacks. New networking functionality can be programmed using a minimal set of APIs (Application Programming Interfaces) to compose high-level services. This idea was proposed as a way to facilitate the network evolution. Some solutions such as Open Signaling [2], Active Networking [28], and Netconf [6], among others, are early programmable networking efforts and precursors to current technologies such as Software Defined Networking (SDN) [11]. In particular, SDN is a programmable networking paradigm in which the forwarding hardware is decoupled from control decisions. SDN proposes three different functionality planes: (1) data plane, (2) control plane and (3) management plane.

The data plane corresponds to the networking devices, which are responsible for forwarding the data. The control plane represents the protocols used to manage the data plane, such as, to populate the forwarding tables of the network devices. Finally, the management plane includes the high-level services and tools, used to remotely monitor and configure the control functionality. Security aspects may have an impact on different plans. For example, a network policy is defined in the management plane, then the control plane enforces the policy and the data plane executes it by forwarding data accordingly.

The idea of using programmable networks for improving security is not new. Some examples include its use for conducting DoS (Denial of Service) attack mitigation [24] and segmentation of malicious traffic [8,17,23]. Programmable networks provide a higher global visibility of the system, which is favorable for attack detection. In addition, a centralized control plane may allow further possibilities to achieve dynamic reconfiguration of network properties, e.g., application of countermeasures.

2.3 Programmable Reflection

Programmable reflection allows a system to adapt itself through the ability of examining and modifying its execution behavior at runtime. Authors in [4,10] proposed to implement programmable networks using reflective middleware platforms. These reflective middleware platforms use reflection in order to configure and adapt in runtime nonfunctional properties like timeliness, resourcing, among others. To achieve this, the architecture is based in different components that may be loaded and unloaded dynamically in order to change the behavior of the platform and structure the programmable network.

As a mitigation technique, programmable reflection has the potential to allow a system to react and defend itself against threats. When a malicious activity is detected, the system can dynamically change the implementation to activate the mitigation techniques to guarantee that the system will continue to work [25]. This kind of approaches has been explored to mitigate attacks against Internet web services [3] using reflection to restore an interface of the system that had been modified in an attack.

3 Preliminaries

We provide in this section some initial preliminaries about our assumptions in terms of system and adversarial models.

3.1 System Model

We assume a system that is already protected from a cyber security point of view. This means that the system has been created considering all the required security mechanisms according to a risk analysis of the system. However, past experience has shown that despite all the prevention actions, attacks are still possible. The proposed approach aims at improving the system resilience and protecting it in a contingency mode after the other security mechanisms failed. This way, major failures in the physical process may be prevented.

We also assume that the CPS is governed by feedback controllers applying, e.g., a closed loop model. As shown in Fig. 1(a), the feedback controller collects the *sensor* measurements y_k to determine the state of the system process. Then, the *feedback controller* determines a control input using the received data and the reference obtained from the model. Finally, it sends a control input u_k to the *plant* so that the *actuators* perform the required actions in the physical process. After this, the sensor obtains new measurements y_k and the process is repeated. The values y_k and u_k are exchanged between the feedback controller and the plant through a network. It means that the data will be forwarded through a set of network forwarding devices to reach the appropriate destination. We assume that this network is a highly distributed, with real time traffic and a dynamic system interconnected using a programmable network that is controller by a *network controller* (e.g., an SDN controller [11]). In addition, we assume a k-resilient network, where k is the number of independent paths that interconnect two nodes.

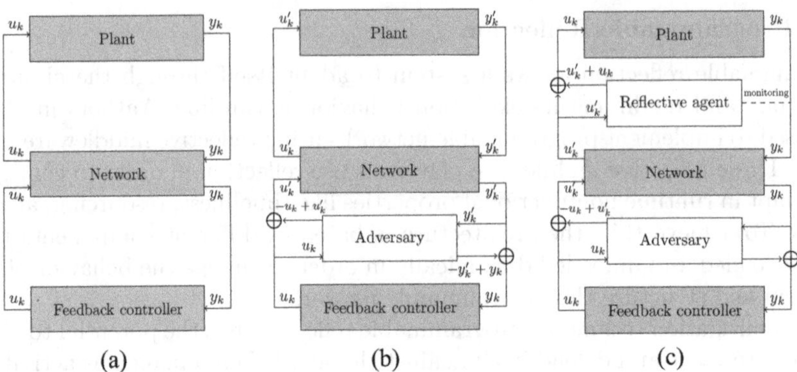

Fig. 1. Feedback control view. (a) Normal operation mode. (b) System under attack. (c) Attack attenuation.

3.2 Adversary Model

Cyber-physical adversaries have different knowledge levels about the system behavior. That knowledge is the main resource in order to build complex attacks and it may even let an adversary remain undetected if the injected data is compatible with the system dynamics. To achieve this, the adversary will try to estimate the model of the physical system and obtain its parameters. Authors in [27] propose a taxonomy of cyber-physical attacks based on the knowledge of the adversaries. Our proposal addresses the cyber-physical injection attacks mentioned in that taxonomy and we assume an insider adversary. To do this, the adversary firstly exploits a cyber vulnerability to gain access in the network channel and be able to insert or modify packets at will. After that, the physical attack to control the physical process starts. To achieve this, the adversary injects a bias in the payload of the packets containing the commands or the measures to manipulate the process. The choice of the introduced modifications depend on the specific impact the adversary wants to produce on the process.

Figure 1(b) depicts an attack against the closed-control loop. We use the traditional representation of a networked-control system. It shows the way how an adversary conducting a cyber-physical attack is represented by the control system community through block diagrams. The $\bigoplus$ symbol in the figure represents a *summing junction*, i.e., a linear element that outputs the sum of a number of input signals. As shown in Fig. 1(b), the adversary modifies the control input u_k to inject a modified u'_k value and affects the system state to disrupt normal operation conditions. Then, the adversary modifies the plant measurements y'_k to send a value y_k to the controller. This way, the controller receives a value y_k that is correlated with the command u_k that it previously sent to the plant. This can be achieved by recording and replicating previous measurements corresponding to normal operation conditions or by injecting some values calculated from the adversary estimated control model of the system.

We also assume that the adversary performs its malicious actions in the cyber-physical system, i.e., at the data layer of the network domain. This means that the adversary is not attacking the programmable network itself, e.g, the control layer. We focus on adversaries that use the network to damage the system. Adversaries that may compromise the physical nodes themselves, to damage the system, are out of the scope of this paper due to this kind of systems usually have good physical protection mechanism implemented.

4 Our Approach

Our proposed approach triggers an attack attenuation for cyber-physical attacks (i.e., disruptive attacks leading to system failures) to remain operational and provide system functionality. We assume a resilient system, capable of reacting and defending itself against known threats. Remediation starts right after attacks are detected. The system dynamically and autonomously changes its behavior to activate an attenuation plan that guarantees work continuation. This is carried out through the cooperation of the feedback controller and the network controller. Although these two controllers have different individual objectives and functionalities, they can work in a coordinated way in order to reach a common goal. Both controllers get connected and coordinate the resilience strategies, e.g., to maintain the resilient properties of the system under failure and attacks.

The proposed resilience strategies try to revert the adversary activity. This is done due to a system capable of modifying its configuration to introduce a new virtual component on-the-fly and dynamically reverting the adversary actions. The solution combines a feedback control technique to detect the attack, programmable reflection for creating the new virtual component that will help the affected feedback controller to bypass the attack and a programmable network in order to neutralize the adversary and sanitize the traffic. The complete process is composed of three main phases: (1) detection, (2) reflection and (3) traffic sanitization.

- **Phase 1 – Detection.** A feedback control detection mechanism is executed in the feedback controller. When an attack is detected, it alerts the network controller to start the coordination of the different components in the system. The physical process in a CPS can be described using an accurate mathematical model that allows to control it and detect deviations from the normal behavior. In addition, it can provide mechanisms to provide attack detection, for example using a physical watermarking that allows to authenticate the correct operation of a control system using a challenge-response detector. In our solution, we used the approach explained in [20,21]. To authenticate the exchanged information, this solution injects a known noise in the physical system signals. It is expected that the effect of that noise is also present in the measured output due to the dynamics of the system. The added noise increases the difficulty associated to the learning process of the adversary. It becomes harder for the adversary to identify the system parameters, hence

decreasing the chances of the adversary to correlate the proper input and output values.
- **Phase 2 – Reflection.** The feedback controller creates a reflective agent, which gets executed within the domain of the network controller. The reflective agent has the control capabilities associated to the victims of the attack. It uses programmable reflection to create, at runtime, a component that executes the same program and equivalent interfaces as the feedback controller. By programmable networking reflection, we refer to the system capability of modifying its networking behavior, i.e., changing accordingly to what is required. For this reason, an on-demand process for loading and unloading components as services could be performed.
- **Phase 3 – Traffic sanitization.** The forwarding elements using network programming capabilities allow to perform a dynamic network traffic sanitizing by modifying the packet containing malicious payloads. The packet affected by the adversary gets sanitized by the reflective agent, which determines what is the correct payload the packet should have. All the network actions required to sanitize the traffic are coordinated by the network controller.

The solution dynamically applies a attenuation technique using the forwarding devices to modify the traffic in order to revert the adversary actions. In a cyber-physical bias injection attack, the physical damage in the system occurs due to modified control commands injected in the plant actions. For this reason, after the traffic is modified by the adversary, the forwarding devices under the command of the network controller intercept those packets and modify them using the reflective agent that knows the physical model of the system and has the ability to determine whether those values in the packets are correct or not. In order to perform the calculations, the reflective agent uses as input the sensor measurements that the plant communicated to the feedback controller previously, since this component executes the same transmission function as the feedback controller, it can determine the correct command values without any model of normal behaviour or historic data of the system. In addition, this node can monitor the measures values, since it is in the network control level and has the potential power to see all what is happening in the network. Moreover, since the network is k-resilient this node can be placed in the most convenient path between the plant and the feedback controller.

Figure 1(c) shows how our attenuation process works in order to handle the attack perpetrated by the adversary. The adversary modifies the command u_k sent from the feedback controller to the plant in order to insert a fake command u'_k. After this, the traffic is modified again to sanitize it with the help of the reflective agent calculations that take as input the monitored sensor values y_k captured from the network. This way, the plant receives the correct u_k command and the physical process is not affected by the adversary actions. When the attack is finished, the normal operation of the system can be restored. The original controller can take over again.

To achieve this solution, the feedback controller is made of two subcomponents: (a) the control component that is in charge of enforcing the dynamical control objectives (fast dynamics are involved); (b) the supervisory component that communicates in a bi-directional way with the network controller. At the data layer of the network domain, we have network probes and effectors, conducting data monitoring—if instructed by the control domain. Network probes monitor the traffic in the data domain and provide the information to the network controller.

The network controller, based on measurements provided by network probes and feedback provided by the feedback controller, is able to detect a possible threat acting on the control path. In response to such a threat, the reflective agent provides a corrective measure to attenuate the impact. The network controller can be seen as a computing entity that is located at an external location (e.g., a kind of Network Operating System [11]). For instance, it provides resources and abstractions to manage the system using a centralized or a decentralized model [20].

Together, both controllers manage the data domain. The feedback controller manages the physical system through physical sensors and actuators deployed at the physical layer. The network controller estimates and manages the data domain through probes and effectors -deployed at the management and control domain.

The network controller analyses the information and forwards control actions to the effectors. Network rules at the control domain are responsible for enforcing such actions. For instance, when a network probe finds tampered traffic in a network path, it provides the tampered information to the control domain. Then, the network controller, located at the control domain, checks for the available resources and helps in order to enforce the action.

5 Experimental Results

We present in this section some experimental results to validate our approach. We use a physical SCADA testbed, for the generation of Modbus-driven CPS data [15]. The testbed consists of *Lego Mindstorms* EV3 bricks [19] and Raspberry Pi [14] boards that control some representative sensors (e.g., distance sensors) and actuators (e.g., dynamic speed accelerators). A sample picture of the testbed is shown in Fig. 2(a). The Modbus SCADA protocol used in the testbed is based on standard Modbus protocol specifications [15] implemented in Java. The testbed implements a kinetic dynamics use case, in which two motion devices perform a deterministic path based on linear motion (backward and forward motion over a bounded square area). We refer the reader to http://j.mp/omnetcps and [22], for additional information and video captures about this testbed. Figure 2(b) depicts a numeric co-simulation complementing the same scenario, using the collected SCADA data to train a CPS programmable simulator. The implementation uses OMNeT++ (Objective Modular Network Testbed in C++) [29,31] and leverages a series of shared APIs (Application

Programming Interfaces) over the INET [30] and SCADASim [18] libraries, to enforce the use of the Modbus protocol over TCP and UDP traffic. All the components (both in the Lego SCADA testbed and the OMNeT++ co-simulation) are synchronized by feedback controllers. Every motion device has a distance sensor in the frontal part, to measure its relative distance to the boundaries of a unit square area. The distance is transmitted to the feedback controllers via Modbus SCADA messages. The feedback controller computes the relative velocity of each motion device, and the Euclidean distance between the two motion devices, in order to guarantee spatial collision-free operations.

The goal of the adversary is to launch an attack at the control level to move the physical process to an undesirable state resulting in the physical collision of the two motion devices. Figure 3(a–b) show the kinetic dynamics of the system during the nominal case (i.e., absence of attacks, left-side); and during the attack (i.e., the moment at which the adversary takes control over the system, right-side). Time is normalized between 0.0 and 1.0, representing the temporal percentage of multiple experimental runs. We can appreciate how the system moves to unstable states, disrupted by the adversary. Some live demonstration videos showing the spatial collision that cause the disruption represented in Fig. 3 are available at http://j.mp/legoscada.

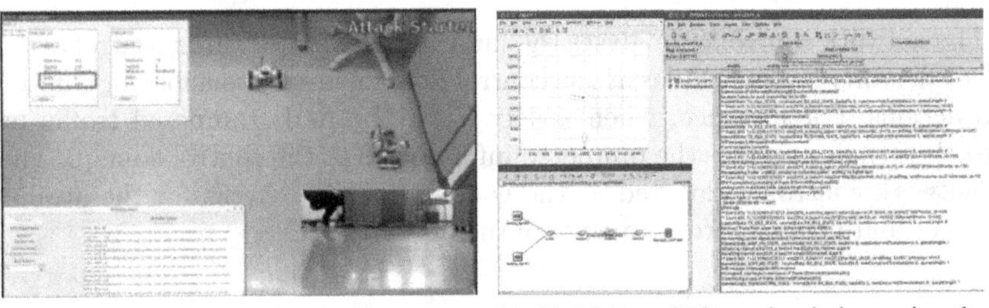

(a) Lego Mindstorms testbed for the generation of SCADA data.

(b) OMNeT++ CPS co-simulation, using the generated data.

Fig. 2. (a) Lego testbed for the generation of SCADA-driven CPS data (cf. http://j.mp/legoscada for live demonstration videos and source code). (b) CPS co-simulation implemented over OMNeT++ (cf. http://j.mp/omnetcps for live demonstration videocaptures and source code).

During the OMNeT++ co-simulation, we analyze the system behavior in the normal operation mode, under attack and using the proposed attenuation approach. In the testbed, the two motion devices follow a trajectory of two meters. The feedback controller coordinates the movement of the motion devices, by sending the relative velocity to the motion device, and receiving back the distance of the motion device to the spatial boundaries. The feedback controller sends a series of Modbus messages to the physical environment of the plant, through a network of traffic programmable forwarders (e.g., SDN switches). The plant contains the physical process itself, the distance sensors and the actuators

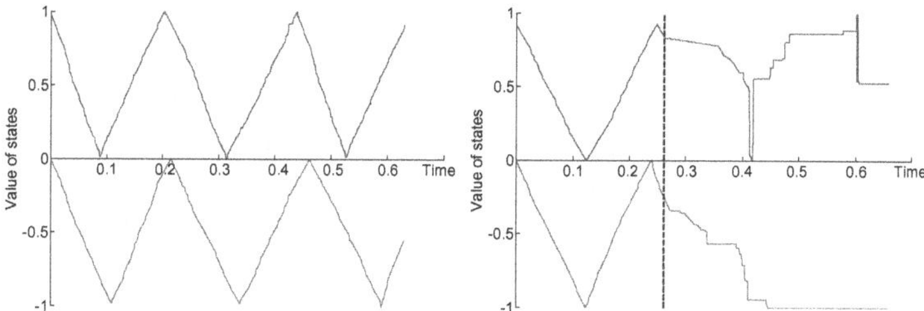

(a) Temporal representation of the CPS kinetic dynamics, associated to the two motion devices (left-side, nominal mode dynamics; right-side, dynamics during the attack).

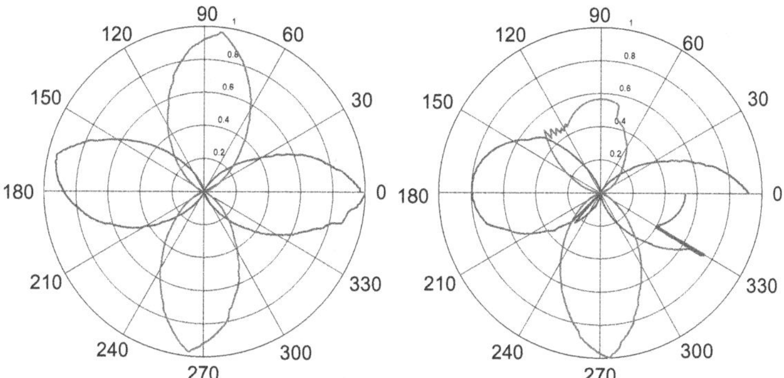

(b) Winding graph of a complete dynamics cycle (left-side, nominal case; right-side, attack case.)

Fig. 3. Lego testbed results (systems dynamics during nominal and attack modes). (a) Temporal representation (the dotted line represents the moment when an attack starts). (b) Winding graph representation of the nominal and attack modes.

that perform the commands (accelerators that increase or decrease the relative velocity of the two motion devices).

The adversary starts the cyber-physical attack by either tampering the controller with fake sensor readings or modifying the control commands sent from the controller. With the OMNeT++ co-simulation, we evaluate the attenuation of the bias injection attack, i.e., by forging tampered control commands from the controller to the plant. For simplicity reasons, we focus only on the physical part of the cyber-physical attack using the network to damage the system. In other words, we assume an adversary that already found a way to hack the cyber layer and gain remote access to the system.

Each co-simulation evaluates fifty Monte Carlo different runs. In addition, according to the sensor specification, the simulation considers a possible error of up to 1 cm w.r.t. the measured distance value. We also model the network delays using the probability distribution in [5]. Figure 4(a) shows the results obtained for the nominal case (i.e., absence of attack), considering the aforementioned possible variation. The plots depict the average Euclidean distance, with 95% confidence intervals, between the motion devices in function of time. The horizontal axis of the plots in Fig. 4(a–d) provides a normalized time between 0.0 and 1.0, representing the temporal percentage prior concluding the simulation runs. The vertical axis of the plots in Fig. 4(a–d) provides the Euclidean distance between the two motion devices, from 0 to 1400 cm. Some further evaluation details are discussed below.

Discussion—During the perpetration of the attacks, the adversary performs a bias injection of cyber-physical data. The adversary uses the network to modify the exchanged packets between the feedback controller and the plant. We assume an adversary recording and learning the system dynamics from commands and sensor outputs. The adversary performs an initial learning phase, in order to eavesdrop data and infer the system dynamics, i.e., the same one used by the feedback controller to guarantee the stability of the system, shown as nominal case in Fig. 4(a).

Let u_k be a feedback controller command sent to the actuator of a motion device at time k. Let u_k^{act} be the command received by the actuator at time k, where $0 \leq k \leq T_s$ and T_s be the full duration of each simulation run. The attack interval T_a is limited to the simulation time T_s, as summarized next:

$$u_k^{act} = \begin{cases} u_k \text{ if } k \notin T_a \\ u'_k \text{ if } k \in T_a \end{cases}$$

For our evaluation, we compare two type of adversaries according to the bias injected in the payload of the packets, i.e, according to the difference between the value u'_k injected by the attacker and the real value u_k sent by the controller. This way, we define two adversary models: an *aggressive adversary* and a *non aggressive adversary*. The aggressive adversary injects in u'_k a bigger difference with respect to the correct command u_k sent by the feedback controller compared to the non aggressive adversary. In consequence, an aggressive adversary will make the system move faster from its nominal state. Figure 4(b) shows the results obtained for the two attack scenarios. The feedback controller loses its control over the system, while the adversary forces the spatial collision of the two motion devices.

During the attenuation process, the system reacts using reflective programmable networking. The reflective agent takes control of the situation, after a hangover of the feedback controller functionality (which moves to the programmable controller domain). This reflective agent takes control over the adversary communications and neutralizes the attack. For each of the defined adversaries, we simulate two scenarios using different values for the time the solution starts working. This is a parameter of the simulation that depends mainly on the time required for the detection mechanism to detect the attack plus the time required to set up and coordinate all the components working in the approach. Figure 4(c)–(d) show how the approach guarantees the controllability property. The first vertical dotted line shows the moment when the attack starts and the second vertical dotted line shows the moment when the technique starts. It is

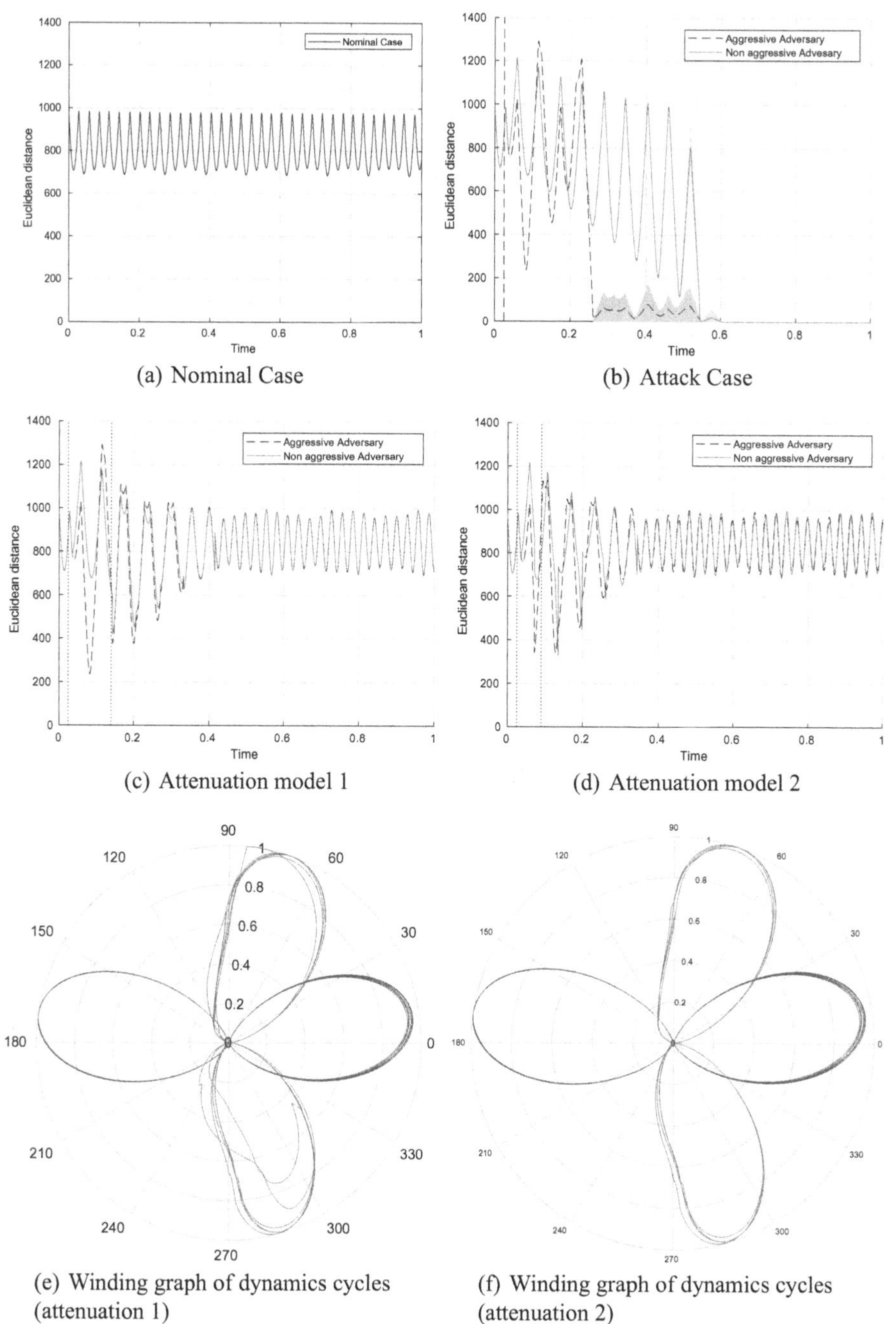

Fig. 4. OMNeT++ results. (a–b) Euclidean distance (with 95% confidence intervals), nominal and attack simulations. (c–d) Euclidean distance, attenuation of two different remediation starting time models. (e–f) Winding graphs, same attenuation models.

possible to appreciate that the attacker introduces a perturbation in the system. As a consequence, the Euclidean distance between the two motion devices starts to oscillate out of the expected behavior (w.r.t. Figure 4(a)).

When the attack is detected, the technique starts working and the reflective agent starts sanitizing the control commands to the moving agents to restore the nominal behavior of the system. Figure 4(e–f) show the winding graph of the motion devices under the approach. The attacked device corresponds to the vertically oriented ellipses. It is possible to observe some perturbations, due to the modifications introduced by the reflective agent when thwarting the adversary actions and recover the stability of the process. As a result, the spatial collision between the two devices is avoided and the system keeps working. Notice that the technique takes control of the physical environment in order to conduct the physical environment from an unstable behavior generated by the attack to a stable and safety behavior, converging to the normal behavior of the physical environment. Figure 4(c–d) show that approach neutralizes the effects of the attack right after a short period of instability. The approach does not eliminate the adversary. However, it contains the effects and reorients the system to the nominal case.

We argue that the solution is reflective since it creates a dynamic component at runtime to help with the function of the attacked control loops. In addition, the component is reflected to the network domain. It gets a greater control of the network than the victim component which has only the possibility to communicate through the network data plane. This is an advantage of the approach compared with other techniques such as redundancy, which implies to have a copy of the same component as a backup. In that case, the adversary may move the attack to the redundant component. For this same reason, routing-based mitigation techniques are not sufficient since the system may find an alternative route but the adversary may move to the new paths. Other solutions that implement mitigation at the node level, such as diversity, are not enough either since the adversary uses the network to perform the malicious activity. Cyber mechanisms to detect packet injection, such as, a Message Authentication Code (MAC), cannot mitigate this kind of attacks. Although they allow to drop modified messages, fail at satisfying real-time constraints. In our approach, the network itself is containing the adversary to revert its actions.

6 Conclusion

We have presented an attenuation approach driven by reflective programmable networking actions, in order to take control of adversarial attacks against Cyber-Physical Systems (CPS). The resulting CPS satisfies self-healing, i.e., during adversarial situations, it continues working in an autonomous way, while ensuring resilience. We have shown and validated the approach via experimental work. We have assumed a cooperation between two different families of controllers (e.g., feedback and reflective programmable networking controllers). Both cooperate together to reach a common goal (e.g, to ensure system stability). The two controller families can have individual objectives (i.e., non-explicit objectives that are not conflicting between them, either). The obtained results are very promising. We plan to go beyond by expanding the analysis with additional controllers and adversaries. Further work will also include the achievement of optimal controller goals in terms of quality of control.

Acknowledgements. The authors acknowledge support from the Cyber CNI chair of the Institut Mines-Télécom. The chair is supported by Airbus Defence and Space, Amossys, EDF, Nokia, BNP Paribas and the Regional Council of Brittany. The chair has been acknowledged by the Center of excellence in Cybersecurity. Authors acknowledge as well support from the European Commission (H2020 SPARTA project), under grant agreement 830892.

References

1. Albert, R., Jeong, H., Barabási, A.-L.: Error and attack tolerance of complex networks. Nature **406**(6794), 378 (2000)
2. Campbell, A.T., Katzela, I., Miki, K., Vicente, J.: Open signaling for ATM, internet and mobile networks (OPENSIG'98). SIGCOMM Comput. Commun. Rev. **29**(1), 97–108 (1999)
3. Cavalli, A.R., Ortiz, A.M., Ouffoué, G., Sanchez, C.A., Zaïdi, F.: Design of a secure shield for internet and web-based services using software reflection. In: Jin, H., Wang, Q., Zhang, L.-J. (eds.) ICWS 2018. LNCS, vol. 10966, pp. 472–486. Springer, Cham (2018). https://doi.org/10.1007/978-3-319-94289-6_30
4. Coulson, G., et al.: Reflective middleware-based programmable networking. In: The 2nd International Workshop on Reflective and Adaptive Middleware, pp. 115–119 (2003)
5. Elteto, T., Molnar, S.: On the distribution of round-trip delays in TCP/IP networks, pp. 172–181, November 1999
6. Enns, R., Bjorklund, M., Schoenwaelder, J., Bierman, A.: Network configuration protocol (NETCONF) - internet engineering task force, RFC 6241, June 2011. http://www.ietf.org/rfc/rfc6241.txt
7. European Union Agency for Network and Information Security Agency (ENISA). Methodologies for the identification of Critical Information Infrastructure assets and services (2015). https://fullreportatwww.enisa.europa.eu/
8. Hachem, N., Debar, H., Garcia-Alfaro, J.: HADEGA: a novel MPLS-based mitigation solution to handle network attacks. In: 31st IEEE International Performance Computing and Communications Conference, IPCCC 2012, Austin, TX, USA, 1–3 December 2012, pp. 171–180 (2012)
9. Jajodia, S., Ghosh, A.K., Swarup, V., Wang, C., Sean Wang, X.: Moving Target Defense: Creating Asymmetric Uncertainty For Cyber Threats, vol. 54. Springer, New York (2011)
10. Joolia, A., Coulson, G., Blair, G., Gomes, A.T., Lee, K., Ueyama, J.: Flexible programmable networking: a reflective, component-based approach (2003)
11. Kreutz, D., Ramos, F.M.V., Verissimo, P.E., Rothenberg, C.E., Azodolmolky, S., Uhlig, S.: Software-defined networking: a comprehensive survey. Proc. IEEE **103**(1), 14–76 (2015)
12. Krotofil, M., Larsen, J.: Rocking the pocket book: hacking chemical plants for competition and extortion. DEF CON, 23 (2015)

13. Kuipers, D., Fabro, M.: Control systems cyber security: defense in depth strategies. Technical report, Idaho National Laboratory (INL) (2006)
14. Lagu, S.S., Deshmukh, S.B.: Raspberry Pi for automation of water treatment plant. In: 2015 International Conference on Computing Communication Control and Automation (ICCUBEA), pp. 532–536, February 2015
15. Modbus Organization. Official Modbus Specifications (2016). http://www.modbus.org/specs.php. Accessed Apr 2019
16. Ogata, K., Yang, Y.: Modern Control Engineering, vol. 4. Prentice-Hall, Upper Saddle River (2002)
17. Piedrahita, A.F.M., Gaur, V., Giraldo, J., Cardenas, A.A., Rueda, S.J.: Virtual incident response functions in control systems. Comput. Netw. **135**, 147–159 (2018)
18. Queiroz, C., Mahmood, A., Tari, Z.: SCADAsim–a framework for building SCADA simulations. IEEE Trans. Smart Grid **2**(4), 589–597 (2011)
19. Rollins, M.: Beginning LEGO MINDSTORMS EV3. Apress, New York (2014)
20. Rubio-Hernan, J., De Cicco, L., Garcia-Alfaro, J.: Event-triggered watermarking control to handle cyber-physical integrity attacks. In: Brumley, B.B., Röning, J. (eds.) NordSec 2016. LNCS, vol. 10014, pp. 3–19. Springer, Cham (2016). https://doi.org/10.1007/978-3-319-47560-8_1
21. Rubio-Hernan, J., De Cicco, L., Garcia-Alfaro, J.: Revisiting a watermark-based detection scheme to handle cyber-physical attacks. In: 2016 11th International Conference on Availability, Reliability and Security (ARES), pp. 21–28. IEEE, August 2016
22. Rubio-Hernan, J., Rodolfo-Mejias, J., Garcia-Alfaro, J.: Security of cyber-physical systems. In: Cuppens-Boulahia, N., Lambrinoudakis, C., Cuppens, F., Katsikas, S. (eds.) CyberICPS 2016. LNCS, vol. 10166, pp. 3–18. Springer, Cham (2017). https://doi.org/10.1007/978-3-319-61437-3_1
23. Rubio-Hernan, J., Sahay, R., De Cicco, L., Garcia-Alfaro, J.: Cyber-physical architecture assisted by programmable networking. Internet Technol. Lett. **1**, e44 (2018)
24. Sahay, R., Blanc, G., Zhang, Z., Debar, H.: Towards autonomic DDoS mitigation using software defined networking. In: SENT 2015: NDSS Workshop on Security of Emerging Networking Technologies, San Diego, CA, USA. Internet society, February 2015
25. Segovia, M., Cavalli, A.R., Cuppens, N., Garcia-Alfaro, J.: A study on mitigation techniques for SCADA-driven cyber-physical systems (position paper). In: Zincir-Heywood, N., Bonfante, G., Debbabi, M., Garcia-Alfaro, J. (eds.) FPS 2018. LNCS, vol. 11358, pp. 257–264. Springer, Cham (2019). https://doi.org/10.1007/978-3-030-18419-3_17
26. Soupionis, Y., Ntalampiras, S., Giannopoulos, G.: Faults and cyber attacks detection in critical infrastructures. In: Panayiotou, C.G.G., Ellinas, G., Kyriakides, E., Polycarpou, M.M.M. (eds.) CRITIS 2014. LNCS, vol. 8985, pp. 283–289. Springer, Cham (2016). https://doi.org/10.1007/978-3-319-31664-2_29
27. Teixeira, A., Shames, I., Sandberg, H., Johansson, K.H.: A secure control framework for resource-limited adversaries. Automatica **51**, 135–148 (2015)
28. Tennenhouse, D.L., Smith, J.M., Sincoskie, W.D., Wetherall, D.J., Minden, G.J.: A survey of active network research. Comm. Mag. **35**(1), 80–86 (1997)
29. The OMNeT++ network simulation framework. http://www.omnetpp.org/. Accessed Apr 2019
30. The OMNeT++/INET framework. http://inet.omnetpp.org/. Accessed Apr 2019
31. Varga, A., Hornig, R.: An overview of the OMNeT++ simulation environment. In: 1st International Conference on Simulation Tools and Techniques for Communications, Networks and Systems & Workshops (Simutools) (2008)

Distributed UCON in CoAP and MQTT Protocols

Athanasios Rizos[1,2(✉)], Daniel Bastos[3(✉)], Andrea Saracino[1], and Fabio Martinelli[1]

[1] Istituto di Informatica e Telematica, Consiglio Nazionale delle Ricerche, Pisa, Italy
{athanasios.rizos,andrea.saracino,fabio.martinelli}@iit.cnr.it
[2] Department of Computer Science, University of Pisa, Pisa, Italy
[3] BT Adastral Park Research Labs, British Telecommunications plc, Ipswich, UK
daniel.bastos@bt.com

Abstract. The Internet of Things (IoT) is playing a key role in consumer and business environments. Due to the sensitivity of the information IoT devices collect and share, and the potential impact a data breach can have in people's lives, securing communication and access to data in IoT has become a critical feature. Multiple application layer protocols are used nowadays in IoT, with the Constrained Application Protocol (CoAP) and the Message Queue Telemetry Transport (MQTT) being two of the most widely popular. In this paper, we propose a solution to increase the security of both CoAP and MQTT based on the distributed Usage Control (UCON) framework. The inclusion of UCON provides dynamic access control to the data shared using these protocols. This occurs by monitoring mutable attributes related to the local protocol nodes and also by sharing data values between remote nodes via the distributed instances of UCON. We present the architecture and the workflow of our approach together with a real implementation for performance evaluation purposes.

Keywords: CoAP · Internet of Things · MQTT · Usage Control

1 Introduction

Internet of Things (IoT) is a world-wide network of interconnected devices, uniquely addressed that interact between each other and exchange information via standard communication protocols [24]. The IoT is already impacting the everyday life of many people and its importance is expected to rise in the next few years [10]. The total number of IoT devices that will be in use in 2020 is

This work has been partially funded by EU Funded projects H2020 NeCS, GA #675320, H2020 C3ISP, GA #700294 and EIT Digital HC&IoT.

S. Katsikas et al. (Eds.): ESORICS 2019 Workshops, LNCS 11980, pp. 35–52, 2020.
https://doi.org/10.1007/978-3-030-42048-2_3

expected to reach 50 billion [6]. The IoT is an inherently complex ecosystem, due to the many different architectures and protocols used, and the different types of hardware and software present in IoT devices. Besides, there are a lot of immature products and cheap devices being released in the market. As a result, several security issues have been identified, such as interception of communications, data compromise by unauthorized parties to collect Personal Identifiable Information (PII), authentication can be brute-forced, credentials can be extracted from device firmware, mobile apps or intercepted at login, and new firmware can be uploaded with malware [2]. Thus, it is of paramount importance to provide techniques that allow secure information exchange between IoT devices.

When it comes to application layer protocols, two of the most widely used are the Constrained Application Protocol (CoAP) and the Message Queue Telemetry Transport (MQTT) [1]. Both protocols were designed for IoT and Machine-to-Machine (M2M) applications. On one hand, CoAP was introduced as a standard by the Internet Engineering Task Force (IETF) in 2014 [25] and its key features are simplicity for constrained environments, very low overhead, and easy interoperability with Hypertext Transfer Protocol (HTTP). Hence, CoAP uses a Client/Server communication pattern, in which *Servers* make resources available and *Clients* interact with resources using REpresentational State Transfer (REST) methods. When a *Client* requests access to a certain piece of information, the access granting decisions are based on the optional use of the Datagram Transport Layer Security (DTLS) library, which provides the security-oriented features of CoAP. On the other hand, MQTT was recently standardized by OASIS[1] and follows the Publish/Subscribe communication pattern. In this pattern, a central entity called *Broker* handles the communication by collecting data, organized by topics, from *Publishers* and distributing it to the set of valid *Subscribers*. According to [1], the MQTT standard provides support for Transport Layer Security (TLS)/Secure Socket Layer (SSL) protocols but offers only a basic authentication feature by default, applied to Publishers/Subscribers during registration. Most of the security solutions developed for MQTT are application-specific or try to leverage TLS/SSL in some way.

In this paper, we propose a security enhancement of both CoAP and MQTT protocols by adding strong authorization capabilities provided by the Distributed Usage Control (UCON). UCON enhances Attribute-Based Access Control (ABAC) models by providing two novelties: Continuity of control and mutability of attributes [20]. Hence, it provides the ability to evaluate policies that have attributes which may change their values during a session. For securing CoAP and MQTT simultaneously we used the distributed version of UCON in [19]. With this solution, we aim to provide dynamic policy enforcement towards more secure data distribution on both protocols at the same time. Moreover, we enhance the interoperability between the protocols, by sharing attribute values via UCON. This work presents the implementation of UCON on top of CoAP and MQTT. We highlight that the presence of UCON does not impact

[1] https://www.oasis-open.org/.

how the protocols work, which means any CoAP and/or MQTT application can support it. To further our approach, we measure the performance of a real implementation.

The rest of the paper is organized as follows: In Sect. 2 we report some background information on IoT protocols, detailing also UCON and its distributed version. Section 3 details the proposed architecture and operative workflow. Section 4 details our implementation and discusses the results of the performance analysis. In Sect. 5 we present a set of related works about security in CoAP and MQTT, and applications of UCON in IoT. Finally, Sect. 6 we offer some conclusions and hint at future directions.

2 Background

In this section we present the main protocols for IoT, motivating the choice to focus on CoAP and MQTT. We also introduce the most important concepts of UCON.

2.1 IoT Protocols

In the area of IoT, the devices are generally constrained in regards to computational power and network availability, so application protocols are usually designed to be very light. The most popular protocols for IoT are CoAP, MQTT, Extensible Messaging and Presence Protocol (XMPP), Advanced Message Queuing Protocol (AMQP), Data Distribution Service (DDS), Websocket and finally for web compatibility HTTP is also sometimes used [15]. The main difference between these protocols is the communication pattern they follow, which can be either Request/Response or Publish/Subscribe. Thus, we focused on two protocols, one for each pattern. The CoAP protocol, that uses the Request/Response pattern, and MQTT that uses the Publish/Subscribe.

CoAP Protocol. Communication in CoAP follows the Client/Server communication pattern. A *Client* sends a request to the *Server* to perform an action on a resource. Each request is composed by a method code (*Get, Post, Put, Delete*) and a Uniform Resource Identifier (URI) which identifies the targeted resource on a *Server*. After receiving the request, the *Server* processes the request and sends a response to the *Client* containing the information acquired by other *Clients* and in accordance with the requested action. A token is used in order to match responses to requests. The response contains a code similar to HTTP ones and, if requested, the respective resource representation.

CoAP offers the ability for a *Client* to follow the updates of a certain resource on a scheduled basis, without sending multiple requests, via a feature called *Observe* [12]. When the *Observe* flag is set on inside a CoAP *Get* request, the *Server* continues to reply after the initial response, streaming resource state changes to the *Client* as long as they occur. After being set, an observation can be cancelled at any point by the *Client* if it wants to stop receiving resource

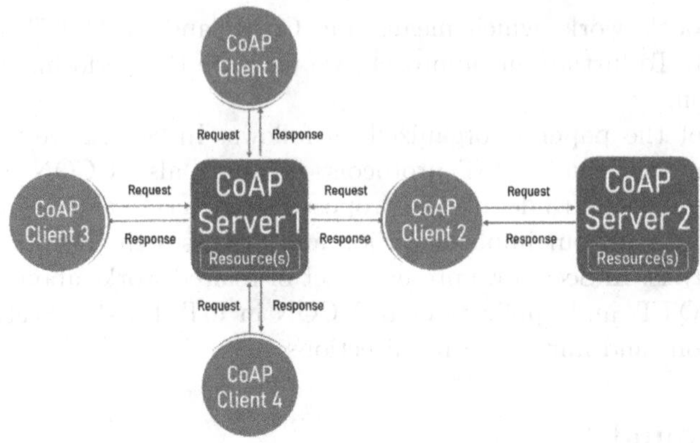

Fig. 1. CoAP architecture

updates. This operation is triggered by sending a request to the *Server* with the *Observe* flag off or by replying to a resource update with a reset message to the *Server.* Figure 1 presents the CoAP architecture, showing a *Server* interacting with multiple clients and, on the right side, a *Client* interacting with other *Server.*

Conversely to HTTP, CoAP uses the User Datagram Protocol (UDP) instead of the Transmission Control Protocol (TCP) for message exchanging. In essence, this means that reliability for message exchange is not guaranteed as UDP doesn't support mechanisms for reliable communications, focusing instead on fast and simple message exchanging. As a result, CoAP implements two request types: Confirmable (CON) and Non-Confirmable (NON). On one hand, CON requests achieve reliable communications by expecting an acknowledgement (ack) message from the *Server* in response to each request. On the other hand, NON requests are "fire and forget" messages that don't expect any confirmation that the request was indeed received by the *Server.* As a result to the previous, CoAP provides two Quality of Service (QoS) levels: *at least once* (using CON requests), and *At most once* (using NON requests). Because CoAP uses UDP it supports multicast requests, where one *Client* can send the same request to multiple *Servers* at the same time. However, a CoAP *Server* always replies in unicast to a multicast request. The CoAP protocol by itself does not provide any security features (e.g. authentication), so security is not designed in the context of the application layer but instead, it is optionally supported at the transport layer [11]. CoAP supports the DTLS protocol [22]. DTLS provides three modes for secure message exchanging: *PreSharedKey, RawPublicKey and Certificate* [9]. These modes allow for strong authentication and data encryption and integrity in transit. However, they don't provide refined authorization capabilities. This work focuses on the CoAP protocol since it is the most constrained one and widely used in the area of IoT. Existing security features of CoAP protocol rely only on the use of DTLS, which does not deal with what happens after the information is shared to the *Client* and does not provide a continuous checking mechanism on the access to the information shared between *Client(s)* and *Server(s)*. Our work addresses this problem by providing continuous verification of access authorization to resources on *Server(s)*.

MQTT Protocol. MQTT is a Publish/Subscribe protocol designed for constrained devices used in telemetry applications. MQTT is designed to be very simple on the client side either this is the *Subscriber* or the *Publisher*. Hence, all of the system complexities reside on the *Broker* which performs all the necessary actions for the MQTT functionality. MQTT is independent from the routing or networking specific algorithms and techniques. However, it assumes that the underlying network provides a point-to-point, session-oriented, auto-segmenting data transport service with in-order delivery (such as TCP/Internet Protocol (IP)) and employs this service for the exchange of messages.

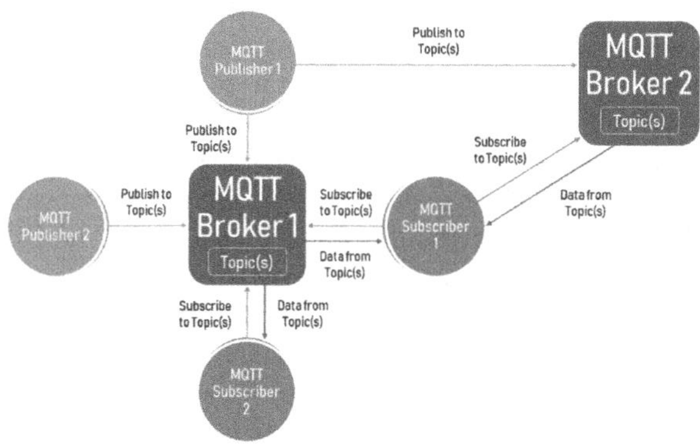

Fig. 2. MQTT architecture.

MQTT is also a topic-based Publish/Subscribe protocol that uses character strings to create and control support of hierarchical topics. It is possible for a *Publisher* to publish to multiple topics and for a *Subscriber* to subscribe to multiple topics at the same time. In Fig. 2, we can see the topology of the protocol. It shows *Publishers* that publish data to topic(s) in the *Broker*. *Subscribers* authenticate with the *Broker* in order to subscribe to topics. The *Broker* is responsible to send value updates for each topic that every *Subscriber* is subscribed to. The *Publishers* and the *Subscribers* can be very constrained devices, especially in the case of *Publishers* which can be simple sensors. Conversely, the *Broker* must provide enough computational power to be able to handle the amount of data being distributed. Depending on how critical is the application, MQTT provides three QoS levels for message delivery [5].

We consider the MQTT protocol for our work since it is the most generic among the IoT protocols described, and libraries are available for all major IoT development platforms, like Arduino, for several programming languages

(C, Java, PHP, Python, Ruby, JavaScript) and for the two major mobile platforms (iOS and Android) [6]. The only security feature MQTT provides is *Publisher/Subscriber* authentication with the *Broker*. They can provide a Username and Password during registration, however this information is optional and it is also transmitted in plain text so in reality no security is provided [18]. A well known effort to add more security to MQTT is proposed in [26], but this solution makes changes to the protocol itself, breaking compatibility as a result, and also does not address changes in *Publisher/Subscriber* which might violate any existing policies. Our proposal addresses this problem by providing continuous control of *Publishers/Subscribers* during both authentication and access.

2.2 Usage Control

The UCON model extends traditional access control models. It is based on the ABAC model and introduces mutable attributes and new decision factors besides authorizations, like obligations and conditions. Mutable attributes represent features of subjects, objects and environment that may change their values during an active session of the usage of an object [8]. These changes lead to the creation of such policies that will be evaluated not only before but also during an active session. The continuous evaluation of a policy when the access is in progress, aims at revoking the access when the execution rights are no longer valid, in order to reduce the risk of misuse of resources. Hence, it is crucial for the UCON model to be able to continuously retrieve the values of attributes. By being aware of any updates which might cause a policy violation, it can promptly react by interrupting the ongoing accesses which are no longer authorized. Architecturally, the UCON framework consists of the following blocks: the *Usage Control System (UCS)*, the *Controlled Systems* and the *Attribute Environment* as they are shown in Fig. 3. For more information about UCON, readers can refer to [16]. The UCS is the core part that takes care of all the requests, the evaluation of the policies, and the attribute retrieval from the *Attribute Environment* which is not controlled by the UCS [4]. On the contrary, policies are enforced by the *Controlled Systems*. The requests from the subjects for access to specific objects and the enforcement of the policy evaluation results are performed by the *Controlled System* to and from the UCS respectively, via a specific component which is called Policy Enforcement Point (PEP).

More in detail, in order for the UCS to provide its functionality, it has its own components which are the following [17]:

`Policy Decision Point (PDP)`: This is where the policy evaluation is happening. It takes as an input a request together with the accompanying policy and attribute values. As a result, it gives back the evaluation result which can be one of the following: *Permit, Deny, Undetermined.*

`Policy Information Point (PIP)`: Application specific interface, so that UCS can communicate with each *Attribute Environment* and receive the values of attributes.

`Session Manager (SM)`: A database which stores all active sessions, with the necessary information to perform monitoring on the status of all the sessions.

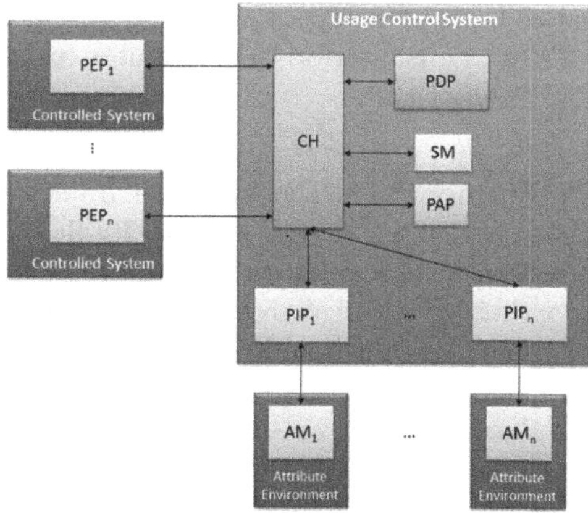

Fig. 3. Usage control framework diagram [17].

`Policy Administration Point (PAP):` Non-mandatory policy storage area.

`Context Handler (CH):` The main part of the UCS and responsible of exchanging information and routing processes among the various components. It receives access requests from the PEP, and enhances the requests the with the attribute values that the PIPs acquire from the Attribute Manager (AM)s. Then sends the enhanced request to the PDP for evaluation, and forwards the result to the PEP and takes the necessary internal actions on the UCS according to the result.

The UCON framework operation is done via the following actions [13]:

`TryAccess:` The first action to happen, it is executed by the PEP that sends an access request to the UCS for evaluation. The UCS, after collecting all the necessary information about the attributes and the policy, responds with *Permit, Deny or Intermediate.* If the answer is *Permit*, the UCS assigns to the response a unique SessionID.

`StartAccess:` It follows a successful *TryAccess* and is sent again by the PEP to the UCS with the previously assigned SessionID as a parameter. It indicates the actual start of the usage of the resources but has again to pass through evaluation from the UCS and only if the response is *Permit*, this session is considered as active until it finishes.

`RevokeAccess:` If, during the continuous re-evaluation, an attribute changes its value, the UCS identifies the change and checks if this change violates the policy. If so, the result is *Deny* and the access has to be revoked via the *RevokeAccess* action. Then, the CH informs both PEP and SM that this session is revoked. On one hand, the SM keeps the session recorded but in an inactive state, whereas, on the other hand, the CH informs the PEP to perform the necessary actions.

`EndAccess:` On the contrary, when the subject wants to terminate an active session, it initiates an action to the UCS to stop a specific session. When this action is received by the UCS, it deletes the session details from the SM and communicates to the PIPs to unsubscribe the attributes related to that session, unless other sessions are using them.

Distributed UCON Framework. The proposed framework is based on a fully distributed Peer-to-Peer (P2P) UCON system [19]. It has been specifically designed to be implemented in IoT architectures and it is based on a group of smart-nodes which have their own logical architecture that can match UCON, as described in the previous section. Each node has its own access directly to *local* attributes that are accessed only by this node. Conversely, there are also the *remote* attributes the values of which can be remotely acquired by other nodes. The policies in the distributed UCON framework consider both attribute types. By using this version of UCON framework, we have the ability to create subsystems that have a standalone UCS with its own PEPs and *local* attributes. At the same time, all of them are connected together in a distributed system which allows access to *remote* attributes [7]. For more information about distributed UCON readers can refer to [19].

UCON in MQTT. For the UCON in MQTT part, our work is based on the existing work that the authors of [14] did. In that setup, an instance of the UCS is installed on the *Broker* of every MQTT system controlling the access of *Subscribers* to the data coming from the *Publishers* over specific *Topics*. The difference between that work and the work presented in this paper is that due to the use of the distributed model of UCON, in our setup the UCS instances that are installed in MQTT systems can share their attributes or retrieve the values of remote attributes from other systems.

3 Introducing Distributed UCON in CoAP and MQTT

In this section we introduce the architecture of the solution we propose including its workflow and implementation.

3.1 Architecture

Taking advantage of the distributed version of the UCON framework [19], we created a similar architecture in our framework in order to combine simultaneous control of accesses using different IoT application layer protocols.

As shown in Fig. 4, we consider a system of interconnected subsystems using different IoT protocols. These standalone subsystems include a set of smart-devices communicating via the same instance of CoAP or MQTT protocol. All of these subsystems work standalone with a separate instance of UCS that is installed accordingly to the protocol each time, enhancing thus their security and continuous monitoring of the access. Thus, all the devices of every system are connected to the same instance of UCS by communicating with their own PEPs.

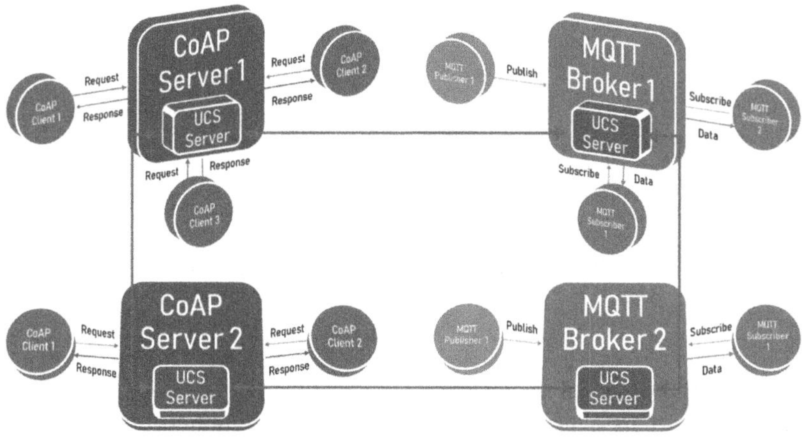

Fig. 4. Architecture diagram of the proposed framework.

For example, we can have the systems (Ci, $i \in \mathbb{N}_{>0}$) that use the CoAP protocol and the systems (Mj, $j \in \mathbb{N}_{>0}$) that use the MQTT protocol. For the sake of simplicity, in Fig. 4 we present only a couple of subsystems for each protocol. Because of the different architecture of each IoT protocol, the PEP component of UCON has to be specifically adjusted to each protocol, whereas the UCS does not change but can be executed in different components according to the protocol used. Every system has their own *local* attributes. In the meantime, each system *(Ci/Mj)* for their local evaluation of access requests may need access to the values of *remote* attributes that belong to another subsystem *(Cx,Mx)*. This communication between different instances of UCS for sharing attribute values gives us the ability to control different protocols without the necessity of the sensors that provide the attributes to use the same protocol for communication. At this point, it is worth re-iterating that the use and functionality of both protocols works as standard despite the addition of UCON.

3.2 UCON in CoAP

CoAP protocol follows the Client/Server model. Each *Client* can either request and/or provide data to the CoAP system. *Clients* could be very constrained devices whereas the *Server* has to provide enough computational power to support all the communications and actions of the CoAP system. The registration and management of the *Clients* is performed by the *Server* that assigns unique tokens to each *Client*. Yet, this model is very simple and does not provide any mechanisms for checking the access during time. All the *Clients* remain connected as soon as they firstly register correctly. In reality, there might occur cases in which sensitive information should not be delivered to specific *Clients*. To achieve such continuous monitoring of the access rights of the *Clients*, the CoAP architecture has been enhanced by the addition of UCON.

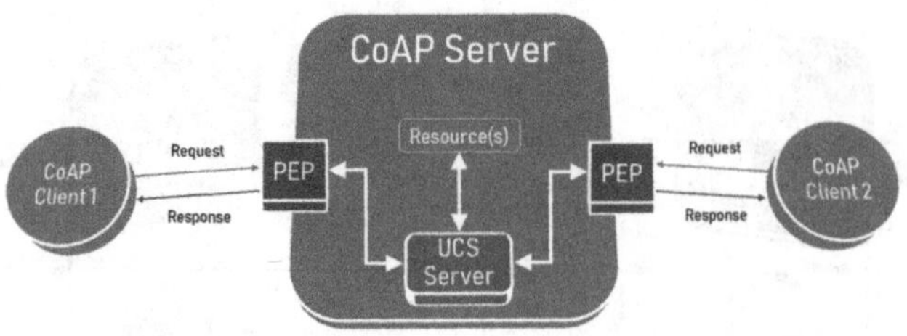

Fig. 5. Architecture diagram of UCON in CoAP protocol.

In Fig. 5 we present the proposed enhancement of the CoAP architecture. The UCS is in the same device with the *Server* of CoAP. UCS can communicate also with other UCSs that can provide the values of remote attributes. The component that performs this communication is the CH. There are various PIPs that are receiving the values from the various AMs regarding subject, resource and environmental attributes. The PEP is also installed in the *Server* and every new request that comes from a *Client* is firstly sent from the *Server* to the PEP to be evaluated by the UCS. For every session of the UCS there is a unique sessionID assigned and stored in the SM. This unique sessionID is matched with the unique token assigned to each *Client* by the CoAP *Server*. The PEP enforces the decision of the UCS by interacting accordingly with the *Server* that manages the subscriptions. Thus, we ensure that there is no chance that a *Client* can be registered in the system without being monitored by UCON. Furthermore, we manage to achieve our goal without making any modification to the *Clients*.

Operative Workflow of UCON in CoAP. In Fig. 6, we report the workflow of an instance of UCON to a system that uses the CoAP protocol. For the sake of simplicity, we will consider a simple system made out of one *Client* that publishes information (CLIENT_P) and another one *Client* that requests for information (CLIENT_R) which is marked with red color on the right part of Fig. 6.

The workflow starts with the request for access by the CLIENT_R to the *Server* (Task 1). When the request arrives to the *Server* it initiates the communication with the local PEP (PEP_L) (Task 2). At this point, we should mention that the components of the local UCS (UCS_L) are marked with green color and have the (L) identification to their names, whereas the components of the remote UCS are marked with light blue color and have the (R) identification to their names. As soon as the request is received by the PEP_L, it communicates with the UCS_L by performing the *TryAccess* action to the CH component of the UCS_L, which is marked in the workflow as CH_L, containing the request and the policy (Task 3). The request has to be enhanced with the attribute values that the CH requests from the various PIPs that take them from the specific AMs (Tasks 4–5). If the value cannot be provided by a local PIP (PIP_L), the CH_L communicates with a remote CH (CH_R) of a remote UCS (UCS_R) (Task 6). CH_R is responsible to acquire the attribute value from PIP_R (Task 7–8) and return it to the CH_L (Task 9). Then all the above are sent to the local PDP (PDP_L) to be evaluated (Task 10) and the PDP_L replies with the result to the CH_L (Task 11). Considering the result is either *Permit* or *Deny*, the request is approved or not accordingly and the CLIENT_R is informed about this (Tasks 12–14).

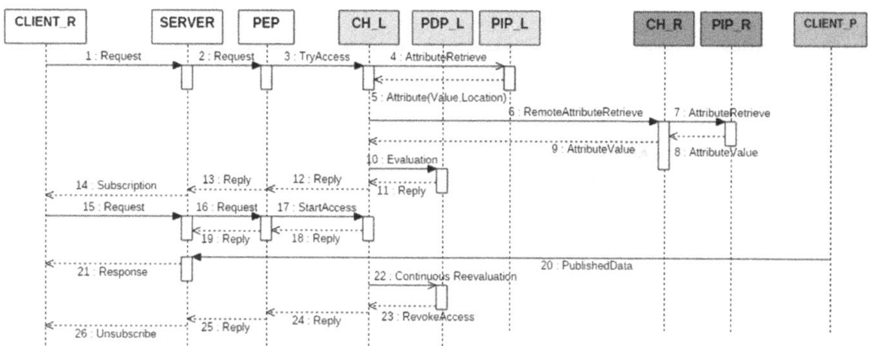

Fig. 6. Workflow diagram of UCON in CoAP protocol.

Then, in the case of a *Permit* in the previous request, the CLIENT_R performs another request to obtain data, which in our case will be provided by the CLIENT_P (Task 15), after the *Server* communicates with PEP_L (Task 16) and gets a *Permit* on that request. For this to happen, PEP_L must perform the *StartAccess* to the CH_L which again passes through evaluation by the PDP_L as previously (Tasks 4–11). Supposing that CLIENT_P starts sending data to the *Server* (Task 20) that must be delivered to CLIENT_R, the *Server* distributes them without any interference by UCON (Task 21). In the meantime, UCS_L is performing a continuous re-evaluation of the attributes (Task 22). In the case there is a policy violation, the access of CLIENT_R should be revoked (Task 23). The CH_L informs the glspep_L (Task 24) and the latter informs the *Server* (Task 25). The *Server* deletes CLIENT_R from its authorized clients and informs it about this fact (Task 26).

4 Experimental Evaluation of Our Framework

In this section we introduce the use cases for our proposed framework and present experiments in both simulated and real environments to help demonstrate our results.

4.1 Example of Use Case

For this use case we consider a scenario of a MQTT system (system M) and a CoAP system (system C) within a smart home. Both systems have a UCS

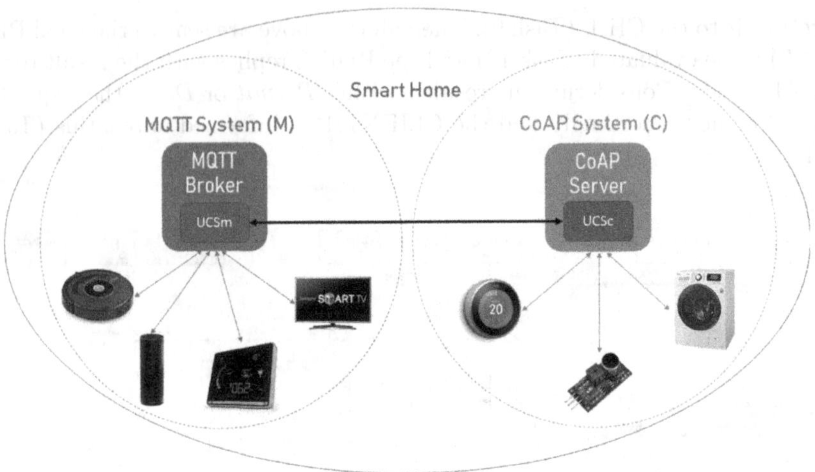

Fig. 7. Use case diagram

installed (UCSm and UCSc respectively). Figure 7 describes the topology of our use case scenario.

In this scenario a smart vacuum cleaner wants to operate. The policy states that it is allowed to operate only if the power consumption and noise levels are within a certain threshold. Some appliances like a smart TV, a smart meter (that measures power consumption) and a smart speaker together with the vacuum cleaner belong to the same system, communicating via MQTT protocol (System M). Furthermore, we consider a smart washing machine, a smart thermostat and a smart noise sensor that are also inside the same home but communicate via CoAP protocol and they belong to a CoAP System (System C). In order for the vacuum cleaner (*Subscriber*) to start cleaning, it must first connect to the *Broker* of system M to subscribe to the power consumption values which are gathered and stored by the smart meter (*Publisher*). The *Broker* receives this request and forwards it to the UCSm. UCSm realizes that in the policy regarding authorization of subscriptions contains a noise level attribute that cannot be retrieved locally by a PIP. Since this value is not local to the system M but belongs to the UCSc of System C, the UCSm contacts the UCSc and asks for access to the value of the noise level from the noise sensor. After receiving the value from the UCSc, the UCSm evaluates the request and forwards the result to the *Broker*, which, in case of "Permit", allows the vacuum cleaner to retrieve the data coming from the smart meter. In parallel, the UCSm continuously checks all the attributes and evaluates the policy. In the event that the value of the noise level or the power consumption rises above policy-defined threshold, the policy is violated and the access of the vacuum cleaner to the data of the smart meter is revoked, which also leads to the cancellation of the subscription from the MQTT system. Thus, without this information the vacuum cleaner will halt its task.

On the other hand, the opposite scenario is happening on System C. The smart washing machine (*Client* C1) wants to receive the data coming from the smart noise sensor (*Client* C2) of System C. In this instance the policy states that the smart washing machine is able to receive the data only if the power consumption is below a certain threshold. The CoAP *Server* of System C forwards this request to UCSc that checks the request conformance with the policy. However, the value of the power consumption belongs to UCSm, which means that the UCSc has to retrieve the attribute value remotely. Thus, UCSc communicates with UCSm, acquires this value, evaluates the request and forwards the result to the *Server* of System C. If the result is "Permit", the *Client* C1 retrieves the data and operates normally. If at any given point the value of the power consumption or the noise level rises above the defined threshold, the policy is violated and the access of C1 to the data is revoked by the UCSc, which leads to the halt of the washing machine task.

4.2 Implementation

The UCS framework was implemented as a Java application. The software used to implement the *Broker* of the MQTT protocol was *Moquette*[2]. This *Broker* is based on the same programming language as the UCS framework which helped making sure that they could be integrated in the same device. Regarding MQTT Subscribers and Publishers we used off the shelf Python-based implementations. These ran as standard, without any modifications. Only the Moquette Broker was partially modified so as to host the PEP and call the UCS when invoking the *TryAccess, StartAccess, EndAccess* actions and wait the response from UCS.

The software used for the CoAP system was *Californium*[3] which is also developed in Java like *Moquette. Californium* is a well-known implementation of CoAP and provides implementation of both *Clients* and *Servers.* Following the same pattern of the MQTT implementation, the Clients of CoAP ran without any modification whereas the *Server* was partially modified in order to host the PEP and the UCS. When a *Client* wants to observe some resource on a *Server*, the PEP calls the UCS invoking the same actions as previously in the case of the Moquette *Broker.* In the case of a negative response, the *Server* returns a message to the *Client* that it was not allowed to observe that resource. If, in the case of both protocols, there is a policy violation, *RevokeAccess* is invoked by the UCS to the PEP and on both cases the session is terminated and the *Subscriber* or the *Client*, depending on the protocol, is removed.

4.3 Testbed and Timing Evaluation

To demonstrate the viability of the proposed approach we examined the overhead of UCON in a real environment. The framework was tested in a virtual machine with Ubuntu 18.04 64-bit powered by an Intel i7-6700HQ using only 4 of its

[2] https://github.com/andsel/moquette.

[3] https://github.com/automote/Califorium.

logical CPUs and 4 GB of RAM. We considered a scenario containing one MQTT and one CoAP system, respectively. In this scenario we intercepted requests of each system considering a constant number of 5 local attributes and a variable number of remote attributes coming from the other system that varies from 0 to 5. In Table 1, we report the detailed timings for each one of the setups described above taking the median of 5 experiments per setup. Firstly we ran the scenario with CoAP system as local and MQTT as remote and vice versa.

Table 1. Timings in milliseconds (ms) for both protocols

Protocol	CoAP						MQTT					
Time (ms)/No. Attrs (Local/Remote)	5/0	5/1	5/2	5/3	5/4	5/5	5/0	5/1	5/2	5/3	5/4	5/5
Subscription time (UCON)	2407	2660	2783	2831	2901	2905	2455	2708	3065	2882	2884	2971
Subscription time (Protocol)	1	1	1	2	2	2	3	4	4	3	3	3
Total subscription time	2408	2661	2785	2832	2903	2907	2458	2712	3070	2885	2887	2974
Revoke time (UCON)	852	917	919	959	985	964	949	980	1155	1069	1058	1064
Unsubscribe time (Protocol)	$\simeq$1	$\simeq$1	$\simeq$1	$\simeq$1	$\simeq$1	$\simeq$1	$\simeq$1	$\simeq$1	$\simeq$1	$\simeq$1	$\simeq$1	$\simeq$1
Total revoke time	853	918	920	960	986	966	949	980	1156	1070	1059	1065

Although the process in CoAP is called observation and in MQTT subscription, we use here the term subscription for simplicity. We appose the subscription time only for UCON which consists of the summary of the times of the *TryAccess* and *StartAccess* actions. We also provide the subscription time that is needed only for the protocol and then we give the total sum of subscription times which is the sum of the previous two times. Considering the subscription time, we recognize that the time in each protocol is very low, especially for CoAP given that CoAP is more constrained. Also, we notice that there is some overhead caused by UCON. But, this overhead of UCON is happening only at the subscription time and there is no overhead in the functionality of each protocol when distributing information after granting permission. Moreover, the ongoing evaluation is happening in the UCS without causing any overhead to the protocol functionality. For unsubscribing (*RevokeAccess*) we consider again two different times for each protocol. The first time is the time of the execution of the *RevokeAccess* action for UCON and the second one is the time for the unsubscription of the components in the protocols (Subscriber and Client for MQTT and CoAP respectively). Again the time of UCON is near one second which produces some overhead comparing to the approximately 1ms of the protocols, but yet again this is not crucial considering real IoT scenarios and it happens only in the revoke time and not during the sessions of the protocols. Finally, when there are not any remote attributes the timings are significantly lower, but as the number of remote attributes increases the timings of UCON also increase although not significantly.

5 Related Work

Over the past few years a number of research works have presented new ways to improve the security of CoAP. Most of these works are focused on reducing the overhead of using DTLS on top of CoAP. In [21], the authors introduced *Lithe* which proposes improvements in the integration between CoAP and DTLS to allow increased performance and more efficient packet sizes and energy consumption. In [28], the authors propose a lightweight security scheme in CoAP using Advanced Encryption Standard (AES) 128 symmetric key algorithm, introducing an object security (payload embedded)-based authentication mechanism with integrated key management. Finally, in [3] the authors introduced RESTful DTLS connections as CoAP resources using Elliptic Curve Cryptography (ECC)-based cryptography, achieving gains in Read Only Memory (ROM) and Random Access Memory (RAM) occupancy. The IETF supports efforts to secure coap, like DTLS for CoAP [9], or the Object Security for Constrained RESTful Environments (OSCORE) group which is developing a mode for protecting group communication over CoAP [27]. The new DTLS standard (1.3) adds improvements in performance and security [23] which CoAP can take advantage. However our solution, provides a continuous control monitoring mechanism, that according to the values of critical attributes, can revoke the access when policy is violated. Moreover, for MQTT protocol, the most significant effort about security, is SMQTT [26]. It adds a security feature based on Key/Ciphertext Policy-Attribute Based Encryption (KP/CP-ABE) that uses lightweight Elliptic Curve Cryptography. This solution produces significant overhead and requires specific *Publishers* and *Subscribers* for encryption and decryption. However, our solution does not require specific *Publisher*s or *Subscriber*s and the overhead is only on the side of the *Broker* hosting the UCS.

The area of IoT includes various protocols and applications that target to a wide range of constrained environments. Thus, the complexity to create security enforcement tools that can handle policies in such environments increases. To this effort, there are other works based on UCON in the area of IoT. In [19], the authors have presented an effort to create a variation of UCON that tries to adapt UCON to the area of IoT, but they do not provide any application to an application layer protocol where the information is shared. There is also another work that tries to address this problem that focuses on how UCON can be integrated in MQTT protocol [15], [14]. This effort focuses on the MQTT protocol highlighting that it is the most generic, since, as they claim, the architecture of MQTT protocol fits nicely with the architecture of UCS. However, this work tries to prove that UCON can fit not only in one protocol, but also in other protocols with different architectures in the same time providing interoperability and attribute sharing among different protocols.

6 Conclusion

To the best of our knowledge, up to now the efforts for policy enforcement and continuous monitoring of the access in IoT application layer protocols are still limited. In this paper, we presented a first and preliminary work on increasing the security of both CoAP and MQTT protocols with dynamic policy enforcement of UCON policies together with the ability of sharing attribute values for access evaluation purposes between protocols. We have demonstrated the general methodology that proves the ability of integrating UCON in a seamless way without modifying the protocols. We have presented also a real implementation of our framework that together with performance evaluation demonstrate the viability of our approach.

As future work, we plan to test our framework to a more complicated testbed that will include other protocols and larger amount of attributes that lead to the creation, evaluation and enforcement of more complex policies.

References

1. Al-Fuqaha, A., Guizani, M., Mohammadi, M., Aledhari, M., Ayyash, M.: Internet of Things: a survey on enabling technologies, protocols, and applications. IEEE Commun. Surv. Tutor. **17**(4), 2347–2376 (2015). https://doi.org/10.1109/COMST.2015.2444095. (Fourthquarter)
2. Bastos, D., Shackleton, M., El-Moussa, F.: Internet of Things: a survey of technologies and security risks in smart home and city environments. In: Living in the Internet of Things: Cybersecurity of the IoT - 2018, pp. 1–7, March 2018. https://doi.org/10.1049/cp.2018.0030
3. Capossele, A., Cervo, V., De Cicco, G., Petrioli, C.: Security as a CoAP resource: an optimized DTLS implementation for the IoT. In: 2015 IEEE International Conference on Communications (ICC), pp. 549–554. IEEE (2015)
4. Carniani, E., D'Arenzo, D., Lazouski, A., Martinelli, F., Mori, P.: Usage control on cloud systems. Future Gener. Comput. Syst. **63**(C), 37–55 (2016). https://doi.org/10.1016/j.future.2016.04.010
5. Chen, D., Varshney, P.K.: QoS support in wireless sensor networks: a survey. In: International Conference on Wireless Networks, vol. 233, pp. 1–7 (2004)
6. Collina, M., Corazza, G.E., Vanelli-Coralli, A.: Introducing the QEST broker: scaling the IoT by bridging MQTT and REST. In: 2012 IEEE 23rd International Symposium on Personal, Indoor and Mobile Radio Communications (PIMRC), pp. 36–41, September 2012. https://doi.org/10.1109/PIMRC.2012.6362813
7. Costantino, G., La Marra, A., Martinelli, F., Mori, P., Saracino, A.: Privacy preserving distributed attribute computation for usage control in the Internet of Things. In: 2018 17th IEEE International Conference on Trust, Security and Privacy in Computing and Communications/12th IEEE International Conference on Big Data Science and Engineering (TrustCom/BigDataSE), pp. 1844–1851, August 2018. https://doi.org/10.1109/TrustCom/BigDataSE.2018.00279
8. Faiella, M., Martinelli, F., Mori, P., Saracino, A., Sheikhalishahi, M.: Collaborative attribute retrieval in environment with faulty attribute managers. In: 2016 11th International Conference on Availability, Reliability and Security (ARES), pp. 296–303, August 2016. https://doi.org/10.1109/ARES.2016.51
9. Gerdes, S., Bergmann, O., Bormann, C., Selander, G., Seitz, L.: Datagram Transport Layer Security (DTLS) Profile for Authentication and Authorization for Constrained Environments (ACE). Internet-Draft draft-ietf-ace-dtls-authorize-07, Internet Engineering Task Force, March 2019. https://datatracker.ietf.org/doc/html/draft-ietf-ace-dtls-authorize-07. (work in Progress)

10. Giusto, D., Iera, A., Morabito, G., Atzori, L.: The Internet of Things. Springer, New York (2010). https://doi.org/10.1007/978-1-4419-1674-7
11. Granjal, J., Monteiro, E., Silva, J.S.: Security for the Internet of Things: a survey of existing protocols and open research issues. IEEE Commun. Surv. Tutor. **17**(3), 1294–1312 (2015)
12. Hartke, K.: Observing Resources in the Constrained Application Protocol (CoAP). RFC 7641, September 2015. https://doi.org/10.17487/RFC7641. https://rfc-editor.org/rfc/rfc7641.txt
13. Karopoulos, G., Mori, P., Martinelli, F.: Usage control in SIP-based multimedia delivery. Comput. Secur. **39**, 406–418 (2013). https://doi.org/10.1016/j.cose.2013.09.005
14. La Marra, A., Martinelli, F., Mori, P., Rizos, A., Saracino, A.: Improving MQTT by inclusion of usage control. In: Wang, G., Atiquzzaman, M., Yan, Z., Choo, K.-K.R. (eds.) SpaCCS 2017. LNCS, vol. 10656, pp. 545–560. Springer, Cham (2017). https://doi.org/10.1007/978-3-319-72389-1_43
15. La Marra, A., Martinelli, F., Mori, P., Rizos, A., Saracino, A.: Introducing usage control in MQTT. In: Katsikas, S.K., et al. (eds.) CyberICPS/SECPRE 2017. LNCS, vol. 10683, pp. 35–43. Springer, Cham (2018). https://doi.org/10.1007/978-3-319-72817-9_3
16. Lazouski, A., Martinelli, F., Mori, P.: Usage control in computer security: a survey. Comput. Sci. Rev. **4**(2), 81–99 (2010). https://doi.org/10.1016/j.cosrev.2010.02.002
17. Lazouski, A., Martinelli, F., Mori, P., Saracino, A.: Stateful data usage control for android mobile devices. Int. J. Inf. Secur., pp. 1–25 (2016). https://doi.org/10.1007/s10207-016-0336-y
18. Locke, D.: MQ telemetry transport (MQTT) v3. 1 protocol specification. IBM developerWorks Technical Library (2010)
19. Marra, A.L., Martinelli, F., Mori, P., Saracino, A.: Implementing usage control in Internet of Things: a smart home use case. In: 2017 IEEE Trustcom/BigDataSE/ICESS, pp. 1056–1063, August 2017. https://doi.org/10.1109/Trustcom/BigDataSE/ICESS.2017.352
20. Park, J., Sandhu, R.: The UCONABC usage control model. ACM Trans. Inf. Syst. Secur. **7**(1), 128–174 (2004). https://doi.org/10.1145/984334.984339
21. Raza, S., Shafagh, H., Hewage, K., Hummen, R., Voigt, T.: Lithe: lightweight secure CoAP for the Internet of Things. IEEE Sens. J. **13**(10), 3711–3720 (2013). https://doi.org/10.1109/JSEN.2013.2277656
22. Rescorla, E., Modadugu, N.: Datagram Transport Layer Security Version 1.2. RFC 6347, January 2012. https://doi.org/10.17487/RFC6347. https://rfc-editor.org/rfc/rfc6347.txt
23. Rescorla, E., Tschofenig, H., Modadugu, N.: The Datagram Transport Layer Security (DTLS) Protocol Version 1.3. Internet-Draft draft-ietf-tls-dtls13-31, Internet Engineering Task Force, March 2019. https://datatracker.ietf.org/doc/html/draft-ietf-tls-dtls13-31. (work in Progress)
24. INFSO D.4 Networked Enterprise and RFID INFSO G.2 Micro and Nanosystem: Internet of Things in 2020, A Roadmap for the Future (2009)
25. Shelby, Z., Hartke, K., Bormann, C.: The Constrained Application Protocol (CoAP). RFC 7252, June 2014. https://doi.org/10.17487/RFC7252. https://rfc-editor.org/rfc/rfc7252.txt

26. Singh, M., Rajan, M.A., Shivraj, V.L., Balamuralidhar, P.: Secure MQTT for Internet of Things (IoT). In: 2015 Fifth International Conference on Communication Systems and Network Technologies, pp. 746–751, April 2015. https://doi.org/10.1109/CSNT.2015.16
27. Tiloca, M., Selander, G., Palombini, F., Park, J.: Group OSCORE - Secure Group Communication for CoAP. Internet-Draft draft-ietf-core-oscore-groupcomm-04, Internet Engineering Task Force, March 2019. https://datatracker.ietf.org/doc/html/draft-ietf-core-oscore-groupcomm-04. (work in Progress)
28. Ukil, A., Bandyopadhyay, S., Bhattacharyya, A., Pal, A., Bose, T.: Lightweight security scheme for IoT applications using CoAP. Int. J. Pervasive Comput. Commun. **10**(4), 372–392 (2014)

Towards the Creation of a Threat Intelligence Framework for Maritime Infrastructures

Nikolaos Pitropakis[1](✉), Marios Logothetis[2], Gennady Andrienko[3], Jason Stefanatos[4], Eirini Karapistoli[5], and Costas Lambrinoudakis[6]

[1] Blockpass Identity Lab, Edinburgh Napier University, Edinburgh, UK
n.pitropakis@napier.ac.uk
[2] INTRASOFT International SA, Luxembourg, Luxembourg
[3] Fraunhofer Institute IAIS, Sankt Augustin, Germany
[4] DNV GL, Oslo, Norway
[5] Cyberlens, Amsterdam, The Netherlands
[6] Department of Digital Systems, University of Piraeus, Piraeus, Greece

Abstract. The maritime ecosystem has undergone through changes due to the increasing use of information systems and smart devices. The newly introduced technologies give rise to new attack surface in maritime infrastructures. In this position paper, we propose the MAritime Threat INtelligence FRAMEwork (MAINFRAME), which is tailored towards collection and analysis of threat intelligence in maritime environments. MAINFRAME combines: (i) data collection from ship sensors; (ii) collection of publicly available data from social media; (iii) variety of honeypots emulating different hardware and software component; (iv) event detection assisted by deep learning; (v) blockchain implementation that maintains audit trail for activities and transactions, and electronic IDs; and (vi) visual threat analytics. To highlight the interdependencies between cyber and cyber-physical threats in autonomous ships, MAINFRAME's operation is evaluated through the liquefied natural gas (LNG) Carrier case study.

Keywords: Maritime · Cybersecurity · Threat Intelligence

1 Introduction

The marine industry is undergoing a digital transformation, implementing new innovative ICT (Information and Communication Technology) tools and services to optimize and further enhance its operations. The advent of new technologies (e.g. Supervisory Control and Data Acquisition - SCADA systems, IoT devices, Big Data) strengthens the maritime industry that currently experiences a new wave of globally connected digital services. The digital transformation has positive implications to the maritime industry processes in operational efficiency, asset management, decision-making and many more. However, recent years have

S. Katsikas et al. (Eds.): ESORICS 2019 Workshops, LNCS 11980, pp. 53–68, 2020.
https://doi.org/10.1007/978-3-030-42048-2_4

convincingly demonstrated that digital transformation comes along with cyber threats.

Malicious parties take the opportunity to expand their activities in different areas. For example, Wannacry ransomware and Petya malware [1] affected many crucial infrastructures such as the United Kingdom's National Health Service (NHS), universities around the globe and the maritime industry causing financial and image loss to companies and public entities. An example is the cyber attack costs of shipping giant Maersk in 2017 which resulted in a loss of around 300 million dollars [2]. In general, cyber attacks in oil and gas industry cost hundreds million dollars per year when at the same time the awareness of cyber security in maritime sector is low to non-existent [3].

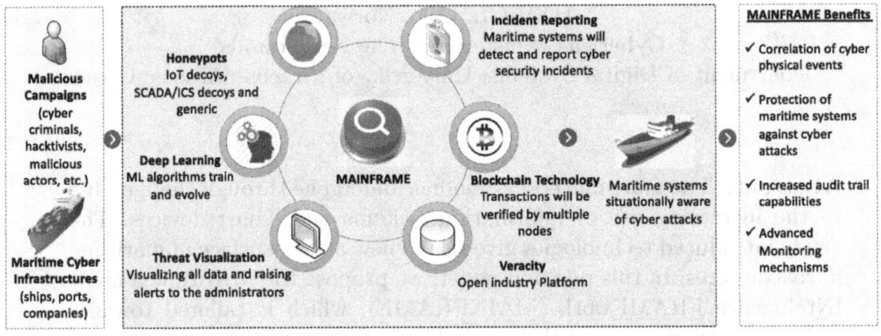

Fig. 1. MAINFRAME approach.

The main cybersecurity challenges faced by maritime industry are related to: (i) *gathering knowledge* related to cyber threats; (ii) *detecting cyber attacks* against maritime systems; (iii) protecting maritime data transactions and creating audit trails; (iv) augmenting maritime systems' robustness against cyber attacks; and (v) increasing cyber security awareness within maritime industry. MAINFRAME (illustrated in Fig. 1) aims to address cybersecurity challenges within the maritime industry increasing its resilience to cyber threats. MAINFRAME orchestrates the *collection* and *correlation* of threat intelligence through an open industry platform. Additionally, blockchain technology and the use of smart contracts will revolutionize the way maritime systems operate as through a single ledger, every transaction will no longer be in the hands of a single party (e.g. a company) and interaction will no longer be limited to closed systems (e.g. centralized maritime ledgers). The proper execution of contracts could be verified by the network of computers connected to the blockchain. In addition to that, blockchain technology will provide the necessary audit trail in case former activities or transactions need to go under intensive check. A Security Information and Event Management (SIEM) adapted for maritime needs and supported by deep learning will detect cyber attacks, while *visual threat analytics* will deliver new insights to the data processing. Every component will share its functionality and collected data through an open industry platform, VERACITY [4] which is specifically designed for maritime industry.

The rest of the paper is organized as follows: Sect. 2 offers some background information about cyber attacks against maritime ecosystem; Sect. 3 introduces the MAINFRAME framework and briefly describes its components while referencing the state of the art practises; Sect. 4 describes MAINFRAME's operation in a LNG carrier use case; and finally, Sect. 5 draws the conclusions giving some pointers for future work.

2 Maritime Security

Modern vessels and ports face various cyber threats affecting:

- *communication systems:* satellite communications, Voice Over IP, wireless local networks);
- *navigation systems:* Global Positioning Systems (GPS), Electronic Chart Display and Information System (ECDIS), Automatic Identification System (AIS), Voyage Data Recorder (VDR), Radar;
- *propulsion and power control systems*;
- *access control systems:* Engine Control Room (ECR), Cargo Control Room (CCR), Closed-Circuit Television (CCTV), Bridge Navigational Watch Alarm System (BNWAS), Ship Security Alert System (SSAS);
- *passenger servicing and management systems*;
- *passenger and crew networks:* WiFi, Local Area Network (LAN);
- *core Information Technology (IT) infrastructure systems:* Router, Firewall, Virtual Private Network (VPN).

One of the most popular cyber attacks that has the largest financial impact on maritime industry is conducted via Business Email Compromise (BEC) [5], a social engineering attack. BEC operators have a solid understanding of various maritime specific operations and they use their knowledge to take advantage of employees with low awareness of cyber attacks. For example, last year researchers from Dell SecureWorks have identified a hacking group called GOLD GALLEON, which is responsible for many wide-scale BEC attacks targeting maritime companies, such as ship management services, port services and cash to master services [6]. Ransomware is another type of cyber threat affecting the maritime industry. An exemplary victim of such cyber attack is COSCO (China Ocean Shipping Company) US branch [7] which was attacked by a ransomware that resulted in the breakdown of their telephone network, email servers, even the US website of the company being offline in July 2018.

One of the most attractive targets in the maritime sector is Industrial Control Systems (ICS), which are critical parts of a vessel's operations. Should cyber attackers bypass the security perimeter of a vessel's IT network they can inject malware to ICS systems. During the last years, several attacks using ICS malware have been reported, with the most recent one targeting Triconex Safety

Instrumented System (SIS) controllers made by Schneider Electric [8]. The malware replaces the Logic of SIS controllers, an action which can: (i) use SIS to shutdown the process, resulting in financial losses due to the process downtime and the plant start-up procedure after the shutdown, (ii) reprogram the SIS to allow an unsafe state, which will increase the risk of a hazardous situation with physical consequences (e.g. impact to equipment, product, environment and human safety) and (iii) reprogram the SIS to allow an unsafe state, while using the Distributed Control System (DCS) to create an unsafe state or hazard, which will have an impact on human safety, the environment, or equipment damage, the extent of which depends on the physical constraints of the process and the plant design. Interestingly, instances of STUXNET have been found on vessels using the same Siemens industrial controllers as the Uranium enrichment plants of Iran [9].

3 MAINFRAME Technologies

The MAINFRAME framework aims at strengthening maritime security situational awareness and preparedness, in terms of *prevention*, *detection* and *response* to cyber threats. MAINFRAME integrates a diverse range of technologies. It will support *visual threat analytics* and include appropriate technologies for the maritime cyber security domain. We envisage that MAINFRAME will be built upon *blockchain* Hyperledger [10] in order to achieve full data supply chain auditing and integrity. It will also make use of *electronic identities* (EIDs) to achieve a robust decentralized identity ecosystem. Yet, a *honeypot* infrastructure with different kinds of honeypots (IoT, SCADA/ICS and generic) will be part of the MAINFRAME framework. Finally, MAINFRAME's *threat detection* will based on machine learning and specifically on statistical learning techniques, such as support vector machines, random forest and logistic regression, while classification benefits from more powerful processing resources, which allow access to big data analysis and deep learning methodologies. We believe that all the above technologies combined in a single framework (illustrated in Fig. 2) that will be integrated to the VERACITY platform, as described below, will provide a robust and scalable cyber security product for maritime security. To clarify the development status of each component, it should be noted that VERACITY is an existing commercially successful product, the Blockchain and SIEM components depend on open source solutions with the exception of deep learning and all of the components of Threat Visualisation that will be developed from scratch.

3.1 VERACITY

The VERACITY platform [4] is an established product delivered by DNV GL with more than 100,000 registered users in the maritime industry. It is a platform that addresses common data challenges such as: (a) Data quality; (b) Incompatible data sets and data trapped in silos; (c) Ownership of asset data; (d) Access control and sharing; and (e) Security. VERACITY includes a marketplace where someone can access all DNV GL's digital services and applications, but also services from third parties such as the security solutions that comprise MAINFRAME. VERACITY also includes a community for developers to make it easier to develop new applications and analytics. On the platform's marketplace, asset owners can subscribe to industrial applications and data analytics services that can help them make better use of data to optimize their safety and performance. These applications will be provided not only by DNV GL, but by a host of other qualified providers of data, data analytics, digital solutions and cyber security tools. VERACITY will make easier the implementation and the interoperability of the rest of the MAINFRAME's components. All of the components will use VERACITY as the main pillar of interaction. For example, VERACITY will be capable to host extra functionalities such as the Event Detection and Event Monitoring components that will orchestrate the cyber threats detection, thus augmenting the existing VERACITY's functionalities.

Data Processing's (DProc) task is the collection of data from a range of sources and silos of the maritime ecosystem. After the data has been ingested, VERACITY checks its quality and then provides the necessary cleaning process. The latter will permit the normalization and aggregation of data from multiple sources in a common format and its addition to the VERACITY's database, where the data is physically protected and encrypted at the same time. This step is quite critical as the maritime industry lacks on standardization when it comes to data acquisition and IT systems on-board vessels. Consequently, the maritime companies can have a better overview of what is really happening in physical and cyber level, allowing the analysis of events and possible correlation between them. For example, access in a restricted area might be correlated with an installed malware that lead to an infection of the systems. Cyber events along with cyber physical events will offer a better understanding of processes in maritime environment, thus increasing the cyber security situational awareness at any given time. Dproc also includes processes that are meant for secure operations, where strong controls are enforced to limit access to trusted personnel only. MAINFRAME, will augment VERACITY's capabilities by reinforcing the cyber security part.

Data Fabric (DFab) offers important services to users. The user can control what data to share, with whom and the amount of time. As the data is extracted from proprietary silos and legacy IT systems, they are being uploaded in a cloud-based infrastructure, giving the ability to perform automated analytics, which can lead to comparisons between assets and benchmarking. The data the user chooses to share on the platform is isolated from other products and other businesses' data unless the user chooses otherwise. Consequently, every maritime business can benefit in terms of training, research and analytics tools. Training and research are focused on cyber security, data quality assessment and reliability of sensor data. MAINFRAME's goal is to strengthen the cyber security part, as the potential user will be able to access to threat intelligence data related to cyber threats and cyber security incidents. The threat intelligence data, correlated with the rest of the collected data from silos and legacy systems, will offer a better view and understanding about all occurred incidents as the physical, cyber and cyber physical approaches will work together towards a common goal. Regarding the analytics tools, the threat detection and threat virtualization components will offer the ability to detect and visualize cyber security incidents. Additionally, the analytics about intrusions and metrics about the robustness of every system will help the potential users strengthen their defences against cyber threats.

3.2 Threat Detection

MAINFRAME includes a SIEM based on open source solution OSSEC [11] which will need to face all the inherent problems of information security on a vessel. This SIEM solution will be configured to accommodate a complete vessel's network detection mechanism which has to meet the needs of the maritime sector. It will monitor all Vessels' IT and OT systems. Event Monitoring (EMon) component will enable monitoring and prompt discovery of cyber threats on vessels. In specific Emon will monitor: (1) Network and Telecom equipment; (2) Incoming and Outgoing connections through the Firewall and log forwarding; (3) All installed operating systems; (4) File integrity; (5) Logs; (6) Processes; (7) System infections; and (8) Most importantly will populate VERACITY's threat intelligence database with all the collected information security related logs. EMon will be offered as a service through VERACITY and will help towards harvesting threat intelligence that will help not only a specific ship, or port but the whole maritime ecosystem by revealing the existence of new threats, thus increasing the awareness and the robustness. The third party role of VERACITY allows for the unbiased collection of information across the entire global fleet

Event Detection (EDec) component is also based on OSSEC [11] and includes: (a) Intrusion Detection; and (b) Threat Intelligence Unification: The Threat Intelligence Unification module will protect vessels assets against known threats, which will be updated frequently and especially each time a new threat or vector of infection is identified through VERACITY; and (c) Alert subsystem: The Alert subsystem module provides an auto alerting system that it is capable to inform all related personnel (IT Department, Security Analysts) with critical events occurred in the network real-time. EDec will be able to detect various threats in: (1) Communication Systems; (2) Bridge Systems, including ECDIS, Propulsion & Power Control; (3) Access Control System; (4) Cargo Management Systems; (5) Passenger Servicing & Management; (6)Passenger-facing Networks; (7) Core Infrastructure Systems; and (8) Admin & Crew Welfare Systems. MAINFRAME will also add two more components which will assist and elevate EDec's detection capability. The first component is a set of honeypots that can attract potential threats before the main systems do and can also permit the contained execution of malicious code, in order to understand its engineering. In addition to that, there is the deep learning component which will help with the detection and classification of cyber and cyber-physical attacks against autonomous systems. It will leverage the cyber and physical features of the autonomous systems for implementing the detection logic and then using lightweight heuristic techniques or advanced deep learning techniques, it will decide whether the autonomous system is in under attack or not. As an extension, it will also employ a method based on Bayesian Networks to determine the domain (cyber or physical) from which the attack originated from. Deep learning component will be a core addition to the SIEM, willing to augment its detection capabilities.

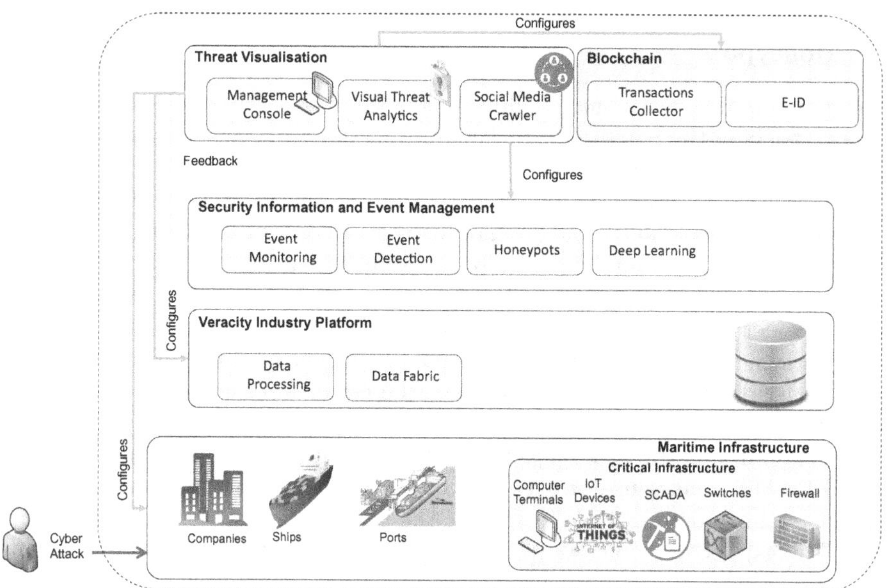

Fig. 2. MAINFRAME architecture.

State-of-the-Art. The incorporation of machine learning in traditional SIEM systems is gaining traction very fast. Traditional SIEM analysts have to deal with large amounts of data manually, and the process of separating meaningful data from various sources is becoming increasingly challenging. Machine learning is attempting to offer intelligent functionality with anomaly detection and classification in order drastically reduce detection and mitigation time of potential threats. Researchers even employ the Graphical Processing Unit to accelerate machine learning methodologies [12]. IBM's Watson [13] is currently being used to augment the functionality of existing cybersecurity intelligent solutions in order to provide better insight on threats. Splunk's user behaviour analytics models combine data analytics with machine learning, to discover abnormalities and unknown threats, which traditional approaches might have missed [14]. The process of detection of cyber threats is traditionally addressed as a classification problem with binary classification evaluating whether there is a threat, and multi-class classification identifying which exact threat it is. Usually high-accuracy multi-class classification is much more demanding in terms of processing and time. For this reason, in systems that have the necessary processing resources, deep learning methods can be employed [15]. Instead, for those systems that are computationally constrained, statistical-based methods are used. For autonomous devices, Bayesian networks have been studied [16], and have been proven as a feasible approach, and presented that they can determine whether the attack has originated in physical or cyber domain.

3.3 Honeypots

Honeypots are decoy systems, deployed alongside production systems with the intent of tricking the potential attackers into breaking the security of the decoy systems. It is a system which value is in getting its security violated. This is one of the few methods available to a security professional to deceive the attackers and study their behaviour. The main objectives of honeypots are to divert malicious traffic away from important systems, get early warning of a current attack before critical systems are hit, and gather information about the attacker and the attack methods. By deceiving an attacker into carrying out his/her attack on a non-critical, well-monitored system, valuable insight can be gained into their attack methods, and information can be gathered for forensic or legal purposes. Deception is so crucial to detecting lateral movement, uncovering privilege escalation, and building threat intelligence, that any kind of honeypots are valuable. MAINFRAME, makes use of a variety of open source honeypots that will be implemented on top of SIEM. In specific the honeypots include: (a) IoT (Internet of Things) decoys: Honeything [17] emulates the TR-069 WAN management protocol, as well as a RomPager web-server, with vulnerabilities. Other IoT decoys can be created by emulating embedded telnet/FTP servers, for example with BusyBox; (b) SCADA/ICS decoys: ConPot [18] emulates a number of operational technology control systems infrastructure, including protocols like ModBus, DNP3 and Bacnet. It comes with a web-server that can emulate a SCADA HMI as well; and (c) Generic: Honeydrive [19] is a GNU/Linux distribution that comes pre-installed with a lot of active defence capabilities. The purpose of MAINFRAME is to cover the majority of the activities in a maritime ecosystem, thus using decoys for IoT devices, SCADA/ICS and general-purpose solutions that will help SIEM to increase its robustness towards a variety of attacks and cyber threats. The SIEM endpoint instance/device will correlate and report back data collected from Honeypots in near real time. Additionally, those data will populate the VERACITY's knowledge base, so as to be used by other clients in favour of their protection.

State-of-the-Art. Honeypots are utilized to increase the security of computer systems and network infrastructures in two ways: (a) the presence of honeypots wastes the attacker's time and resources and (b) once the attacker compromises a honeypot, the network administrator can analyze all of the attacker's actions in great detail. First, attackers spend time and resources in honeypots until they understand that this is not a real system. Second, the attackers leave traces behind, thus an analysis of the attack is feasible that could lead to effective counter measurements, e.g. patches, attack signatures, antivirus design but also assist network forensic investigations. Attacks on honeypots can also serve as an early warning system for administrators, providing more time to react to attacks in progress. Honeypots have been popular in traditional IT systems and the community has tried to maximize their use. Jasek et al. [20] stated that it is feasible to use honeypots in order to detect APT campaigns. In a similar way of thinking, Pitropakis et al. [21] suggested the use of honeypots in combination with the creation of virtual personas willing to achieve cyber attack attribution. However, the use of honeypots is not so popular in the maritime ecosystem. In 2013 Solomon [22] suggested the use of honeypots that can act as a trap against malicious parties. Bou-Harb et al. [23] in 2017 also suggested the use of honeypots as a countermeasure of cyber physical systems which can be attacked in maritime transportation. Honeypots can be monitored either internally or externally an activity that is of paramount importance. Being deployed inside the monitored honeypots, internal monitoring mechanisms are able to provide a semantic-rich view on various aspects of system dynamics (e.g., system calls). However, their very internal existence makes them visible and tangible [24]. On the other hand, external honeypot monitoring systems are invisible to cyber attackers by they are not capable of capturing any internal activity such as system calls. While Sebek is one of the most important honeypot monitoring system used in a variety of high-interaction honeypots internally, the authors in [24] proposed an external virtualisation-based system, called VMscope, which is able to monitor the system internal events of VM-based honeypots from outside the honeypots. The authors also provided a proof-of-concept prototype by leveraging and extending one key virtualization technique called binary translation. Based on their experiments with real-world honeypots, VMscope is proved robust against advanced countermeasures that can defeat existing internally-deployed honeypot monitors.

3.4 Blockchain

In MAINFRAME, the deployment of blockchain is based on the open source Hyperledger Fabric (HLF) project [10] which is a global open source collaborative initiative to advance cross-industry distributed ledger and is hosted by the Linux Foundation. Hyperledger Fabric is a platform for distributed ledger solutions underpinned by a modular architecture delivering high degrees of confidentiality, resiliency, flexibility and scalability. It is designed to support pluggable implementations of different components and accommodate the complexity and intricacies that exist across the economic ecosystem. It also allows secure & private transactions between businesses in supply chains and other use cases. MAINFRAME implements a smart contract engine with a greater focus on this enterprise-by-design concept than in other smart contract engines such as Ethereum [25]. It delivers greater scalability than other blockchain solutions by allowing for consensus mechanisms which meet the requirements of the business, meaning fewer nodes are needed to validate transactions while still maintaining practical byzantine-fault tolerance. This implementation allows full data supply chain auditing as the use of this type of technology prevents malicious actors from editing the transaction history, which can help to identify the group responsible in case of a breach.

With data breaches and identity theft becoming more sophisticated and frequent, companies need a way to take ownership of their identity, thus making blockchain technology and protocols well suited for Enabling Decentralized IDs (DID). Additionally, blockchain offers a secure encrypted digital hub (ID Hubs) that can interact with user's data while honouring user privacy and control, resulting in Privacy by design, built in from the ground up. Traditional identity systems are mostly geared toward authentication and access management. A self-owned identity system will add a focus on authenticity and aid maritime community to establish trust. In a decentralized system trust is based on attestations: claims that other entities endorse – which helps prove facets of one's identity. In addition to that DIDs and ID Hubs will enable developers to gain access to a more precise set of attestations while reducing legal and compliance risks by processing such information. Finally, the proposed solution will result in a robust decentralized identity ecosystem that is accessible to all users, as it will be built on top of standard, open source technologies, protocols, and reference implementations.

State-of-the-Art. During the last decade, the popularity of the blockchain has been increasing and has reached important notoriety not only in scientific and IT journals but also in general public media. Since Blockchains began attracting the attention of the financial, security and IT communities, several other blockchain implementations have appeared (e.g. Ethereum [25]). As an alternative to Bitcoin and Ethereum, The Linux Foundation has proposed a new blockchain project called Hyperledger. This project is a blockchain framework to develop new services and applications based on a permissioned ledger. Even though Hyperledger can be used for a wide spectrum of applications, one of the most popular is for Smart Contracts development. The Hyperledger project consists of five blockchain frameworks: Fabric, Iroha, Sawtooth, Burrow and Indy (not released yet). In the case of Sawtooth, the implementation considers a new consensus algorithm called Proof of Elapsed Time (PoET) that solves the power consumption issue that Bitcoin has. On the other hand, Iroha is a simple blockchain scheme designed to be easy to use for multiple business applications. A more sophisticated blockchain implementation is Burrow. This blockchain implementation is a smart contract machine based on the Ethereum Virtual Machine (EVM) specifications. Finally, Fabric is a blockchain modular framework that gives the flexibility to change different components by plug and play. Moreover, the blockchain replication process between the nodes is cost-efficient and capable to process about 3.500 tps [10], thanks to their consensus algorithm based on Practical Byzantine Fault Tolerant. This makes Hyperledger Fabric one of the best options for customizing a blockchain implementation.

3.5 Threat Visualization

The MAINFRAME Management Console (MC) component constitutes a vital part of the MAINFRAME Threat Visualization component. Given the heterogeneity and complexity of the data related to cyber threats, the visual analysis is imperative to be communicated through a simple intuitive interface allowing for the effective representation of the identified issues. MAINFRAME will employ an interactive user-friendly visualization dashboard displaying real-time information acquired from the SIEM and Social Media Crawler (SMC) components, as well as from VERACITY, after conducting big data analysis. The dashboard will be capable of supporting visual analytics with several security-oriented data transformations and representations, including but not limited to network intrusion graphs, traffic histographs, temporal charts, location maps, and 3D visualizations, in an effort to simplify the highly complex data and provide a meaningful threat analysis. The main goal is to provide a highly customisable environment for the users, attempting achieve a balance between automation and control. Therefore, the dashboard is built upon a tier-based architecture, where the higher-level tiers will present a general overview of the data and the lower-level tiers will display more detailed representations, allowing users to pull up information and drill down into specific details when needed. Finally, the graphical user interfaces built for the configuration of the core MAINFRAME components provides users with the opportunity to handle and manage the operation of the MAINFRAME framework.

The MAINFRAME Visual Threat Analytics (VTA) component is another step towards the visualization of threats against maritime systems. Although MAINFRAME makes use of a SIEM, there are more features that can be used, which will not only augment SIEM's capability but at the same time lead the way towards the visualization of threat management. The goal of VTA is to support informed decision making on cyber security incidents by supporting users in exploring data quality, identifying problems and limitations, and enabling understanding of functionality of pattern detection methods and their dependence on data properties and method parameters. The latter is a functionality that nor traditional Intrusion Detection Systems support and neither does VERACITY. This will result in raising the trust of operators to the methods and, eventually, to the improved recognition of attacks along with the already standard detection functionalities, maximizing the usability of the threat intelligence gathered. In addition to that, maritime ecosystem by making use of visual analytics, will be able to create another line of defence against the Advanced Persistent Threats, the most carefully orchestrated campaigns, which cannot be detected by conventional SIEMs.

The MAINFRAME Social Media Crawler (SMC) aims to monitor a number of crawl points corresponding to social media sources in an automatic and continuous fashion, with the goal to discover and collect information related to maritime industry. The crawling process will be carried out using open-source tools, such as Apache Nutch, as well as social media Application Programming Interfaces (APIs) adapted where appropriate, so as to deliver the expected outcome.

The collected data will be subject to linguistic analysis and go through a series of processes employing a pipeline of tools in the following order: sentence-breaking, tokenization, local grammars, lexicons, part of speech tagging, text normalization, and eventually parsing. Additionally, there will be an extended use of "Regular Expressions", which are expected to have a significant impact on the quality of the results, whereas specialized gazetteers of relevant entities will also aid the extraction. SMC aims at combining the social media concepts/named entities extracted in a smart and scalable way, given the large and highly heterogeneous nature of the data structure. These information will further feed VERACITY's threat intelligence database with more data. It should be noted that the whole process will be carried out on publicly available data respecting always the users' privacy.

State-of-the-Art. Visual Analytics (VA) is defined as a science of analytical reasoning facilitated by interactive visual interfaces [26]. VA focuses on the tight integration of computational and visual techniques through supporting both the reasoning capabilities of both the human factor and the machine. Critical to this approach is that the computer algorithms are controlled and interpreted by the user through intuitive interactive visual interfaces. Visualization is used to graphically convey cyber threat related information, while interaction methods help the users to navigate between different configurations of the rest of the components, thus comparing and contrasting alternatives in complex, heterogeneous data sources. The methods and graphics developed in this field aim to present threat information in a thorough and clear way increasing analysts awareness.

A recent trend in visual analytics has been proposed in [27]. Authors propose a process that includes:

- visually-supported assessment of data quality, data properties and identification of limits of applicability of potentially useful computational methods (see, for example, [28] for mobility data)
- visually-driven application of pattern detection methods and exploration of detected patterns, also known as informed machine learning (see [29] for a comprehensive review)
- visually-steered model building, critical evaluation, uncertainty assessment, continuous monitoring, and incremental model improvement [27]

Cyber security is an important domain for applying visual analytics techniques and has already shown to support many tasks that have become a necessity to administrators and security experts [30]. Relevant tasks such as spotting anomalies and trends, relating multiple metrics, and observing real-time changes are often effectively supported by visualization [31]. Applications in network security include anomaly behavior analysis in netflow data, malware behaviors [32], etc. Techniques such as parallel coordinates, time series visualization and graph visualizations are commonly used in this domain. Traditional sequential and timeline based methods cannot easily address the complexity of temporal and relational features of user behaviors, therefore a map-like visual metaphor is proposed for identifying user behavior patterns [33]. However, despite all these activities, little has been done on improving visual threat analytics capabilities of SIEMs specifically and informed decision making is vital for specific domain needs.

4 Liquefied Natural Gas Carrier

An LNG carrier is a tank ship designed for transporting liquefied natural gas (LNG). As the LNG market grows rapidly, the fleet of LNG carriers continues to experience tremendous growth. In order to facilitate transport, natural gas is cooled down to approximately 163°C at atmospheric pressure, at which point the gas condenses to a liquid. The tanks on board an LNG carrier effectively function as giant thermoses to keep the liquid gas cold during storage. No insulation is perfect, however, and so the liquid is constantly boiling during the voyage. LNG carriers have complex systems with many IT, OT components, IoT and SCADA ICS devices, thus having a broad attack surface that makes them a very attractive target for malicious parties. Compared to oil, there is less public concern over spillage of Liquid Natural Gas (LNG) carrying vessels. However, there is concern about collisions which are rare but possible. Any collision that may happen with an LNG carrier may lead not only to environmental issues but there is a high possibility to affect even the human life. LNG carriers like a lot of modern ships make use of a lot of autonomous components, one of them being auto navigation component.

In this scenario, illustrated in Fig. 3, an attacker wants to take control of the LNG carrier and drive it to a collision as an act of terrorism, causing environmental disaster along with human casualties. As part of his plan, he launches a scan attack **(1. Scan Attack)**, trying to find vulnerable devices that he can take advantage to reach the autonomous navigation component. After having found a poorly updated IoT device, meant for temperature control **(2. Gain Access)**, he continues his attack finding the autonomous identification system **(3. Escalate Privileges)**, which is the tracking system used on ships. The attacker's final goal is to manipulate the tracking readings, thus misdirecting the LNG carrier from its course and navigating it onto another ship creating a collision.

As described in the MAINFRAME's specifications, a variety of honeypots (IoT, SCADA/ICS and generic), are on purpose outdated in terms of firmware to attract possible attacks. Consequently, the attacker finds a honeypot IoT device and proceeds into a honeypot autonomous navigation replica **(4. Enter Honeypot)**. As the attack escalates the SIEM's monitoring system tracks down every action of the attacker inside the honeypot system **(5. Monitoring)**. Right afterwards the SIEM's detection component assisted by deep learning correlates the attack traces **(6. Correlation)**. Right afterwards, the dashboard is notified about the attack detected in the honeypot system **(7. Attack Detection)**. The admin team considers any patterns detected by the VTA **(8. VTA Supported Detection)** that will help in case the same attacker manages to penetrate the real LNG carrier's systems **(9. Stop Attack)**.

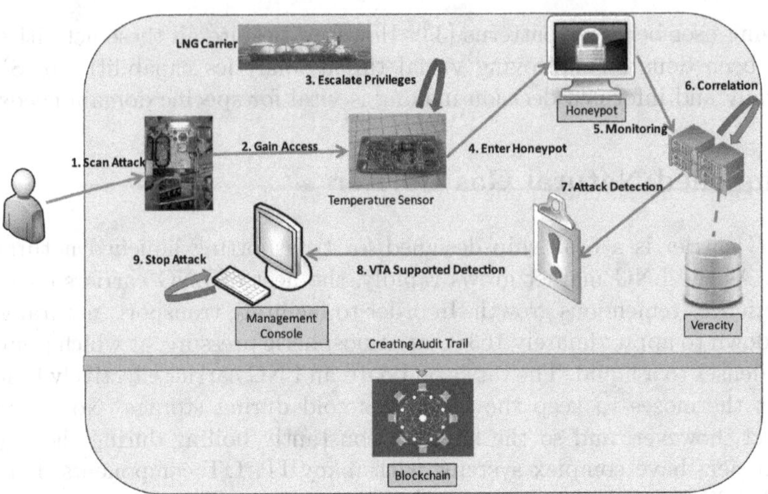

Fig. 3. Liquefied Natural Gas carrier use case of MAINFRAME.

5 Conclusion

Driven by the increasing use of ICT systems in maritime environments and the lack of focus on the cyber threats, we proposed a new framework, whose goal is to aid threat intelligence collection and analysis in the maritime ecosystem. Our solution is built on top of a commercially successful product, strictly designed for maritime needs. On top of it, we suggested the addition of up to date intrusion detection solutions, honeypot systems and visualization approaches that will maximize the utilization of the previous components. Willing to secure the big amount of transactions, our solutions makes also use of hyperledger blockchain technology to achieve that, while enabling the use of EIDs.

The process of integrating so many different components, especially when some of them have to be developed is a very challenging task. However, this is not the end, rather than the beginning of systematic orchestration of defensive mechanics that will help to protect the cyber maritime infrastructures against malicious parties. MAINFRAME through the LNG Carrier case study will also highlight the interdependences that exist between cyber and cyber-physical threats as autonomous ships become more popular over the years. The key to securing cyber maritime infrastructures remains the same and is the threat intelligence gathering and sophisticated analysis.

Acknowledgments. This work has been partially supported by the Research Center of the University of Piraeus.

References

1. Greenberg, A.: The untold story of NotPetya, the most devastating cyberattack in history. Wired, August 2018
2. Taddeo, M., Floridi, L.: Regulate artificial intelligence to avert cyber arms race. Nature **556**(7701), 296–298 (2018)
3. Apostolou, B., Apostolou, N., Schaupp, L.C.: Assessing and responding to cyber risk: the energy industry as example. J. Forensic Investig. Account. **10**(1) (2018)
4. DNVGL: Veracity. https://www.dnvgl.com/data-platform/index.html/. Accessed 09 Feb 2019
5. Mansfield-Devine, S.: The imitation game: how business email compromise scams are robbing organisations. Comput. Fraud Secur. **2016**(11), 5–10 (2016)
6. O'Donnell, L.: Gold galleon hacking group plunders shipping industry. https://threatpost.com/gold-galleon-hacking-group-plunders-shippingindustry/131203/. Accessed 09 Feb 2019
7. Shapo, V.: Cybersecurity implementation aspects at shipping 4.0 and industry 4.0 concepts realization. J. Sci. Perspect. **2**(4), 1–12 (2018)
8. Johnson, B., Caban, D., Krotofil, M., Scali, D., Brubaker, N., Glyer, C.: Attackers deploy new ICS attack framework "TRITON" and cause operational disruption to critical infrastructure. Threat Research Blog (2017)
9. Marks, P.: Why the Stuxnet worm is like nothing seen before. News Science (2010)
10. Cachin, C.: Architecture of the hyperledger blockchain fabric. In: Workshop on Distributed Cryptocurrencies and Consensus Ledgers, vol. 310 (2016)
11. OSSEC: Ossec. https://www.ossec.net/. Accessed 09 Feb 2019
12. Pitropakis, N., Lambrinoudakis, C., Geneiatakis, D.: Till all are one: towards a unified cloud IDS. In: Fischer-Hübner, S., Lambrinoudakis, C., Lopez, J. (eds.) TrustBus 2015. LNCS, vol. 9264, pp. 136–149. Springer, Cham (2015). https://doi.org/10.1007/978-3-319-22906-5_11
13. IBM: Artificial intelligence for a smarter kind of cybersecurity. https://www.ibm.com/security/artificial-intelligence/. Accessed 09 Feb 2019
14. Carasso, D.: Exploring Splunk. CITO Research, New York (2012)
15. Wei, J., Mendis, G.J.: A deep learning-based cyber-physical strategy to mitigate false data injection attack in smart grids. In: Joint Workshop on Cyber-Physical Security and Resilience in Smart Grids (CPSR-SG), pp. 1–6. IEEE (2016)
16. Bezemskij, A., Loukas, G., Gan, D., Anthony, R.: Detecting cyber-physical threats in an autonomous robotic vehicle using Bayesian networks, pp. 98–103 (2017)
17. IBM: Honeything. https://www.ibm.com/security/artificial-intelligence/. Accessed 09 Feb 2019
18. Conpot: Conpot. http://conpot.org/. Accessed 09 Feb 2019
19. BruteForce Lab: HoneyDrive. https://bruteforcelab.com/honeydrive/. Accessed 09 Feb 2019
20. Jasek, R., Kolarik, M., Vymola, T.: APT detection system using honeypots. In: Proceedings of the 13th International Conference on Applied Informatics and Communications (AIC 2013), pp. 25–29. WSEAS Press (2013)
21. Pitropakis, N., Panaousis, E., Giannakoulias, A., Kalpakis, G., Rodriguez, R.D., Sarigiannidis, P.: An enhanced cyber attack attribution framework. In: Furnell, S., Mouratidis, H., Pernul, G. (eds.) TrustBus 2018. LNCS, vol. 11033, pp. 213–228. Springer, Cham (2018). https://doi.org/10.1007/978-3-319-98385-1_15
22. Solomon, J.F.: Maritime deception and concealment: concepts for defeating wide-area oceanic surveillance-reconnaissance-strike networks. Naval War Coll. Rev. **66**(4), 87 (2013)

23. Bou-Harb, E., Kaisar, E.I., Austin, M.: On the impact of empirical attack models targeting marine transportation. In: 2017 5th IEEE International Conference on Models and Technologies for Intelligent Transportation Systems (MT-ITS), pp. 200–205. IEEE (2017)
24. Jiang, X., Wang, X.: "Out-of-the-Box" monitoring of VM-based high-interaction honeypots. In: Kruegel, C., Lippmann, R., Clark, A. (eds.) RAID 2007. LNCS, vol. 4637, pp. 198–218. Springer, Heidelberg (2007). https://doi.org/10.1007/978-3-540-74320-0_11
25. Wood, G.: Ethereum: a secure decentralised generalised transaction ledger. Ethereum Proj. Yellow Pap. **151**, 1–32 (2014)
26. Keim, E.D., Kohlhammer, J., Ellis, G.: Mastering the information age: solving problems with visual analytics. Eurographics Association (2010)
27. Andrienko, N., et al.: Viewing visual analytics as model building. In: Computer Graphics Forum. Wiley Online Library (2018)
28. Andrienko, G., Andrienko, N., Fuchs, G.: Understanding movement data quality. J. Locat. Based Serv. **10**(1), 31–46 (2016)
29. Endert, A., et al.: The state of the art in integrating machine learning into visual analytics. In: Computer Graphics Forum, vol. 36, pp. 458–486. Wiley Online Library (2017)
30. Shiravi, H., Shiravi, A., Ghorbani, A.A.: A survey of visualization systems for network security. IEEE Trans. Vis. Comput. Graph. **18**(8), 1313–1329 (2012)
31. Fischer, F., Keim, D.A.: NStreamAware: real-time visual analytics for data streams to enhance situational awareness. In: Proceedings of the Eleventh Workshop on Visualization for Cyber Security, pp.65–72. ACM (2014)
32. Chen, S., Guo, C., Yuan, X., Merkle, F., Schaefer, H., Ertl, T.: OCEANS: online collaborative explorative analysis on network security. In: Proceedings of the Eleventh Workshop on Visualization for Cyber Security, pp. 1–8. ACM (2014)
33. Chen, S., et al.: User behavior map: visual exploration for cyber security session data (2018)

Connect and Protect: Requirements for Maritime Autonomous Surface Ship in Urban Passenger Transportation

Ahmed Amro[1(✉)], Vasileios Gkioulos[1], and Sokratis Katsikas[1,2]

[1] Norwegian University of Science and Technology, Gjøvik, Norway
{ahmed.amro,vasileios.gkioulos,sokratis.katsikas}@ntnu.no
[2] Faculty of Pure and Applied Sciences, Open University of Cyprus, Nicosia, Cyprus
sokratis.katsikas@ouc.ac.cy

Abstract. Recent innovations in the smart city domain include new autonomous transportation solutions such as buses and cars, while Autonomous Passenger Ships (APS) are being considered for carrying passengers across urban waterways. APS integrate several interconnected systems and services that are required to communicate in a reliable manner to provide safe and secure real-time operations. In this paper, we discuss the APS context, stakeholders, regulations, standards and functions in order to identify communication and cybersecurity requirements towards designing a secure communication architecture suitable for APS.

Keywords: Autonomous ship · Communication system · Communication security · Cyber security

1 Introduction

According to the most recent report from the Norwegian Shipowners' Association, exactly half of the global shipping companies will implement autonomous ships by 2050, while Rolls-Royce aims to operate autonomous unmanned ocean-going ships by 2035 [25]. In this direction, the International Maritime Organization (IMO) started to address the regulatory scope for autonomous ships [8]. Norway is leading the autonomous shipping industry by opening several testing areas for the development of this technology, in addition to the production of Yara Birkland, the worlds first all-electric and autonomous cargo ship [27], and other projects aiming to operate autonomous passenger ferries in different locations [5,28]. Many other initiatives all around the globe are taking place towards the development of autonomous ships; for instance, in 2018, Rolls-Royce and a Finish ferry operator demonstrated the world's first fully autonomous ferry in Finland [26].

The Norwegian Forum for Autonomous Ships (NFAS) has provided definitions for autonomous ships, their context, and functions in [33]. A classification of autonomous maritime systems was suggested, depending on the operational

S. Katsikas et al. (Eds.): ESORICS 2019 Workshops, LNCS 11980, pp. 69–85, 2020.
https://doi.org/10.1007/978-3-030-42048-2_5

area (underwater or surface), the control mode (remote control or autonomous) and the manning levels (from continuously manned to continuously unmanned). This paper is targeting a specific autonomous maritime system which is the Maritime Autonomous Surface Ship (MASS) with a specific application for passenger transportation in urban waterways, to which we refer to as Autonomous Passenger Ship (APS). A comprehensive definition for a ship is suggested by NFAS: "a vessel with its own propulsion and steering system, which execute commercially useful transport of passengers or cargo and which is subject to a civilian regulatory framework". Consequently, an autonomous ship is defined as "a ship that has some level of automation and self governance". The typically expected operational mode of autonomous ships that is appropriate for APS is called "autoremote" and refers to a ship operating in a fully autonomous mode with the ability for a human intervention in case of emergency to take over full control of the ship operations [19].

With the increased research in the maritime industry focused at autonomous ships, the technological improvements were directed toward benefiting the development of smart cities through the smart transportation domain. The city of Trondheim which was recently stamped by EU as smart city [10] has opened the Trondheim Fjord as the world's first testing area for autonomous ships [39]. The idea behind the development of a smart city includes suggesting solutions for improving the citizens quality of life [38]. In this direction, the city of Trondheim is considering the application of a new technology i.e the autonomous ferry (*Autoferry*) [1] through the Trondheim canal to improve residents' life as an alternative to a high-cost bridge [40]. In this paper we focus on this new type of autonomous ships that will be used for passenger transportation in urban waterways.

Operating an autonomous passenger ship in a highly congested area is challenging for many reasons. Such a ship is expected to require the development of new technologies, while maintaining security and safety for the surrounding environment, the ship itself, and its passengers. Designing a suitable communication architecture is a crucial factor for safe operations, since improper communications is considered a primary factor for maritime casualties [11]. Additionally, according to ship owners, the most significant challenges for the usage of unmanned ships are rules and regulations, in addition to competence, compatible ports and fairways, and cyber security [27]. Therefore, the APS' communication architecture should satisfy certain requirements, deriving from the applicable rules and regulations and should be compatible with the views of the stakeholders of the APS ecosystem. Accordingly, this paper aims to identify requirements for a secure communication system in the specific case of APS. To this end, we identify the APS's stakeholders and their views and goals; we analyze existing regulations, guidelines and standards governing the design and operation of autonomous vessels; and we consider the functionality that such vessels should have to be able to operate safely.

The remaining of the paper is organized as follows: In Sect. 2 we review relevant research works. In Sect. 3 we discuss the APS's context, stakeholders, functions, relevant regulations, standards and guidelines. In Sect. 4 we present the identified requirements for the APS secure communication architecture. Finally, in Sect. 5, we summarize our conclusions and we present directions for future work.

2 Related Work

Several studies targeted the design and development of autonomous vessels. A master thesis proposed a design for a small autonomous passenger ferry that aims to be used for transporting passengers across the Trondheim city canal [22]. Another work proposes a technique for carrying out autonomous vessel steering tasks in coastal waters by implementing an agent system; each agent is deployed to perform specific tasks controlled by an agent platform installed on a computer on shore [24]. Neither of these works discussed communication or cybersecurity in their design proposals. Reliable communication capabilities are considered crucial toward the development of autonomous passenger vessels [22,24]. The literature is rich in various works targeting the communication architecture for autonomous ships, focusing on different operational areas, vessel types, and functional requirements. Furthermore, several navigation solutions known as e-navigation have been introduced by IMO in order to reduce human and traditional machine errors, and improve safety related to navigation on board ships, toward better protection for passengers, crew, maritime systems and the environment [30]. The e-navigation solutions targeted SOLAS (International Convention for the Safety of Life at Sea)-based ships, making them inapplicable to the APS. Nonetheless, a previous work discussed the integration of e-navigation solutions for non-SOLAS manned ships [12].

Moving toward autonomous ships, Maritime Unmanned Navigation through Intelligence in Networks (MUNIN) was a project that targeted the technical aspects in the operation of unmanned merchant vessels, and the assessment of their technical, economic and legal feasibility [31]. The project produced many deliverables, including the ship and communication architecture, remote bridge, autonomous engine room, and shore control center. The MUNIN project also produced a communication architecture for unmanned merchant ships, also suggesting communication and legal requirements to carry out unmanned operations in close to shore areas [32]. The MUNIN communication architecture is expected to influence the design and implementation of the communication architecture for the APS. Bureau Veritas, a member of the maritime classification society, published a document providing guidelines for suggested functions and components in autonomous ships [15]. The document aimed to provide guidelines for achieving the most essential functionality and improved reliability, being helpful in the process of studying related communication and cybersecurity requirements. The document also provided communication requirements for functionality and increased reliability. Although the document focused on satellite communications, which is not relevant for urban passenger transportation, the proposed considerations can be adjusted to radio frequencies in close to shore operations.

Although the guidelines exclude ships smaller than 20m, we believe that the suggested guidelines related to communication are relevant for the APS. Additionally, DNV GL published several documents discussing aspects of autonomous ships. In their position paper they discussed the expected change in navigation, the regulatory scope, safety assurance, and social and ethical assurance [21]. Another related document from DNV GL is the class guidelines for autonomous and remotely operated ships [19]. In this document, DNV GL discussed several aspects including navigation functions, communication functions and cybersecurity considerations.

Several works discuss the lack of a regulatory framework that governs the operation of autonomous ships and suggests solutions to adapt to such technology. The Danish maritime authorities published a report on the regulatory barriers to the use of autonomous ships, suggesting suitable steps toward tackling these barriers, such as creating new laws for autonomous ships or amending existing ones [17]. Another work surveyed relevant regulations that might affect the operational capacity of autonomous ships [23]. The authors discussed regulations like SOLAS, COLREGS (International Regulations for Preventing Collisions at Sea), and others in detail, and pointed out that the regulations in their current form limit the deployment of autonomous ships. The work presented in [23] suggested generic communication requirements in order to satisfy certain regulations such as the availability of delay-free, reliable, fast and secure communication between the ship and control center.

3 The APS Ecosystem

3.1 System Context

A general system context for the operation of a MASS as shown in Fig. 1 was suggested by NFAS. A brief description of the context components and their relevance to the APS is given below:

- **Remote Control Center (RCC):** The implementation of such controlling entity is common across most works involving autonomous ships. Some

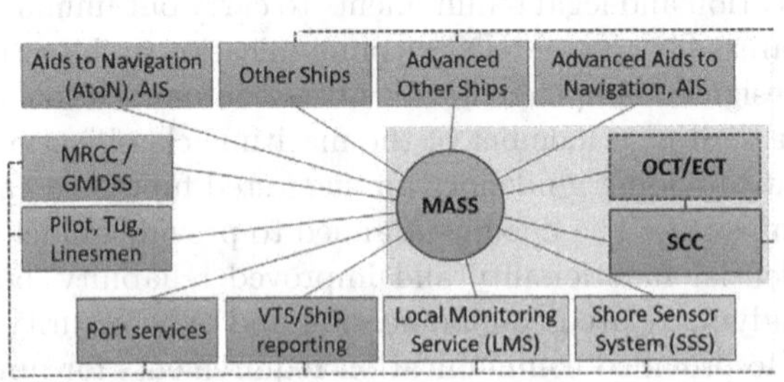

Fig. 1. Context diagram for autonomous ship operation [33].

refer to this entity as Shore Control Center (SCC), others as Remote Control Center (RCC); herein we adopt the latter term. An RCC functions as an observer, by monitoring the APS status, but in some cases it might be forced to take control of the ship in order to avoid accidents. For this reason, it was concluded that certain manning requirements are important for the RCC to operate [36]. Additionally, a single or a chain of RCCs might be expected to serve several ships concurrently. The location of the RCC might be on shore or it can reside on-board another vessel (e.g. an escort vessel).
- **Emergency Control Team (ECT):** a team which is expected to intervene in case of emergencies endangering the passengers or the surrounding environment. For instance, a passenger falling into water, or the ship not responding to remote commands and heading on a collision course.
- **Shore Sensor System (SSS):** A collection of sensors are expected to be mounted on shore to aid some functions of the APS. For instance, ship automatic docking, charging, and other functions related to passenger embarking and disembarking.
- **VTS/RIS:** Ships are expected to establish contact with Vessel Traffic Services (VTS) for guidance and reporting. Moreover, the European Parliament has defined activities towards establishing harmonized River Information Services (RIS) for inland waterways to facilitate navigation [13].
- **Aids to Navigation (AtoN):** Collection of systems expected to provide real-time information for the ship navigation system regarding weather, other ships, location awareness, etc. Examples of such systems are the Automatic Identification System (AIS), the Global Navigation Satellite System (GNSS), Radar, LIght Detection and Ranging (Lidar), etc.
- **Other Ships:** The APS is expected to communicate with other ships in the area for sharing navigational information using several agreed upon communication systems, such as Very high frequency (VHF), the more advanced VHF Data Exchange System (VDES) or AIS.
- **Port Services:** Some services, such as electric charging, maintenance, passenger embarking and disembarking, might be provided to the APS at the port or quay.

Other components in Fig. 1, such as the Maritime Rescue Coordination Centre (MRCC), Global Maritime Distress and Safety System (GMDSS), and Service vessels (Pilot, tug, etc.) are less relevant to the case of the APS, due to the smaller size of its operational area.

3.2 APS Stakeholders

It is important for the development of the APS communication system to grasp an overview of all the system's stakeholders and understand their requirements. Several works discussed the stakeholders of autonomous ships; some focused on the regulator's perspective [17], whilst others provided an overview of all stakeholders from the shipping industry perspective [41]. In the context of APS, we identified seven categories of stakeholders, as shown in Fig. 2. Detailed descriptions of each stakeholder category, their interactions and their interest in the system are provided below:

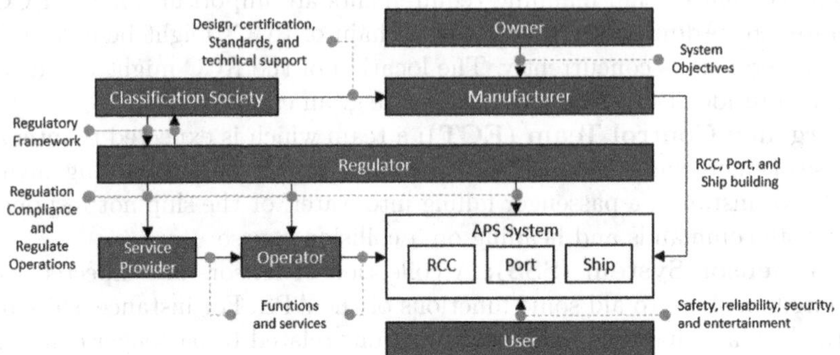

Fig. 2. APS stakeholders and their interactions

- **Owner:** The entire APS or parts of it might be owned by one or several entities. Usually, system owners dictate the objectives to be realized by the manufacturer.
- **Manufacturer:** All entities involved in the design and the implementation of APS, RCC, and port systems and facilities. Such entities are expected to follow standards and requirements related to functionality, reliability, safety, cybersecurity set by the classification society.
- **Classification Society:** Entities that contribute to the maritime domain, including through providing recommendations and suggesting relevant standards for ship manufacturers. The International Association of Classification Societies (IACS) consists of twelve members (including Bureau Veritas and DNV GL) that contribute to the classification design, construction, and rules and standards compliance for more than 90% of the world's ships. IACS is also recognized by IMO as the principal technical advisor [3].
- **Regulator:** A crucial component for the operation of APS is a relevant civilian legal framework. While such a framework does not exist at the time of writing this paper, its development is an ongoing task carried out by IMO [8], assisted by several other entities [19]. Additionally, the operations of APS are expected to be regulated through ship registration and instructions from several entities such as local maritime authorities and traffic regulators (VTS, RIS, etc.). Ensuring regulatory compliance is another task performed by some regulatory entities.
- **Operator:** All entities responsible for realizing the functions of the different components of the APS ecosystem; these are mainly the RCC, ship, and port. It must be noted that in some cases the system might be operated by its owner.

- **Service providers:** Supporting entities that provide additional functions and services for the system's operators. Services may include maintenance, connectivity, insurance, technical support, ship movement in and outside water, etc.
- **User:** Passengers constitute an important component of the APS ecosystem. Their safety and well being is the top priority when designing and operating the ship. Passengers expect such a ship to be safe, reliable, secure, and entertaining.

3.3 Regulations, Standards, and Guidelines

As mentioned earlier, the definition of a ship includes a regulatory framework that governs its operation, mainly to ensure safety, security and protection of the environment. Internationally, such responsibility falls upon the IMO, while regional or national regulatory entities are entitled to issue their own regulations within their jurisdiction [21]. Several international regulations need to be considered while moving forward toward autonomous ships. The identified international regulations and their applicability to APS is depicted in Table 1.

Table 1. International Regulations and Standards relevant to APS

Regulations			
Title	Section/Chapter	Scope	APS Applicaple
SOLAS		International voyages	✗
	ISM		✗
	ISPS		✗
	GMDSS		✗
UNCLOS		Sea	✗
STCW			✗
MARPOL			✗
SAR			✗
COLREG		Sea Connected	✓*
Standards			
IEC 61162	1 (NMEA 0183)	Serial Communication	✓
	3 (NMEA 2000)		✓
	450	Ethernet	✓
	460	Ethernet and Security	✓
IEC 61850	90-4	LAN Engineering	✓
MSC.252	83	Integrated Navigation System	✓
IEC 62443	3-3	Security of Industrial Control Systems	✓
ISO/IEC 27000	27001	Information Security Management Systems	✓
	27002		✓
IEC 62940		Communication between on-board systems and external computer systems	✓

✓*: Require modifications

In the case of APS in urban transportation, the most related regulations are the Convention on the International Regulations for Preventing Collisions at Sea

(COLREG) which applies to all vessels operating at sea or waterways connected to the sea and accessed by seagoing vessels [29]. This can apply to APS operating in rivers and canals linked to the sea. An important regulation that affects the core functionality of the autonomous vessels to operate safely at water is Rule 5 in COLREG. The rule basically requires that the ship shall maintain proper lookout by proper means to avoid collision [29]. Considering that 48.9% of 1522 reported maritime accidents in the Republic of Korea between 2013–2017 were related to improper lookout, [41] it is evidently crucial to address this issue in autonomous ships. Additional regulations concerning passenger vessels differ between regions and countries. The European Union enforces several regulations regarding the cybersecurity of ships and ports like the NIS directive (EU 2016/1148) and the General Data Protection Regulation (GDPR) for processing data of EU citizens, in addition to some other regulations that are related to ships in international voyages. In the Nordic region, each country specifies the passenger vessel types that require an operation certificate. Finland and Norway require all vessels of all sizes to acquire certificates, whilst in Sweden and Denmark certificates are required only for vessels carrying more than 12 passengers. Additionally, all passenger vessels that require certificates must comply with the regulations set by the maritime administration in that country. In Norway, for instance, such administration is the Norwegian Maritime Authorities (NMA) [4]. IACS [2,6,7], DNV GL [19], and Bureau Veritas [15], the most referenced standards that are suggested to be followed are also depicted in Table 1. Additionally, the most referenced guidelines to be considered in providing cybersecurity protections for autonomous ships come from the National Institute of Standards and Technology (the NIST Framework) [37], from IMO in resolution MSC.428(98) (MSC-FAL.1/Circ.3) [16], and from the French National Cybersecurity Agency (ANSSI) [14].

3.4 APS Functions

In order for the APS to operate safely, it must support functions that include navigation, machinery and passenger management, and communications. In this paper we focus on the communication functions and cybersecurity considerations for the APS to perform its intended functions, with an increased focus on navigation. DNV GL discussed the navigation functions that are expected of a vessel in autoremote operation [19]. These are listed below:

- **Voyage Management:** This function includes tasks such as the planning, updating, and recording of voyage data.
- **Condition Detection and Analysis:** This function includes tasks such as proper lookout and situational awareness (e.g determination of position)
- **Contingency Planning:** A critical safety feature that is expected of any APS is referred to as Minimum Risk Condition (MRC). MRC is a state with the lowest possible risk where the ship should be programmed to enter in case of abnormal situation during operations such as the loss of communication links [19]. MRC can also be referred to as fail-safe condition.

- **Safe Speed:** The human in control or in supervisory mode must receive sufficient information regarding the situational awareness to keep the ship's speed within regulated limits.
- **Maneuvering:** To enable maneuvering for collision avoidance or voyage route change, an effective two way communication to provide sufficient situational awareness for either the autonomous system or the RCC in control to make correct decisions.
- **Docking:** An effective two way communication with the docking stations on board and on the shore (e.g. SSS).
- **Alert Management:** An alerting functionality through a Central Alert Management system (CAM) is crucial to achieve safety.

To realize such functions, a combination of systems are expected to be integrated within the APS. These systems require a certain level of connectivity and cybersecurity protection, which should be provided by the communication functions and protected using cyber security controls.

4 Communication and Cybersecurity Requirements

Based on [15,19] and on our analysis of the APS ecosystem in Sect. 3, this section presents the extracted communication and cybersecurity requirements of the APS to perform its expected functions (cf Sect. 3.4). These requirements derive from the perspective of each stakeholder (cf Sect. 3.2), and their presentation is organized accordingly.

4.1 Requirements Deriving from the Regulators' Perspective

At the time of writing this paper there exist no specific regulations that govern the operations of autonomous ships. Nevertheless, the main aim of the regulators of APS is to ensure safety, security and environmental protection. This implies that autonomous ships must achieve a level of safety and security that is at least equivalent to that of a traditional ship.

4.2 Requirements Deriving from the Classification Society's Perspective

Both DNV GL [19] and Bureau Veritas [15] have offered communication and cybersecurity requirements for autonomous ships to operate in compliance with the related regulations, especially COLREG and SOLAS. Bureau Veritas suggested requirements focusing on the functionality and reliability of autonomous ships, whereas DNV GL focused more on safety. An overarching requirement is that *An efficient and secure communication network should be implemented to enable communication between internal and external systems of the autonomous ship.*

In the sequel, we discuss in detail the requirements for (efficient) and (secure) communication in the APS case. Three main communication categories have been identified for the APS to perform its intended functions: 1. External communication including connection with the RCC and external systems and stakeholders; 2. internal communication between on-board ship components; and 3. communication with other vessels in the vicinity. This subsection discuss the communication requirements for each communication category in addition to general requirements that apply across all categories. Additionally, this subsection discusses cybersecurity requirements mapped to the relevant NIST framework function as suggested by Bureau Veritas [15]. Each requirement in this section is titled with a three level coding scheme. The first level is related to the domain (communication (C) or Cybersecurity (S)). The second level is related to the sub-domain. The communication sub-domains are external (X), internal (N), with other ships (O) or general (G). The cybersecurity sub-domains are identification (I), protection (P), detection (D), response and recovery (R). The third level refers to the relative numbering of the requirement within its category.

Communication Requirements: This subsection discusses external and internal communication requirements, in addition to the communication with other ships and other general communication requirements.

- External Communication
  First, *a dedicated physical space must be allocated separately from the controlled vessel*, which can be on the shore or on-board another ship. The required level of reliability, availability, and security of the communication link will increase with increased control of the RCC over the APS, depending on the latter's autonomy level. Additional communication with off-ship systems is required. Examples of off-ship systems that are leveraged for operational purposes are SSS, AtoN, VTS and RIS communication (cf Sect. 3.1). Additionally, other systems may require access to the ship's systems, to provide services such as maintenance, processing insurance claims, etc. Communication with external stakeholders is expected by the APS either by automated systems on the vessel itself, or by the personnel on the RCC. The requirements for the aforementioned communication are discussed below:
  - **C-X-1:** *The link's minimum acceptable network latency and maximum required bandwidth should be calculated, documented and implemented.* MUNIN provided minimum accepted requirements of latency and bandwidth [34]. In total 4 Mbps accumulated link is considered the minimum link bandwidth for ship to shore communication. The required bandwidth is expected to be larger in the case of APS due to the implementation of new technologies with high data requirements such as the lidar. For instance, the targeted lidar for implementation in the *Autoferry* project [1] requires local transfer rate between 9–20 Mbps. Although the amount of data to be transmitted to the RCC is expected to be much less, in case of an increased control of the RCC over the vessel, the full lidar data might be expected for transmission. Additionally, the accepted latency suggested by MUNIN ranges from 0.05 s for ship to ship communication up to 2.5 s for HD video.

- **C-X-2:** *A dedicated, permanent and reliable link for emergency push buttons for passengers should exist.* Such button should be used to indicate passenger related emergency and is expected to initiate intervention of the available ECT (cf Sect.3.1) in the area or to change the autonomy level to provide the RCC full control of the APS if appropriate.
- **C-X-3:** *The link with the RCC should be fault-tolerant so that it operates at full capacity even in case of failure in a single component.*
- **C-X-4:** *Traffic in the link with the RCC should be prioritized according to a pre-defined prioritization policy to enable traffic with higher priority to be forwarded in case of reduced bandwidth.* DNV GL suggested a prioritization policy so that the traffic is prioritized in the following order, from highest to lowest priority: 1. Control messages for emergency (e.g. MRC activation); 2. commands for remote control of key vessel functions; 3. situational awareness data for remote control of key vessel functions; 4. supervision data; 5. maintenance data.
- **C-X-5:** *The operator should be able to seamlessly switch and distribute different vessel data between the different communication channels without a negative effect on the operations* e.g. situational awareness data on one channel, the rest on another.
- **C-X-6:** *Communication links should operate according to appropriate QoS requirements and adapt with signal degradation.* The QoS requirements are case dependent based on the implemented systems on board the APS. For instance, a rule could be established that delay sensitive systems (i.e. collision avoidance) should be carried through an appropriate communication channel that provides the lowest delay whereas delay tolerant systems (i.e. HD video) could be channeled through a communication channel with higher but still appropriate delay.
- **C-X-7:** *The network should integrate monitoring and notification systems for real-time or near real-time link quality analysis, based on data collection and aggregation subsystems which satisfy intrinsic and contextual Quality of Information requirements to support such real-time/near real-time situational awareness and incident response.* The notification functionality is expected to be integrated within the ship's CAM.
- **C-X-8:** *The operator should have independent troubleshooting capabilities over each one of the communication links.* Troubleshooting one link should not interrupt the operations of another.
- **C-X-9:** *Communication link with RCC should be established using redundant communication channels, including main and backup channels, preferably using different communication technologies and service providers.* The communication architecture presented by MUNIN was mainly focusing on deep sea operations. This entails the application of satellite communication for carrying ship to shore operations as a primary communication channel; this is different compared to inland or short sea shipping such as the APS, where high communication requirements are needed. In this case, mobile communication or Wi-Fi channels can be primarily used [35].

- Internal Communication
  - **C-N-1:** *The Communication network design should comply with the applicable requirements in the relevant standards* (cf Table 1).
  - **C-N-2:** *A Segregated network design should exist to avoid failure cascading.* DNV GL suggested a specific network arrangement that applies network segregation [19]. They suggested that the following systems should not be connected to the same network: 1. Navigation system; 2.Communication system; 3. Machinery control and monitoring system; 4. Safety systems; 5. Control systems that serve redundant vessel services; 6. Auxiliary systems not related to vessel key functions; 7. Other systems from different system suppliers. Suggested network segmentation methods include air-gap, VLAN, firewalls etc.
  - **C-N-3:** *A redundant network design should exist with automatic transition/activation/restoration between the main and backup system components.*
  - **C-N-4:** *It should be possible to divert connectivity to local resources upon loss of remote resources.* (e.g in case of distributed network or cloud services providing data storage, backup local storage for critical data are expected to be implemented).
  - **C-N-5:** *Connectivity to several systems on-board, such as passenger management system, alert system (CAM), log book, and local sensors should exist.* The passenger management system provides certain services to the passengers on-board such as voice communication, trip status, and internet-access. Local sensors may include weather sensors, positioning sensors and others.
  - **C-N-6:** *If several wireless communication links are expected to operate closely on-board with a risk of interference, a frequency coordination plan should be made and documented and then tested on board.*
- Communication with other vessels
  - **C-O-1:** *The APS should be able to communicate with other vessels. For such communication, line of sight (LOS) communication system mainly based on AIS or digital VHF with range of at least two kilometers should be used.* This communication includes position and route advertisement which is essential for safe navigation and collision avoidance.
- General Communication Requirements
  - **C-G-1:** *Important communicated data should be recorded and logged to be analyzed when needed.* DNV GL proposed the minimum data that is required to be recorded [19]: 1. The status of the vessel's key functions including the communication links; 2. Alerts; 3. Manual orders or commands; 4. All input and output data to or from the decision support and automation systems. In case the data is recorded on board, an early alert should be raised in case storage capacity exceeds a certain threshold and it should be possible for it to be transferred to shore.
  - **C-G-2:** *The network components and equipment should be type-approved in compliance with the related certification policy.* For technologies implemented in autonomous vessels to be certified by DNV GL, type approval

is discussed in a specified class program for cybersecurity [20]. Type approval according to Bureau Veritas includes compliance with the IEC 61162 standards (all parts) and the MSC.252(83) performance standards.

- **C-G-3:** *The transmission protocol in each link should comply with a relevant international standard*, for example, 802.11 or 802.15 series for wireless communication.
- **C-G-4:** *Wireless data communication should employ an internationally recognized system with the following features:* 1. Message integrity including fault prevention, detection, diagnosis, and correction; 2. Device configuration and authentication by permitting the connection only for devices that are included in the system design; 3. Message encryption to maintain message confidentiality; 4. Security management to protect network assets from unauthorized access.
- **C-G-5:** *A coverage-analysis of the different wireless communication systems must be performed in order to determine its effectiveness.* To this end, a wireless communication testbed that simulates or emulates the communication architecture of the APS can be leveraged.
- **C-G-6:** *All protocols and interfaces implemented in the communication links should be documented.*

Cybersecurity Requirements: This section discusses requirements for the cybersecurity of the APS communication system. A recognized framework should be applied to prevent or mitigate cybersecurity incidents, and in this paper we approach and discuss the identified cybersecurity requirements in the context of the NIST framework [37].

- Identification
  - **S-I-1:** *An up-to-date cybersecurity management framework should exist to govern the operations of cyber systems. It should include necessary policies, procedures and technical requirements.* According to the IMO resolution MSC.428(98), ship owners/operators must address cybersecurity risks in their management systems [16]. This can be achieved through an Integrated Ship Security and Safety Management System (IS3MS).
  - **S-I-2:** *A regularly updated map of the IT installations and the network architecture should be established with a list of the equipment specified by model number and software specified by software version number.*
  - **S-I-3:** *Network user accounts should be inventoried with the associated privileges, reflecting actual authorization.*
- Protection
  - **S-P-1:** *User access management should exist and support the best practices in secure authentication, avoidance of generic and anonymous accounts, secure password and password change policies.*
  - **S-P-2:** *Regular network software updates must be performed, according to an update policy that includes a list of components, responsibilities, means of obtaining and assessing updates, updates verification, and a recovery processes in case of failure.*

  - **S-P-3:** *The network should be protected using secure protocols*, e.g. encrypted transmission, and/or authentication as appropriate.
  - **S-P-4:** *Protection from malware should be implemented to prevent spreading between systems or network segments.*
  - **S-P-5:** *Any personnel who shall access the system should be trained on relevant cybersecurity policies.* It has been determined that a major cause of cybersecurity incidents is the lack of awareness [19].
  - **S-P-6:** *Software-based components should go through regular security analysis with suitable update policy.*
- Detect
  - **S-D-1:** *Monitoring capabilities should be put in place to detect abnormal events.* Abnormal events such as several log-in failures, or massive data transfer. Monitoring capabilities might include Intrusion Prevention Systems, Firewalls, etc. Additionally, such monitoring capabilities should adapt to the existence of encrypted traffic through utilizing best practices such as SSL/TLS proxies and/or anomaly detection.
- Response and Recovery
  - **S-R-1:** *An incident response plan should be formulated, including the isolation of infected components and detailed reporting.* First action after the isolation of all infected machines from the network, for each detected incident a feedback should be documented, and lessons learned sessions should be arranged, to improve defensive measures for similar events in the future.
  - **S-R-2:** *Availability of backup facilities for essential information should be made available with a suitable backup plan.*

4.3 Requirements Deriving from the Service Providers' Perspective

Additional cybersecurity considerations should be given regarding the service providers, especially in the case of them being provided from an external party rather than the systems operators. A list of identified possible service providers categories and their related cybersecurity considerations is given below:

- **Ship Registry:** secure authentication controls should exist for ship certification and revocation of certificates.
- **IT Service Providers:** controls regarding authorization and access control should exist.
- **System installation:** controls to verify proper and secure systems installation according to a defined list of configuration parameters should exist.
- **Maintenance:** access to the system to provide software and/or hardware maintenance services should be controlled, monitored, and verified.
- **Financial services:** controls should exist to protect processes related to passengers payments.
- **Insurance services:** controls should exist to secure access or disclosure of certain data in case of accidents.

4.4 Requirements Deriving from the Users' Perspective

Essentially, passengers safety should be guaranteed by all means during trips. Communication solutions for passengers to communicate with the ship operators and vise versa should be made available. Additionally, certain regulations exist to protect passengers privacy, for instance in Europe, compliance with GDPR is expected and in Norway there exist regulations including Privacy Law and personal data act that are set forth by The Norwegian Data Protection Authority (Datatilsynet) [9] governing tracking (The use of WiFi, Bluetooth, beacons and intelligent video analytic.), video surveillance and anonymity [18]. So, passengers should be protected against tracking, and their information should be processed with privacy considerations.

5 Conclusion and Future Work

A special type of autonomous ships is the Autonomous Passenger Ship. APSs operating in urban waterways constitute a case of increased interest when it comes to the design and implementation of their communication system. In order to define communication and cybersecurity requirements in this case, we defined and analyzed the APS ecosystem in terms of context, stakeholders, regulations, standards, and functions. By leveraging this analysis, we extracted communication and cybersecurity requirements that need to be satisfied so as the APS may perform its required functions. This work is part of an ongoing project called *Autoferry* [1]. Our future work will design and implement a communication architecture and an IS3MS for the *Autoferry* as a use case of an APS system, according to the requirements defined in this paper.

References

1. Autonomous all-electric passenger ferries for urban water transport. https://www.ntnu.edu/autoferry
2. IACS Rec 164 - communication and interfaces - new Nov 2018. IACS
3. International association of classification societies. http://www.iacs.org.uk/
4. Nordic boat standard. https://www.sdir.no/en/guides/nordic-boat-standard/
5. Projects carried out by members of NFAS. http://bit.ly/NFASProjects
6. IACS Rec 158 - physical security of onboard computer based system - new Oct 2018. http://www.iacs.org.uk/download/8782
7. IACS Rec 159 - network security of onboard computer based systems - new Sept 2018. http://www.iacs.org.uk/download/8652
8. IMO takes first steps to address autonomous ships. http://bit.ly/IMOAutonomous
9. Tracking in public spaces. http://bit.ly/DatatilsynetTracking
10. Trondheim blir smartby. http://bit.ly/Trondheimkommune
11. Focus on risks 2018, November 2017. http://bit.ly/sdirRisks2018
12. An, K.: E-navigation services for non-solas ships. Int. J. e-Navig. Marit. Econ. **4**, 13–22 (2016)
13. Andrés, S., Piniella, F.: Aids to navigation systems on in land waterways as an element of competitiveness in ULCV traffic. Int. J. Traffic Transp. Eng. **7**(1) (2017)

14. ANSSI: Information systems defence and security: France's strategy (2011)
15. Bureau Veritas: Guidelines for autonomous shipping (2017). http://bit.ly/BureauVeritas641NI2017
16. TMS Committee: Maritime cyber risk management in safety management systems (2017)
17. Danish Maritime Authority: Analysis of regulatory barriers to the use of autonomous ships. Danish Maritime Authority, Final Report, December 2017
18. Datatilsynet: The anonymisation of personal data. http://bit.ly/DatatilsynetAnonymisation
19. DNV GL: DNVGL-CG-0264: Autonomous and remotely operated ships (2018)
20. DNV GL: DNVGL-CP-0231: Cyber security capabilities of control system components (2018)
21. DNV GL - Maritime: Remote-controlled and autonomous ships position paper (2018)
22. Havdal, G., Heggelund, C.T., Larssen, C.H.: Design of a small autonomous passenger Ferry. Master's thesis, NTNU (2017)
23. Komianos, A.: The autonomous shipping era. Operational, regulatory, and quality challenges. TransNav: Int. J. Mar. Navig. Saf. Sea Transp. **12** (2018)
24. Łebkowski, A.: Design of an autonomous transport system for coastal areas. TransNav: Int. J. Mar. Navig. Saf. Sea Transp. **12** (2018)
25. Levander, O., Marine, R.R.: Ship intelligence-a new era in shipping. In: The Royal Institution of Naval Architects, Smart Ship Technology, International Conference Proceedings, pp. 26–27 (2016)
26. MI News Network: Rolls-Royce and Finferries demonstrate world's first fully autonomous ferry, December 2018. http://bit.ly/marineinsightRollsRoyce
27. Norwegian Shipowners' Association: Maritime outlook 2018. Technical report, Norwegian Shipowners' Association (2018)
28. Olsen, S.: Autonom ferge ballstadlandet. http://bit.ly/lofotenmatpark
29. IM Organization: Convention on the international regulations for preventing collisions at sea. COLREGS (1972)
30. Patraiko, D.: The development of e-navigation. TransNav Int. J. Mar. Navig. Saf. od Sea Transp. **1**(3) (2007)
31. Porathe, T., Burmeister, H.C., Rødseth, Ø.J.: Maritime unmanned navigation through intelligence in networks: the MUNIN project. In: 12th International Conference on Computer and IT Applications in the Maritime Industries, COMPIT 2013, Cortona, 15–17 April 2013, pp. 177–183 (2013)
32. Rødseth, Ø., Burmeister, H.: MUNIN deliverable d10.1: impact on short sea shipping (2015). http://www.unmanned-ship.org/munin/wp-content/uploads/2015/10/MUNIN-D10-1-Impact-on-Short-Sea-Shipping-MRTK-final.pdf
33. Rødseth, Ø., Nordahl, H.: Definitions for autonomous merchant ships. In: Norwegian Forum for Unmanned Ships (2017)
34. Rødseth, Ø.: Munin deliverable 4.3: evaluation of ship to shore communication links (2012). http://www.unmanned-ship.org/munin/wp-content/uploads/2014/02/d4-3-eval-ship-shore-v11.pdf
35. Rødseth, Ø.J., Kvamstad, B., Porathe, T., Burmeister, H.C.: Communication architecture for an unmanned merchant ship. In: 2013 MTS/IEEE OCEANS-Bergen, pp. 1–9. IEEE (2013)
36. Rødseth, Ø.J., Tjora, Å.: A system architecture for an unmanned ship. In: Proceedings of the 13th International Conference on Computer and IT Applications in the Maritime Industries (COMPIT) (2014)

37. Sedgewick, A.: Framework for improving critical infrastructure cybersecurity, version 1.1. Technical report, National Institute of Standards and Technology (2019)
38. Sikora-Fernandez, D., Stawasz, D., et al.: The concept of smart city in the theory and practice of urban development management. Rom. J. Reg. Sci. **10**(1), 86–99 (2016)
39. SINTEF: Test site opens for unmanned vessels. http://bit.ly/sintefTestSites
40. Skille, A., Lorentzen, S.: Foreslår førerløs passasjerferge i Trondheim. http://bit.ly/nrkTrondheim
41. Yoon, I.: Technology assessment - autonomous ships, September 2018. https://doi.org/10.13140/RG.2.2.36778.88009

Simulation-Based Evaluation of DDoS Against Smart Grid SCADAs

Damjan Gogic[1], Bojan Jelacic[1], and Imre Lendak[1,2](✉)

[1] Faculty of Technical Sciences, University of Novi Sad, Novi Sad, Serbia
lendak@uns.ac.rs

[2] Faculty of Informatics, Eötvös Loránd University, Budapest, Hungary

Abstract. The goal of this paper is to simulate the effects of different Distributed Denial of Service (DDoS) attack scenarios which might be launched against smart grid Supervisory Control and Data Acquisition systems, i.e. SCADAs. We will analyze attacks which are launched from compromised Remote Terminal Units (RTUs) located in the process environment. We created an ICS testbed and industrial DDoS simulator environment consisting of a single C&C server and a configurable number of bots. We simulated scenarios with different numbers of hacked RTUs trying to overwhelm the SCADA with unwanted messages. We analyzed the effects of DDoS-type attacks against SCADAs with different internal queue architectures used to manage the incoming messages, i.e. no queues, single queue and separate queue for each connected RTU.

Keywords: Distributed Denial of Service (DDoS) · Supervisory Control and Data Acquisition (SCADA) · Process environment · SCADA queue architecture · Remote Terminal Unit · Distributed Network Protocol Version 3 (DNP3)

1 Introduction

Information and cyber security in Industrial Control Systems (ICS) is receiving exemplary focus ever since the 2010 Stuxnet cyberattacks against the Iranian nuclear facility in Natanz, which was launched from the cyber domain, but resulted in physical destruction of centrifuges used in nuclear fuel processing. The 2015 and 2016 cyber-attacks against selected elements of the Ukrainian electric power system further emphasized that trend. In the 2015 Ukraine attacks the perpetrators managed to gain a foothold in the information technology (IT) environment of the targeted distribution system operators (DSOs), laterally moved into the ICS networks belonging to the operational technology (OT) domain and managed to turn off electricity for $\sim$225,000 customers for a duration of 1 to 6 h. Subsequent attacks incorporated more sophisticated tools and higher levels of attack automation, e.g. automatic enumeration of ICS devices and/or eavesdropping on OT networks relying on industrial communication protocols.

With the above background in mind, the goal of this paper is to present a simulation-based assessment of various distributed denial of service (DDoS) attack

S. Katsikas et al. (Eds.): ESORICS 2019 Workshops, LNCS 11980, pp. 86–97, 2020.
https://doi.org/10.1007/978-3-030-42048-2_6

scenarios originating from malevolently manipulated intelligent electronic devices (IED) in the process environment sending torrents of unsolicited measurement values to the ICS.

The paper is structured into five sections. The introduction is followed by the review of related works and problem definition. The ICS testbed and DDoS simulator are described in Sect. 4. Our experiments are presented in Sect. 5, which is followed by our concluding remarks.

2 State-of-the-Art Review

In our review of the state-of-the-art we analyze the latest developments in ICS security, denial of service attacks in ICS, as well as ICS security simulation testbeds.

2.1 ICS Security

ICS security entered the limelight in the 2010s, following the most publicized ICS attacks, e.g. the 2010 Stuxnet and the 2015 and 2016 attacks against (electric power) distribution system operators (DSOs) in Ukraine. The Stuxnet attack was the first well-known attack in which attackers succeeded to start an attack from the cyber domain which resulted in the physical destruction of equipment. The advanced persistent threat (APT) actors managed to install malware in an Iranian nuclear facility which replaced legitimate control software and code in an air-gapped ICS [17]. In the 2015 Ukraine attacks the attackers utilized spear phishing to obtain an initial foothold, followed up by lateral movement from the information technology (IT) to the operational technology (OT) environment to hijack operators' control sessions and issue illicit commands via the SCADA and turn off electricity for up to ~225,000 customers [18]. Even before the above attacks, ICS security was a hot research topic. Different authors listed and analyzed the different cybersecurity challenges arising in the latest SCADA solutions [13, 15, 21]. It became mainstream knowledge that the historically closed and proprietary SCADA solutions opened up via their transition to TCP/IP and their interconnections with external systems [6]. A study published in 2007 analyzed different SCADA solutions for the electric power sector and found that vendors did not implement adequate security measures in their products [5]. Specific security strategies were developed for SCADA networks [4], which became necessary as soon as ICS networks started using the TCP/IP protocol stack. ICS-specific intrusion detection techniques were developed for detecting anomalous network traffic [3]. Others refer to a move from "islands of automation" towards "totally integrated computer environments" in which it is necessary to (at least logically) separate the operational from the administrative (i.e. IT) environment [8]. The authors in [9] list potential vulnerabilities, known and possible threats in SCADA systems and describe security strategies for remediation. A comparative analysis of relevant SCADA security standards is presented in [29]. A very detailed listing of SCADA vulnerabilities is listed in [21]. A cyber warfare-sensitive overview of the latest threat sources (i.e. potential adversaries), threats, flaws, exploits, risks and mitigation strategies in the area of SCADA security is presented in [22]. In the latest publications the authors usually generalize and mostly focus on ICS instead of the SCADA only. Reference [16] surveys the latest cybersecurity risk measurement methods and research in ICS. Attack detection is discussed in [24]. More specifically, the authors present a mathematical framework, monitoring limitations and centralized and distributed attack detection and identification. The Distributed Network Protocol's security features are assessed in [25].

2.2 Denial of Service

Denial of service (DoS) and distributed denial of services (DDoS) attacks aim to disrupt the third element of the confidentiality-integrity-availability (CIA) triad, namely availability. Their goal is to interrupt the availability of data or services by deleting data or overloading/crashing services. DDoS attacks usually attempt to overload critical services by sending unsolicited messages from multiple sources, resulting in service unavailability due to depleted memory (RAM) or processor (CPU) time. An assessment of a class of denial-of-service (DoS) attack models in the optimal control for a discrete time, linear dynamical system is presented in [1]. An assessment of different DoS scenarios on load frequency control (LFC) in smart grids is evaluated in [19]. Others simulate the stochastic process of packet delay jitter and loss under local network and non-local network DoS attacks [20]. DoS attacks can be classified as either weak or strong. Mitigation strategies for both types of attacks and experiments involving a DC motor controlled via a network under DoS attack are presented in [23]. Yuan et al explain in their paper [33] that DoS attacks might lead to severe delays and degradation of control capabilities in cyber-physical systems (CPS). They go on to present a design of DoS-resilient CPS control systems. They illustrate their design principles on a power system example.

2.3 ICS Testbeds

Some authors concluded that it was necessary to build large scale SCADA testbed requirements, deployment strategies and potential hurdles as early as 2007 [6]. Others were focusing on developing specific testbeds for assessing the vulnerabilities introduced by using general-purpose communication networks (i.e. TCP/IP) and possible threats grouped into the following three categories: terrorist groups/adversarial nation states, malicious insiders and script kiddies, whom they describe as individuals with great hacking skills utilizing off-the-shelf hacking tools [7]. Wang et al describe an extensible SCADA simulation environment including a simulated enterprise net-work, OPC clients and servers, SCADA, RTU, as well as actuators and sensors [32]. A power system-specific experiment was conducted at Iowa State, where a cyber-physical system (CPS) security testbed was used to implement and evaluate cyberattacks against Automatic Generation Control (AGC) [2]. The authors evaluated the effects of an attack targeting the integrity of tie-line and frequency measurements. It was concluded that such attacks could result in under frequency conditions and unwanted load shedding. A systematic smart grid testbed research conducted by Qasim et al. [26] consists of (1) an overview of electrical power grid SCADA system vulnerabilities and threats, (2) testbed research areas, implementation, and design approaches, and (3) a scalable and reconfigurable SCADA cybersecurity testbed proposal. Early SCADA testbeds [10] usually had a simple system architecture not yet aligned with the IEC 62443 layered security model [14]. The PowerCyber testbed was designed to closely resemble real-life power grid communications and was therefore equipped with field devices and SCADA software. It was designed to support both education and research purposes [11]. The authors of a 2015 survey on ICS testbeds explains that the extreme availability requirements of real-life ICS make it challenging to conduct security tests in practice, i.e. on systems already deployed in industrial settings. They argue that this is the reason why researchers and practitioners turn to ICS testbeds and go on to identify and asses 30 such testbeds [12]. An open, virtual testbed for ICS is presented in [28]. The authors of [27] build a modular testbed, mimicking a SCADA network and controlling real sensors and actuators via the Modbus protocol. The authors use their testbed to evaluate the effects of different DDoS scenarios on SCADA operations. An ICS cybersecurity testbed written in Python and consisting of virtual devices and process de-vices is presented in [28]. The Smart City Testbed (SCT) developed at the Washington State University (WSU) was used to analyze potential cyber intrusions and anomaly detection systems (ADS) in substations, which are key components of smart grids [30]. The scalable and reconfigurable, virtual SCADA security testbed presented in [31] was used to evaluate the effects a DDoS-type false data injection attack would have on normal SCADA operation.

3 Problem Definition

The primary goal of this research is to develop an ICS testbed for investigating the potential effects of DDoS attacks originating from the process (i.e. operational technology - OT) environment. The secondary goal is to investigate the impact of DDoS attacks against different SCADA queue management solutions.

It was the authors' intention to investigate the extent of impact a few hijacked RTUs could have on the operational performance of complex ICS, which consisted of additional services consuming data forwarded by the SCADA. It was planned to specifically analyze the behavior of those services, which require high CPU, RAM and/or storage capacities. One such service is the calculation engine present in electric power systems, which runs energy and/or distribution management system functions (EMS/DMS), e.g. topology analysis, load flow, contingency analysis, short circuit calculations.

4 System Architecture

4.1 Smart Grid ICS Testbed

The software architecture of the experimental expert system environment is presented in the below figure. All elements were developed by the authors or their team members as part of a joint project. The solution development was closely monitored by senior software engineers and professors who participated in the creation of multiple industry-grade ICS solutions sold on international markets.

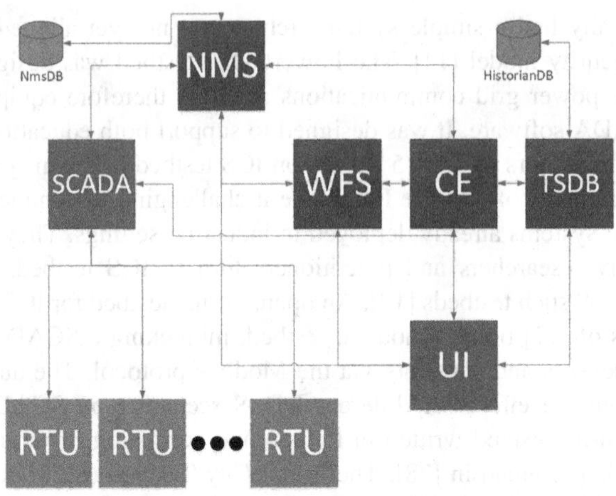

Fig. 1. Simplified smart grid ICS architecture

The key elements of the ICS environment presented in Fig. 1 were the following:

- The Supervisory Control and Data Acquisition (SCADA) service collects, transforms and visualizes data from the process environment and allows operators to issue commands.
- The Network Model Service (NMS) is the single source of truth for the electric power system's network model, which it serves to the other services whose functionality depends on having up-to-date network model information.
- The Weather Forecast Service (WFS) collects and serves weather forecast information to the other elements of the system.
- The Calculation Engine (CE) extends the SCADA with network optimization functionality, e.g. topology analysis, load flow, contingency analysis, short circuit calculations. It relies on data collected from the NMS, SCADA and WFS.
- The Time Series Database (TSDB) stores and provides access to historical values, e.g. all past measurements, commands and network model changes.
- Remote Terminal Units (RTU) are industrial computers deployed inside the process environment, which collect measurement values from sensors and forward control commands to actuators.
- The User Interface (UI), or the Human Machine Interface allows the operators to monitor and control the underlying physical process.

4.2 SCADA Architecture

We experimented with different internal message queue management solutions inside the SCADA service. More specifically, we implemented the following three message queue solutions inside our SCADA service:

1. No message queues. In this SCADA architecture (cf. Fig. 2) a single thread is assigned to each RTU, which accepts messages, does engineering unit transformations, checks values for alarms and notifies subscribed parties about the received values.

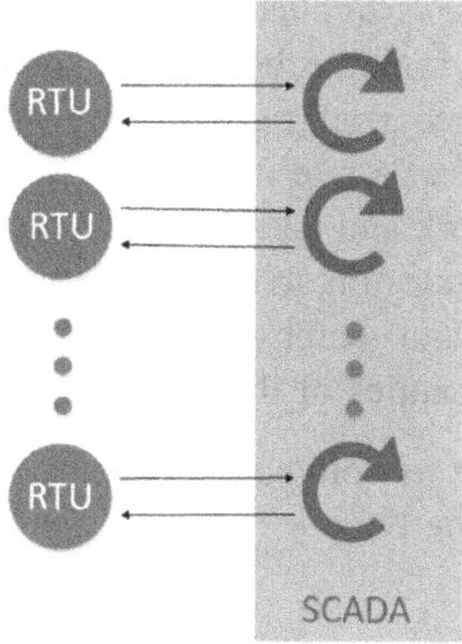

Fig. 2. SCADA with no message queues

2. Single message queue. This architecture assigns one thread to each RTU to accept messages, which are stored in a single, internal message queue. When the RTU threads put the received messages into the single queue, they notify a single message processing thread to take over and process the content.
3. Multiple message queues. SCADA solutions in this group assign a separate message queue and two threads to each RTU (Fig. 3). One thread is tasked to receive messages, and the other does the data processing.

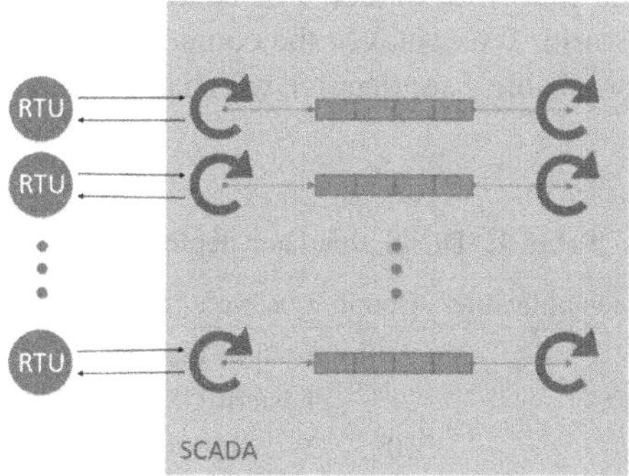

Fig. 3. SCADA with multiple message queues

4.3 ICS DDoS Simulator

The main goal of the ICS-specific DDoS simulator was to simulate multiple hacked RTUs, located in the process environment and sending unsolicited (i.e. unwanted) Distributed Network Protocol Version 3 (DNP3) messages to the central ICS solution, (usually) deployed in a control center.

We chose the centralized DDoS architecture, which consisted of a single command and control server (C&C) and multiple bots which report to the C&C and receive command from it. We developed configurable bots, which received the target's IP address and the (unwanted) message rate used. It was envisaged that the bots will be connected to the SCADA network and take over the roles of regular RTUs during the reconnect cycles, i.e. when reconnecting to the SCADA service. The bots were capable to send valid DNP3 messages and thereby the SCADA could not differentiate them from regular RTUs. The core features of the C&C server were the following:

- Maintain a list of bots under its command.
- Send configuration data to the bots.

5 Experiments

All three SCADA architectures were implemented in the C# programming language. The DDoS simulator was also programmed in C#. The inter-bot communication and bot to C&C communications were implemented via duplex Windows Communication Foundation (WCF) channels. Each RTU was configured with 100 analog measurement values, i.e. they were capable to send 100 different values to the SCADA. We decided to use C# code in simulating industrial devices, as we considered that the attackers would substitute the IEDs with simple, general purpose computers capable to be programmed in C#.

We deployed our DDoS simulation environment in the Microsoft Azure Cloud Computing Platform. The following numbers of elements were deployed in different data centers around the world. We deployed the components of our system in different geographical locations (see Table 1 for details), which allowed us to simulate a realistic distributed system.

Table 1. DDoS simulator deployment.

Service/application	Count	Location
C&C	1	Central France
SCADA	1	Eastern USA
Bot	10	W/N Europe + E. USA
RTU	10	W/N Europe + E. USA

We performed three specific experiments, described shortly in the next sub-sections.

5.1 Experiment #1: Zero Bots

In our first experiment we measured the baseline load of the ICS shown in Fig. 1. There were no malicious RTUs in this scenario. We measured CPU load and RAM use with all three SCADA queue architectures listed. RAM use was constant as well as CPU load, which varied periodically, but without significant anomalies. The results of our 5-hour-long measurements are shown in the Fig. 4 below.

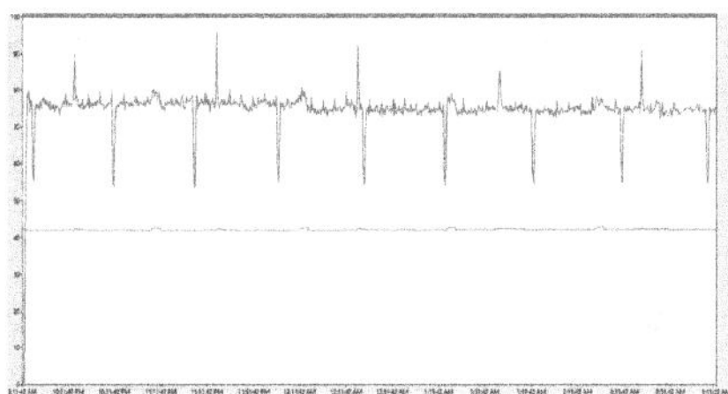

Fig. 4. Baseline ICS loads: CPU and RAM

During the test all ICS services operated regularly and there were no visualization delays in the SCADA human-machine interface (HMI) and it was available to receive and forward (operator-issued) commands. All messages were processed by the SCADA service in a timely manner. All values were forwarded to the Historian and stored. The calculation engine executed all calculations in a timely manner.

5.2 Experiment #2: 1 Bot

In the second experiment we measured the ICS load in the presence of a single bot, i.e. one malicious element introduced instead of a regular RTU. The bot was configured to continuously send measurement value changes for all 100 configured SCADA points. The bots were configured to generate unwanted measurement changes every 5 s. This rate was configurable from the C&C via the WCF interface of the bots.

We analyzed the behavior of all three SCADA queue management architectures. We observed a failure in the ICS which was configured with a SCADA with no message queues. The first component to fail was the calculation engine, followed by the SCADA service after 2 h of continuous bombardment with unsolicited messages (see Fig. 5 for details). We analyzed the SCADA logs and found out that although the SCADA with no queues was operational, it was losing data, i.e. it was not able to process all messages and forward them to the other services in a timely manner.

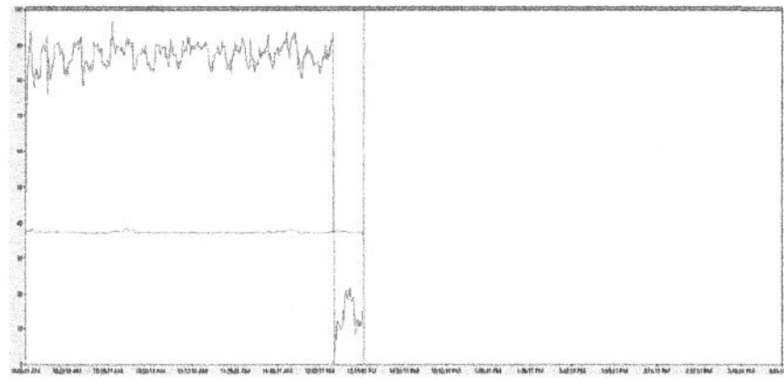

Fig. 5. 1-bot ICS loads: CPU and RAM

We analyzed the logs of the SCADA with a single message queue and observed that its message queue of messages waiting for processing contained 1000 messages in the 10th min of the simulation. After one hour, there were 7800 messages in the message queue, i.e. all those messages were delayed. None of the services failed, but the values were visualized with delay in the SCADA HMI. The length of the message queue was sufficient, so there were no messages lost. All messages were archived in the Historian.

The behavior of the SCADA with multiple message queues was similar to the single-queue architecture. Message processing delays were shorter, as we observed maximum queue length of 2800 at the end of the 5-hour simulation run.

5.3 Experiment #3: 5 Bots

In the third experiment we measured the ICS load in the presence of 5 bots introduced instead of regular RTUs. The bots were configured to send measurement value changes for all 100 configured SCADA points continuously.

The ICS solution configured with a no-queue SCADA failed as in the previous experiment. The one-queue SCADA proved to be more resilient, but its message queue was ~5,000-long after only 10 min and contained 145,000 messages at the end of the 5-hour simulation run. The calculation engine failed after 2 h and it was restarted manually. The SCADA did not fail. We observed varying CPU load and a continuous rise in RAM use in this scenario - see Fig. 6 for details.

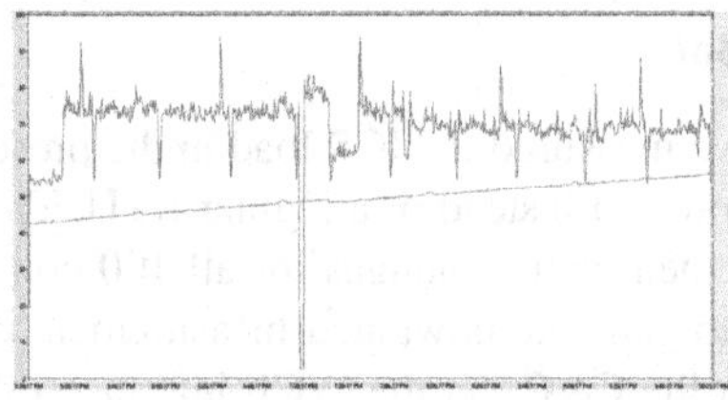

Fig. 6. 5-bot ICS loads: CPU and RAM

Even the multiple-queue SCADA failed to properly respond to the data loads generated in the 5-bot simulation scenario. At the end of the 5-hour simulation, the messages queues handling the bots were up to 80,000 message-long. CPU load rose by 14\%. The calculation engine failed after 2 h, similarly to the previous scenario. It was manually restarted, and the simulation run was not interrupted.

6 Conclusion

This paper presents an Industrial Control System (ICS) testbed and DDoS simulator used for investigating the potential effects of attacks originating from one or more manipulated Remote Terminal Units (RTUs) in the process environment.

The presented testbed consisted of RTUs, SCADA and other services running in the operational technology (OT) environment. The DDoS simulator had a centralized system architecture consisting of a single command and control server and a configurable number of bots. The bots were designed to impersonate regular RTUs during the RTU to SCADA reconnect phase. The ICS communication protocol used was DNP3.

The experiments conducted by the authors suggest that the presence of a single manipulated or malfunctioning RTU has significant negative impact on the operational capabilities of ICS. The negative impact is more pronounced for simple SCADA architectures without an adequate message queuing solution. We showed that a SCADA with no message queuing capabilities is incapable to respond to message flooding from even a single RTU. Even a SCADA with a dedicated message queue for each connected RTU would struggle if it would be bombarded from multiple manipulated RTUs, as shown in our 5-bot experiment.

Additionally, we showed that even if the SCADA was capable to process the unwanted messages resulting from a DDoS attack, the services consuming real-time data received from the SCADA would eventually fail. In our experiments the calculation engine running power system analyses (e.g. topology analysis, load flow, contingency analysis) was usually the first to fail.

As the DDoS simulator relies on a well-known ICS communication protocol, it can be potentially modified, extended and used in the simulation of other attack scenarios. Additionally, it can be extended with more elaborate DDoS traffic generation schemes which could more easily avoid detection by firewalls and/or intrusion detection systems.

The authors intend to extend this research and incorporate the results into a real-life cyber-physical testbed, consisting of a mix of virtual and physical components, e.g. sensors and actuators.

Acknowledgment. This work was supported by the Ministry of Education, Science and Technological Development of the Republic of Serbia under grants III-42004 and TR33013. The authors received funding from the EU's Education, Audiovisual and Culture Executive Agency (EACEA) under the Erasmus+ Capacity Building in the Field of Higher Education (CBHE) grant number 586474-EPP-1-2017-1-RS-EPPKA2-CBHE-JP.

References

1. Amin, S., Cárdenas, A.A., Sastry, S.S.: Safe and secure networked control systems under denial-of-service attacks. In: Majumdar, R., Tabuada, P. (eds.) HSCC 2009. LNCS, vol. 5469, pp. 31–45. Springer, Heidelberg (2009). https://doi.org/10.1007/978-3-642-00602-9_3
2. Ashok, A., Wang, P., Brown, M., Govindarasu, M.: Experimental evaluation of cyber attacks on automatic generation control using a CPS security testbed. In: 2015 IEEE Power & Energy Society General Meeting, pp. 1–5. IEEE (2015)
3. Barbosa, R.R.R., Pras, A.: Intrusion detection in SCADA networks. In: Stiller, B., De Turck, F. (eds.) AIMS 2010. LNCS, vol. 6155, pp. 163–166. Springer, Heidelberg (2010). https://doi.org/10.1007/978-3-642-13986-4_23

4. Chandia, R., Gonzalez, J., Kilpatrick, T., Papa, M., Shenoi, S.: Security strategies for SCADA networks. In: Goetz, E., Shenoi, S. (eds.) ICCIP 2007. IIFIP, vol. 253, pp. 117–131. Springer, Boston (2008). https://doi.org/10.1007/978-0-387-75462-8_9
5. Chikuni, E., Dondo, M.: Investigating the security of electrical power systems SCADA. In: IEEE AFRICON 2007, Windhoek, South Africa, pp. 1–7. IEEE (2007)
6. Christiansson, H., Luiijf, E.: Creating a European SCADA security testbed. In: Goetz, E., Shenoi, S. (eds.) ICCIP 2007. IIFIP, vol. 253, pp. 237–247. Springer, Boston (2008). https://doi.org/10.1007/978-0-387-75462-8_17
7. Davis, C.M., Tate, J.E., Okhravi, H., Grier, C., Overbye, T.J., Nicol, D.: SCADA cyber security testbed development. In: 2006 38th North American Power Symposium, pp. 483–488. IEEE (2006)
8. Ericsson, G.N.: Cyber security and power system communication—essential parts of a smart grid infrastructure. IEEE Trans. Power Deliv. **25**(3), 1501–1507 (2010)
9. Fernandez, J.D., Fernandez, A.E.: SCADA systems: vulnerabilities and remediation. J. Comput. Sci. Coll. **20**(4), 160–168 (2005)
10. Giani, A., Karsai, G., Roosta, T., Shah, A., Sinopoli, B., Wiley, J.: A testbed for secure and robust SCADA systems. SIGBED Rev. **5**(2), 4 (2008)
11. Hahn, A., et al.: Development of the PowerCyber SCADA security testbed. In: Proceedings of the Sixth Annual Workshop on Cyber Security and Information Intelligence Research, p. 21. ACM (2010)
12. Holm, H., Karresand, M., Vidström, A., Westring, E.: A survey of industrial control system testbeds. In: Buchegger, S., Dam, M. (eds.) Nordic Conference on Secure IT Systems, vol. 9417, pp. 11–26. Springer, Cham (2015). https://doi.org/10.1007/978-3-319-26502-5_2
13. Igure, V.M., Laughter, S.A., Williams, R.D.: Security issues in SCADA networks. Comput. Secur. **25**(7), 498–506 (2006)
14. International Electrotechnical Commission (IEC): Industrial communication networks - Network and system security - Part 3-3: System security requirements and security levels. IEC 62443-3-3, Geneva, Switzerland (2013)
15. Johnson, R.E.: Survey of SCADA security challenges and potential attack vectors. In: 2010 IEEE International Conference for Internet Technology and Secured Transactions, London, United Kingdom, pp. 1–5. IEEE (2010)
16. Knowles, W., Prince, D., Hutchison, D., Disso, J.F.P., Jones, K.: A survey of cyber security management in industrial control systems. Int. J. Crit. Infrastruct. Prot. **9**, 52–80 (2015)
17. Kushner, D.: The real story of Stuxnet. IEEE Spectr. **3**(50), 48–53 (2014)
18. Lee, R.M., Assante, M.J., Conway, T.: Analysis of the Cyber Attack on the Ukrainian Power Grid. Defense Use Case, SANS ICS (2016)
19. Liu, S., Liu, X.P., El Saddik, A.: Denial-of-Service (DoS) attacks on load frequency control in smart grids. In: 2013 IEEE PES Innovative Smart Grid Technologies Conference (ISGT), Washington DC, USA, pp. 1–6. IEEE (2013)
20. Long, M., Wu, C.H., Hung, J.Y.: Denial of service attacks on network-based control systems: impact and mitigation. IEEE Trans. Ind. Inform. **1**(2), 85–96 (2005)
21. Nazir, S., Patel, S., Patel, D.: Assessing and augmenting SCADA cyber security: a survey of techniques. Comput. Secur. **70**, 436–454 (2017)
22. Nicholson, A., Webber, S., Dyer, S., Patel, T., Janicke, H.: SCADA security in the light of Cyber-Warfare. Comput. Secur. **31**(4), 418–436 (2012)
23. Pang, Z.H., Liu, G.P., Dong, Z.: Secure networked control systems under denial of service attacks. IFAC Proc. Vol. **44**(1), 8908–8913 (2011)
24. Pasqualetti, F., Dörfler, F., Bullo, F.: Attack detection and identification in cyber-physical systems. IEEE Trans. Autom. Control **58**(11), 2715–2729 (2013)

25. Patwardhan, M.: DNP3: security and scalability analysis. Sacramento. California State University (2012)
26. Qassim, Q.S., Jamil, N., Daud, M., Hasan, H.C.: Towards implementing scalable and reconfigurable SCADA security testbed in power system environment. Int. J. Crit. Infrastruct. **15**(2), 91–120 (2019)
27. Queiroz, C., Mahmood, A., Hu, J., Tari, Z., Yu, X.: Building a SCADA security testbed. In: Third IEEE International Conference on Network and System Security, Gold Coast, Queensland, Australia, pp. 357–364. IEEE (2009)
28. Reaves, B., Morris, T.: An open virtual testbed for industrial control system security research. Int. J. Inf. Secur. **11**(4), 215–229 (2012)
29. Sommestad, T., Ericsson, G.N., Nordlander, J.: SCADA system cyber security—a comparison of standards. In: IEEE PES General Meeting, Minneapolis, Minnesota, USA, pp. 1–8. IEEE (2010)
30. Sun, C.C., Hahn, A., Liu, C.C.: Cyber security of a power grid: state-of-the-art. Int. J. Electr. Power Energy Syst. **99**, 45–56 (2018)
31. Tesfahun, A., Bhaskari, D.L.: A SCADA testbed for investigating cyber security vulnerabilities in critical infrastructures. Autom. Control Comput. Sci. **50**(1), 54–62 (2016)
32. Wang, C., Fang, L., Dai, Y.: A simulation environment for SCADA security analysis and assessment. In: 2010 IEEE International Conference on Measuring Technology and Mechatronics Automation, Changsha, China, pp. 342–347. IEEE (2010)
33. Yuan, Y., Zhu, Q., Sun, F., Wang, Q., Başar, T.: Resilient control of cyber-physical systems against denial-of-service attacks. In: 2013 6th International Symposium on Resilient Control Systems (ISRCS), San Francisco, USA, pp. 54–59. IEEE (2013)

Identifying Safety and Human Factors Issues in Rail Using IRIS and CAIRIS

Amna Altaf[1(✉)], Shamal Faily[1], Huseyin Dogan[1], Alexios Mylonas[1], and Eylem Thron[2]

[1] Bournemouth University, Fern Barrow, Poole, UK
{aaltaf,sfaily,hdogan,amylonas}@bournemouth.ac.uk
[2] Ricardo Rail, 30 Eastbourne Terrace, London, UK
eylem.thron@ricardo.com

Abstract. Security, safety and human factors engineering techniques are largely disconnected although the concepts are interlinked. We present a tool-supported approach based on the Integrating Requirements and Information Security (IRIS) framework using Computer Aided Integration of Requirements and Information Security (CAIRIS) platform to identify the safety and human factors issues in rail. We illustrate this approach with a case study, which provides a vehicle for increasing the existing collaboration between engineers in security, safety and human factors.

Keywords: Security by design · Safety hazards · Human factors · IRIS

1 Introduction

As the rail information infrastructure becomes integrated with operational technology, new vulnerabilities are introduced together with the new threats that exploit them. As such attacks are directly or indirectly responsible for compromising safety, cyber security has become a new concern for rail safety engineers. Poor design decisions made during security engineering may lead operators to make human errors or mistakes where rules are intentionally disobeyed [14], which may eventually affect system safety. Therefore, rail infrastructures can only be made safe and secure if along with safety and security, the human factors engineers contribute to its design and evaluation.

In this paper, we illustrate such an approach where the core concepts from the Integrating Requirements and Information Security (IRIS) framework are used to define an intersecting model, based on a proposed relationship between different security-by-design and usability techniques. This approach is tool-supported using the open-source Computer Aided Integration of Requirements and Information Security (CAIRIS) platform[1].

[1] https://cairis.org.

S. Katsikas et al. (Eds.): ESORICS 2019 Workshops, LNCS 11980, pp. 98–107, 2020.
https://doi.org/10.1007/978-3-030-42048-2_7

A key contribution of this work is the use of Human Factors Analysis and Classification System (HFACS) to augment IRIS framework and CAIRIS platform to identify safety and security issues. This helps rail stakeholders better understand the safety and human factors implications of security concerns, and also helps discover inter-dependencies between security, safety and human factors engineering techniques.

In Sect. 2, we describe the related work upon which our approach is based, followed by the explanation of our approach in Sect. 3. We illustrate this approach with a case study example in Sect. 4, before concluding and discussing future directions for our work in Sect. 5.

2 Related Work

2.1 Security and Safety Challenges in Rail Infrastructure

The rail infrastructure has long been managed in accordance with health and safety standards, working within legislative requirements such as in United Kingdom the Railway Act 2005, under guidance and supervision from bodies like Railway Safety and Standards Board (RSSB) and Office of Rail Regulation (ORR). More recently, the shift to digitalisation stipulated by the European Railway Traffic Management System (ERTMS) imposed by European Union has seen the introduction of the Common Safety Method for Risk Evaluation and Assessment (CSM-REA) in addition to UK specific safety concepts such as 'As Low As Reasonably Practicable' (ALARP) in managing safety risks.

The evolving nature of the cyber threats have imposed a greater challenge for security experts in rail [12]. As a result, the rail infrastructure needs to be supported by codes of practice (CoPs) throughout its life cycle as a combination of security and safety [6]. Security should be infused with safety at a design phase by ensuring a combined risk assessment approach.

Similarly, the strong linkage between the human intent to violate rules and imposed safety hazards described by [3] highlights the value of combining safety with human factors. The Human Factors Analysis and Classification System (HFACS) is a framework for eliciting possible accident and incident contribution factors based on taxonomy of active and latent failures caused by human interactions in rail [17]. The HFACS have been used by rail stakeholders to determine the human error sources behind accidents and incidents. However, to date, there has been no work on how it can be used to consider safety or security attributes of rail system.

2.2 Bridging Security, Safety, and Human Factors

Hazards and accidents may occur due to security breaches, and dependability – delivering services that can justifiably trusted – encompasses safety and some major elements of security [5]. Safety is an attribute of dependability, with availability, reliability, integrity and maintainability; security refers to the availability and integrity attributes and to confidentiality [13]. Thus the risk factors (probability of chances of damage) along with the dependability (trust and reliance on system) are triggered by safety and security issues. Both safety and security engineering communities are now working to better bridge their communities [11], e.g. safety engineering consideration of *security mindedness* [6].

Previous work has considered human error as an intersecting concept between cyber security and safety. Humans may cause harm by making mistakes (active failures) or by inducing errors within system (latent failures) [7], with human intent as a differentiating factor. If humans are benevolent (unintentional), they may alert the safety engineers by causing hazards and accidents; if malevolent (intentional), they may carry out threats and exploit vulnerabilities that compromise system security [16], thereby leading to a risk instigating a safety hazard.

2.3 IRIS and CAIRIS

The Integrating Requirements and Information Security (IRIS) process framework [8] was devised to understand how design concepts associated with security, usability, and software engineering could be aligned. It is complemented by the Computer Aided Integration of Requirements and Information Security (CAIRIS) platform, which acts as an exemplar for tool-support to manage and analyse design data collected when applying an IRIS process. IRIS and CAIRIS have been used in several real-world case studies, including the development of security policies for critical infrastructure systems [9].

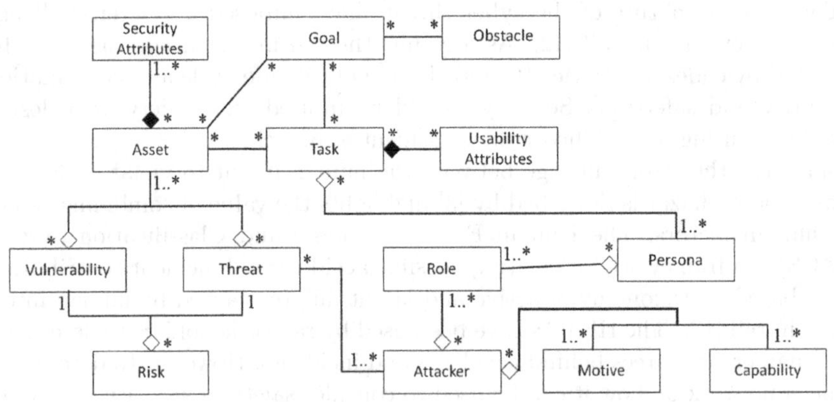

Fig. 1. UML class diagram of IRIS

The core IRIS concepts are illustrated in the UML class diagram in Fig. 1. Vulnerabilities and threats contribute to potential risks, and threats are contingent on attacker's intent. This intent helps analysts identify the tasks and goals they carry out or exploit, which can help determine human factors issues in the form of human errors (active failures). Consequently, although not explicitly designed with safety in mind, IRIS provides a foundation for integrating security, safety and human factors.

3 Approach

We have devised an approach based on the IRIS framework, which leverages security and usability engineering approaches to better understand the safety implications of rail infrastructure under design. This approach is tool-supported using CAIRIS. The approach takes input from security and human factors engineers, as well as from rail stakeholders with safety expertise.

3.1 Asset Modelling and Their Associations

The approach begins with a security analysis of the system and its environment by identifying the possible assets [10]. These assets and their relationships are modelled using UML class diagrams. Each asset is defined in a particular environment, and categorised by asset types. The security attributes for assets like confidentiality, integrity, availability are defined and values (Low, Medium, High) are assigned, based on priorities defined by the rail stakeholders.

3.2 Roles and Attacker Personas

The roles are defined based on stakeholder roles in rail like driver, manager, ticketing staff, signaller etc. The roles are further used to identify specific personas describing the archetypical behaviour of system actors. Attacker personas are created by following the approach described in [4]; this approach entails using qualitative data analysis and argumentation models to form the basis of personas characteristics. *Factoids* underpinning the personas are elicited by categorising data about attackers, and thematically analysing these factoids based on affinity groups. CAIRIS facilitates online affinity diagramming, and allows annotated factoid lists to be imported into CAIRIS as personas characteristic argumentation models. These argumentation models are based on Toulmin's model of argumentation, such that each characteristic is justified by one or more *grounds* that evidence the persona's validity, *warrants* that act as inference rules connecting the grounds to the characteristic, and *rebuttals* that act as counterarguments for the characteristic. A model qualifier is also used to describe the confidence in the validity of the personas characteristic. Attacker personas narratives are then specified based on these personas characteristics.

3.3 Vulnerabilities Identification and Threat Modelling

The vulnerabilities are weaknesses of the system, which, if exploited, leads to a security breach [8]. While identifying vulnerabilities, the assets open to attack are identified. Personas support this exercise by providing an insight into an attacker's mind, given that an attacker's model of the system may be different from a security engineer's model of the same system. Attacker's motivation and capabilities play an important role in threat identification. Tasks and goals fulfilled by attackers also provide an insight during threat modelling. The threats identified are assigned security properties based on the goals of attacker.

3.4 Risk Analysis

Vulnerabilities and threats contribute to the identification of potential risks [8]. Using risk analysis, the likelihood and severity of an incident is determined based on the ability of an attacker, and the value of assets that need to be protected. CAIRIS generates visual risk models based on this analysis, which are used as the basis for further analysis.

3.5 Task and Goal-Obstacle Modelling

Based on asset modelling and risk analysis, the concerned tasks and goals are elicited. These form the basis of system and user level goals. Tasks and goals are identified from the attacker's perspective and also form the basis for *obstacles* that model obstructions to system goals. Goal and task models can help the security engineers to better understand the system threat model.

3.6 Identification of Safety Hazards

The risk model generated by CAIRIS determines the safety hazards, by showing the linkage between the assets with their associated security attributes, vulnerabilities, emergent threats and the possible risks. The main purpose of this type of modelling is to identify the possible safeguards to be taken and minimise the chances of occurrence of any hazardous events.

3.7 Human Factors Analysis

Our approach uses HFACS as a multi-level framework defining human factors in four main categories [15]: unsafe acts of operations, preconditions for unsafe acts, unsafe supervision and organizational influences. In lieu of a standardised methodology for determining the human error sources using HFACS, each vulnerability, threat and risk identified as part of threat model is analysed against the human factors definitions according to HFACS. The value with the closest possible explanation for human error is labelled as the desired human factors issue.

4 Case Study - Polish Tram Incident

We illustrate our approach by applying it to a real life incident where a security breach occurred by exploiting a system vulnerability, leading to the compromise of passenger safety[2]. The 2008 incident was logged as *School Boy Hacks into Polish Tram System* in the 'Repository of Industrial Security Incidents' [2].

We gathered open source intelligence as an input to our approach. This was based on several online articles written about the particular Polish Tram Incident. We supplemented publicly available data with the Operational Concept for European Railway Traffic Management System (ERTMS); this was used to understand the system architecture, application levels, operating modes, signalling principles and control. We also obtained feedback on the emerging CAIRIS model from safety and human factors experts at Ricardo, who were representative of the rail stakeholder that might provide input to our approach.

4.1 Asset Modelling and Their Associations

Two working environments were defined: *Morning* and *Night shift.* The *Morning Shift* is based on assumption that it is expected to be much busier in terms of passenger numbers, compared to operations that take place during *Night Shift.* 51 assets were identified, based on types of software, hardware, information and people. Assets were modelled by taking an attacker's perspective of the tram system, thus helping the security engineers to understand the relevant vulnerabilities. Asset modelling was not limited to the early stages of the process; at later stages asset associations were also defined. For instance, during attacker personas definition three assets namely *Infrared Remote Control*, *Public Libraries* and *Internet Codes* were identified. These assets formed the basis for determining the capabilities of an attacker who learned the coding for building infrared remote control from the Internet.

4.2 Roles and Attacker Personas

The analysis about the rail infrastructure lead to the recognition of 11 roles. The most notable was the role of *Attacker.* Based on online articles and incident records, we concluded that the attacker did not wish to intentionally cause harm. Instead, attacks were exploratory in nature with no consideration given to the consequences. The role of attacker further motivated us to understand the intent and capability behind the cyber attack with the help of personas.

We created an attacker persona *Adam* based on relevant sources for the Polish Tram incident, which provided different perspectives of the incident. *Adam* was built based on 18 argumentation models used to specify 18 complementary personas characteristics, underpinned by 47 factoids. For example, the persona characteristic *Working Knowledge about Railways* describes how *Adam* gained access to the rail network based on his skills and knowledge; he recorded and replayed signals using a universal remote control. Based on this, we identified a system vulnerability, i.e., the *1970s Switching System* on which Poland Tram System was operating, and the subsequent threat of *Unauthorised Access into Poland Railway Signalling System.*

[2] The final model created, including references to online sources used, is available from: https://bit.ly/2KSocEg.

4.3 Vulnerabilities Identification and Threat Modelling

By exploring the attacker motives, 4 vulnerabilities were identified namely, *Poor Architectural Design and Lack of Risk Assessment, 1970s Switching System, Reported Problems with Signalling System* and *Fautly Track Points.* These vulnerabilities were responsible for compromising the security of 6 assets.

We also identified 3 threats: *Poland Railway Network Intrusion, Replay Attack* and *Switch Splitting.* The anticipation of possible threats and cyber-attacks at design level is the work of security engineers, but considering *Adam's* perspective helped identify exploitable vulnerabilities. For example, the threat *Poland Railway Network Intrusion* was based on our interpretation of *Adam's* ability to exploit *Faulty Track Points.*

4.4 Risk Analysis

Within an environment of *Morning Shift*, 4 risks were defined using vulnerabilities and threats. These form the basis of the risk analysis, the results of which are illustrated in Fig. 2. The threat of *Switch Splitting* based on vulnerability of *Faulty Track Points*, could lead to risk of *Train Derailment.* On the basis of this risk, security design decisions that minimise the chances of occurrence of this risk can be taken. The risk analysis also contributed towards the better understanding of visible safety hazards and human factors issues based on their occurrence and likelihood ratios.

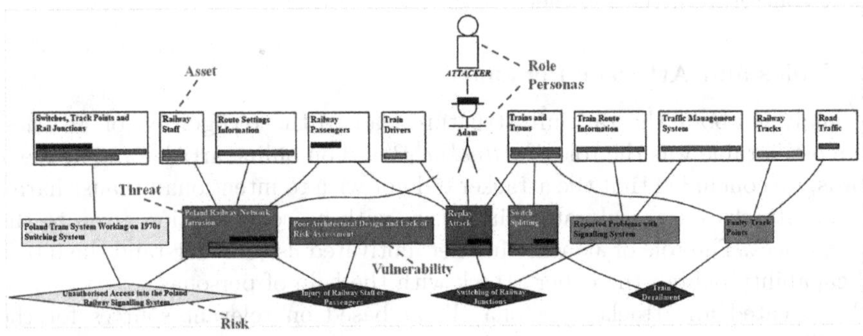

Fig. 2. Risk modelling in CAIRIS

4.5 Task and Goal-Obstacle Modelling

The narrative of attacker personas formed the basis for responsibility modelling which comprised of identification of 4 tasks performed by attacker to conduct the cyber-attack. Adam *learned coding skills* from his class and the internet before he *built an infrared device* by modifying a universal remote control. Adam used that infrared device to *record signals and replayed* them to *switch track points.*

The completion of these tasks lead to the satisfaction of system goals (*Modify TV Remote Control*, *Access Railway Network* and *Redirect Railway Trams*) on the part of attacker.

The attack was conducted by exploiting system loop-holes. The exploitation of these loop-holes were active failures on the part of security engineers. For example, the vulnerability *Reported Problems with Signalling System* led to the human factors issue of *Violations* as the operation and performance of signalling system was not compliant with secured protocols and standards. This allowed the attacker to perform the task of *Record Signals*, fulfilling the system goal *Access Railway Network*. In this case, the major security goal defined by security engineers which would have acted as an obstacle for attacker would have been the use of *Advanced Train Control Protocol System* which would have denied *Adam* an unauthorised access into the railway network. Thus, it would have mitigated the cyber-attack, and ensured the safety of passengers.

4.6 Identification of Safety Hazards

For explanation purposes, we consider the risk of *Switching of Railways Junctions* that is due to the threat of *Replay Attacks*. The realisation of this risk might cause *Collisions* between two or even more than two trains, which compromises the safety of passengers and staff present in train. Table 1 represents the identification of potential safety hazards from risk modelling elements (vulnerabilities, threats, risks) based on the Risk Assessment Log presented by Randstad Rail [1]. The documentation of Randstad Rail includes the activities and tasks in the railway sector which may lead to catastrophic hazards. The identified risks were used to categorise these safety hazards. Knowledge of these potential safety hazards is helpful for alerting safety engineers dealing with critical infrastructures.

4.7 Human Factors Analysis

Table 1 shows how the vulnerabilities, threats and risks identified can be categorised to determine the human factors issues based on HFACS along with safety hazards. These human factors issues also help us to verify the system usability for risks, by the satisfaction of user goals depending on certain procedures, competencies, permissions and training needs analysis (TNA) to achieve those goals and complete defined tasks.

For example, the risk of *Injury of Railway Staff or Passenger* which is linked to threat of *Poland Railway Network Intrusion*, may lead to safety hazard of *Loss of Life*. In this case, the human factors issue observed using the HFACS framework is the poor design of *Technological Environment* due to *Poor Architectural Design and Lack of Risk Assessment*, which has life-threatening consequences. This illustrates how the timely evaluation of technological environment using checklists and task factors can minimise the chances of risk occurrence.

Table 1. Human factors issues based on HFACS

Vulnerabilities	Threats	Associated risks	Safety hazards	Human factors
Faulty Track Points	Switch Splitting	Train Derailment	Life Threatening for Staff and Passengers in Train as well as near Train	Failed to Correct Known Problems
Reported Problems with Signalling System	Replay Attack	Switching of Railway Junctions	Collision (Between Two Trains or Even More Than Two Trains)	Violations
Poland Tram System working on 1970s Switching System	Poland Railway Network Intrusion Threat	Unauthorised Access into the Poland Railway Signalling System	Disruption of Train Services or Emergency Stop	Inadequate Supervision
Poor Architectural Design and Lack of Risk Assessment	Poland Railway Network Intrusion Threat	Injury of Railway Staff or Passengers	Loss of Life	Technological Environment

5 Discussion and Conclusion

In this paper, we presented a tool-support approach for identifying safety and human factor issues, based on core concepts from IRIS and CAIRIS. The scientific novelty has been the methodological application to safety and human factors engineering in rail. We carried out a preliminary evaluation of this approach by applying it to a case study where inter-dependencies between safety, security, and human factors were present. In doing so, we have made three contributions. First, our approach shows how asset modelling and their associations, can be used to identify security attributes namely, confidentiality, integrity, availability of assets as prioritised by rail stakeholders. Second, we have shown how building models of attackers not only rationalises attacker assumptions, but also helps to identify system vulnerabilities. Both lead to the identification of threats which, with the support of scenarios, rationalises risks and the identification of several safety hazards. On the basis of these hazards, root causes of active failures (human errors) like *violations* and *inadequate supervision* could be determined using HFACS. Finally, we have shown how building the personas for other roles like driver and signaller helps rail stakeholders determine the task scenarios in more detail. These task scenarios can be used by human factors engineers to inform hierarchical and cognitive task analysis which can predict the reliability of systems in different environments.

We are evaluating our approach on a project where the representative rail stakeholders will be closely involved when considering the risks, roles, tasks, goals, requirements, dependencies and obstacles between the humans and systems. In future work, we will present a refined process-framework based on best practices from safety, security and human factors engineering. For this purpose, further categorisation of tasks at system, design or operator levels using ERTMS specifications may have the potential to determine broader design weaknesses. A more thorough task analysis exercise could provide more detailed insights into human factors, and subsequent security and safety concerns. The resultant process-framework will be translated into tool-support for implementation in rail and other critical infrastructures.

Acknowledgements. The work described in this paper was funded by the BU studentship *Integrating Safety, Security, and Human Factors Engineering in Rail Infrastructure Design & Evaluation.* We are also grateful to Ricardo for their support.

References

1. Randstad Rail - Generic Risk Assessment Log. https://www.randstad.co.uk
2. RISI - The Repository of Industrial Security Incidents (2008). https://www.risidata.com
3. Alper, S.J., Karsh, B.T.: A systematic review of safety violations in industry. Accid. Anal. Prev. **41**(4), 739–754 (2009)
4. Atzeni, A., Cameroni, C., Faily, S., Lyle, J., Flechais, I.: Here's Johnny: a methodology for developing attacker personas. In: 2011 Sixth International Conference on Availability, Reliability and Security, pp. 722–727. IEEE, Vienna (August 2011)
5. Avizienis, A., Laprie, J.C., Randell, B., Landwehr, C.: Basic concepts and taxonomy of dependable and secure computing. IEEE Trans. Dependable Secure Comput. **1**(1), 11–33 (2004)
6. Bloomfield, R., Bishop, P., Butler, E., Stroud, R.: Security-informed safety: supporting stakeholders with codes of practice. Computer **51**(8), 60–65 (2018)
7. Brostoff, S., Sasse, M.A.: Safe and sound: a safety-critical approach to security, p. 10 (2001)
8. Faily, S.: Designing Usable and Secure Software with IRIS and CAIRIS. Springer, Cham (2018). https://doi.org/10.1007/978-3-319-75493-2
9. Faily, S., Flechais, I.: User-centered information security policy development in a post-stuxnet world. 2011 Sixth International Conference on Availability, Reliability and Security, pp. 716–721. IEEE, Vienna (August 2011)
10. Gollmann, D.: Computer Security, 2nd edn. Wiley, Hoboken (2007)
11. Jonsson, E., Olovsson, T.: On the integration of security and dependability in computer systems, p. 6 (1998)
12. Boudi, Z., Koursi, E.M.E., Ghazel, M.: The new challenges of rail security. French Institute of Science and Technology for Transport, Development, and Networks IFSTTAR-COSYS-ESTAS (2016). University of Lille Nord de France, F-59000 Lille, Villeneuve d'Ascq, France. Journal of Traffic and Logistics Engineering
13. Piètre-Cambacédès, L., Bouissou, M.: Cross-fertilization between safety and security engineering. Reliab. Eng. Syst. Saf. **110**, 110–126 (2013)
14. Reason, J.: Human Error. Cambridge University Press, Cambridge (1990)
15. Wiegmann, D.A., Shappell, S.A.: A Human Error Approach to Aviation Accident Analysis: The Human Factors Analysis and Classification System, 1st edn. Routledge, Aldershot (2003)
16. Young, W., Leveson, N.G.: An integrated approach to safety and security based on systems theory. Commun. ACM **57**(2), 31–35 (2014)
17. Zhou, J.L., Lei, Y.: Paths between latent and active errors: analysis of 407 railway accidents/incidents' causes in China. Saf. Sci. **110**, 47–58 (2018)

SECPRE Workshop

How Not to Use a Privacy-Preserving Computation Platform: Case Study of a Voting Application

Jan Willemson[1,2(✉)]

[1] Cybernetica AS, Ülikooli 2, 51003 Tartu, Estonia
jan.willemson@cyber.ee
[2] STACC, Ülikooli 2, 51003 Tartu, Estonia

Abstract. We present an analysis of a recent proposal by Dang-awan *et al.* who develop a remote electronic voting protocol based on secure multi-party computation framework Sharemind. Even though Sharemind comes with provable security guarantees and an application development framework, the proposed protocol and its implementation contain a number of flaws making the result insecure. We hope this case study serves as a good educational material for future secure computation application and voting protocol developers.

Keywords: Secure computation · Electronic voting · Protocol analysis

1 Introduction

Data processing is a field offering both threats and opportunities. On one hand, having access to larger amount of high-precision data allows to take better-informed policy decisions and as a result increase the quality of life of the whole society. On the other hand, having access to personal information may give rise to malicious profiling, manipulation, blackmailing or other types of misuse.

Thus a balance is required between the two extremes of making all data public (destroying individual privacy) and closing all data up (destroying data utility).

One possible equilibrium is provided by *secure computation* mechanisms that allow to generate aggregate results while still protecting the individual records. Being originally proposed in early 1980s, the respective methods have evolved over the decades, resulting in a number or practically applicable frameworks. Some of the currently actively developed examples include Sharemind [7], SPDZ [9], ObliVM [21], Chameleon [26], etc.

Unfortunately, building an application on top of such a framework does not yet guarantee that the application itself is secure. There are many places where things can go wrong if done carelessly.

A tempting area to deploy secure computation mechanisms is electronic voting. At the first sight, its problem setting closely resembles the one of secure

S. Katsikas et al. (Eds.): ESORICS 2019 Workshops, LNCS 11980, pp. 111–121, 2020.
https://doi.org/10.1007/978-3-030-42048-2_8

computation. A potentially large number of voters each have their private input (political preference), and their joint interest is to compute an aggregate end result (the tally).

The major approach to join the two worlds has been using homomorphic encryption which has been studied and developed since 1980s [3,4]. However, this approach is quite limited in the choice of voting protocols it is able to implement. Since homomorphic encryption allows performing only one kind of protected operation (say, addition), the resulting protocols can not go much further from simple vote counting. Implementing more involved paradigms like preferential voting or supporting more complex ballots becomes very challenging.

Deploying a fully-fledged secure computation framework as a basis for a flexible electronic voting solution is a natural idea. However, until recently there have been only a few incomplete attempts in this direction. In [13], Gang merely states the basic idea, and in [24], Nair *et al.* implement a simple Java application to add secret-shared votes. Gjøsteen and Strand take a different approach utilising recent advances in fully homomorphic encryption [16]. However, fully homomorphic encryption is still too inefficient to be applied on a large scale.

The first fully functional solution for secure computation based electronic voting was proposed and implemented by Dang-awan *et al.* in 2018 [10]. They have built their proof-of-concept application on top of Sharemind[1] [7], an established secure computation platform with good development tools, including high-level SecerC programming language for creating secure applications [6]. Regrettably, Dang-awan *et al.* made a number of mistakes in several stages of design and development, resulting in a completely insecure application.

In this paper, we will be going over their main flaws. Besides the direct protocol-analytic value, we find the result also very educational for the developers of both secure computation and electronic voting applications.

The paper is organised as follows. We begin with a short overview of the state of the art in both secure computation and electronic voting in Sect. 2, followed by a general overview of the system architecture of Dang-awan *et al.* [10] in Sect. 3. Next we analyse both the voting and tallying processes in Sects. 4 and 5, respectively. Finally, we draw some conclusions in Sect. 6.

2 State of the Art

Both secure computation and electronic voting domains have been actively studied for decades.

The idea and first protocols for secure computation come from Yao in early 1980s [30]. Yao built his protocols around the garbled circuits paradigm. In the later research, also other algebraic primitives like secret sharing [28] and fully homomorphic encryption (FHE) [14] have been proposed as the basis for secure computation. We refer to [8] and [23] for good recent surveys on the respective topics.

---

[1] https://sharemind.cyber.ee/.

Even though FHE, in principle, supports outsourcing of arbitrary computations, the implied overhead of current implementations is still too large for even medium-size computations [2]. Garbled circuits are much faster, but assume a lot of bandwidth between the computing nodes. All in all, secret-sharing-based secure computation frameworks provide currently the best trade-off between performance and security properties [2].

The idea of using electr(on)ic means for vote recording is almost as old as human usage of electricity. On June 1, 1869, Thomas A. Edison was awarded U.S. Patent number 90,646 for an "electrographic vote-recorder" which he envisioned to be used in U.S. Congress elections. In 1870s, several proposals to use electric machinery to record votes were made in France [19]. Since then, mankind has experimented with various vote casting assistants including Direct Recording Electronic machines and Internet voting. We refer to Robert Krimmer's PhD thesis for a good historical overview of all the relevant developments and their societal context [19].

By early 2000s, Internet had become the primary means of data transfer. It was a natural question to ask whether votes could also be cast via Internet during elections. For example, there was such an experiment performed in 2000 Arizona presidential primaries [1]. The first legally binding country-wide elections with Internet voting as an option were organised in Estonia in 2005 [22]. Since then, several countries (e.g. Norway, Switzerland and Australia) have experimented with various approaches.

One of the main challenges with any kind of elections is ensuring integrity of the result. To achieve this, all of the processes must be transparent and independently auditable, preserving vote privacy at the same time. There is an inherent contradiction between these two requirements, making finding a trade-off a delicate task (see e.g. [25] for a good overview of recent research in this direction).

The scheme of Dang-awan *et al.* [10] also tries to establish an equilibrium between privacy and verifiability. Unfortunately, it achieves neither of these properties.

3 System Architecture

Remote electronic voting systems generally comprise of the following components.

- **Client software** working in the voter's environment and being responsible for displaying the options, getting the voter preference and securing it (by encrypting, signing and/or other means).
- **Voting server** being responsible for collecting and storing the votes (typically in a secured state).
- **Tallying server** is where the votes are opened (e.g. decrypted) and tabulated.

To prove that the required security properties of the system hold, frequently various **auditing components** are implemented in addition. In a more general sense, we can also consider operating systems, network connections, local legislation, etc. to be part of the picture, but out treatment will not go into these details.

Dang-awan *et al.* [10] start from the observation that securing the voting and tallying servers is a critical prerequisite for a trustworthy remote electronic voting system. Indeed, a breach in a server-side component has a potential to allow for a large-scale vote manipulation attack to be implemented unnoticed [29].

In order to decrease the need to rely on a single server, Dang-awan *et al.* propose to distribute the voting server between different parties and run secure multi-party computation (SMC) protocols between them to achieve the required functionality [10].

On the high level, a representative-based architecture is used [12] (see Fig. 1).

In this architecture, voters act as (input) parties submitting their votes in a secret shared form to computation servers (also called *nodes*), of which there are three in the standard configuration of Sharemind. Each server also has a database back-end to store the shares, and a Node.js front-end to implement communication routines with the other parties.

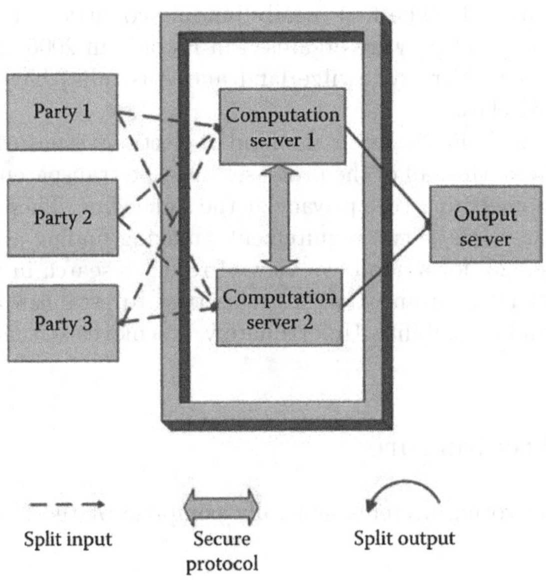

Fig. 1. Representative-based architecture for SMC [12]

Running applications in the distributed environment is managed by a special controller library. One example of such an application is the tally triggered by the election organiser, with the aggregated end result designated for the output server. Note that the end result is computed and reaches the output server in secret shared form. In order to tabulate the result, it must be explicitly *declassified*, i.e. the shares of the output are combined according to the underlying secret sharing scheme to give the open aggregated tally.

Declassification operation is security-critical. In principle, it can also be applied on intermediate results or even input values, thus violating their privacy. On the other hand, this operation is required to obtain human-readable output of the computations, so we can not just prohibit it. Thus, declassification has to be invoked with great caution.

4 Voting

In the system proposed by Dang-awan *et al.*, vote casting is implemented via a Javascript library loaded into the browser. The library secret shares the vote (even though this operation is repeatedly confused with encryption in [10]) and sends the shares to Sharemind computing nodes.

The first problem we observe is that integrity of the votes is not protected by signatures or any other strong cryptographic mechanism. Instead, the authors propose a naïve cast-as-intended verification protocol.

The vote (consisting of the voter ID, position ID and candidate ID) is check-summed using CRC32, and this check sum is then hashed with SHA-1. The resulting hash is displayed to the voter as a receipt. After the vote shares are received by the Sharemind nodes, they perform the same operation and the resulting SHA-1 hash is returned to the voter for comparison. If the comparison succeeds, the voter should be assured of correct casting.

There are many flaws in this protocol. Perhaps the biggest conceptual problem is that all the communication between the voter and the central system (including displaying the check-sums) is performed through a single web browser. While this is definitely convenient, it creates a single point of attack. When the browser gets compromised (a scenario that is unfortunately very much possible), it can manipulate the displayed information arbitrarily. As a result, the voter can not distinguish whether the hash-check-sum displayed to her really matches the vote stored on the servers, or has it been maliciously changed before being shown to her.

It is exactly for this reason that remote cast-as-intended verification needs and independent channel. It may be implemented in various ways like the code sheets plus SMS as in Norway [15], or using an independent auditing device as in Estonia [17]. In any case it is clear that just relying on one medium for both vote casting and verification is not sufficient.

Second, applying SHA-1 after CRC32 does not add any security as SHA-1 is a deterministic function (but it does make the hashes longer, thus more difficult to compare by a human).

Third, no random salt is added before hashing. This means that the pre-images can be easily found by full inspection. To give some back-of-the-envelope estimates, let's consider the university student council election given as a use case by the authors of [10]. There would probably be about few thousand voters (say, up to 10,000), a few positions (say, about 10), and a few dozens of candidates (say, up to 100).

All in all, a vote has in the order of magnitude 10 million possible values. Since both CRC32 and SHA-1 are designed to be very fast to evaluate, pre-computing a table of 10 million hashes is an easy task. As all the hashes are put on a publicly accessible bulletin board (basically a webpage) for verification purposes, anyone with the pre-computed table can efficiently find out how everyone of the voters voted. This is definitely something that a well-designed election system should avoid in order to counter vote selling and other coercion attacks.

The double hashing proposed in [10] also leads to other problems. Note that the output of CRC32 is just 32 bits long and

$$\sqrt{2^{32}} = 2^{16} = 65536\,.$$

This means that whenever the number of possible vote options

$$\#voters \times \#positions \times \#candidates$$

is roughly equal to or larger than 65536, there is a significant probability (50% or larger) of a collision due to the birthday paradox. Again, re-hashing the output with SHA-1 is useless against such collisions resulting already from CRC32.

What this means is that the server can present the same receipt to several voters whose choices happen to give a collision. This defeats the whole purpose of the cast-as-intended verification.

Ironically, the collisions may give some coercion-resistance to the scheme, but only in the case that the voter's true preference and the coercer's preference give the same CRC32 hash, which is in turn a very unlikely situation.

The way server-side verification hash is computed is also significant. Dangawan *et al.* present the actual SecreC snippet that they have used (see Fig. 2). Note that curly brace mismatch comes already from [10]; confusion of secret sharing and encryption is also evident here.

Note that all the vote components are explicitly declassified before computing the CRC32 hash. What this operation does is to make all these private values accessible to all the computing nodes. This defeats the whole purpose of using a secure computation platform in the first place, and thus constitutes the biggest flaw in the whole paper. Declassification should only happen in the very last stage of computation, i.e. only on the tally results.

The authors of [10] refer to unavailability of other hash functions on Sharemind platform other than CRC32 as the main reason for using it. All the above-mentioned problems away, it is unclear why they did not decide to at least use a privacy-preserving version of it in their implementation.

Limitations of the out-of-the-box API are, in general, a poor excuse for using insecure primitives. CRC32 was never intended as a cryptographic hash functions, it can merely capture stochastic transmission errors, but it can not withstand active collision and pre-image attacks. In case stronger cryptographic primitives (hash functions, signatures, etc.) are needed, Sharemind provides the developers with various tools (like SecerC domain-specific language [6]) for extending the API. Of course, there would be some performance overhead, but this is inherent in the case of secure computations.

```
/***************************************
app_save_vote.sc:
How sent encrypted values are saved
***************************************/
for (uint i = 0; i < size(candidateId); ++i) {
    table = arrayToString(
     declassify(electionId[i]));
     tdbInsertRow(datasource, table,
         {voterId, positionId[i],candidateId[i]});
     print("ROW INSERTED");
     message = bl_str(
      arrayToString(declassify(voterId))
      +arrayToString(declassify(positionId[i]))
      +arrayToString(declassify(candidateId[i])));
     hash[i] = CRC32(message); // hashes returned
    }
}
```

Fig. 2. Vote recording script

5 Tally

The tallying procedure of elections is essentially a histogram computation, and this Dang-awan *et al.* actually implement in a privacy-preserving manner. However, privacy is not the only requirement of the tally process. Perhaps even more important is integrity, i.e. making sure that vote counting was not manipulated by anyone.

The biggest problem in [10] is using Sharemind in its out-of-the-box, three-server passive security mode. What passive security means here is the ability to withstand an attacker who is only observing one of the computing nodes, but is not trying to actively interfere with it. However, this model is too weak for the voting use case.

Just to give a small illustrating example, recall that standard Sharemind uses additive secret sharing [7], i.e. a value $x \in \mathbb{Z}_{2^{32}}$ is divided into shares $x_1, x_2, x_3 \in \mathbb{Z}_{2^{32}}$ so that

$$x_1 + x_2 + x_3 = x \bmod 2^{32} ,$$

where the share x_i is held by the computing party P_i. What a malicious party can do is e.g. increasing his share of one of the votes and decreasing another at the same time, resulting in the same change in the values of the vote sums. This would lead to a serious voting result trustworthiness violation as any computing node would be able to manipulate it undetected.

Of course, tally integrity concerns are inherent in any election system. This is why a large variety of approaches towards verification have been proposed in the research community (see, e.g. [18] for a good overview). Ideally, tally correctness should be checkable by everyone, or at least by a large number of designated independent auditors. The proposal by Dang-awan *et al.* does not foresee any of such mechanisms.

Ironically, the ability to find pre-images of hashes displayed on the bulletin board gives a way for anyone to compute the tally independently. However, this happens with the price of total vote privacy loss, which is something we do not want either.

If a multi-party computation engine like Sharemind is used to implement the voting server, measures ensuring security against active manipulation attacks should be deployed [11,20].

On top of that, modern electronic voting systems target *software independence*, a state of affairs where verifying security properties of the system should not rely on assumptions about the underlying software platform [27]. A practical way of approaching this target is requiring strong independently verifiable cryptographic audit trail of all the critical operations.

In the case of vote tallying, there are two main approaches proposed and implemented that can achieve this property. First, homomorphic tallying allows combining votes under encryption so that the end result is the encryption of the final count. Second, votes can also be directly decrypted giving non-interactive zero-knowledge proofs of decryption. To facilitate independent auditing and protect vote privacy at the same time, mix-nets need to be applied in this case. We refer to [5] for a recent overview on these techniques.

Secure computations on top of secret sharing can actually be implemented in a homomorphic way. In fact, the tally routine of Dang-awan *et al.* makes use of homomorphic properties of Sharemind's additive secret sharing. But the missing piece of the puzzle is a software-independent cryptographic trail that can be verified for integrity by independent auditors. Developing such a component is a necessary prerequisite for a voting system to be considered secure in late 2010-s.

6 Conclusions

Implementing a secure computation application is tricky, even if you have access to a well-established platform with provable security guarantees like Sharemind.

First of all, it is crucial to understand all the security aspects of the application domain. Electronic voting is an especially complicated area, since there are a number of different and partly even contradicting requirements. Failure to take some of them (like coercion-resistance or tally integrity) into account will result in an insecure system.

It is also important to fully specify and understand the threat model. In case on remote electronic voting, the biggest vulnerabilities are inflicted by the weaknesses of the client platform. The protocol of Dang-awan *et al.* relies on a web browser as the sole voter device. If the attacker manages to gain the control of it, he can leave the voter with the impression that her vote was cast fine, whereas in reality it has been modified or blocked altogether. To counter this threat, a verification procedure utilising an independent channel is unavoidable.

Third, using a secure computation platform does not automatically imply security of the application. On one hand, there are several definitions of security. And on the other hand, there are simple programming flaws like declassifying values too early that render the whole framework useless. As declassification is a necessary part of secure computation protocols, it can not just be prohibited. It is inherently the responsibility of the application developer to use it only when absolutely necessary.

Secure computation platforms are in fast development and their functionality is expanding all the time. Nevertheless, it may sometimes happen that a desired API call is missing. In that case it is a bad idea to search through the API documentation for something remotely similar. CRC32 was never designed to be a cryptographic hash function (even though check-summing is sometimes also called hashing). Its collisions are easy to find and it is easy to invert. Confusing the design with an extra layer of cryptographic hashing does not improve the situation.

And last but not least – even the strongest cryptographic guarantees do not protect against poor overall protocol design. Hashing values from a relatively small domain without extra entropy leads to easy pre-image-finding even if the hash function would be implemented securely. In case of electronic voting applications, this leads to large-scale privacy violation and potential coercion attacks.

Learning is a process that involves making mistakes, and before a person is able to build something strong, he/she has to acquire knowledge of potentially weak places. We hope that this paper has served as a good study use case for the future architects of both secure computation and voting applications.

Acknowledgments. The research leading to these results has received funding from the Estonian Research Council under Institutional Research Grant IUT27-1 and the European Regional Development Fund through the Estonian Centre of Excellence in ICT Research (EXCITE) and the grant number EU48684.

References

1. Report of the National Workshop on Internet Voting: Issues and Research Agenda (March 2001), Internet Policy Institute. https://www.verifiedvoting.org/downloads/NSFInternetVotingReport.pdf
2. Archer, D.W., Bogdanov, D., Pinkas, B., Pullonen, P.: Maturity and performance of programmable secure computation. IEEE Secur. Priv. **14**(5), 48–56 (2016). https://doi.org/10.1109/MSP.2016.97
3. Benaloh, J.C., Fischer, M.J.: A robust and verifiable cryptographically secure election scheme (extended abstract). In: 26th Annual Symposium on Foundations of Computer Science, Portland, Oregon, USA, October 21–23, 1985, pp. 372–382. IEEE Computer Society (1985). https://doi.org/10.1109/SFCS.1985.2
4. Benaloh, J.C., Yung, M.: Distributing the power of a government to enhance the privacy of voters (extended abstract). In: Halpern, J.Y. (ed.) Proceedings of the Fifth Annual ACM Symposium on Principles of Distributed Computing, Calgary, Alberta, Canada, August 11–13, 1986, pp. 52–62. ACM (1986). https://doi.org/10.1145/10590.10595

5. del Blanco, D.Y.M., Alonso, L.P., Alonso, J.A.H.: Review of cryptographic schemes applied to remote electronic voting systems: remaining challenges and the upcoming post-quantum paradigm. Open Math. **16**(1), 95–112 (2018)
6. Bogdanov, D., Laud, P., Randmets, J.: Domain-polymorphic language for privacy-preserving applications. In: Proceedings of the First ACM Workshop on Language Support for Privacy-enhancing Technologies, PETShop 2013, pp. 23–26. ACM, New York (2013). https://doi.org/10.1145/2517872.2517875
7. Bogdanov, D., Laur, S., Willemson, J.: Sharemind: a framework for fast privacy-preserving computations. In: Jajodia, S., Lopez, J. (eds.) ESORICS 2008. LNCS, vol. 5283, pp. 192–206. Springer, Heidelberg (2008). https://doi.org/10.1007/978-3-540-88313-5_13
8. Cramer, R., Damgård, I.B., Nielsen, J.B.: Secure Multiparty Computation and Secret Sharing. Cambridge University Press, Cambridge (2015)
9. Damgård, I., Pastro, V., Smart, N., Zakarias, S.: Multiparty computation from somewhat homomorphic encryption. In: Safavi-Naini, R., Canetti, R. (eds.) CRYPTO 2012. LNCS, vol. 7417, pp. 643–662. Springer, Heidelberg (2012). https://doi.org/10.1007/978-3-642-32009-5_38
10. Dang-awan, R., Piscos, J.A., Chua, R.B.: Using Sharemind as a tool to develop an internet voting system with secure multiparty computation. In: 2018 9th International Conference on Information, Intelligence, Systems and Applications (IISA), pp. 1–7. IEEE (July 2018)
11. Eerikson, H., Orlandi, C., Pullonen, P., Puura, J., Simkin, M.: Use your brain! Arithmetic 3PC for any modulus with active security. Cryptology ePrint Archive, Report 2019/164 (2019). https://eprint.iacr.org/2019/164
12. Frikken, K.B.: Secure multiparty computation. In: Atallah, M.J., Blanton, M. (eds.) Algorithms and Theory of Computation Handbook, Volume 2: Special Topics and Techniques, pp. 14:1–14:16. CRC Press, Boca Raton (2009)
13. Gang, C.: An electronic voting scheme based on secure multi-party computation. In: 2008 International Symposium on Computer Science and Computational Technology, vol. 1, pp. 292–294 (December 2008)
14. Gentry, C.: Fully homomorphic encryption using ideal lattices. In: Mitzenmacher, M. (ed.) Proceedings of the 41st Annual ACM Symposium on Theory of Computing, STOC 2009, Bethesda, MD, USA, May 31–June 2, 2009, pp. 169–178. ACM (2009). https://doi.org/10.1145/1536414.1536440
15. Gjøsteen, K.: The Norwegian Internet voting protocol. In: Kiayias, A., Lipmaa, H. (eds.) Vote-ID 2011. LNCS, vol. 7187, pp. 1–18. Springer, Heidelberg (2012). https://doi.org/10.1007/978-3-642-32747-6_1
16. Gjøsteen, K., Strand, M.: A roadmap to fully homomorphic elections: stronger security, better verifiability. In: Brenner, M., et al. (eds.) FC 2017. LNCS, vol. 10323, pp. 404–418. Springer, Cham (2017). https://doi.org/10.1007/978-3-319-70278-0_25
17. Heiberg, S., Willemson, J.: Verifiable Internet voting in Estonia. In: Krimmer, R., Volkamer, M. (eds.) 6th International Conference on Electronic Voting: Verifying the Vote, EVOTE 2014, Lochau/Bregenz, Austria, October 29–31, 2014, pp. 1–8. IEEE (2014). https://doi.org/10.1109/EVOTE.2014.7001135
18. Jonker, H., Mauw, S., Pang, J.: Privacy and verifiability in voting systems: methods, developments and trends. Comput. Sci. Rev. **10**, 1–30 (2013). https://doi.org/10.1016/j.cosrev.2013.08.002
19. Krimmer, R.: The evolution of e-voting: why voting technology is used and how it affects democracy. Ph. D. thesis, Tallinn University of Technology, doctoral Theses Series I: Social Sciences (2012)

20. Laud, P., Pankova, A., Jagomägis, R.: Preprocessing based verification of multiparty protocols with honest majority. PoPETs **2017**(4), 23–76 (2017). https://doi.org/10.1515/popets-2017-0038
21. Liu, C., Wang, X.S., Nayak, K., Huang, Y., Shi, E.: ObliVM: a programming framework for secure computation. In: 2015 IEEE Symposium on Security and Privacy, SP 2015, San Jose, CA, USA, May 17–21, 2015, pp. 359–376. IEEE Computer Society (2015). https://doi.org/10.1109/SP.2015.29
22. Madise, Ü., Martens, T.: E-voting in Estonia 2005. The first practice of country-wide binding Internet voting in the world. In: Krimmer, R. (ed.) Electronic Voting 2006: 2nd International Workshop, Co-organized by Council of Europe, ESF TED, IFIP WG 8.6 and E-Voting.CC, August 2–4, 2006, Castle Hofen, Bregenz, Austria. LNI, vol. 86, pp. 15–26. GI (2006). http://subs.emis.de/LNI/Proceedings/Proceedings86/article4547.html
23. Martins, P., Sousa, L., Mariano, A.: A survey on fully homomorphic encryption: an engineering perspective. ACM Comput. Surv. **50**(6), 83:1–83:33 (2017). https://doi.org/10.1145/3124441
24. Nair, D.G., Binu, V.P., Kumar, G.S.: An improved e-voting scheme using secret sharing based secure multi-party computation (2015)
25. Puiggalí, J., Cucurull, J., Guasch, S., Krimmer, R.: Verifiability experiences in government online voting systems. In: Krimmer, R., Volkamer, M., Braun Binder, N., Kersting, N., Pereira, O., Schürmann, C. (eds.) E-Vote-ID 2017. LNCS, vol. 10615, pp. 248–263. Springer, Cham (2017). https://doi.org/10.1007/978-3-319-68687-5_15
26. Riazi, M.S., Weinert, C., Tkachenko, O., Songhori, E.M., Schneider, T., Koushanfar, F.: Chameleon: a hybrid secure computation framework for machine learning applications. In: Proceedings of the 2018 on Asia Conference on Computer and Communications Security, ASIACCS 2018, pp. 707–721. ACM, New York (2018). https://doi.org/10.1145/3196494.3196522
27. Rivest, R.L.: On the notion of 'software independence' in voting systems. Philos. Trans. R. Soc. A Math. Phys. Eng. Sci. **366**(1881), 3759–3767 (2008)
28. Shamir, A.: How to share a secret. Commun. ACM **22**(11), 612–613 (1979)
29. Springall, D., et al.: Security analysis of the Estonian Internet voting system. In: Proceedings of the 2014 ACM SIGSAC Conference on Computer and Communications Security, pp. 703–715. ACM (2014)
30. Yao, A.C.: Protocols for secure computations (extended abstract). In: 23rd Annual Symposium on Foundations of Computer Science, Chicago, Illinois, USA, November 3–5, 1982, pp. 160–164. IEEE Computer Society (1982). https://doi.org/10.1109/SFCS.1982.38

A Proposed Privacy Impact Assessment Method Using Metrics Based on Organizational Characteristics

Eleni-Laskarina Makri(✉), Zafeiroula Georgiopoulou(✉), and Costas Lambrinoudakis(✉)

Department of Digital Systems, University of Piraeus, 18532 Piraeus, Greece
{elmak, clam}@unipi.gr, roulageorgio@ssl-unipi.gr

Abstract. The assessment of the potential impact for an organization from a privacy violation incident is important for three main reasons: the organization will have a justified estimate of the cost (financial, reputation or other) that may be raised, will facilitate the selection of the appropriate technical, procedural and organizational protection mechanisms and also will be compliant with the new General Data Protection Regulation that will be in effect from May 2018. Today, there are several methods to do a Privacy Impact Assessment but none of these quantifies the results according to specific metrics and thus can be significantly affected by various subjective parameters. Furthermore, the specific organizational characteristics (size, activities, number of clients, type of offered services etc.) are very rarely accounted, a fact that also affects the accuracy of the results. In this paper, a privacy impact assessment method that explicitly takes into account the organizational characteristics and employs a list of well-defined metrics as input, is presented.

Keywords: Privacy impact assessment · Risk analysis · Privacy principles · Privacy metrics · Privacy enhancing technologies

1 Introduction

As IT applications are steadily increasing, via the Internet, more and more people are using them failing to estimate the positive, or even worse neglecting the potential negative consequences. Thus, the major problem that arises is how companies can protect both customers' and employees' personal data in order to avoid privacy breaches [36]. This is an interesting field of study which should be thoroughly researched due to the fact that a huge amount of personal information is collected, stored, edited, communicated and published on the Internet [1, 6]. More specifically, when using the Internet-based applications the users risk their privacy, since their personal data may be exposed to others.

In order to prevent privacy breaches, several laws, standards, regulations and directives [2] have been applied to most developed countries. The intent is to compel organizations to fully inform their users and obtain their prior consent before collecting, storing or processing their personal data in any way. At the same time, privacy

S. Katsikas et al. (Eds.): ESORICS 2019 Workshops, LNCS 11980, pp. 122–139, 2020.
https://doi.org/10.1007/978-3-030-42048-2_9

principles [3], privacy requirements [4, 5] and security requirements [4, 5], are also helpful since they assist the development of an integrated security and privacy protection framework.

It is therefore necessary to have mechanisms that facilitate the assessment of the impact of modern IT systems and applications on customers' privacy. This assessment should be carried out during the design stage of an IT system or application, and definitely throughout its lifecycle. Scientists have been working towards this direction, proposing methodologies that can assist organizations to measure the impact of privacy breaches. However, there is still a definite lack of reliable metric systems that companies can adopt.

Considering that there is still no effective method for the quantification of privacy breach impact, the contribution of this paper is that it introduces an approach for assessing the privacy level of a system. If the impact of a privacy breach is quantified, the personal data can be effectively protected, thus supporting individuals against the digital age challenges and helping them to minimize possible intrusions in their private lives. An additional objective is to facilitate a uniform management of security and privacy requirements in the sense that specific security countermeasures can also assist in the satisfaction of privacy requirements. To this respect the proposed methodology integrates the results of risk analysis methods (i.e. CRAMM, Octave, VSRisk etc.) in terms of the criticality of the data assets and of their potential impact on the organization if a security incident (loss of confidentiality, integrity, availability) occurs.

The paper is organized as follows: Sect. 2 provides an overview of the literature on privacy impact assessment methodologies. Based on the literature review, Sect. 3 provides an overview of the different types of data sets maintained by organizations, together with the associated privacy principles and requirements. It continuous with the description of the proposed Privacy Impact Method together with the derived metrics for the quantification of the criticality of the privacy principles for an organization. Section 4 draws the conclusions giving some pointers for future work.

2 Literature Review

In the advent of computer science era, individuals use computers on a daily basis to satisfy their "digital needs", for instance to perform electronic transactions via the net. To do so, they do not hesitate to provide the personal data required for accessing the applications. Yet, can people be really protected when they "offer" their personal data so willingly? To answer this question, it is first necessary to estimate the consequences from a potential privacy breach, employing a *Privacy Impact Assessment (PIA)* method. Having estimated the impact, the stakeholders may adopt remedial actions for eliminating or minimizing the consequences [7]. Furthermore, failure to apply a PIA method may result in a breach of privacy laws - regulations.

The adoption of a PIA method can certainly benefit both individuals and organizations [7, 11, 29]. As far as individuals are concerned, the first and most important advantage is that they can ensure that companies processing their personal data are compliant with standards, laws and guidelines. In addition, individuals can determine how their information is collected, stored and processed, ensuring transparency. On the other hand, there are also benefits for organizations applying a PIA method, as they protect their clients, mitigating privacy breaches and ensuring compliance with the legal framework. Furthermore, when organizations offer privacy-oriented services, they build both their customers and employees' trust. Last but not least, the financial benefits should not be neglected. By reducing the ongoing costs of a project through the minimization of the amount of information collected or processed, where possible [11], the organization can obviously become more profitable.

Along with the positive aspects of applying a PIA method, there are also some negative ones [29]. The implementation and the following publication of PIA results may assist opponents to exploit them, putting the individuals' privacy at risk. Besides, a PIA method may impose delays and additional costs when a new project is implemented. Another important concern is the limitation of the organizations' flexibility. That, in practical terms, means that organizations are committed to take actions in a specific way, based on laws and regulations, without alternative choices, which, for instance, would help them to finish specific tasks more quickly. However, the advantages far outweigh the disadvantages, since a PIA is by all means a really good way to protect users' privacy and mitigate privacy risks.

Considering the aforementioned PIA benefits, it can be inferred that through the application of a PIA method the most widely known privacy principles are maintained. In 1980 [3] the OECD organization proposed eight privacy principles, which were globally accepted, namely: purpose specification principle, collection limitation principle, data quality principle, use limitation principle, openness principle, individual participation principle, accountability principle, security safeguards principle. Their aim was to minimize the risk of personal data disclosure and consist the basis of privacy protection [12]. Cavoukian [13–15] strongly supports the notion of privacy-by-design, according to which privacy should be maintained throughout the entire life-cycle of an IT system, from the conception of a new system up to its implementation. According to Oetzel and Spiekermann [16, 17] the notion of privacy-by-design is really important in a PIA method as PIAs try to follow these privacy principles in order to achieve privacy-by-design, which is one of the most crucial concerns of today's privacy community.

In order for an organization to protect the personal data of an individual, Privacy Enhancing Technologies (PETs) are employed to satisfy privacy requirements (data protection, anonymity/ pseudonymity, unlinkability and unobservability), along with the privacy principles mentioned above. PETs are various technical and procedural measures that can prevent unnecessary or unwanted processing of users' personal data and can thus protect their privacy [12, 18].

The idea of a PIA method is relatively new. UK was the first European country to use the PIA handbook which was developed and published by the Information Commissioner's Office (ICO) in December 2007, followed by a revised edition in June 2009 [7, 9, 19]. In the ICO publication the basic stages of a PIA method were explained in detail. In May of the same year, the European Commission's Recommendation on radio frequency identification (RFID) tags followed, where the Member States called to ensure that industry, in collaboration with relevant civil society stakeholders, will develop a framework for privacy and data protection impact assessment, providing input to the Article 29 Data Protection Working Party [7, 10]. The above provide clear evidence that recently the need for applying a PIA method is gaining ground and that it provides the foundation for taking privacy into consideration [27].

Recently, the European Commission co-funded the project PIAF (A Privacy Impact Assessment Framework for data protection and privacy rights), which aims to encourage the EU and its Member States to adopt a PIA policy [23]. The 22-month-project was completed in December 2012 and resulted in a step-by-step guide to privacy impact assessment so that privacy issues could be better addressed and personal data could be more effectively protected from unwanted processing [24]. This project highlights how important the application of a PIA method is in IT systems and that it is mandatory to all EU Member States.

In May 2013, ICO conducted further research on the PIAs which led to the publication of the "Privacy impact assessment and risk management", in which specific improvements were suggested, the most important of which was the better integration of PIAs with existing project management and risk management processes [20]. One year later, in February 2014 [21], ICO published the Privacy Impact Assessment (PIA) Code of Practice, which was updated in January 2017 to help organizations comply with their data protection law obligations when changing the way they use personal data [22].

In May 2017, the International Organization for Standardization (ISO) and the International Electrotechnical Commission (IEC), which form the specialized system for worldwide standardization, published a standard related to privacy impact assessment defining PIAs [8], which is not significantly different from David Wright's and Paul De Hert's definition [7]. Specifically, it will support that a PIA is more than a tool and will be defined as a process beginning at the earlier stages of a system and continuing throughout its development life cycle, thus achieving privacy-by-design [8]. The aim of the International Standard will be to provide guidelines on the process for conducting a PIA method and on the structure and content of a PIA report. According to the official published draft [8] "*it will be relevant to those involved in designing or implementing projects, including the parties operating data processing systems and services that process PII*". In addition, it will be applicable to all public and private bodies.

Prior to the upcoming standard, ISO produced a standard for PIAs in financial services [28]. The aim of ISO 22307:2008 standard was to act as a tool for the internal editing of personal data during the development of a proposed financial system (PFS). It is used to mitigate the risks which appear when an organization processes the financial data of customers and consumers, business partners as well as citizens.

Except for organizations such as ICO and ISO/IEC, eminent scientists have made research on PIA methodologies. They have proposed PIA methodologies, which can be easily applied by an organization, giving accurate results at the same time. In 2012 [16] and 2013 [17], Oetzel Marie Caroline and Spiekermann Sarah proposed a systematic method for privacy impact assessment. Their PIA method, based on NIST security risk assessment process (2002) [31] and the UK PIA process (ICO, 2009) [9], reduces the complexity of the privacy laws landscape for practitioners, helping them to take privacy management decisions for their applications. Furthermore, it defines privacy targets, evaluates the level of protection they need, identifies threats and proposes controls.

Throughout the years, the rapid improvement of PIA methodologies highlights their importance on privacy and data protection. However, there is no explicit way to quantify the privacy impact. In 2011, Wright [25, 29] highlighted this need, by stating that "*Making privacy impact assessments mandatory is not the end of the story. Audits and metrics are needed to make sure that PIAs are actually carried out and properly so and to determine if improvements to the process can be made*". More recently, in 2013, Wadhwa and Rodrigues [26] agreed with David Wright's statement, which practically means that the specific need still exists.

One of the main reasons that organizations adopt PIAs is to gain users' trust. A number of PIA tools, like AIPCA/CICA privacy risk assessment tool, the Security and Privacy Impact Assessment (SPIA) tool of the University of Pennsylvania, the GS1 RFID Privacy Impact Assessment (PIA) tool, the Vienna University intelligent PIA tool for RFID applications and the Privacy Impact Assessment Tool for Cloud Computing proposed by Tancock, Pearson, and Charlesworth [37], have been proposed in order to assist companies assess privacy risks. However, none of them employs metrics to quantify the impact of a privacy breach.

In July 2016, Agarwal [30] highlighted the fact that although there are a series of modular and well-structured online PIA tools (GS1 tool, iPIA tool, SPIA tool, etc.), they all fail to provide a metric to assess progress in the implementation of privacy controls. In his research, he developed a structured metric to measure privacy risk. Before Agarwal, Oetzel and Spiekermann [16, 17], had already proposed a qualitative metric (low, medium, high) for measuring privacy risks, but their effort was quite unstructured and difficult to measure explicitly [30]. In order to evaluate privacy risk, Agarwal defined it as the product of impact and likelihood. To be more specific, Agarwal assessed the impact using Solove's taxonomy and the likelihood using Lipton's work. For the calculation of the impact, he used four different dimensions of privacy, splitting them into categories and subcategories. For the likelihood, he used actors (companies, 3rd parties, others) and data characteristics (amount of data, sensitivity of data, value of data involved). This paper proposed a structured privacy risk metric, but failed to delve deeper into the organizations' characteristics which can have a considerable negative impact on the users' privacy.

In June 2015, Commission Nationale de l'Informatique et des Libertés (CNIL) published a PIA methodology, which is in line with EU's General Data Protection Regulation (GDPR) [2]. According to CNIL [34], the PIA methodology rests on two pillars: firstly, the fundamental principles and rights and, secondly, the management of data subjects' privacy risks. To be more specific, the methodology consists of four steps: the definition and description of the content of the processing of personal data under consideration, the identification of existing or planned controls, the evaluation of privacy risks and the decision to validate the manner in which it is planned to comply with privacy principles and treat the risks, or review the preceding steps. In December 2017, CNIL published a free and open source PIA software [35] in order to help data controllers to follow their methodology.

In conclusion, it can be inferred that an effective way to measure the privacy impact is by using metrics. Metrics can help organizations to calculate the significance of threats and lead them to take measures to mitigate the risks. Despite the remarkable efforts to define metrics by various researchers [16, 17, 30], so far, there has been no detailed PIA method to use metrics and, at the same time, take into account the organization characteristics. Furthermore, there is no method that integrates security and privacy assessment.

3 The Proposed Security and Privacy Impact Assessment Method

3.1 Scope of the Proposed Method

The proposed method aims to assist organizations to protect the privacy of their users and the security of the data that they store and process. Users may be the customers of the organization (people using the offered services) or the employees (users who operate the systems of the organization).

The novelty of the method is that it handles security and privacy requirements simultaneously, since it utilizes the results of risk analysis together with those of a PIA. A further novelty of the method is that it introduces metrics for the quantification of the requirements and also that it takes into account the specific characteristics of the organization.

It should be stressed that we do not aim to propose a specific method for information security or privacy risk management, but instead to allow an organization to utilize an existing methodology for risk management and privacy impact assessment while, at the same time, to facilitate the integration of the derived security and privacy requirements with the privacy principles dictated by the legal and regulatory framework. All of that in the context of the specific organization (i.e. taking into account the specific characteristics, perceptions and wills of the organization). As demonstrated in Fig. 1 later in the paper, independent methodologies for the elicitation of the security and privacy requirements can be utilized producing the risk factor (both in terms of security and privacy) for the system assets. This risk factor 'feeds' the proposed method (through the security safeguards principle) in order to calculate the overall criticality for the specific organization (taking into account the privacy principles and the organizational characteristics).

Our approach is therefore very similar to the one of ISO 27005 that does not provide any specific method for information security risk management but it simply allows the organization to adopt any methodology under the framework of the standard.

3.2 Theoretical Background

3.2.1 Data Sets Definitions

A huge amount of data is stored and processed in information systems and/or portable devices such as mobile phones or tablets. However, the criticality of the data is not always the same. For instance, some applications may only use publicly available data, others may involve personal data (like names, addresses etc.) and others may also process sensitive data (like health data). Clearly, its case exhibits different criticality and must be handled differently [36]. To facilitate that, through the proposed method, the data that an organization stores/process either internally (e.g. employees' data) or externally (e.g. users' data) are classified in the following categories:

- **Personal Data**: There are several approaches to define personal data. The Data Protection Act [32] defines the personal data as data relating to a living individual who is or can be identified either from the data directly or in conjunction with other information that is in, or is likely to come into, the possession of the data controller. The EU Data Protection Directive (REGULATION (EU) 2016/679) [2] defines the personal data as any information relating to an identified or identifiable natural person ('data subject'); an identifiable natural person is one who can be identified, directly or indirectly, in particular by reference to an identifier such as a name, an identification number, location data, an online identifier or to one or more factors specific to the physical, physiological, genetic, mental, economic, cultural or social identity of that natural person. For the needs of the proposed method, this data set category will host data that an organization stores and processes in its systems and are related to an identified or identifiable natural person. Some indicative examples of personal data are: name, surname, age, address, telephone number, email, education.
- **Sensitive Personal Data**: The sensitive personal data can be considered a subcategory of personal data. Sensitive personal data, according to the legal framework, need high protection. They are defined in Sect. 2 of the Data Protection Act [32] as personal data consisting of information relating to the data subject with regard to racial or ethnic origin, political opinions, religious beliefs or other beliefs of a similar nature, trade union membership, physical or mental health or condition, sexual life, the commission or alleged commission by the data subject of any offence, or any proceedings for any offence committed or alleged to have been committed by the data subject, the disposal of such proceedings or the sentence of any court in such proceedings. For the needs of the proposed method, this data set category will host data that an organization stores and processes in its systems and are related to an identified or identifiable natural person and belong to any of the aforementioned sub-categories.
- **Operational Data**: Operational data are the data that an organization stores and processes, as a result of the use of its information systems. More specifically, this data set category includes data generated by the information system itself, like logging users' actions. For instance, a log file may contain details about the attempts of a user log in, for how long she was connected, the timeframe that she used a specific application etc.
- **Financial Data**: This data set includes all the financial data of an organization (related to its employees and/or users). Similarly to the operational data, they are not provided by users or employees but, instead, they are "created" by the organization on behalf of its users and/or its employees. More specifically, the financial data are classified in two sub-classes: (a) Data related to the payroll of the organizations' employees, (b) Data related to payments by organization's users for the provided services. It should be stressed, that the financial data, for both sub categories, are generated by the organization.

- **Other Data**: Any data that cannot be classified in any of the above categories will be considered under this final data set. However, the type, use and criticality of the data should be explicitly defined.

3.2.2 The Role of Privacy Principles, Privacy and Security Requirements

The privacy principles together with all privacy requirements, must be satisfied by the organization in order to claim "privacy-preserving" services. Undoubtedly, equally important is the satisfaction of the security requirements. In [4], an integrated methodology for facilitating organizations to specify the appropriate security and privacy preserving measures for their information systems has been proposed (depicted in Fig. 1). More specifically, Fig. 1 identifies the steps that the organization should go through in order to identify the security and privacy requirements, for the system under study, taking into account the privacy principles, as well as the stage at which the organization should select the appropriate safeguards for satisfying the aforementioned requirements. Clearly, the selection of the safeguards is based on the identified security and privacy requirements and, in fact, comes to satisfy the "Security Safeguards" Principle.

In addition to that, in [5] a four-level classification of the existing privacy principles, based on their significance and on the sequence that a potential audit procedure should be carried out, has been proposed (depicted in Fig. 2). All the steps are interdependent and should be followed in strict order since failure to audit any step implies that it is meaningless to continue the audit procedure. At the same time, it has been identified that there is need for certain privacy principles to be maintained throughout the entire auditing procedure.

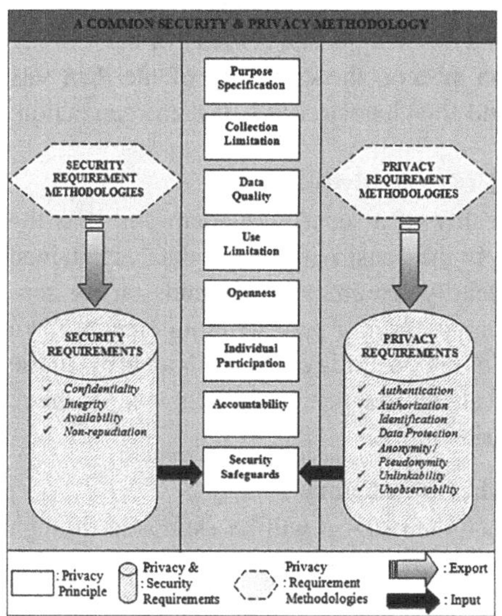

Fig. 1. A common security and privacy methodology [4]

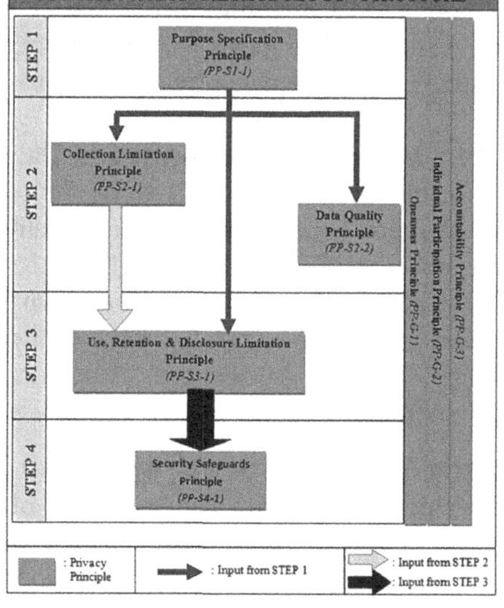

Fig. 2. Privacy audit methodology structure [5]

More specifically, the first step is the most important one since the "Purpose Specification Principle" defines the scope of data collection and use. If this privacy principle is not satisfied the other privacy principles will not be applied in the right way, violating the data privacy. The second step includes the satisfaction of "Data Collection Limitation Principle" and "Data Quality Principle". If the purpose from the step 1 has been specified, the data collection and use must be limited and related to the purpose. Moreover, the collected data should be accurate and kept updated. If these privacy principles are not satisfied the upcoming privacy principles will not be applied in the right way, violating the data privacy. The third step includes the satisfaction of "Use, Retention and Disclosure Principle". If the privacy principles from the step 2 have been satisfied, the data should be limited used, retained and disclosed according to organizations' policies. If the privacy principle in the third step is not satisfied the upcoming privacy principles will not be applied in the right way, violating the data privacy. The fourth and last step includes the satisfaction of "Security Safeguards Principle".

The other privacy principles include the satisfaction of "Openness Principle", "Individual Participation Principle" and "Accountability Principle". These privacy principles should be satisfied throughout the entire methodology.

Based on the hierarchy of the steps (as depicted in Fig. 2), Step 1 is the most important one, Step 2 is more important than Step 3 and Step 3 is more important than Step 4. The other privacy principles should be applied throughout the entire process.

3.3 Quantification of Security and Privacy Requirements

In order to facilitate auditors to "measure" the degree to which security and privacy requirements have been addressed by an organization, it is necessary to introduce metrics that will be utilized for the quantification of the requirements. The proposed method introduces metrics that have been based on the type and severity of the security and privacy requirements for the information system, the criticality of the data sets involved, the applicable privacy principles and the characteristics of the organization.

3.3.1 Security Requirements and Data Sets' Sensitivity

The main criterion for determining the criticality of a security incident and thus the potential consequences for the organization, is the sensitivity of the data maintained and processed. Clearly, the weight of the security requirements depends on the sensitivity of the data sets; i.e. more sensitive data raise *harder* security requirements. On a second level, in order to judge the sensitivity of the data it is essential to identify all the different subsets (subcategory) of data and valuate independently each one of them. A description of the identified valuation metrics follows.

Metric 3.3.1.1: The Sensitivity of Each Data Subcategory

Description of Metric: The sensitivity of each data subset will be estimated through the use of a risk analysis method, like CRAMM [33]. The outcome of the risk analysis will be a numeric value known as risk factor. The classification of data to different subcategories will be based on the fact that all data belonging to a specific subset should exhibit a similar sensitivity level for the organization. Some indicative data subcategories are:

- Personal Data (Data which uniquely identify a person using IDs, personal or marital status, business activities etc.)
- Sensitive Personal Data (Medical Data, convictions etc.)
- Financial Data (Data related to financial transactions, yearly tax etc.)
- Operational Data (Data generated during the execution of a service, i.e. cookies, private log files of the organization etc.)
- Other Data

As already mentioned, the estimation of the organization's data sensitivity, through risk analysis, will be based on the impact that could be caused to the organization by a potential security incident on an independent data subcategory. The overall impact for the organization will depend on the partial impact caused by each data subcategory, adopting in all cases the worst-case scenario.

Input to Metric: The organization's Data Set, classified in data subcategories DS1, DS2 … (DSn).
Formulation: Through Risk Analysis the risk factor for each data subcategory is calculated, depending on the impact that a security incident could cause to the organization.

Level 1 – Very Low *:Minimal impact (Risk Factor Value = 1)*
Level 2 – Low *:Small Impact (Risk Factor Value = 2)*
Level 3 – Medium *:Medium Impact (Risk Factor Value = 3)*
Level 4 – High *:Significant Impact (Risk Factor Value = 4)*
Level 5 – Very High *:Organization's viability in danger (Risk Factor Value = 5)*

Final Output: *A metric "SeveritySubCatDSx" for each data subcategory x (where x = 1, 2, …, n) is calculated, representing the impact that could be caused for the organization by a security incident that affects the data subcategory DSx.*

Metric 3.3.1.2: The Overall Data Set's Sensitivity

Description of Metric: The overall sensitivity (risk factor) of the organization's data, calculated through the risk factors of each independent data subcategory (metric 3.3.1.1). The way to calculate the overall sensitivity is the following:

- If all organizational data have been classified in one category the overall sensitivity will be equal to the sensitivity of that specific data category.
- If the organizational data have been classified in several data subcategories, the overall sensitivity of organizations' data will be equal to the maximum sensitivity of the data subcategories. This is because the maximum sensitivity level covers all data subcategories.

The above calculation principle is depicted in Fig. 3.

Input to Metric: The severity of each data subcategory (Metric 3.3.1.1)
Formulation:
SeverityDS = max (SeveritySubCatDS1, …, SeveritySubCatDn)
<u>Cases:</u>
if (n = 1) then SeverityDS = SeveritySubCatDS
if (n = 2) then SeverityDS = max (SeveritySubCatDS1, SeveritySubCatDS2)
…
if (n = n) then SeverityDS = max (SeveritySubCatDS1, …, SeveritySubCatDn)
Final Output: *A metric "Severity DS" is calculated, representing the overall severity of the organization's data.*

If the organization has several distinct data sets, each one divided in different data subcategories, the above Severity DS metric will be computed separately for each data set. The risk treatment process will start considering the data set that exhibits the biggest severity first, and then the data sets with smaller severities.

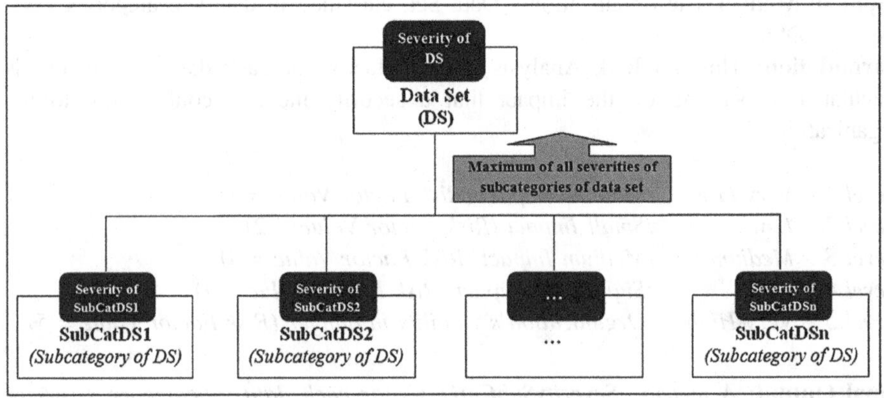

Fig. 3. The overall data set sensitivity

3.3.2 Privacy Requirements and Principles

In addition to the security requirements, it is important to consider and quantify the privacy requirements. For the purposes of this paper, we assume that the privacy requirements have been considered together with the security requirements, thus covered by the already defined metrics, and thus here we simply evaluate the related privacy principles. As explained in [4, 5], the privacy principles are classified in a hierarchy of steps (Figs. 1 and 2). Metrics, estimating the impact for the organization, in cases where one or more steps are not satisfied, will be defined.

The definition of these metrics is much more complex, as compared to the ones used for the data sets' sensitivity. More specifically, the metrics for the privacy principles depend on the hierarchical level (step) of the principle, which is a constant value, and on the characteristics of the organization, which is a variable that depends on the organization type and activities.

Metric 3.3.2.1: Hierarchical Level of Each Privacy Principle

Description of Metric: The privacy audit method proposed in [5] has pre-defined steps. The specific metric reflects the criticality of the hierarchical level that a privacy principle belongs to, the most critical being Step 1.

Input to Metric: The hierarchical levels (steps) of the privacy audit method proposed in [5].

Formulation: According to the hierarchical level (step) that a privacy principle is associated with, a constant weighting factor "app" (where pp = privacy principle) is given to the principle. The weight reflects the importance of the specific step, and thus of the privacy principles associated with it, for the organization. The minimum weighting factor has been assumed to be 1. In addition, the weight associated with each step highlights the *criticality difference* among the various privacy principles. More specifically:

Step 1 – PP of very high importance (Weighting factor = 3)
Step 2 – PP of high importance (Weighting factor = 2)
Step 3 – PP of medium importance (Weighting factor = 1)
Step 4 – (Weighting factor = Severity DS)
The weighting factor for the Security Safeguards Principle (Step 4) is the only one that is not constant and thus not aligned with the hierarchical level that the principle is associated with. The reason is that the importance of the specific principle largely depends on the severity of the data set under consideration which is reflected by the Severity DS value (Metric 3.3.1.2) calculated through the risk analysis/PIA.
Horizontal Steps – PP of high Importance (Weighting factor = 2)

Final Output:
A metric "app - Weighting Factor" for each Privacy Principle, which is:

- Weighting Factor for the Purpose Specification Principle = 3
- Weighting Factor for the Collection Limitation Principle = 2
- Weighting Factor for the Data Quality Principle = 2
- Weighting Factor for the Use, Retention and Disclosure Principle = 1
- Weighting Factor for the Security Safeguards Principle = Severity DS
- Weighting Factor for the Openness Principle = 2
- Weighting Factor for the Individual Participation Principle = 2
- Weighting Factor for the Accountability Principle = 2

Metric 3.3.2.2: Organizational Characteristics

Description of Metric: Each organization has its own type, activities, peculiarities etc. These characteristics may affect the potential impact/consequences for the organization in case of a privacy violation incident.

A vector "$z_{1..N}$" is being used for modelling the organization's characteristics. Each characteristic has its own scale, depending on how it affects the organization in case of a security or privacy violation incident. For instance, the characteristic "Data Volume" has importance α if the organization manages a very low volume of personal data, while its importance is β (where $\beta > \alpha$) if the organization maintains and processes a considerable amount of sensitive data.

Input to Metric: The characteristics of the organization.
Formulation: According to the organization's characteristics a vector will be used to assess their impact on the security and privacy issues.

$$
\begin{aligned}
z_{1..N} = &[\text{a numeric value for CH1 from the range : } \mathbf{Value1\ Value2 \ldots ValueN}] \\
&[\text{a numeric value for CH2 from the range : } \mathbf{Value1\ Value2 \ldots ValueN}] \\
&[\ldots] \\
&[\text{a numeric value for CHN from the range : } \mathbf{Value1\ Value2 \ldots ValueN}]
\end{aligned}
$$

where: indicative CHs and VALUEs are presented in Table 1 next.

Table 1. Indicative characteristics and values of the organization

No	CH 1, 2 … N	Range of values
1	Data Volume	1: Few
		2: Many
2	Data Life Time	1: No data is not kept at all
		2: Data are kept for specific period of time
		3: Data are kept forever
3	Data Type	1: Public Data
		2: Private Data
		3: Sensitive Personal Data
4	Way of Data Collection	1: With written consent of subject
		2: With electronic consent (e.g. accepting "terms and conditions")
		3: Through another entity (legal or illegal)
5	Organization Size	1: Small-Medium Company
		2: Large Company - nationwide
		3: Multinational company
6	Number of Users	1: Under 100 users
		2: 100-1.000 users
		3: 1.000 users - …
7	Legal Framework of country the organization is established	1: Comply with the laws
		2: Deviations from Legal Framework exist
8	Legal Framework of country the organization operates	1: Comply with the laws
		2: Deviations from Legal Framework exist
9	Awareness/Culture of Employees	1: They are aware
		2: They are not aware
10	Incident History	1: Maintained
		2: Not maintained

Final Output: A metric "Vector $z_{1..N}$", providing the importance of each organizational characteristic.

Metric 3.3.2.3: Customization of Organizational Characteristics
Description of Metric: The Vector $z_{1..N}$ metric, defined above, provides a generic assessment of the way various organizational characteristics may influence the impact on the organization, in case of a privacy violation incident. However, each organization may, depending on the data that it processes and the type of its activities, judge the importance of each characteristic differently. To allow each organization to customize the importance of its characteristics, a *priority percentage* is given to each characteristic.
Input to Metric: Vector $z_{1..N}$ (Output of metric 3.3.2.2)
Formulation: Applying the *priority percentages* in Vector $z_{1..N}$ a new metric is derived:

$$k_i = Priority\,percentages * Vector\,z_{1..N}$$

Example:

$$k_i = (20\% * CH1) + (18\% * CH2) + (15\% * CH3) + (12\% * CH4) + (10\% * CH5) + (8\% * CH6) + (6\% * CH7) + (5\% * CH8) + (4\% * CH9) + (2\% * CH10)$$

where: CH1,2,…,10: Characteristics 1,2,…,10 (e.g. Data Volume, Data Type, etc.)

Final Output: *A metric "k_i" is defined, representing the customized (specific to the organization) criticality of its characteristics on privacy issues.*

Metric 3.3.2.4: Severity of Privacy Principles
Description of Metric: The severity of each distinct Privacy Principle depends on two factors: the "a_{pp} - *Weighting Factor*" for each Privacy Principle (Sect. 3.3.2.1) and the criticality of the organizational characteristics (metric "k_i" defined in Sect. 3.3.2.3).
Input to Metric: The "a_{pp}" weighting factor, the "k_i" metric
Formulation: The value of "*Severity PP*" metric is calculated from the "a_{pp}" weighting Factor and the "k_i" metric.

$$Severity\,PP = a_{pp} * k_i$$

Final Output: *A metric "Severity PP", representing the overall severity of each privacy principle.*

3.4 The Proposed PIA Method

Having defined the aforementioned metrics, it is now possible to use them in order to deduce the criticality of each privacy principle for every different data set of the organization. The value of each *Table Cell* in the following table is calculated in accordance to the following formula:

$$Table\,Cell = Severity\,DS + Severity\,PP$$

It should be stressed that the derived table cell value for a specific privacy principle and a specific data set, will not be necessarily the same for different organizations, since it depends on the calculated k_i value which is related to specific organizational characteristics (Table 2).

Table 2. The proposed PIA method

<table>
<tr><td></td><td>Severity DS</td><td>[1...7]</td><td>[1...7]</td><td>...</td><td>[1...7]</td></tr>
<tr><td>Severity PP =
a_{pp} * ki =</td><td>Data Sets
Privacy Principles</td><td>DATA SET 1
SeverityDS1</td><td>DATA SET 2
SeverityDS2</td><td>...</td><td>DATA SET N
SeverityDSn</td></tr>
<tr><td>[3] * k_1</td><td>Purpose Specification Principle
SeverityPSP</td><td colspan="4" rowspan="8"><u>LEVEL OF PRIVACY & SECURITY CRITICALITY</u>

Range of values for each Table Cell =
[(Severity DSi) + (a_{pp}*ki_{min})
...
(Severity DSi) + (a_{pp}*ki_{max})]</td></tr>
<tr><td>[2] * k_2</td><td>Collection Limitation Principle
SeverityCLP</td></tr>
<tr><td>[2] * k_3</td><td>Data Quality Principle
SeverityDQP</td></tr>
<tr><td>[1] * k_4</td><td>Use, Retention and Disclosure Limitation Principle
SeverityURDLP</td></tr>
<tr><td>[2] * k_5</td><td>Security Safeguards Principle
SeveritySSP</td></tr>
<tr><td>[2] * k_6</td><td>Openness Principle
SeverityOP</td></tr>
<tr><td>[2] * k_7</td><td>Individual Participation Principle
SeverityIPP</td></tr>
<tr><td>[2] * k_8</td><td>Accountability Principle
SeverityAP</td></tr>
</table>

<u>Where:</u>

- Severity DS (risk factor for each data set)
- Severity PP (privacy principles, privacy and security requirements, characteristics of the organization)
- Severity PP = a_{pp} * k_i
- a_{pp} = weighting factor of each privacy principle
- ki = 100% * Vector zi (Characteristics)
- z_i = characteristics of the organization

To summarize, the final value of each *Table Cell* highlights the criticality of each privacy principle for every data set maintained by the organization. The method employed for the calculation of that criticality level, as already explained in the previous sections, takes into account the consequences that the organization may experience in case of a security or privacy violation incident on a specific data set, the weighting of each privacy principle and the unique characteristics of each organization (Table 1).

The resulting table values offer a strong indication of the security measures and privacy enforcement mechanisms that the organization should adopt in order to effectively protect its data. More specifically the value of each table cell can be compared with the minimum or/and maximum value that the specific cell can take, depending on the characteristics of the organization (Table 1), and if it is found to be near to the maximum cell value the criticality of the privacy principle for the specific data set is considered to be very high.

4 Conclusions

This paper has presented a Privacy Impact Assessment method that employs metrics and takes into account the peculiarities and other characteristics of the organization. The aim is to assist the organizations to estimate the criticality of potential privacy breaches and, thus, to select the appropriate security measures for the protection of the data that they collect, process and store. As far as the identification and assessment of the risks, it is performed through the risk management or/and PIA methodology that the organization decides to use while for the mitigation of the risks it is in our plans for future work to develop a feedback channel that will enhance the proposed method in a way that it will be able to recalculate the criticality by taking into account the suitability/effectiveness of the implemented mitigation techniques. We will thus support the Plan-Do-Check-Act (PDCA) model of the ISO 27000 standard.

Additionally, we are considering the integration of the requirements set by the new Data General Protection Regulation (GDPR).

Acknowledgment. This work has been partially supported by the Research Center of the University of Piraeus.

References

1. Hong, W., Thong, J.Y.L.: Internet privacy concerns an integrated conceptualization and four empirical studies. MIS Q. **37**(1), 275–298 (2013). https://papers.ssrn.com/sol3/papers.cfm?abstract_id=2229627
2. Regulation (EU) 2016/679 of the European Parliament and of the Council: The European Parliament and the Council of the European Union, 27 April 2016. http://eur-lex.europa.eu/legal-content/EN/TXT/PDF/?uri=CELEX:32016R0679&qid=1485368166820&from=en
3. OECD Privacy Principles: OECDprivacy.org, 1980. http://oecdprivacy.org/

4. Makri, E.L., Lambrinoudakis, C.: Towards a common security and privacy requirements elicitation methodology. In: Jahankhani, H., Carlile, A., Akhgar, B., Taal, A., Hessami, A., Hosseinian-Far, A. (eds.) ICGS3 2015. CCIS, vol. 534, pp. 151–159. Springer, Cham (2015). https://doi.org/10.1007/978-3-319-23276-8_13
5. Makri, E.L., Lambrinoudakis, C.: Privacy principles: towards a common privacy audit methodology. In: Fischer-Hübner, S., Lambrinoudakis, C., López, J. (eds.) TrustBus 2015. LNCS, vol. 9264, pp. 219–234. Springer, Cham (2015). https://doi.org/10.1007/978-3-319-22906-5_17
6. Bélanger, F., Crossler, R.E.: Privacy in the digital age: a review of information privacy research in information systems. J. MIS Q. **35**(4), 1017–1042 (2011). http://dl.acm.org/citation.cfm?id=2208951
7. Wright, D., De Hert, P.: Introduction to privacy impact assessment. In: Wright, D., De Hert, P. (eds.) Privacy Impact Assessment. Law, Governance and Technology Series, vol. 6, pp. 3–32. Springer, Dordrecht (2012). https://doi.org/10.1007/978-94-007-2543-0_1
8. ISO/IEC FDIS 29134: Information technology—Security techniques—Privacy impact assessment—Guidelines, Target publication, 30 May 2017. http://www.iso.org/iso/catalogue_detail.htm?csnumber=62289, https://www.iso.org/obp/ui/#iso:std:iso-iec:29134:dis:ed-1:v1:en
9. Information Commissioner's Office (ICO): Privacy Impact Assessment Handbook, Wilmslow, Cheshire, December 2007, Version 2.0, June 2009
10. European Commission: Recommendation on the implementation of privacy and data protection principles in applications supported by radio-frequency identification, C (2009) 3200 final, Brussels, 12 May 2009. http://eur-lex.europa.eu/legal-content/EN/TXT/PDF/?uri=CELEX:32009H0387&from=EN
11. Information Commissioner's Office (ICO): Data Protection Act, Conducting privacy impact assessments code of practice, February 2014. https://ico.org.uk/media/for-organisations/documents/1595/pia-code-of-practice.pdf
12. Wang, Y., Kobsa, A.: Privacy-Enhancing Technologies (2008). http://www.cs.cmu.edu/afs/cs/Web/People/yangwan1/papers/2008-Handbook-LiabSec-AuthorCopy.pdf
13. Cavoukian, A.: Creation of a Global Privacy Standard, November 2006. http://www.ipc.on.ca/images/Resources/gps.pdf
14. Cavoukian, A., Taylor, S., Abrams, M.E.: Privacy by design: essential for organizational accountability and strong business practices. In: Identity in the Information Society, Springer (2010). http://link.springer.com/article/10.1007/s12394-010-0053-z
15. Cavoukian, A.: Privacy by design – the 7 foundational principles, Technical report, Information and Privacy Commissioner of Ontario, January 2011. (revised version)
16. Oetzel, M.C., Spiekermann, S.: Privacy-by-design through systematic privacy impact assessment - a design science approach. In: ECIS 2012 Proceedings, Paper 160 (2012). http://aisel.aisnet.org/ecis2012/160
17. Oetzel, M.C., Spiekermann, S.: A systematic method for privacy impact assessments: a design science approach. Eur. J. Inf. Syst. **23**(2), 1–25 (2013)
18. van Blarkom, G.W., Borking, J.J., Olk, J.G.E.: PET, Handbook of Privacy and Privacy-Enhancing Technologies, The Case of Intelligent Software Agents (2003). ISBN 90-74087-33-7. http://www.andrewpatrick.ca/pisa/handbook/Handbook_Privacy_and_PET_final.pdf
19. Information Commissioner's Office (ICO): Privacy Impact Assessment Handbook, Wilmslow, Cheshire, Version 1.0, December 2007
20. Information Commissioner's Office (ICO): Privacy impact assessment and risk management, May 2013. https://ico.org.uk/media/1042196/trilateral-full-report.pdf

21. Information Commissioner's Office (ICO): Conducting privacy impact assessments code of practice, February 2014. https://ico.org.uk/media/for-organisations/documents/1595/pia-code-of-practice.pdf
22. Information Commissioner's Office (ICO): The Guide to Data Protection, January 2017. https://ico.org.uk/media/for-organisations/guide-to-data-protection-2-7.pdf
23. European Commission PIAF: A Privacy Impact Assessment Framework for data protection and privacy rights, January 2011–October 2012. http://www.piafproject.eu/Index.html
24. Wright, D., Wadhwa, K.: A step-by-step guide to privacy impact assessment, Second PIAF workshop, Sopot, 24 April 2012. http://www.piafproject.eu/ref/A_step-by-step_guide_to_privacy_impact_assessment-19Apr2012.pdf
25. Wright, D.: Should privacy impact assessments be mandatory? Commun. ACM **54**(8), 121–131 (2011). https://doi.org/10.1145/1978542.1978568. http://cacm.acm.org/magazines/2011/8
26. Wadhwa, K., Rodrigues, R.: Evaluating privacy impact assessments. Innov.: Eur. J. Soc. Sci. Res. **26**(1–2), 161–180 (2013). http://www.tandfonline.com/doi/abs/10.1080/13511610.2013.761748, http://www.tandfonline.com/doi/pdf/10.1080/13511610.2013.761748?needAccess=true
27. Brooks, S., Nadeau, E.: Privacy Risk Management for Federal Information Systems, Information Technology Laboratory, NIST, Internal Report 8062, May 2015. http://csrc.nist.gov/publications/drafts/nistir-8062/nistir_8062_draft.pdf
28. Ferris, J.M.: The ISO PIA standard for financial services. In: Wright, D., De Hert, P. (eds.) Privacy Impact Assessment. Law, Governance and Technology Series, vol. 6, pp. 307–321. Springer, Dordrecht (2012). https://doi.org/10.1007/978-94-007-2543-0_14
29. Wright, D.: Should privacy impact assessments be mandatory? Trilateral Research & Consulting, 17 September 2009. http://www.ics.forth.gr/nis09/presentations/18-wright.pdf
30. Agarwal, S.: Developing a structured metric to measure privacy risk in privacy impact assessments. In: Aspinall, D., Camenisch, J., Hansen, M., Fischer-Hübner, S., Raab, C. (eds.) Privacy and Identity 2015. IAICT, vol. 476, pp. 141–155. Springer, Cham (2016). https://doi.org/10.1007/978-3-319-41763-9_10
31. NIST (National Institute of Standards and Technology): Risk management guide for information technology systems, NIST Special Publication 800-30 (2002)
32. Data Protection Act (1998). http://www.legislation.gov.uk/ukpga/1998/29/contents, http://www.legislation.gov.uk/ukpga/1998/29/pdfs/ukpga_19980029_en.pdf
33. European Union Agency for Network and Information Security (ENISA): CRAMM (CCTA Risk Analysis and Management Method). https://www.enisa.europa.eu/topics/threat-risk-management/risk-management/current-risk/risk-management-inventory/rm-ra-methods/m_cramm.html
34. Commission Nationale de l'Informatique et des Libertés (CNIL), Privacy Impact Assessment (PIA) Methodology (how to carry out a PIA), June 2015. https://www.cnil.fr/sites/default/files/typo/document/CNIL-PIA-1-Methodology.pdf
35. Commission Nationale de l'Informatique et des Libertés (CNIL): The open source PIA software helps to carry out data protection impact assessment, January 2018. https://www.cnil.fr/en/open-source-pia-software-helps-carry-out-data-protection-impact-assesment
36. De Capitani, S., di Vimercati, S., Foresti, G.L., Samarati, P., Privacy, D.: Definitions and techniques. Int. J. Uncertainty, Fuzziness Knowl.-Based Syst. **20**(6), 793–818 (2012)
37. Tancock, D., Pearson, S., Charlesworth, A.: A privacy impact assessment tool for cloud computing. In: Second IEEE International Conference on Cloud Computing, pp. 667–676. Indiana University, USA (2010)

A Conceptual Redesign of a Modelling Language for Cyber Resiliency of Healthcare Systems

Myrsini Athinaiou(✉), Haralambos Mouratidis, Theo Fotis, and Michalis Pavlidis

University of Brighton, Brighton BN2 4GJ, UK
M.Athinaiou@brighton.ac.uk

Abstract. Security constraints that enforce security requirements characterize healthcare systems. These constraints have a substantial impact on the resiliency of the final system. Security requirements modelling approaches allow the prevention of cyber incidents; however, the focus to date has been on prevention rather than resiliency. Resiliency extends into the detection, mitigation and recovery after security violations. In this paper, we propose an enhanced at a conceptual level that attempts to align cybersecurity with resiliency. It does so by extending the Secure Tropos cybersecurity modelling language to include resiliency. The proposed conceptual model examines resiliency from three viewpoints, namely the security requirements, the healthcare context and its implementational capability. We present an overview of our conceptual model of a cyber resiliency language and discuss a case study to attest the healthcare context in our approach.

Keywords: Security · Resiliency · Modelling language · Healthcare

1 Introduction

Security covers an increasingly broad range of domains that rarely interplay in other contexts. For example, a healthcare system's security design should address, not just hardware and software vulnerabilities, but also other issues, such as equipment failures, human errors, dependencies of healthcare services. In this sense, it essential to provide a common language to address and manage this heterogeneity within the security context. Such a language will allow the specification of a broad range of security requirements of different stakeholders within the healthcare setting. Moreover, it can allow the analysis of their resiliency as part of their security requirements elicitation, meaning as early as possible in their design.

Healthcare systems stand for the organization of interacting elements arranged to accomplish one or more healthcare purposes (based on [1]). Examples of healthcare systems are implantable cardiac medical devices; medical ventilator and robotic X-ray. Long life-cycles characterize healthcare systems. Over the usable lifespan of health-care, their design and development methods change [47]. While an understanding of the preventive security aspects of healthcare systems' design is essential, issues

S. Katsikas et al. (Eds.): ESORICS 2019 Workshops, LNCS 11980, pp. 140–158, 2020.
https://doi.org/10.1007/978-3-030-42048-2_10

associated with other requirements and constraints when incidents occur are of more significant concern for life-critical and context-aware systems. Healthcare systems are increasingly networked, interconnected and software-dependent. With limited resources and an ever-evolving threat landscape, any new insight into the cyber resiliency of healthcare systems and their design and implementation becomes crucial [22].

Cyber resiliency (also termed resilience) stands according to NIST SP 800-160, V.2. for "*the ability to anticipate, withstand, recover from, and adapt to adverse conditions, stresses, attacks, or compromises on systems that use or are enabled by cyber resources.*" [40]. Based on the context (e.g., supply chain, environmental, psychological, technological) with which it associates, resiliency can approach different types of problems. In this paper, we focus only on cybersecurity resiliency, excluding other contexts of resiliency.

One approach to allow the by-design cyber resiliency of maintaining security requirements is the Model-driven engineering (MDE) [10, 47]. For healthcare systems that have the patient-in-the-loop, model-based frameworks that explicitly model an MCPS's interaction with the environment and with the patient can contribute towards safer development [5]. Similarly, modelled-based security approaches have shown the benefits of considering security requirements from the early stages of systems development [32, 34]. Such modelling approaches can potentially facilitate the development of healthcare systems that consider the full cyber resiliency life-cycle (i.e., preparation, identification, containment, eradication, recovery, lessons learned) [13].

Many security requirements modelling approaches are based on *Goal-oriented Requirements Engineering* (GORE). Typically, they analyze a system considering its organizational, operational and technical environment; to identify issues and opportunities. High-level goals are then modelled refined to address such issues and meet the opportunities [15, 20]. In Security Requirements Engineering (SRE), relevant requirements are then elaborated to meet those goals [2, 32, 34]. MDE and SRE may be used in combination to support the resilience of healthcare systems and in particular, to improve the awareness of redesign and reconfiguration capabilities of a healthcare system, before its actual construction. After all, any of such activities, if not well studied in advance, can harm the patients. Such cases contradict with the fundamental medical goal of "at least not harm" [5], and hence, they should not be ignored in healthcare systems engineering.

The main aim of this paper is to explore the consideration of cyber resiliency under conditions of uncertainty where incidents challenge the achievement of a healthcare system's goals. In this paper, we present the first step towards the modelling language, which will be part of a framework: redesigning a metamodel. Notice that we do not offer a modelling language, but we do present underlying conceptual considerations that led to the redesign of the language.

The research outcomes presented here aim to enhance the resilience management of cybersecurity by proposing a cybersecurity-resilience unified model. Mainly, the contribution of this paper comprises of:

- a combination of resiliency in the cybersecurity domain, extending the Secure Tropos approach to cover resiliency concepts. We focus on the design of systems considering cyber resiliency from the stage of requirements engineering;

- the proposed conceptual model presented as a UML class diagram, useful for the development of other cybersecurity artefacts that support cyber resiliency. Such artefacts can include processes, algorithms and tools. Such artefacts can support the semi-automation of a cyber resiliency analysis;
- the demonstration of the pertinence of the conceptual model in regard to the healthcare context, through a case study.

2 Background

Existing research indicates areas where more domain-specific research is needed. It is possible to form a structured approach for cyber resiliency with the current technical means. But validation and evaluation approaches for the assessment of resiliency plans and their resilience capability is limited [12, 14, 16, 18, 44]. Restrictions in the form of time, security capabilities, actors' skills, responder's motivation, financial resources and heterogeneity among systems are also addressed [11, 14, 18, 21, 30, 45] showing the need for a holistic approach. The technological heterogeneity that introduces complexity associated with the healthcare context yields a technical conflict [7, 23]. Specifically, security mechanisms exist for security [44], but research related to their cyber resiliency, let alone in regard to healthcare systems is very limited [23]. This is coupled with the challenges of incident quantification [17] and cyber resiliency assessment [14], enforcement of resiliency plans and security practices during response [18, 44]. Additionally, the lack of cybersecurity expertise results in outsourced resilience that does not correspond to healthcare contextual needs [14, 21]. Hence more research is required in the field where cybersecurity, resiliency and healthcare intersect.

2.1 Healthcare Cyber Resiliency

Concerning healthcare and cyber resiliency, Jalali et al. conducted a systematic review of journal articles that focus on cyber resiliency in healthcare [23]. They identified the need to evaluate and improve incident response strategies. The existing literature, in regard to the different phases of resiliency offers some guidance. For example, for preparation phase of cyber resiliency in healthcare, the literature addresses the need for more resources referring not only to financial but also to other types such as human availability and systems' redundancies [14, 16, 44]. It also identifies the need for security policies [12, 16, 44], identification capability of critical information, systems, actors and the dependencies among them [43–45].

The literature related to the cyber resiliency phase of detection and analysis, shows that independently from preparedness and preventive security mechanisms, incidents can still occur. When that happens a root cause analysis (RCA)is suggested [11, 14] to guide incident categorization [16, 17, 21]. When an incident does occur, existing works are concerned with the need of healthcare organizations to maintain communication with internal and external parties, which will be also used for compliance with legally required notifications [14, 16–18, 23]. Forensic analysis is essential at all phases and at this phase it supports incident classification, prioritization and damage assessment of the affected entities [12, 16, 23].

At the phase of containment, eradication and recovery, according to the literature, incident response teams (IRTs) need to contain an incident initially. Containment requires the availability of relevant technical and legal expertise [14]. At this phase incident, IRTs want to eliminate any further damage [16]. They can achieve that through a diverse set of control mechanisms to initially neutralize an attack, using incident response systems, segmentation of networks, disconnection of affected devices and algorithmic recovery support to name a few [11, 23]. These are all relevant with downtime procedures, vulnerabilities patching and forensic evidence preservation [16, 23].

For the implementation of these controls and activities, what seems to be essential is the way with which IRTs prioritize restoration activities [17]. This prioritization seems in case studies to be a straight forward ability, and current ad hoc practices seem to indicate that [14]. However, within healthcare organizations, there are various people, processes and technologies that are prioritized differently under different circumstances [14, 16]. Thus an ad hoc mentality is not optimal as attacks are sophisticated, and they can introduce delays and further vulnerabilities that can allow more attacks, more significant impact or increased costs [11, 14].

Lastly, at the phase of post-incident activity that follows the demobilization of the emergency operations command center, healthcare organizations need to take actions to prevent an incident's recurrence [17, 43]. Regulatory oversight might be necessary in cases of health sector-wide digital changes, following an incident [18]. To list and initiate the necessary changes as well as to determine how wide they need to be, the identification of what went wrong is necessary. After debriefing takes place based on reports of incident occurrence and severity resulted from the previous phases, assessments are conducted [14, 44].

After this knowledge has been collected, it needs to be redistributed back to the healthcare organization [21, 23]. Essential part of this process is the documentation of the recommendations and lessons learned that commonly take the form of a after action report (AAR) [14, 16, 17, 23].

2.2 Security-Oriented Modelling Languages

There are plenty of existing security-oriented modelling languages. Each one of the addresses relevant concerns from a different viewpoint. Usually, they extend existing modelling languages to cover security concerns. For example, Misuse Cases [42] and Abuse Cases [29], extend the use case diagrams, to elicit threats and vulnerabilities that adversaries could target. SecureUML [28] also extends UML diagrams centering on authorization constraints for access control goals. UMLsec [24] is another approach that extends UML, providing security data to UML diagrams. SecureUML and UMLsec address security at the design level and they do not concentrate on assets and early security requirements.

Other examples are extensions of the i* goal-oriented approach [46], an extension of Tropos [19]. KAOS, which is also goal-oriented, addresses security concerns by perceiving attacks as anti-goals [26]. Anti-goals stand for adversarial purposes that obstruct security goals. Abuse Frames have also been used to frame a security problem's scope with anti-requirements and their usage to aid the formation of security requirements and the examination of relevant vulnerabilities and threats [27].

The Secure Tropos [34] approach is also an extended Tropos [9] version, which provides means to elicit and analyze security requirements. It allows the expression of a wide range of security, privacy and trust requirements in the form of constraints. Secure Tropos is well-known for being a robust language for defining secure systems at the organizational level. Its organizational approach to security allows its extension to cover the healthcare context considering attacks that can have beyond cyber also physical impact. Furthermore, existing automatic tools (i.e., SecTro [36]) ease the design activities using this metamodel and can also be extended accordingly.

3 Redesign Decisions and Challenges

The Secure Tropos metamodel inspired the first design attempt of a cyber resiliency modelling language for healthcare [34]. The initial design of the metamodel can be found in [6]. The decision of a redesign stemmed from interviews with experts from the Brighton and Sussex University Hospitals and MedStar Health as well as the application of small case studies. From there, it became apparent that the metamodel needed some enhancements. As a group, we agreed into three main redesign enhancements: the incident, the healthcare context and the inclusion of constructs related to resiliency. These enchantments led to the design of a second version of the metamodel, presented in Fig. 1. The following subsections report on how this metamodel was redesigned.

3.1 Justification for the Use of Secure Tropos

We consider that the Secure Tropos metamodel is suitable to achieve the following purposes that relate to our research:

1. Supports the analysis and design activities in the software development process, capturing early and late requirements, modelling the environment of the system and the system itself respectively. Hence it can be used for healthcare systems representing the unique environment in which they operate.
2. It takes into account the relationship between security controls and security requirements [38]. This aspect forms an important base for the assessment of a security design when controls fail to achieve security requirements (i.e., when successful attacks do occur).
3. It is based on the principle that security should be taken into consideration from the early stages of the software system development process instead of been added as an afterthought. Resiliency also needs to be considered from early development stages, and a relevant conceptual extension might be useful.
4. Provides a modelling language, a process and a set of reasoning automation to support security analysis. The overall approach is well known and peer-reviewed, and any extension does not need to establish fundamental constructs but focus only to those constructs that are related to cyber resiliency and are not currently covered.

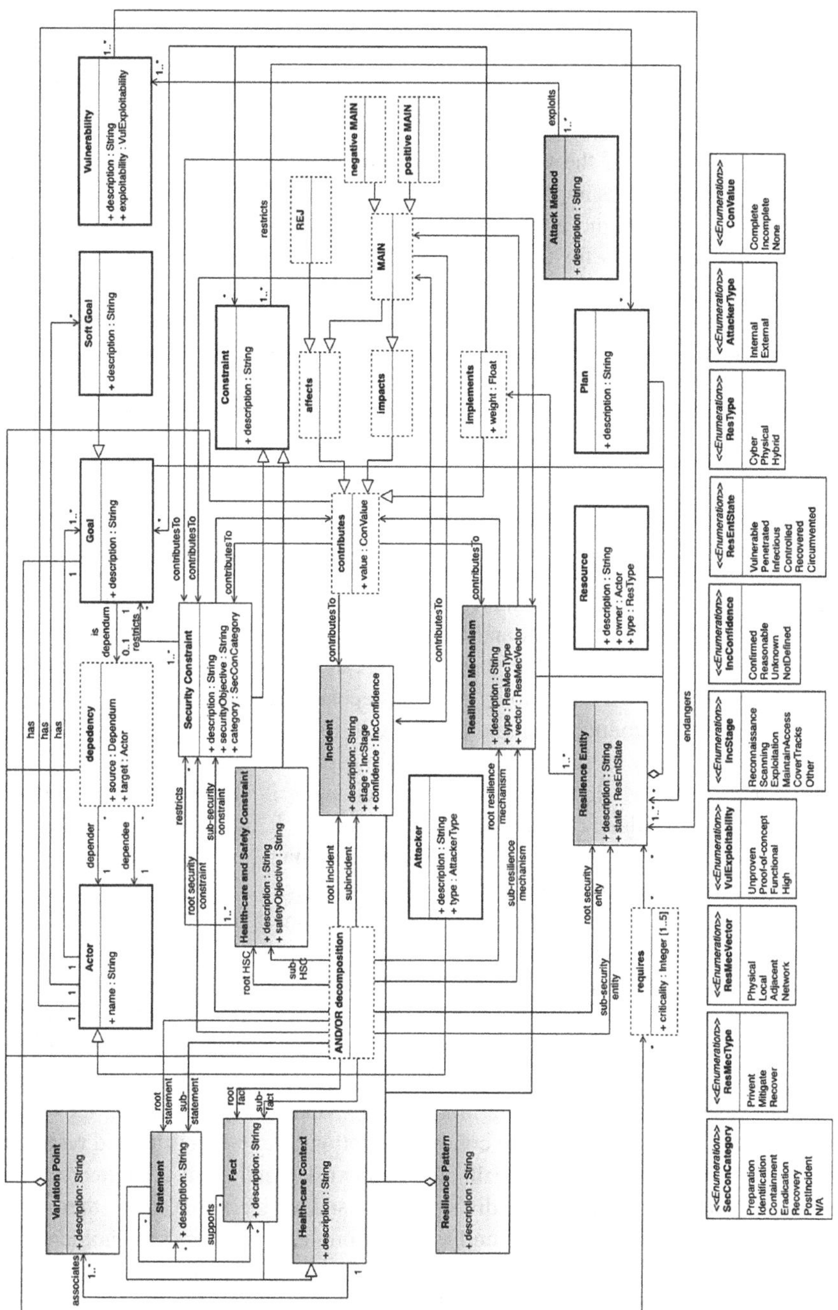

Fig. 1. Redesigned metamodel.

5. Secure Tropos, has been already extended to cover different types of systems (e.g., cloud security requirements [33], trust [37], business processes [4]). Following this paradigm, an extension can take place addressing the unique characteristics of healthcare systems in relation to their cyber resiliency.

Having identified some of the advantages of extending Secure Tropos, coincide with other security requirements approaches (e.g., KAOS [25], CORAS [8], SQUARE [31], GBRAM [3]). However, these approaches tend to focus on the preventive aspect of security. Resiliency stands for the ability to prepare for, respond to and recover from cyber incidents. It helps a healthcare infrastructure to prepare for incidents, defend against, limit their severity and ensure the continuation of operations despite an incident. Cyber resiliency has emerged as traditional cybersecurity measures are challenged, especially in the case of APTs [35]. When incidents do occur, the systems need to be able to keep up with the changes and continue to pursue critical goals and functions.

3.2 Redesign Challenges

The redesign of the modelling language with resiliency in the healthcare context is a challenging and critical task. Typically, cybersecurity languages are well structured and technical. Requirements engineers and technology-oriented stakeholders use the same vocabulary having a technological focus. They can follow deterministic approaches using security models as the technological interdependencies are known. However, the healthcare context introduces unique challenges for a language redesign. Such a redesign requires a way to capture the healthcare aspect to be able to express relevant processes and services. However, this is not enough. It also needs to show how cybersecurity and resiliency affect and are affected by it too. There classical deterministic approaches do not suffice. Because on the one hand, incidents cannot be easily analyzed and managed, nor cyber resiliency engineering is yet well studied and understood to be able to determine with certainty responses and their negative impact on infrastructure's operational or security capability.

Semantic level differences intensify these difficulties as the language has a multidisciplinary focus. Different interpretations of the same term or different terms with the same meaning are common, which the literature review indicates. Nevertheless, the language needs to ensure that all the involved stakeholders share and understand the terminology used. However, this terminology expands far beyond the technology constructs commonly applied for the conceptualization of cybersecurity and resiliency. Social aspects integrated into the healthcare context demand from a language to also consider the values that underpin a diverse set of stakeholders that holds them might prioritize and appreciate them differently. For example, healthcare stakeholders commonly focus on systems functionalities that enhance the health and wellbeing of patients and do not cause harm. Naturally, they prioritize safety over security and understand the necessity for cyber resiliency differently from security and resiliency engineers. For example, they prioritize availability over maintenance and practice with medical equipment over participation in the incident response capability testing of their department. To redesign a language that combines cybersecurity features with resiliency, we realized that there was a need to form constructs that support their unification. Though, there was no clear way derived from the literature to support us into making such a decision. Consequently, to face this obstruction, we plan to involve practitioners for validation of the redesigned language.

3.3 Healthcare Cyber Resiliency Challenges

Healthcare services are dependent not only to computer systems and hospital equipment but also to devices attached to or even implemented in the human body. Thus, the healthcare context introduces unique challenges in the design of a language. For cybersecurity and resiliency, this means that any configuration can have not only cyber impact but also kinetic. This context sets implementational barriers of conventional cybersecurity approaches. For example, the time and duration of security and resiliency are affected. They need to consider what healthcare processes are ongoing when an incident occurs and how they can pursue security requirements attainment even when an attack has successfully compromised other healthcare systems of the same infrastructure (e.g., hospital, biomaterials facility).

Moreover, healthcare systems are diverse and have different challenges and limitations based on their type. For instance, the security challenges for a healthcare system where the user has device control capabilities, raise cybersecurity challenges related to the design of an interface that recognizes cases of patient's misuse [39]. However, in healthcare systems that sense and actuate without user involvement, the challenges are different and not user-related. They relate to the systems decision process design, the establishment of secure communications among system's components given hardware limitations, and even the alert system that will inform that security configurations are undertaken and can change the system's behavior and are within the patient's body [39]. It becomes clear through these simple examples that healthcare challenges cannot be excluded from the cyber resilience design because that can cause much more than just systems malfunctions. The patient is in the loop of this system, along with all the other users of such devices and ultimately the society as a whole. Please note that the first paragraph of a section or subsection is not indented. The first paragraphs that follows a table, figure, equation etc. does not have an indent, either.

3.4 Conceptual Metamodel Redesign

The basic idea of redesigning a metamodel is that the initial metamodel is the source that produces the redesigned metamodel. Before presenting an overview of the redesigned model, let us clarify that we have a model engineering perspective. In other words, we want to elaborate redesign decisions with the help of metamodels. Model engineering suggests that we have to start by identifying an existing metamodel for a redesign. Such a metamodel abstracts and collects the changes. In our redesign, we use the UML class diagram for the formulation of redesign models. Consequently, the redesigned model is a UML model. The class diagram in Fig. 2 presents the three parts of the redesigned model. Incident constructs are in the middle, healthcare constructs in the left, and resiliency constructs in the right. The model also expresses generalization and associations among the various constructs.

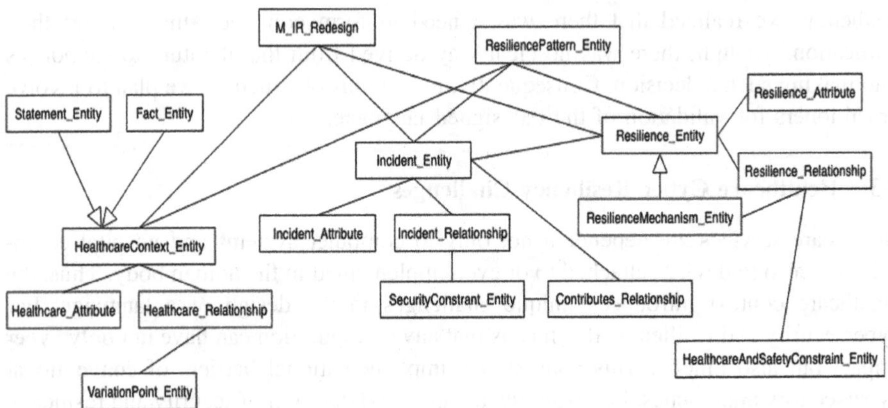

Fig. 2. Early version of the redesigned metamodel of Secure Tropos.

The main semantic changes reflected in the three parts of the redesigned model resulted from a systematic review of the scientific and standardization literature. The purpose of the review was the sound derivation of a conceptual model. Here we cannot present in detail the review process, but we discuss the main findings that resulted in the redesign of the modelling language at a conceptual level. Every construct has a variety of functions and implications, which can change over time and context. The conceptual unification of cybersecurity and resiliency starts with the identification of the basic constructs of the problem to be treated. The common terms identified in the relevant literature are incident, healthcare, response and security. We briefly present how they have been interpreted, offering useful components for the design of a conceptual model of a modelling language.

The set of collected papers interprets the term incident in four different ways. The majority of papers (7) consider an event such as updates, hardware failures, emergencies, human errors, natural disasters, misuse and abuse cases as occurrences of incidents [12, 14, 17, 21, 30, 44, 45]. In 4 papers an incident interpreted as a cybersecurity attack like hacking, ransomware and advanced persistent threat (APT) [7, 11, 12, 43]. Two (2) papers use the NIST SP 8000-61 definition either explicitly or implicitly [16, 23] and 1 paper focuses on the effects of an occurrence on systems functions and society as an incident [18]. Here it seems that an incident definition exists, and each study chooses to focus on an aspect of an incident. Other studies seem to choose a wider scope, that of event that also includes incidents and subsequently cybersecurity incidents.

Healthcare overall appeared to have five different meanings. In 3 papers coincides with the term hospital [16, 17, 44], in 6 papers with a form of a system, including medical cyber-physical systems, electronic medical records systems and healthcare information systems [7, 11, 14, 30, 43, 45], in 3 papers as a healthcare critical infrastructure or a particular type (e.g. NHS) [7, 18, 45], in 2 papers addressed healthcare organizations in general [21, 23] and 1 was focusing on healthcare information [12]. From the above, it can be observed that the majority of papers interpret the term healthcare as a type of healthcare system. It is important here to clarify, that the reason the number of papers corresponding to meanings (15) is greater than the set of papers collected (13) is that in some papers the same term is used but is given multiple meanings. The same holds for the rest of the terms and the corresponding number of papers with similar interpretations.

When it comes to response, 4 papers address specific aspects/phases like detection, forensics and post-incident activities [7, 12, 21, 30] 3 papers refer to all the phases of incident response [14, 16, 43], 2 papers analyze response overarching manner ranging from reactive on the one end and on the other to proactive adaptable responses to incident characteristics [11, 44], in 2 papers response is studied within the planning context in the form of an incident response plan (IRP) along with other types of plans like emergency plan and business continuity plan [17, 23]. Response is also considered closely associated with resilience and recovery in [45] and with management in [18]. The selected set of papers studies response from many aspects, usually related either with its phases individually or as a whole and in other studies as broader positioning of response within healthcare organizations.

The concept of security is one that is commonly associated with safety. Within this set of papers that was the case only in [16] and even there, the proposed security approach adjusts to feet cybersecurity needs. Examining relevant papers, it also seems that security mostly in the past but also in the present focuses on information security and confidentiality, integrity and availability properties [12, 16, 21, 30, 44, 45]. However, in more recent studies, cyber-physical aspects are studied as well as moving from information technology-security to what is referred to in the broader literature as operational technology-security [7, 18].

Specific aspects of security are also studies in the relevant literature. The conceptualization of security as vulnerable [45], the adaptability of security [11, 45] are two such examples. Moreover, security is addressed from a socio-technical perspective [43], as organization wide [14, 17]. In some cases, defense [44] and forensics [12] as important elements of security are studied based on risk plans [23]. Thus, security evolves as cyber risks do. The cyber risks become more sophisticated and dynamic, and security interpretations and understanding reflect these changes.

3.5 Incident Redesign

While most people have an intuitive idea of what an incident is when asked to define it explicitly, there are large numbers of correct answers. From early incident response research, we learn that incidents have typically been defined as including the concepts of a set of security constraints imposed to goals within an infrastructure, that are impacted from actual attacks or are exposed to potential threats. An incident has been defined from NIST SP.800-61r2 as "*a violation or imminent threat of violation of computer security policies, acceptable use policies, or standard security practices.*" [13]. Based on the above definitions and our interviews with experts an incident stands for a negative occurrence that happens or is thought of as happening and leads to the failure of security constraints maintenance.

This definition similar to NIST SP.800-61r2 is quite subtle because it not only allows that an incident can be something that actually happened in the real world, but also that it can be imaginary and does not really occur. The example of a false positive alarm of an intrusion detection system can be treated as an incident even though it did not occur. The second meaning describes incidents that occur in computer systems. In this way, the term incident corresponds to incidents as a threat or as an actual attack.

An incident can be better understood through its likelihood and severity. In our framework, we consider likelihood as evidence that maintains or rejects the occurrence of an incident (MAIN and REJ). For example, the resilience entity *all the actions the surgeon takes should be recorded with nonrepudiation capability* in the telesurgery robotic system will help to enforce (MAIN) the security constraint *protect against any reasonably anticipated uses or disclosures of patient's health-care data* and discard (REJ) the incident *modify messages while packets are in-flight*.

On the other hand, severity is introduced as the influence of an incident to a security constraint. This relation allows us to model situations where a single incident impacts on more than one security constraints. The occurrence of an incident contributes to security constraint maintenance. In other words, a system under normal circumstances achieves a security constraint. When an incident occurs, the system wants to maintain security constraint achievement. The occurrence of an incident contributes to a security constraint's negatively in regard to its maintenance. Since the severity of an incident restrains a security constraint when it occurs, in our model, we use only MAIN relations between an incident and security constraints. This relation stands for the maintenance of an incident and can result in a positive or negative contribution to a security constraint's maintenance.

On the other hand, a *resilience mechanism* is a tool or technique that can be adopted in order to either prevent, mitigate or recover from an incident or is meant to implement a security constraint. A resilience mechanism might operate by itself, or with others, to provide a particular service. When an incident stands for a threat, then the preventive aspect of a resilience mechanism is meaningful, whereas in cases where an incident is an actual attack, then the mitigating and recovery aspects are relevant.

A *healthcare and safety constraint* (HSC) is a safety condition that the system has to achieve and restricts a security constraint in order not to endanger a patient's health and/or well-being. In the modelling process, HSC constraints are modelled as variation points of a resiliency plan. They are imposed by a healthcare actor that restricts the achievement of a security constraint. HSC constraints are within the control of an actor. This association with actors means that, differently than security constraints, HSC constraints are conditions that an actor wishes to introduce to protect the patient in the loop that characterizes healthcare systems. However, HSC constraints are examined based on how they affect security entities and thus contribute towards the analysis of resilience security requirements. HSC constraints can also be grouped according to the safety objective towards the achievement they contribute. Safety objectives are broader descriptions of safety principles or rules such as sterilization, calibration and interoperability.

3.6 Healthcare Redesign

Healthcare services are dependent not only to computer systems and hospital equipment but also to devices attached to or even implemented in the human body. Thus, the healthcare context introduces unique challenges in the design of a language. For cybersecurity and resiliency, this means that any configuration can have not only cyber impact but also kinetic (e.g., physical harm to a patient). This context sets implementational barriers of conventional cybersecurity approaches. For example, the time and duration of security and resiliency are affected. They need to consider what healthcare processes are ongoing when an incident occurs and how they can pursue security requirements attainment even when an attack has successfully compromised other healthcare systems of the same infrastructure (e.g., hospital, biomaterials facility).

Moreover, healthcare systems are diverse and have different challenges and limitations based on their type. For instance, the security challenges for a healthcare system where the user has device control capabilities, raise cybersecurity challenges related to the design of an interface that recognizes cases of patients' misuse [39]. However, in healthcare systems that sense and actuate without user involvement, the challenges are different and not user-related. They relate to the systems decision process design, the establishment of secure communications among system's components given hardware limitations, and even the alert system that will inform that security configurations are undertaken and can change the system's behavior and are within the patient's body [39]. It becomes clear through these simple examples that healthcare challenges cannot be excluded from the cyber resilience design because that can cause much more than just systems malfunctions. The patient is in the loop of this system, along with all the other users of such devices. Text can be associated with AND/OR decomposition, contribution and dependency.

3.7 Resiliency Redesign

Resilience mechanisms are central to the process of determining the impact of an incident on the security constraint satisfaction. For instance, the incident *ransomware attack* can obstruct the satisfaction of the security constraint *patients' data availability*. However, the severity of this incident can be reduced with the use of the resilience mechanisms *use different credentials for backup storage*, *maintain complete visibility of healthcare IT infrastructure* and *leverage different file systems for backup storage*. The vulnerability is a critical component that defines the weakness of the designed healthcare system or the structure that can be exploited from one or more attack methods (e.g., unpatched equipment, insecure communication protocols). Attack methods are needed to distinguish between the ways an attacker can utilize to harm the system and how this harm is manifested. For example, a social engineering attack method manifests as an information breach threat. Each attack method is linked to one or more system vulnerabilities.

Another relevant construct to an incident is the *resilience entity* that represents any resilience-related goal, soft goal, plan, resource, resilience mechanism of the system. We extend the meaning of the security entity to cover resilience. For that purpose, we use the concept as an overarching term to cover especially decomposition, requires and endangers relations.

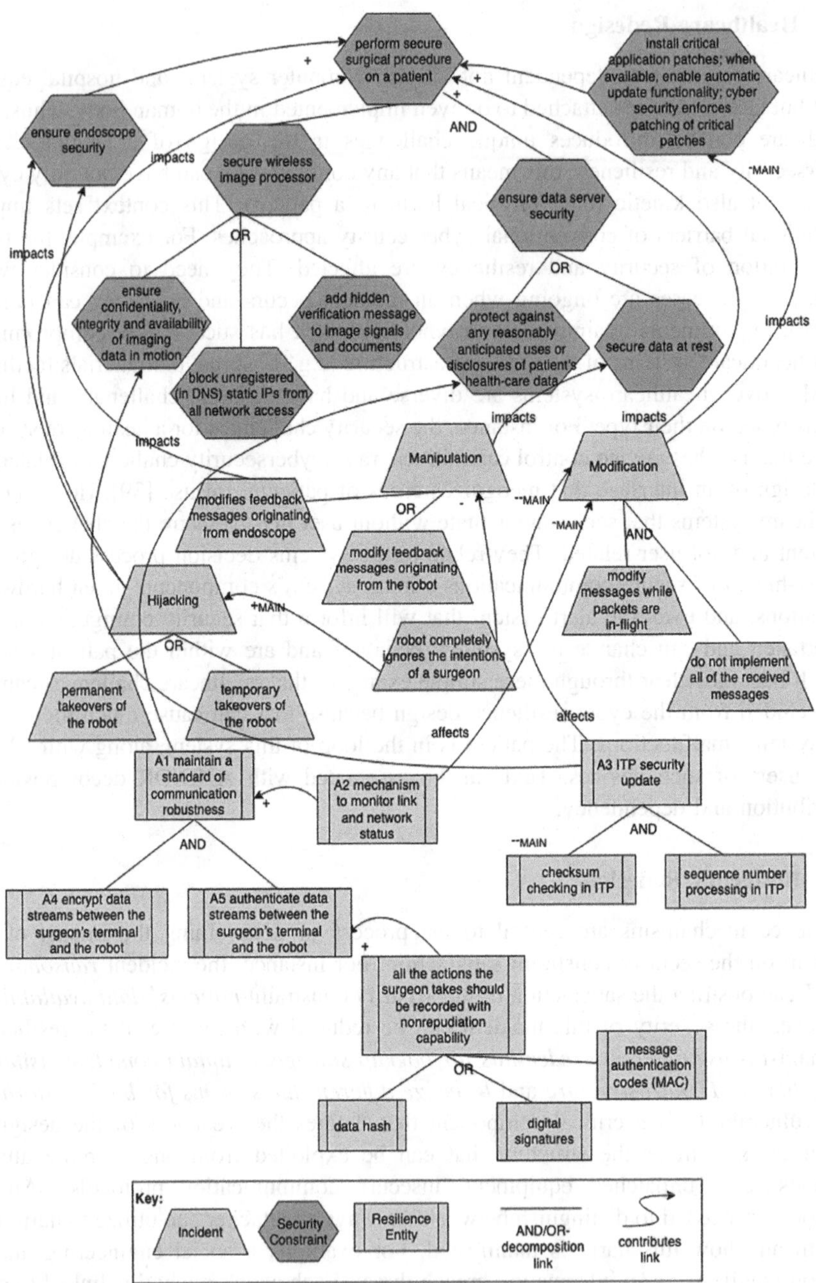

Fig. 3. Example of security model.

We understood that detecting simple mishandling incidents is a critical issue. However, heading off incidents before they occur requires detecting patterns as they are happening. Patterns of resilience can be used to detect situations where resilience is likely to result in an unwanted impact. A *resilience pattern* can be extracted based on the pattern definition given from Schumacher [41]. In general terms, a *Resilience pattern* is a template that specifies resilience objects called instances of the pattern. According to a security ontology introduced from Schumacher [41] a security pattern aggregates the concepts: context, problem and solution. In our modelling language following the same pattern ontology, we aggregate under a resilience pattern the concepts: health-care context, incident and resilience mechanism as defined in this document. The construct incident stands for a specific and observable adversarial action that violates or poses an imminent threat of violation of security constraints (based on NIST SP.800-61r2 [13]). It is a negative occurrence that happens or is thought of as happening.

The general structure of resilience patterns is identical to traditional patterns. They have a descriptive name, a context, a problem and a solution. There are relations to other resilience patterns as well. Nevertheless, specific resilience concepts can be assigned to these structural pattern elements. An example of such a pattern is teleoperation that is subject to hijacking and to be resilient for such attacks it is designed with non-persistence (i.e., generating and retaining resources within needs and time constraints).

4 Case Study

We take a scenario where a surgical system performs a surgical procedure (e.g., biopsy) on a patient with manipulators and an endoscope. An endoscope is a long, thin, flexible tube that has a light source and camera at one end. In our scenario, the surgical system comprises a surgical robot, including a station, four robot arms mounted on the station and a console for controlling the surgical robot. The surgical system also comprises a data server for storing information from diagnostic imaging modalities (e.g. MRI, CT, X-ray) which have been captured from a patient with the use of an ultrasonic diagnostic device mounted on the distal end of a robot arm and a display unit. The display unit simultaneously displays an endoscopic image and acquired from the endoscope and an ultrasonic image acquired by the ultrasonic diagnostic device. This scenario provides a simplified view of the stakeholders in the surgical system, the healthcare services supported, and the concepts involved when a healthcare service is provided.

Due to space limitations in Figs. 3 and 4 we present a partial view that captures the security and healthcare context, respectively. Particularly Fig. 4 depicts the healthcare context along with goals, security constraints and resilience entities. The process starts taking the security constraints from Secure Tropos and forming a conjunctive security constraints tree (where the relation between sub-security constraints represents conjunctive or disjunctive sub-security constraints). We have developed a simple security constraints structure with parent goal "perform surgical procedure on a patient" that has an AND decomposition (both of them need to be achieved for the parent goal to be achieved) with the sub-goals "use console to control the surgical robot" and "utilize patient data from the data server". From the high-level security constraint "perform a secure surgical procedure on a patient", we can also extract leaf security constraints that must be satisfied by resilience entities within the system. In our example, we prefer to keep simplicity at this point, because the AND/OR decomposition are well known in the existing literature.

Given ongoing attacks and expected incidents, we derive what security constraints are relevant to these incidents and consequently, what are the security entities that we need to consider. These considerations take the form of a three-layered incident model that connects security constraints, incidents and resilience entities, as shown in Fig. 3. This model is then used as input for the instantiation of Fig. 4. Moreover, by reviewing healthcare process documents and relating them with resilience entities, different points where a response will need to adjust to the ongoing conditions are specified. In our example, some of such points are "ergonomic settings", "laparoscopic procedure" and "change device settings". Taking one of these points, let us say "laparoscopic procedure" a security practitioner that considers implementing a resilience entity such as "encrypt data streams between the surgeon's terminal and the robot" has to consider if a laparoscopic operation is taking place at the same time. If so, the overhead or other complication that encryption might result from having to be valued in relation to the potential impact the response can have to the ongoing healthcare process and ultimately, the patient.

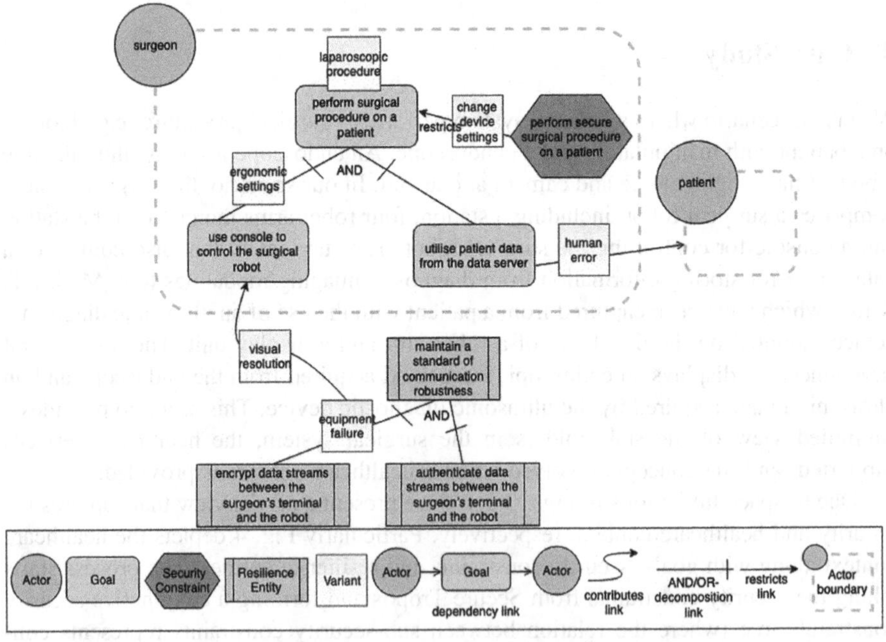

Fig. 4. Example of healthcare context variations model.

With this simple case, we were able to demonstrate one of the additional capabilities that the enhanced design can offer to cybersecurity practitioners of healthcare environments. In particular, we looked at the constructs that relate to the healthcare context and described at a high-level process through which such models can be instantiated.

5 Conclusions

This paper focuses on cyber resiliency in relation to incidents that have recently arisen or may arise for healthcare systems. The critical result of this revision of the modelling language was the update of the metamodel to define more accurately the constructs related to incidents, healthcare and resiliency. These enhancements were made to allow security engineers to define a structure to support the resiliency of specific applications relevant to their healthcare systems and incident conditions they face or prepare to manage. In a case study for a robotic surgical system, we were able to demonstrate one aspect of the application of the modelling language extensions. A detailed validation needs to take place in future work. Because of the wide variety of physical and digital capabilities of healthcare systems along with the potential impact they can have, we believe that their cybersecurity needs to be studied further.

References

1. ISO/IEC/IEEE 15288:2015. https://www.iso.org/standard/63711.html. Accessed 12 July 2019
2. Li, T., Horkoff, J., Mylopoulos, J.: Integrating security patterns with security requirements analysis using contextual goal models. In: Frank, U., Loucopoulos, P., Pastor, Ó., Petrounias, I. (eds.) PoEM 2014. LNBIP, vol. 197, pp. 208–223. Springer, Heidelberg (2014). https://doi.org/10.1007/978-3-662-45501-2_15
3. Antón, A.I., Earp, J.B.: Strategies for developing policies and requirements for secure and private electronic commerce. In: Ghosh, A.K. (ed.) E-Commerce Security and Privacy. Advances in Information Security, vol. 2, pp. 67–86. Springer, Boston (2001). https://doi.org/10.1007/978-1-4615-1467-1_5
4. Argyropoulos, N., Mouratidis, H., Fish, A.: Advances in Conceptual Modeling. Springer, Cham (2015). https://doi.org/10.1007/978-3-642-33999-8
5. Arney, D., Pajic, M., Goldman, J.M., Lee, I., Mangharam, R., Sokolsky, O.: Toward patient safety in closed-loop medical device systems. In: Proceedings of the 1st ACM/IEEE International Conference on Cyber-Physical Systems - ICCPS 2010, pp. 139–148. ACM Press, Stockholm (2010)
6. Athinaiou, M., Mouratidis, H., Fotis, T., Pavlidis, M., Panaousis, E.: Towards the definition of a security incident response modelling language. In: Furnell, S., Mouratidis, H., Pernul, G. (eds.) TrustBus 2018. LNCS, vol. 11033, pp. 198–212. Springer, Cham (2018). https://doi.org/10.1007/978-3-319-98385-1_14
7. Boddy, A., Hurst, W., Mackay, M., Rhalibi, A.E.: A study into data analysis and visualisation to increase the cyber-resilience of healthcare infrastructures. In: Proceedings of the 1st International Conference on Internet of Things and Machine Learning - IML 1917, pp. 1–7. ACM Press, Liverpool (2017)

8. Den Braber, F., Hogganvik, I., Lund, M.S., Stlen, K., Vraalsen, F.: Model-based security analysis in seven steps a guided tour to the CORAS method. BT Technol. J. **25**(1), 101–117 (2007)
9. Bresciani, P., Perini, A., Giorgini, P., Giunchiglia, F., Mylopoulos, J.: Tropos: an agent-oriented software development methodology. Auton. Agents Multi-Agent Syst. **8**(3), 203–236 (2004)
10. Chapurlat, V., et al.: Towards a model-based method for resilient critical infrastructure engineering how to model critical infrastructures and evaluate ist resilience? How to model critical infrastructures and evaluate its Resilience? In: 2018 13th Annual Conference on System of Systems Engineering (SoSE), pp. 561–567. IEEE, Paris (2018)
11. Chen, Q., Lambright, J.: Towards realizing a self-protecting healthcare information system. In: 2016 IEEE 40th Annual Computer Software and Applications Conference (COMPSAC), pp. 687–690. IEEE, Atlanta (2016)
12. Chernyshev, M., Zeadally, S., Baig, Z.: Healthcare data breaches: implications for digital forensic readiness. J. Med. Syst. **43**(1), 7 (2019)
13. Cichonski, P., Millar, T., Grance, T., Scarfone, K.: Computer Security Incident Handling Guide: Recommendations of the National Institute of Standards and Technology. Technical report NIST SP 800-61r2, National Institute of Standards and Technology (2012)
14. Cooper, T., Collmann, J., Neidermeier, H.: Organizational repertoires and rites in health information security. Camb. Q. Healthc. Ethics **17**(4), 441–452 (2008)
15. Dardenne, A., van Lamsweerde, A., Fickas, S.: Goal-directed requirements acquisition. Sci. Comput. Program. **20**(1–2), 3–50 (1993)
16. DeVoe, C., Rahman, S.S.M.: Incident response plan for a small to medium sized hospital. Int. J. Netw. Secur. Appl. **5**(2), 1–20 (2013)
17. Genes, N., Chary, M., Chason, K.W.: Case study. An academic medical centers response to widespread computer failure. Am. J. Disaster Med. **8**(2), 145–150 (2013)
18. Ghafur, S., Grass, E., Jennings, N.A., Darzi, A.: The challenges of cybersecurity in health care: the UK National Health Service as a case study. Lancet Digit. Health **1**(1), e10–e12 (2019)
19. Giorgini, P., Massacci, F., Zannone, N.: Security and trust requirements engineering. In: Aldini, A., Gorrieri, R., Martinelli, F. (eds.) FOSAD 2004-2005. LNCS, vol. 3655, pp. 237–272. Springer, Heidelberg (2005). https://doi.org/10.1007/11554578_8
20. Giorgini, P., Mylopoulos, J., Sebastiani, R.: Goal-oriented requirements analysis and reasoning in the Tropos methodology. Eng. Appl. Artif. Intell. **18**(2), 159–171 (2005)
21. He, Y., Johnson, C.: Challenges of information security incident learning: an industrial case study in a Chinese healthcare organization. Inf. Health Soc. Care **42**(4), 393–408 (2017)
22. Lee, I., et al.: Challenges and research directions in medical cyberphysical systems. Proc. IEEE **100**(1), 75–90 (2012)
23. Jalali, M.S., Russell, B., Razak, S., Gordon, W.J.: EARS to cyber incidents in health care. J. Am. Med. Inf. Assoc. **26**(1), 81–90 (2019)
24. Jürjens, J.: UMLsec: Extending UML for Secure Systems Development. In: Jézéquel, J.-M., Hussmann, H., Cook, S. (eds.) UML 2002. LNCS, vol. 2460, pp. 412–425. Springer, Heidelberg (2002). https://doi.org/10.1007/3-540-45800-X_32
25. van Lamsweerde, A.: Goal-oriented requirements engineering: a guided tour. In: Proceedings Fifth IEEE International Symposium on the Requirements Engineering, pp. 249–262. IEEE Computer Society, Toronto (2000)
26. van Lamsweerde, A., Letier, E.: From object orientation to goal orientation: a paradigm shift for requirements engineering. In: Wirsing, M., Knapp, A., Balsamo, S. (eds.) RISSEF 2002. LNCS, vol. 2941, pp. 325–340. Springer, Heidelberg (2004). https://doi.org/10.1007/978-3-540-24626-8_23

27. Lin, L., Nuseibeh, B., Ince, D., Jackson, M., Moffett, J.: Introducing abuse frames for analyzing security requirements. J. Lightwave Technol. 371–372 (2003). IEEE Comput. Soc, Monterey Bay, CA, USA
28. Lodderstedt, T., Basin, D., Doser, J.: SecureUML: a UML-based modeling language for model-driven security. In: Jézéquel, J.-M., Hussmann, H., Cook, S. (eds.) UML 2002. LNCS, vol. 2460, pp. 426–441. Springer, Heidelberg (2002). https://doi.org/10.1007/3-540-45800-X_33
29. McDermott, J., Fox, C.: Using abuse case models for security requirements analysis. In: Proceedings 15th Annual Computer Security Applications Conference (ACSAC 1999), pp. 55–64. IEEE Computer Society, Phoenix (1999)
30. McGlade, D., Scott-Hayward, S.: ML-based cyber incident detection for Electronic Medical Record (EMR) systems. Smart Health **12**, 3–23 (2019)
31. Mead, N.R., Stehney, T.: Security quality requirements engineering (SQUARE) methodology. ACM SIGSOFT Softw. Eng. Notes **30**(4), 1 (2005)
32. Meland, P.H., Paja, E., Gjre, E.A., Paul, S., Dalpiaz, F., Giorgini, P.: Threat analysis in goal-oriented security requirements modelling. In: Computer Systems and Software Engineering: Concepts, Methodologies, Tools, and Applications, pp. 2025–2042. IGI Global (2018)
33. Mouratidis, H., Argyropoulos, N., Shei, S.: Security requirements engineering for cloud computing: the secure tropos approach. In: Karagiannis, D., Mayr, H., Mylopoulos, J. (eds.) Domain-Specific Conceptual Modeling, pp. 357–380. Springer, Cham (2016). https://doi.org/10.1007/978-3-319-39417-6_16
34. Mouratidis, H., Giorgini, P.: Secure tropos: a security-oriented extension of the tropos methodology. Int. J. Softw. Eng. Knowl. Eng. **17**(02), 285–309 (2007)
35. Mwiki, H., Dargahi, T., Dehghantanha, A., Choo, K.-K.R.: Analysis and triage of advanced hacking groups targeting western countries critical national infrastructure: APT28, RED October, and Regin. In: Gritzalis, D., Theocharidou, M., Stergiopoulos, G. (eds.) Critical Infrastructure Security and Resilience. ASTSA, pp. 221–244. Springer, Cham (2019). https://doi.org/10.1007/978-3-030-00024-0_12
36. Pavlidis, M., Islam, S., Mouratidis, H.: A CASE tool to support automated modelling and analysis of security requirements, based on secure tropos. In: Nurcan, S. (ed.) CAiSE Forum 2011. LNBIP, vol. 107, pp. 95–109. Springer, Heidelberg (2012). https://doi.org/10.1007/978-3-642-29749-6_7
37. Pavlidis, M., Islam, S., Mouratidis, H., Kearney, P.: Modeling trust relationships for developing trustworthy information systems. Int. J. Inf. Syst. Model. Des. **5**(1), 25–48 (2014)
38. Pavlidis, M., Mouratidis, H., Panaousis, E., Argyropoulos, N.: Selecting security mechanisms in secure tropos. In: Lopez, J., Fischer-Hübner, S., Lambrinoudakis, C. (eds.) TrustBus 2017. LNCS, vol. 10442, pp. 99–114. Springer, Cham (2017). https://doi.org/10.1007/978-3-319-64483-7_7
39. Ransford, B., Clark, S.S., Kune, D.F., Fu, K., Burleson, W.P.: Design Challenges for Secure Implantable Medical Devices. In: Burleson, W., Carrara, S. (eds.) Security and Privacy for Implantable Medical Devices, pp. 157–173. Springer, New York (2014). https://doi.org/10.1007/978-1-4614-1674-6_7
40. Ross, R., Graubart, R., Bodeau, D., McQuaid, R.: Systems Security Engineering Cyber Resiliency Considerations for the Engineering of Trustworthy Secure Systems. Technical report, NIST (2018)
41. Schumacher, M.: Toward a security core ontology. In: Security Engineering with Patterns: Origins, Theoretical Models, and New Applications, pp. 87–96. no. 2754, LNCS, Springer, New York (2003). https://doi.org/10.1007/b11930

42. Sindre, G., Firesmith, D.G., Opdahl, A.L.: A reuse-based approach to determining security requirements. Requirements Eng. **10**, 34–44 (2004)
43. Sittig, D., Singh, H.: A socio-technical approach to preventing, mitigating, and recovering from ransomware attacks. Appl. Clin. Inf. **07**(02), 624–632 (2016)
44. Wiant, T.L.: Information security policy's impact on reporting security incidents. Comput. Secur. **24**(6), 448–459 (2005)
45. Williams, P.A.H.: Is cyber resilience in medical practice security achievable? In: Proceedings of the 1st International Cyber Resilience Conference, pp. 105–111. Edith Cowan University, Perth (2010)
46. Yu, E.S.K.: Modeling strategic relationships for process reengineering, Ph.D. thesis, University of Toronto, Canada (1995)
47. Jiang, Z., Pajic, M., Mangharam, R.: Cyberphysical modeling of implantable cardiac medical devices. Proc. IEEE **100**(1), 122–137 (2012)

Shaping Digital Identities in Social Networks: Data Elements and the Role of Privacy Concerns

Thanos Papaioannou[1,2(✉)], Aggeliki Tsohou[1], and Maria Karyda[3]

[1] Ionian University, Corfu, Greece
{thanospapa, atsohou}@ionio.gr
[2] PDM&FC, Lisbon, Portugal
thanos.papaioannou@pdmfc.com
[3] University of the Aegean, Samos, Greece
mka@aegean.gr

Abstract. Individuals today shape a digital identity through which they "introduce" themselves to others in Social Network Sites (SNS). SNS embody features that enable users to customize their digital identity at will and to disclose desirable elements of their personality. The processes by which users shape their digital identity through information disclosure are largely unknown, including the role of privacy concerns. In this paper we identify the data elements that users consider important for shaping their digital identity in SNS and how privacy concerns shape this process.

In order to explore the above, we conducted an online survey research with 759 participants. Our findings reveal the elements that users consider as important for shaping their digital identity. They also demonstrate that users' privacy concerns do not seem to affect the amount of information users choose to publish when shaping their digital identity. Finally, we show that particular characteristics of social networking platforms affect the way that users shape their digital identity and privacy behavior.

Keywords: Digital identity · Privacy concerns · Social networks

1 Introduction

Identity is a complex and multifaceted concept due to the dynamic way it is formed and redefined in space and time, as well as due to the complexity that characterizes interpersonal interaction as to how it is perceived by oneself and others (Subrahmanyam and Šmahel 2011; Delahunty 2012).

Within classical anthropological theories, human identity is considered as static: a distinct personality that corresponds to the physical body of a human being (Stone 1996). However, in practice people experience identity in a completely different way than this conceptualization; they choose how to present oneself differently depending on the context in which they act and their target audience each time (Goffman 1959). Nowadays, social, cultural, economic and technological developments suggest that

S. Katsikas et al. (Eds.): ESORICS 2019 Workshops, LNCS 11980, pp. 159–180, 2020.
https://doi.org/10.1007/978-3-030-42048-2_11

identity is a "fluid" concept and takes shape within a social context equally fluid and changing (Papacharissi 2010; Kimmons 2014). It is also argued that there is no substantial or real identity, but multiple identities or "versions" of the identity that represent respectively the multiple "selves" of the individual (e.g. private and professional) (Subrahmanyam and Šmahel 2011; Barbour and Marshall 2012; Ramírez and Palu-ay 2015). These "selves" are formed and activated within unique timeframes (Gee 1999). Thus, the term "identity" relates to the point of view that one has of himself/herself or the way in which the views of oneself are presented in various aspects of art and the media (Marwick 2013). Many studies examine the meaning of identity as the way in which someone "introduces" himself to other people in contexts enabled by Web 2.0 technologies (Canary et al. 2003; Baym 2010; Boyd 2010).

A "digital identity" refers to the way in which individuals choose to introduce themselves when they communicate and interact on the Internet (Canary et al. 2003; Delahunty 2012; Michikyan et al. 2015). The use of the term "digital identity" compared to the term "identity", implies a distinction between the way users would present themselves on the Internet and in the real life. However, people nowadays communicate with other people they know in real life and through social networks and are continuously online through mobile devices; thus, it makes sense that they choose to disclose for themselves true identity data (Marwick 2013). Especially within Web 2.0 and social network contexts individuals are supposed to voluntary create a virtual presentation of themselves (Baym 2010; Subrahmanyam and Šmahel 2011; Fieseler et al. 2014; Junco 2014). Considering that social media users constantly present themselves online in various roles (e.g. user as: self-creator through posted content, member of specific groups expressing social belonging, information-seeker, audience of other users' activities, self-presenter), they are expected to maintain these presentations as unique personal identities (Fieseler et al. 2014; Bareket-Bojmel et al. 2016). When it comes to real-life representations (e.g. personal and professional), it is easier for the individual to identify himself or herself, try changes to his public profile and get feedback without risk (Belk 2013; Junco 2014). On the contrary, online identities are more complex to create and change. Social Networking Sites (SNS) comprise of virtual collections of user profiles that are used to maintain ties and can be shared with other users (Hughes et al. 2012). Thus, a digital identity comprises of the information that an individual share publicly, but it also includes the conclusions drawn by other users. People form an opinion for someone by looking at and interpreting every aspect of his/her online profile, activity and interaction with others (Delahunty 2012; Marwick 2013; Wang 2013; Kimmons 2014; Hodkinson 2017).

Through the creation of virtual profiles, the use of SNS has led to the collection and storage of huge amounts of information about people, part of which may refer to personal and sensitive data (Zhang et al. 2010). Although users provide their information for specific purposes and expect that it would be shared only with specific recipients, in reality personal information shared in SNS is often used for commercial and advertising interests or become the target of malicious attacks (Gross and Acquisti 2005; Barnes 2006), raising issues of privacy violations (Krishnamurthy and Wills 2008). This exploitation of SNS data reveals a key contradiction that users face: While information disclosure is a prerequisite for anyone who wants to build a strong online profile and take full advantage of the networking capabilities offered by the SNS, as the philosophy and operation of SNS depends on information sharing (Joinson 2008; Joinson et al. 2010), information sharing, at the same time, entails significant threats, such as illegal monitoring, slanderous defamation and interception of economic interest information (Zhang et al. 2010; Joinson et al. 2010).

Although the process of digital identity formation is continuous, related literature hasn't yet studied how people conceptualize their own digital identities and which identity elements they perceive to be part of their presentation of oneself. This paper builds on the assumption that users decide which elements constitute their digital identity dynamically and per context (i.e., different elements constitute identity on one SNS and different in another SNS) to investigate this formation process. We draw upon previous studies to identify common identity elements and we examine how users perceive their digital identities, as well as which elements they consider to be part of their virtual presentation. Further, we argue that privacy concerns are an essential part of the digital identity formation process, especially because these concerns may prohibit information disclosure. Relevant studies however fail to provide a clear picture with regard to the relationship between the personal information users choose to disclose and their concerns about privacy violations: some studies argue that privacy concerns make users reluctant to reveal information and use SNS to their full potential (Krasnova et al. 2009; Shin 2010; Madden 2012; Zhang et al. 2010) while other studies conclude that either users do not have significant privacy concerns due to lack of awareness (Gross and Acquisti 2005) or that these concerns do not affect information disclosure (Dwyer et al. 2007; Tufekci 2008). Forming a digital identity is a process influenced by various aspects of personality and everyday life of the individual and interpreted by various fields of science, thus, the study of the phenomenon is complicated and requires in depth investigation. Consequently, it is important to understand how privacy concerns influence individuals' information disclosure and, ultimately, the formation of digital identities, to gain deeper and clearer insights on this inner process.

Different SNS platforms aim at different purposes and are associated with different patterns of use. The above explains, firstly, why many people keep accounts in two or more social networks at the same time and, secondly, why different SNSs have become very popular at different times and in different countries (Skeels and Grudin 2009). Related research indicates that users differentiate how they present themselves in each one of them and how they deal with possible privacy violations (van Dijck 2013; Karapanos et al. 2016). For example, on popular social networking platforms that are not based on the disclosure of personal information and do not mainly aim at creating and/or maintaining social relationships (like Twitter), users form digital identities with little or no personal information. This implies that certain characteristics of SNS platforms may influence privacy concerns and finally the users' disclosure behavior and need further investigation.

This paper explores the issues identified above: we (a) investigate how SNS users conceptualize their personal digital identity and what are the data elements that shape this meaning, and (b) we explore whether information disclosure is different depending on privacy concerns and depending on the characteristics of SNS platforms. We have designed and executed a survey to identify which elements are considered essential for a digital identity by SNS users (e.g., photos). This paper provides evidence that different individuals consider different elements as essential of their digital identities depending on the SNS. We did not find evidence that privacy concerns prohibit users from disclosing the information that they believe are part of their digital identities.

Section 2 presents background studies through which we have identified the data elements that comprise digital identities and we have formulated our hypotheses regarding digital identity shaping and the role of privacy concerns and social network site. Section 3 presents our research strategy including the design of the survey. In Sect. 4 we present the results of the empirical analysis and our findings, while Sect. 5 concludes the paper.

2 Forming Digital Identities in Social Networks

Many researchers argue that the formation of digital identity resembles the process of "public self-presentation" (Larsen 2007; Mehdizadeh 2010; Subrahmanyam and Šmahel 2011; Wang 2013; Michikyan et al. 2015; Ramírez and Palu-ay 2015) and refers to the way in which the users choose to introduce themselves when they communicate and interact on the Internet (Canary et al. 2003; Hodkinson 2017). Building a digital identity and disclosing personal information is part of the modern social networking philosophy. The typical practices of communication, interaction and self-presentation in social media have also been described as the usage of an "identity-kit" (Belk 2013). Zhao et al. (2008) explored the formation of digital identity in online environments that favor - or even require - a correspondence with the real identity. Their findings suggest that people nowadays tend to *show* rather than *say* things about themselves. According to this view, digital identity is not a personal trait but a social "product", which is not only shaped by what is shared by the users but also by what other users are sharing or stating about them. The above is also confirmed by research findings suggesting that young people use their digital literacy skills to construct their digital identity (Alvermann et al. 2012; Subrahmanyam and Šmahel 2011).

The *real name* of an individual is a crucial element of digital identity in SNS (Larsen 2007; Zhao et al. 2008). Furthermore, SNS users whose digital identity corresponds to the real one, are considered more trustworthy and, therefore, they broaden their networking easier and faster. SNS encourage individuals to use their real name to prevent frauds and to guarantee security. On the other hand, this allows SNS to exploit users' personal data for commercial purposes (Marwick 2013).

Relevant studies also suggest that, in addition to the use of their real name, the digital identity of users is also formed by disclosing a series of personal data directly related to their real identity (such as *gender*, *job position, interests*) and *habits* of one's everyday life (Stutzman 2006; Pempek et al. 2009; Ismail 2010; Shafie et al. 2012; Marwick 2013). *Photos* are an essential element of a SNS digital identity; they act as links between the past and the present self and therefore represent identity (Salimkhan et al. 2010; Ismail 2010). Photos can transfer messages that the user wants to communicate. They show a desirable image of the users (Tufekci 2008) and hence users choose to upload the photos that help them highlight positive traits and cover any negative ones (Zhao et al. 2008). Another element of digital identity is the users' level of *social connectivity* and *popularity*, which is calculated based on the number of online friends, posts and participation in groups (Gross and Acquisti 2005; Zhao et al. 2008; Hoy and Milne 2010; Shafie et al. 2012).

Besides explicit elements that form a digital identity, such as hobbies, interests, opinions, favorite music, movies and so on, there are also implicit ones. Research shows that even the *fonts* and *pseudonyms* that users choose may symbolize aspects of their identity that make them stand out from others especially when they use them to enter new interest groups (Ismail 2010; Papacharissi 2010; Shafie et al. 2012; Marwick 2013; van Dijck 2013; Cover and Doak 2015; Hodkinson 2017).

Thus, a digital identity encompasses a wide range of offline authentication attributes (e.g. name, gender, age etc.), combined with several online elements and behaviors (e.g. profiles, usernames, passwords, shared or published content etc.) (Wessels 2012; Ramírez and Palu-ay 2015; Eastin et al. 2016). All these attributes, elements and behaviors create clear links and common references between social and technological interpretation of identity (Wessels 2012).

Although existing literature does not examine digital identity elements per se, there are various studies that help us specify the information that users commonly choose in order to form their digital identities, including their names, photos, etc. In the next sections, we examine aspects of the digital identity formation process and analyze some factors that may influence this process.

Conclusively, personal data disclosure is part of the digital identity formation process which is associated with popularity: the digital identity of popular users is characterized by high percentage of other people's involvement in shaping it (Zhao et al. 2008; van Dijck 2013). This creates a dilemma for the user: limiting third-party access to personal information will eventually limit the digital identity formation and, therefore, the user's popularity. This dilemma in its extreme means that not participating in social media leads to a cost, which is equivalent to the lack of a digital identity and a complete absence of the user from the online realm (Raynes-Goldie 2010); Turkle (2011) state "online networks can lead to isolation anxiety" and Cover and Doak (2015) argue that "identity construction is becoming increasingly relational, built on high quantity, low quality interactions".

3 Research Design

3.1 Research Hypotheses

Modern SNS encourage users to disclose real data in order to form a strong digital identity. Users, on the other hand, are concerned about the protection of their privacy (Zhang et al. 2010; Raynes-Goldie 2010; Joinson et al. 2010; Marwick 2013). Once users choose to share an information in the SNS it becomes accessible and the individual no longer has control over the entities who can access it (Buchanan et al. 2007; Tufekci 2008; Krasnova et al. 2009; Ross et al. 2009; Hoy and Milne 2010; Shin 2010; Zhang et al. 2010; Xu et al. 2011; Madden 2012). Users are concerned not only about who accesses their information shared on SNS, but also how they use them (Gross and

Acquisti 2005; Krasnova et al. 2009; Youn 2009; Shin 2010; Xu et al. 2011). The concerns expressed by users themselves are related to various aspects of their private and social life. Besides concerns on the information that a user chooses to disclose, users also express concerns about the lack of control on information that others share about them (Krasnova et al. 2009; Shin 2010; Madden 2012). This is related to possible feelings of embarrassment or shame if that content becomes visible to people outside the close friendly environment (Krasnova et al. 2009; Zhang et al. 2010).

Relevant research shows that users may choose pseudonyms or multiple profiles as a mechanism for privacy protection, although they express that this may be ineffective given that their real identity can be revealed through dozens of other ways, such as social networking lists or other media posts that refer to them (Raynes-Goldie 2010).

Interestingly, there are mixed conclusions if privacy concerns affect users' information disclosure behavior. While some studies argue that privacy concerns do not affect users' disclosure behavior (Stutzman 2006; Madden et al. 2007; Tufekci 2008), others show that users actually reduce the amount of information they disclose due to privacy concerns and adjust their SNS presence depending on perceived privacy invasion threats (Krasnova et al. 2009; Raynes-Goldie 2010; Madden 2012).

From our point of view, if privacy concerns determine information disclosure behavior, this eventually affects the digital identity formation. Thus, we formulate the following research hypothesis:

H1: Increased privacy concerns lead to reduced identity-shaping information disclosure.

Taking advantage of the features that each SNS offers, users can publish their information, communicate with friends and share common interests. Different SNS platforms offer different services and functionalities (Papacharissi 2009; Hughes et al. 2012; van Dijck 2013), which can explain why some SNS became more popular than others during time or in different regions (Skeels and Grudin 2009). According to Karapanos et al. (2016) and van Dijck (2013) these differences alter the overall user experience that the individual gains from each SNS. It is not only the social interaction functionalities by themselves (e.g., provision of chat), but also the user interface that affect the user experience. Especially because of these unique features the various SNS platforms offer, it has become common the last few years for the majority of people to be subscribers of more than one SNS (Brandtzaeg 2012).

Therefore, we expect that the SNS would be a determinant factor for information a user discloses (and thus the respective privacy concerns) and the formation of digital identity and assume that:

H2: The SNS that an individual use, determines the formation of digital identity.

H3: The SNS that an individual use, affects their privacy concerns.

3.2 Research Model

Our research model and hypotheses are presented in Fig. 1.

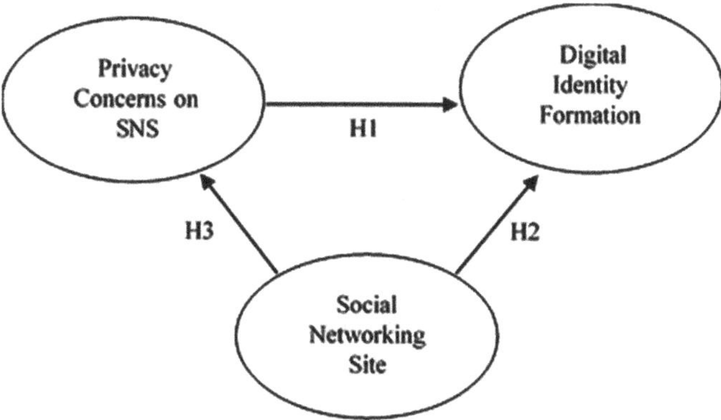

Fig. 1. Research model and hypotheses

3.3 Survey Design

The questionnaire used for the survey consisted of an introductory part (participant information sheet) and two major sections. In the first major section, the users completed demographic data, indicated which SNS platforms they use and were asked to choose a SNS platform according to which they will proceed with the questions of the second section. The second major section included questions about privacy concerns and the amount of data the user discloses on the chosen SNS, as well as questions about the digital identity elements they reveal. Answers to all questions were obligatory to minimize invalid responses. All questions were closed-ended and in 5-point Likert-type scale, except the questions on SNS type and the selection of identity information they disclose in their profile, which were binary (Y/N replies). The research constructs were measured in the questionnaire as shown in Table 1:

Table 1. Research constructs

Constructs	Items	Sources
General Privacy concerns (5-point Likert scale)	PC1: In general, how concerned are you about your privacy while you are using the internet? PC2: Are you concerned about online organizations not being who they claim they are? PC3: Are you concerned about people online not being who they say they are? PC4: Are you concerned that you are asked for too much personal information when you register or make online purchases?	Buchanan et al. (2007)

(continued)

Table 1. (*continued*)

Constructs	Items	Sources
Privacy Concerns – Social Threats (5-point Likert scale)	PCS1: I am often concerned that I don't have control over the actions of other users PCS2: I am often concerned that someone might purposefully embarrass me on SNS PCS3: It often worries me that other users might purposefully write something embarrassing about me on SNS PCS4: I am often concerned that other users might take advantage of the information they learned about me through SNS	Krasnova et al. (2009)
Privacy Concerns – Organizational Threats (5-point Likert scale)	PCO1: I am often concerned that the SNS provider could store my information for the next couple of years PCO2: I sometimes feel anxious that the SNS provider might know too much about me PCO3: I am often concerned that the SNS provider could share the information I provide with third parties (e.g. marketing, HR or government agencies) PCO4: It often worries me that third parties (e.g. marketing, HR, government agencies) could use the information they have collected about me from the SNS for commercial purposes	Krasnova et al. (2009)
Digital Identity perception (5-point Likert scale)	IDP: How much does each piece of profile information below help you to express who you are to others in SNS? Name, Gender, Photo, Friend List, Email Address, Physical Address, Country, Phone Number, Birthday, Hometown, Relationship Status, Major, Sexual Orientation, Academic Classification, Academic Status, School Information, Job/Occupation, Political beliefs, Group Affiliation, Interests, Favorite Music, Favorite Books, Favorite Movies, Favorite TV Shows, Personal Statement, Web page	Pempek, et al. (2009)
Identity information disclosure – Amount (5-point Likert scale)	IDA1: I have a comprehensive profile on SNS IDA2: I find time to keep my profile up to date IDA3: I keep my friends updated about what is going on in my life through SNS IDA4: When I have something to say, I like to share it on SNS	Krasnova et al. (2009)

(*continued*)

Table 1. (*continued*)

Constructs	Items	Sources
Identity information disclosure – Honesty (5-point Likert scale)	IDH1: I am always honest in the information I provide on SNS IDH2: I am always truthful when I write about myself on SNS	Krasnova et al. (2009)
Identity information disclosure (Yes/No)	CIE: In my SNS profile I disclose: Name, Gender, Photo, Friend List, Email Address, Physical Address, Country, Phone Number, Birthday, Hometown, Relationship Status, Major, Sexual Orientation, Academic Classification, Academic Status, School Information, Job/Occupation, Political beliefs, Group Affiliation, Interests, Favorite Music, Favorite Books, Favorite Movies, Favorite TV Shows, Personal Statement, Web page	Stutzman (2006) Zhao et al. (2008) Pempek et al. (2009) Ismail (2010) Shafie et al. (2012)

We utilized the construct Privacy Concerns on SNS, adapted from Krasnova et al. (2009). The construct includes two dimensions: (a) Concerns about Organizational threats, which refer to users' concerns on how SNS' organizations may use their information and (b) Concerns about Social threats which refer to possible negative outcomes from an undesired exploitation of users' information from their social environment. In this study we included the most popular SNS in terms of traffic (ALEXA 2017), namely Facebook, Twitter, LinkedIn, Google+, Tumblr, Instagram, Pinterest, YouTube.

3.4 Sampling and Survey Execution

We disseminated our questionnaire via emails and SNSs (sharing on Facebook, Twitter and Google+) to users across Greece between 19th December 2016 and 10th May 2017, following a random sampling technique. The questionnaire was written in Greek and addressed to the general population of Greece with age as the unique limitation, as most SNS report that legal users are considered adolescents and adults over 13 years of age. All data were submitted anonymously, since the questionnaire did not allow participants to provide their names, to ensure that no ethical or privacy issues arise. We clarified that the survey should not be considered as a means of promotion, advertising or mandatory adoption of SNS.

3.5 Research Validation

Prior to analyzing the results, we grouped together the questions that measure each of the variables pertaining to privacy concerns and digital identity formation (honesty and amount of information disclosed). We used factor analysis to determine the contribution of each question to the construct configuration. The constructs of digital identity perception and digital identity elements are excluded, as they are structured in a different way and they were used for descriptive conclusions. The results confirmed our grouping. The quality criteria of the constructs are shown in Table 2.

During the analysis of the results, all responses were examined in two ways. The entire set of responses was the first basis for drawing conclusions, especially fields related to demographic statistics, and then this set was split into smaller individual subsets, nine in total, one for each user-preferred SNS, as the one they use most and is selected in order to complete the questionnaire.

Concerning the construct that measures privacy concern (PC), the first question (PC1) shows a lower contribution to the formation of the variable. This is due to the variation of responses from one SNS to another. If the answers for a specific SNS, such as Facebook, are isolated, the question rate (PC1) increases exponentially.

To test H2 hypothesis, responses were analyzed in two different ways to ensure the validity of the result. In order to illustrate how digital identity is being formed, users were asked to state which Common Identity Elements they disclose in their SNS profile. A checkbox list of answers was given, with 27 available options, including "something else" option. At first, all the responses were transformed into an absolute number that represents the number of items they disclose. In the One-Way Analysis of Variance, the dependent variable was the number of items disclosed by the user and the predictive factor was the SNS. Subsequently, the answers to this question have been coded in four categories so as to create a rating scale for the disclosure of digital identity data. Users with little or no disclosed data were ranked in the first group (0–5 elements), those who disclosed several data were ranked in the second group (6–12 elements), then those who disclosed many elements (13–19 elements) and, finally, the users with the maximum number of disclosed data (20–26 elements). These four groups were created from a basis of 30 different options. 26 items were given to the question, 3 new items were declared by the users (Foreign Languages, Nickname and Sporting Team), and zero option (no items disclosed) is also included. Responses ranged from 0 to 26 choices. Chi Square control was then applied.

For the third research hypothesis (H3) we initially used a comparative table of the averages of variables related to privacy concerns. Then, we performed three variance analyses with one factor, one for each of the privacy variables, and the categorizing factor was the SNS.

The participants replied to the questionnaire according to a specific SNS they use, in order to study the possible impact of each platform on how users form their digital identity. It would be interesting to also study the possible differentiation of the same user's behavior among different SNS. However, in this case the extent of the questionnaire would make its completion unattainable, with the risk of low participation. As not all users all the SNSs, or the same combination of them, the collected data would not be comparable. Our findings are also bounded by the self-report limitations that apply to human behavior studies which use surveys.

Table 2. Quality criteria of the constructs

Construct	Mean	Standard deviation	Standardized item loadings	Cronbach's alpha
Privacy Concerns (PC)	*3,57*	*,94*		*,827*
PC1	3,20	1,265	,453	
PC2	3,63	1,152	,822	
PC3	3,76	1,180	,820	
PC4	3,70	1,036	,630	
Privacy Concerns Social threats (PCS)	*2,67*	*1,11*		*,890*
PCS1	2,74	1,262	,627	
PCS2	2,53	1,289	,857	
PCS3	2,57	1,306	,891	
PCS4	2,86	1,274	,699	
Privacy Concerns Organizational threats (PCO)	*3,22*	*1,18*		*,923*
PCO1	3,26	1,310	,787	
PCO2	3,23	1,353	,827	
PCO3	3,13	1,333	,855	
PCO4	3,27	1,274	,834	
Identity Information Disclosure Amount (IDA)	*2,44*	*,88*		*,782*
IDA1	3,00	1,184	,642	
IDA2	2,75	1,190	,815	
IDA3	1,94	1,035	,841	
IDA4	2,08	1,099	,770	
Identity Information Disclosure Honesty (IDH)	*3,77*	*1,14*		*,845*
IDH1	3,70	1,244	,901	
IDH2	3,85	1,206	,906	

4 Analysis of Survey Results

We obtained 759 observations (N = 759), of whom 59,8% were women and 40,2% were men. The first three age categories recorded the majority of respondents; 36,9% were between 26 and 35 years old, 29,1% were between 36 and 45 years old and 21,7% were younger than 25 years old. 67.3% of the participants were graduates of a higher education institution (BSc, MSc, PhD). Regarding the demographics of SNSs user base, Facebook holds the first place, with 97,2% of the respondents, followed by YouTube and Instagram.

The distribution of SNS's in the sample is presented in the Fig. 2.

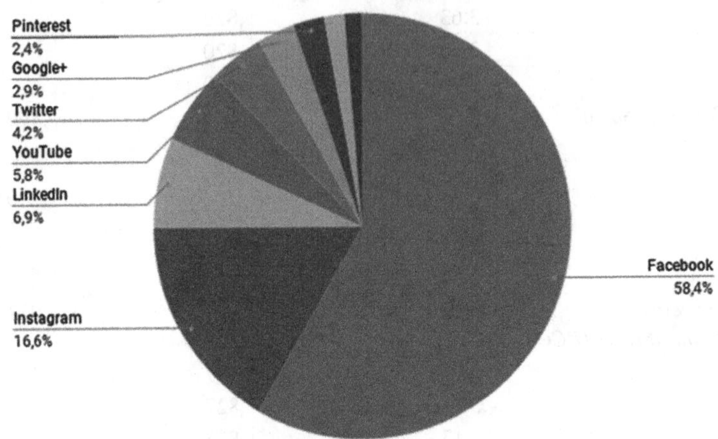

Fig. 2. Distribution of SNSs used by respondents

4.1 Users' Understanding of Digital Identity

A first important finding of this research is the classification of the information that helps users to show to others who they are on SNSs (Fig. 3).

Our findings indicate that the elements that individuals use to present themselves in real life, are not equally used to form their digital identity. For example, in real life, political beliefs and sexual orientation are two representative elements of identity, (Van Bavel and Pereira 2018; D'Augelli 1994). However, in the survey results these attributes appear in the last positions of the ranking. This conclusion is in line with the findings of similar studies (Pempek et al. 2009).

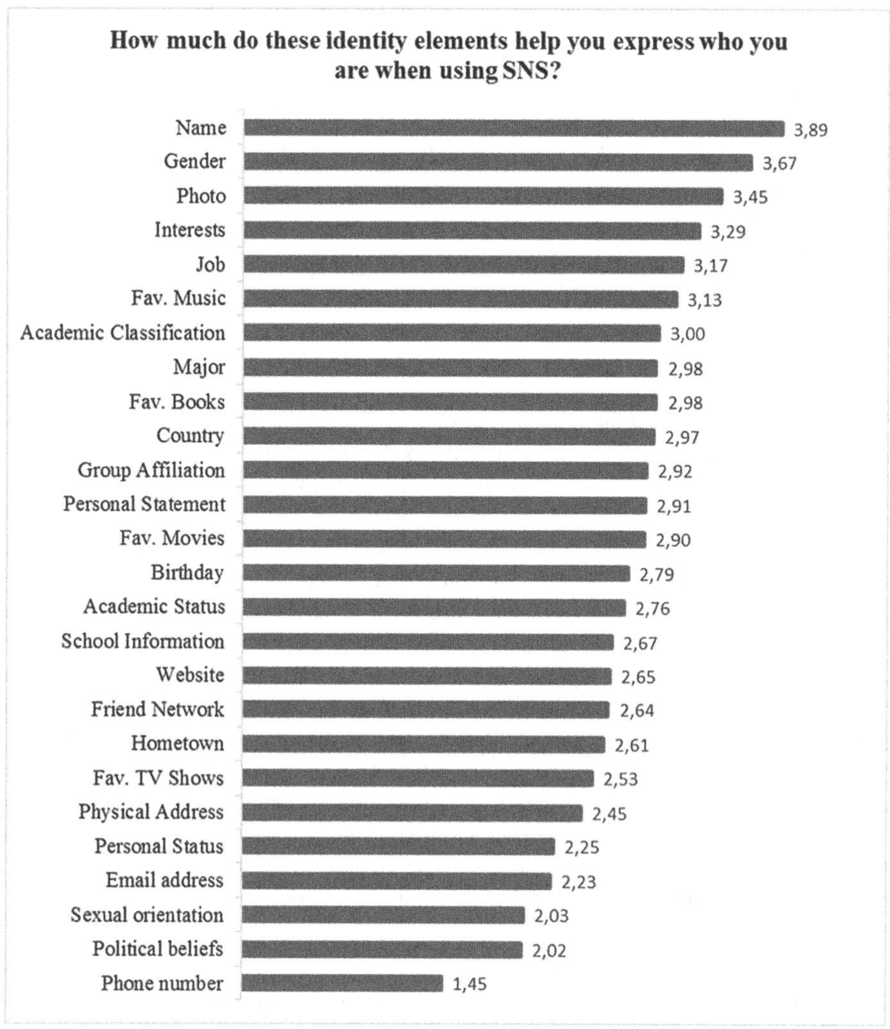

Fig. 3. Digital identity elements' ranking (means)

4.2 Findings on H1: The Effect of Privacy Concerns on Digital Identity Formation

For the research hypothesis H1, linear regression showed that there is significant statistical difference between the amount of information disclosed by users and privacy concerns, but only regarding social "threats" (PCS). However, their correlation is low. Therefore, our empirical data do not support H1 hypothesis. According to the above, we did not find evidence that users' privacy concerns affect the amount of information users disclose on SNS. These results are in line with what is referred to as the "privacy paradox" (Norberg et al. 2007) (Table 3).

Table 3. Linear regression for research hypothesis H1

Coefficients[a]					
Model	Unstandardized coefficients		Standardized coefficients	t	Sig.
	B	Std. Error	Beta		
1 (Constant)	2,107	,082	,160	25,691	,000
Privacy Concerns-Social Threats(PCS)	,126	,028		4,465	,000

a. Dependent Variable: Identity Information-Amount (IDA)

Although we expected that privacy concerns affect the amount of information users disclose on SNS (H1), nonetheless our findings do not support this. There are studies that also did not find a strong relationship among them (Acquisti and Gross 2006; Stutzman 2006; Dwyer et al. 2007; Tufekci 2008). They explained this finding based on the unpredictable way in which human perceptions are transformed into actual behavior (Tufekci 2008). As an example, there is a rhetorical statement in an interview from a user who wondered why to keep a profile SNS active if it does not give enough information for its owner and ultimately does not fulfill its role, which is effective networking (Tufekci 2008). Facing this scenario, a common users' reaction is to limit the audience in which information is visible, despite the amount already disclosed. On the users' side, this explanation is also due to the prevailing norms on the use of SNS. People who use SNS in their everyday life, adopt a set of behaviors, which in this case are related to the disclosure of personal information. A paradoxical reason for this behavior is also suggested by Palen and Dourish (2003), who argue that someone can increase the amount of information they disclose in order to restrict the target audience; by stating specific details about personality and preferences, those who are not interested or do not agree distance themselves.

4.3 Findings on H2 and H3: Social Network Influence on Digital Identity Formation and Privacy Concerns

Investigating research hypothesis H2, the One-Way Analysis of Variance results showed that there is significant statistical difference between the SNSs examined, when the dependent variable was the amount of identity elements disclosed. In particular, Facebook and LinkedIn differ significantly from all other networks other than Google+. The second SNS in the amount of responses, Instagram, appears to differ statistically from Google+ and Tumblr. However, Twitter, YouTube, and less Pinterest, show statistically significant differences only with Facebook and LinkedIn. Their different orientation, as described in a previous chapter, with regard to the purpose of adoption and use, seems to confirm these deviations.

The Chi Square test was applied, and its results confirm the H2 hypothesis, as it appears that SNS affects users in forming their digital identity in terms of the amount of identity information they disclose. Our findings confirm that SNS affects the way users

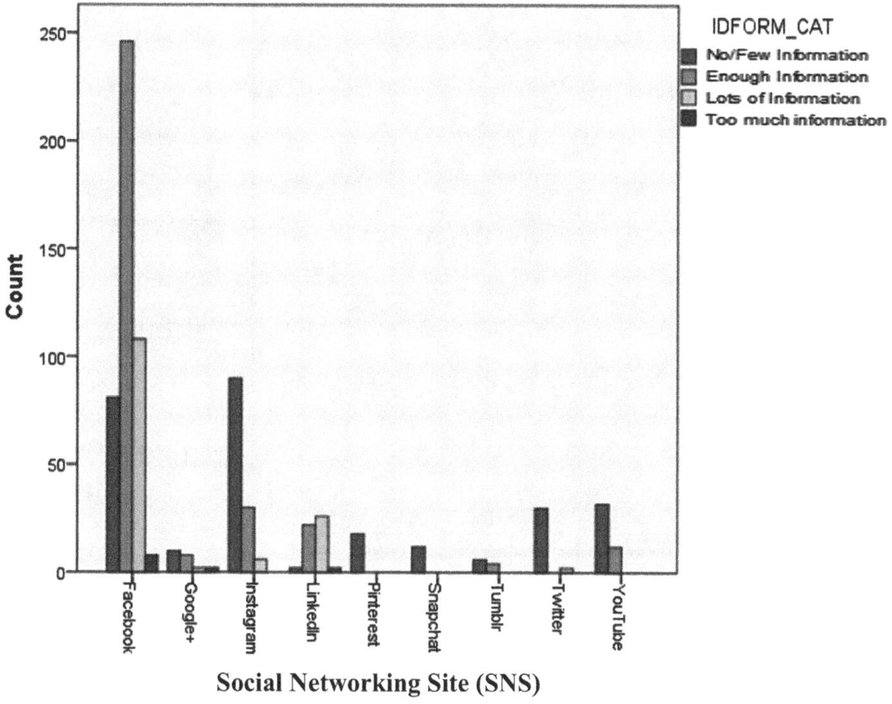

Fig. 4. Type of SNS's influence on digital identity formation

choose to introduce themselves to other users of the platform and hence the formation of their digital identity. On Fig. 4, the distribution of responses for each social network in relation to the amount of published information, is demonstrated.

Concerning H3 research hypothesis, there was a large difference in average values between some SNS platforms. For example, Facebook's average on each of the three privacy-related variables is significantly higher than those on LinkedIn, Twitter, YouTube, Instagram and Pinterest. Figure 5 shows the average of the three variables for each SNS. From the line graph we conclude that the average for the variable of general privacy concerns is considerably higher than those of the other two variables, independently of the SNS. It also appears that privacy threats related to the social environment are considerably lower, also regardless of the used SNS. Finally, the SNS that seems to raise most privacy concerns is Facebook, while LinkedIn appears to raise less privacy concerns.

Analysis of variance results showed that there are statistically significant variations with all three combinations, when the dependent variable was each of the three constructs of privacy concerns. Statistically significant differences are again observed in the same pairs of SNS. In the variable of privacy concerns regarding social threats, we notice the lowest averages among all SNS. The same variable has the largest deviations from the highest to the lower limit (Facebook and LinkedIn respectively.

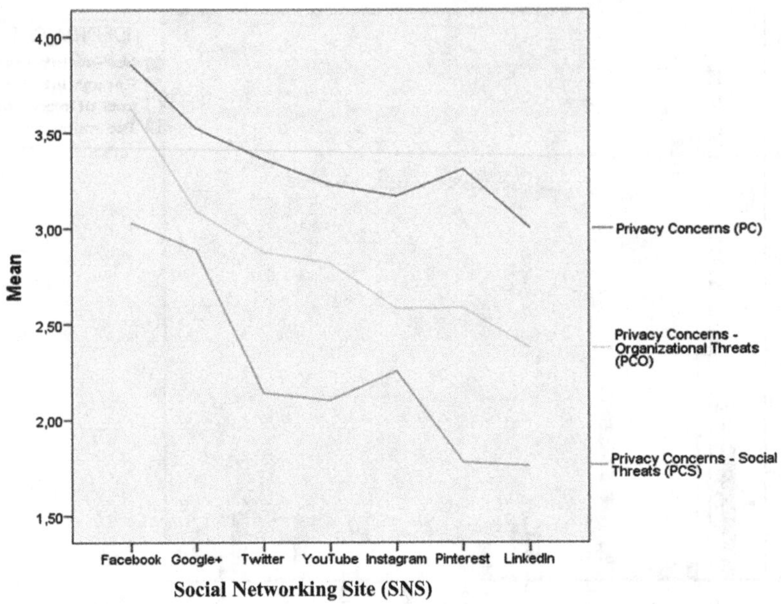

Fig. 5. SNS's influence on users' level of privacy concerns

Overall, we can conclude that the SNS that the user utilizes affects users' privacy concerns. The platforms that users trust to disclose much and honest identity information, such as LinkedIn, are ranked very low in privacy concerns rating. This finding seems expected if we consider the reason why someone uses a network like LinkedIn. The information provided by the user should be complete and accurate for job-oriented networking to be effective. On the contrary, Facebook collects vast amounts of information and seems to worry users about privacy violations. Although the platform integrates privacy protection tools, concerns about privacy issues record the highest averages. The support of H3 research hypothesis is also reinforced by the differentiation of the contribution of questions in the formation of each variable. The contribution factors of each question, separately for each SNS, are higher than those recorded in the aggregate results.

5 Discussion

This paper explores digital identities' formation in SNSs, by identifying the elements that users perceive as constituents of their digital identities, as well as the role of privacy concerns for forming them. As identification and analysis of the data elements that constitute digital identities in SNS is scarce in the literature, this study provides an understanding of how users perceive and form these identities.

Results of this research show that users perceive as pillar information for their digital identity, in sequence of significance: their name, gender, photo, interests, job, favorite music, academic classifications, and others (see Fig. 2). Our findings demonstrate that privacy concerns do not seem to affect the information that users disclose when they form their digital identities. The paradox of this finding can be explained by the unpredictable nature of the human personality and the way it is expressed. This fluidity of human behavior in general, and especially in terms of privacy behaviors, was reflected in the research that led to the formulation of the privacy paradox. From a psychological viewpoint, the privacy paradox occurs when users realize that they must trade-off between their privacy concerns and impression management (Utz and Kramer 2009). This gives us an indication of why users in our research differentiate the personal data they disclose when privacy concerns related to their social environment are mediated. The ability of people to adapt to the circumstances and their tendency to make choices in pursuit of the best desired result outline those cases where the user ignores presumable negative effects.

Through this research we have also identified how users' perceptions and behaviors differentiate across different SNS, including the diversity of information that users choose to publish for shaping their digital identity in them. The SNS was found to be determinant for both the information users choose for their digital identity and for their privacy concerns. The large number of social networking platforms available today can confirm the validity of this finding. Each of the SNS brings together specific features and targets different audiences. The usage purpose, the user interface and the trust of the user to the platform are factors that play an important role in shaping the conditions, under which users adopt a social network. Furthermore, each SNS offers a different combination of personal identity elements, from which the user can choose what to disclose in order to form a unique digital identity. Consequently, users behave online in a specific context, different for each social networking platform.

To the best of our knowledge, this is the first paper that examines digital identity formation in SNS in relation to the type of SNS and privacy concerns. As mentioned in the introduction, shaping digital identity using social networks is an internal process, which is then influenced by such factors. Literature mentions as determinants of identity formation, inter alia, user self-esteem/self-confidence (Forest and Wood 2012; Emery et al. 2014; Marshall et al. 2015), the "Big Five" model of personality (Marshall et al. 2015), narcissism (Mehdizadeh 2010), perceived benefits (Xu et al. 2013; Khan and Shaikh 2007; Forman et al. 2008; Boyd and Ellison 2007), privacy sensitivity (Yang and Wang 2009; Xu et al. 2013), information control (Xu et al. 2013) and subjective rules such as social culture, trust and intimacy with other users (Lewis et al. 2008; Xu et al. 2013). However, these are factors that have been already researched and validated by previous works. The combination of social media chosen by the user and privacy concerns as regulators of shaping the digital identity is proposed in this paper for the first time. The aforementioned factors can be further studied in the future, in combination with those proposed in the present research, with a view to drawing more detailed conclusions about human behavior online.

There are also limitations in our research. First, participants answered the questions according to the SNS they chose. In a more advanced research approach, we could study the differentiation of every user's behavior among the social networks that they use. However, in this case other methodological problems would arise, as the large extent of the questionnaire would take a long time to complete, at the risk of low participation. Moreover, all users do not use all social networks, nor the same combination of them, which would lead to the collection of a very large number of different cases that are not comparable to each other. Second, in our research, responses for specific SNSs had few answers because they are not popular in Greece. Snapchat, Tumblr and Flickr had less than 2% of the sample and therefore could not provide evidence to support or not the corresponding findings of the literature.

6 Conclusions and Further Research

Overall, the results of this research are consistent with findings in relevant literature and contribute with new insights: Whilst privacy concerns about "social threats" affect the amount of personal information disclosure, we have found that this is not the case with general privacy concerns and those related to "organizational threats". As Tufekci (2008) argues, it seems that users are more concerned about being honest with their real friends and prefer to keep unwanted audiences away using privacy settings. Moreover, users tend to disclose a lot of their personal information, overcoming their privacy concerns, in order to state their preferences clearly and avoid misconceptions. In the same time, we need to consider a possible lack of concern about organizations, government etc., comparing to the social environment. The findings of this study can motivate further research in users' online behavior and can be of value for SNS designers as they reveal the difficulty to understand the role of privacy within social networking.

Further, we provide evidence that users have different privacy concerns per SNS platform and choose different elements to formulate their digital identity in each one of them. This finding can provide significant insights for the SNS providers and the protective mechanisms that they enable. This study indicates that users worry differently about their privacy depending on the type of SNS. SNS providers can benefit from this finding by differentiating their authentication methods to reassure their users (e.g., our data implies that Facebook would benefit by enforcing stronger authentication mechanisms as a remedy for the increased privacy concerns).

We also examined the role of privacy concerns for individuals' perception and information disclosure. Our findings confirm that users do have privacy concerns when using SNS, which can be a useful finding for entities that design privacy awareness campaigns (e.g., ENISA). These privacy concerns however were not found to prohibit users from disclosure information that they perceive as important for expressing who they are in SNS platforms.

Findings of this study can also trigger future research in the understanding of human behavior across SNS. It would be interesting to examine how the same user may differentiate her digital identity formation when moving from one SNS to another.

Acknowledgement. This research has been partially supported by the SECREDAS project, which is co-funded by the ECSEL Joint Undertaking of the European Union under grant agreement number 783119 and PDM&FC.

References

Acquisti, A., Gross, R.: Imagined communities: awareness, information sharing, and privacy on the Facebook. In: Danezis, G., Golle, P. (eds.) PET 2006. LNCS, vol. 4258, pp. 36–58. Springer, Heidelberg (2006). https://doi.org/10.1007/11957454_3

Alexa Web Search: The top 500 sites on the web: Global (2017). Accessed 11 Apr 2017

Alvermann, D.E., Marshall, J.D., McLean, C.A., Huddleston, A.P., Joaquin, J., Bishop, J.: Adolescents' web-based literacies, identity construction, and skill development. Lit. Res. Instr. **51**(3), 179–195 (2012)

Barbour, K., Marshall, D.: The academic online: constructing persona through the World Wide Web. First Monday **17**(9) (2012). https://doi.org/10.5210/fm.v0i0.3969

Bareket-Bojmel, L., Moran, S., Shahar, G.: Strategic self-presentation on Facebook: personal motives and audience response to online behavior. Comput. Hum. Behav. **55**, 788–795 (2016)

Barnes, S.B.: A privacy paradox: social networking in the United States. First Monday **11**(9) (2006). https://firstmonday.org//article/view/1394/1312

Baym, N.K.: Personal Connections in the Digital Age. Polity, Malden (2010)

Belk, R.W.: Extended self in a digital world. J. Consum. Res. **40**(3), 477–500 (2013)

Boyd, D.: Social network sites as networked publics: affordances, dynamics, and implications. In: Papacharissi, Z. (ed.) A Networked Self: Identity, Community, and Culture on Social Network Sites, pp. 39–58. Routledge, New York (2010)

Boyd, D.M., Ellison, N.B.: Social network sites: definition, history, and scholarship. J. Comput.-Mediat. Commun. **13**(1), 210–230 (2007)

Brandtzaeg, P.B.: Social networking sites: their users and social implications-A longitudinal study. J. Comput.-Mediat. Commun. **17**(4), 467–488 (2012)

Buchanan, T., Paine, C., Joinson, A.N., Reips, U.D.: Development of measures of online privacy concern and protection for use on the Internet. J. Am. Soc. Inf. Sci. Technol. **58**(2), 157–165 (2007)

Canary, D., Cody, M., Manusov, V.: Interpersonal Communication: A Goals-Based Approach, pp. 2–49. Bedford/St. Martin's, Boston (2003)

Cover, R., Doak, S.: Identity offline and online. In: International Encyclopedia of the Social & Behavioral Sciences, pp. 547–553. Elsevier (2015)

Delahunty, J.: 'Who am I?': exploring identity in online discussion forums. Int. J. Educ. Res. **53**, 407–420 (2012)

Dwyer, C., Hiltz, S.R., Passerini, K.: Trust & privacy concern within social networking sites: a comparison of Facebook & MySpace. In: AMCIS 2007 Proceedings (2007)

D'Augelli, A.R.: Identity development and sexual orientation: toward a model of lesbian, gay, and bisexual development. In: Trickett, E.J., Watts, R.J., Birman, D. (eds.) The Jossey-Bass Social and Behavioral Science Series. Human Diversity: Perspectives on People in Context, pp. 312–333. Jossey-Bass, San Francisco (1994)

Eastin, M.S., Brinson, N.H., Doorey, A., Wilcox, G.: Living in a big data world: predicting mobile commerce activity through privacy concerns. Comput. Hum. Behav. **58**, 214–220 (2016)

Emery, L.F., Muise, A., Dix, E.L., Le, B.: Can you tell that I'm in a relationship? Attachment and relationship visibility on Facebook. Pers. Soc. Psychol. Bull. **40**, 1466–1479 (2014)

Fieseler, C., Meckel, M., Ranzini, G.: Professional personae-how organizational identification shapes online identity in the workplace. J. Comput.-Mediat. Commun. **20**(2), 153–170 (2014)

Forest, A.L., Wood, J.V.: When social networking is not working: individuals with low self-esteem recognize but do not reap the benefits of self-disclosure on Facebook. Psychol. Sci. **23**, 295–305 (2012)

Forman, C., Ghose, A., Wiesenfeld, B.: Examining the relationship between reviews and sales: the role of reviewer identity disclosure in electronic markets. Inf. Syst. Res. **19**(3), 291–313 (2008)

Gee, J.: An Introduction to Discourse Analysis: Theory and Method. Routledge, Abingdon (1999)

Goffman, E.: The Presentation of Self in Everyday Life. Doubleday, New York (1959)

Gross, R., Acquisti, A.: Information revelation and privacy in online social networks. In: Proceedings of the 2005 ACM Workshop on Privacy in the Electronic Society, Alexandria, VA, November 2005, pp. 71–80 (2005)

Hodkinson, P.: Bedrooms and beyond: youth, identity and privacy on social network sites. New Media Soc. **19**(2), 272–288 (2017)

Hoy, M.G., Milne, G.: Gender differences in privacy-related measures for young adult Facebook users. J. Interact. Advert. **10**(2), 28–45 (2010)

Hughes, D.J., Rowe, M., Batey, M., Lee, A.: A tale of two sites: Twitter vs. Facebook and the personality predictors of social media usage. Comput. Hum. Behav. **28**(2), 561–569 (2012)

Ismail, S.: An evaluation of students' identity-sharing behavior in social network communities as preparation for knowledge sharing. Int. J. Adv. Sci. Arts **1**(1), 14–24 (2010)

Joinson, A.N.: "Looking at", "Looking up" or "Keeping up with" people? Motives and uses of Facebook. In: Proceedings of CHI. ACM, New York (2008)

Joinson, A., Reips, U., Buckhanan, T., Paine Schofield, C.: Privacy, trust and self-disclosure online. Hum.-Comput. Interact. **25**, 1–24 (2010)

Junco, R.: Engaging Students Through Social Media: Evidence-Based Practices for Use in Student Affairs, p. 113. Wiley, Hoboken (2014)

Karapanos, E., Teixeira, P., Gouveia, R.: Need fulfillment and experiences on social media: a case on Facebook & WhatsApp. Comput. Hum. Behav. **55**, 888 (2016)

Khan, J.I., Shaikh, S.S.: Computing in social networks with relationship algebra. J. Netw. Comput. Appl. **31**, 862–878 (2008)

Kimmons, R.: Social networking sites, literacy, and the authentic identity problem. TechTrends **58**(2), 93–98 (2014)

Krasnova, H., Gunther, O., Spiekermann, S., Koroleva, K.: Privacy concerns and identity in online social networks. Identity Inf. Soc. **2**(1), 39–63 (2009)

Krishnamurthy, B., Wills, C.E.: Characterizing privacy in online social networks. In: Proceedings of the First Workshop on Online Social Networks, pp. 37–42, Seattle, WA, August 2008 (2008)

Larsen, M.C.: Understanding social networking: on young people's construction and co-construction of identity online. Internet Res. **8**, 18–36 (2007)

Lewis, K., Kaufman, J., Christakis, N.: The taste for privacy: an analysis of college student privacy settings in an online social network. J. Comput.-Mediat. Commun. **14**, 79–100 (2008)

Madden, M., Fox, S., Smith, A., Vitak, J.: Digital Footprints: Online Identity Management & Search in the Age of Transparency. Pew Internet & American Life Project, Washington, DC (2007)

Madden, M.: Privacy management on social media sites. Pew Internet Report, pp. 1–20 (2012)

Marshall, T.C., Lefringhausen, K., Ferenczi, N.: The Big Five, self-esteem, and narcissism as predictors of the topics people write about in Facebook status updates. Pers. Individ. Differ. **85**, 35–40 (2015)

Marwick, A.: Online identity. In: A Companion to New Media Dynamics, pp. 355–364. Blackwell Publishing Ltd. (2013)

Mehdizadeh, S.: Self-presentation 2.0: narcissism and self-esteem on Facebook. Cyberpsychol. Behav. Soc. Netw. **13**(4), 357–364 (2010)

Michikyan, M., Dennis, J., Subrahmanyam, K.: Can you guess who I am? Real, ideal, and false self-presentation on Facebook among emerging adults. Emerg. Adulthood **3**(1), 55–64 (2015)

Norberg, P.A., Horne, R., Horne, A.: The privacy paradox: personal information disclosure intentions versus behaviors. J. Consum. Aff. **41**(1), 100–126 (2007)

Palen, L., Dourish, P.: Unpacking "privacy" for a networked world. In: Proceedings of the ACM Conference on Human Factors in Computing Systems, pp. 129–136. Association for Computing Machinery, New York (2003)

Papacharissi, Z.: The virtual geographies of social networks: a comparative analysis of Facebook, LinkedIn and ASmallWorld. New Media Soc. **11**(1–2), 199–220 (2009)

Papacharissi, Z.: A Networked Self: Identity. Community and Culture on Social Network Sites. Routledge, Abingdon (2010)

Pempek, T.A., Yermolayeva, Y.A., Calvert, S.L.: College students' social networking experiences on Facebook. J. Appl. Dev. Psychol. **30**(3), 227–238 (2009)

Ramírez, G., Palu-ay, L.: "You don't look like your profile picture": the ethical implications of researching online identities in higher education. Educ. Res. Eval. **21**(2), 139–153 (2015)

Raynes-Goldie, K.: Aliases, creeping and wall cleaning: understanding privacy in the age of Facebook. First Monday **15**(1–4) (2010). https://firstmonday.org/article/viewArticle/2775/2432

Ross, C., Orr, E.S., Sisic, M., Arseneault, J.M., Simmering, M.G., Orr, R.R.: Personality and motivations associated with Facebook use. Comput. Hum. Behav. **25**(2), 578–586 (2009)

Salimkhan, G., Manago, A., Greenfield, P.: The construction of the virtual self on MySpace. Cyberpsychol.: J. Psychosoc. Res. Cyberspace **4**(1) (2010). https://cyberpsychology.eu/article/view/4231/3275

Shafie, L., Nayan, S., Osman, N.: Constructing identity through Facebook profiles: online identity and visual impression management of university students in Malaysia. Soc. Behav. Sci. **65**, 134–140 (2012)

Shin, D.H.: The effects of trust, security and privacy in social networking: a security-based approach to understand the pattern of adoption. Interact. Comput. **22**(5), 428–438 (2010)

Skeels, M., Grudin, J.: When social networks cross boundaries: a case study of workplace use of Facebook and LinkedIn. In: Proceedings of the GROUP 2009, pp. 95–104 (2009)

Stone, A.A.: The War of Desire and Technology at the Close of the Mechanical Age. MIT Press, Cambridge (1996)

Stutzman, F.: An evaluation of identity-sharing behavior in social network communities. Int. Digit. Media Arts J. **3**(1), 10–13 (2006)

Subrahmanyam, K., Šmahel, D.: Constructing identity online: identity exploration and self-presentation. In: Subrahmanyam, K., Smahel, D. (eds.) Digital Youth. Advancing Responsible Adolescent Development, pp. 59–80. Springer, New York (2011). https://doi.org/10.1007/978-1-4419-6278-2_4

Tufekci, Z.: Can you see me now? Audience and disclosure regulation in online social network sites. Bull. Sci. Technol. Soc. **28**(1), 20–36 (2008)

Turkle, S.: Alone Together: Why We Expect More from Technology and Less from Each Other. Basic Books, New York (2011)

Utz, S., Kramer, N.: The privacy paradox on social network sites revisited: the role of individual characteristics and group norms. Cyberpsychol. J. Psychosoc. Res. Cyberspace **3**(2) (2009). Article 1. https://cyberpsychology.eu/article/view/4223/3265

Van Bavel, J.J., Pereira, A.: The partisan brain: an identity-based model of political belief. Trends Cogn. Sci. **22**(3), 213–224 (2018)

Van Dijck, J.: 'You have one identity': performing the self on Facebook and LinkedIn. Media Cult. Soc. **35**(2), 199–215 (2013)

Wang, S.S.: "I share, therefore I am": personality traits, life satisfaction, and Facebook check-ins. Cyberpsychol. Behav. Soc. Netw. **16**(12), 870–877 (2013)
Wessels, B.: Identification and the practices of identity and privacy in everyday digital communication. New Media Soc. **14**(8), 1251–1268 (2012)
Xu, H., Dinev, T., Smith, J., Hart, P.: Information privacy concerns: linking individual perceptions with institutional privacy assurances. J. Assoc. Inf. Syst. **12**(12), 798 (2011)
Xu, F., Michael, K., Chen, X.: Electron. Commer. Res. **13**(2), 151–168 (2013)
Yang, S., Wang, K.: The influence of information sensitivity compensation on privacy concern and behavioral intention. Data Base Adv. Inf. Syst. **40**(1), 38–51 (2009)
Youn, S.: Determinants of online privacy concern and its influence on privacy protection behaviors among young adolescents. J. Consum. Aff. **43**(3), 389–418 (2009)
Zhang, C., Sun, J., Zhu, X., Fang, Y.: Privacy and security for online social networks: challenges and opportunities. IEEE Netw. **24**(4), 13–18 (2010)
Zhao, S., Grasmuck, S., Martin, J.: Identity construction on Facebook: digital empowerment in anchored relationships. Comput. Hum. Behav. **24**, 1816–1836 (2008)

GDPR Compliance: Proposed Technical and Organizational Measures for Cloud Providers

Zafeiroula Georgiopoulou(✉), Eleni-Laskarina Makri, and Costas Lambrinoudakis

Department of Digital Systems, University of Piraeus, 18532 Piraeus, Greece
roulageorgio@ssl-unipi.gr, {elmak, clam}@unipi.gr

Abstract. The process of GDPR compliance for cloud computing environments may turn out to be a demanding process in terms of the technical, organizational and procedural measures that should be adopted. This paper identifies the requirements and the appropriate countermeasures for GDPR compliance in cloud environments. Furthermore, it describes the necessary GDPR related roles and separates the requirements and measures in accordance to the cloud architecture (IAAS, PAAS, SAAS).

Keywords: Cloud computing · GDPR · Data controller · Data processor · IAAS · SAAS · PAAS

1 Introduction

Cloud computing is a technology with huge spread in many aspects and areas of ICT. A lot of research has been conducted over the past years on security, privacy and trust issues of cloud environments and especially on shared clouds. This research is still open, imposing, even today, obstacles in the adoption of cloud. In addition to that, from May 2018 cloud providers should comply with GDPR. The General Data Protection Regulation (GDPR) has a clear goal: to introduce a higher, more consistent level of personal data protection across the European Union, which will give citizens back control over their personal data and simplify the regulatory environment for business. The regulation, applies to all companies that hold or process EU residents' data, including cloud computing users, providers and their sub-contractors. The existing National legal framework, based on the 95/46 EU Data Protection Directive, has not achieved harmonization of personal data protection rules between member states. These variations, and at times conflicting rules, are complicating businesses' requirements and procedures, especially as data increasingly flows across borders in today's digital age. By implementing it as a regulation, the GDPR aims to ensure that the same data protection rules will apply uniformly across the EU. In addition, while many of the GDPR's concepts and principles have been based on the 95/46 Data Protection Directive, it introduces significant new rules and enhancements. The emphasis is on how personally identifiable information (PII) is handled and protected by institutions within the EU—and, in certain cases, outside the EU. For the cloud providers, the new

S. Katsikas et al. (Eds.): ESORICS 2019 Workshops, LNCS 11980, pp. 181–194, 2020.
https://doi.org/10.1007/978-3-030-42048-2_12

obligations are extensive and challenging. The purpose of this paper is to give a brief guidance on what a cloud provider should consider and what further actions to take in order to comply with GDPR [2].

Section 2 describes in detail the requirements for GDPR compliance of cloud computing environments. Section 3, presents the GDPR roles (data controller and data processor) in a cloud environment and discusses the applicability of GDPR compliance requirements for each cloud architecture (IAAS, PAAS, SAAS). Furthermore, Sect. 3 proposes countermeasures for satisfying the aforementioned requirements. Section 4 concludes the paper.

2 GDPR Requirements

During the process of conforming with GDPR in cloud computing environments several requirements of the regulation should be considered. On the following section we present a detailed description of the previous.

2.1 Material and Territorial Scope

GDPR applies to cloud 'controllers' (who decide how and why personal data is processed) and 'processors' (who process personal data on controller's behalf). More specifically an EU based cloud controller or processor should comply to GDPR requirements. To the previous add clouds which are not based in EU but offer services to European Union citizens or include monitoring actions that take place in the European Union.

As a check of whether a cloud needs to fulfill GDPR requirements or not, it is suggested to implement an audit-alert mechanism that will check if a cloud user (Software as a service) or the data uploaded/processed in the cloud (Infrastructure as a Service) falls under GDPR. When an alert is triggered specific automatic or/and manual actions with technical and organizational measures, as described below, should be taken to ensure GDPR compliance.

2.2 Data Protection Principles

Cloud providers must ensure the following GDPR principles: lawfulness, fairness and transparency, purpose limitation, data minimization, accuracy, storage limitation, integrity and confidentiality, accountability. More specifically the personal data of the data subject must be processed according to the law requirements, in a fair and transparent manner. The specific requirement highlights the need for the data controller to adopt privacy policies that are friendlier to data and thus promoting privacy rights. Cloud providers should collect, store and process personal data for specific and legitimate purposes, prohibiting any processing that lies outside the initial scope. The only window that GDPR leaves open for further processing is under the aspect of public interest and scientific research. Furthermore, to comply with the principle of minimization, personal data stored in cloud premises should be adequate, relevant and limited to what is necessary in relation to the purpose for which they have been collected. Cloud controllers must keep personal data accurate and up to date. When the data are not any more required, in relation to the initial processing purpose, they should be immediately erased, thus conforming to the storage limitation principle. Finally, integrity and confidentiality should be reassured to avoid unauthorized or unlawful processing or/and accidental loss, destruction or damage.

To conform with the above cloud providers must maintain full documentation of personal data held, where it came from and with whom they are shared with, including the reason of processing. Data minimization should be considered in the organization and the purpose of collecting information should be defined in the security policy. Scheduled data re-evaluation should be performed periodically. Furthermore, to ensure purpose limitation it is necessary to perform periodic audits to cloud clients and employees. Also, periodic data accuracy compliance checks should be done. Finally, vital for cloud providers is to apply storage limitation scan mechanisms and transfer restriction. To ensure integrity and confidentiality, data encryption, encrypted networks, firewall, data fragmentation, and anonymization techniques should be utilized. Pseudoanonymization, a privacy enhancing technique, should also be implemented if possible, avoiding immediate linkability of data to the data subjects. In terms of accountability and lawfulness of processing, appropriate audit mechanisms on data operations (access, edit, delete, export etc.) are proposed to be implemented. The legitimate interest should be documented and included with accurate, clear and specific terms in the Service Level Agreement – SLA.

2.3 Consent

Cloud providers that collect/process any form of personal data need always a legal basis. In certain cases this legal basis can be the consent of the data subject. In other words, the cloud controller needs at any time to be able to demonstrate that the data subject has consented to the processing of his or her personal data. If the data subject's consent is given in the context of a written declaration which also concerns other matters, the request for consent shall be presented in a manner which is clearly distinguishable from the other matters, in an intelligible and easily accessible form, using clear and plain language. Any part of such a declaration which constitutes an infringement of this Regulation shall not be binding. The data subject shall have the right to withdraw his or her consent at any time. The withdrawal of consent shall not affect the lawfulness of processing based on consent before its withdrawal. Prior to giving consent, the data subject shall be informed thereof. It shall be as easy to withdraw as to give consent.

The consent management mechanisms should be supported through some software application which will support the provision, updating, revoking and maintaining of users' consents. Restriction on clear and plain language consent should be included in order to be intelligible and easily accessible (e.g. native language of data subject). Alerting for updating the users' consents will be necessary when a change in the purpose or manner of personal data processing is happening.

2.4 Children – Parental Consent

In case that a cloud service is offered directly to a child under 16 years old, parental consent is required (Article 6(1)). The specific consent is considered to be lawful only if it is given or has been authorized by the holder of parental responsibility over the child.

Cloud providers that have as users children, should enforce mechanisms for parental control. Alert mechanism that will require further actions should be implemented when a child is trying to use cloud or his parents are giving rights to store and process its data. After the alert is generated an authentication mechanism should be generated to make sure that the legitimate parent is giving the consent and the language of consents should be children friendly in order to make children's able to understand that parental approval is required. Software like the one described in Sect. 2.3 should be used but having also the above functions.

2.5 Sensitive Data and Lawful Processing

According to GDPR sensitive data are the ones revealing:

- Racial or ethnic origin
- Political opinions
- Religious or philosophical beliefs
- Trade union membership
- Genetic data
- Biometric data for uniquely identifying a natural person
- Data concerning health or a natural person's sex life and/or sexual orientation

Cloud providers that collect/process such data categories should take further actions in order to satisfy GDPR requirements.

To this extend, the types of sensitive data that are processed should be identified and analytically described in the security policy of the cloud, providing also the reasoning for their necessity. In technical terms, it will be vital to implement a cloud-perimeter protection mechanism that will perform file and data scan, especially in cases of hardware as a service architecture where data storage is offered as a service.

2.6 Information Notices

Cloud providers must provide information through their privacy policy and/or upon request of the data subjects about the:

- Identity and contact details of the controller
- Data involved, purpose of processing and legal basis
- Recipient or categories of recipients
- Details of data transfer outside EU
- Data retention period
- Right of individuals

Regarding information notices a suggestion is to adopt some tool for generating and automatically sharing, template documents for the information notices, requests and responses.

2.7 Subject Access, Rectification and Portability

Cloud providers should provide to the data subjects confirmation whether his/her personal data are being processed, access the data and supplemental information regarding rectification or reassure, source of data and portability.

Full reporting and document templates are required. Techniques of alerts and corresponding deletion or non-availability of data that are subject to retention should be used. Cloud providers must be able to export data mechanism in a safe manner and in a common format/technology that can be widely adopted to support portability (e.g. xml, tab, csv). They should also be able to provide mechanism for validity of the request of the data subject. Provide a mechanism to respond to requests on personal data access. Maintain the technological ability to trace and search personal data.

2.8 Rights to Object

Cloud providers must give data owners the right to object against a data processing in an easy and safe way. In terms of technical proposal this can be converted to a mechanism applied for data subject objection and automated further actions.

2.9 Right to Erasure and Right to Restriction of Processing

Erasure or restriction of processing must be applied in cloud when any of the below is valid:

- Data are no longer necessary for the purpose for which they were collected or processed.
- Individuals withdraw their consent.
- Controllers cannot demonstrate that there are overriding legitimate grounds
- Unlawful processing.

When data are put in public domain the cloud provider need to notify the other controllers that the data owner want to restrict the access or that his data need to be erased.

Cloud providers must have in place special eraser software to make sure that data cannot be retrieved from the hard disk of storages. Also, in cases where the information is required to be kept for some period it is necessary to have restriction mechanisms in place that will not have available the information, blocking the data to a different system.

2.10 Profiling and Automated Decision-Taking

Profiling consists of three aspects: Automated processing (processing using computers) of personal data with the aim of evaluating personal aspects relating to a person or group of people (including analysis or prediction). The guidelines make it clear that the definition is very broad and that the processing does not need to involve inference to be caught – "simply assessing or classifying individuals based on characteristics such as their age, sex, and height could be considered profiling, regardless of any predictive purpose" [7]. The guidelines describe profiling as having three distinct stages each of which fall within the GDPR definition of profiling: (1) data collection (2) automated analysis to identify correlations and (3) applying the correlation to an individual to identify characteristics of present or future behavior. A decision based solely on automated processing is a decision with no human involvement in the decision process. The guidelines warn that involving a human in the process to circumvent the rules on solely automated decision making would not work, as the human involvement must be meaningful and not just a token gesture. The individual needs to have the authority to change the decision considering all the information available.

Individuals must be told when a decision has been taken solely using automated decision making and they must have the right to request a review of the decision. The review should be done by a person with appropriate authority and capacity to change the decision and should involve a thorough review of all relevant data and any additional information provided by the individual. Organizations using automated decision making should also carry our regular reviews and use appropriate procedures to prevent errors.

2.11 Accountability, Security and Breach Notification

GDPR's article 24 codifies the accountability obligation. It requires controllers to:

- Implement appropriate technical and organizational measures (including the introduction of data protection by design and by default principles where relevant) to ensure and be able to demonstrate that data processing is performed in accordance with the GDPR
- Review and update measures where necessary through notably internal and external assessment such as privacy seals. Those measures should take into account the nature, scope, context and purposes of processing and the risk to the rights and freedoms of natural persons.

In the case of a personal data breach, the controller shall without undue delay and, where feasible, not later than 72 h after having become aware of it, notify the personal data breach to the supervisory authority competent in accordance with Article 55, unless the personal data breach is unlikely to result in a risk to the rights and freedoms of natural persons. Where the notification to the supervisory authority is not made within 72 h, it shall be accompanied by reasons for the delay.

Thus, cloud providers should have in place mechanisms for network protection, encryption and notification to the supervisory authorities and the data subjects [1].

3 Countermeasures Depending on the Cloud Architecture

3.1 GDPR Roles and Cloud Architectures

Cloud participants, in GDPR terms, can be separated into two main roles: the data processors and the data controllers. Most of the times, cloud providers act as data processors on behalf of their customers/users who are the data controllers.

"Data processor means a natural or legal person, public authority, agency or other body which processes personal data on behalf of the controller." (Article 4 – (8)) "Controller means the natural or legal person, public authority, agency or other body which, alone or jointly with others, determines the purposes and means of the processing of personal data; where the purposes and means of such processing are determined by Union or Member State law, the controller or the specific criteria for its nomination may be provided for by Union or Member State law". (Article 4 – (7)).

Cloud can appear in three main architectures/models:

- Infrastructure as a Service (IaaS): Provides hardware resources as computing facility, storage, memory etc. Known provider of IaaS is Amazon with EC2 and S3.
- Platform as a Service (PaaS): The term platform is related to systems (e.g. operating system) that can be used to develop and build custom applications. Known provider of PaaS is Microsoft Azure.
- Software as a Service (SaaS): Provides any type of software (application or service) through cloud. Known provider of SaaS is Salesforce.

In the following sections we will attempt to separate the countermeasures required depending on the cloud architecture.

3.2 Infrastructure as a Service

A cloud provider who offers Infrastructure as a service falls under GDPR, as most of the times acts as a data processor.

An IaaS cloud provider needs to support material and territorial scope in specific terms. More specifically, the storage location of personal data should be available at any moment, with full transparency, from the IaaS cloud providers [9]. It will be very useful to also support data transfer functionality and options for auditing the geographical flow of information [4].

An IaaS provider needs to have in place incident response mechanisms to promptly identify/respond incidents that create suspicion and indicate unauthorized access but only on the infrastructure level. Data protection principles are only partially applicable to IaaS cloud providers. An IaaS cloud service provider does not need to do anything about the lawfulness of processing since he has not a direct relationship with the data subjects, nor has knowledge on the data that his customer (data controller) has collected from the data subjects. However, they should have in place measures designed to identify the root cause of the Personal Data Breach, mitigate any possible adverse effects and prevent a recurrence.

Personal data processing should be done only for supporting GDPR purposes and to serve daily operation like security, attacks on systems networks, bots, administration of daily processes and comply with local legislations. The above processing can be shared with sub-contractors only if the IaaS publishes the list of subcontractors accompanied with full documentation and reasoning of sharing.

To support the transparency principle, audit mechanisms must be provided by cloud providers, recording in an automatic way the requested resources, the users and the sources of activity.

Purpose limitation in an Infrastructure as a Service cloud architecture can be supported by splitting the infrastructure into individual clusters. Cloud hardware resources provided to a data controller, should be isolated to avoid flow of personal data information. Cloud providers should also be able to offer to their customers the ability to create virtual cloud networks and thus facilitate communication between the isolated resources and at the same time supporting isolation from public internet.

Accuracy, from the side of an IAAS cloud provider, should be supported by offering relevant tools to their customers (data controllers). Software scanning must be enabled to actively monitor data content, integrity and automatically generate alerts to customer for malicious data. Encryption techniques can also help in the accuracy.

"GDPR can support integrity and confidentiality to ensure that the appropriate security of personal data against unauthorized or unlawful processing and against accidental loss, destruction or damage…" Article 5(1)(f). Hardware and network level access control in a cloud infrastructure is proposed to comply with GDPR with the concept of least privilege. Encryption on storage can also help in security of personal data applying encryption on block level, object level and metadata with separate keys and up to date technologies.

An IaaS is not obliged to have the consent of data subjects since they do not have direct relationship with the service offered. The same logic applies to parental consent. The only part that could be related to but without any required obligation is to take extra measures in the authentication process to mitigate the unauthorized access especially for non-adults.

In terms of Sensitive data an IaaS cloud provider should comply with all the aforementioned data protection measures and have in place a software for scanning data files in order to quickly identify sensitive information stored in their datastores.

Information notices is not an obligation of GDPR for cloud providers. Only for the offered marketing and client support services they could employ a mechanism for generating automatically templates for the documents that the cloud controllers need to provide to authorities and to data subjects.

Subject access rectification and portability falls under IaaS oligarchy to GDPR. IaaS providers must provide information regarding the data processed, the possible data transfers with the relevant recipients, including information regarding rectification and reassure. To support this, providers needs to have in place mechanisms for supporting data portability through the appropriate export mechanisms.

The right to object, erasure and restriction is mostly relevant to cloud processors and not providers-controllers themselves. The only case that an IaaS provider may request a cloud processor to embed network restrictions and isolations for specific parts of the infrastructure is after a data subject objects to a cloud processor. Also, a software for secure erasure must be in place in the Infrastructure used.

Profiling and automated decision-taking is out of scope for an IaaS Cloud provider.

Finally, an IaaS cloud provider is subject to accountability, security and breach notification. A cloud provider is obliged to have installed firewalls and network protection measures. Incident management mechanisms and procedures should also be in place to actively monitor potential data breaches in order to be able to notify the supervisory authority in 72 h and to minimize the impact of the data breach. Standard certification of the infrastructures provided could help (e.g. ISO 27001) (Table 1).

Table 1. Applicability of GDPR requirements for IaaS.

GDPR requirement	Applicability for cloud provider
Material & territorial scope	Obligation
Data protection principles	Obligation
Consent	Recommended
Children – parental consent	Recommended
Sensitive data & lawful processing	Recommended
Information notices	Recommended

3.3 Platform as a Service

Platform as a Service cloud providers should comply with GDPR. This Section describes, one by one, the measures that a PaaS provider must or should offer to its customers in order to comply with GDPR or to help them to do so in favor of shared responsibilities.

Analytic information regarding the geographical source, flow and process of information should be available from the PaaS provider at any time. This information should be available online, by mail alert and official documentation. Besides the informative part, PaaS providers must help their customer to maintain their data in specific geographic location accepting relevant terms in their SLAs [5].

Data protection principles should be maintained in a stricter way compared to IaaS cloud providers. PaaS helps cloud customers to protect and safeguard their data, including personal data, in support of organizational security commitments and GDPR compliance requirements. The employment of several service-level security measures for ensuring the confidentiality, integrity and availability of the processed data is strongly recommended. The security measures should be multilayered in physical, logical and data levels, indicatively including: 24-h restricted access to datacenters, multiple authentication processes (such as badges, smart cards, and biometric scanners) for physical access, on-premises security guards, monitoring using video surveillance, motion sensors, and security breach alarms, automated fire prevention and extinguishing systems, access control lists, IPsec policies on hosts, restrictive firewall rules and host-based firewall rules, edge router security, network segmentation to provide physical separation of critical back-end servers and storage devices from public-facing interfaces, strict control of admin access to customer data, antimalware software, data isolation using Active Directory authorization, role-based access controls and workload-specific isolation mechanisms, use of encryption and other cryptographic security measures.

Data subject consent management is not a requirement that a PaaS cloud provider should comply with. Some big PaaS providers offer supporting tools to collect consent. Parental consent is also not required.

PaaS cloud providers must employ tools for sensitive data identification and relevant measures for classifying and protecting them. Data retention tools may be also necessary. Rule based controls could be also provided to alert the administrators of the cloud processor that a PaaS user stores information that has been classified as sensitive. Regarding sensitive date it is strongly recommended to have audit controls against global data privacy standards such as ISO 27018.

In terms of information notices, PaaS providers need to maintain full documentation of their platforms and of the security mechanisms they employ to support requests for information notices from authorities.

PaaS Cloud users maintain the right of access, rectification and portability under the enforcement of GDPR. All information hosted in PaaS environments must be exportable in a universal and readable way through tools that the cloud service provider will supply.

Right to object is also applicable to PaaS providers and they must provide tools for restriction of data storage, retention or deletion after the data subject objects.

Profiling and automated decision-taking is out of scope for a PaaS Cloud provider.

Furthermore, a PaaS cloud provider is subject to accountability, security and breach notification. In the security measures, it is imperative to include firewalls and network protection tools. Incident management should be also in place to actively monitor data breaches and thus to support the notification of supervisory authorities in 72 h. Standard certification of the infrastructures provided could help (e.g. ISO 27001) (Table 2).

Table 2. Applicability of GDPR requirements for PaaS.

GDPR requirement	Applicability for cloud provider
Material & territorial scope	Obligation
Data protection principles	Obligation
Consent	Recommended
Children – parental consent	Recommended
Sensitive data & lawful processing	Obligation
Information notices	Recommended
Subject access, rectification and portability	Recommended

3.4 Software as a Service

Under the GDPR, SaaS cloud providers face direct obligations relating to data processing activities. They will need to ensure that their product agreements with customers comply with the upcoming data regulations. Failure to do so could result in customers, their customer's customers, and local data protection authorities imposing fines against them. The data controller and data processor co-exist and they both have responsibilities, requirements and rights.

A SaaS provider needs to maintain documentation of data location and information flow. It is proposed to have in place a mechanism that will generate alerts to software administrators when EU citizens are using the software to notify software owners that they should comply to GDPR [8].

Data protection principles to SaaS cloud providers apply to all layers of cloud from physical protection, infrastructure and up to software data protection. Measures regarding physical protection must cover unauthorized access of personnel in the data centers, including physical access control mechanisms like cards, cameras and biometrics. On network level, encryption mechanisms are suggested, and it is necessary to use firewalls, Intrusion Detection and Intrusion Prevention controls. Furthermore, network segregation is required, mac filtering and network access control. Storage encryptions techniques should be on level of hardware applying also on the same level software scan tools. On the software data level, the best practices proposed by global standards should be applied. Vulnerability assessments of the software and penetration testing must be periodically conducted. Software must include audit mechanisms to log and alert for data view, usage and edit with alert customization rules. It is also imperative to apply encryption between communication and storage levels in terms of database and hardware itself. Pseudonymization and anonymization is also proposed when applicable [6].

Software delivered in form of SaaS is not necessary to embed consent management techniques. It would be useful and probably recommended, but it is not obligatory since it is out of the scope of the software itself. The same applies to children consent but it would be useful to have a way for parental consent.

Sensitive data and relevant documentation of where it could be stored from software partition level, up to physical infrastructure required would be more than obligatory. It is also required to have in place encryption techniques and all the measures referred above on data protection levels.

In terms of information notices there is a need to maintain full documentation of their platforms and security mechanisms applied to support requests for information notices from authorities.

Subject access, rectification and portability must be fully documented by data controllers, but SaaS data processors must give to controller's tools to maintain this information. It is also imperative to have mechanisms for data export to support portability in universal formats.

SaaS providers should avoid profiling users based on their sensitive information whether these are directly collected from them or inferred as part of their undergoing automated profiling. Data minimization principle should drive service design as data controllers should be able to understand the minimum amount of data you will need for it. The best way for doing that is to consider Data Protection by Design and by Default, building services always examining what data are strictly needed, how to use them and why. Do not experiment with algorithms and training models by collecting first data and then decide how to use them, but rather only use well tested models that you know will suffice to your scope, before deploying them [3].

Accountability, security and breach notification notices should be raised from SaaS providers to let know the data controller about the leakage. Intrusion detection must be included in the infrastructure of SaaS and relevant DPO must react. Full documentation of data leakage and audit information should also be included (Table 3).

Table 3. Applicability of GDPR requirements for SaaS.

GDPR requirement	Applicability for cloud provider
Material & territorial scope	Obligation
Data protection principles	Obligation
Consent	Recommended
Children – parental consent	Recommended
Sensitive data & lawful processing	Obligation
Information notices	Recommended
Subject access, rectification and portability	Obligation

4 Conclusions

The following Table 4 provides a summary of the requirements for cloud providers acting as data Processors.

Table 4. Recommended and obligatory measures for data processors

Requirements	IaaS	PaaS	SaaS
Material & territorial scope	◩	◩	◩
Data protection principles	◩	◩	◩
Consent	■	■	■
Children – Parental Consent	■	■	■
Sensitive data & lawful processing	■	◩	◩
Information notices	■	■	■
Subject access, rectification and portability	■	■	◩

◩ Recommended/ Obligatory

■ Recommended

The following Table 5 provides a summary of the requirements for cloud providers acting as data Controllers.

Table 5. Recommended and obligatory measures for data controllers

Requirements	IaaS	PaaS	SaaS
Material & territorial scope	■	■	■
Data protection principles	■	■	■
Consent	■	■	■
Children – Parental Consent	■	■	■
Sensitive data & lawful processing	■	■	■
Information notices	■	■	■
Subject access, rectification and portability	■	■	■
■ Obligatory			

This paper has provided an overview of the security measures that could be engaged in the process of GDPR compliance in cloud computing environments. For future work we plan to research on what level trust management can influence GDPR.

Acknowledgment. This work has been partially supported by the Research Center of the University of Piraeus.

References

1. Bird & Bird, Guide to the General Data Protection Regulation, January 2017

2. Cloud Security Alliance, Code of Conduct for GDPR Compliance, November 2017. https://downloads.cloudsecurityalliance.org/assets/research/gdpr/CSA_Code_of_Conduct_for_GDPR_Compliance.pdf
3. Regulation (EU) 2016/679 of the European Parliament and of the Council, The European Parliament and the Council of the European Union, 27 April 2016. https://eur-lex.europa.eu/legal-content/EN/TXT/PDF/?uri=CELEX:32016R0679&qid=1485368166820&from=en
4. Microsoft, Accelerate GDPR compliance with the Microsoft Cloud, July 2017
5. Amazon Web Services, Navigating GDPR Compliance on AWS (2018)
6. Google Cloud Whitepaper, General Data Protection Regulation (GDPR), May 2018
7. Deloitte, Data Privacy in the cloud, September 2015
8. LexisNexis, GDPR and codes of conduct in SaaS, January 2019
9. Oracle Cloud Infrastructure, Oracle Cloud Infrastructure and the GDPR, European Union General Data Protection Regulation, April 2018

On the Applicability of Security and Privacy Threat Modeling for Blockchain Applications

Dimitri Van Landuyt(✉), Laurens Sion, Emiel Vandeloo, and Wouter Joosen

imec-DistriNet, KU Leuven, 3001 Leuven, Belgium
{dimitri.vanlanduyt,laurens.sion,emiel.vandeloo,
wouter.joosen}@cs.kuleuven.be

Abstract. Elicitative threat modeling approaches such as Microsoft STRIDE and LINDDUN for respectively security and privacy use Data Flow Diagrams (DFDs) to model the system under analysis. Distinguishing between external entities, processes, data stores and data flows, these system models are particularly suited for modeling centralized, traditional multi-tiered system architectures.

This raises the question whether these approaches are also suited for inherently decentralized architectures such as distributed ledgers or blockchains, in which the processing, storage, and control flow is shared among many equal participants.

To answer this question, we perform an in-depth analysis of the compatibility between blockchain security and privacy threat types documented in literature and these threat modeling approaches. Our findings identify areas for future improvement of elicitative threat modeling approaches.

Keywords: Threat modeling · STRIDE · LINDDUN · Blockchain

1 Introduction

Threat modeling [24,25,29] involves the systematic investigation of threats to software-intensive systems, and is performed by evaluating generic and well-known threat types or threat categories. Threat elicitation approaches such as Microsoft's STRIDE [25] and LINDDUN [8] act upon an end-to-end system model encoded in a Data Flow Diagram (DFD) and rigorously examine the applicability and likelihood of threat types at an intricate level of granularity in a software architecture. Given their versatility, these methods are increasingly adopted in practice, and different tool implementations are in existence [19,24,26]. Essentially distinguishing between user entities, processing elements, data storage elements, and data flows, DFDs are created with abstractions that are particularly well-aligned to traditional, centralized, multi-tier architectures.

This raises the key question whether existing threat elicitation methods and tools can be applied successfully to more contemporary decentralized architectures. In this paper, we evaluate this question in the context of distributed

S. Katsikas et al. (Eds.): ESORICS 2019 Workshops, LNCS 11980, pp. 195–203, 2020.
https://doi.org/10.1007/978-3-030-42048-2_13

ledger architectures, also called *blockchains*. Blockchain as an architectural style is built upon a complex security model that integrates cryptographic principles with game-theoretic aspects to maintain incentive compatibility of all participants in an open peer-to-peer based participation model. Emerging from the context of financial systems and crypto-currencies, the architectural principles of blockchain are increasingly being adopted for decentralized transaction-based data storage and processing across diverse applications [5].

We adopt the following approach: in a first step, we gather existing knowledge on blockchain security and privacy threat and attack types through literature review and existing survey studies [6], and cluster these into broader threat types specific to blockchain. In a second step, we explore the notion of *compatibility* between these threat types and the STRIDE and LINDDUN threat elicitation frameworks. We more precisely assess the extent to which the blockchain-specific threats can or *could* be identified by means of these approaches. To this end, we define an objective and categorical assessment scale. The findings and implications of this study allow us to highlight open challenges and define a roadmap for ongoing threat modeling research.

The considerable amount of attention spent on blockchain systems has led to the identification a wide range of blockchain-specific attacks and threat types [6]. Since these threat types mainly focus on crypto-currencies such as Bitcoin [20], most of the threat types discussed in this article focus on Bitcoin by intent, but are nonetheless applicable in the wider context of proof-of-work (PoW)-based distributed ledgers. Different types of blockchain systems (e.g., involving *smart contracts*) are not explicitly studied, and the investigation of threat types specific to these technologies is considered part of future work.

Recently emerging threat modeling approaches such as ABC [1] are specifically tailored for crypto-currency systems. Such alternative approaches represent a departure from threat modeling approaches that are meant to be versatile and applicable in a technology- and domain-agnostic context.

This paper is structured as follows: Sect. 2 discusses the necessary background on threat modeling and blockchain systems. Then, Sect. 3 lists the most prominent categories of security and privacy threats, whereas Sect. 4 presents an assessment of the compatibility of these threat types with the existing models of STRIDE and LINDDUN. Section 5 finally concludes the paper.

2 Background

This section first introduces threat modeling, and then provides a brief introduction to the main principles behind blockchains and distributed ledgers.

Threat Modeling. Threat modeling refers to a number of architecture-centric analysis approaches to identify security- and privacy-related design flaws, potential threats to the correct and fair workings of a software-intensive system.

STRIDE [25] and LINDDUN [8] are acronyms[1] of *threat categories* for respectively security and privacy. There threat categories are further refined into more concrete *threat types* in so-called *threat trees*. In these elicitative threat modeling approaches, the system under analysis is modeled as a Data Flow Diagram (DFD) constituting of *external entities*, *processes*, *data stores*, and *data flows* between these. Every element in a DFD is systematically investigated for each of the threat types via a *mapping table* that indicates whether a threat type of a specific threat category is applicable to an element of a DFD model element type.

Threat modeling is widely used in industry as a cornerstone of secure development life-cycles (SDLs) and the importance of security- and privacy-by-design principles is increasingly recognized. Existing tool implementations [19,26] highlight and exploit the *elicitative* nature of these approaches; i.e. they systematically iterate over the architectural elements encoded in the system DFD and the threat trees to identify and generate concrete threats (this is the *threat elicitation* step). In practical implementations, distinction is made between *per-element* [8,25] and *per-interaction* [25,27] threat elicitation, in which threats are identified respectively at the level of individual DFD elements or specifically at the level of interactions in the system (data flows).

Blockchain Architecture and Principles. Blockchain architectures are decentralized data stores in which many participants (nodes) hold a copy of shared data structure, and cooperate in a peer-to-peer fashion to reach consensus on a linked list of transactions (a digital transaction history, also called a *ledger*). Emerging from the context of digital crypto-currencies (and it best-known instance Bitcoin [20]), a blockchain is a shared data store among many participants, that is incrementally maintained and kept consistent through transactions. Individual participants (nodes) collect and validate transactions and package them in *blocks*.

To accept a block on the blockchain, distributed consensus is to be attained. In proof-of-work (PoW) based blockchain systems, this consensus is reached via the mechanism of mining. Miner participants are financially incentivized to solve mathematical and computationally-intensive problems. This in turn provide them with authority to append a new block to the blockchain, which is then shared in gossip-style among all peers in the peer-to-peer network.

3 Blockchain Threat Types

To ensure integrity, consistency, and availability at the level of data transactions, blockchain architectures implement a security model that is rooted upon a complex interplay of tactics and principles, involving distributed consensus

[1] STRIDE: Spoofing, Tampering, Repudiation, Information Disclosure, Denial of Service, Elevation of Privilege;
LINDDUN: Linkability, Identifiability, Non-repudiation, Detectability, Disclosure of information, Unawareness, Non-compliance.

Table 1. Classification and overview of the blockchain-specific security and privacy threat types identified in literature.

Threat type	Enactment	Root cause	Risks/Consequences	Ref.
SECURITY THREAT TYPES				
Double spending	Block races	Consensus protocol Mining	Tampering Dishonest profits Disadvantage participants Wasting resources	[15] [12]
Mining Mining pools	Block races Deviating mining strategy Economic incentives	Consensus protocol Mining activity Incentive-incompatibility	Double spending Disproportional gains Wasting resources 51%-attack	[11] [23] [7] [17]
P2P network	Identification & connection of peers Deploying a large number of nodes	Decentralization Internet overlay	Isolating nodes Denial of service Double spending Selfish mining	[14]
PRIVACY THREAT TYPES				
Blockchain analysis	Transaction, address & user network Clustering heuristics Combining with off-chain data Active execution of transactions Behavior-based clustering	Transparency Public nature Pseudonimity	Linking transactions to each other Identification of participant	[22] [18] [21] [2] [9]
Network analysis	Anomalies in relay patterns Propagation of IP addresses and transactions TOR attacks via DoS-protection	P2P network	Linking transactions to IP addresses	[16] [3] [4]
Key management	Bloomfilters in SPV Extraction of private keys	Cryptographic basis	Linking transactions - to each other - to IP addresses	[21] [13] [10]

mechanisms, providing economic incentives to participants, and cryptography. In their purest implementation (e.g., Bitcoin), blockchains are open and public ecosystems and participants are free to join and contribute. This gives rise to a number of security and privacy issues that in turn can be generalized to threat categories that should be considered when building blockchain-based applications. The survey study of Conti et al. [6] provides an exhaustive and in-depth analysis of blockchain threat types. We shortly discuss the most prominent threat types below.

Security Threat Types. The root causes of the identified security threats include human and economic incentives of rational miners that maximize their benefits by grouping mining resources in mining pools, weaknesses of the network infrastructure upon which the P2P network is built, and issues caused by practical deployment.

The top half of Table 1 presents the most relevant security threat types. These represent attacks to the core principles of blockchain transaction processing:

(i) exploiting race conditions in the consensus protocol, (ii) colluding among participants (miners) to obtain disproportional gains or to gain control over the network (51% attacks), and (iii) attacks to the network itself (denial of service, isolating nodes, etc).

Privacy Threat Types. Blockchains are essentially public, transparent, and shared data stores onto which transactions are processed in a pseudonymous manner (at the basis of addresses). The public nature leads to a number of privacy threat types related to identifying, linking, and accumulating information about how these addresses are used. As shown in the bottom half of Table 1, we distinguish between threats that act upon the information on the blockchain (blockchain analysis threats), upon transaction meta-data (e.g., addresses or pseudonyms used), and privacy threats related to key management.

Table 2. Categorical scale defined to assess the compatibility of STRIDE and LINDDUN with the identified blockchain-specific threat types.

Score	Compatibility	Meaning
0	Problematic	The system model has to be created with a-priori and explicit knowledge of the threat type
1	Problematic	The threat type is not covered by one of the existing threat categories
2	Problematic	Threat type can be mapped to an existing threat category, but element- or interaction-based elicitation does not suffice
3	Intermediate	Threat type can be mapped to an existing threat category, but the category definition has to be revised or broadened
4	Positive	Threat type can be mapped onto an existing threat category but is not covered by a leaf in an existing threat tree
5	Positive	There is a direct match between the threat type and a leaf in a threat tree. As such the threat can directly be found with current threat modeling frameworks

4 Compatibility Assessment

To systematically investigate the compatibility of the existing threat modeling frameworks with the threat types discussed in the previous section, we have established the categorical scale presented in Table 2.

These criteria specifically aim at identifying (i) issues related to the expressivity of the DFD notation and incompatibilities that may arise in threat elicitation itself (scores 0, 2), (ii) the a-priori compatibility of the threat categories of STRIDE, respectively LINDDUN (scores 1, 3), or more specifically, (iii) compatibility with the existing threat trees (scores 4, 5).

Based on extensive expertise with the STRIDE and LINDDUN threat modeling approaches, and our assessment of the impact on existing tooling efforts [28],

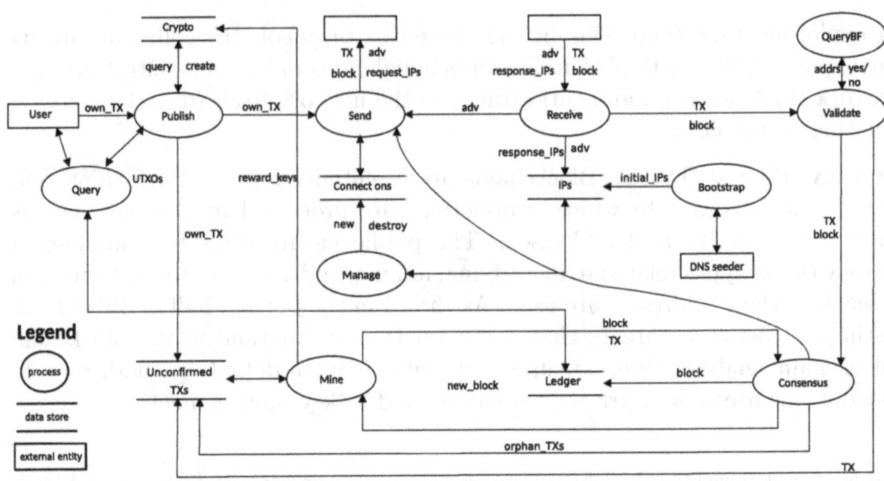

Fig. 1. DFD of miner activities. Empty entities represent different participants (peers) in the distributed ledger.

Table 3. Results of compatibility assessment results of the blockchain threat types.

Threat type	Discussion	Score
Blockchain analysis	Analysis of transactions in the blockchain corresponds to Linkability of the ledger (a Data Store)	5
Network analysis	The attack of Biryukov et al. [3] is an *Information Disclosure*, threat but can only be identified against a collection of peers	2
DoS TOR	Separating Tor-relays and blockchain servers can be considered a *Denial-of-Service* threat enacted towards an Tor relay as external entity	4
MitM TOR	Corresponds to *Spoofing*, but traditional interpretation does not consider a valid participant, but an attacker over an unsafe channel	3
SPV	- A bloomfilter attack in a Simplified Payment Verification (SPV) context can be considered an *Information Disclosure* threat	4
	- The DFD model does not allow expressing the unlimited ability of an attacker to perform queries	0
Crypto	Corresponds with an *Information Disclosure* threat on the Crypto data store in the DFD	5
Double spending	Can be considered as a *Tampering* threat, applied to the ledger	3
Selfish mining	- Does not correspond to an existing threat category	1
	- The affected assets (all other miners) are difficult to identify using traditional elicitation techniques	2
Block withholding	- Does not correspond to an existing threat category	1
	- It is difficult to model a *mining pool* (i.e., colluding miners) in a DFD	2
Bribery attack	Does not correspond to an existing threat category	1
Eclipse attack	This threat type corresponds to *Spoofing* of the incoming and outgoing data flows	4

we explicitly value these scores, ranging from problematic to positive. These labels indicate our assessment of the discrepancy to the existing threat modeling frameworks.

To assess the compatibility, a DFD was created that models the essential blockchain functionality from the point of view of a typical Bitcoin-alike miner. This DFD is presented in Fig. 1. This DFD is then used in a threat modeling exercise, applying both STRIDE and LINDDUN. Comparing the outcome threat catalog with the threat types in Table 1 allows up to assess the extent to which the threat types from literature can or could be elicited with current threat modeling tools and frameworks. Table 3 summarizes the results of compatibility assessment per threat type.

5 Conclusion

We have explored the compatibility between two established elicitative threat modeling frameworks that rely on DFD models, specifically STRIDE and LINDDUN, and distributed ledgers or blockains –an architectural style representative of a contemporary decentralized storage systems. Our results confirm that for some threat types, there is a discernible gap. In our assessment, these incompatibilities are mainly caused by (i) limited expressivity of the DFD notation, (ii) the per-element or per-interaction elicitation paradigm that does not allow identifying threats that occur under more specific system context conditions, and finally (iii) the agnostic nature of these approaches, in terms of incentives and game-theoretic aspects that are essential to the blockchain security model.

In future work, we will address these issues through (i) extending the DFD notation with support for modeling concepts such as mining pools and large clusters of participants (potentially colluding adversaries), (ii) tool support for more sophisticated threat elicitation approaches, and (iii) tighter integration with modeling approaches (e.g. goal-driven threat assessments, game-theoretic models, etc) that allow reasoning about attacker capabilities, incentive compatibility and aid at determining game-theoretic equilibria in such threat models.

Acknowledgments. This research is partially funded by the Research Fund KU Leuven and the imec-ICON BOSS research project.

References

1. Almashaqbeh, G., Bishop, A., Cappos, J.: ABC: a cryptocurrency-focused threat modeling framework. arXiv preprint arXiv:1903.03422 (2019)
2. Androulaki, E., Karame, G.O., Roeschlin, M., Scherer, T., Capkun, S.: Evaluating user privacy in bitcoin. In: Sadeghi, A.-R. (ed.) FC 2013. LNCS, vol. 7859, pp. 34–51. Springer, Heidelberg (2013). https://doi.org/10.1007/978-3-642-39884-1_4
3. Biryukov, A., Khovratovich, D., Pustogarov, I.: Deanonymisation of clients in Bitcoin P2P network. In: Proceedings of the 2014 ACM SIGSAC Conference on Computer and Communications Security, pp. 15–29. ACM (2014)

4. Biryukov, A., Pustogarov, I.: Bitcoin over Tor isn't a good idea. In: 2015 IEEE Symposium on Security and Privacy, pp. 122–134. IEEE (2015)
5. Carson, B., Romanelli, G., Walsh, P., Zhumaev, A.: Blockchain beyond the hype: what is the strategic business value. McKinsey & Company (2018)
6. Conti, M., Kumar, E.S., Lal, C., Ruj, S.: A survey on security and privacy issues of Bitcoin. IEEE Commun. Surv. Tutorials **20**(4), 3416–3452 (2018)
7. Courtois, N.T., Bahack, L.: On subversive miner strategies and block withholding attack in Bitcoin digital currency. arXiv preprint arXiv:1402.1718 (2014)
8. Deng, M., Wuyts, K., Scandariato, R., Preneel, B., Joosen, W.: A privacy threat analysis framework: supporting the elicitation and fulfillment of privacy requirements. Requirements Eng. **16**(1), 3–32 (2011)
9. DuPont, J., Squicciarini, A.C.: Toward de-anonymizing Bitcoin by mapping users location. In: Proceedings of the 5th ACM Conference on Data and Application Security and Privacy, pp. 139–141. ACM (2015)
10. Eskandari, S., Clark, J., Barrera, D., Stobert, E.: A first look at the usability of Bitcoin key management. arXiv preprint arXiv:1802.04351 (2018)
11. Eyal, I., Sirer, E.G.: Majority is not enough: Bitcoin mining is vulnerable. Commun. ACM **61**(7), 95–102 (2018)
12. Finney, H.: Best practice for fast transaction acceptance-how high is the risk (2011)
13. Gervais, A., Capkun, S., Karame, G.O., Gruber, D.: On the privacy provisions of bloom filters in lightweight Bitcoin clients. In: Proceedings of the 30th Annual Computer Security Applications Conference, pp. 326–335. ACM (2014)
14. Heilman, E., Kendler, A., Zohar, A., Goldberg, S.: Eclipse attacks on Bitcoin's peer-to-peer network. In: 24th USENIX Security Symposium (2015)
15. Karame, G.O., Androulaki, E., Capkun, S.: Double-spending fast payments in bitcoin. In: Proceedings of the 2012 ACM Conference on Computer and Communications Security, pp. 906–917. ACM (2012)
16. Koshy, P., Koshy, D., McDaniel, P.: An analysis of anonymity in Bitcoin using P2P network traffic. In: Christin, N., Safavi-Naini, R. (eds.) FC 2014. LNCS, vol. 8437, pp. 469–485. Springer, Heidelberg (2014). https://doi.org/10.1007/978-3-662-45472-5_30
17. Kwon, Y., Kim, D., Son, Y., Vasserman, E., Kim, Y.: Be selfish and avoid dilemmas: fork after withholding (FAW) attacks on Bitcoin. In: Proceedings of the 2017 ACM SIGSAC Conference on Computer and Communications Security. ACM (2017)
18. Meiklejohn, S., et al.: A fistful of Bitcoins: characterizing payments among men with no names. In: Proceedings of the 2013 Conference on Internet Measurement Conference, pp. 127–140. ACM (2013)
19. Microsoft Corporation: Microsoft Threat Modeling Tool 2016 (2016). http://aka.ms/tmt2016
20. Nakamoto, S., et al.: Bitcoin: a peer-to-peer electronic cash system (2008)
21. Nick, J.D.: Data-driven de-anonymization in Bitcoin. Master's thesis, ETH-Zürich (2015)
22. Reid, F., Harrigan, M.: An analysis of anonymity in the Bitcoin system. In: Altshuler, Y., Elovici, Y., Cremers, A., Aharony, N., Pentland, A. (eds.) Security and Privacy in Social Networks, pp. 197–223. Springer, New York (2013). https://doi.org/10.1007/978-1-4614-4139-7_10
23. Rosenfeld, M.: Analysis of bitcoin pooled mining reward systems. arXiv preprint arXiv:1112.4980 (2011)
24. Shevchenko, N., Chick, T.A., O'Riordan, P., Scanlon, T.P., Woody, C.: Threat modeling: a summary of available methods (2018)

25. Shostack, A.: Threat Modeling: Designing for Security. Wiley Publishing, Indianapolis (2014)
26. Sion, L., Van Landuyt, D., Yskout, K., Joosen, W.: SPARTA: security & privacy architecture through risk-driven threat assessment. IEEE (2018)
27. Sion, L., Wuyts, K., Yskout, K., Van Landuyt, D., Joosen, W.: Interaction-based privacy threat elicitation. In: International Workshop on Privacy Engineering (2018)
28. Sion, L., Yskout, K., Van Landuyt, D., Joosen, W.: Solution-aware data flow diagrams for security threat modelling. In: SAC 2018: Proceedings of the 33rd Annual ACM Symposium on Applied Computing, pp. 1425–1432, April 2018. https://doi.org/10.1145/3167132.3167285
29. Tuma, K., Calikli, G., Scandariato, R.: Threat analysis of software systems: a systematic literature review. J. Syst. Softw. **144**, 275–294 (2018)

Privacy, Security, Legal and Technology Acceptance Requirements for a GDPR Compliance Platform

Aggeliki Tsohou[1(✉)], Manos Magkos[1], Haralambos Mouratidis[2], George Chrysoloras[3], Luca Piras[2], Michalis Pavlidis[2], Julien Debussche[4], Marco Rotoloni[5], and Beatriz Gallego-Nicasio Crespo[6]

[1] Ionian University, Corfu, Greece
atsohou@ionio.gr
[2] University of Brighton, Brighton, UK
[3] University of the Aegean, Samos, Greece
[4] Bird & Bird, Brussels, Belgium
[5] ABI Lab, Rome, Italy
[6] Atos, Madrid, Spain

Abstract. GDPR entered into force in May 2018 for enhancing user data protection. Even though GDPR leads towards a radical change with many advantages for the data subjects it turned out to be a significant challenge. Organizations need to make long and complex changes for the personal data processing activities to become GDPR compliant. Citizens as data subjects are empowered with new rights, which however they need to become aware of and understand. Finally, the role of data protection authorities changes as well as their expectations from organizations. GDPR compliance being a challenging matter for the relevant stakeholders calls for a software platform that can support their needs. The aim of the Data govErnance For supportiNg gDpr (DEFeND) EU Project is to deliver such a platform. To succeed, the platform needs to satisfy legal and privacy requirements, be effective in supporting organizations in GDPR compliance, and provide functionalities that data controllers request for supporting GDPR compliance. Further, it needs to satisfy acceptance requirements, for assuring that its users will embrace and use the platform. In this paper, we describe the process, within the DEFeND EU Project, for eliciting and analyzing requirements for such a complex platform, by involving stakeholders from the banking, energy, health and public administration sectors, and using advanced frameworks for privacy requirements and acceptance requirements. The paper also contributes by providing elicited privacy and acceptance requirements concerning a holistic platform for supporting GDPR compliance.

Keywords: GDPR · Compliance · Software requirements · Prioritisation

S. Katsikas et al. (Eds.): ESORICS 2019 Workshops, LNCS 11980, pp. 204–223, 2020.
https://doi.org/10.1007/978-3-030-42048-2_14

1 Introduction

Since May 2018 the General Data Protection Regulation (GDPR) has become the center of attention for practitioners, researchers, States, and citizens. The General Data Protection Regulation enforces significant changes on the way that personal data is being processed, the way that data protection authorities guide and audit data controllers and on the individual rights of data subjects. Further, GDPR altered the territorial scope of the European Data Protection framework, enforcing changes to service providers who serve data subjects living in European member states.

For entities that process personal data (i.e., data controllers or data processors) the enforcement of GDPR means the implementation of organizational and technical changes, including the deployment of tools that allow demonstration of GDPR compliance, the appointment of Data Protection Officers, the conduction of privacy impact assessments, the training of staff, the implementation of data de-identification techniques, and so on. According to the first official report on implementation of the GDPR, provided by the European Data Protection Board (European Data Protection Board 2019), most organizations have increased their financial budget allocated to personal data protection (30%–50%), increased the personnel allocated, while a total of 206.326 legal cases have been presented to the authorities from 31 member states (complaints, data breaches, etc.). Reuters (2019) reports that organizations are still not ready in terms of GDPR compliance, and many of them know very little about the Regulation and whether or how it will affect them. A report by ISACA also presents a similar view (approximately 65% of organizations reported not ready in terms of GDPR compliance in May 2018) and elaborates on the technical, regulatory and legislative tools that should be implemented to assist organizations in their compliance efforts (ISACA 2019).

We aim to address this research and industrial gap through the development of a GDPR compliance platform that will deliver tools for organizations and interfaces for data protection authorities and citizens to interact with the organizations that process personal data. We do so, through the Data govErnance For supportiNg gDpr (DEFeND) EU Project (Innovation Action) that is dedicated into delivering such a platform. Ten organizations collaborate for the provision of the platform from Spain, UK, Italy, Portugal, Bulgaria, Greece and France. The DEFeND platform will guide organizations in fulfilling GDPR compliance through Privacy by Design and by Default tools, and in supporting consent management, privacy analysis, security risk assessment, and data breach management. The platform will also support citizens concerning personal data management, awareness and breach notifications. Finally, it will support the interaction of organizations with the respective data protection authorities.

In this paper, we present the software engineering methodology and results that were followed to capture the needs of users and model the software requirements for a GDPR Compliance Platform. Our software engineering approach spanned into multiple aspects of user needs, including functional, security, privacy, legal and acceptance requirements. We collected user needs focusing on four industrial sectors; namely financial, health, public administration and energy management. In this paper however we will emphasize on the financial sector and the respective lessons learned.

The paper is structured into seven sections. Following this introduction, Sect. 2 provides a review of state of the art to reveal the industrial and academic needs associated with a GDPR compliance platform. Section 3 presents our software engineering approach and Sect. 4 presents our methodology to collect data for capturing software requirements. Section 5 presents indicative software requirements that resulted and Sect. 6 provides the knowledge that was learnt from this process and could be informative for similar endeavors. Finally, Sect. 7 concludes the paper.

2 The Defend Project and Its Position in the Industry

2.1 Industry State of the Art

The evolution of European organizations' readiness for GDPR compliance before May 25, 2018 until today shows that, although there is significant progress achieved since that date, there is still a long way to go. A recent research report by TrustArc (2018) shows that 27% of the organizations in Europe (excluding the UK), 21% in the UK and 12% in the U.S. reported believing to be compliant. These numbers show a significant increase in comparison to the situation in 2017 and the research report forecast is that 93% of the companies expect to be compliant by the end of 2019.

Organizational compliance towards GDPR is expected to impact in significant expenditures. A PwC survey, conducted in 2016, predicted that 40% of large organization will spend more than 10 million dollars on GDPR compliance (Pulse Survey 2017). Also, Gartner (2017) predicted that 65% of all data loss prevention buying decisions will be driven by GDPR through 2018. The situation one year after, as described by the participants in TrustArc's report shows that 68% of the organizations already have spent more than six figures on GDPR compliance and 67% expect to spend an additional six figures by the end of 2018 in order to reach full compliance.

Investing in technology has become a popular strategy among companies in Europe to achieve compliance with regulations such as the Data Protection Directive (95/46) and EU's General Data Protection Regulation. According to TrustArc's report, 87% of the companies assessed needed third party support and 94% used technology to help them in their GDPR implementation projects. There are many products already in the market that support organizations in managing their privacy requirements and according to IAPP (2018), the number of vendors providing privacy management technologies has doubled in one year and some of the existing ones have enhanced their offering with new services. Despite the remarkable increase in the market offering, the report also highlights that "there is no single vendor that will automatically make an organization GDPR compliant".

2.2 Literature State of the Art

The DEFeND Platform will be built around three axes of privacy protection, all related to the general obligations for controllers and processors for GDPR compliance.

Privacy by Design (PbD). Data should be protected by design and by default (ar. 25, GDPR), in the sense that privacy should be proactively adopted, be embedded into the design phase of new systems and services, and also be enforced as a default setting (Cavoukian 2011; Kurtz and Semmann 2018). While a number of methodologies for privacy by design have been proposed during the last decade (e.g., (Kalloniatis et al. 2011; Deng et al. 2011; Faßbender et al. 2014; Notario et al. 2015), recent surveys (e.g., (Kurtz and Semmann 2018)) exhibit a lack of technologies and/or tools to implement the PbD principle in a holistic way. PbD principles have not yet gained adoption in the engineering practice, mainly because a mismatch between the legal and technological mindsets (Martin and Kung 2018) with the result being that engineers are mostly relied on privacy policies for compliance.

The DEFeND project advances state-of-the-art by facilitating organisations to implement a privacy management approach that takes into account the PbD principles, enabling them to (re)design their processes with respect to their privacy requirements, at an operational level.

Consent Management. Until recently, users were supposed to read privacy policies or notices before giving their consent to the data controller for processing their data, but in reality users never read them (McDonald and Cranor 2008). The cost of reading privacy policies. ISJLP, 4, 543.), in which case consent becomes not informed (Tsohou and Kosta 2017). Even if the users read the privacy policies, it is usually difficult to follow the legal and technical terminology inside (often, lengthy) policy texts and notices. With GDPR's more strict requirements on: (a) the consent being specific; (b) getting parents' consent for processing children data; (c) respecting data subjects' rights to revoke their consent, technologies and tools should provide users the possibility to withdraw consent as easily as they gave it. State of the art technologies and/or tools to implement the Lawfulness of Processing (ar. 6, GDPR) principle in a holistic way do not exist or are still immature (Politou et al. 2018; Priyadharshini and Shyamala 2018).

The DEFeND project approaches consent management in a holistic way, delivering a Privacy Data Consent (PDC) to users which will act as a contract among the data controller and data subject, encapsulating all the necessary information regarding the consent of the processing to their personal data. At operational level, the platform, based on the PDC, will monitor and enforce data subject's preferences, and will notify users if any inconsistency will be identified.

Privacy Impact Assessment (PIA). The execution of PIAs (ar. 35, GDPR) should ideally be supported by an information security risk management system to identify and reduce the privacy risks of data subjects when their personal data are processed by data controllers. Given that the guidelines of ISO/IEC 27005:2011do not include PIAs, and that data protection standards such as BS 10012:2017, ISO/IEC 29151:2017, ISO/IEC 27018:2014, require PIA in addition to conducting information security risk assessments, in 2017 ISO issued the ISO/IEC 29134:2017 standard with guidelines for PIA, superseding ISO 22307:2008 ("Financial services - Privacy impact assessment") and related guidelines (WP29 Guidelines on Data Protection Impact Assessment 2017).

The DEFeND project will advance the current state of the art in Data Protection Impact Assessment by providing an in-depth processing analysis based on a recognized methodology and based on international standard. This analysis will be performed in an easy and user-friendly interface and it will not need a specific knowledge and expertise in security and/or risk analysis to be performed.

2.3 The DEFeND Project

The DEFeND Platform is an innovative data privacy governance platform, which will facilitate scoping and processing of data and data breach management and will support organisations towards GDPR compliance.

In order to comply with the GDPR, organisations have to implement in their processes, at a very low-level, different tools, solutions, and practices, as to inherently integrate privacy in these ones. Therefore, it is important that DEFeND will provide a solution that not only supports compliance of the relevant GDPR articles, but will also fulfill special characteristics of needs that organisations might have. DEFeND will go beyond current products that offer general solutions and need special expertise and effort in order to cover the requirements of the organizations.

DEFeND will be adaptable enough so that organisations with budget restrictions can still make use of it. We plan to achieve this by following a modular strategy providing different services to users and supporting both planning and operational stages. This allows two innovative aspects: on one hand the solutions will be more specific to the needs of the organization and, on the other hand, the modules of DEFeND could be extended with new solutions. The DEFeND platform will support not only organisations to comply with GDPR but also professional advisors (legal and/or technical).

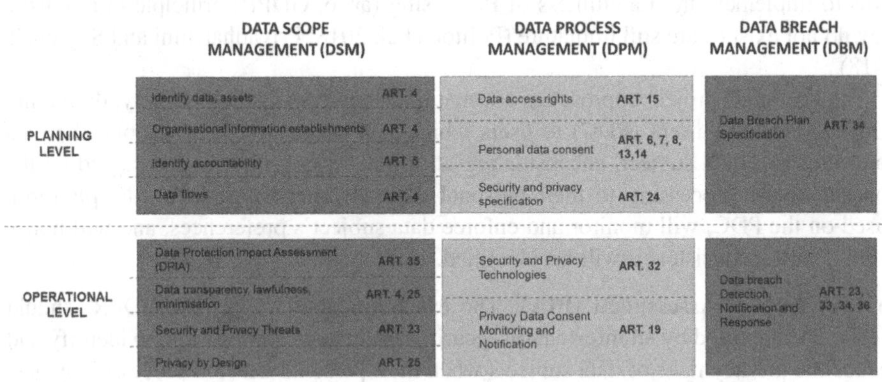

Fig. 1. Three management areas of the DEFeND platform

The project will achieve its aim by introducing a new paradigm, which we call Model-Driven Privacy Governance (MDPG). Such paradigm enables building (from an abstract to a concrete level) and analysing privacy related models following a Privacy-by-Design approach that spans over two levels, the Planning Level and the Operational

Level, and across three management areas, i.e. Data Scope, Data Process and Data Breach as shown in Fig. 1.

More specifically, at the planning level, the platform will support the development of models of the organisational data that capture information required for GDPR compliance such as identification of data and assets (art. 4), Organisational Info and establishments (art. 4), Data Transparency, Lawfulness and Minimisation (art. 25), personal data consent (art. 6, 7, 8, 13, 14) and data breach information (art. 34). Concretely, the DEFeND platform will support the transformation of planning models to operational models that are employed to perform analysis that supports Data minimisation, Data Protection, Impact Assessments (art. 35) and Privacy-by-Design and Privacy-by-Default principles (art. 25). At the operational level, the project will bring together security and privacy methodologies, encryption and anonymization tools and policy enforcers.

These management areas could be seen as the main services that the platform will provide to organizations and relevant stakeholders. Each one of these services assists organisations to collect, analyse and operationalise different aspects and articles of the GDPR and provide appropriate reporting capabilities.

To support those services, the platform consists of five (5) back-end components: Data Assessment Component, Data Privacy Analysis Component, Privacy Specification Component, Privacy Implementation and Monitoring Component, Data Breach Component. Each component includes a number of modules aiming to deliver functionalities (Fig. 2). The modules will be developed by enhancing software tools, services and frameworks of the project partners. Moreover, the platform includes a dashboard, which works as the main front-end between the platform and its users.

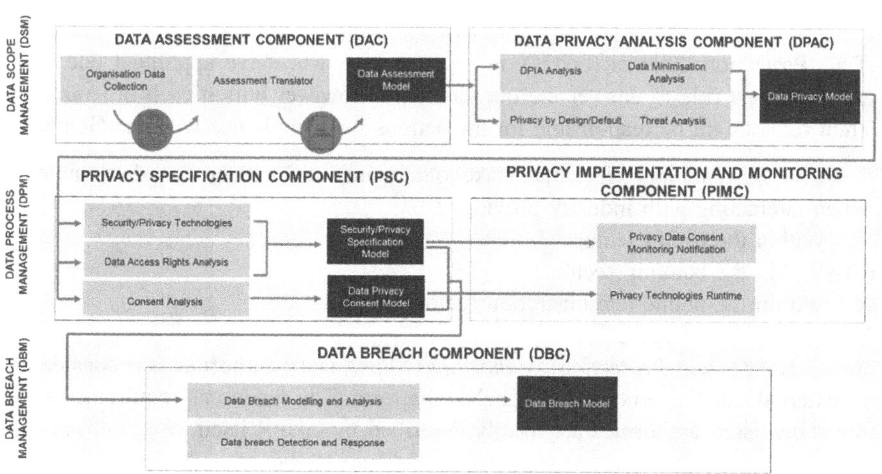

Fig. 2. DEFeND platform modules

3 An Holistic Engineering Approach: Functional, Privacy, Security, Legal and Acceptance Needs

3.1 Stakeholder Analysis

A stakeholder is an entity that can be influenced by the results of the DEFeND project. In this task we were interested on key stakeholders possibly engaged and committed to use the DEFeND platform, i.e., operate or depend on it. Different DEFeND users may have different expectations on the functionalities of the DEFeND platform, the services and support which will be provided, as well as on the importance of the security and privacy aspects of the GDPR compliance (e.g., for a citizen's role, breach notification and managing user consent) and the visualization of such compliance within the platform.

There are different roles that could provide functional requirements, which would reflect different perspectives. It was considered as very crucial to cover a diverse cross-section of different stakeholders, so that the produced list of user needs and requirements are not skewed towards a particular direction. The most critical is the perspective of the roles regarding compliance and auditing (e.g., DPO). The consortium identified the possible users in different scenarios and classified them, according to their types:

1. *Internal Stakeholders:* Stakeholders who are responsible for activities regarding the GDPR compliance in an organization. Candidate roles were:
   (a) Data Protection Officer (DPOs)
   (b) Chief of the Organization
   (c) Chief Data Officer
   (d) IT manager/technician
   (e) Risk Assessment Officer
   (f) Audit Officer

   Data Protection Officers (DPOs), in organizations who have appointed one, represented the best role to answer the questionnaire; however within each organization different roles might be responsible for the actions for compliance with the GDPR.

2. *External Stakeholders:* External stakeholders included citizens as data subjects when interacting with industry providers:
   (a) Within the health sector
   (b) Within the banking sector
   (c) Within the public administration sector
   (d) Within the energy sector
3. *Supervisory (Data Protection) Authorities:* Supervisory authorities are considered as external stakeholders of the DEFeND platform. The functional requirements for the supervisory authorities are mostly described by GDPR itself.

3.2 Privacy and Security Needs

The DEFeND platform will support privacy-by-design development of new services and systems, to allow natural integration of security and privacy of data in organizations. To achieve that, the project is dedicated to the rigorous definition of pilot scenarios, user privacy and compliance requirements using a systematic approach for end-users and citizens' security/privacy and functional needs collection, analysis and translation in prioritized requirements, to be included in the platform.

Furthermore, the DEFeND project will use, as part of the Data Privacy Analysis Component (DPAC), state-of-the-art requirements engineering methodologies, on top of modeling languages and methodologies and tools for security by design and privacy by design that partners have performed, such as the Secure Tropos (Mouratidis and Giorgini 2007) security-aware software systems development methodology and related tool (SecTro), which is used in the DEFeND project to elicit, model and analyse the privacy and security requirements of the platform, and which will also be extended to include human factors during the privacy/security requirements engineering level. The resulted tools will support organisations in understanding security and privacy requirements, and design systems and services that fulfill those requirements.

The functional requirements of the platform will be identified, defined and formalized in terms of use case diagrams and SRS (software requirements specification) as established by related standards[1], while a priority will be associated which each requirement.

3.3 Legal Needs

Building a platform for GDPR compliance necessarily requires evaluating all aspects from a legal perspective. Indeed, any tool or functionality of a particular GDPR compliance platform, including the DEFeND platform, needs to be assessed in light of the specific requirements imposed by the legislation (i.e. the GDPR). This necessitated a careful evaluation of each relevant article, including of its conditions and exceptions, and the interaction it may have with other articles and Recitals of the GDPR. Failing to perform such investigation of the legal requirements would lead to building a platform that would not sufficiently encapsulate the obligations enshrined in the GDPR and thus be incomplete or inaccurate.

3.4 Technology Acceptance Needs

Acceptance requirements are non-functional requirements that consider psychological, cognitive, sociological factors to take into account for individuating strategies stimulating the user to accept to use a software system, particular system features or new technological methods (Piras 2018; Piras et al. 2016, 2017, Piras et al. 2019). In fact, it happens often that, when the user starts using a new system, she has some difficulties, gets bored in relation to repetitive software tasks or due to complex procedures, and the result is that the user leaves the system. Therefore, in order to favor the acceptance and the usage of a system, acceptance requirements need to be considered and elicited starting from the early stages of any software engineering process by performing an acceptance requirements analysis. This is particularly relevant here because the DEFeND platform is expected to serve the needs of different heterogeneous actors with different expertise, interests and motivations (e.g., Data Controllers, Data Processors, Data Subjects, IT technicians, lawyers, etc.). The platform must support functionalities that are appreciated, accepted and used by all types of users involved.

[1] IEEE Guide for Software Requirements Specifications, IEEE Std 830-1984.

4 A Methodology to Elicit Software Requirements for a GDPR Compliance Platform

Towards defining the requirements necessary to be used as basis for building the DEFeND platform, we used a *Human-Centered design* (HCD), where incorporating the user's perspective into software development is considered of paramount importance in order to achieve a functional and usable system (Maguire 2001). Based on widely accepted methodologies that have been proposed in the area of user-adaptive systems development, user data have been collected using *questionnaire-based* and *interviews-based* approaches in order to assist *the elicitation of requirements* for the platform. Further, focus groups were realized in order to validate the data collection instruments and the elicited requirements. In particular, DEFeND partners identified the *key stakeholders*, and for each user category, a questionnaire was prepared, aiming at capturing the DEFeND user needs concerning various aspects; legal, functional, security, privacy and acceptance aspects. In sequence, user needs were translated into software requirements for all levels of the DEFeND platform, i.e., Data Scope Management (DSM), Data Process Management (DPM), and Data Breach management (DBM). The overall approach is depicted in Fig. 3.

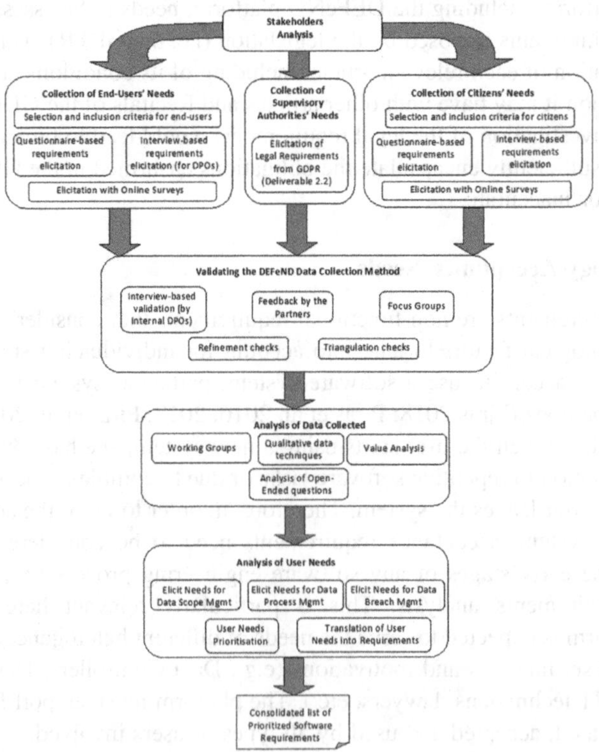

Fig. 3. Methodological approach for eliciting software requirements for DEFeND platform

4.1 Preparation of Questionnaires

To discover and validate that we have identified the stakeholders' need(s), and thus build the right product to satisfy these need(s), we combined two approaches: First, we followed the approach established in (Blank 2007) for customer development, which includes three main steps:

Customer Segmentation. A relevant action point was to consider the possibility of different questionnaire versions depending on the role of the participant in end-user organizations. In addition, each participant citizen completed the questionnaire having in mind only his/her personal data being processed by one sector (i.e., health organization or public administration or energy or bank organization). This was considered as important in order to register any number of different requirements per sector. Customer segmentation is supported by questionnaire's[2] section regarding user information, questions 1–5 and background information, questions 6–15.

Problem Discovery and Validation. The second category of questions aimed at validating the hypotheses about the problem(s) and challenges that the DEFeND platform aims at dealing with, as depicted in DEFeND's proposal, but also at learning about new problems and challenges as conceived by the interviewees. This category is supported by questions 16–22.

Product Discovery and Validation. The third category of questions aims at validating the hypotheses about the usefulness of the specific features envisaged for the DEFeND platform, but also at learning about new features as conceived by the interviewees. This category is supported by questions 23–36, regarding features of an ideal GDPR tool, functional, privacy and security features of the DEFeND Platform, as well as usability, reliability and performance features.

Our second approach involved selecting questions that span over the two levels (planning and operational) and the three management areas (Data Scope Management, Data Process Management and Data Breach Management), to follow the Privacy by Design approach as envisaged by the project. To this end, questions included in the questionnaires for the interviews with both the end-users and citizens have been selected to depict the privacy-by-design approach and to capture the users' needs for the different components of the platform.

4.2 Validation of Questionnaires

The initially prepared questionnaire was commented by the Data Protection Officer (DPO) of each partner in the project consortium. The inputs received by all partners' DPOs have helped to significantly alter the initial questionnaire and/or the information collection process. All feedback was collected and processed by the technical partners.

One of the major requirements gathering objectives was to receive opinions or comments from members of a specific sector about the questionnaire. One partner of the project has sent the questionnaire to the banking sector stakeholders who would

2 https://ec.europa.eu/eusurvey/runner/DEFeNDEndUser.

participate in a focus group during a subsequent partners meeting. Indeed, DPOs and IT managers from various organizations in the banking sector have participated either physically or via conference call. The session included an initial introduction by one partner of the project, a round table discussion with the participants and a final part with question and responses. The objective of this session was to gather feedback from this group of end-users on the questionnaire (with respect to structure, text of the questions, format of the questions/answers, language used, etc.) which was shared with them in advance. The result of this stage was a consolidated draft of the questionnaire for the end users.

4.3 Data Collection Approach

We collected data regarding the needs of the platform's users by participants from seven European countries (i.e., Italy, Greece, Spain, Bulgaria, France, Portugal, UK), spanning the two main user roles; organizations and citizens. The profile of participants for organizational needs, was described as an individual responsible for the coordination and monitoring of activities regarding the GDPR compliance. The profile of participants for citizens' needs was described as any individual, since any identified or identifiable natural person is a data subject. In order to ensure that we gained insights into the understanding of multiple citizens' perspectives we targeted to include individuals with different characteristics (i.e., representation of males and females; of different age groups; of different education levels; of different GDPR awareness level). Given that many researchers were involved in the data collection and analysis process, we developed a data collection guidance document, which provided the steps to follow and necessary instructions. Further, in order to ensure ethical principles, we developed an information participant sheet and a consent form the participants signed. Further, we provided a privacy policy that described our processing rules for the participants' personal data.

For organizational needs the data collection was conducted using semi-structured interviews and one online survey. The interviews were used to ensure in-depth analysis of needs of DPOs who are the main expected user role for the platform. The online survey was utilized for the collection of needs from multiple stakeholders. For the online survey we used the EU Survey platform (https://ec.europa.eu/eusurvey/). For citizens' needs we used an online survey, using the same survey platform.

The interviews were semi-structured and were conducted based on an interview protocol. Semi-structured interviews use incomplete scripts, allowing for flexibility, improvisation, and openness (Myers and Newman 2007). We also used the technique of mirroring (Myers and Newman 2007), according to which the interviewer uses the interviewees' words and phrases to construct subsequent questions.

For organizational needs we collected information from 10 individuals via interviews and 31 individuals via online survey, representing the energy, education, banking, health, public administration and information technology consultancy sectors. For citizens' needs we collected data from 174 individuals.

4.4 Data Analysis Approach

In order to elicit requirements from the data that were collected during the data collection phase, we followed a four iterative stage approach. The first 2 stages were held during a three-day workshop.

In the first stage, each working group analyzed collectively the responses resulting from the different numerical questions and from the open text contents. They deducted potential requirements for the DEFeND platform from these analyses. The resulting elicited requirements were aggregated into a single document acting as a first round of elicited requirements.

In the second stage, all partners acted as a single working group, reviewed the first round of requirements and refined them. This resulted in the second round of elicited requirements. The consortium during the first two stages used qualitative data analysis techniques and in particular open coding (Bryman 2008; Juristo et al. 2006).

In the third stage, which was fulfilled through collaborative work partners we divided into various groups depending the type of requirements and their expertise. Regarding the end users' requirements, the technical partners of the consortium were divided into two working groups and each group was allocated with the responses corresponding to a level of the questionnaire (i.e., planning level, operational level). Regarding the citizens' requirements, the pilot partners of the consortium were allocated with analyzing the requirements resulting from the responses corresponding to five questions of the questionnaire. The above work resulted in the third round of elicited requirements.

In the fourth and final stage, the third round of elicited requirements was distributed to all partners for further refinement, resulting in the fourth round of elicited requirements.

During the first two stages the requirements were considered raw and acted as first level requirements. During the next two stages, the consortium agreed to follow a common way in expressing the requirements which was decided prior to the beginning of the third stage. The guidelines were as simple as possible in order to enable all partners, including non-technical ones, to give feedback. This approach allowed a consistent transformation of raw requirements. For example:

Raw requirement (stage 1 or 2):

"Dashboard showing overview of obligations and notifications to select which ones I want to be notified of", Question 25(d).

Refined requirement following consortium guidelines (stage 4):

Fun.REQ01.01: Platform shall utilize notifications on data breach.

Fun.REQ01.02: Citizens shall be able to customize preferences about breach notifications.

Regarding the closed ended questions, the consortium used the average value given by the participants for each question of the online questionnaires in order to prioritize the requirements.

5 Eliciting Requirements for a GDPR Compliance Platform

5.1 Functional and Privacy/Security Requirements

During the analysis of end users' needs at the planning level, a number of important outcomes were recorded:

- At the Data Scope Management area, most end users believed that a tool for data inventory and mapping would be the most critical and less difficult to achieve.
- At the Data Process Management area, end users believed that the most important features of a platform would be to guarantee the separation of duties to prevent fraud and error when processing personal data, and also to allow them to review compliance activities and keep records for internal/external reporting to demonstrate compliance.
- At the Data Breach Management, most end users pointed out the criticality of a tool that allows them to define and review information security policies and incident response plans to comply with the GDPR obligations for reporting a breach.

During the analysis of stakeholders needs at the operational level, important outcomes included:

- At the Data Scope Management area, the assessment of organization's readiness for the GDPR was seen as the most important feature by the end users. Other features that were highlighted as mostly important was the ability of the tool to measure the privacy level that the organization achieves and to analyze and select the security measures for risk mitigation.
- At the Data Process Management area, the most important feature according to the end-users was to provide support for implementing security and privacy controls (e.g., anonymisation, encryption and authorisation).

At the Data Breach Management, end users pointed out the criticality of the real-time notification of the data subjects about privacy violations.

During the analysis of citizens' needs, user-friendliness of the DEFeND platform and relevant interfaces was considered as mostly important, followed by the need to include a functionality that allows transparent management of users' consent.

Some indicative functional requirements are presented in Table 1.

Table 1. Indicative functional and security requirements

Fun.REQ04	Area: data scope management
Fun.REQ04.01	The DEFeND platform shall assess the GDPR compliance readiness of the organization based on the GDPR self-assessment
Fun.REQ04.10	The DEFeND platform shall support the activity of DPIA
Sec.REQ01	Correct control and management of access to the system
Sec.REQ01.02	The DEFeND platform should include an authorization mechanism based on need-to-know profiling
Sec.REQ01.04	The DEFeND platform should include least privilege principle

5.2 Legal Requirements

In terms of legal requirements, the DEFeND platform will offer to organizations several tools, components and functionalities to enable compliance with the numerous obligations imposed by the GDPR. In order to ensure that such tools, components and functionalities correspond to what is foreseen by the legal text of the GDPR, they need to be designed and developed on the basis of a list of legal privacy and security requirements. Accordingly, a list of requirements has been extracted and transposed on the basis of the legal text of the GDPR. The list of privacy and security legal requirements is structured around the following 12 themes of the DEFeND platform: Developing a GDPR privacy plan, Creating a third party management program, Implementing privacy by design/privacy engineering, Managing privacy complaints and individual rights, Data de-identification/anonymization, Creating data inventory and maps, Conducting privacy risk assessments (PIAs/DPIAs), Meeting regulatory reporting requirements, Obtaining and managing user consent, Managing privacy incidents and breach notification, Addressing international data transfers, and Selection of appropriate security technical and organisational measures.

Towards defining the privacy and security legal requirements necessary to be used as basis for building the DEFeND Platform, the project relied on a desk research comprising of an analysis of the core legal text at the basis of the entire project (i.e. the GDPR), and of the 12 core themes of the DEFeND platform. In this context, a "privacy or security legal requirement" is to be understood as a single obligation extracted from one or more provisions of the GDPR that concern an organisation (i.e. a controller and/or processor), and which require that organisation either to do or to abstain from doing something in order to reach compliance or to document certain events or a reasoning to demonstrate compliance and which can be to a lesser or greater extent addressed through a technical solution corresponding to one or more of the 12 themes of the DEFeND Platform.

In order to define the privacy and security legal requirements, a thorough methodology has been followed, comprising of the following 7 steps.

The first three steps of the methodology played an important role in determining which parts of the GDPR could be included or not in the DEFeND platform. Indeed, certain Chapters, Sections and Articles of the GDPR are not and cannot form part of a GDPR compliance platform due to their specific content or their purpose. Accordingly, the initial steps aimed to determine the relevance of each Chapter, Section and Article of the GDPR to the DEFeND Project. In order to determine such relevance, a three-step test composed of three cumulative criteria was applied. The first criterion related to the question whether the Chapter, Section or Article concerns an organisation (i.e. a controller and/or processor). The second criterion related to the question whether the Chapter, Section or Article requires the organisation either to do or to abstain from doing something or to document certain events or a reasoning to demonstrate compliance. The third and final criterion related to the question whether the Chapter, Section or Article corresponds to one or more of the 12 themes of the DEFeND Platform. Where all of the three criteria could be answered negatively for a particular Chapter, Section or Article it was concluded that it was not relevant to the DEFeND Project and therefore that no requirement could be extracted. Where the responses to at least one of the three criteria were (even partially) positive for a Chapter, we moved to step 2, in which the specific Sections of that Chapter were examined in terms of relevance applying the same three-step test. Where the responses to at least one of the three criteria were (even partially) positive for a Section, we moved to step 3, in which the individual Articles of that Section are examined in terms of relevance applying the same three-step test.

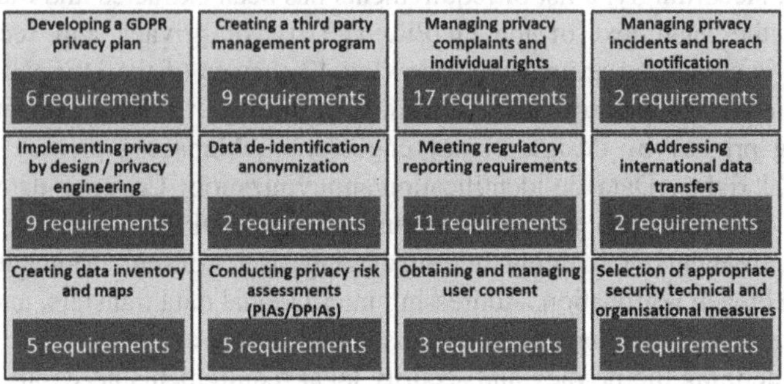

Fig. 4. Distribution of legal requirements

Ultimately, the project has identified concrete, practical privacy and security legal requirements that should ideally be met in relation to each theme of the DEFeND platform for it to be able to support organisations in complying with the GDPR. Considering both the 12 themes of the DEFeND platform and the GDPR requirements, 74 legal requirements have been compiled and distributed as depicted in Fig. 4.

Table 2. Indicative legal requirements

Leg.REQ0l	Developing a GDPR privacy plan	GDPR reference
Leg.REQ01.04	The DEFeND Platform should provide tools to enable an organisation to draw reports in order to demonstrate compliance with its GDPR obligations and to compose the organisation's accountability file	Art. 5(2), 24(1)
Leg.REQ02	Creating a third party management program	GDPR reference
Leg.REQ02.01	The DEFeND Platform should allow an organisation, when acting as a controller, to identify and map its relationships with processors	Art. 28
Leg.REQ02.06	The DEFeND Platform should provide tools to assist an organisation, acting as controller, to keep track of data processing agreements	Art. 28(3)

Some indicative legal requirements in the areas 'Developing a GDPR privacy plan' and 'Creating a third party management program' are presented below in Table 2.

5.3 Acceptance Requirements

The analysis of the questionnaire responses, in particular the questions targeting the elicitation of acceptance requirements, provided us with information to characterize the different users of the DEFeND platform.

Regarding the citizen role, we discovered that male citizens, young citizens, socializers who are not obliged to use the system, are more prone to accept the DEFeND platform. Further, we identified acceptance requirements which will assist in designing and enhancing the DEFeND platform architecture, in a way that it can really support and motivate all the stakeholders, by supporting usability, ease of use, awareness of the framework and guidance. Among the most important aspects pertaining the acceptance requirements is the need of users for social interaction and collaboration with other users. Such requirements provide insights into platform features, such as the integration of a social, collaborative forum to enable user communities, where the users can share their experiences, describe the advantages in using the platform to the other users, suggest to use functions of the platform, to give and receive suggestions, guidance, help and support using the platform. Some indicative acceptance requirements are presented in Table 3.

Table 3. Indicative acceptance requirements

XFun.REQ0l	Acceptance requirements
NFun.REQ01.03	The DEFeND platform shall offer a wide user acceptance and appreciation about it's features
NFun.REQ06.02	The DEFeND platform shall make the citizen to perceive that the platform is useful in terms of the effectiveness of enabling her in managing her personal data and in having her rights fulfilled
NFun.REQ06.04	The DEFeND platform shall make the citizen aware that the platform is promoted largely at the social level, for instance by important institutions and by the promoters of the platform

6 Requirements' Engineering for a GDPR Compliance Platform: Lessons Learned

In this section we present the requirements engineering challenges that the consortium faced, the innovations that were applied, and the lessons learned from the process of eliciting and consolidating requirements for a GDPR compliance platform.

6.1 Academic Implications

During the preparation and validation of the data collection questionnaire we received significant feedback by DPOs working in the financial sector, as well as DPOs working within the organizations participating in the consortium; where two trends emerged. One trend was that the questionnaire was not adequate to capture completely all the needs. DPOs commented that questions should allow for open text as much as possible in order to allow relevant stakeholders to express their needs. In addition, interviews were highlighted as of paramount importance, which would need to include follow up questions. This feedback reveals the complexity of capturing requirements for a GDPR compliance platform. A second trend was that the questionnaire would require a lot of time to be completed by a participant and therefore should include only multiple-choice questions. This request can be explained by the DPOs' busy schedule and lack of time to complete the questionnaire. Therefore, a hybrid approach was followed which included interviews and a multiple-choice questionnaire. Interviews would be selected only when the GDPR compliance representative could afford to dedicate significant effort and time, while multiple choice questionnaire would allow receiving information from multiple stakeholders even if they did not have lots of time to devote.

Conducting effective requirements elicitation interviews is challenging. Some of the consortium partners were novice interviewers. Empirical evidence has shown that the methodological soundness and correct conduct of interviews is important (Davis et al. 2006). Therefore, to overcome this challenge a detailed interview protocol was developed and followed during the interviews. The interview questions were designed to allow the participants to openly express their expert opinion and needs on a subject matter. In several cases, the response of the participant triggered a new question or a more in-depth question. In these cases, we used the technique of mirroring (Myers and Newman 2007), according to which the interviewer uses the interviewees' words and phrases to construct subsequent questions. This proved to be very successful as it established a common understanding and reduced the use of leading questions.

The needs of the citizens from a GDPR compliance platform were collected using an instructed questionnaire completion technique. In order to receive as detailed as possible responses, citizens were instructed to complete the questionnaire in the context of an online service that they are using from the four sectors that the project is interested in. This resulted in the collection of more meaningful responses and justified explanations by the citizens.

In contrast with the DPOs', citizens contributed a lot less in open-ended questions, this was expected due to the wide audience that the consortium sent the questionnaire to, and the challenges a citizen faces in fully understanding GDPR in this early stage that the regulation is enforced. Nevertheless, they highly expressed towards a platform that (i) enables them to clearly verify whether the basic GDPR principles and their rights are complied with when their data is processed by third parties, (ii) is user friendly and (iii) enables them to define their consent.

6.2 Industrial Implications

It is a widespread opinion that the implementation of the GDPR had led the financial sector to improve tools and methods for managing personal information in an optimized way, also increasing the awareness on the major repercussions on business processes and IT architectures. In other words, from a certain point of view the recent regulatory developments may be viewed as an opportunity for banks, raising the attention in establishing good practices in various data management areas. With this in mind, many banks have been working rapidly over recent years in improving incident monitoring, governing security and managing IT risks. This means that in the last years, the banks had implemented several tools and procedures to ensure compliance with the GDPR.

In this context, the value of a unique platform like DEFeND could be in the possibility of supporting a continuous GDPR Maturity Assessment, in order to identify the most critical areas of compliance, plan the improvement actions and convey specific reports to different actors, also considering the existing standard and the evolution of best practices. However, our requirements elicitation process revealed that to leverage those opportunities, it is important that the GDPR platform represents a sort of orchestration engine, able to enforce a presidium on the different data protection processes and able to seamlessly integrate with all the other systems and procedures that the bank has already put in place. To this extent, the possibility to have a modular solution is paramount.

7 Conclusions

In this paper, we have presented the process that was followed to elicit and analyze requirements for a GPDR compliance platform. The complexity of the process was high as it included the involvement of stakeholders from four different sectors, banking; energy; health; and public administration. The process is composed of several requirements engineering activities that were adapted in order to specify the requirements for a GDPR compliance platform including functional, non-functional, security, privacy, legal and acceptance requirements. Finally, the challenges and lessons learned from this process were summarized and presented.

Acknowledgments. This paper has received funding from the European Union's Horizon 2020 research and innovation programme under grant agreement No. 787068.

References

Blank, S.G.: Four Steps to the Epiphany: Successful Strategies for Products that Win, Palo (2007)

Bryman, A.: Social Research Methods, 3rd edn, p. 2008. Oxford University Press, Oxford (2008)

Cavoukian, A.: Privacy by Design. The 7 Foundational Principles, Implementation and Mapping of Fair Information Practices (2011). https://iab.org/wp-content/IAB-uploads/2011/03/fred_carter.pdf

Davis, A., Dieste, O., Hickey, A., Juristo, N., Moreno, A.M.: Effectiveness of requirements elicitation techniques: empirical results derived from a systematic review. In: 14th IEEE International Requirements Engineering Conference (RE 2006), pp. 179–188. IEEE (2006)

Deng, M., Wuyts, K., Scandariato, R., Preneel, B., Joosen, W.: A privacy threat analysis framework: supporting the elicitation and fulfillment of privacy re-quirements. Re-quirements Eng. **16**(1), 3–32 (2011)

European Data Protection Board: First overview on the implementation of the GDPR and the roles and means of the national supervisory authorities (2019). https://edpb.europa.eu/sites/edpb/files/files/file1/19_2019_edpb_written_report_to_libe_en.pdf

Faßbender, S., Heisel, M., Meis, R.: Problem-Based Security Requirements Elicitation and Refinement with PresSuRE. In: Holzinger, A., Cardoso, J., Cordeiro, J., Libourel, T., Maciaszek, L.A., van Sinderen, M. (eds.) ICSOFT 2014. CCIS, vol. 555, pp. 311–330. Springer, Cham (2015). https://doi.org/10.1007/978-3-319-25579-8_18

Gartner: Forecast Analysis: Information Security, Worldwide, 1Q17 Update, August 2017 (2017). https://www.gartner.com/en/documents/3889055

IAPP: 2018 Privacy Tech Vendor Report v.2.4e (2018). https://iapp.org/resources/article/2018-privacy-tech-vendor-report/

ISACA: GDPR The End of the Beginning (2019). http://www.isaca.org/Knowledge-Center/Documents/2018-GDPR-Readiness-Survey-Report.pdf

Juristo, N., Moreno, A.M., Dieste, O., Davis, A., Hickey, A.: Effectiveness of requirements elicitation techniques: empirical results derived from a systematic review. In: 14th IEEE International Requirements Engineering Conference (RE 2006) (RE), Minneapolis/St. Paul, Minnesota, USA, 2006, pp. 179–188 (2006)

Kalloniatis, C., Belsis, P., Gritzalis, S.: A soft computing approach for privacy requirements engineering: the PriS framework. Appl. Soft Comput. **11**(7), 4341–4348 (2011)

Kurtz, C., Semmann, M.: Privacy by Design to Comply with GDPR: A Review on Third-Party Data Processors (2018)

Maguire, M.: Methods to support human-centred design. Int. J. Hum.-Comput. Stud. **55**(4), 587–634 (2001)

Martin, Y.S., Kung, A.: Methods and tools for GDPR Compliance Through Privacy and Data Protection Engineering. In: 2018 IEEE European Symposium on Security and Privacy Workshops (EuroS&PW), pp. 108–111. IEEE (2018)

McDonald, A.M., Cranor, L.F.: The cost of reading privacy policies. ISJLP **4**, 543 (2008)

Mouratidis, H., Giorgini, P.: Secure tropos: a security-oriented extension of the tropos methodology. Int. J. Softw. Eng. Knowl. Eng. **17**(02), 285–309 (2007)

Myers, M.D., Newman, M.: The qualitative interview in IS research: examining the craft. Inf. Organ. **17**(1), 2–26 (2007)

Notario, N., et al.: PRIPARE: integrating privacy best practices into a privacy engineering methodology. In: 2015 IEEE Security and Privacy Workshop, pp. 151–158. IEEE, May 2015

Piras, L.: Agon: a gamification-based framework for acceptance requirements. Ph.D. dissertation, University of Trento, 2018 (2018)

Piras, L., Dellagiacoma, D., Perini, A., Susi, A., Giorgini, P., Mylopoulos, J.: Design thinking and acceptance requirements for designing gamified software. In: 13th IEEE International Conference on Research Challenges in Information Science (RCIS), IEEE, Bruxelles (BE), 2019 (2019)

Piras, L., Giorgini, P., Mylopoulos, J.: Acceptance requirements and their gamification solutions. In: 24th IEEE International Requirements Engineering Conference (RE), 2016. IEEE, Beijing (2016)

Piras, L., Paja, E., Giorgini, P., Mylopoulos, J.: Goal models for acceptance requirements analysis and gamification design. In: Mayr, H.C., Guizzardi, G., Ma, H., Pastor, O. (eds.) ER 2017. LNCS, vol. 10650, pp. 223–230. Springer, Cham (2017). https://doi.org/10.1007/978-3-319-69904-2_18

Politou, E., Alepis, E., Patsakis, C.: Forgetting personal data and revoking consent under the GDPR: challenges and proposed solutions. J. Cybersecurity **4**(1), tyy001 (2018)

Priyadharshini, G., Shyamala, K.: Strategy and solution to comply with GDPR: guideline to comply major articles and save penalty from non-compliance. In: 2018 2nd International Conference on I-SMAC (IoT in Social, Mobile, Analytics and Cloud) (I-SMAC), pp. 190–195. IEEE (2018)

Pulse Survey: GDPR budgets top $10 million for 40% of surveyed companies, October 2017 (2017). https://www.pwc.com/us/en/services/consulting/library/general-data-protection-regulation-gdpr-budgets.html

Reuters, T.: Study finds organizations are not ready for GDPR compliance issues (2019). https://legal.thomsonreuters.com/en/insights/articles/study-finds-organizations-not-ready-gdpr-compliance-issues. Accessed 5 Apr 2019

TrustArc: GDPR Compliance Status. A Comparison of US, UK and EU Companies, July 2018 (2018)

Tsohou, A., Kosta, E.: Enabling valid informed consent for location tracking through privacy awareness of users: a process theory. Comput. Law Secur. Rev. **33**(4), 434–457 (2017)

WP29 Guidelines on Data Protection Impact Assessment. Guidelines on Data Protection Impact Assessment (DPIA) and determining whether processing is “likely to result in a high risk” for the purposes of Regulation 2016/679 (2017). https://ec.europa.eu/newsroom/article29/item-detail.cfm?item_id=611236

Uncertainty-Aware Authentication Model for IoT

Mohammad Heydari[1(✉)], Alexios Mylonas[1], Vasilis Katos[1], Emili Balaguer-Ballester[1], Amna Altaf[1], and Vahid Heydari Fami Tafreshi[2]

[1] Department of Computing and Informatics, Bournemouth University, Bournemouth, UK
{mheydari,amylonas,vkatos,eb-ballester, aaltaf}@bournemouth.ac.uk

[2] School of Computing and Digital Technologies, Staffordshire University, Stoke, UK
v.heydari@staffs.ac.uk

Abstract. Handling the process of authentication for the hundred million of computer embedded devices in Internet of Things (IoT) is not achievable without considering inherent IoT characteristics like scalability, heterogeneity, dependency and dynamism. In one hand, traditional and emerging access control models cannot handle indeterminate data access scenarios in IoT by applying deterministic access policies. On the other hand, moving towards resilient access control paradigms needs new attitudes and current manual risk analysis methods that rely on vulnerability calculations do not fit in IoT. This holds true as considering vulnerability as the key player in risk assessment is no longer efficient way to tackle with indeterminate access scenarios due to complicated dependency and scalability of IoT environment. Moreover, most of the IoT devices are not patchable so by discovering new vulnerabilities the vulnerable devices need to be replaced. Therefore, IoT needs agile, resilient and automatic authentication process. This work suggests a novel authentication method based on our previous work in which uncertainty was introduced as one of the neglected challenges in IoT. Uncertainty in authentication derived from incomplete information about incident happening upon authenticating an entity. Part of IoT characteristics makes such an uncertainty worse. Therefore, we have proposed an uncertainty-aware authentication model based on Attribute-Based Access Control (ABAC). Our prediction model is able to consider the uncertainty factor of mobile entities as well as fixed ones in authentication. In doing so, we have built our prediction model using boosting classifiers (AdaBoost and Gradient Boosting algorithms) besides voting classifier. We have compared the results with our previous work. Our designated model (AdaBoost) can achieve authentication performance with 86.54% accuracy.

Keywords: Uncertainty · Authentication · Internet of Things · Supervised learning · Prediction model

S. Katsikas et al. (Eds.): ESORICS 2019 Workshops, LNCS 11980, pp. 224–237, 2020.
https://doi.org/10.1007/978-3-030-42048-2_15

1 Introduction

Internet of Things (IoT) covers a wide range of connectivity from human-to-machine to machine-to-machine communication. It offers large scale integration of heterogeneous networks and devices, which apart from the obvious opportunities, introduces great security and privacy challenges. These challenges are not new, as they have been well-studied in the relevant literature in different IoT domains (such as e-Health, Smart City, Smart Grid) [1–3]. Among the various security challenges in IoT, access control is deemed to be of great significance and remains an open challenge [4]. This holds true as the volume, velocity and variety of data produced by IoT-enabling technologies introduce new challenge for data access. Amongst the characteristics inherent to IoT this work considers that scalability, heterogeneity, interoperability, dynamism and resource sharing exaggerate the security challenges that are related to the field of access control. Scalability roots in the exponential growth of IoT devices which also increases network connectivity demands. Heterogeneity and interoperability in IoT derive from the different technologies and networks (such as RFID, WSN, GSM) that exist in IoT. In such a heterogenous environment not only achieving a secure and seamless integration of different platforms is a challenge, but also data access control becomes more cumbersome. Dynamism in IoT stems from the need for real-time access of interconnected things in which interactions require fast responses in a timely manner. For this, access control as well as any context-aware services are directly influenced. Resource sharing in IoT improves the performance with the minimum investment. However, it comes at a risk of insider threats and permission misuses. Data communication loss in the event of a network or device failure is inevitable, which might render the data inaccurate or incomplete in IoT. Incompleteness inherent in the above-mentioned sources can hinder precise access control decisions. In all of the mentioned cases, the lack of information caused by the inability of tracking those changes results in uncertainty. In summary, uncertainty in authentication comes to play where an access decision needs to be made based on incomplete information. To address this challenge, we consider our definition of uncertainty in authentication by considering the "likelihood of an incident occurring" per each authentication request and then try to measure the uncertainty and build a data-driven model to handle the uncertainty in authentication.

The rest of the paper is organized as follows. In Sect. 2 background and related work are presented. In Sect. 3 our proposed model is presented. Our methodology is thoroughly discussed in Sect. 4. Section 5 consists of the results that come from the conducted experiments. It also discusses the results. Finally, Sect. 6 contains our conclusion and future work.

2 Background and Related Work

Access control is defined as a mechanism to govern the access to the resources in a way that such resources can be used only by authorized entities. Access control consists of the three functions: Authentication, Authorization and Auditing [5]. In this research we focus on uncertainty aspect of the authentication phase of the access control.

Authentication is a verification process to check whether the credentials of an entity is valid [5]. From studied characteristics for access control systems like delegation, revocation, granularity, flexibility, scalability, lightweight, heterogeneity and context-aware, some are more important in dynamic, scalable and heterogenous environments like IoT [6]. For this reason, in order to build an access control model for IoT the following specifications must be taken into considerations [7]:

1. **Scalability:** Scalability in access control must be evaluated by three dimensions, namely: *(a) Subject/Object (entities) scalability* if increasing the number of entities does not lead to an overhead in processing time or workload, *(b) Policy rules scalability:* if increasing the number of access rules does not lead to overhead in terms of processing time or workload., and *(c) Extensibility* if it has the ability to extend its structure to cover more sub-systems and domains. The third form of scalability can be achieved through using a de-centralized structure - rather than centralized structure - in scalable environments like IoT.
2. **Heterogeneity/Interoperability:** In IoT entities have dependencies and their workflows are tightly convergent, which increases complexity. For this reason, any access control breach in IoT can be more disruptive compared to traditional networks. Furthermore, as IoT is composed by different platforms, enabling technologies and domains, designing an access control model to regulate access inter/intra domains or technologies is a needed.
3. **Dynamism:** If the access decision must change, due to the changes in the subject, object or environment attributes, while the access is granted, then, the access control system is classified as dynamic. Otherwise, if the changes do not affect the access decision, then the access control system is considered as static. Considering dynamism in IoT access control models is important, due to the rapid changes of contextual parameters that occur in this paradigm.
4. **Context-Aware:** It refers to the ability of the access control system to take contextual attributes to make an access decision. Considering contextual parameters in access decision brings flexibility in terms of tracking subject, object and environment changes if those changes have impacts on the decision.

The above evaluation criteria uncover limitations in the both traditional access control models like DAC, MAC, RBAC and emerging access control models like CapBAC, ABAC and making them inapplicable to any scalable, dynamic and heterogenous environment like IoT [8–10].

In unpredicted access scenarios that consist of indeterminate factors like uncertainty, the models are not capable of making resilient and accurate access decisions either. For this reason, three resilient paradigms were suggested to deal with indeterminate data access scenarios. These paradigms include (i) Break-The-Glass (BTG) Access Control (ii) Optimistic Access Control, and (iii) Risk-Aware Access Control (RAAC) [11, 12]. Ferreira [13] proposed BTG to allow unanticipated access to be provided in emergency situations. The main application of this method is in the healthcare system [14]. BTG suffers from scalability issue in terms of policy overriding. In other words, by increasing the number of policy overriding, the access monitoring and misuse detection become impossible [15]. Optimistic access control system was proposed to prioritize the openness and availability [16]. In this paradigm, most access requests are assumed as legitimate requests therefore it allows the subject to exceed their normal access rights. This approach suffers from the same problem as BTG called the lack of scalability in terms of policy rules. Risk-Aware access control was proposed to assess the risk of the authentication request to determine whether the access to a resource should be granted [17]. A number of studies suggested using RAAC. Bijon et al. [18] incorporated the concept of risk awareness in RBAC. The role in the introduced RBAC model will be activated only if the total risk of its active roles does not exceed a threshold. Furthermore, the threshold is determined dynamically in an adaptive manner. Baracaldo et al. [19, 20] used trust and risk concepts on RBAC to deal with insiders. In this method, each user is assigned a trust level and each access permission is associated with a risk value. The risk of each role is calculated by the total risk of all direct and indirect permissions enabled by its activation. In this method, a role is activated if the user meets the minimum trust level required for that role. The value of the trust is determined based on the amount of risk exposed by activating the role. Dimmock et al. [21] proposed a method based on [22] to enhance the RBAC with trust and risk. To meet this goal trust and cost evaluation measures are added to the OASIS policy language. This method introduced a risk evaluation expression language to calculate the risk based on the given values and make an access decision based on that calculation. Atlam et al. [23] developed an adaptive RAAC model for IoT. This model accepts real-time attributes including user context, resource sensitivity, action severity and risk history as input and estimates the overall risk value associated with each access request. The major concern about this work is that the authors did not validate their proposed model. Nogoorani et al. [24] proposed an access control framework for grid environment to address the misuse of resource in virtual organizations. This method offers both risk and trust analysis in authorization to assess the subject's actions. The trust model uses feedback to calculate user's trust degree in a probabilistic approach. On the other hand, the risk model is utility-based and uses the user's trust degree to calculate the probability of fulfilment of obligations. The proposed model was evaluated using simulation. The results show that it is scalable in terms of the number of entities, the number of policy rules and extensibility. Nurse et al. [25] argue that IoT-related characteristics such as scalability, heterogeneity and dynamism make the current risk assessment approaches inadequate due to the following reasons: (i) Doing periodic assessment in highly scalable and dynamic environments like IoT is impossible, (ii) It is difficult to gather information about all entities participating in various IoT scenarios due to the scalability of such an environment and (iii) Interoperability brings new challenges in terms of dependencies among IoT entities and makes the risk analysis a challenging task.

3 Proposed Model

Uncertainty needs more attention as a challenge in authentication in the context of IoT than the other challenges like scalability, heterogeneity, interoperability and dynamism that have been studied in the relevant literature, such as [1–3, 26, 27].

For this reason, we consider uncertainty in authentication in order to make resilient access decision in the context of IoT. If the authentication relies on crisp and deterministic rules regardless of the uncertainty concept, it does not fit in dynamic environment like IoT. As discussed in [28] and [7], uncertainty is caused by the lack of information about the likelihood of an incident occurring. Therefore, we define uncertainty in authentication as the incompleteness of information regarding the likelihood of whether the acceptance of an authentication request leads to an incident. "Uncertainty" and "Risk" have similarity. In one hand, risk is measured by analysing the likelihood of occurrence of a harmful circumstance or event besides assessing the adverse impact that would arise if that circumstance or event occurs [29]. On the other hand, in order to measure uncertainty, the likelihood of adverse event occurring is considered so the "likelihood of event occurring" is common between these two concepts.

Our uncertainty-aware data-driven model is based on the extension of ABAC. In order to build our model, we consider three attributes from authentication request namely as: time of the request, location in which the request comes from and the credential provided by the user who sends the request. As shown in Fig. 1, we have proposed an architecture based on the generic architecture of XACML [30]. According to our proposed architecture in [28], (1) users send authentication requests to the Policy Enforcement Point (PEP). (2) PEP as the interface between the system and the user is responsible to forward the request to Policy Decision Point (PDP). PDP gathers policy related to the specified resource from Policy Administration Point (PAP). (3) PDP asks for policy from PAP. (4) PAP provides requested policy to PDP. (5) P also queries for subject, object and environment attributes related to the request from Policy Information Point (PIP). (6) PIP gathers requested attributes and makes it available to PDP. (7) PDP forwards the gathered information to Indeterminacy Estimation Point (IEP) and asks the uncertainty engine to calculate the uncertainty values associated to the authentication request. (8) IEP queries the uncertainty engine to calculate the value of uncertainty associated with the authentication request. (9) Uncertainty engine returns the calculated the overall value for the uncertainty using our data-driven prediction model which will be discussed in Sect. 4.2. (10) IEP sends the calculated value of uncertainty to PDP. (11) PDP makes final access decision using related policy and the value of indeterminacy which is provided by IEP. Then the decision will be forwarded to PEP. (12) PEP fulfils the obligations based on the decision.

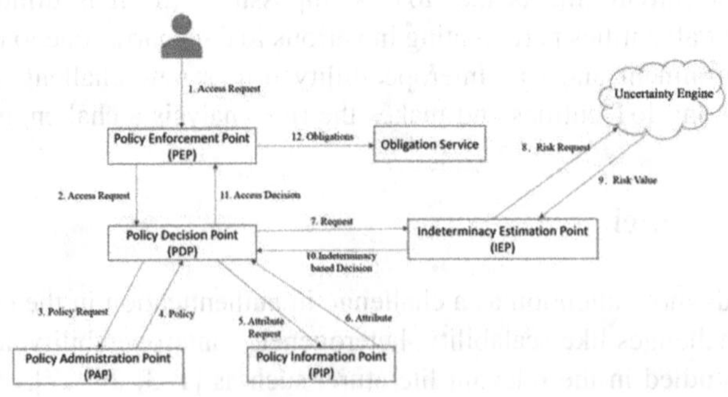

Fig. 1. Architecture of the proposed model based on the XACML architecture [28]

4 Methodology

As discussed earlier, one of the building blocks of architecture is uncertainty engine. Uncertainty engine is a prediction model which is created using supervised binary classification algorithm to predict the class label for authentication: Access or Deny. In this research we applied Boosting and Voting algorithms namely AdaBoost, Gradient Boost and Voting algorithm. The process of building our data-driven model consists of two parts: *(i)* Generating an authentication dataset and *(ii)* applying above-mentioned algorithms in order to create and validate the data model. We have synthetized our dataset based on the state-of-the-art researches using Probability Distribution Functions (PDFs) in MATLAB, Mathworks inc., 2019a). The process of generating our dataset is discussed in [28]. For the second part of the research we have used scikit-learn library (version 0.20.2) with python (version 3.7.1) to apply classification algorithms. We have also used the hardware with the following specifications: 17 GPUs (Asus Geforce 1080 Ti) and dual CPUs (Intel Core i7-8700K) with 64 GB RAM. In the rest of this chapter, we first discuss about the dataset synthesis and then prediction models will be presented.

4.1 Dataset Synthesis

One of the big obstacles in conducting a research in the field of authentication is the lack of publicly available dataset. Those datasets that are publicly available like LANL [31] and Bank Note [32] don't consist of our required attributes. As a result, we generated a dataset consisting of required attributes. The dataset was used for both training and the robust testing of our uncertainty-aware authentication approach. As mentioned earlier, our ABAC based model consists of the following attributes: (i) Time of the request (ii) Location of the request and (iii) Credentials provided by the user. Having synthesized the uncertainty values for these attributes, we will come up with the overall uncertainty value per user request using our uncertainty engine.

The uncertainty values for each of these attributes will be generated by probability distribution functions (PDFs) because in real word scenario these attributes derived from stochastic processes, so they follow a mixture of PDFs. In doing so, each attribute has been studied separately to determine the PDFs that represents the uncertainty in authentication. PDFs is responsible to present the likelihood of the incident occurrence for a selected attribute if the requested is accepted. The outcome of the dataset synthesis process is a matrix consisting of generated uncertainty values for these three attributes (Fig. 2). As we have discussed the whole process of generating the dataset in details in [28]. For our dataset, we have generated 5000 authentication requests in terms of time, location (mobile and fixed) and credential. We briefly explain the process in the reminder of this section.

	Time	Location	Credential	Access (0/1)
Authentication Request #1	0.1	0.54	0.05	1
Authentication Request #2	0.1	0.78	0.05	0
Authentication Request #3	0.1	0.28	0.05	1
Authentication Request #4	0.8	0.28	0.05	1
Authentication Request #5	0.1	0.28	0.05	1
.	.	.	.	.
.	.	.	..	..
Authentication Request #N	0.1	0.28	0.5	1

Fig. 2. Uncertainty matrix consisting of generated uncertainty values

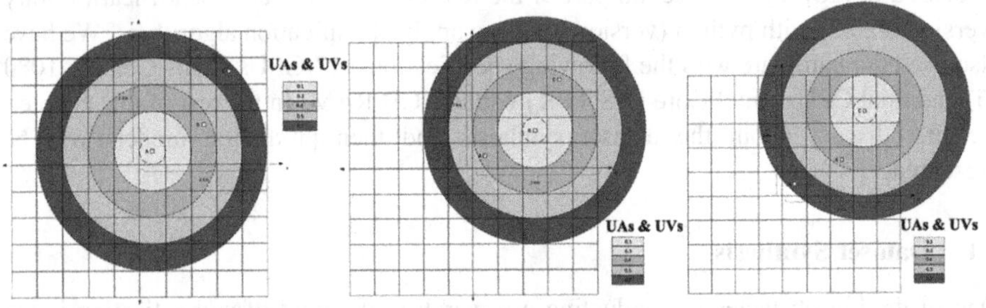

Fig. 3. Uncertainty areas for three defined PoIs, from PoI_1 to PoI_3 from left to right

Time. **(i)** The pattern for the time of authentication request depends on the business model of the service in which the authentication process is embedded. For services are deployed to be accessible 24 h a day, 7 days a week like Email service generally no restriction is defined for the sake of access in terms of time. In such a case, time of the authentication requests follows uniform distribution. In order to make the scenario for dataset more challenging we consider a service which is mostly demanded during a specific time period like work hours (e.g. 9 AM to 5 PM) then we should take those time preferences into consideration and find the corresponding PDFs. **(ii)** According to our assumption for this case study, the majority of users send authentication requests during work hours (9 AM to 5 PM) and the number of requests before 9 AM and after 5 PM plummeted gradually. We also suppose that the number of requests between 12–13 decreases due to the rest/lunch time. **(iii)** We have broken the time of the authentication requests into 11 timeslots due to the above considerations. Based on the likelihood of making authentication request, we assign a weight in terms of probability for each timeslot. For example, the probability of receiving an authentication request between 9 AM to 12 AM and 13 PM to 17 PM is higher than the other timeslots. We have also defined an uncertainty value for each timeslot. In doing so, we determine values in a way that authentication requests made during work hours supposed to be less risky than any request which is made out of work hours therefore the value of uncertainty is lower during work hours and such a value for the requests out of the work hours increases gradually. We have also assumed the least value of uncertainty for all authentication requests during work hours because of the potential threat of insiders. **(iv)** In order to generate the values for the time of authentication request, we have applied two PDFs. Multinomial distribution was used to randomly generate the samples for timeslots in which the request comes from. In doing so we used the assigned weights. Then a uniform distribution was similarly applied to randomly determine the time of the request within nominated timeslot. Finally, uncertainty values for the generated request times were assigned based on the records of Table 1.

Table 1. Timeslots and associated probabilities and uncertainty values

Time-slot	Weight (probability)	Uncertainty value
[1–5)	0.005	0.80
[5–7)	0.006	0.75
[7–8)	0.01	0.60
[8–9)	0.04	0.50
[9–12)	0.35	0.10
[12–13)	0.10	0.20
[13–17)	0.40	0.10
[17–18)	0.06	0.40
[18–19)	0.02	0.50
[19–23)	0.007	0.70
[23–1)	0.002	0.90

Location. As thoroughly discussed in [28], one of the attributes of our ABAC based model is the location. Our approach can consider the location in which the authentication request comes from in order to make accurate access decision. It can also handle the uncertainty of mobile users as well as fixed ones in authentication. The need for considering mobility in authentication is on the rise the number of security and privacy incidents caused by them is rapidly increasing [33]. We have taken the following points into considerations to generate uncertainty values for the location of the requests: **(i)** We have applied the mixture of Gaussian PDF to generate data for any specific location of the mobile user in a two-dimensional grid, (X: longitude and Y: latitude) based on a number of studies which suggested normally distributed locations of mobile users in communication [34–37]. **(ii)** In order to make our case study more challenging, we have defined a scenario consisting of three Point of Interests (PoI). The number of PoIs may vary from one case study to another. According to above-mentioned assumptions our PDF consists of three Gaussian factors (because of our three Point of Interests) in which each of them has a weight and each PDF belongs to one PoI respectively:

$$G_T = \alpha G_1 + \beta G_2 + \gamma G_3 \tag{1}$$

We expect that most of the authentication requests to be sent from or around the first PoI (which is generated using G_1) such that the magnitude of α coefficient was chosen in a way that reflects this fact. Next, the second PoI generates the second highest number of requests (using G_2) and the magnitude of β was chosen in a way that it is lower than α whist the third PoI should generate the smallest number of authentication request associated with location (using G_3) and the magnitude of γ was determined as the lowest value to represent this fact that the least of the authentication requests to be sent from or around the third PoI. So that:

$$\alpha > \beta > \gamma \quad (2)$$

(iii) We have generated our samples in terms of location (mobile and fixed) along with a map of area 2000 m * 2000 m, which contains three PoIs namely PoI_1, PoI_2 and PoI_3. Figure 3 shows the corresponding map in detains. The assigned values as gaussian parameters μ and σ for our three gaussian factors are shown in Table 2. These values were used to generate random values in both dimensions X and Y. **(iv)** We have defined five different Uncertainty Areas (UAs) for each PoI and determined uncertainty values for each of these areas respectively (Fig. 3). In order to define UAs for each PoI, five circles were drawn with the PoI point as the center and with (2n + 1)*r as radius (n = 0, 1, 2, 3… and r = 200 m). The number of circles and the length of the radius may vary from one case study and thus is considered a system parameter. **(v)** The process of generating samples for the authentication request in terms of location are as follows: First, in order to randomly choose a PoI from three PoIs a multinomial PDF was applied using nominated weights (α, β, γ) as probabilities. Then, corresponding Gaussian PDF was applied to generate the X and Y points of the location. Third, according to the location of the generated point like A on the map, an Uncertainty Value (UV) was calculated using the following formula:

$$\begin{aligned} \text{Uncertainty Value of } (A) &= \alpha * (\text{UV assigned by PoI\_1 to A}) \\ &+ \beta * (\text{UV assigned by PoI\_2 to A}) + \gamma * (\text{UV assigned by PoI\_3 to A}) \end{aligned} \quad (3)$$

The value assigned by each given PoI in the above formula depends on the uncertainty area (UA) in which the point has fallen.

Table 2. Assigned values for Gaussian PDFs parameters

PoI_1	PoI_2	PoI_3
$\mu_x = 200$, $\sigma_x = 50$	$\mu_x = 1000$, $\sigma_x = 200$	$\mu_x = 1400$, $\sigma_x = 300$
$\mu_y = 200$, $\sigma_y = 50$	$\mu_y = 600$, $\sigma_y = 150$	$\mu_y = 1400$, $\sigma_y = 200$
$\alpha = 0.65$	$\beta = 0.20$	$\gamma = 0.15$

Credential. The most common form of credential is username and password. We have considered this information as the credential for this research. We have taken the following points into considerations to generate uncertainty values for credentials: **(i)** Usernames and passwords entered by users makes three possibilities: (i) both username and password provided by the user are correct (ii) only the username is correct and (iii) both username and password is incorrect. Data for the three possible states was generated form a multinomial PDF as described below. **(ii)** Generally, most users enter username and password correctly. Otherwise, most users enter the username correctly but enter the password incorrectly. These were considered when assigning probability values and associated uncertainty values listed in the Table 3 for these three states.

Access Decision. After generating the uncertainty values for each attribute in the matrix shown in Fig. 2 the final uncertainty value is calculated for each request in order to make an authentication decision. The final value for each authentication request was calculated by averaging the uncertainty values of time, location and credential. Generally, credential is the most important authentication attribute in comparison with time and location. We have added weights to the generated uncertainty values to show the priority and importance of the attributes. The magnitude of these weights may vary based on the research priorities. Therefore, we have calculated the weighted arithmetic mean by averaging of weighted uncertainty values (weight values: Time = 2, Location = 3 and Credential = 5). Finally, for labelling the dataset we have used the final uncertainty value for each request as the probability for binomial distribution to determine the class of the result: {0: Deny and 1: Access}.

Table 3. Assigned values for credential associated PDF and corresponding uncertainty values

Username & password are correct	Username is correct but password	Username & password are incorrect
Probability: 0.85	Probability: 0.10	Probability: 0.05
Uncertainty: 0.05	Uncertainty: 0.70	Uncertainty: 0.95

4.2 Prediction Models for Authentication

In this research we have applied three supervised classification algorithms namely as AdaBoost, Gradient Boost and Voting classifiers to build our prediction models besides other models created in our previous contribution [28] using other classifiers.

Boosting Classifiers. The idea behind boosting approach is to lower the bias of the classifiers by focusing on the misclassification samples. For this reason, each training data sample is assigned by a weight and different classifiers are trained with these weighted samples. In this method, future models are based on the previous ones, so it is assumed that errors from misclassified samples arise from the bias of the classifiers. Therefore, by increasing the weights of misclassified samples and applying new classifiers the bias decreases [38]. We have applied two popular boosting algorithms namely as *AdaBoost* and *Gradient Boost* classifiers.

AdaBoost algorithm is a popular machine learning algorithm used to build strong classifier by combining weak classifiers (tree-based classifiers). By employing a vast number of weak classifiers, the rate of misclassification will be reduced significantly [39]. Gradient Boost algorithms is another type of boosting method and consists of a set of classification and regression trees. Like AdaBoost, Gradient Boost is built incrementally by adding new trees and minimizing the misclassification error of the previous model [40].

Voting Classifier. Voting algorithm (soft vote) conceptually aggregates different classifiers to predict the class label (Access/Deny) based on the average predicted probabilities by each classifier whereas voting classifier in 'hard vote' mode predicts the class label based on the majority of the labels predicted by each individual classifier [41]. We have applied both soft and hart vote modes in this research.

We have discussed other classifiers including decision tree, SVM, logistic regression and Naïve Bayes in [28].

Validation. In order to validate the data model, Cross-Validation process has been used by each of the applied classifier. Cross validation is the widely used method to evaluate the generalizability of proposed models [42]. In doing so, 10% of dataset was assigned to the test split (10-fold cross validation). In order to increase the chance of finding the best fit model and improve the generalizability of the generated model we also used the shuffling feature.

5 Results and Discussion

Figure 4 summarizes the performance of the prediction models developed in the research in terms of accuracy, precision, recall and F1. The results are after running cross-validation process. The results were also aggregated and presented using a clustered column chart. As shown, the accuracy of the AdaBoost classifier is the highest (86.54%) and the model which was created using decision tree shows the lowest performance in terms of accuracy (78.20%). According to our observation which is summarized in Fig. 4 the results for SVM and gradient Boost in terms of accuracy, precision, recall and f1 were exactly the same. This was expected, because SVM tries to maximize the minimum margin and Gradient Boost tends to do the same by minimizing a cost function related to the margin. We have also applied a sensitivity analysis using Receiver Operator Characteristic (ROC) curve [43]. As shown in Fig. 5, ROC curves for AdaBoost and Naïve Bayes have the most Area Under the Curve (AUC) which shows that these two models are better in distinguishing between Access and Deny classes than the others. Moreover, the ROC curves for AdaBoost and Voting (soft vote) models dominates the other curves. According to [44] a curve dominates in ROC space if and only if its precision dominates in precision space. For this reason, model created using AdaBoost is chosen as our designated model because its precision rate is higher than the model which was created using Voting classifier.

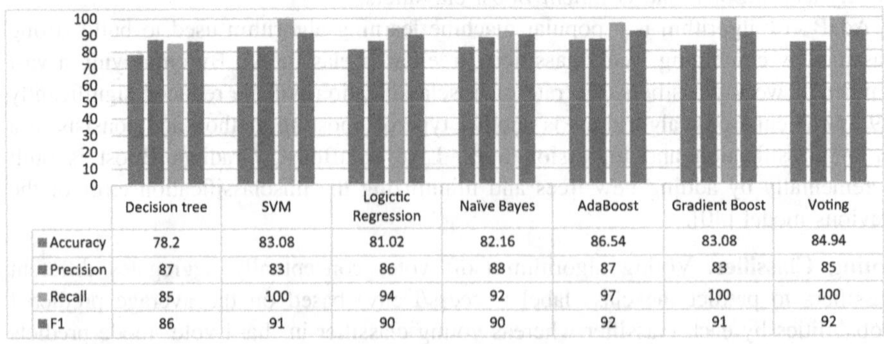

	Decision tree	SVM	Logictic Regression	Naïve Bayes	AdaBoost	Gradient Boost	Voting
Accuracy	78.2	83.08	81.02	82.16	86.54	83.08	84.94
Precision	87	83	86	88	87	83	85
Recall	85	100	94	92	97	100	100
F1	86	91	90	90	92	91	92

Fig. 4. Performance of prediction models applied to uncertainty problem in authentication

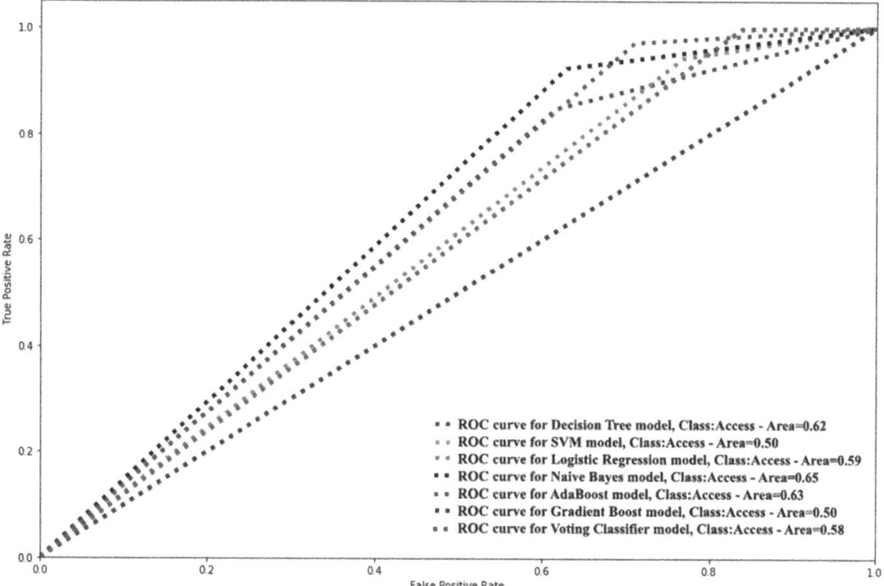

Fig. 5. Aggregated ROC curves for prediction models

6 Conclusion and Future Work

In this paper we have reviewed the state-of-the-art access control models suggested for IoT. According to our findings, applying pre-defined access policies included in traditional and emerging access control models do not result in accurate access decision for indeterminate access scenario in IoT. We have also stressed on uncertainty as a neglected challenge in the authentication for IoT environment which is exaggerated by IoT characteristics like scalability, dynamism and heterogeneity. We have also reviewed the resilient access control proposed in the literature. We found that proposed RAAC methods in literature are inadequate for the IoT. We have also proposed an uncertainty-aware authentication model based on ABAC. Our model was built based on the dataset that we have synthesized based on the state-of-the-art researches. We have built uncertainty-aware authentication models using Boosting and voting classifiers. The results indicated that the model created using AdaBoost shows better performance in terms of higher accuracy and precision together than the performance of the other models. The future step of this work is to focus on ambiguity in authentication.

References

1. Zhou, W., Jia, Y., Peng, A., Zhang, Y., Liu, P.: The effect of IoT new features on security and privacy: new threats, existing solutions, and challenges yet to be solved. IEEE Internet Things J. **6**(2), 1606–1616 (2018)

2. Bertino, E., Choo, K.-K.R., Georgakopolous, D., Nepal, S.: Internet of Things (IoT): smart and secure service delivery. ACM Trans. Internet Technol. **16**(4), 22–29 (2016)
3. Restuccia, F., D'Oro, S., Melodia, T.: Securing the Internet of Things in the age of machine learning and software-defined networking. IEEE Internet Things **5**(6), 4829–4842 (2018)
4. Zhang, C., Green, R.: Communication security in Internet of Thing: preventive measure and avoid DDoS attack over IoT network. In: IEEE Symposium on Communications & Networking (2015)
5. Stallings, W.: Access control. In: Computer Security, Principles and Practice. Pearson (2017)
6. Ouaddah, A., Mousannif, H., Abou, A., Abdellah, E.: Access control in the Internet of Things: big challenges and new opportunities. Comput. Netw. **112**, 237–262 (2017)
7. Heydari, M., Mylonas, A., Katos, V., Gritzalis, D.: Towards indeterminacy-tolerant access control in IoT. In: Dehghantanha, A., Choo, K.-K.R. (eds.) Handbook of Big Data and IoT Security, pp. 53–71. Springer, Cham (2019). https://doi.org/10.1007/978-3-030-10543-3_4
8. Rizvi, S.Z.R., Fong, P.W.L.: Interoperability of relationship - and role-based access model. In: Proceedings of the Sixth ACM Conference on Data and Application Security and Privacy (2016)
9. Kaiwen, S., Lihua, Y.: Attribute-role-based hybrid access control in the Internet of Things. In: Han, W., Huang, Z., Hu, C., Zhang, H., Guo, L. (eds.) APWeb 2014. LNCS, vol. 8710, pp. 333–343. Springer, Cham (2014). https://doi.org/10.1007/978-3-319-11119-3_31
10. Biswas, P., Sandhu, R., Krishnan, R.: Attribute transformation for attribute-based access control. In: Proceedings of the 2nd ACM International Workshop on Attribute-Based Access Control (2017)
11. Savinov, S.: A dynamic risk-based access control approach: model and implementation. Ph.D. thesis, University of Waterloo (2017)
12. Salim, F.: Approaches to access control under uncertainty. Ph.D. thesis, Queensland University of Technology (2012)
13. Ferreira, A., Cruz-Correia, R., Antunes, L.: How to break access control in a controlled manner. In: 19th IEEE International Symposium on Computer-Based Medical Systems (2006)
14. Maw, H.A., Xiao, H., Christianson, B., Malcolm, J.A.: BTG-AC: break-the-glass access control model for medical data in wireless sensor networks. IEEE J. Biomed. Health Inform. **20**(3), 763–774 (2016)
15. Schefer-Wenzl, S., Strembeck, M.: Generic support for RBAC break-glass policies in process-aware information systems. In: 28th Annual ACM Symposium on Applied Computing (2013)
16. Povey, D.: Optimistic security: a new access control paradigm. In: ACM Workshop on New Security Paradigms (1999)
17. Molloy, I., Dickens, L., Morisset, C., Cheng, P.C., Lobo, J., Russo, A.: Risk-based security decisions under uncertainty. In: Proceedings of the Second ACM Conference on Data and Application Security and Privacy (2012)
18. Bijon, K.Z., Krishnan, R., Sandhu, R.: Risk-aware RBAC sessions. In: Venkatakrishnan, V., Goswami, D. (eds.) ICISS 2012. LNCS, vol. 7671, pp. 59–74. Springer, Heidelberg (2012). https://doi.org/10.1007/978-3-642-35130-3_5
19. Baracaldo, N., Joshi, J.: A trust-and-risk aware RBAC framework: tackling insider threat. In: ACM Proceedings of the 17th Symposium on Access Control (2012)
20. Baracaldo, N., Joshi, J.: An adaptive risk management and access control framework to mitigate insider threats. J. Comput. Secur. **39**, 237–254 (2013)
21. Dimmock, N., Belokosztolszki, A., Eyers, D., Bacon, J., Moody, K.: Using trust and risk in role-based access control policies. In: ACM Symposium on Access Control Models and Technologies (SACMAT) (2014)

22. Bacon, J., Moody, K., Yao, W.: A model of OASIS role-based access control and its support for active security. ACM Trans. Inf. Syst. Secur. **5**(4), 492–540 (2002)
23. Atlam, H.F., Alenezi, A., Walters, R.J., Wills, G.B., Daniel, J.: Developing an adaptive risk-based access control model for the Internet of Things. In: IEEE International Conference on Internet of Things (2017)
24. Nogoorani, S.D., Jalili, R.: TIRIAC: a trust-driven risk-aware access control framework for grid environments. Future Gener. Comput. Syst. **55**, 238–254 (2016)
25. Nurse, J.R.C., Creese, S., De Roure, D.: Security risk assessment in Internet of Things systems. IT Prof. **19**(5), 20–26 (2017)
26. Ghorbani, H.R., Ahmadzadegan, M.H.: Security challenges in Internet of Things: survey. In: IEEE Conference on Wireless Sensors (ICWiSe) (2017)
27. Frustaci, M., Pace, P., Aloi, G., Fortino, G.: Evaluating critical security issues of the IoT world: present and future challenges. IEEE Internet Things J. **5**(4), 2327–4662 (2017)
28. Heydari, M., Mylonas, A., Katos, V., Balaguer-Ballester, E., Tafreshi, V.H.F., Benkhelifa, E.: Uncertainty-aware authentication model for fog computing in IoT. In: The Fourth IEEE International Conference on Fog and Mobile Edge Computing, Rome, Italy (2019)
29. Gallagher, P.D.: NISP SP800-30 guide for conducting risk assesment. In: NIST (2012)
30. Moses, T.: Extensible access control markup language (XACML). In: OASIS (2013)
31. User-Computer Authentication Associations in Time. Los Alamos National Laboratory. https://csr.lanl.gov/data/auth/. Accessed 13 Feb 2019
32. Lohweg, V.: Banknote authentication data set. Center for machine learning and intelligent systems, University of California. https://archive.ics.uci.edu/ml/datasets/banknote+authentication. Accessed 13 Feb 2019
33. Premarathne, U.S., Khalil, I., Atiquzzaman, M.: Location-dependent disclosure risk based decision support framework for persistent authentication in pervasive computing applications. Comput. Netw. **88**, 161–177 (2015)
34. Marcus, P., Linnhoff-Popien, C.: Efficient evaluation of location predicates for access control systems. In: IEEE Sixth UKSim/AMSS European Symposium on Computer Modeling and Simulation (2012)
35. Chandrasekaran, G., Wang, N., Hassanpour, M., Xu, M., Tafazolli, R.: Mobility as a service (MaaS): a D2D-based information centric network architecture for edge-controlled content distribution. IEEE Access **6**, 2110–2129 (2018)
36. Ekman, F., Keranen, A., Karvo, J., Ott, J.: Working day movement model. In: ACM Proceedings of the 1st ACM SIGMOBILE Workshop on Mobility Models (2008)
37. Keränen, A., Ott, J., Kärkkäinen, T.: The ONE simulator for DTN protocol evaluation. In: ACM Proceedings of the 2nd International Conference on Simulation Tools and Techniques (2009)
38. Aggarwal, C.C.: An introduction to data mining. Data Mining, pp. 1–26. Springer, Cham (2015). https://doi.org/10.1007/978-3-319-14142-8_1
39. Hu, W., Hu, W., Maybank, S.: AdaBoost-based algorithm for network intrusion detection. IEEE Trans. Syst. Man Cybern. Part B (Cybern.) **28**(2), 577–583 (2008)
40. Punmiya, R., Choe, S.: Energy theft detection using gradient boosting theft detector with feature engineering-based preprocessing. IEEE Trans. Smart Grid **10**(2), 2326–2329 (2019)
41. Raschka, S., Mirjalili, V.: Combining different models for ensemble learning. In: Python Machine Learning. Packt Publishing, pp. 219–233 (2017)
42. Ian, H., Frank, E., Hall, M.A., Pal, C.J.: Data mining: practical machine learning tools and techniques. Morgan Kaufmann Series in Data Management Systems (2016)
43. Fawcett, T.: An introduction to ROC analysis. Pattern Recogn. Lett. **27**(8), 861–874 (2006)
44. Davis, J., Goadrich, M.: The relationship between precision-recall and ROC curves. In: Proceedings of the 23rd International Conference on Machine Learning, ICML 2006 (2006)

From ISO/IEC 27002:2013 Information Security Controls to Personal Data Protection Controls: Guidelines for GDPR Compliance

Vasiliki Diamantopoulou[1(✉)], Aggeliki Tsohou[2], and Maria Karyda[1]

[1] Department of Information and Communication Systems Engineering, University of the Aegean, Samos, Greece
{vdiamant,mka}@aegean.gr

[2] Department of Informatics, Ionian University, Corfu, Greece
atsohou@ionio.gr

Abstract. With the enforcement of the General Data Protection Regulation (GDPR) in EU, organisations must make adjustments in their business processes and apply appropriate technical and organisational measures to ensure the protection of the personal data they process. Further, organisations need to demonstrate compliance with GDPR. Organisational compliance demands a lot of effort both from a technical and from an organisational perspective. Nonetheless, organisations that have already applied ISO27k standards and employ an Information Security Management System and respective security controls need considerably less effort to comply with GDPR requirements. To this end, this paper aims to identify the controls provisioned in ISO/IEC 27001:2013 and ISO/IEC 27002:2013 that need to be extended in order to adequately meet, if/where possible, the data protection requirements that the GDPR imposes. Thus, an organisation that already follows ISO/IEC 27001:2013, can use this work as a basis for compliance with the GDPR.

Keywords: General Data Protection Regulation · ISO/IEC 27001:2013 · ISO/IEC 27002:2013 · Security controls · Data protection controls · Compliance

1 Introduction

The ubiquitous presence of information technology in people's daily routine poses challenges regarding the protection of the information they share. Social media, fora, instant messaging, mobile applications and e-commerce activities are some of the most popular technologies that heavily rely on personal data being collected and exchanged, for the provision of the respective services. One of the most valuable types of data managed by companies is personal information, i.e. information that can be linked to persons. Personal data that people share

S. Katsikas et al. (Eds.): ESORICS 2019 Workshops, LNCS 11980, pp. 238–257, 2020.
https://doi.org/10.1007/978-3-030-42048-2_16

online, exchanged on a broad scale, constitute one of the driving forces of modern enterprises [20]. Online activities of individuals produce data that are of value for enterprises which base their business models on such data to provide personalised services, exploiting targeting marketing. For this reason, the protection of personal data has seen a major upheaval during the last decades, concentrating the attention of politicians, developers, public and private organisations, legislators, authorities, as well as the general public. Personal data protection legislation has attempted to pose restrictions to the uncontrollable use of such data, by governments, enterprises, etc. However, different national laws had substantially different characteristics [18], allowing organisations to take advantage of such blurred territories of legislation and proceed with the exploitation and processing of such data. Before May 2018, European Union (EU) Member States applied national privacy laws, following the EU Directive 95/46 [1] each Member State of the EU had its national privacy law that the organisations had to comply with. With the General Data Protection Regulation (hereafter, GDPR or Regulation) [2], EU adopted a unified privacy law, aiming to protect and regulate the massive usage of personal data. The GDPR aims at the regulation and the management of personal data, defining strict fines to the data controllers that do not comply.

Compliance with the GDPR comprises a challenging project for organisations for a series of reasons; the complexity of business activities and the duplication of data (in different information flows or even entire departments within an organisation) are the most important ones. In addition, even if organisations need to comply with the GDPR, they lack guidelines that could help them into complying with these requirements. There are already products being developed that can facilitate the compliance with the GDPR, however, none of the current technical solutions is able to capture the current personal data protection status of an organisation, identify the gaps, assess the criticality of the processing activities and the personal data they use, provide concrete solutions tailored to each organisation to finally fortify its processes and guarantee the protection of individuals' personal data [12].

We argue that the ISO 27k standard series can form a useful baseline for businesses to build their "towards-compliance" strategy upon, dealing with topics such as risk definition and assessment, continuous evaluation and appropriate documentation. ISO/IEC 27001:2013 [16] (hereafter, ISO 27001) and GDPR aim both to strengthen data security and mitigate the risk of data breaches, and they both require organisations to ensure the confidentiality, integrity and availability of data. Recital 83 of the GDPR states *In order to maintain security and to prevent processing in infringement of this Regulation, the controller or processor should evaluate the risks inherent in the processing and implement measures to mitigate those risks, such as encryption.* The information-risk-driven approach, which is also described in the GDPR, consists a fundamental perspective for ISO 27001. ISO 27001 provides detailed best practices while Article 24 of the GDPR specifies that adherence to codes of conduct and approved certifications can be used as an element for demonstrating compliance. There are several similarities as they both aim to cultivate a culture of protecting processes/assets/data and shaping the organisation's philosophy in this direction. Therefore, we argue that for organisations that base their information security frameworks on ISO 27001, compliance with the GDPR requires limited (or at least less than the one required if no such certification exists) effort, as many processes and controls should already be in place, as should be the organisation's attitude towards protecting (processes/assets/data). Towards this direction, the authors in [7] have identified synergies by analysing the ISO 27001 standard and the GDPR by extracting the main concepts from both texts, and have proposed best practices for compliance. The aim of this paper is to further extend the previous work, by focusing on the security controls level, rather than on security management practices that the ISO/IEC 27002:2013 [15] (hereafter, ISO 27002) provides and in order to meet GDPR requirements, by focusing on data protection actions.

The rest of the paper is structured as follows. Section 2 presents an overview regarding the acceptance of the GDPR by organisations one year after its application. Section 3 provides insights of the ISO 27001 certification and the ISO27k standards, explaining potential benefits for organisations adopting a certification schema. Section 4 analyses the ISMS framework of ISO 27001 and identifies synergies with the GDPR compliance efforts. Insights of the corresponding controls described in detail in ISO 27002 of each module of the ISMS are provided, in order for the reader to realise the effort they have to put to reach GDPR compliance. Section 5 focuses on the enhancement of the ISMS framework with personal data protection risk management. Finally, Sect. 6 concludes the paper by providing overall conclusions and issues for further research.

2 Background Information: Challenges in Personal Data Protection in the GDPR Era

Through the GDPR, EU regulators aim to enforce significant changes on the way that organisations process data subjects' personal information. Even though these changes are expected to bring significant advantages for the data subjects, it is a reality that it has become a significant challenge for organisations to make the considerable shifts on their information technology, culture, business processes, and generally the way they function. Some of these challenges have been documented by organisations, academic papers or by European Commission reports, highlighting the particular aspects of the GDPR that appear troublesome.

Since May 2016 GDPR entered into force, reports were released revealing that organisations are not ready and compliance will be a challenging issue. Gartner in 2017 [11] argues that organisations are unprepared and highlights the responsibility of organisations outside the EU. Similarly, the report by Ernst & Young in 2018 [9], states that only 33% of responding organisations had a plan to address GDPR compliance at the time the survey (between October and November 2017) was conducted and 39% of respondents indicated that they are not at all familiar with the GDPR. This picture does not seem to change much after the GDPR came into force. A recent Thomson Reuters article [21] highlights that evidence show that organisations are still not fully aware of the GDPR's potential impact and are not ready for the GDPR compliance issues. In a survey [13] among privacy professionals which was published in 2019 by the International Association of Privacy Professionals (IAPP), it appears that less than half of respondents said they are fully compliant with the GDPR. Interestingly, nearly 20% of the privacy professionals who participated argues that full GDPR compliance is truly impossible.

Among the reported challenges [6], it seems that organisations are battling on the way to satisfy the data subjects' right to erasure ("right to be forgotten") (GDPR, Article 17). This was cited by 53% of the survey respondents as the biggest challenge on achieving compliance with the GDPR. Data protection-by-design and -by-default (GDPR, Article 25) follows with 42% and "records of processing activities" (GDPR, Article 30) with 39%. IAPP [14] has published a Data Protection Officer's (DPO) experience on the GDPR a year after it entered into force also highlights that managing and addressing data subjects' requests was the biggest challenge.

3 ISO27001 Certification and the ISO27k Standards

ISO 27001, entitled "Information technology - Security techniques - Information security management systems - Requirements" aims at the provision of recommendations on good practices for information security management, risk management and taking security measures, within the context of an Information Security Management System (ISMS). It belongs to the ISO27k family standards that provide details (e.g., ISO/IEC 27005 about the information security risk management and ISO/IEC 27018 for the protection of personally identifiable information in public clouds), while other ISO and non-ISO standards and resources provide much more information and, in some cases, propose alternative or complementary approaches and controls. Specifically, ISO 27001 specifies the requirements for establishing, implementing, operating, monitoring, reviewing, maintaining and improving a documented ISMS within the context of the organisation's overall business risks. The objective of the standard is to thoroughly describe an ISMS, to provide definitions on the fundamental terms of information security, and on terms that are referenced in the family of ISO27k. This standard is addressed to all types of organisations and businesses of any business sector, size, and activity.

ISO 27002, entitled "Information technology - Security techniques - Code of practice for information security controls" provides a list of controls and good practices that can be used as guides when selecting and implementing measures to achieve information security. Annex A' of ISO 27001 is totally in line with ISO 27002. They present the security modules, control objectives and controls that an ISMS shall cover at minimum. The structure of security controls includes 14 modules that expand in 35 security objectives and 114 security controls to achieve the objectives. However, the difference between those two standards is the level of detail they present the controls, as ISO 27001 dictates a short description of each control, while ISO 27002 explains each control in detail, providing good practices for their successful implementation.

The application of ISO 27001 supports organisations in creating better business efficiency, safeguards valuable assets such as personal data or hardware, protects staff and organisations' reputation, and simultaneously facilitates the attainment of compliance objectives. Organisations have always sought some short of certification for one or more of their business activities. Regarding information security, 39,501 ISO 27001 certificates were issued to organisations, worldwide, in 2017[1]. Given its wide recognition and acceptance, and in the absence of a GDPR compliance certification, ISO 27001 makes a good candidate to be considered as the baseline upon which organisations can work on in order to reach GDPR compliance. Furthermore, there is a lot of common ground between ISO 27001 and GDPR, which additionally strengthens the previous statement.

4 From Information Security Controls to Personal Data Protection Controls

Juxtaposing ISO 27001 and the GDPR we have identified that they are based on common ground. Despite the fact that they have different perspectives, both ISO 27001 and the GDPR focus on the minimisation of risk that can be realised when a data breach occurs. ISO 27001 focuses on reducing risks to information security by compelling organisations to produce ISMS that are continuously maintained and improved. GDPR aims at the preservation of privacy of individuals, providing them with rights against organisations that process their personal data. GDPR also promotes accountability, by placing clear data protection responsibilities to the corresponding organisations processing such data. The aforementioned accountability lies on the implementation of appropriate technical and organisational measures to ensure a level of security appropriate to the risk (GDPR, Article 32).

Both GDPR and ISO 27001 request that organisations focus on the empowerment of knowledge which is communicated to the leadership, and develop awareness within the whole organisation regarding the protection of data, exploiting security measures [12]. The GDPR provisions numerous personal data protection settings and controls, many of which are also recommended in ISO/IEC 27001:2013, ISO/IEC 27002:2013, and other "ISO27k" standards. Organisations that currently have an ISMS are likely to satisfy many of the GDPR requirements already, needing a few adjustments to be made. In this section we analyse the ISMS framework of ISO 27001 and identify synergies with the GDPR compliance efforts. In the following subsections the fourteen control modules of Annex A' of ISO 27001 are presented, focusing on the level of the proposed controls that can be implemented. At this level, we extend the information security controls to personal data protection controls, analysing and describing the

[1] https://www.iso.org/the-iso-survey.html.

necessary additional actions that an organisation is required to implement, in relation to the aforementioned controls, towards GPDR compliance. Finally, we provide suggestions to the organisations that are already certified according to the ISO 27001, on the following actions they have to conduct to also comply with the requirements of the GDPR. Each paragraph describes the obligations that ISO 27001 and 27002 impose to organisations, and compared to them, we propose the additional actions that an organisation has to conduct towards GDPR compliance.

4.1 Enhancing Information Security Policies with Data Protection Policies

The first control module of ISO 27001 and ISO 27002 includes one control related with the management direction for information security. The objective is the provision of management direction and support for information security in accordance with business requirements, and relevant laws and regulations. For the realisation of this module, two controls have been identified; the first refers to policies for information security, while the second imposes review of the aforementioned polices.

Actions Towards GDPR Compliance: The organisation shall be based on the information security policy that has already developed in order to establish a Data Protection Policy. The Data Protection Policy describes the set of rules that define how the organisation protects personal data, so that it complies with the GDPR and protects the privacy of the data subjects. The purpose of the Data Protection Policy is to provide strategic guidance to the organisation's management and staff for the protection of personal data when processing them. The Data Protection Policy applies to all operational processes that involve the processing of personal data. Moreover, it applies to all employees and associates of the organisation who are directly or indirectly involved in the processing of personal data. This policy should be distinct from the information security policy [17] and should provide information on new processes that regulate organisational aspects pertaining to the way the organisation:

- Manages consent
- Fulfils data subjects' rights
- Makes transfers of personal data to third countries
- Manages collaborating third parties - data processors
- Manages transfer or disclosure of personal data
- Responds to incidents that may lead to a personal data breach
- Monitors measures personal data processing activities and supporting assets, to continuously ensure compliance with the regulation
- Manages personnel awareness and training of specialised personnel (in order to ensure that they have the knowledge and skills to apply the data protection policy)
- Implements data protection-by-design and -by-default principles regarding information systems the organisation develops in-house or through procurement

Regarding the second control of this module, similarly to the information security policy, the Data Protection Policy is not static but should be kept as up to date as possible and adjusted in line with the changes of information systems and the technical and social environment. The Data Protection Policy should be updated periodically and this process should be documented. In addition, it should also be updated in the event of major changes to the organisation or its IT systems. The senior management of the organisation assigns the responsibility for reviewing the Data Protection Policy to the Data Protection Officer.

4.2 Extending Organisation of Information Security with Personal Data Protection Structures and Roles

This control module includes two categories, (i) the internal organisation, and (ii) the mobile devices and teleworking. This control module aims at the establishment of a framework for the administration on the implementation and operation of security within the organisation, and the protection of security related with the information accessed, processed and/or stored at teleworking sites, and the use of portable devices.

The category Internal Organisation consists of six controls. The first refers to information security roles and responsibilities, mentioning that all information security responsibilities shall be defined and allocated. The second refers to segregation of duties, where conflicting duties and areas of responsibility should be segregated to reduce opportunities for unauthorised or unintentional modification or misuse of the organisation's assets. The third refers to contact with authorities, where appropriate contacts with relevant authorities should be maintained. The fourth refers to contact with special interest groups, where appropriate contacts with special interest groups or other specialist security forums and professional associations should be maintained. Finally, the fifth control refers to information security in project management, where information security should be addressed in project management, regardless of the type of the project.

Actions Towards GDPR Compliance: The organisation is responsible for implementing an organisational framework according to which there are roles with responsibilities for the protection of personal data. The framework should include the role of the Data Protection Officer; in cases required. The role of the Data Protection Officer should be designated by the senior management, assigning this responsibility to a competent person reporting directly to the senior management without receiving any instructions on how to perform his/her tasks. Senior management needs to ensure that the Data Protection Officer is not dismissed or penalised for performing his/her tasks. The organisational structure of the organisation reflects the distinct role of the Data Protection Officer. A Data Protection Officer should be appointed, if (i) the processing is carried out by a public authority or body, except for courts acting in their judicial capacity, (ii) the data controller's main activities require regular and systematic monitoring of the data subjects on a large scale, and (iii) the data controller's main activities are large scale processing of specific categories of personal data (GDPR, Article 37). The organisation should appoint necessary responsibilities to the Data Protection Officer, as described in GDPR (Article 39).

Regarding contact with authorities, the data controllers need to cooperate with the supervisory authorities when a data breach occurs (GDPR, Article 33), informing them without undue delay, when the personal data breach affects the rights and freedoms of the corresponding natural persons. When the data controller realises that the data breach may pose a high risk to their rights and freedoms, they should also inform the data subjects for the violation of their data (GDPR, Article 34), choosing the most appropriate means for communication (e.g., email, newsletter, press release, etc.) according the number of the affected natural persons and the severity of the data breach.

Regarding contact with special interest groups, in order for a data controller to be able to guarantee the protection of the personal data they process, they need to conduct a Data Protection Impact Assessment (DPIA) when particular types of processing is likely to result in a high risk to the rights and freedoms of natural persons (GDPR, Article 35). The data controller carries out DPIA in case of (i) systematic and extensive evaluation of personal aspects relating to natural persons which is based on automated processing, including profiling, (ii) processing on a large scale of special categories of data, (iii) systematic monitoring of a publicly accessible area on a large scale.

Finally, regarding information security in project management, organisations should establish a code of conduct (GDPR, Article 40). Codes of conduct can contribute to the proper application of the GDPR, taking account of the specific features of the various processing sectors and the specific needs of micro, small and medium-sized enterprises. They are related to associations and other bodies that represent data controllers or data processors. To this direction, data controllers and data processors are encouraged by the GDPR to be certified with a certification mechanism (GDPR, Article 42). Such mechanisms may be established for the purpose of demonstrating the existence of appropriate safeguards provided by controllers or processors. They enable the mandatory monitoring of compliance either by the supervisory authority, or by an accredited organisation (demonstrating independence and expertise). Codes of conduct can be drawn up by organisations that represent data controllers or data processors and approved either by the supervisory authority of a member state or by the European Data Protection Board.

4.3 Expanding Controls on Human Resources Security to Protect Personal Data Handled by Employees

The human resources security module consists of three sub categories, (i) information security prior to employment; (ii) during employment, and (iii) termination and change of employment. Information security prior to employment contains two controls, i.e. screening and terms and conditions, during employment the controls refer to the management responsibilities, information security awareness, education and training and disciplinary process, while in the termination and change of employment the organisation should take care of the information security responsibilities that remain valid after termination or change of employment.

Actions Towards GDPR Compliance: Further actions should be taken regarding the protection of personal data that an organisation processes by its employees. The organisation should take appropriate measures and controls related with the management of their employees, so that they protect the personal information (of the personal data of natural persons that the organisation keeps, e.g., personal data of customers, suppliers) that they process within the scope of their occupation. Specifically, before the employment of their employees, an organisation should take appropriate measures to ensure that the employees are fit to handle personal data, e.g., by a screening process and by informing them about possible legal consequences during the exercising of the work activities (regarding personal data misuse, etc.). During employment, the organisation should review the already existing contracts of their employees who have access to personal data, and make sure that they include specific clauses for confidentiality, with legal bindings. Finally, after the employment, the organisation should remove access rights to personal data the corresponding employees had access to.

4.4 Enhancing Asset Management with Personal Data Management

Asset management's module contains three controls: (i) responsibility for assets; (ii) information classification; and (iii) media handling. The objective for the first control is the identification of the organisational assets, and the definition of appropriate protection responsibilities. Regarding the information classification, the organisation needs to ensure that information receives appropriate level of protection in accordance with its importance. Regarding the media handling control, the organisation is responsible for preventing unauthorised disclosure, modification, removal or destruction of information stored on media. This control includes securely disposing of media on which information is stored when it is no longer required.

Actions Towards GDPR Compliance: The aim of this clause is to develop and maintain appropriate safeguards for the protection of organisational assets. Towards this direction, GDPR requires that data controllers and processors alike maintain records of their processing activities regarding personal data and special categories of personal data (GDPR, Articles 5, 7, 9, 30). Taking into account that personal data and special categories of personal data also consist a valuable asset, the organisation, acting as a data controller, needs to keep records of the categories of data subjects; the categories of the collected data; the types of processing activities that have occurred or are likely to take place; the legal grounds related with the processing (this point is also related with the consent that the organisation should obtain by the data subject); potential recipients of data disclosures; potential transfer of data to non-EU countries, accompanied with information regarding the appropriate safeguards these countries have, ensuring an adequate level of protection; retention period of the data; and security measures the organisation applies. When an organisation acts as a data processor the records of the processing activities contain contact details of the data processor or processors and of each data controller on behalf of which the data processor is acting, and where applicable, the contact details of the Data Protection Officer; the categories of processing activities; potential transfer of data to non-EU countries and information regarding technical and organisational security safeguards the organisation applies. The organisation shall keep documented records of processing activities.

Additionally, organisations should develop appropriate procedures that allow provision of information to the data subject related to the aforementioned personal data they keep (GDPR, Articles 13, 14).

4.5 Implementing Data Protection-by-Design and -by-Default in Access Control

Access control module contains four controls: (i) business requirements of access control; (ii) user access management; (iii) user responsibilities; and (iv) system and application access control. All these controls are related with specific guidelines about the management of access of the users to information, with the prevention of unauthorised access to systems and services and with the accountability for safeguarding organisation's authentication information. According to user access management control, organisations should have systems for the (de)registration of the users, enabling thus access right assignments; they also should have processes for users' authentication and revoking access; and finally, organisations should be careful regarding access rights when a collaboration is terminated. According to system and application access control, organisations should apply secure log-on procedures for the authentication of users to information and application systems.

Actions Towards GDPR Compliance: Taking the above actions as a basis, the organisation should implement a process through which the data subjects can either correct, or request correction (GDPR, Article 16) of the personal data the organisation holds for them or erase, or request the erasure (GDPR, Article 17) of such data. Automated access, rectification, and erasure should be established by the security team. Additionally, with respect to Recital 63[2], the organisation should be able to generate records of the data subjects' requests and the timeliness of the organisation's response. This functionality can also facilitate the measurement of the performance of the organisation to a data subject's request, ensuring that the appropriate information is provided to data subjects upon request in a secure way.

Additionally, the organisation should develop their systems with respect to data protection-by-design and -by-default principles (GDPR, Article 25) in order

[2] Provision of remote access to a secure system that would provide the data subject with direct access to their personal data.

to protect users' privacy. This means that when designing the access control safeguards the organisation should not take into account only the security requirements (e.g., identification, accountability), but also take into account privacy requirements and principles (e.g., data minimisation).

4.6 Employing Cryptography

The control module Cryptography contains one control, i.e. cryptographic controls, which aims at ensuring proper and effective use of the technological measure of cryptography in order to protect the confidentiality, authenticity and/or integrity of information.

Actions Towards GDPR Compliance: Encryption and pseudonymisation are the two technical measures that the GDPR proposes (GDPR, Article 32). Based on [8], using encryption, privacy is preserved by keeping personal data confidential, and thus, unauthorised users are not allowed to have access to it. Moreover, for the satisfaction of the data subjects' right to data portability (GDPR, Article 20), the organisation is encouraged to apply encryption to securely communicate the corresponding personal data to other organisations. Based on the criticality of the data and on the risk for an organisation, encryption can be applied to protect equipment, databases, partitions or containers, standalone files, emails, communication channels [5].

We should note that when anonymisation, which differs from pseudonymisation [19] as it enables the data subject to remain unidentifiable, is applied to a data set, this data set is exempted from GDPR obligations (GDPR, Recital 26). Therefore, anonymisation is a method that can minimise the risk for an organisation when a requirement to store a data subject's identity no longer exists (e.g., keeping data for statistical results). According to [5], an organisation should determine what has to be anonymised, based on the nature of the data and the risk create for the organisation. Next, organisations can either permanently anonymise the data, or can choose tools (e.g., partial deletion, encryption, hashing, index, etc.) that are closer to their requirements.

4.7 Enhancing Communications Security with Personal Data Protection Objectives

This control module contains two controls: network security management and information transfer. The objective is to ensure the protection of information in networks and its supporting information processing facilities and to maintain the security of information transferred within an organisation and with any external entity. Information transferred to an external party, i.e. a customer, a supplier, a partner, etc., should be secured appropriately, subject to agreements addressing security and consistent with formal policies, procedures and appropriate controls.

Actions Towards GDPR Compliance: Taking the above controls as a basis, an organisation can further focus on the design and development of the communication security, protecting thus personal data of any party in its network requesting access to personal data (GDPR, Article 26). This can be extended to the international transfers, where the organisation, before transferring the requested personal data, should have received appropriate safeguards ensuring an adequate level of protection of the corresponding country, the territory, or one or more specified sectors within that third country.

Additionally, appropriate roles should be given to the corresponding employees who have access to personal data, accompanied with specific responsibilities. This functionality promotes accountability and transparency, while it consists a basis for the accurate response of the organisation, either to any request received by a data subject regarding the processing of their data (GDPR, Articles 13–22), or to the supervisory authority, when a data breach occurs (GDPR, Articles 31, 33). In this way, the organisation is able to locate and retrieve securely the personal data it keeps.

4.8 Acquiring, Developing and Maintaining Systems Following Data Protection Principles

The control module of system acquisition, development and maintenance consists of three controls, (i) security requirements of IS, (ii) security in development and support process, and (iii) test data. This module refers to the development process of IS that an organisation has to follow. It is worth noting that this is the only control module in ISO 27001 and 27002 that covers requirements regarding software development. Organisations should be able to choose their working environment (framework, language, operating system, to name a few parameters) in relation to the criticality of the product they wish to develop.

Actions Towards GDPR Compliance: The requirements of these controls guide the organisation to design and develop their IS following security-by-design principles. With respect to Article 25 of the GDPR, the organisations should also apply data protection-by-design principles [4]. The protection of personal data and users' privacy can be improved and enhanced by designing information systems in a way that reduces the degree of invasion in privacy. One of the measures that the Regulation proposes is data minimisation. In this way, organisations minimise the data they collect to the minimum level demanded for their processing activities. In this area belong a series of methodological frameworks and tools that help analysts, designers and developers to develop ISs that privacy will be a built-in and not an add-on feature. To this end, privacy, in order to be included as a concept in the software development cycle, should be transformed into a technical requirement.

In addition, the organisation should estimate/assess the profit in relation to the cost (cost-benefit analysis) of managing a new system related to the lawful processing of data (GDPR, Article 6). This should also be covered in the risk assessment and management, in general, and taken under consideration when designing or upgrading systems and processes. This assessment may indicate, for example, that some personal data processing residual risk may be accepted, or this risk should be further mitigated by applying one or more security controls.

Also, the organisation should be able to identify and assess the special categories of personal data they process. Information risks could be avoided, where feasible, by assessing the usefulness of the personal and special categories of personal data they keep. Towards risk minimisation, the aggregation of such data is also accepted (GDPR, Articles 9, 11).

In addition, in order to satisfy the right of data subjects to know the outcome of requests related with the correction, completion, erasure, restriction of their personal data (GDPR, Article 19), the organisation should inform the requestor on the above, also providing that this process/application form is easy for insiders and outsiders of the organisation to follow.

4.9 Managing Supplier Relationships While Protecting Personal Data

The module Supplier Relationships aims to manage the relationship of the organisation with its suppliers, or any other third party that has access to the organisation's assets, and to set up and agree a level of information security and service delivery. It consists of two controls, (i) information security in supplier relationships, and (ii) supplier service delivery management.

Actions Towards GDPR Compliance: This control module sets the basis for the establishment of a security framework among an organisation and the external parties it collaborates with, ensuring the protection of the transferred information. GDPR sets specific requirements regarding the management of the relationship of the data controller with its processors. If an organisation uses one or more third parties to process personal information ("processors"), it must ensure they too are compliant with the GDPR (GDPR, Articles 27, 28). Towards this direction, data controllers should conduct continuous evaluation of their processors and suppliers, and use approved certification mechanisms in order to demonstrate that they ensure an adequate level of protection with respect to data protection-by-design and -by-default principles.

Moreover, organisations need to ensure the privacy and other information security aspects of their business partners. This might contain aspects such as jointly investigating and resolving privacy incidents, breaches or access requests, to name a few. These requirements are applied to any relationship the organisation has with external parties, such as ISPs and CSPs, and any other third party that the organisation has exchanged (personal) data with, for example external payroll or marketing companies.

Finally, when data is transferred outside EU, involved organisations should ensure the level of protection of the involved natural persons. Consequently, organisations located outside Europe that interact with European organisations must formally nominate privacy representatives inside Europe if they meet certain conditions (GDPR, Article 27).

4.10 Including Data Breach Notification in Incident Management

The control module Information Security Incident Management consists of one category which is realised through seven controls. The objective of this category is to ensure a consistent and effective approach to the management of information incidents.

Actions Towards GDPR Compliance: The organisation that has already established incident management procedures has allocated responsibilities to each employee, and has developed a policy that has been communicated to all involved parties (employees, external parties) presenting the actions that have to be taken in a potential security incident. For the satisfaction of the Article 33 of the GDPR, the organisation should implement process in order to be able to notify the supervisory authority. Specifically, when a potential data breach occurs, and provided there is a risk for natural persons, the organisation, when acting as a data controller, must inform the competent supervisory authority *without delay and, if possible, no later than 72 hours from the time it occurred*, and the data subjects (GDPR, Article 35), if it is required. The organisation, when acting as a data processor, should promptly notify the data controller for the violations. This notice must be "immediate" to help the data controller comply with the time commitments. If the organisation acts as a data processor and offers services to more than one data controllers, it must report the incident and details about it, to each of them. As the requirement for timely notification to the supervisory authority is too demanding, the organisation should implement procedures for timely notification (i.e. what types of data the organisation should provide (GDPR, Article 33, paragraph 3)) and for communication to data subjects, when necessary.

4.11 Enhancing Compliance to Satisfy Lawfulness of Processing

The module compliance consists of two categories, (i) compliance with legal and contractual requirements, and (ii) information security reviews. This module aims at the avoidance of any kind of breaches related to information security and of any security requirements and to ensure that the information security is implemented and operated in accordance with the organisational policies and procedures.

Actions Towards GDPR Compliance: In order to comply with the GDPR, organisations should follow these six privacy principles (GDPR, Article 5):

1. Lawfulness, fairness, and transparency: Regarding lawfulness, the processing shall fulfil the described tests in the GDPR. Fairness means that the processed data must much the description. Transparency is achieved by informing the data subject what data processing is to be done.
2. Purpose limitations: Personal data can be acquired only for *specified, explicit and legitimate purposes*. This data may only be used for a specific purpose of processing of which the subject is made aware and no other, without acquiring further consent.

3. Minimisation of data: Collected data on a data subject shall be *adequate, relevant and limited to what is necessary in relation to the purposes for which they are processed.* Only the minimum amount of data is to be kept for the purposes of specific processing.
4. Data accuracy: Data shall be *accurate and where necessary kept up to date.* Proper protection and measures against identity theft can be taken through baselining. Holders of data have to build processes for rectification into data management/archiving activities regarding the data subject.
5. Limitations of storage: It is expected by the data controller that personal data is *kept in a form which permits identification of data subjects for no longer than necessary.* The data that is no longer required, should be deleted.
6. Confidentiality and integrity of data: It is required from the data controllers or data processors that data be handled *in a manner [ensuring] appropriate security of the personal data, including protection against unlawful processing or accidental loss, destruction, or damage.*

The organisation must ensure that the above six principles are followed regarding the processing of personal data. However, in order for a processing to be lawful, the organisation should have ensured that at least one of the following applies:

1. The data subject has provided their consent regarding the processing of their personal data.
2. Performance of a contract to which the data subject takes part.
3. Processing is necessary for compliance with a legal obligation of the data controller.
4. Processing is necessary for the protection of vital interests of natural per-sons.
5. Processing is necessary for the performance of a task related with public interest
6. Processing is necessary for the purposes of the legitimate interests pursued by the controller or by a third party.

In order to satisfy the above requirements, the organisation should follow a specific procedure for identifying the types of data processed (personal, special categories, convictions) and be able to prove that the way the data is processed complies with the applicable processing instructions for each type. Moreover, it should document the legal basis for the processing of the data. When consent is the legal basis for the transfer/storage of personal data, special attention should be given in order for consent to be provided by the data subject freely, is specific and clear, and the data subject has been already informed about the processing purposes.

4.12 Modules that Support GDPR Compliance

The following three modules are also part of the Annex A' of the examined ISO, however they have no direct application to the GDPR, but they can help an organisation develop a culture that will assist towards reaching GDPR compliance. Moreover, these modules are included in our study for the sake of completeness.

Enhancing Physical and Environmental Security for GDPR Compliance: This control module concerns two controls: secure areas and equipment. The identification of secure areas can prevent unauthorised physical access, damage and interference to the organisation's information and information processing facilities, while the safeguarding of the equipment of the organisation prevents loss, damage, theft or compromise of assets and interruption of organisation's operation.

Actions Towards GDPR Compliance: This section applies to the general requirement of the GDPR to the organisations for implementing appropriate technical and organisational measures to ensure the level of security appropriate to the risk (GDPR, Articles 24, 25, 28, 32).

Enhancing Operations Security for GDPR Compliance: This control module contains seven controls: (i) operational procedures and responsibilities, (ii) protection from malware, (iii) back up, (iv) logging and monitoring, (v) control of operational software, (vi) technical vulnerability management, and (vii) information systems audit considerations. The objective of this section is to ensure correct and secure operations of information processing facilities, protection against malware and data loss, to record events and generate evidence, to ensure the integrity of operational systems, to prevent exploitation of technical vulnerabilities and to minimise the impact of audit activities on operational systems.

Actions Towards GDPR Compliance: Similarly to the previous section of "physical and environmental security", an organisation is able to demonstrate that they have implemented they appropriate technical and organisational measures to safeguard the personal data they keep. Additionally, the organisation should implement procedures related with the management of the satisfaction of the data subjects' rights (GDPR, Articles 12–22) and for the process of the provision of consent of the data subjects (GDPR, Articles 7).

Extending Business Continuity Management to Support GDPR Compliance: This control module contains two controls: (i) information security continuity, and (ii) redundancies. The objective is the establishment of a business continuity and disaster recovery plan. The continuity of operations is indented to restore the operation of the organisation's systems within a reasonable time. In addition, staff training is required in the continuity plan, while its efficiency must be tested and managed properly.

Actions Towards GDPR Compliance: As a general direction for the satisfaction of the GDPR, an organisation should implement appropriate technical and organisational measures to ensure the level of security appropriate to risk (GDPR, Articles 24, 25, 28, 32).

5 Enhancing the ISMS Framework with Personal Data Protection Risks Management

As it has already been mentioned in the introduction, one of the fundamental perspectives of ISO 27001 is the information-risk-driven approach, which has not been described as a control per se, but it is part of the ISMS framework. Specifically, according to the clause 6 of ISO 27001, the countermeasures applied by an organisation are not only those described in Annex A', but also those that are the outcome of the security risk assessment that is conducted to establish and maintain information security risk criteria, and to identify the information security risks. After risk assessment and the evaluation of the aforementioned outcomes, the organisation is able to select the appropriate information security risk treatment options, based on both the Annex and results of the risk assessment.

Accordingly, in order for an organisation to be compliant with the GDPR, they may need to conduct a data protection impact assessment (GDPR, Article 35) to extend the implemented countermeasures in a way that can demonstrate the appropriateness of the measures taken for each processing activity. Specifically, an organisation may be required to carry out an assessment of the impact of their processing activities in order to protect personal data during its processing, as well as to protect computer or other supporting resources that support processing. To this end, data protection impact assessment is a risk assessment related to the impact that business operations or technologies associated with the processing of personal data, may have. According to Article 35 of the GDPR, data protection impact assessment is conducted when particular types of processing is likely to result in a high risk to the rights and freedoms of natural persons. These types of processing are summarised in the following bullets:

- When systematic and extensive evaluation of personal aspects relating to natural persons is based on automated processing (including profiling), is carried out.
- When processing on a large scale of special categories of data is conduct-ed.
- When systematic monitoring of a publicly accessible area on a large scale is conducted.

In order for an organisation to satisfy the requirement for data protection impact assessment, the core actions they have to follow are (i) to create a list of classified corporate information - including personal data, and (ii) to implement an appropriate methodology, and to establish policies and procedures for carrying out an impact assessment. In the literature there are quite a few risk analysis methodologies [3,10,23], however, Working Party 29 has released criteria for acceptable data protection impact assessment [22] that an organisation can follow, where they also suggest EU generic frameworks as well as sector-specific ones.

6 Conclusions

The new regulation for the protection of the personal data, GDPR, provisions numerous settings and controls focused on the management and the protection of such data. Many of these controls are also provisioned in ISO/IEC 27001:2013, ISO/IEC 27002:2013, and other "ISO27k" standards. Thus, organisations that currently have developed an ISMS are likely to satisfy many of the GDPR requirements already, needing a few adjustments to be made. Other organisations might decide to apply an ISMS as a general framework for the management of the personal data of data subjects that they process, in the context of: (i) the broader management of the information risks; (ii) the security of the data they process, either in hard copy or in a digital version, as well as the relevant compliance; (iii) the incident management; and (iv) addressing business continuity issues. This work describes the necessary additional actions that an organisation is required to implement since they have already an ISMS in place to reach compliance with the GDPR. Specifically, the fourteen control modules of Annex A' of ISO 27001 are presented, focusing on the lower level of analysis presented in the ISO/IEC 27002 and providing extension of the corresponding controls, in order to meet GDPR requirements, by focusing on data protection actions. That means that if organisations already have an ISO 27001 framework in place, compliance with GDPR requirements will not be necessitated a duplication of the demanded effort. In addition, compliance to the GDPR is mandatory, whereas ISO 27001 certification is not. Organisations can start from ISO 27001 certification and reach GDPR compliance, or vice versa.

This work provides guidelines for practitioners of the domain of information security and protection of privacy, since it presents a roadmap on how to design a "towards GDPR compliance" project, contributing also to the awareness regarding the protection of personal data of an organisation.

Future work of this study includes the validation of the proposed guidelines to-wards GDPR compliance by a number of ISO 27001 certified organisations that have also reached GDPR compliance. The analysis of such feedback will further validate (or provide other perspectives to) the findings of this work. Moreover, data protection officers could also be involved in this process, providing their experiences regarding the demanded effort to reach GDPR compliance for an already ISO 27001 certified organisation.

References

1. European Commission: Directive 95/46/EC of the European parliament and of the council. http://eur-lex.europa.eu/legal-content/EN/TXT/?uri=CELEX:31995L0046. Accessed 14 May 2017
2. European Parliament: Regulation (EU) 2016/679 of the European parliament and of the council of 27 April 2016 on the protection of natural persons with regard to the processing of personal data and on the free movement of such data, and repealing directive 95/46/EC (general data protection regulation) (2016)

3. Alberts, C., Dorofee, A., Stevens, J., Woody, C.: Introduction to the octave approach. Technical report, Software Engineering Institute, Carnegie-Mellon University Pittsburgh, PA (2003)
4. Cavoukian, A., et al.: Privacy by design: the 7 foundational principles. Information and Privacy Commissioner of Ontario, Canada 5 (2009)
5. CNIL 2018: Privacy impact assessment (PIA) - knowledge bases. Technical report (2018)
6. CSA 2018: GDPR preparation and challenges survey report from cloud security alliance (CSA). Technical report (2018). https://cloudsecurityalliance.org/articles/gdpr-preparation-and-challenges-survey-report/. Accessed 09 July 2019
7. Diamantopoulou, V., Tsohou, A., Karyda, M.: General data protection regulation and ISO/IEC 27001:2013: synergies of activities towards organisations' compliance. In: Gritzalis, S., Weippl, E.R., Katsikas, S.K., Anderst-Kotsis, G., Tjoa, A.M., Khalil, I. (eds.) TrustBus 2019. LNCS, vol. 11711, pp. 94–109. Springer, Cham (2019). https://doi.org/10.1007/978-3-030-27813-7_7
8. ENISA: Recommended cryptographic measures - securing personal data. Technical report (2013)
9. Ernst & Young 2018: Global forensic data analytics survey. Technical report (2018). https://www.ey.com/Publication/vwLUAssets/ey-how-can-you-disrupt-risk-in-an-era-of-digital-transformation/%24FILE/ey-how-can-you-disrupt-risk-in-an-era-of-digital-transformation.pdf. Accessed 09 July 2019
10. Fredriksen, R., Kristiansen, M., Gran, B.A., Stølen, K., Opperud, T.A., Dimitrakos, T.: The CORAS framework for a model-based risk management process. In: Anderson, S., Felici, M., Bologna, S. (eds.) SAFECOMP 2002. LNCS, vol. 2434, pp. 94–105. Springer, Heidelberg (2002). https://doi.org/10.1007/3-540-45732-1_11
11. Gartner 2017: Gartner says organizations are unprepared for the 2018 European data protection regulation. Technical report (2017). https://www.gartner.com/en/newsroom/press-releases/2017-05-03-gartner-says-organizations-are-unprepared-for-the-2018-european-data-protection-regulation. Accessed 09 July 2019
12. IAAP: Privacy tech vendor report. Technical report (2018)
13. IAPP 2018: Annual governance report. Technical report (2018). https://iapp.org/resources/article/iapp-ey-annual-governance-report-2018/. Accessed 09 July 2019
14. IAPP 2019: GDPR one year later: looking backward and forward. Technical report (2019). https://iapp.org/news/a/gdpr-one-year-later-looking-backward-and-forward/. Accessed 09 July 2019
15. ISO/IEC: ISO 27001:2013 information technology - security techniques - code of practice for information security controls. Technical report (2013)
16. ISO/IEC: ISO 27001:2013 information technology - security techniques - information security management systems - requirements. Technical report (2013)
17. Lambrinoudakis, C.: The general data protection regulation (GDPR) era: ten steps for compliance of data processors and data controllers. In: Furnell, S., Mouratidis, H., Pernul, G. (eds.) TrustBus 2018. LNCS, vol. 11033, pp. 3–8. Springer, Cham (2018). https://doi.org/10.1007/978-3-319-98385-1_1
18. Palmieri III, N.F.: Data protection in an increasingly globalized world. Ind. LJ **94**, 297 (2019)
19. Pfitzmann, A., Hansen, M.: A terminology for talking about privacy by data minimization: Anonymity, unlinkability, undetectability, unobservability, pseudonymity, and identity management (2010)
20. Spiekermann, S., Acquisti, A., Böhme, R., Hui, K.L.: The challenges of personal data markets and privacy. Electron. Mark. **25**(2), 161–167 (2015)

21. Thomson Reuters 2019: Study finds organizations are not ready for GDPR compliance issues. Technical report (2019). https://legal.thomsonreuters.com/en/insights/articles/study-finds-organizations-not-ready-gdpr-compliance-issues. Accessed 09 July 2019
22. Working Party 29: Guidelines on data protection impact assessment. Technical report (2019)
23. Yazar, Z.: A qualitative risk analysis and management tool-CRAMM. In: SANS InfoSec Reading Room White Paper, vol. 11, pp. 12–32 (2002)

SPOSE Workshop

On the Trade-Off Between Privacy and Utility in Mobile Services: A Qualitative Study

Yang Liu[1,2](✉) and Andrew Simpson[3]

[1] College of Computer Science and Technology, Harbin Institute of Technology (Shenzhen), Shenzhen, China
liu.yang@hit.edu.cn
[2] Cyberspace Security Research Center, Peng Cheng Laboratory, Shenzhen, China
[3] Department of Computer Science, University of Oxford, Oxford, UK
andrew.simpson@cs.ox.ac.uk

Abstract. While the widespread use of mobile services offers a variety of benefits to mobile users, it also raises serious privacy concerns. We report the results of a user study that investigated the factors that influence the decision-making process pertaining to the trade-off between privacy and utility in mobile services. Through two focus groups, 16 individual interviews and a questionnaire survey involving 60 participants, the study identified awareness and knowledge of privacy risks, trust in service providers, desire for mobile services, and belief of cyber privacy as four factors that contribute to the perceived trade-off. The results also suggest that, with appropriate adoption, privacy-preserving tools can positively influence the privacy trade-off. In addition, our findings explore the cultural differences regarding privacy between participants from western countries (with the UK as the main representative) and China. In particular, the results suggest that participants from China are more likely to be comfortable with a government department protecting their individual privacy, while participants from western countries are more likely to wish to see such responsibility reside with some combination of individuals and non-governmental organisations.

Keywords: Privacy · Mobile services · Human aspects

1 Introduction

It is well understood that, almost every time people attempt to use mobile services, they are making a decision to exchange their privacy for benefits. For example, people often need to provide their location to obtain a real-time weather forecast or share their interests to acquire accurate recommendations for goods or activities. Indeed, the economic model behind most free mobile services is based on such trade-offs: when using mobile services provided by Facebook or Google, users do not directly pay the service providers money to download or

S. Katsikas et al. (Eds.): ESORICS 2019 Workshops, LNCS 11980, pp. 261–278, 2020.
https://doi.org/10.1007/978-3-030-42048-2_17

use their mobile services; rather, the mobile platforms collect a vast amount of users' personal data by analysing users' in-app behaviour. The personal data is then used to sell highly targeted ads.

People's attitudes towards such privacy issues vary significantly. Some users would be prepared to abandon the benefits provided by mobile services to protect their personal data. According to a survey of 2,000 Americans conducted by the Pew Research Center [6], 54% of mobile users have decided to not install an app when they discovered how much personal information they would need to share in order to use it and 30% of mobile users have uninstalled an app after discovering it was collecting personal information that they did not wish to share. Some others would enjoy the benefits without considering the potential privacy risks. A field experiment [5] showed that about 93% of participants are willing to provide personal data about their date of birth and monthly income for a 1 Euro discount for purchasing DVDs.

Various privacy-preserving technologies, with examples including permission management tools [10,13], app analysing tools [2,26] and privacy-preserving frameworks in specific fields [17,27], have been proposed to help people decrease their privacy risks when using mobile devices. While the theoretical advantages of such privacy-preserving technologies are clear, little adoption has been observed in practice [4].

Online users' privacy concerns may vary depending on the situation [25]. In terms of mobile services, factors such as perceived convenience [20], perceived financial cost [18], expected degree of information disclosure and potential privacy risks [12] all play important roles and lead people to varying decisions. However, many questions still remain unanswered in this context. Such questions include: what factors influence people's decision-making processes?; what are the benefits of, and barriers to, using privacy-preserving technologies in this context?; what direction might be followed to foster adoption of such technologies?; and do cultural differences play a role?

To start to address these questions, we conducted a qualitative study by combining the methods of focus group sessions (two groups with five participants each), individual interviews (16 participants), and a questionnaire survey (60 participants). The objectives of this study were: to investigate the human factors influencing decision-making pertaining to the trade-off between privacy and utility in mobile services; to explore the direction that might be followed to foster adoption of privacy-preserving technologies that could help mobile users to balance privacy and utility in more effective ways; and to study the impact of cultural differences regarding the protection of privacy.

The paper contributes to the debate surrounding mobile privacy issues and to research into the adoption of privacy-preserving technology. It does so by presenting a detailed description of human factors influencing mobile users' decision making, and by presenting theoretical and practical guidelines for developers who are responsible for designing privacy-aware mobile services and for researchers who are interested in designing privacy-preserving mobile tools.

2 Motivation and Background

Compared to the huge benefits received by users, the cost of mobile services is, on the face of it, extremely cheap. However, users pay with their personal information instead of cash. According to AppBrain [1], by the end of 2017 only about 222,600 of the total 3.5 million apps on Google Play were paid apps, meaning that more than 3.3 million apps were free to download. In addition, only about 275,700 of these free apps offer in-app purchases—most of the rest are totally free to use and rely on in-app ads. The free app business model results in the collecting of a vast amount of users' personal data, as these apps need individuals' data to make the in-app ads highly targeted.

The highly involved mobile services and the free app ecosystem regularly lead mobile users into situations requiring them to make decisions. Almost every time they attempt to use a mobile service, they are making a decision to exchange their privacy (in terms of their personal information (e.g. age, location, monthly income, etc.)) for benefits. The utility of a mobile service is the measure of the worth or value it provides. Attitudes towards the trade-off between privacy and utility vary significantly. The results of a survey conducted by Marketing Land [19] suggest that close to half (46%) of respondents indicated either a neutral or unconcerned reaction to being retargeted by retailers, while the rest have concerns about the potential privacy risks.

Individuals behave inconsistently: not only do different people's attitude vary, but the same user may choose different strategies to handle the trade-offs when using different mobile service as various factors might be involved in their decision-making process. For instance, when facing the trade-off between receiving the benefits of a mobile coupon and giving up personal information, factors such as perceived value and 'coupon proneness' could positively affect the user's acceptance of related apps, whereas perceived fees and perceived privacy risks might impact negatively [15].

The inconsistency between people's privacy attitudes and their final decisions makes for a complicated state of affairs. Deciding to use an app does not necessarily indicate a lack of concern about privacy. Users might take a number of steps such as clearing their browsing and searching history or turning off the location-tracking feature on their mobile devices to protect their personal information before enjoying mobile services. On the other hand, users who claim they have a serious concern about privacy risks might also share their personal information willingly for certain benefits. People's observed behaviour being inconsistent with their reported attitude to privacy is usually termed the *Privacy Paradox* [3].

Our aim is to understand how human factors can impact upon the decision-making process pertaining to the trade-off between privacy and utility in mobile services. We are also interested in understanding whether certain privacy-preserving technologies can positively influence such a trade-off. In addition, we want to explore the impact of cultural differences.

Table 1. Participants description

Group (N)	Type	Description
Cyber security doctoral students (5)	Focus group	Cyber security doctoral students in a university in the UK, between 26–45
Non-technical (5)	Focus group	Adults of various countries, various occupation, and various ages; two members between 26–35, three others between 36–45
Young British adults (8)	Individual interview	Young British citizens, between 26–35
Young Chinese adults (8)	Individual interview	Young Chinese citizens, between 26–35

This research presented several challenges:

1. **Privacy paradox.** Despite the various levels of privacy awareness and knowledge of participants in this study, people's stated attitudes may be influenced by the so-called privacy paradox. As such, users' observed actions should also be used to infer the level of privacy concern [23].
2. **Cultural differences.** Privacy concerns and related approaches of protecting privacy vary between cultures [7]. The interview subjects of our study (26 participants in total) were drawn from diverse cultures and backgrounds (38% were British, 38% were Chinese, and 24% were participants from other countries).
3. **A complex array of factors.** People's decision-making can be affected by a complex array of factors. It is important to declare that the human factors we discuss in this study cannot fully explain the decision-making process. In addition, these factors and their importance to the participants are relatively subjective.

3 Methodology

We now introduce the qualitative approaches adopted in our study and present details of the scenarios and the design of questions.

3.1 Study Approaches and Participants

This study was conducted in Oxford, UK, in February 2017. Two primary qualitative approaches were adopted: focus group interviews (10 participants) and individual interviews (16 participants). In addition, a questionnaire survey (60 participants) also provided auxiliary data.

Focus groups are useful for gathering detailed information about both personal and group feelings [14]. A broader range of information can also be collected from the interaction and discussion among the participants. By contrast, individual interviews are helpful for researchers to probe more deeply on each topic and get information from non-verbal responses [9].

Two groups based on participants' technology backgrounds were selected for the current study. Members of the first group were doctoral students in the field of system and software security. Instead of the strong knowledge of security technology, the second group was internationally diverse: the members are adults from five different countries with different occupational backgrounds. The focus groups were set up in such a way to ensure appropriate interaction within each group and to provide a clear contrast between different groups, enabling us to better discuss how awareness and knowledge of privacy risks might affect the decision-making process.

The participants of individual interviews were also categorised into two groups to investigate the similarities and differences between attitudes between young British citizens and young Chinese citizens. The interviews with Chinese residents were conducted via Skype in the language of Chinese. The individual interview groups were set up in such a way to collect comments from participants from different cultures.

The group size of each focus group session was 5 and the size of each individual interview category was 8. The total number of interview subjects was 26. All participants were asked to complete a questionnaire[1], which was used to deduce participants' privacy attitudes, as a pre-survey before they attended the interview.

Participant recruitment was conducted by posting posters on Facebook and Wechat Moments (social networking), and by circulating advertisements through the mail lists of different departments, colleges, and clubs of Oxford University. All of the subjects were offered a £10 Amazon gift voucher for their time. The distribution of participants is shown in Table 1.

3.2 Scenarios and Data Collection

Wash *et al.* [29] argued that the result reflected by users' actual behaviours is more accurate than that collected by their self-reports when studying certain user decisions. To better measure participants' actual behaviours, a card-exchanging game was applied in the focus group sessions to start off the discussion.

Participants were asked to play the roles of "mobile users" and "service providers" in a two-round card-exchanging game. Five cards representing personal information (including gender, location and contacts list) were issued to "mobile users" and five cards representing mobile services (e.g. real-time weather forecast, recommendations of interested activities and a £5 Amazon voucher)

[1] Full survey text can be accessed here:
https://yangliu.typeform.com/to/OEPM6f (English Version),
https://yang46.typeform.com/to/PR3oWD (Chinese Version).

were issued to "service providers". In the first round, "mobile users" were asked to select between zero and five information cards they can afford to disclose, then exchange them with the corresponding number of service cards decided by "service providers". In this round, "mobile users" were not able to figure out the service cards they could obtain before the trade was finally made. In the second round, "service providers" were asked to show all their service cards before performing the trade. Therefore, "mobile users" were able to choose the particular service cards, and then exchange them with self-selected information cards.

Compared to traditional approaches (e.g. interview or focus group), the card game has an advantage in collecting users' actual behaviours. In the first round, participants are blind to the exact services they might receive, whereas, in the second round, participants are able to exchange specific service with self-selected personal information. Participants' actual behaviours under different conditions are observed and recorded during the game. In addition, the card game served as an icebreaker and helped participants to build mental associations with privacy and utility exchange.

Apart from the card game, the same scenarios were applied in both the focus group sessions and the individual interview sessions to collect participants' comments. At the beginning of each session, five scenarios that mobile users typically encountered in their everyday lives were presented. The aim was to explore participants' experience with balancing privacy and utility related to mobile services. The scenarios were:

- **Scenario 1.** Experience of exposing personal information actively: imagine that you are posting stories or photos on Facebook or Instagram.
- **Scenario 2.** Experience of interacting with mobile system providers: imagine that you are downloading an app from the official Android or iOS app stores.
- **Scenario 3.** Experience of receiving targeted recommendation services: imagine that you are visiting an unfamiliar place and you receive recommendations for useful information such as tourist attractions, hotels and restaurants on your mobile device.
- **Scenario 4.** Experience related to financial activities: imagine that you are doing online shopping on your mobile device.
- **Scenario 5.** Experience related to personal events: imagine that you are managing calendar events on your mobile device.

For each scenario, participants were requested to think about and comment on the following topics.

1. *What type of personal information do you think is being collected in this scenario?* (To explore participants' understanding of privacy leakage.)
2. *Who do you think is collecting your personal information? Where do you think your personal information will end up?* (To explore participants' perceptions of the leakage path of their personal information.)
3. *How do you think they collect or deduce your information?* (To explore participants' knowledge of the different personal information-collecting technologies.)

4. *In what ways do you think your personal information will be used? Do you see any potential risks?* (To explore participants' understanding of privacy risks.)
5. *What utility do you think is obtained in this scenario? Do you think it is worth the cost?* (To explore participants' feelings of, and attitudes toward, the trade-off between privacy and utility.)

They were then presented with a brief introduction to the Privacy-Preserving Targeted Mobile Advertising (PPTMA) framework [17] as an example technology. The framework was applied to the five scenarios to showed how privacy-preserving technologies could help mobile users to take control of their sensitive information. The example also introduced the possibility of taking advantage of mobile services without compromising users' privacy.

After showing the examples, participants were requested to think about and comment on the following topics.

1. *What do you see as the benefits of using such privacy-preserving technologies?*
2. *What do you see as the barriers to using such privacy-preserving technologies?*
3. *Do you think such privacy-preserving technologies could influence your decision-making process with regards to making trade-offs between privacy and utility in mobile services?*
4. *Who do you think should be responsible for certifying that such privacy-preserving technologies do what they say?*

4 Results

The initial results indicate that the focus group members, individual interview members and questionnaire survey participants demonstrated a degree of consistency with regards to their mobile service use. For example, about 80% of them spend more than 60 min on mobile services per day, with more than half of the total participants spending more than 120 min. The devices are mostly used for services such as social networking (90%), searching for information (88%), creating and checking emails (63%), and online shopping (53%). Furthermore, most of the participants had some experience in making decisions involving the trade-off between privacy and utility in mobile services.

4.1 Factors Contributing to the Trade-Off

Awareness and Knowledge of Privacy Risks. It is clear that the awareness and knowledge of privacy leakage is an important factor that strongly influences people's decision-making processes. The differences with regards to this factor between the groups was greater than expected. The findings suggest that the influences vary significantly due to the participants' various backgrounds.

Pötzsch [22] argued that privacy awareness enables people to make informed decisions about the disclosure of data. Our findings suggests that people with limited awareness and knowledge of privacy leakage are more likely to exchange their personal information for mobile services:

Table 2. Auxiliary data: awareness and knowledge of privacy leakage

Questionnaire: To the best of your knowledge, which of the following information is technically possible to be collected/deduced by an app provider when you use an app? (Multiple choices)

Item	China (43 participants)	Western Countries (17)	Frequency in total (60)
Your geographical location	38	16	54
Your phone number	29	15	44
Your contacts	26	12	38
Time of usage	20	17	37
Your email address	23	13	36
Your network operator	20	13	33
The list of apps installed on your phone	17	14	31
⋮	⋮	⋮	⋮
The retail price of your phone	4	7	11

"If I know my privacy is compromised I would not make the trade-off. The key problem is that in many cases I didn't realise my personal information is being collected." (I2P6, Chinese, Female, Individual interview, Semi-skilled worker)

"I personally feel safe. Maybe because that I don't consider myself that important or special. I can't see why they want my information. So if Google requires my location details to provide services I'll give it without thinking about the trade-off" (G2P3, Finnish, Female, Focus group, House person)

On the other hand, many interviewees stated that they refused to make such trade-offs when sensitive information is required for exchanging services.

"Yes, I have refused to install apps that ask for very specific information. I tried to find substitutes in that case." (G2P1, British, Female, Focus group, Professional and managerial occupation)

"I didn't pay for using the apps so I understand they need my information to make money by some means. But for most apps, I would only use them if they promise that the data would only be used in aggregate form." (G1P4, American, Male, Focus group, Cyber security doctoral student)

The findings suggests that limited awareness and knowledge of privacy leakage could positively affect the user's acceptance of mobile services with risks of disclosing personal information. It is noteworthy that some interviewees acknowledged that they normally consider themselves to have serious privacy concerns in a pre-survey; however, in the subsequent card-exchanging game (personal information cards versus mobile services cards), they unconsciously ignored the privacy risks and decided to make the trade-offs.

In addition, our findings show that, while most participants could identify the risks of privacy leakage about the information with a high exposure rate from public media (e.g. geographical location, phone number and contacts), certain personal information that seems difficult to collect (but, in fact, is not) is rarely considered by the users. Take *"the retail price of your mobile"* in Table 2 as an example: it is straightforward to obtain the information of the phone model. The phone model then leads to a precise retail price, which can then be used to deduce the spending power of the phone owner. Overall, participants showed relatively low awareness of such privacy leakage.

Trust in Service Providers. Earp and Baumer [8] found that, if a site or a company is well-known, consumers would be more likely to disclose information to it. Similar comments received in our study suggests that trusting the reputation of a company would weaken users' awareness of privacy risks from such a company and positively impact the adoption of the trade-off. The following representative comment indicates how *trust* can affect users' privacy awareness and subsequently influences decision-making:

> "I feel safe to use some mobile services because the companies like Google or Facebook are famous and so many people are using their services. Furthermore, the government can help to monitor them." (I2P4, Chinese, Female, Individual interview, House person)

However, the extent that *trust* affects *privacy awareness* may vary according to users' knowledge of privacy risks. Although a good reputation is viewed positively by participants with more privacy knowledge, such participants show stronger concerns under the same situation: We also know no

> "I think I'm more scared of potential recruiters or potential employers looking at my profile on Facebook and use it to take advantage of me. So I never post anything public. ... We also know no matter I post it in public or private Facebook is going to get the information. I believe in Facebook as a company, but what about their employees. We all know stories like software engineer may hack into company's servers to steal others' personal information, which happened in Google previously. In addition, company like Facebook may share our profile with countless cooperative advertisers. Can we trust these advertisers as well? All these factors make me feel hesitate to use their services." (G1P5, Chinese, Male, Focus group, Cyber security doctoral student)

Desire for Mobile Services. As already discussed, *awareness and knowledge of privacy risks* clearly influences the decision-making process. We predicted that, in general, a user with a relatively weak awareness of privacy risks is more likely to 'make the deal'. However, our findings suggest that a strong desire for specific mobile services may also enable users with strong knowledge of privacy

Table 3. Auxiliary data: impact of trade-off situations

Questionnaire: What might encourage you to give the information to an app? (Multiple choices)

Item	China (43 participants)	Western Countries (17)	Frequency in total (60)
In exchange for access to the main functions of the app	30	15	45
The app provides a statement regarding how the information is going to be used	18	11	29
If there is no substitute for the app	16	7	23
In exchange for a useful recommendation	10	7	17
If the data would only be used in aggregate form	5	11	16
In exchange for valued-added service	10	3	13
In exchange for a small discount or coupon	3	3	6

leakage to bear the risks. For example, a statement made by a participant shows the ineluctability of using mobile service such as Facebook:

> "I rarely post pictures or comments to Facebook and I'm careful with what I post and where from. However, as a small business, (to advertise my business) I have no choice about being on Facebook. If I didn't have to be I would avoid it." (I1P8, British, Female, Individual interview, Professional and managerial occupation)

Another statement made by a cyber security doctoral student with relatively strong knowledge of privacy risks also indicates how the *desire for mobile services* may work in this context.

> "It's such pain to type in my address or my credit card details every time to shopping online. So I use Amazon app all the time. Because it already got my credit card details, already got my post address. If my friend recommends me a book I can buy it with one click and get it by tomorrow. I know Amazon is collecting my information, that's fine. I chose to have a business relationship with them. I'm happy that they have my address, my credit card details, my purchasing habits. Because I got good recommendation and also get cheaper items from them. I feel like they have more duty not to sell my information because they already got money from me." (G1P2, British, Male, Focus group, Cyber security doctoral student)

These statements suggest that, in some situations, the strong desire for mobile services may overcome the awareness of privacy risks and encourage users to disclose their information. For example, there is no substitute for the Facebook app, and the Amazon app may provide significant benefits—such as useful recommendations. The auxiliary data of Table 3 shows some factors that might encourage users to give personal information to an app.

Beliefs of Cyber Privacy. In addition to the particular situations introduced in Table 3, there is another encouraging factor that can be easily noticed: the common belief that cyber privacy does not exist or that "I've got nothing to hide".

Phelan *et al.* [21] found that the belief that nothing is private online is often used by people as a reference frame to assess marginal risk in the context of privacy concerns related to online data collection. A significant number of participants made similar statements in our study.

> "The services is worth the cost. Because, in fact, there is no so-called 'privacy' in the cyber world nowadays. We're going to give out our privacy anyway, why not exchange it for some benefits?" (I2P1, Chinese, Male, Individual interview, Professional and managerial occupation)

> "Our personal information is not only exposed by mobile. From this aspect, we don't need to feel so sensitive. We are surrounding by internet, who can escape?" (I2P7, Chinese, Female, Individual interview, Semi-skilled worker)

> "There are many ways to use our information. Maybe to improve the service to make you use it more or maybe they just want to sell it or use with advertisers. If we think too much we'll have no app to use, because every app is doing this." (I1P6, British, Male, Individual interview, Student)

4.2 Desired Adoption of, and Trust in, The Privacy-Preserving Technologies

Various types of privacy-preserving technologies have been proposed to help users handle the privacy and utility dilemma [13,17,26]. While the theoretical advantages of such tools are clear, little adoption has been observed in practice [4]. Some researchers have started to explore the direction that might be followed to foster adoption of privacy-preserving technologies [24]. Others (e.g. [16]) have provided foundations for future research on designing incentive schemes for privacy-sensitive users by proposing models to capture the interactions between businesses and consumers in the context of targeted advertising. In this study, we discuss our participants' attitudes with regards to importing privacy-preserving technologies in this context.

Perhaps unsurprisingly, participants' responses suggest that they were in favour of privacy-preserving technologies that can provide utility for users to manage their personal information in mobile devices and can help users to increase their awareness when using mobile services. Such technologies have the

Table 4. Auxiliary data: trust in the privacy-preserving technologies

Questionnaire: Who do you think is responsible to certify such technologies do what they say? (multiple choices)

Item	China (43 participants)	Western Countries (17)	Frequency in total (60)
Government department	22	4	26
Don't know	15	9	26
Organisations	3	5	8
Famous companies	3	1	4
Others	0	1	1

potential to decrease users' privacy concern and establish a win-win situation for both users and mobile service providers.

> "Yes, if I thought any technology could give me better service as a result of more fine-grained information I'd probably agree that such technology would influence my decision making process." (G2P4, Korean, Female, Focus group, white collar worker)

> "Such technologies would make me more likely to download an app if coarse-grained data was collected only." (I1P4, British, Female, Individual interview, Student)

In addition, the same participants' different behaviours observed during the two-round card-exchanging game also echo the adoption of personal information management tools. Compared to the first round of the game, participants suggested that, in the second round—when they could clearly figure out what services they might obtain and when they were able to decide which part of their personal information should be submitted to the service providers—a better decision could be made.

While the necessity for privacy-preserving technologies is clear, participants expressed their concerns about the potential trouble caused by adopting such technologies. For example, some participants worried about the costs of learning how to use such tools. Some provided comments pertaining to their previous experience of receiving disturbing notifications caused by uninterrupted reminders from such tools.

> "It's useful. But I think it's difficult for my parents to learn how to use it. They are not good at IT stuff." (I2P6, Chinese, Female, Individual interview, Semi-skilled worker)

> "I get a bit annoyed once you use some apps and then you start to get notifications (from the privacy-preserving tools) reminding you to protect your data." (G2P5, Australian, Male, Focus group, white collar worker)

Participants also provided comments on basic requirements for decreasing such barriers, including configurability, easy deployment, privacy by default, and automatic activation. In addition to these requirements, there is a major concern about trust in such tools. Many people are still confused about the monitor in this context: who is responsible for certifying that such technologies do what they say? What if a privacy-preserving technology provider steals users' information under the guise of protecting it?

> "It's tricky with electronic stuff. What's that to do with my data? ... If you have that stamp, then we know you follow the rules. That might be easier. But whose job is it (to give the stamp)?" (G2P2, Chinese, Female, Focus group, House person)

A noteworthy percentage (43%) of the participants cannot determine a suitable entity to play this supervisory role. Most of the remainder would be prepared to see an appropriate government department take the role (Table 4):

> "Government should publish related policies, and companies with high reputation should help to implement the policies and monitor related technologies." (I2P5, Chinese, Female, Individual interview, Semi-skilled worker)

> "Maybe the government but can they be trusted? I hope that third party standards exist but I'm not sure if they do and how or who could regulate them." (G2P1, British, Female, Focus group, Professional and managerial occupation)

> "To some extent the person downloading the app is responsible for checking what data will be taken from them, because when he accesses the (Android) app store, the app to be downloaded has already told the him what permission it needs and what information it will collect." (I1P4, British, Female, Individual interview, Student)

Responses on this topic tended to differ between participants from different cultures, which we will explore further in the next subsection.

4.3 Privacy Concerns Across Cultures

Kayes *et al.* [11] argue that users' privacy concerns vary between cultures. Specifically, users from individualistic countries[2] tend to give more weight to privacy protection when compared with those from collectivistic countries[3]. Our study explored the influences of cultural differences regarding the protection of privacy.

The first interesting result emerged when we review the responses associated with "Trust in privacy-preserving technologies". While more than half of Chinese participants (22 out of 43) stated that a government department should

[2] Individualistic countries emphasis on prioritization of self over the group.

[3] Collectivistic countries emphasis on prioritization of the group over self.

play a role in monitoring technology providers, the corresponding figure for participants from western countries was about 24% (4 out of 17). From a different aspect, our findings suggest that users from collectivistic countries are more likely to be comfortable with a government department protecting their individual privacy, while users from individualistic countries are more likely to see the responsibility reside with some combination of individuals and non-governmental organisations. Representative comments from each groups are as follows:

> "I go for the government. Because companies and organisations may take advantage of the monitor position for their own benefits. ... (when asked about the possibility of government surveillance) Maybe, but it's better to put my information in the hands of the government rather than in those of some companies." (I2P2, Chinese, Female, Individual interview, White collar worker)

> "I rely on information from groups such as ORG (Open Rights Group, a UK-based organisation that works to protect the rights to privacy and free speech online) at the moment, but all options such as government, organisations or famous companies are problematic." (I1P8, British, Female, Individual interview, Professional and managerial occupation)

We also saw some similarities between participants from different cultures. For example, with regards to the question "Who is collecting your information? Where will the information end up?", most of the participants from western countries and China both mentioned advertisers, software developers, social network platform such as Facebook and Instagram (mentioned by participants from western countries), or Weibo (mentioned by Chinese participants). None of the 43 Chinese participants mentioned the government, whereas 2 of the 17 participants from western countries proposed the possibility of government surveillance.

It is important to declare that the size of participants was relatively small and the comments made by participants were relatively subjective. However, to a certain extent, our finding suggests that the Chinese participants tend to rely on the government to protect their privacy and mainly care about invasions of privacy by big corporations. The participants from western countries, by contrast, were concerned about the disclosure of personal information to corporations, as well as to government.

5 Discussion

We have reported the results of a user study that investigates the trade-off between privacy and utility in mobile services. The research explored the human factors that influence the decision-making process pertaining to the trade-off and reported the major concerns of adopting privacy-preserving technologies. In addition, the research explored the cultural differences regarding the protection of privacy with participants from the UK and China as an example. Our findings enhanced the theoretical understanding of privacy concerns in this emerging area and provided practical suggestions for stakeholders involved in this context.

Our findings suggest that human factors such as users' understanding of privacy risks, users' trust of service providers, users' desire for mobile services, and their belief of cyber privacy are all important contributing items of the decision-making process. Meanwhile, users are also encouraged to share their information in particular situations.

Most participants expressed a strong desire for adopting privacy-preserving technologies in this context. While there is a potential to establish a win-win situation for users and mobile service providers, participants also showed their concerns about the potential trouble that might be caused by adopting such technologies, including learning cost, frequent reminders, and—a major concern—the need for a governing body to monitor the activities of technology providers. Most Chinese participants stated that government should play such a role; this was less popular with western participants.

This study confirms several findings from the existing research on privacy issues of mobile services. First, this research presented and investigated the human factors that influence the decision-making process pertaining to the trade-off between privacy and utility in mobile services. This advances our understanding of mobile users' behaviour and the potential causes of the privacy paradox. Future research can expand and weigh the factors to build related models. Second, our findings suggested that, although users are aware of their privacy leakage, an appropriate compensation mechanism could still encourage them to get involved in the privacy-trading process. To this end, if users are given corresponding rewards, as well as the ability to make independent choices with regards to releasing specific parts of their personal information, they are more likely to adopt the exchanging relationship with service providers. From this perspective, future research can explore potential strategies to provide mutual benefits for both sides of the trade. Third, this research enhanced the theoretical understanding of the differences of privacy concerns from cross-cultural dimensions. Future research can be conducted to further study the effects of culture on privacy concerns.

This study provides guidelines for mobile service providers who are interested in improving trust to help recruit more privacy-sensitive users. It also shows the direction that might be followed to foster adoption of privacy-preserving technologies to help mobile users in their attempts to balance privacy and utility. First, practical suggestions for mobile service providers or app developers can be provided by examining the factors discussed in this paper. For example, strategies such as providing a statement regarding how users' information is going to be used in apps, using data in only aggregate form, or providing valued-added service and coupons can effectively encourage users to release the information and apply the related mobile services. Second, the findings suggested that more attention should be paid to enhancing users' trust in privacy-preserving technologies. Although the benefits of applying such technologies are clear, users' distrust can negatively affect the adoption. Third, our findings suggested that, with regards to the role of supervising privacy-preserving technologies, none of the government departments, non-governmental organisations or large companies can in isolation obtain users' trust. It would appear that a mechanism that involves all of these stakeholders would be most palatable.

As with any empirical research, our study has limitations. First, the number of participants is relatively small and the participants themselves have a degree of imbalance: the total number of participants is 60, with 17 participants from western countries and 43 participants from China. (Although there are precedents: in a previous study, 22 people working in the IoT field were interviewed in Finland and in China (11 people respectively) to investigate their different personal perspectives on individual privacy in the IoT [28].) Second, the main participants in our research are young adults—most of whom had received undergraduate or post-graduate education. A future study will give consideration to a broader range of users. Third, the factors and their importance provided by participants are relatively subjective. Again, a larger sample in future work will inevitably help to mitigate such subjectiveness.

Acknowledgments. The authors thank the participants of the survey for their valuable comments. We are grateful to the reviewers for their constructive and helpful comments. We also wish to thank Norbert Nthala, Emma Osborn and Aaron Ceross for discussions that helped to improve this work. This work is partly supported by the National Key Research and Development Program of China (2017YFB0802204), Key Research and Development Program for Guangdong Province, China (2019B010136001), and Basic Research Project of Shenzhen, China (JCYJ20180507183624136).

References

1. AppBrain. Google Play Stats (2017). http://www.appbrain.com/stats. Accessed Dec 2017
2. Bal, G., Rannenberg, K., Hong, J.: Styx: design and evaluation of a new privacy risk communication method for smartphones. In: Cuppens-Boulahia, N., Cuppens, F., Jajodia, S., Abou El Kalam, A., Sans, T. (eds.) SEC 2014. IAICT, vol. 428, pp. 113–126. Springer, Heidelberg (2014). https://doi.org/10.1007/978-3-642-55415-5_10
3. Barnes, S.B.: A privacy paradox: social networking in the united states. First Monday **11**(9) (2006). https://doi.org/10.5210/fm.v11i9.1394
4. Benenson, Z., Girard, A., Krontiris, I.: User acceptance factors for anonymous credentials: an empirical investigation. In: Workshop on the Economics of Information Security (WEIS 2015) (2015)
5. Beresford, A.R., Kübler, D., Preibusch, S.: Unwillingness to pay for privacy: a field experiment. Econ. Lett. **117**(1), 25–27 (2012)
6. Boyles, J.L., Smith, A., Madden, M.: Privacy and data management on mobile devices, vol. 4. Pew Internet & American Life Project (2012)
7. Cooper, R., Assal, H., Chiasson, S.: Cross-national privacy concerns on data collection by government agencies. In: Proceedings of the 15th International Conference on Privacy, Security and Trust (PST), pp. 28–30 (2017)

8. Earp, J.B., Baumer, D.: Innovative web use to learn about consumer behavior and online privacy. Commun. ACM **46**(4), 81–83 (2003)
9. Gorden, R.L.: Interviewing: Strategy, Techniques, and Tactics. Dorsey Press, Homewood (1969)
10. Holavanalli, S., et al.: Flow permissions for Android. In: Proceedings of the 28th IEEE/ACM International Conference on Automated Software Engineering (ASE 2013), pp. 652–657. IEEE, Palo Alto (2013)
11. Kayes, I., Kourtellis, N., Quercia, D., Iamnitchi, A., Bonchi, F.: Cultures in community question answering. In: Proceedings of the 26th ACM Conference on Hypertext & Social Media (HT 2015), pp. 175–184. ACM (2015)
12. Keith, M.J., Thompson, S.C., Hale, J., Lowry, P.B., Greer, C.: Information disclosure on mobile devices: re-examining privacy calculus with actual user behavior. Int. J. Hum Comput Stud. **71**(12), 1163–1173 (2013)
13. Kern, M., Sametinger, J.: Permission tracking in Android. In: Proceedings of the 6th International Conference on Mobile Ubiquitous Computing, Systems, Services and Technologies (UBICOMM 2012), Barcelona, Spain, pp. 148–155 (2012)
14. Kitzinger, J.: Qualitative research: introducing focus groups. BMJ: Br. Med. J. **311**(7000), 299 (1995)
15. Liu, F., Zhao, X., Chau, P.Y., Tang, Q.: Roles of perceived value and individual differences in the acceptance of mobile coupon applications. Internet Res. **25**(3), 471–495 (2015)
16. Liu, Y., Simpson, A.: Privacy-preserving targeted mobile advertising: formal models and analysis. In: Livraga, G., Torra, V., Aldini, A., Martinelli, F., Suri, N. (eds.) DPM/QASA -2016. LNCS, vol. 9963, pp. 94–110. Springer, Cham (2016). https://doi.org/10.1007/978-3-319-47072-6_7
17. Liu, Y., Simpson, A.C.: Privacy-preserving targeted mobile advertising: requirements, design and a prototype implementation. Softw.: Pract. Exp. **46**(12), 1657–1684 (2016)
18. Luo, X., Li, H., Zhang, J., Shim, J.P.: Examining multi-dimensional trust and multi-faceted risk in initial acceptance of emerging technologies: an empirical study of mobile banking services. Decis. Support Syst. **49**(2), 222–234 (2010)
19. Marvin, G.: Survey: 3 out of 4 consumers now notice retargeted ads (2016). http://marketingland.com/3-out-4-consumers-notice-retargeted-ads-67813. Accessed July 2017
20. Okazaki, S., Mendez, F.: Exploring convenience in mobile commerce: moderating effects of gender. Comput. Hum. Behav. **29**(3), 1234–1242 (2013)
21. Phelan, C., Lampe, C., Resnick, P.: It's creepy, but it doesn't bother me. In: Proceedings of the 2016 CHI Conference on Human Factors in Computing Systems (CHI 2016), pp. 5240–5251. ACM (2016)
22. Pötzsch, S.: Privacy awareness: a means to solve the privacy paradox? In: Matyáš, V., Fischer-Hübner, S., Cvrček, D., Švenda, P. (eds.) Privacy and Identity 2008. IAICT, vol. 298, pp. 226–236. Springer, Heidelberg (2009). https://doi.org/10.1007/978-3-642-03315-5_17
23. Preibusch, S.: Guide to measuring privacy concern: review of survey and observational instruments. Int. J. Hum. Comput. Stud. **71**(12), 1133–1143 (2013)
24. Sabouri, A.: On the user acceptance of privacy-preserving attribute-based credentials – a qualitative study. In: Livraga, G., Torra, V., Aldini, A., Martinelli, F., Suri, N. (eds.) DPM/QASA -2016. LNCS, vol. 9963, pp. 130–145. Springer, Cham (2016). https://doi.org/10.1007/978-3-319-47072-6_9
25. Sheehan, K.B.: Toward a typology of internet users and online privacy concerns. Inf. Soc. **18**(1), 21–32 (2002)

26. Taylor, V.F., Martinovic, I.: Securank: starving permission-hungry apps using contextual permission analysis. In: Proceedings of the 6th Workshop on Security and Privacy in Smartphones and Mobile Devices, SPSM 2016, pp. 43–52. ACM, New York (2016)
27. Toubiana, V., Narayanan, A., Boneh, D., Nissenbaum, H., Barocas, S.: Adnostic: privacy preserving targeted advertising. In: Proceedings of the 17th Annual Network and Distributed System Security Symposium (NDSS), San Diego, CA, USA, p. 2010 (2010)
28. Virkki, J., Chen, L.: Personal perspectives: individual privacy in the IoT. Adv. Internet Things **3**(02), 21 (2013)
29. Wash, R., Rader, E., Fennell, C.: Can people self-report security accurately?: agreement between self-report and behavioral measures. In: Proceedings of the 2017 CHI Conference on Human Factors in Computing Systems (CHI 2017), pp. 2228–2232. ACM (2017)

Analysis of Automation Potentials in Privacy Impact Assessment Processes

Jan Zibuschka(✉)

Robert Bosch GmbH, 70465 Renningen, Stuttgart, Germany
jan.zibuschka@de.bosch.com
http://www.bosch.com/research

Abstract. With the recent introduction of the EU's General Data Protection Regulation (GDPR), privacy impact assessments (PIA) have become mandatory in many cases. To support organisations in correctly implementing those, researchers and practitioners have provided reference processes and tooling. Integrating automation features into PIA tools can streamline the implementation of compliant privacy impact assessments in organizations. Based on a general reference architecture and reference process based on guidance by authorities, this contribution offers a systematic analysis of which process steps show the most promise with regard to this, and discusses impediments to this approach and directions for future research.

Keywords: Data protection · Privacy impact assessment · Model-based engineering · Business processes

1 Introduction

In its Article 35, the recent European General Data Protection Regulation mandates the controller performs a privacy impact assessment where processing of personal information is likely to result in a high risk to the rights and freedoms of individuals [15]. Specifically, this applies to cases of profiling, surveillance of public places, or large-scale processing of personal information [3]. Similar requirements are set forth by other international regulators, e.g. for governmental information processing in Canada [18]. Organizations across Europe have established processes to perform such privacy impact assessments, across all business sectors, including industry, telecommunications, and electronics [19]. Whether those were implemented in response to the new legal requirement or existed previously, in any case the processes need to be reviewed in light of new regulation.

Enterprise information systems are proven tool to integrate and extend business processes [21], and also offer the chance to prescribe specific processes. While this effect may be detrimental to organisation if it is not employed consciously [7], implementing enterprise systems supporting privacy impact analysis holds

S. Katsikas et al. (Eds.): ESORICS 2019 Workshops, LNCS 11980, pp. 279–286, 2020.
https://doi.org/10.1007/978-3-030-42048-2_18

the promise to ensure compliance. Additionally, offering tool support for PIA[1] processes reduces time and effort organizations need to spend, which have been cited as main arguments against mandatory PIAs [18].

This contribution reviews a process [4] and tooling [5] proposed by some European data protection authorities, identifying subprocesses that are not currently supported by tools, but offer a significant potential to be supported by automation features in next generation tools.

The rest of the paper is structured as follows: In the following section, we provide related work, including processes and tooling for privacy impact assessments as well as related disciplines, specifically security engineering and model-based engineering. After this, we introduce some assumptions about tool architecture and capabilities, which form the basis for the following section, which holds a step-by-step analysis of automation potentials in a specific PIA process. We conclude by discussing our findings and next steps.

2 Related Work

There is a significant body of work on privacy impact assessments. PIA support has been identified as one of the essential functions of systems supporting implementation of the GDPR [16]. Several processes for PIA have been documented in literature [1,4,18]. We base our analysis on Bieker et al. [4], as it is based on the (mandatory) European General Data Protection Regulation, captures legal requirements as it is authored by legal professionals, and is provided by members of a data protection authority. It also itself is based on a review of several earlier process models.

In addition to a process model, which is one of the ones reviewed by [4], French data protection authority CNIL also provide a tool for PIA [5] that produces standardized documentation based on a questionnaire and knowledge base. The knowledge base that comes with the tool covers both legal and technical aspects, aiding in the characterization of assessed systems. A wide range of modelling approaches for the meta-information used in such PIA exists [6].

As privacy impact analysis processes mirror security engineering processes within organizations [12] – for example with regard to threat analysis [20] – we can also draw upon ideas from the security engineering domain. Originally also based on questionnaire approaches [17], model-based security engineering a long-running trend [2]. Tooling has emerged that automates part of threat modelling based on system models, e.g. Microsoft's Threat Modelling Tool or OWASP Threat Dragon [12]. In other domains, model-based engineering has lead to a large degree of automation [13]. Automation potentials have also been explored for security engineering, identifying both potentials and restrictions in automation of security controls [9]. It is the aim of this contribution to offer a similar analysis for the case of PIAs.

---

[1] we use the terms privacy impact assessment and data protection impact assessment interchangeably.

3 Envisioned System Architecture

While an investigation of automated security controls can build on extensive standards [9], tools for privacy impact assessments are less standardized. To avoid confusion, we provide a coarse-grained overview of our fundamental perspective and terminology regarding tooling for PIA in this section.

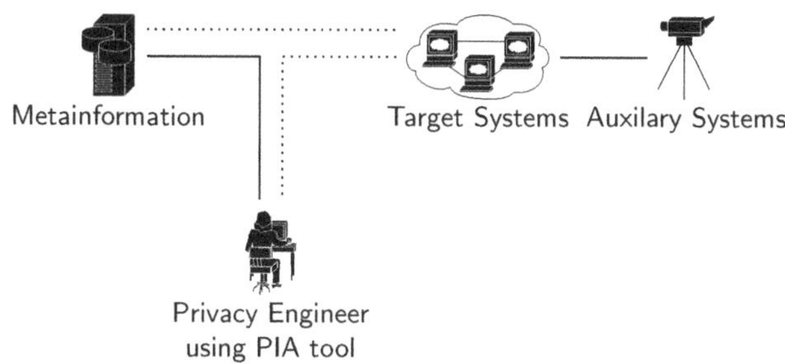

Fig. 1. System overview (solid lines: current-gen (metainformation), dotted lines: next-gen (system access).)

We differentiate three maturity levels, roughly reflecting no automation, current generation tooling and current research in related fields, and automation going beyond the capabilities of current approaches:

1. **No Tooling:** The baseline of our analysis; an organization that does not use any tooling for privacy impact assessments.
2. **Current-Gen:** PIA tools need access to meta-information about the target system and its environment to generate the documentation required as a result of the PIA process [3]. Current generation tools (such as CNIL PIA [5]) leverage questionnaires and selection from pre-defined knowledge bases to elicit this information, mirroring approaches from the security engineering space [17]. PIAs can also benefit from the use of conventional project management software for projecting the assessment, and threat modelling tools [12] can also be used in the process, i.e. for identification of relevant protection goals.
3. **Next-Gen:** Next generation tools could offer direct integration with the target system, enabling both access to information, specifically personal information, within the system during PIA, and derivation of meta-information from the current state of the system. The motivation for developing tooling in this direction is founded in existing behavioural and business research: one of the main impediments to security operations in contemporary organizations is lack of access to systems and information [14], automation in privacy processes has been shown to be preferred by end users [22], and synchronization between models and real systems, i.e. round-trip engineering, could avoid errors resulting from incorrect meta-information, and has proven

valuable in many domains where model-based engineering is employed [13]. We also assume today's capabilities regarding automation functions, e.g. security automation as described in [9].

Figure 1 gives an overview of the resulting reference architecture that underlies the analysis in this contribution: a privacy engineer uses a PIA tool that has access to meta-information about the target system. In a more sophisticated setup, the tool also has access to the target system, and meta-information can be read directly from the target system. However, the target system my still have auxiliary systems that cannot be accessed by the PIA tooling directly, though information about them may be present in the target system.

4 Process Analysis

This section provides a step-by-step walk-through of PIA subprocesses based on the PIA process proposed by [4]. For each subprocess, it gives an analysis of existing tooling and automation potential.

4.1 Preparation Stage

During preparation of a PIA, current tools mainly support in projecting the assessment (step A2 according to [4]). Those are not specialized privacy engineering tools; rather, generic project management software can be used.

Our proposed next generation tooling can support, first and foremost in describing the target system (step A3). System structure, data within the system, and data flows could be detected automatically. This enables automatic generation of system models for the PIA process.

In addition, information derived from the system may also support the decision whether a PIA is necessary, and documentation of the motivation for this decision (step A1). Once again, it could be automatically detected whether the system holds sensitive personal information. Tracing of the system structure can also aid in deciding whether development has progressed so much that a renewed PIA process has to be triggered.

It should be noted that an initial PIA needs to be performed before a mechanism for collecting or processing personal information is implemented. Collecting meta-information from information technology may still be useful, as infrastructural systems that are envisioned to be used for processing of personal information may already be present, or the future target system may even already be running on dummy information.

Overall, the role of next-generation tooling in the preparation stage would be to offer a basis for identification of organizational stakeholders, concerned individuals, and relevant legal requirements based on a model that would still be in part provided by a privacy engineer answering questionnaires, but would also in part be automatically derived from the target system, as can be seen from our illustration in Fig. 2.

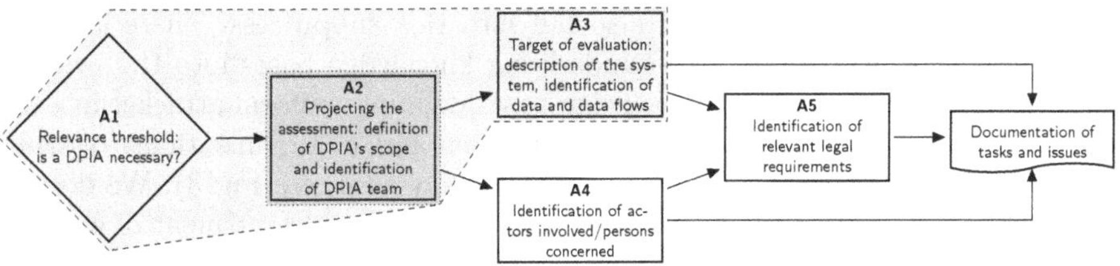

Fig. 2. Tooling in preparation stage [4] (dotted dark: current-gen tooling; dashed light: next-gen automation potentials.)

4.2 Evaluation Stage

During the evaluation of the target system, privacy engineers can already use threat modelling tools from the security space, which can derive protection goals (step B1) from a model of the system and its stakeholders, considering communication between subsystems and trust boundaries, and research also has provided approaches taking into account an overall risk level [12]. The models underlying those tools can be extended with privacy-specific threats and risks, as illustrated by CNIL's PIA tool [5].

In addition, to support a consistent assessment of various target systems within an organization and beyond, organizations, data protection authorities or standardization bodies could build knowledge bases of attacker models and evaluation criteria for various domains and systems, which could then serve as a basis for tooling in identification and characterization of potential attackers and evaluation benchmarks (steps B2 and B3). These steps can also be supported by business process information [8], that can be accessed by e.g. integrating ERP systems, which may already be accessible via the project management software (cmp. step A2, Sect. 4.1).

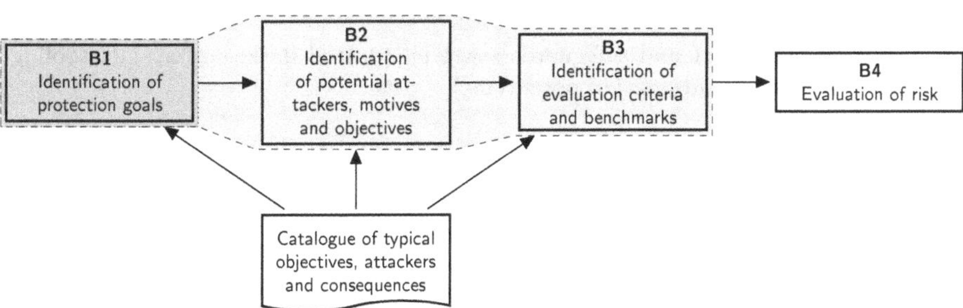

Fig. 3. Tooling in evaluation stage [4] (dotted dark: current-gen tooling; dashed light: next-gen automation potentials.)

Overall, tooling during the evaluation stage, especially threat modelling tools, are already common in the security space, and the most advanced functions provided by current PIA tooling also fall into this subprocess. There is additional potential for extending the underlying knowledge bases into the privacy space and offering specialized knowledge bases defining uniform attacker models and evaluation benchmarks for various domains and/or organizations, offering a standardized basis for the evaluation of risk (step B4, see Fig. 3). We do not envision the automation of the evaluation of risk itself, as assessment of e.g. the proportionality of processing typically performed in this step [4] can hardly be performed in an unsupervised fashion.

4.3 Report and Safeguards Stage

Following the evaluation, in the final stage of the PIA process, a report describing the evaluation results is created and appropriate safeguards are selected and implemented. Current generation tools for PIA (such as [5]) can generate standardized reports as an output, which is the main artefact used to demonstrate that a PIA has been performed.

As a continuation of the evaluation stage, next-gen PIA systems could also support developers in the selection of appropriate safeguards (step C1, see Fig. 4); research approaches have already made first steps in this direction [8]. We do not, however, consider the actual implementation of those controls (C4) as amenable to automation, as this would require complex orchestration even for most technical controls, and seems entirely implausible for organizational measures.

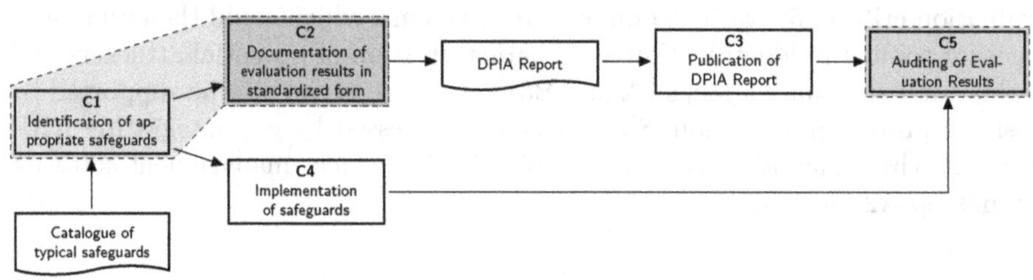

Fig. 4. Tooling in report and safeguards stage [4] (dotted dark: current-gen tooling; dashed light: next-gen automation potentials.)

While an automatic publication of the PIA report is certainly possible, as organizations may want to scrutinize the report for business secrets before a sanitized version is published [4], we do not see this as a next gen-feature.

On the other hand, generating the report (step C2) in a machine-readable manner could also the basis for automation in auditing of the target system with regard to the report (step C5). In this case, the user of the tool would not be a project privacy engineer, but an auditor reviewing the report resulting from a PIA. Automated auditing measures could also help in determining when a new PIA cycle needs to be started based on identified deviations between the state of the target system and the current PIA report. This closes the PIA loop described in [4], as a new preparation stage begins (see Sect. 4.1).

5 Discussion

There are clear directions for future research. We do not offer a complete system architecture implementing automation in privacy impact assessments. Clearly, integrating existing project management, privacy impact assessment, and threat modelling tools, and providing integration with the target system has the promise of significantly lowering efforts for PIA implementation, addressing one of the core arguments of its opponents [18]. To address additional effort caused by the need to model the target system, we propose automatic generation of the model, with the long term goal of round-trip engineering, a proven approach from other model-driven engineering domains [13]. Experience from security response centres also suggests that tooling giving access to target systems can address many pain points in day-to-day operations [14].

The less technical nature of determining the privacy impact, compared to more technical security engineering approaches, may pose additional problems for concrete implementations due to the interdisciplinary nature of privacy analyses, covering legal, economic, and societal in addition to technical aspects [11]. We need to avoid codifying in technology [7], and specifically automating, things that do not necessarily apply in all cases from a legal perspective [10]. In addition, adding automation in privacy impact assessments may reduce the awareness for privacy issues generated by a manual privacy impact assessment [19]. This concern may already apply to the current-gen CNIL tool, which we do not envision to replace but merely extend.

We offer this contribution as a basis for discussion of the merits and flaws of such systems. To evaluate the real-world applicability of our approach, it should be evaluated what does and does not work for various target systems, and which part of typical target systems would remain auxiliary and inaccessible by PIA tools.

References

1. Ahmadian, A.S., Strüber, D., Riediger, V., Jürjens, J.: Supporting privacy impact assessment by model-based privacy analysis. In: Proceedings of the 33rd Annual ACM Symposium on Applied Computing, pp. 1467–1474. ACM Press (2018)
2. Baskerville, R.: Information systems security design methods: implications for information systems development. ACM Comput. Surv. **25**(4), 375–414 (1993)
3. Bieker, F., Bremert, B., Hansen, M.: Die Risikobeurteilung nach der DSGVO. Datenschutz Datensicherheit DuD **42**(8), 492–496 (2018)
4. Bieker, F., Friedewald, M., Hansen, M., Obersteller, H., Rost, M.: A process for data protection impact assessment under the European general data protection regulation. In: Schiffner, S., Serna, J., Ikonomou, D., Rannenberg, K. (eds.) APF 2016. LNCS, vol. 9857, pp. 21–37. Springer, Cham (2016). https://doi.org/10.1007/978-3-319-44760-5_2
5. CNIL: PIA Software (2019). https://www.cnil.fr/en/open-source-pia-software-helps-carry-out-data-protection-impact-assesment/. Accessed 26 June 2019

6. Dewitte, P., et al.: A comparison of system description models for data protection by design. In: Proceedings of the 34th ACM/SIGAPP Symposium on Applied Computing, pp. 1512–1515. ACM Press (2019)
7. Gosain, S.: Enterprise information systems as objects and carriers of institutional forces: the new iron cage? J. AIS **5**(4), 6 (2004)
8. Kokolakis, S., Demopoulos, A., Kiountouzis, E.: The use of business process modelling in information systems security analysis and design. Inf. Manag. Comput. Secur. **8**(3), 107–116 (2000)
9. Montesino, R., Fenz, S.: Information security automation: how far can we go? In: Sixth International Conference on Availability, Reliability and Security, pp. 280–285. IEEE (2011)
10. Pagallo, U., Durante, M.: The pros and cons of legal automation and its governance. Eur. J. Risk Regul. **7**(2), 323–334 (2016)
11. Radmacher, M., Zibuschka, J., Scherner, T., Fritsch, L., Rannenberg, K.: Privatsphärenfreundliche topozentrische Dienste unter Berücksichtigung rechtlicher, technischer und wirtschaftlicher Restriktionen. In: 8 Internationale Tagung Wirtschaftsinformatik 2007 - Band 1, pp. 237–254 (2007)
12. Sion, L., Van Landuyt, D., Yskout, K., Joosen, W.: SPARTA: security & privacy architecture through risk-driven threat assessment. In: 2018 International Conference on Software Architecture Companion, pp. 89–92. IEEE (2018)
13. Streitferdt, D., Wendt, G., Nenninger, P., Nyßen, A., Lichter, H.: Model driven development challenges in the automation domain. In: 32nd Annual Computer Software and Applications Conference, pp. 1372–1375. IEEE (2008)
14. Sundaramurthy, S.C., McHugh, J., Ou, X., Wesch, M., Bardas, A.G., Rajagopalan, S.R.: Turning contradictions into innovations or: how we learned to stop whining and improve security operations. In: SOUPS 2016, pp. 237–251. USENIX Association, Denver (2016)
15. Tikkinen-Piri, C., Rohunen, A., Markkula, J.: EU general data protection regulation: changes and implications for personal data collecting companies. Comput. Law Secur. Rev. **34**(1), 134–153 (2018)
16. Tsohou, A., et al.: Privacy, security, legal and technology acceptance requirements for a GDPR compliance platform. In: SECPRE Workshop at ESORICS 2019. Springer, Luxembourg (2019)
17. Vermeulen, C., Von Solms, R.: The information security management toolbox - taking the pain out of security management. Inf. Manag. Comput. Secur. **10**(3), 119–125 (2002)
18. Wright, D.: Should privacy impact assessments be mandatory? Commun. ACM **54**(8), 121 (2011)
19. Wright, D.: The state of the art in privacy impact assessment. Comput. Law Secur. Rev. **28**(1), 54–61 (2012)
20. Wuyts, K., Scandariato, R., Joosen, W.: Empirical evaluation of a privacy-focused threat modeling methodology. J. Syst. Softw. **96**, 122–138 (2014)
21. Xu, L.D.: Enterprise systems: state-of-the-art and future trends. IEEE Trans. Ind. Inform. **7**(4), 630–640 (2011)
22. Zibuschka, J., Nofer, M., Zimmermann, C., Hinz, O.: Users' preferences concerning privacy properties of assistant systems on the Internet of Things. In: Proceedings of the Twenty-fifth Americas Conference on Information Systems, AIS (2019)

An Insight into Decisive Factors in Cloud Provider Selection with a Focus on Security

Sebastian Pape(✉) and Jelena Stankovic

Chair of Mobile Business and Multilateral Security, Goethe University Frankfurt, Frankfurt, Germany
sebastian.pape@m-chair.de

Abstract. In the last ten years cloud computing has developed from a buzz word to the new computing paradigm on a global scale. Computing power or storage capacity can be bought and consumed flexibly and on-demand, which opens up new opportunities for cost-saving and data processing. However, it also goes with security concerns as it represents a form of IT outsourcing. We investigate how these concerns manifest as a decisive factor in cloud provider selection by interviews with eight practitioners from German companies. As only a moderate interest is discovered, it is further examined why this is the case. Additionally, we compared the results from a systematic literature survey on cloud security assurance to cloud customers' verification of their providers' security measures. This paper provides a qualitative in-depth examination of companies' attitudes towards security in the cloud. The results of the analysed sample show that security is not necessarily decisive in cloud provider selection. Nevertheless, providers are required to guarantee security and comply. Traditional forms of assurance techniques play a role in assessing cloud providers and verifying their security measures. Moreover, compliance is identified as a strong driver to pursue security and assurance.

Keywords: Cloud provider selection · Security assurance · Interviews

1 Introduction

Cloud Computing has been emerging as the new computing paradigm in the last ten years, enabling consumers to purchase computing power and storage capacity on-demand, conveniently and cost efficiently from specialized providers. Recent studies claim that cloud computing has left the hype phase behind and can already be considered the norm for IT [10].

Besides the potential economic benefits of cloud adoption, it also goes with security concerns as it represents a form of IT outsourcing and exhibits technological peculiarities concerning size, structure and geographical dispersion [35]. With rising adoption rates of cloud services, security concerns remained

S. Katsikas et al. (Eds.): ESORICS 2019 Workshops, LNCS 11980, pp. 287–306, 2020.
https://doi.org/10.1007/978-3-030-42048-2_19

unchanged or even rose as well. On the other hand, many technical reports also reveal benefits to security in the cloud. It is argued that a cloud provider (CP) enjoys economies of scale in terms of security as well, being able to invest more and thereby achieve a higher security level on a much larger scale than most client companies would with an in-house data centre [24,29]. Thus, in either case, one would expect companies to incorporate security into their provider selection and cloud use.

We investigate organizations' practises when selecting a secure CP: *"What role does security play in CP selection?"*. Despite expected "inherent differences in such things as the intended purpose, assets held, legal obligations, exposure to the public, threats faced, and tolerance to risk" between different companies or organizations [29], we expected to verify the importance of security. Under that assumption there would be an incentive for providers to invest in security measures, as potential customers might make their choice based on this characteristic [24]. Moreover, in order to prevent a market for lemons in cloud computing [1], we expected cloud service providers and customers to come up with quality/security assurance methods. Thus, we intended the follow-up question: *How are the providers' security measures verified?* – if security is a selection criteria. Or respectively: *Why is security not considered in CP selection?*

In order to find answers for the underlying research questions a qualitative approach is taken. Practitioners from eight German companies who are associated with CP selection are interviewed and questioned about their companies' provider selection and ways to establish assurance.

2 Related Work

Our research questions can be related to contributions on provider selection, the role of security and security assurance. Security concerns, which are seen as the inhibiting factor of cloud adoption, can be easily related to well researched issues. A bunch of issues is related to technical properties of cloud computing, i.e. the complex architecture [29], multi-tenancy in connection with isolation failures [24,29], and network vulnerabilities The list of risks also includes the threat of a malicious insider on the CP's side [9], who may abuse his privileges. However, this is a general outsourcing issues due to a loss of governance which can bear dangers for the cloud customers [24]. Therefore, focus in this section is on measures for the CP to assure the security level of its service (corresponding to our extended research question). Assurance is also often necessary from a legal and compliance perspective since most companies underlie a variety of legal obligations, depending on the sector and the type of data they handle.

Since we follow the qualitative content analysis method which is considered hermeneutic and uses deductive examination (cf. Sect. 3.2), an inherent understanding of the topic was necessary in order to interpret the material. Therefore, we conducted a systematic literature survey on security assurance measures.

Table 1. Reviewed contributions

Assurance	Contribution	Model proposals
SLAs	Lee et al. [40], Luna et al. [44]	Casola et al. [11], Kaaniche et al. [31], Nugraha and Martin [53]
Monitoring	Ismail et al. [27]	Ba et al. [8], Deng et al. [17], Fernando et al. [21], Kanstrén et al. [32], Rios et al. [62], Zhang et al. [71,72]
Testing		Sotiriadis et al. [67], Stephanow and Khajehmoogahi [68], Tung et al. [70]
Auditing	Ryoo et al. [64]	Ghutugade and Patil [22], Jakhotia et al. [28], Jiang et al. [30], Lins et al. [42,43], Ma et al. [45], Majumdar et al. [47], Meera and Geethakumari [48], More and Chaudhari [50], Parasuraman et al. [55], Pasquier et al. [56], Rashmi and Sangve [59], Rewadkar and Ghatage [61], Thendral and Valliyammai [69]
Certification	Di Giulio et al. [18], Di Giulio et al. [19], Polash and Shiva [57], Schneider et al. [65]	Anisetti et al. [3–5], Anisetti et al. [6], Katopodis et al. [33], Krotsiani and Spanoudakis [34], Lins et al. [41], Munoz and Mafia [51]
Other		Henze et al. [25], Mohammed and Pathan [49], Ramokapane et al. [58], Rizvi et al. [63], Sen and Madria [66]

2.1 Security Assurance

We rely on a survey from Ardagna et al. [7] which covers contributions on security measures and assurance techniques until 2014 and followed their methods and definitions as close as possible to update it for our recent research. Due to space limitations, we can not show the results in detail, but only give a brief summary and list them in Table 1.

Almost all contributions reasoned with customers' security concerns as the main inhibiting factor of cloud adoption and that a contribution might provide the needed transparency to resolve that issue. A further justification for new contributions on security assurance were the "special properties" of the cloud which raise new requirements for that topic. Clearly each contribution presented the benefits of its solution, some also covered the challenges, but the drawbacks of certain assurance techniques could only be found in a few contributions from adjacent categories. Certification and security SLAs were presented as the more accessible and convenient measures. In these contributions the customer is clearly involved in the negotiation and provider choice. On the contrary, contributions on auditing, monitoring and testing are mostly technical models or frameworks.

It might be difficult to apply these technical models and is it not clear if they are practical in reality and who would implement them.

2.2 CP Selection

In this section qualitative research which determined relevant criteria for CP selection will be discussed. The presented contributions suggest a formal and systematic selection process of a CP and identify security as a relevant criterion. They pursue similar research questions and use a qualitative approach like we do. Nevertheless, their results are narrowed down into compact lists, where security is identified as a requirement but not further discussed. We aim to close this gap, by giving further insight into experts' answers and the role of security.

Repschläger et al. [60] develop a CP classification model with a focus on infrastructure as a service (IaaS). The relevant target dimensions are determined as a result of expert interviews and validated and expanded through a literature review. The authors conduct five interviews with experts providing different perspectives on common objectives in cloud computing.

Similarly, Hetzenecker et al. [26] derive a model of requirements to support the user in evaluating CPs. Their model consists of six categories with in total 41 requirements. "Information security" is derived as a category with 15 requirements, such as integrity, availability, data disposal, encryption or scalability. All requirements are only presented by a title but not further elaborated.

Lang et al. [39] conduct a Delphi study with 19 decision makers in order to determine relevant selection criteria with a high abstraction level. Security is only identified as a component of the highest rated criterion "functionality" which does not permit to make any statements about the importance of security at all. The authors call for further research to investigate their identified requirements on a lower abstraction level.

2.3 Security, Threat Models and Compliance

Following the CSA top threats to cloud computing [12–15] as shown in Table 2 one can see that most of the threats are related to security and that data breaches soon evolve as the top threat. In an extensive survey Kumar and Goyal [37] map the threats also to requirements, vulnerabilities and countermeasures. Alhenaki et al. [2] investigate some of the threats mentioned by the CSA, do also a mapping to countermeasures and additionally identify the relevant cloud service models (Saas, PaaS, IaaS) which are concerned by the threats. Mahesh et al. [46] elaborate aspects of cloud computing that need special attention, i.e. by audits. They also list most prominent frameworks and working groups that are widely accepted across industries and describe some approaches from industry practices.

3 Methodology

In this section we briefly describe how the interviews were conducted and how the data was analysed.

Table 2. Top threats to cloud computing identified by CSA [12–15]

#	2010	2013	2016	2019
1	Abuse and nefarious use of cloud computing	Data breaches	Data breaches	Data breaches
2	Insecure application programming interfaces	Data loss	Weak identity, credential and access management	Misconfiguration and inadequate change control
3	Malicious insiders	Account hijacking	Insecure APIs	Lack of cloud security architecture and strategy
4	Shared technology vulnerabilities	Insecure APIs	System and application vulnerabilities	Insufficient identity, credential, access and key management
5	Data loss/leakage	Denial of service	Account hijacking	Account hijacking
6	Account, service & traffic hijacking	Malicious insiders	Malicious insiders	Insider threat
7	Unknown risk profile	Abuse of cloud services	Advanced persistent threats (APTs)	Insecure interfaces and APIs
8	–	Insufficient due diligence	Data loss	Weak control plane
9	–	Shared technology issues	Insufficient due diligence	Metastructure and applistructure failures
10	–	–	Abuse and nefarious use of cloud services	Limited cloud usage visibility
11	–	–	Denial of service	Abuse and nefarious use of cloud services
12	–	–	Shared technology issues	–

3.1 Sample Selection and Conduction of Interviews

We conducted semi-structured interviews with practitioners engaged in the selection of a CP, e.g. with the role of network or cloud architect or a management position. With semi-structured interviews we were able to get answers to a set of predetermined questions but were still flexible enough to include spontaneous questions arising from the discussion with the practitioners.

Since we could not offer financial compensation, we tried to get in touch with relevant practitioners at the Cloud Expo Europe 2018 and completed the set of interviewees with contacts from our personal network. The process of the invitation and the interviews was as follows: When inviting the participants, we already included the information that we were looking for experts in the field of cloud computing to find out which criteria were considered when choosing a CP and which requirements were imposed on the provider. Ideally, the participants should either be involved in such a decision. In order to be able to verify security as a criterion without revealing it beforehand, the research focus on security was not given in the invitation.

We first conducted a pilot interview to test and validate the interview guidelines. Respondents Ra and Rb were from the financial sector and related secu-

Table 3. Respondents' profiles

Respondents	Relation to the cloud	Sector	Employees	Expert's position
Ra/Rb	User	Financial Services	>1000	Infrastructure Specialists
R1	Consultant	IT Consulting	>100000	Cloud Advisory Sen. Manager
R2	Provider	IT	<50	CEO
R3	User	Financial Services	>10000	Network Architect
R4	User	Energy Supply	>10000	Cloud Architect
R5	User	Automotive	>100000	Solution Architect
R6	User	Financial Services	>1000	IT Security Manager
R7	User	Metal Processing	>1000	Project Manager (IT Infrastr.)
R8	User	Fintech	<50	CTO

rity closely to compliance, i.e. regulations imposed by the national supervisory authority BaFin. Therefore, the remaining interviews were further enriched by the question whether there was the intrinsic motivation or personal responsibility to select a secure provider. Afterwards, from October to December 2018, we interviewed eight respondents (cf. Table 3) face to face and in German. In order to maintain continuity all interviews were conducted by the same interviewer . Interviews had an average duration of around 37 min.

Due to space limitations, we describe the interview guideline only briefly. After the warm-up, the second block of questions addressed the provider selection. According to the research questions if respondents claimed to consider security when selecting a CP they were asked about possible assurance techniques their company used. In case security was not mentioned, the respondents were asked about the importance of security. Although security was not among the first criteria mentioned, it was present in most discussions. Eventually this lead to covering both sides of the decision tree in most of the interviews. Finally, the transparency on the cloud market was addressed to generate additional ideas for possible improvements to a non-transparent market.

3.2 Data Analysis

The interviews were transcribed word by word and analyzed with MAXQDA following the qualitative content analysis method from Kuckartz [36], since it suited the data collected in the semi-structured interviews and allowed to analyze the data with regard to the research questions. To get well acquainted with

Table 4. Coding frame for assurance techniques

Assurance techniques	Respondents talk about how they establish security assurance
Certification	Respondents talk about certification. The topic is either which ones they consider important or the advantages and drawbacks of certificates
Audits	Respondents audit their providers or talk about auditing. Statements are also included if they are about financial auditing
Contractual agreements	User and provider agree contractually on certain requirements the provider has to fulfill or on the right of the user to audit
Data center visits	Respondents place a value on being allowed to visit the provider's data center
Documentation	Respondents place a value on checking the providers' documentation on processes or technical measures
Penetration tests	The respondents run penetration tests as a mean of assurance
Cloud risk process	Companies' own process for risk assessment
Questionnaire on security measures	A company uses a questionnaire (comparable to CSA's CAIQ) in order to obtain information from a provider
Skepticism	Respondents express skepticism towards some assurance techniques, or the sense of assurance in general

the material, in the first phase of analysis each interview was summarized and the peculiarities of the given answers were noted. Next, master-codes were developed and tested on the first three interviews before coding the whole material. These codes were generated mostly deductively out of the interview questions. For instance, the codes "Provider Selection" and "Assurance Techniques" were rather straight forward, as these where the main research questions. The result of this phase was a list of master-codes. After coding the whole material with the master-codes, all passages coded with the same master-code were grouped and reread. At this point the aim was to differentiate the master-codes by inductively deriving sub-codes for each master-code. While proceeding from one interview to the next, the generated sub-codes were revised and sorted. The final product was a list of sub-codes which differentiated the master-codes. A sample of the derived coding can be found in Table 4.

4 Interview Results

The interviews and the data analysis were conducted with regard to the initial research questions. This resulted in a coding frame of five master-codes from which three address our research questions directly. In the next subsections, we briefly show the results of the role of security in CP selection, reasons for a moderate interest in security, and the verification of providers' security measures. Since in most of the interviews compliance was strongly connected with security, we also investigated the role of the General Data Protection Regulation (GDPR).

4.1 The Role of Security in CP Selection

The respondents were asked which criteria or requirements they considered when choosing a CP, instead of directly being asked about the role of security. Analogously, the master code "Provider Selection" was extracted from the material with several security related and unrelated sub-codes. The results were selection criteria, of which the ones unrelated to security will only be presented shortly. The most discussed selection criteria were costs (addressed by 5 respondents), size of provider (4) followed by ease of use (3).

Trust: In three interviews the providers' image came up in relation to their trustworthiness, which revealed divided opinions. R1 and R3 provided statements indicating that the image could serve as a proxy for security considerations. *R1: In our region Google did not manage to gain ground, which in my opinion can be contributed to the fact that we are a little bit more sensitive with regard to security and privacy than other countries. So many people shy away when they hear the name "Google" considering them a "data collector"*. Similarly, R3 stated that he would consider any large provider except for the Chinese Alibaba cloud. R2 provided the contrary provider's view on this idea. His small company was able to benefit from the image of the local German cloud in the beginning.

Compliance: Non surprisingly, need for security because of compliance appeared referring to regulation authorities, e.g. BaFin or BNetzA (R4, R6, R8).

Availability: Also a great value was placed on the availability of services (R1, R2, R4, R8) in particular over different time zones and with a certain force. Additionally, the statement of R4 even exceeded availability by considering business continuity of the provider to be able to plan for the future.

Confidentiality: The respondents R3 and R4 considered security for the sake of confidentiality of their users' data. *B3: It is about customer data which is located somewhere and one cannot be sure who has access to it. Of course one would like to use cloud services and algorithms to generate an added value out of this data. But on the other hand, one wants to protect the customer from an unauthorized party to gain access to it. I think this is incredibly difficult.* This statement was the only one in the sample expressing a concern for confidentiality apart from any business goals.

Besides selection criteria, several respondents provided insights on how their organisations selected their current CPs. These additionally provided circumstances matter for understanding the provider selection in its context.

Multiple Providers: Among others, it was stressed that current environments consisted of more than one main provider for the sake of independence, availability and freedom of choice (R3, R4). The decision which project or task was done with which provider was a per case decision, depending on the properties of the data and the provider (R4).

Hierarchy: R7 and R5 revealed that the provider decision was made on a higher hierarchical level. Particularly in the case of R7 a provider selection was unnecessary as the company had a strategic partnership with Microsoft.

Convenience: Several respondents admitted that the choice for a CP was partly made by chance, e.g. simply chose a convenient provider to make the first steps in the cloud (R1, R5), because a developer already had some experience (R4) or the company had a voucher (R8). In individual cases these first steps of conveniently testing out a new provider even contradicted corporate requirements and constituted a shadow IT. Despite these tendencies, a security analysis was done retrospectively (R4, R5). Even if it was done retrospectively, the analysis was not only formal but could have changed the decision. *R5: Basically the cloud risk process could have stopped the decision for the product.*

4.2 Reasons for Moderate Interest in Security

The respondents could not be asked why security was only of moderate interest, as security was sooner or later addressed in all the discussions. Nevertheless, most of the answers could be related to "coping with risk". The related topics came up when the respondents were asked about the role of trust or whether they had possible concerns about confidentiality. Most respondents agreed that these concerns do exist but revealed different "coping mechanisms".

Mitigation: Two ways of mitigating the risk raised by respondents were the choice of a large provider and a national or EU-located data centre. In four interviews the location of a data centre came up as a signal of a trustworthy or preferable provider (R2, R3, R4, R5). The assumption, that especially large providers are secure and trustworthy was found in all the interviews except the one with R3. Most respondents argued that large providers invested more in security and thereby also provided a higher level of security than even possible in the own company, which is in line with academic findings [23,38]. Another benefit was stressed by R6 and R8, namely that large companies were also more likely to cover high compensations than small providers in case of a breach.

Responsibility: R2, R5, R7 and R8 agreed that security was not only the responsibility of the CP, but rather a shared one. R2 stressed the differences compared to traditional technologies with regard to responsibility. *R2: Who bears which responsibility often changes in the cloud compared to traditional methods.[...] Before, I either used to run an in-house data centre or I outsourced it.*

R5 stressed the importance of creating awareness in-house for the new technology and its specific risks.

Encryption: Four respondents reported encryption as a mean to secure the cloud. R6 and R8 attached great importance on encrypting their outsourced data and R1 and R2 reported on means of encryption implemented by their clients. Additionally, R2 pointed out the potential drawbacks for the cloud customer. *R2: When we provide the infrastructure only, encryption is mostly in the hands of the customer. But then he has to manage the keys, which represents an additional complexity he has to handle.*

Data Criticality: In addition, some users saw security relatively to the criticality of data they placed into the cloud. R1 and R6 stated that business critical-data was preferably not outsourced at all. *R1: In my opinion, it will always be the case that for a certain part the companies say: "These are my crown jewels, which I don't give away. No matter how much I trust a provider, I want to have these with me".*

Trust: As the opposite side of mitigation, ideas were raised resonating with trust towards the provider. Maybe the most prominent statement to this topic was given by R1: *I believe that many give their providers a few laurels in advance. "Okay they do this on such a large scale and I either I do not trust them per se. In this case I address encryption and other topics. Or as I said, I give them laurels in advance and say, yes this is going to work out"*, assuming that many users trust their providers without any proof. R2, R4, R5 and R8 expressed their belief that the incentives for providers were set in such a way that they cannot afford to make mistakes with customers' data.

Personal Responsibility: R2 tried to explain the popularity of Amazon with the "IBM Effect". *R2: Well I can rely on them (AWS), at least at most times. And when there is a service failure, it applies to everyone and one can say: "Yes, you know it, AWS just had an outage". So it's the IBM effect: "No one ever got fired for buying IBM", applies to AWS nowadays.* R3 agreed with this idea. Finally, independently of mitigation or trust one question had to be included in light of the given answers concerning the importance of security. Throughout some discussions one could have gotten the impression that some companies simply avoided being held accountable in case of a data breach. Therefore the respondents were asked whether there was a personal responsibility or even an intrinsic motivation to pursue security conscientiously. Consequently, the code "Personal Responsibility" was covered with six respondents.

Compliance: The resulting discussions with R1 and R2 were leaned on the fulfillment of GDPR and compliance requirements and both respondents revealed the belief that the choice of a secure provider is rather extrinsically motivated by the need to comply. They also agreed that the regulating authorities still have not drawn any consequences but most likely would do so in the future in order to set an example. *R1: [...] I believe that many (companies) still wait until the first penalties are issued, as surprisingly it (GDPR) did not have that* *many impact yet. [...] I think the first time something happens and jurisdiction is drawn, and a company really has to pay for it, many others will have a second awakening.* R4 and R6 agreed that compliance is decisive for the final choice. However, according to R4 intrinsic motivation is individual and depends on the employee's training. *R4: Well it depends on who is dealing with the topic. As I already said, the energy sector has very high security requirements, so if a classic energy economist deals with it, then security and compliance are in his blood. [...] If it is a developer, he may not care. He only asks where to put the data, but does not really think about it himself.* However, R4 adds that in recent years the awareness has risen among all the employees.

4.3 Verification of Providers' Security Measures

The first part of the interviews showed that although security was not the top criterion when selecting a CP, it was present as a requirement. For this reason, it could not be directly asked how the respondents compared different providers with regard to security beforehand, but it could be discussed whether they verified the security levels of their CPs.

Certification: The probably most discussed assurance technique in this sample was certification. According to R1, R2, R4, R6 and R8 two kinds of certification seemed to be of importance when a provider was checked. This was either certification after the ISO norm 27001 or the C5 by BSI (R1, R2, R4, R6), a German governmental agency, which among others incorporates the ISO norm and is combined with an audit. R1 expressed his doubts about C5 being attractive to providers who want to achieve global standardization, as it was a German norm. R4 and R6 agreed that certification in general provided a solid basis for trusting a provider, as for one thing certification institutions could be considered credible and for the other their certification process was very demanding. R2 as well stressed the convenience of certificates but later on also warned of misunderstandings, as one always had to look closely at the coverage. *R2: Another important thing is that certificates are often misunderstood. For instance a 9001 certificate can be done for different domains of my company. I could only certify the administration and in that case a production- or data center is not covered at all.* Moreover, R2's small company could not be certified as the formalization of processes was not possible in the dynamic environment of a start-up. These aspects were also picked up by R8 who criticized exactly that certification was for the most parts focused on processes on paper, which in his view would not provide real security.

Audits: Another assurance technique discussed was external auditing, although it has to be said that the audits most respondents considered were not of technical but rather a financial nature. R6 and R7 for instance stated to have sent public accountants or financial auditors to their providers who apparently only in the broadest sense verified provider security. R1 admitted that he did not know of anyone who really audited their CPs and predicted it rather as a future trend after the clients had made some experiences in the cloud. R7 and R8 stressed the benefits of a third party audit, namely that an expert was checking the status of a system and giving advice on how to improve it, which was according to R8 an advantage compared to certificates. While R4 doubted the competence of some auditors, R8 pointed out the conflict of interest. *R8: Exactly, it depends on what kind of auditor you get. You can entrust someone who issues an affirmation for you: "Audit accomplished", or you can entrust someone who works conscientiously. The only problem is that the ones who work conscientiously, are often those who are not well received and afterwards have trouble reselling. There is a slight conflict of interest.*

Contracts: It was often discussed in connection to assurance that respondents had contractual agreements with their providers (R4 and R6). R6 added the possibility to contractually seal where data is located and processed. R2 pointed out that contractual agreements were often not only an option but a requirement in light of GDPR, while R4 and R6 gave the important reason for having a contractual agreement, namely that in case of non-fulfillment a compensation was ensured. R1, R2 and R4 mentioned the possibility to contractually include the users' right to visit the data center in person. According to R2 such a clause may be necessary or important to a client, who handles personal data. Nevertheless, the respondents admitted that in reality such a visit hardly ever happened. Additionally, R2 doubted the sense of sending company representatives to visit a data center. *R2: If someone like you or me went there, what would we be supposed to see? If the door is not open somewhere or a cable hanging loosely, we would have no idea how secure this is and whether it is in accordance to the norm.* R1 added that the providers tried to avoid such visits as they considered the interior of their data centre as a company secret. Additionally, checking technical documentation or documentation of processes was found in the interviews (R4, R6, R7).

Tests: Additionally, R4 and R6 talked about security tests as a mean of assurance. *R6: That means that for a cloud service we will not check whether it is externally attackable, as most data centres must have tested this already for about five-, six-, seven-, eight hundred times. What we check is whether the access point we have to the data centre is secure enough.* R4 also stressed that the tests were not done on the CPs' side but on the final application, which was supposed to run in the cloud or as a hybrid application. Both respondents pointed out some drawbacks of penetration-testing, first the costliness and second that such tests could only be run for known cases.

Two respondents stood out with their companies' specific assurance techniques. R5 reported of his companies' own cloud risk process which helped evaluating a provider with regard to the risk he poses to the company and its data. The process incorporated some of the already presented techniques, like demanding a certification and contractually sealing requirements, but more than this, it was a spreadsheet for assessing the likeliness of scenarios and finally presenting the risk imposed by a provider. Finally, the management was in charge of deciding whether this risk was acceptable or not. The other individual measure was taken by R4's company, which had designed their own questionnaire for CPs comparable to the CAIQ by the CSA.

Finally, besides all the collected assurance techniques it has to be mentioned that several respondents also expressed scepticism when talking about assurance. According to R3 there was no gain from SLAs and contracts, as even if there was a written agreement one had to suffer in case of a data breach in terms of data loss. R4 pointed out the drawback of a third party audit, by telling his own experience with auditors who believed him anything he told them. R7 had doubts about assurance in general and pointed out how the need to control or verify everything although one had outsourced brought unnecessary costliness. Similarly, R8 criticized that certificates do not show real security.

4.4 Compliance and the General Data Protection Regulation

Due to the previous answers, we also elaborate how the GDPR influenced the decisions and to what extent interviewees reported about German and European cloud services which do not transfer data outside of the European Union.

GDPR: According to R2 and R6, a result of the GDPR is that more attention is turned to data protection. R2 claims that the GDPR allows to ensure technical and organisational measures by SLAs more easily.

R1 and R2 agree that since so far data protection authorities have not punished companies by a fine, most companies will assume the first cases will hit large companies and wait for that. R2 was more concerned about written warnings from competitors. R7 reported that his company's data security officer answered to a request about using cloud services that an agreement of the parent company (in Great Britain) with the cloud provider is seen as valid for all subsidiary companies. In contrast, R4 reported that the regulation requires data centres in the EU, which still did not work out for them, because of US employees with access to the stored data. However, they use a CP in Switzerland for non business critical data.

Localisation of CPs: Statements on the localisation of CPs were ambivalent. On the one hand, R3 was concerned about US industrial espionage facilitated by war on terror laws and thus demands a German/European solution with all components (software, hardware) built and run in Germany/EU. This is in line with the report of a "Robin Hood" bonus for a localised offer (R2).

On the other hand R1 and R2 report that at the beginning localisation seemed important, but then lost importance due to data centres in Germany (from the large CPs) and due to observations of other companies seemingly running their cloud services GDPR-compliant with non-EU CPs. An additional argument was that the advantages of localisation can not compensate higher costs (R3, R4, R7), missing features (R1, R2) or development tools (R3) for the German version, customers in the US (R1), and missing trust in the continuity of the service (R4). Many interviewees (R1, R2, R3, R4, R7) were referring to the "German cloud", a cooperation between Telekom and Microsoft which was ended last year[1].

5 Discussion

Role of Security: With regard to the original question on the role of security in cloud provider selection the collected findings are ambiguous. Selection criteria like usability and costs were expressed straightforwardly and matched the findings of the related work [26,60]. Security however, was never the first answer the respondents extensively engaged in. Neither could they provide concrete security requirements comparable to those found in the related contributions. On the other hand, security as a requirement was present in all the discussions. Moreover, availability and in rare cases confidentiality could be extracted as goals. Two respondents revealed that although security had not been a selection criterion, it was considered in retrospect in some cases, where the companies analysed the services after having tested them first. Moreover, the findings from this sample challenge the idea of a systematic provider selection suggested in related works. In this sample it was rarely the case that providers were compared and evaluated in advance with regard to certain criteria.

Moderate Interest in Security: Some respondents assessed the situation and acted in accordance to the mitigation measures proposed in cloud organizations' technical reports. For instance, one could identify the awareness of the separation of duties and the willingness to employ encryption on the user side. These users were aware that security in the cloud was not only the cloud provider's duty and took own responsibility. On the other hand, namely the capability of a provider to grant compensations speaks however again for a financial interest rather than an intrinsic motivation to establish security. The initial assumption that the requirement on security is extrinsically motivated by compliance was clearly supported by the respondents' answers on personal responsibility. The answers revealed as well a different side to the client provider relationship, which was a great amount of trust towards the cloud provider and the acceptance of risk to a certain extent. The idea that an "IBM effect" exists when choosing Amazon's services indicates that this could be a way for decision makers to be exonerated from responsibility.

Security Assurance: Overall, the respondents revealed to rely on certification, audits, contractual agreements and testing as common means of assurance. Besides those assurance techniques, two respondents presented own company-specific methods. The results from this sample show that except for C5 which is a cloud-specific certificate and audit, the companies rather rely on traditional forms of assurance than cloud-specific ones. Especially contractual agreements are considered a convenient method in order to establish compliance and guarantee for a compensation in case of non-fulfillment. Surprisingly, contractually agreed measures like data center visits are not often undertaken. These findings

[1] https://heise.de/-4152650.

are one more indicator that security and also assurance are overshadowed by compliance, but that at the same time regulation may miss out on establishing real and not only paper-based assurance.

In comparison to the findings from academic literature cloud-specific assurance techniques seemed to have not really thrived in practice. Certification which was most present in the literature review was similarly well accepted among the practitioners as a convenient assurance technique. Testing in terms of application security was also present in both, literature and interviews. However, it is striking but not surprising that neither monitoring nor auditing, which offered many cloud-specific frameworks in literature, were present among the respondents. Contractual agreements could be compared to security SLAs with regard to how they work, except that there are no actual metrics agreed upon but rules.

5.1 Threats to Validity and Limitations

One of the major challenges of conducting the interviews turned out to be finding the right respondents. The ideal respondent given the research questions would have been someone in a C-Level position, who was involved in cloud adoption and knowledgeable about the processes in IT and security. Such persons were difficult to reach or to find time to schedule a face to face interview. In the current sample, respondents from the financial industry are a bit overrepresented and it would have been beneficial to have more respondents from small and medium enterprises. In particular, R8 answered from a perspective of a start-up and could contribute some new ideas. Thus, the interviews should be considered as a first insight and be extended by further interviews with representatives from small- and middle sized companies. Most respondents eventually talked about infrastructure- or platform providers, most likely because in the case of Software-as-a-Service one would rather talk about service- than provider selection.

6 Conclusion

Previous research identified security as a requirement considered by CP customers. Our sample indicates that security may not always be a selection criterion and neither the most decisive one. If considered in the CP selection, then mostly in terms of availability and for the sake of compliance. Especially the focus on compliance it not surprising as it has been observed in other sectors as well [16,54]. Nevertheless, it is certainly a requirement companies have, which manifests itself in cloud use. This is indicated by retrospective analysis and considerations of multiple providers.

CP Selection Process: In our sample we could rarely find any elaborated process of eliciting requirements and then coming to a rational decision which CP to select. Instead, CP were chosen based on vouchers, by chance (just pick on CP for 'testing', but then stick with it), by the management because of established relationships, or because of previous experience from a developer. Even more, some companies make use of many CPs in an unstructured way, e.g. each department decides by its own. Another pattern we could identify was that companies often try to 'first get into the cloud' and then optimise costs and sometimes security (lift and shift) or try to sort out the collection of different CPs. Further research would be desired to investigate why the methodology proposed by research seems to be rarely used in practise.

For that purpose the different roles in the requirements/decision making process should be investigated in detail and elaborated at which step the relevant methodologies from research were not considered and why.

Assurance: The respondents reported on using more than one assurance technique, combined models from the literature were not present at all. Additionally, they saw flaws in the existing assurance techniques and may not even be acquainted with possible cloud-specific assurance. Thus, the noteworthy finding of this comparison is a divergence between the assurance methods adopted in practice and the cloud-specific ones proposed in literature. It can be speculated whether some academic approaches to assurance have never exceeded their theoretical approach or if they were not able to gain ground in practice yet.

Company Size: Although the results uncover many dimensions and patterns of cloud security, they are not complete. As mentioned earlier, no saturation of interviews could be reached among small and unregulated companies. In contrast, large regulated companies were well represented and most likely contributed to a strong focus on compliance in this analysis. Future work could examine on a larger scale whether and how companies have incorporated security into their provider selection and in particular investigate commonalities and differences between smaller and larger companies.

Big CPs vs. Localisation: It seems that the big CPs are in general trusted by the companies and the idea of a German cloud failed. Companies are trying to setup a compliant way to work with the big CPs. However, one interviewee was concerned about industrial espionage and strongly voted for a European or German CP with all components made in the EU. Further research should unfold the different dimensions of trust, and also investigate to which extent regulations or agreements as the EU–US Privacy Shield influence it.

Gaps Between Research and Practise: In the requirement elicitation and decision making process and in the use of assurance technologies there seems to be a gap between research and practise. This gap is something which seems to be quite common in a lot of areas [52]. Further work should investigate whether this is just a typical finding and already existing ideas can be applied to bridge it [20] or if it is a context specific problem and new ideas are needed.

References

1. Akerlof, G.A.: The market for "lemons": quality uncertainty and the market mechanism. In: Uncertainty in Economics, pp. 235–251. Elsevier (1978)
2. Alhenaki, L., Alwatban, A., Alahmri, B., Alarifi, N.: Security in cloud computing: a survey. Int. J. Comput. Sci. Inf. Secur. (IJCSIS) **17**(4), 67–90 (2019)

3. Anisetti, M., Ardagna, C.A., Damiani, E.: A certification-based trust model for autonomic cloud computing systems. In: 2014 International Conference on Cloud and Autonomic Computing, pp. 212–219 (2014)
4. Anisetti, M., Ardagna, C.A., Damiani, E.: A test-based incremental security certification scheme for cloud-based systems. In: 2015 IEEE International Conference on Services Computing, pp. 736–741 (2015)
5. Anisetti, M., Ardagna, C.A., Damiani, E., Gaudenzi, F., Veca, R.: Toward security and performance certification of open stack. In: 2015 IEEE 8th International Conference on Cloud Computing, pp. 564–571 (2015)
6. Anisetti, M., Ardagna, C.A., Gaudenzi, F., Damiani, E.: A certification framework for cloud-based services. In: Proceedings of the 31st Annual ACM Symposium on Applied Computing, SAC 2016, pp. 440–447. ACM (2016)
7. Ardagna, C.A., Asal, R., Damiani, E., Vu, Q.H.: From security to assurance in the cloud: a survey. ACM Comput. Surv. **48**(1), 2:1–2:50 (2015)
8. Ba, H., Zhou, H., Bai, S., Ren, J., Wang, Z., Ci, L.: jMonAtt: integrity monitoring and attestation of JVM-based applications in cloud computing. In: ICISCE, pp. 419–423 (2017)
9. Bleikertz, S., Mastelic, T., Pape, S., Pieters, W., Dimkov, T.: Defining the cloud battlefield - supporting security assessments by cloud customers. In: IC2E, pp. 78–87 (2013)
10. Briggs, B., Lamar, K., Kark, K., Shaikh, A.: Manifesting legacy: looking beyond the digital era. Technical report, 2018 Global CIO Survey, Deloitte (2018)
11. Casola, V., Benedictis, A.D., Rak, M., Villano, U.: SLA-based secure cloud application development: the SPECS framework. In: SYNASC, pp. 337–344 (2015)
12. CSA: Top threats to cloud computing v1.0. Technical report, Cloud Security Alliance (2010). https://cloudsecurityalliance.org/topthreats/csathreats.v1.0.pdf
13. CSA: The notorious nine: cloud computing top threats in 2013. Technical report, Cloud Security Alliance (2013). https://cloudsecurityalliance.org/download/artifacts/the-notorious-nine-cloud-computing-top-threats-in-2013/
14. CSA: The treacherous 12 - cloud computing top threats in 2016. Technical report, Cloud Security Alliance (2016). https://downloads.cloudsecurityalliance.org/assets/research/top-threats/Treacherous-12_Cloud-Computing_Top-Threats.pdf
15. CSA: Top threats to cloud computing the egregious 11. Technical report, Cloud Security Alliance (2019). https://cloudsecurityalliance.org/download/artifacts/top-threats-to-cloud-computing-egregious-eleven/
16. Dax, J., et al.: IT security status of German energy providers (2017). https://arxiv.org/abs/1709.01254
17. Deng, L., Liu, P., Xu, J., Chen, P., Zeng, Q.: Dancing with wolves: towards practical event-driven VMM monitoring. In: Proceedings of the 13th ACM SIGPLAN/SIGOPS International Conference on VEE, pp. 83–96. ACM (2017)
18. Di Giulio, C., Kamhoua, C., Campbell, R.H., Sprabery, R., Kwiat, K., Bashir, M.N.: IT security and privacy standards in comparison: improving FedRAMP authorization for cloud service providers. In: CCGrid, pp. 1090–1099 (2017)
19. Di Giulio, C., Sprabery, R., Kamhoua, C., Kwiat, K., Campbell, R.H., Bashir, M.N.: Cloud standards in comparison: are new security frameworks improving cloud security? In: CLOUD, pp. 50–57 (2017)
20. Ferguson, J.: Bridging the gap between research and practice. Knowl. Manag. Dev. J. **1**(3), 46–54 (2005)
21. Fernando, R., Ranchal, R., Bhargava, B., Angin, P.: A monitoring approach for policy enforcement in cloud services. In: CLOUD, pp. 600–607 (2017)

22. Ghutugade, K.B., Patil, G.A.: Privacy preserving auditing for shared data in cloud. In: CAST, pp. 300–305 (2016)
23. Gupta, P., Seetharaman, A., Raj, J.R.: The usage and adoption of cloud computing by small and medium businesses. Int. J. Inf. Manag. **33**(5), 861–874 (2013)
24. Haeberlen, T., Dupré, L.: Cloud computing - benefits, risks and recommendations for information security. Technical report, ENISA (2012)
25. Henze, M., et al.: Practical data compliance for cloud storage. In: 2017 IEEE International Conference on Cloud Engineering (IC2E), pp. 252–258 (2017)
26. Hetzenecker, J., Kammerer, S., Amberg, M., Zeiler, V.: Anforderungen an cloud computing Anbieter. In: MKWI (2012)
27. Ismail, U.M., Islam, S., Islam, S.: Towards cloud security monitoring: a case study. In: Cybersecurity and Cyberforensics Conference (CCC), pp. 8–14 (2016)
28. Jakhotia, K., Bhosale, R., Lingam, C.: Novel architecture for enabling proof of retrievability using AES algorithm. In: ICCMC, pp. 388–393 (2017)
29. Jansen, W., Grance, T.: SP 800-144. Guidelines on security and privacy in public cloud computing. Technical report, NIST (2011)
30. Jiang, T., Chen, X., Ma, J.: Public integrity auditing for shared dynamic cloud data with group user revocation. IEEE Trans. Comput. **65**(8), 2363–2373 (2016)
31. Kaaniche, N., Mohamed, M., Laurent, M., Ludwig, H.: Security SLA based monitoring in clouds. In: IEEE EDGE, pp. 90–97 (2017)
32. Kanstrén, T., Lehtonen, S., Savola, R., Kukkohovi, H., Hätönen, K.: Architecture for high confidence cloud security monitoring. In: IC2E, pp. 195–200 (2015)
33. Katopodis, S., Spanoudakis, G., Mahbub, K.: Towards hybrid cloud service certification models. In: IEEE International Conference on Services Computing, pp. 394–399 (2014)
34. Krotsiani, M., Spanoudakis, G.: Continuous certification of non-repudiation in cloud storage services. In: 2014 IEEE 13th International Conference on Trust, Security and Privacy in Computing and Communications, pp. 921–928 (2014)
35. Krutz, R.L., Vines, R.D.: Cloud Security: A Comprehensive Guide to Secure Cloud Computing. Wiley, Hoboken (2010)
36. Kuckartz, U.: Qualitative Inhaltsanalyse: Methoden, Praxis, Computerunterstützung. Beltz Juventa (2016)
37. Kumar, R., Goyal, R.: On cloud security requirements, threats, vulnerabilities and countermeasures: a survey. Comput. Sci. Rev. **33**, 1–48 (2019)
38. Lacity, M.C., Reynolds, P.: Cloud services practices for small and medium-sized enterprises. MIS Q. Exec. **13**(1), 31–44 (2014)
39. Lang, M., Wiesche, M., Krcmar, H.: What are the most important criteria for cloud service provider selection? A Delphi study. In: ECIS (2016)
40. Lee, C., Kavi, K.M., Paul, R.A., Gomathisankaran, M.: Ontology of secure service level agreement. In: 2015 IEEE 16th International Symposium on High Assurance Systems Engineering, pp. 166–172 (2015)
41. Lins, S., Grochol, P., Schneider, S., Sunyaev, A.: Dynamic certification of cloud services: trust, but verify!. IEEE Secur. Priv. **14**(2), 66–71 (2016)
42. Lins, S., Schneider, S., Sunyaev, A.: Trust is good, control is better: creating secure clouds by continuous auditing. IEEE Trans. Cloud Comput. **6**(3), 890–903 (2018)
43. Lins, S., Thiebes, S., Schneider, S., Sunyaev, A.: What is really going on at your cloud service provider? Creating trustworthy certifications by continuous auditing. In: 48th HICSS, pp. 5352–5361 (2015)
44. Luna, J., Suri, N., Iorga, M., Karmel, A.: Leveraging the potential of cloud security service-level agreements through standards. IEEE Cloud Comput. **2**(3), 32–40 (2015)

45. Ma, M., Weber, J., van den Berg, J.: Secure public-auditing cloud storage enabling data dynamics in the standard model. In: DIPDMWC, pp. 170–175 (2016)
46. Mahesh, A., Suresh, N., Gupta, M., Sharman, R.: Cloud risk resilience: investigation of audit practices and technology advances-a technical report. Int. J. Risk Conting. Manag. (IJRCM) **8**(2), 66–92 (2019)
47. Majumdar, S., Madi, T., Wang, Y., Jarraya, Y., Pourzandi, M., Wang, L., Debbabi, M.: User-level runtime security auditing for the cloud. IEEE Trans. Inf. Forensics Secur. **13**(5), 1185–1199 (2018)
48. Meera, G., Geethakumari, G.: A provenance auditing framework for cloud computing systems. In: SPICES, pp. 1–5 (2015)
49. Mohammed, M.M.Z.E., Pathan, A.K.: International center for monitoring cloud computing providers (ICMCCP) for ensuring trusted clouds. In: IEEE 11th International Conference on Ubiquitous Intelligence and Its Associated Workshops, pp. 571–576 (2014)
50. More, S.S., Chaudhari, S.S.: Secure and efficient public auditing scheme for cloud storage. In: CAST, pp. 439–444 (2016)
51. Munoz, A., Mafia, A.: Software and hardware certification techniques in a combined certification model. In: SECRYPT, pp. 1–6 (2014)
52. Norman, D.A.: The research-practice gap: the need for translational developers. Interactions **17**(4), 9–12 (2010)
53. Nugraha, Y., Martin, A.: Towards the classification of confidentiality capabilities in trustworthy service level agreements. In: IC2E, pp. 304–310 (2017)
54. Pape, S., Pipek, V., Rannenberg, K., Schmitz, C., Sekulla, A., Terhaag, F.: Stand zur IT-Sicherheit deutscher Stromnetzbetreiber (2018). http://dokumentix.ub.uni-siegen.de/opus/volltexte/2018/1394/
55. Parasuraman, K., Srinivasababu, P., Angelin, S.R., Devi, T.A.M.: Secured document management through a third party auditor scheme in cloud computing. In: ICECCE, pp. 109–118 (2014)
56. Pasquier, T.F.J., Singh, J., Bacon, J., Eyers, D.: Information flow audit for PaaS clouds. In: IEEE IC2E, pp. 42–51 (2016)
57. Polash, F., Shiva, S.: Building trust in cloud: service certification challenges and approaches. In: 9th International Conference on Complex, Intelligent, and Software Intensive Systems, pp. 187–191 (2015)
58. Ramokapane, K.M., Rashid, A., Such, J.M.: Assured deletion in the cloud: requirements, challenges and future directions. In: CCSW, pp. 97–108. ACM (2016)
59. Rashmi, R.P., Sangve, S.M.: Public auditing system: improved remote data possession checking protocol for secure cloud storage. In: iCATccT, pp. 75–80 (2015)
60. Repschläger, J., Wind, S., Zarnekow, R., Turowski, K.: Developing a cloud provider selection model. In: EMISA (2011)
61. Rewadkar, D.N., Ghatage, S.Y.: Cloud storage system enabling secure privacy preserving third party audit. In: ICCICCT, pp. 695–699 (2014)
62. Rios, E., Mallouli, W., Rak, M., Casola, V., Ortiz, A.M.: SLA-driven monitoring of multi-cloud application components using the MUSA framework. In: IEEE 36th ICDCSW, pp. 55–60 (2016)
63. Rizvi, S.S., Bolish, T.A., Pfeffer III, J.R.: Security evaluation of cloud service providers using third party auditors. In: Second International Conference on Internet of Things, Data and Cloud Computing, pp. 106:1–106:6 (2017)
64. Ryoo, J., Rizvi, S., Aiken, W., Kissell, J.: Cloud security auditing: challenges and emerging approaches. IEEE Secur. Priv. **12**(6), 68–74 (2014)

65. Schneider, S., Lansing, J., Gao, F., Sunyaev, A.: A taxonomic perspective on certification schemes: development of a taxonomy for cloud service certification criteria. In: HICSS, pp. 4998–5007 (2014)
66. Sen, A., Madria, S.: Data analysis of cloud security alliance's security, trust & assurance registry. In: ICDCN, pp. 42:1–42:10. ACM (2018)
67. Sotiriadis, S., Lehmets, A., Petrakis, E.G.M., Bessis, N.: Unit and integration testing of modular cloud services. In: AINA, pp. 1116–1123 (2017)
68. Stephanow, P., Khajehmoogahi, K.: Towards continuous security certification of software-as-a-service applications using web application testing techniques. In: AINA, pp. 931–938 (2017)
69. Thendral, G., Valliyammai, C.: Dynamic auditing and updating services in cloud storage. In: International Conference on Recent Trends in Information Technology, pp. 1–6 (2014)
70. Tung, Y., Lin, C., Shan, H.: Test as a service: a framework for web security TaaS service in cloud environment. In: 2014 IEEE 8th International Symposium on Service Oriented System Engineering, pp. 212–217 (2014)
71. Zhang, H., Manzoor, S., Suri, N.: Monitoring path discovery for supporting indirect monitoring of cloud services. In: IEEE IC2E, pp. 274–277 (2018)
72. Zhang, H., Trapero, R., Luna, J., Suri, N.: deQAM: a dependency based indirect monitoring approach for cloud services. In: IEEE SCC, pp. 27–34 (2017)

Discrete Event Simulation of Jail Operations in Pursuit of Organizational Culture Change

Hugh D. Lester[1] and Martin J. Miller[2](✉)

[1] Urbahn Architects, PLLC, 306 W. 37th St, 9th Fl, New York, NY 10018, USA
lesterh@urbahn.com
[2] Decision Analytics, LLC, Tampa, FL, USA
Marty@TheDecisionAnalytics.com
http://www.thedecisionanalytics.com

Abstract. Justice facilities such as jails are complex adaptive systems. They are people-driven, whether by the organizational culture of those that operate them, or by inmate culture. The development of organizational culture is organic and based on buy-in at all levels, or the lack thereof. Organizational culture evolves, including in response to attempted interventions from within or without. Physical and electronic security's relationship to detention operations and detainee supervision involves similar dynamics.

In this paper, we explore jail operations. We model human use of a housing unit and associated support spaces via discrete-event simulation. We simulate this system to understand the capacity and limits on human use of building spaces. We explore how this sociotechnical system responds when stressed. We thereby validate the design within limits that correspond to planned operational capacity. The goal of the research is to design spaces and environments that support improved outcomes via improvements in organizational culture.

We introduce the specifics of jail operations via this model while exploring the full range of applications for this type of simulation in the built environment.

Keywords: Jail operations · Justice design · Organizational culture · Discrete-event simulation · Sociotechnical systems

1 Introduction

1.1 Conditions of Confinement and Facility Operations

Conditions of confinement and facility operations impact society. The overwhelming majority of those incarcerated return to society. The negative impacts of those experiences will color their interactions upon their return. Therefore, society benefits from improvements in conditions of confinement; efficient, safe, and just facility operations; and improved outcomes for the formerly incarcerated.

1.2 Jail Versus Prison

Jails and prisons are not synonymous. Prisons are for those convicted and sentenced. Jails are for the accused awaiting trial. Prisoners' levels of need and security

S. Katsikas et al. (Eds.): ESORICS 2019 Workshops, LNCS 11980, pp. 307–322, 2020.
https://doi.org/10.1007/978-3-030-42048-2_20

classifications are well known. Jail detainees' security risk and levels of needs are less well known. Prison stays are lengthy. Jail stays are short. For these reasons, and others, jails are more difficult to design and operate than prisons.

1.3 Drivers of Jail Design

Jail designers know that their designs must address the truism that "if it can happen, it will happen." Infrastructure in the form of physical barriers and secured openings persist, but almost all other factors impacting jail outcomes, such as organizational culture, detainee characteristics, the jail census, and justice system drivers such as criminal law, prosecutorial and judicial discretion, case processing speed, rules surrounding discovery, parole violation terms, and societal mores evolve over time. The Sheriff that built the jail often has one attitude towards how it should be operated, while the next Sheriff may have other priorities and under-resource and neglect the jail.

1.4 The New York City Jail System

In New York City, the jail system consists of eight jails on Rikers Island, two borough-based jails, and one jail barge. The system housed over 22,000 detainees in 1992, but the current census is 7,000 following years of downward trends in criminality combined with justice system reforms at the local and state level. The policy of the City of New York is to close Rikers and replace the entire system with four new borough-based high-rise jails with a combined rated capacity of 4,000 beds by mid-2026. Due to the need for classification, accommodation of peaking, and the need to maintain cells, 4,600 beds in four 1,150-bed jails are planned.

1.5 Factors Driving the Conceptual Design (See Appendix A, Fig. 1)

The conceptual design of one of these facilities is the subject of this paper. The policy of the NYC Department of Corrections is to house in single cells. Direct supervision of detainees is proposed. This means that the correctional officer within the housing unit directly interacts with the detainees without any physical barriers, relying on proactive behavior management, social cues, communication, and immediate sanctions to maintain institutional order. Outcomes for direct supervision facilities are superior to other forms of supervision, by significant margins, over all known metrics [1–3]. In order to balance security compartmentalization, span of control, operational effectiveness, and staffing efficiency mini-jails of 300 detainees are broken into five 60-bed housing units in the design [4]. One such unit and its associated services are modeled in order to optimize operations and space planning for all 20 housing units.

1.6 Operational Validation (See Appendix A, Fig. 5)

The approach taken was discrete-event simulation, which models the evolving state of a system over time. That system involves entities which move through a process, seizing and releasing limited resources. For example, when a detainee cannot seize a sallyport (e.g., because it is occupied by another detainee), they wait in queue while the simulation advances forward in time. Eventually, the sallyport becomes available and the detainee leaves the queue, seizes the sallyport and continues moving through the process. Meanwhile, the simulation tracks 'time in system,' resource utilization, and many more performance metrics. Simulation is a technique for the explicit discovery and analysis of process bottlenecks. It incorporates real-world situations, such as variations in activity times, resource constraints and downtimes. Detainee goal directed behavior is defined algorithmically. The simulation establishes parameters for movement, tracks the state of spaces (number of occupants) and controlled openings (open or closed), while defining schedules and operational norms.

1.7 How We Proceeded

The conceptual design of the facility was developed independently of any attempt to model human use. Early discrete-event simulation runs helped point out issues with the design and allowed us to test alternative spatial layouts. Vague notions of operational policy, procedures, and staffing patterns were necessarily made explicit in order to incorporate them into the model, increasing its validity.

2 Conceptual Design

2.1 Housing Unit Layout (See Appendix A, Figs. 3 and 4)

The housing unit has a capacity of 60 beds, which the designer arrayed in three tiers. Each tier hosts 20 cells (ten on a side). Between the cells are the dayroom and the adjacent indoor recreation area. The size of the dayroom is slightly larger than the 60×35 square feet per detainee required by the *American Correctional Association Local Adult Detention Facility Standards*. The size of indoor recreation is based on accommodating half-court basketball, providing enough space beyond the three-point line for it to function for pickup games or shooting baskets. The layout barely accommodates this use. Half-court basketball is a superior form of recreation because it involves vigorous large muscle exercise, which significantly improves brain chemistry and lowers the propensity for aggressiveness and violence, compared to lower intensity or passive recreation.

2.2 Glazed End Wall (See Appendix A, Figs. 10, 11, 12 and 13)

The end of the dayroom/indoor recreation footprint is a glazed wall. The triple tier design has the benefit of allowing natural light to penetrate deeply into the building interior. This has both health and energy conservation benefits. Access to natural light is important for human health, whether related to the production of Vitamin D or the regulation of circadian rhythms, and has the added benefit of limiting the use of artificial light, which both uses electricity and produces heat which must be removed by air conditioning systems which also use electricity. The feeling of openness and the expansive views provided by the glazed wall are psychologically relevant, as they mitigate the institutional nature of jail.

2.3 Mezzanine Walkways and Stairs (See Appendix A, Figs. 3, 4, 12 and 13)

The second and third tier cells are accessed by mezzanine walkways. These walkways are enclosed by no-climb fence fabric. This eliminates any safety concerns associated with the height of the mezzanines above finished floor. The mezzanine walkways form a "U" at the far end, adjacent to the glazed wall, allowing two means of egress from any point on the mezzanine (a code requirement). The mezzanines terminate in rated stair towers which allow movement between tiers. The stair towers each include an elevator for vertical movement by those who are not able bodied (1 in 10 cells is handicapped accessible). The use of rated stair towers eliminates some of the concerns associated with open straight stairs typical in dayrooms, including the potential for injury associated with falling down or jumping off a long run of 16 or 17 stairs, occlusion of sightlines by the stairs themselves, and the amount of additional floor space required for any portion of the space under the stair where head height is less than 7'-6" above finished floor. Were a detainee to fall (or throw him or herself down) a run of stairs, change in elevation is limited to 4'-1"—reducing the potential for serious injury. Rated egress stairs already required by code in a high-rise make typical dayroom stairs (and their cost) duplicative.

2.4 Housing Support (See Appendix A, Figs. 3 and 4)

Support spaces associated with the housing unit include meeting rooms on Tier 2 and 3. These meeting rooms are sized for twelve detainees and are intended for detainee led meetings such as study groups, bible study, AA or NA, interest groups, etc. based on availability of supervisory custody staff. They are accessible from either stair tower, thereby maintaining two means of egress. Since the meetings occur inside the housing unit perimeter and only involve custodial staff, there is no need for detainees to be searched afterwards.

On Tier 1 and 2, spaces off the stair towers are available for storage or utility spaces. These spaces have not yet been allocated. On Tier 3 these same spaces serve as combination search rooms and sallyports for entering and exiting the Services Mall.

On Tier 1, dual sallyports provide separate ingress and egress at the dayroom. A non-contact visitation stall is provided for professional visits, allowing these to be used without the need for the detainee to be searched. This will greatly facilitate attorney visits, as these can occur on the attorney's schedule instead of having to be pre-scheduled.

Additionally, outside the housing unit perimeter there are two large storage rooms at each end of the 1st tier circulation system of corridors and sallyports. These support the five housing units that make up the mini-jail. Probable items to be stored are extra mattresses and additional furniture for special use, like correctional grade folding tables.

2.5 Contact Visitation (See Appendix A, Fig. 3)

Visitors are screened in the lower levels of the building and proceed upstairs to the housing units for contact visitation (yellow in Fig. 3). The Contact Visitation space is opposite the vertical circulation cores from the Dayroom/Indoor Recreation areas, which means there is one contact visitation space per housing unit. The space is sized to allow five detainees to visit simultaneously, with each detainee allowed six visitors (adults or children) each. The space is directly supervised by a correctional officer. Following the visit, detainees must proceed up the detainee elevator to the Services Mall (see Fig. 4) and be searched prior to any contact with detainees inside or outside the secure perimeter of the housing unit. The visitation area includes shelving for storage of toys, books and games. Two ADA accessible unisex restrooms serve each visitation space. The simulation assumes that a visit lasts 50 min.

2.6 Services Mall (See Appendix A, Fig. 4)

At the third tier level, a "Services Mall" provides spaces to support detainee reentry like the "Jails to Jobs" program, individual psychological assessment and therapy, skills classes, meetings that help connect detainees to services in the community offered by the providers themselves, and positive behavior change classes. The spaces (green in Fig. 4) are distributed as follows: six classrooms of up to twelve detainees each with a single unisex restroom each, twelve single detainee therapy offices in suites of three with a single unisex restroom per suite, two flexible rooms with loose furniture for group therapy or other less structured programs with a single unisex restroom each, a space for commissary via vending machines, and a space for doing personal laundry (an important life skill).

Staff and volunteer-related spaces include four elevator lobbies (grey in Fig. 4) so that non-custodial staff and volunteers can gather and be efficiently dispatched to their staffing locations at the start of the day, as well as one open plan break room, not yet configured but likely to include several restrooms and a kitchenette.

2.7 Rated Stair Towers (See Appendix A, Fig. 2)

It is important to note that there are no sightlines into rated stair towers (purple in Fig. 2) at any level. Stair towers must therefore be traversable by a single detainee at a time. In order to accomplish this, all the doors associated with a stair tower must be electronically interlocked, meaning only one door can be opened at a time. Thus:

1. access control readers on both sides of doors,
2. remotely operated, electromagnetic locks and a closer at each opening, and
3. cameras with digital analytics to detect tailgating and wrong way movement.

These measures, in combination with interior motion detection, confirm that only a single detainee is inside a stair tower at a time—or conversely—trigger an alarm at central control. They also ensure that travel through the stair tower is complete prior to another detainee entering. If only one detainee is allowed in a stair tower at a time, then detainee on detainee violence is not possible.

3 A Different Approach

3.1 Detainee Movement (See Appendix A, Figs. 6, 7 and 8)

The point that ***detainee movement is inherently safe when limited to a single detainee at a time*** is a critical driver of both the design—and the desired outcomes—of this concept. Conventional correctional design involves escorted movement, meaning that a correctional officer escorts a detainee or detainees from point A to point B [5]. On Rikers Island, this means two things: One, the detainee is placed in restraints (handcuffs at a minimum, but often additional restraints; typical when groups are escorted) which is both time consuming (increasing staffing levels and cost) and something that reinforces detainee 'dangerousness' and (feelings of) confinement. Two, the opportunity for violence exists during escorted movement. Many use-of-force incidents in the NYC jail system are associated with escorted movement. Furthermore, use-of-force incidents and other security related issues result in housing units being locked down, meaning that detainees are confined to their cells, preventing beneficial use of day space, movement to programs or visitation, and severely impacting operations [6]. Any design that eliminates routine escorted movement, restricts detainee transitions through spaces to a single detainee at a time (unescorted movement), and ensures that detainees come in contact with other detainees, non-custodial staff or volunteers, visitors, or custodial staff *only in direct supervision settings*—will increase safety and reduce levels of stress experienced by everyone. Reduced stress is a foundation of organizational culture change.

3.2 Why a New Approach

The NYC Department of Correction (NYC DOC) is violent, overly punitive, and neglectful [7]. NYC DOC fell under the **Nunez v. City of New York**, U.S.D.C. (S.D. NY), Case No. 1:11-cv-05845-LTS-JCF federal consent decree on October 22, 2015. In the three years following, full-time correctional officers increased 689 to 10,226 and full-time civilians increased 404 to 2,151. This means that the NYC DOC staff to detainee ratio increased from approximately **1.15:1** to approximately **1.6:1**, which is *5x higher* than one of the highest performing facilities nationwide, Arlington County, VA, which has a staff to detainee ratio of 0.33:1. Still, ***use of force incidents rose*** from 4,074 to 5,175—***a 27% increase***.

Culture change is a critical issue for the replacement jail system in NYC. Allowing this culture to be transplanted into new facilities would undermine this 'once in a generation opportunity' and the massive investment in new facilities. The goal is nothing less than to reinvent corrections in the City of New York and become a model for jurisdictions everywhere. This will not happen unless design supports culture change and the maintenance of the new organizational culture.

3.3 Institutional Culture in the Jails

Institutional culture (a combination of organizational culture and detainee culture) is the primary driver of outcomes, not architectural design. Policies, procedures, and post orders are the guardrails of organizational culture [8]. Staff/detainee communication and proactive goal-directed engagement are indicators of a healthy institutional culture, as these are in alignment with the principles of direct supervision [9].

3.4 Psychological Drivers in Jails

Psychological drivers can be even more critical. If organizational culture is the baseline for mitigating the negatives inherent in institutional operations [10], then psychological drivers are fulcrums that have the potential to magnify positives or negatives, proportionally driving outcomes.

Staff Vigilance. The primary psychological driver of outcomes is staff vigilance. Correctional officers maintain effective control; it is their raison d'être. However, facility design either promotes or undermines staff vigilance. For example, in linear intermittent facilities, correctional officers are only able to surveil detainees during guard tours, and only to the extent the design allows. The detainees effectively run the facility between tours, and staff vigilance, to the extent it exists, is wasted. Direct supervision provides no physical security barriers between detainees and a single correctional officer. Staff vigilance is assured because anything less than complete situational awareness and proactive engagement with detainees will eventually result in a detainee-on-staff assault. Detainees keep the staff under counter-surveillance; line staff know this, and because it is in their best interest to avoid being victimized, vigilance levels are high. In true direct supervision, operations are based on the officer being mobile, which at a minimum keeps the situation dynamic and opportunities for initiating a violent attack fleeting.

Covert Indicators of Brain Chemistry. The other primary psychological driver of outcomes is real-time detainee characteristics: stress levels, aggression, and other indicators of brain chemistry. Individual mental states are revealed only through behavior. Direct supervision has the advantage of providing staff with multiple sensory modalities in order to detect issues and proactively deal with them: sight and sound predominating. Body language can be mined for information, as can how far or near detainees stand in proximity [11], as well as in which groups. Aural information is also telling.

Managing Brain Chemistry. Regarding management of this psychological driver, the best tool that operators have is large muscle exercise. Vigorous exercise or labor changes the equation for the better, in terms of detainee brain chemistry. Post-exercise β-endorphins, dopamine, norepinephrine, and serotonin balance stress hormones like adrenaline [12]. This cocktail is eventually replaced with generalized fatigue, a lower state of arousal than simple physiological homeostasis. Consequently, daily large muscle exercise lowers levels of psychological and physiological arousal, reducing the likelihood of stress or aggression.

Triggers of Aggression. Bad news, on the other hand, increases stress, and resulting aggression. Most bad news arrives during visitation (personal or professional,) and especially during phone calls. For this reason, inmate phones should be placed proximate to staff stations, so custody staff can better monitor body language and behaviors that result from such calls. Early intervention on the staff member's part can break the cycle that otherwise begins with the bad news received, continues with transferred aggression, and ends with a violent outburst or an assault.

A Call for Action. Jail is an extreme situation that places detainees and staff under stress. Extreme situations demand extreme solutions, even in the no-beta-testing culture of detention and corrections. Under such circumstances, drivers that otherwise might not be salient are revealed, allowing design and operational mitigation strategies to manage inmate behavior [13]. The contribution of psychological drivers to the successful outcomes demonstrated by direct supervision [14] should eventually provide practitioners with evidence-based design guidelines that balance facility design and operational integration for best outcomes at the lowest capital and operational cost.

4 Simulations for Design that Helps Generate Positive Organizational Culture

4.1 Validity of Simulations (See Appendix A, Fig. 5)

This paper does not attempt to explain the inner workings of the simulation. Because the designer and the systems engineer are both motivated to have the simulation and modeling effectively guide the design and eventually produce measurable improvements in outcomes, all decisions regarding model construction, parameter selection and modification, and other levers that shift the results of simulation runs were made with that goal in mind. This is a form of pseudo-validity. Actually validating the model would have to wait for operationally generated data once the building is done. Even that would only occur if the real-world data mirrored the simulation generated data. Although positive outcomes would be welcome regardless of causality, the City of New York would be best served if data collection protocols were generated in parallel with design and construction of the new high-rise jails. Early simulation runs have pointed to issues that either design or operations will have to address. These will be addressed in turn.

4.2 Stair Tower Bottlenecks (See Appendix A, Figs. 2, 6, 7 and 8)

The stairs appear to be the biggest bottleneck in the housing unit model, as detainees move between tiers accessing the dayroom for meals and the Services Mall for programs during subsequent (counterflow) movement. Detainees housed on upper tiers are delayed getting to the dayroom for their meals. The last arrivals were about 30 min past the hour. One possible mitigation strategy is staggering meal start times. This could take the form of even numbered cells (on all tiers) starting meals at the top of the hour, while odd numbered cells start meals at half past the hour. In-cell personal hygiene would occur in the non-meal portion of the three hours per day designated for these purposes.

4.3 Adjusting Model Parameters

Alternatively, adjustment of model parameters, such as the duration of certain events during discrete event simulation could mitigate bottlenecks. For example, if the overall rate of detainee movement (a global parameter) were to be increased, the reduction in transition time would be significant in aggregate. However, such adjustments must be reasonable, as discussed in the section on validity above. Another event, the duration of time between presentation of credentials to the access control reader and the cycling of the lock when there is nothing else impinging upon that action is approximately 500 ms. Within the framework of the simulation, when time steps are 30 s, this becomes a non-event. The first simulation runs we attempted allocated a full-time step to the authentication process. This was discovered as we brainstormed how to deal with apparent bottlenecks at the stair towers.

4.4 Log Jams (See Appendix A, Figs. 3, 4, 6, 7 and 8)

Because unescorted movement spaces such as mezzanines, stairs and sallyports can only contain one detainee at a time, "log jams" or "check mates" sometimes arose. These occurred when detainees on either side of a controlled opening were headed in opposite directions. Carefully laying out architectural spaces and predetermining detainee pathways may eliminate log jams. One approach might be to have security electronics software algorithms reserve the entire pathway between a detainee's starting location and his or her ending location before starting that sequence of movement. This would have the advantage of ensuring no other detainees block that movement sequence. However, such an approach would only be able to support simultaneous movement of detainees when their paths do not overlap. Whether the system could support temporal instead of location-based conflict avoidance is a critical issue in terms of overall efficiency. If all movement paths that conflict must be serially sequenced (location-based) instead of supporting simultaneous but staggered (temporal) movement, efficiency will suffer.

4.5 Direction of Movement (See Appendix A, Figs. 6, 7 and 8)

The system doesn't necessarily need to reserve pathways in both directions. Downstream flows are when detainees follow each other in the same direction. The detainees move in a "pace line," seizing spaces one at a time, as the detainee in front clears that space. Upstream flows, conversely, are when detainees reserve the entire pathway in the opposite direction. One way to visualize it is to think about the circulatory system in the human body. It never reverses direction because it is a loop (also because its 'secured openings' include valves that only allow one-way movement). If all detainee movement could occur in a closed loop, conflicts would only be temporal, not spatial. However, the redundancy and resilience of the human circulatory system is limited, thus myocardial infarctions and strokes.

4.6 Additional Mitigation Strategies

Additional mitigation strategies to reduce bottlenecks might include staggered start times for programs, meta level scheduling, such as emphasizing inclusion of recreation the hour prior to mealtimes/hygiene time, etc. We are just at the beginning of our explorations. The simulation model can test (and quantify) the impact of each strategy to determine which will work, which won't, and perhaps what trade-offs exist. This requires key performance indicators, or KPIs.

4.7 Key Performance Indicators (See Appendix A, Fig. 9)

We currently have some notion of what KPIs will be appropriate for this model.

Wait time – Aggregate wait time at controlled openings (elapsed time from presentation of credentials to lock cycling) – at the mean of the distribution and at the 95% percentile (two deviations from the mean).

% Compliance – How many detainees in the simulation succeed in receiving five hours per day of education, vocational, and therapeutic programming, a goal of the City of New York [15].

% Utilization – The amount of time a space is utilized during the hours it can be utilized, which varies based on the space. This metric helps uncover potential overutilization in the form of bottlenecks or instances of underutilization, where multi-use spaces might be considered.

Additional KPIs will be considered and some subset of these will be included as simulation-generated data based on how informative they might be, especially over large numbers of simulation runs.

4.8 Future Work

The team intends to explore how the finalized architectural design and associated model and simulation will respond to adverse events. Adverse events could include anything that prevents a space from being used. The prime adverse event we want to explore is what happens when a detainee refuses to leave a stair tower. Another would be if a detainee has a medical crisis while transiting a mezzanine walkway. The list is endless and range from the micro to the meso, from events involving a single detainee to group actions like riots, to acts of God like an airplane crashing into the building, causing a multi-alarm fire. Basically, we intend to start small and study how the KPIs respond when we "throw a wrench into the system" so we can understand the levels of resilience and redundancy extant in the design and operations as currently conceived.

5 Conclusions

The City of New York is dramatically reforming its justice system [16]. The new policy is to minimize the use of detention and close Rikers Island [17]. Towards that end, four new high-rise jails are proposed. A central concern is the high probability of transference of NYC DOC's dysfunctional organizational culture to these new facilities. To address this issue, policy, staffing, and administrative measures have been proposed, and the best minds [7] are actively engaged with the issue. This paper outlines an approach which explores the design of mini-jails and housing units that actively mitigate or eliminate the possibility of negative interactions between all actors, limiting human interaction to spaces under direct supervision. To support such design and operational integration, discrete event simulation is employed to refine the design, to fine tune the scheduling, to facilitate operations in the form of unescorted movement, and to pseudo-validate the modeling and simulation so employed. Although the work continues, the results to date suggest that architectural design, systems integration, operational integration, and discrete event simulation and modeling all have a role to play in pursuit of culture change and positive outcomes.

Appendix A

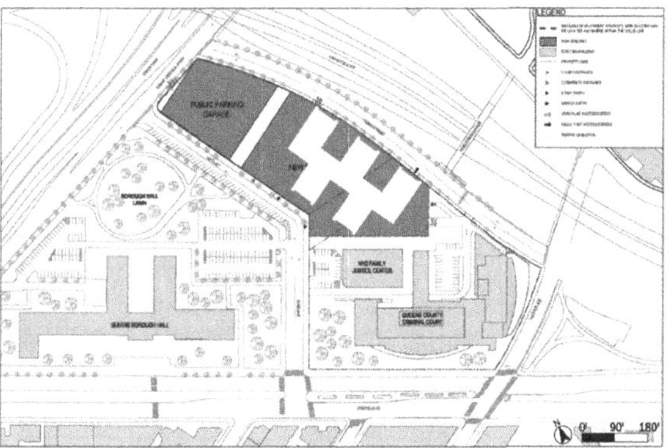

Fig. 1. Site plan with conceptual housing towers

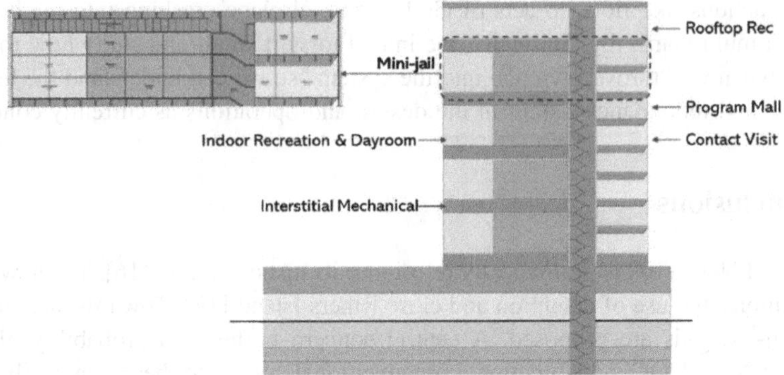

Fig. 2. Building section

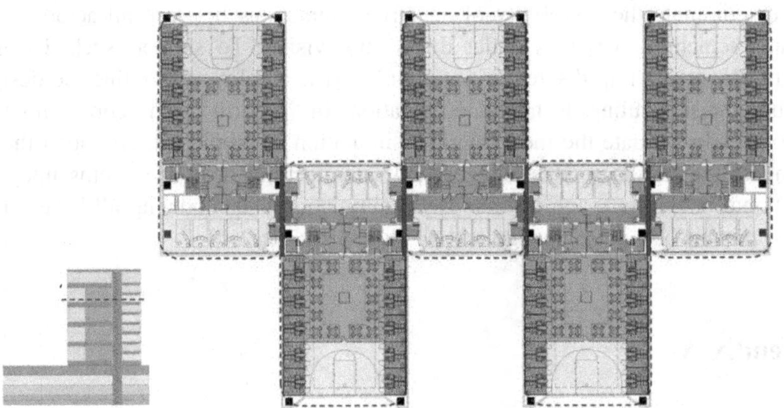

Fig. 3. Dayroom, indoor recreation, and contact visitation

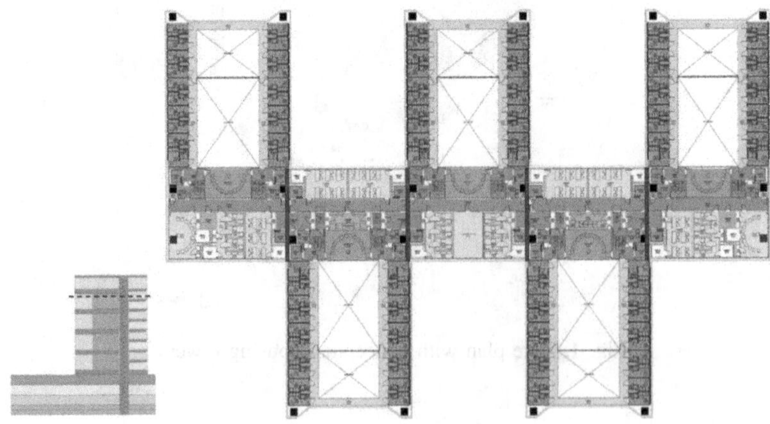

Fig. 4. Services mall

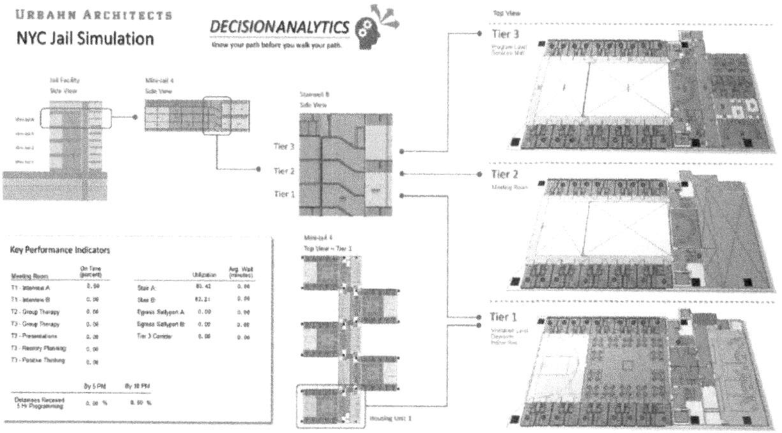

Fig. 5. NYC jail simulation

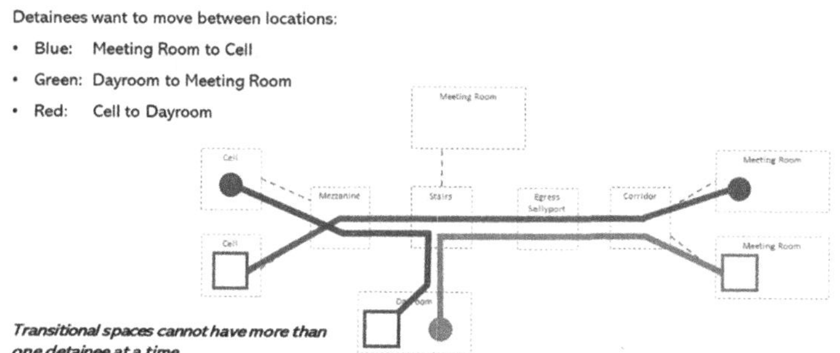

Fig. 6. Detainee movement goal states

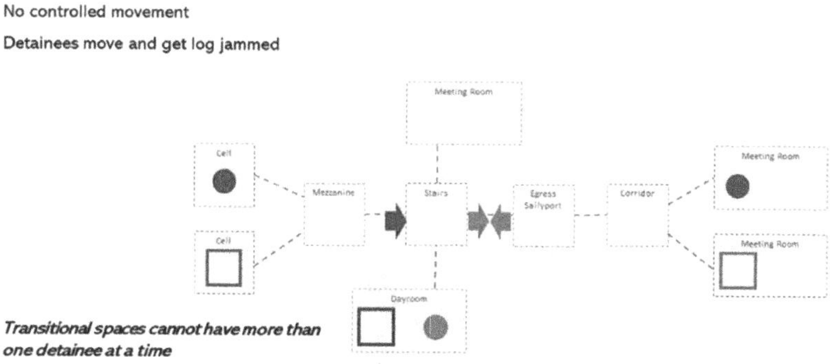

No controlled movement

Detainees move and get log jammed

Meeting Room

Cell

Meeting Room

Mezzanine

Stairs

Egress Sallyport

Corridor

Cell

Meeting Room

Dayroom

Transitional spaces cannot have more than one detainee at a time

Fig. 7. Logjammed detainee movement

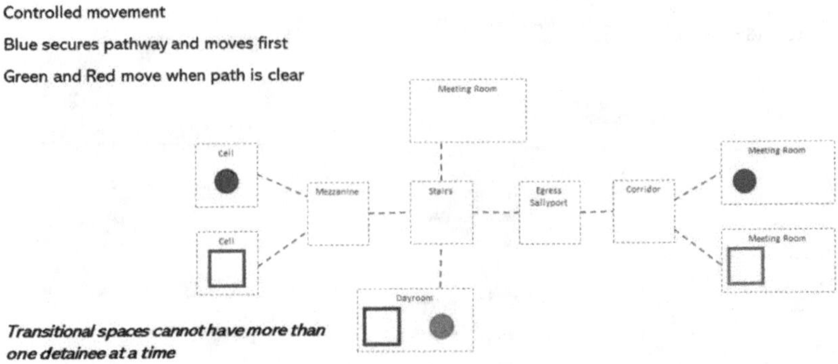

Controlled movement

Blue secures pathway and moves first

Green and Red move when path is clear

Meeting Room

Cell

Mezzanine

Stairs

Egress Sallyport

Corridor

Meeting Room

Cell

Meeting Room

Dayroom

Transitional spaces cannot have more than one detainee at a time

Fig. 8. Detainee controlled movement

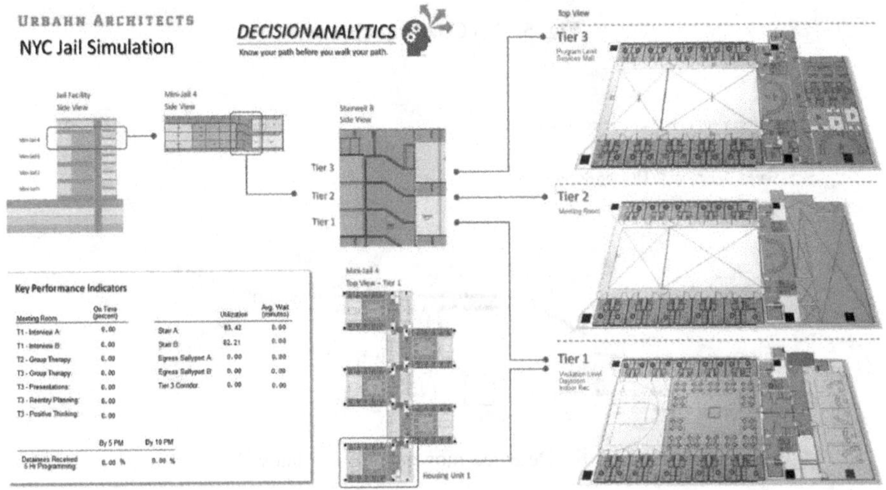

Fig. 9. Key performance indicators

Fig. 10. Housing tower concept, view 1

Fig. 11. Housing tower concept, view 2

Fig. 12. Dayroom to indoor recreation interior elevation, view 1

Fig. 13. Indoor recreation to dayroom interior elevation, view 2

References

1. Carter, S.: Career extensions: the footprints of David Parrish. Correct. News **14**(7), 19–21 (2008)
2. Farbstein, J., Wener, R.: A Comparison of "Direct" and "Indirect" Supervision Correctional Facilities. National Institute of Corrections, Washington, DC (1989)
3. Tartaro, C., Levy, M.: Density, inmate assaults, and direct supervision jails. Crim. Justice Policy Rev. **18**(4), 395–417 (2007)
4. Lester, H., McKay, G., Lester, E.: Sociotechnical systems for high rise detention. In: 26th ISTE International Conference on Transdisciplinary Engineering (TE 2019) Conference Proceedings. IOS Press, Amsterdam (2019, Forthcoming)
5. Ricci, K., Greene, F., Genevro, R.: What Jails Can't Do. Urban Omnibus, New York (2017)
6. New York City Board of Correction: Annual Lockdown Report. Board of Correction, New York (2019)
7. Jacobson, M., DeWolf, E., Egan, M., Hafetz, D.: Beyond the Island: changing the culture of New York City jails. Fordham Urban Law J. **45**(2), 373–436 (2018)
8. Drapkin, M.: Developing Policies and Procedures for Jails. United Book Press, Baltimore (1996)
9. American Jail Association: Resolution: Direct Supervision Jails [Principles of Direct Supervision]. Adopted by the Board of Directors on November 14, 1992. Re-affirmed on May 3, 2008, by the AJA Board of Directors in Sacramento, CA. Amended on October 17, 2013, by the AJA Board of Directors in St. Louis, MO. https://www.americanjail.org/files/About%20PDF/_AJA%20Resolutions%20-%20January%202017.pdf. Accessed 12 Aug 2019
10. Kerle, K.: Exploring Jail Operations. American Correctional Association, Hagerstown (2003)
11. Hall, E.: The Hidden Dimension. Doubleday, Garden City (1966)
12. Craft, L., Perna, F.: The benefits of exercise for the clinically depressed. Prim. Care Companion J. Clin. Psychiatry **6**(3), 104–111 (2004)
13. Hutchinson, V.: Managing inmate behavior in jails. Correct. Today **67**(5), 28–31 (2005)
14. Parrish, D.: The evolution of direct supervision in the design and operation of jails. Correct. Today **62**(6), 84–88 (2000)
15. Mayor's Office of Criminal Justice: Justice Implementation Task Force Culture Change Working Group Meeting #1. Mayor's Office of Criminal Justice, New York (2017)
16. Mayor's Office of Criminal Justice: Breaking the Frame? Remaking the Criminal Justice System in New York City. Mayor's Office of Criminal Justice, New York (2019)
17. Glazer, E.: Progress on Closing Rikers Island. New York City Council's Committee on Fire and Criminal Justice Services, New York (2017)

ADIoT Workshop

A Basic Theory of Lightweight Hierarchical Key Predistribution Scheme

Deepak Kumar Dalai(✉)

School of Mathematical Sciences,
National Institute of Science Education and Research, HBNI,
Bhubaneswar 752 050, Odisha, India
deepak@niser.ac.in

Abstract. Key management is a basic requirement for any security solution. Lightweight key predistribution schemes (KPS) that establish symmetric secrets are best suited for resource constraint devices of low cost Internet of Things (IoT), sensors of Wireless Sensor Networks (WSN). Although there exist numerous elegant KPS, an appropriate hierarchical proposal is absent. To design such a scheme, we propose a combinatorial tool *hierarchical set system/design*. As an application of such a tool, we propose a deterministic lightweight hierarchical KPS (HKPS) that achieves the desirable design criteria:

- *decentralized hierarchy* of a fixed number of depths (l);
- *resilient* against compromise of (i) any number of lower level nodes; and (ii) a threshold number of nodes of same level in the hierarchy;
- *non-interactive* which saves bandwidth and energy;
- *deterministic* KPS which implies the nodes in the network have predictable behaviour of key rings;
- *efficient* as it uses hash chains rather than any public key based key exchange or bilinear maps;
- *free* to choose any basic KPS at any level/depth of hierarchy as per the requirement of that level;
- *simplicity* in design.

To enhance the resilience of the HKPS, we exploited the hash chain idea. Further, we instantiate the HKPS with a very efficient KPS Sensornet. The studies presented here are theoretical and does not contain any experimental and comparative results.

Keywords: Low cost IoT · Wireless Sensor Network · Security · Key predistribution scheme · Hash function · Combinatorial set design

1 Introduction

Internet of Things (IoT) is an emerging technology that has been recently incorporated into our life to make it more comfortable. Resource constraint (low power, computation power, memory etc) devices such as sensors, systems-on-chips, microcontrollers are basic devices low cost IOT. These devices need to

S. Katsikas et al. (Eds.): ESORICS 2019 Workshops, LNCS 11980, pp. 325–340, 2020.
https://doi.org/10.1007/978-3-030-42048-2_21

communicate for networking. Some communications need to be secure and communicated data needs to encrypted. In this paper, we will discuss resource constraint Wireless Sensor Networks. Same would be applied for communication in a resource constraint network.

Wireless Sensor Networks (WSN), a typical low cost prototype of IoT are widely used to connect various smart devices. WSN consists of numerous resource starved sensory devices (sensor or nodes) that deal with sensitive IoT data. These homogeneous nodes are battery powered with a tiny processor, small memory and a wireless transceiver. Networks may either have a flat topology with these identical nodes or a decentralized hierarchy achieved by introducing nodes at the different depth(s). The nodes at lower depth are having more computational power, storage capacity, energy and security than the nodes at a higher depth. Therefore, a node at a lower depth (e.g., a parent) can store more number of keys and perform more computation than a node at higher depth (e.g., the children). Moreover, the parent nodes are more secure against the compromise of nodes than the children node.

1.1 Motivation

Constraints in resources (i.e., energy, storage and computation) of IoT devices, like sensors of WSN, forbids implementations of public key cryptosystems for secure communication in them. Therefore, relatively inexpensive symmetric key cryptosystems (SKC) are adapted in these low cost networks. As the SKC require the end parties to possess the same encryption-decryption key(s), the scheme requires the implementation of an adequate key predistribution scheme (KPS). Several existing approaches to KPS are available [10,12–16,19,24] in literature. See Sect. 2.1 for a brief survey of some prominent KPS and their limitations in adapting to low cost hierarchical setups.

The situation becomes more critical when the number of nodes increases and the network of the organization is already in hierarchical in nature; forcing us to implement a hierarchy via labeling of special nodes that decentralizes the network. Practical instances of such networks are ad-hoc networks that have volatile inter nodal communications or an internal network of a multinational company which has its offices all across the world. More critical applications include military networks or health care or automated processes that must always be ready for an emergency.

Such networks may be well served by a protocol that ensures pair-wise shared key(s) for a node at same as well as different levels. Of course, due to the large (and growing) size of the network and limited storage in each node, subsets of users must share some common key(s). For example, for a military network, during a normal course of action, regiment heads are responsible for their team member's (child's) performance. Being fewer, they may well be given extra physical protection and be allowed to listen in all their children's communications. All existing works [5,13,17,18] are designed to support such systems.

Time of emergency may demand children of various subdivision to securely collaborate among themselves. Involvement of respective parents (or even worse, the root central authority) in such interactions may not be feasible due to practical constraints like distance and traffic overload. These practical instances are not captured by existing works [3–6,8,12,13,15–18,21,22] and motivate our hierarchical key predistribution proposal. In fact solutions with hierarchy provided by state-of-the-art protocols like [13,17,21] relies on random graph theory [11], identity-based key agreement protocol of Sakai et al. [20] and PBIBD [19] respectively. These have some issues of practicality which are briefly discussed in Sect. 2.1.

1.2 Our Contribution

The primary contribution in this paper is a proposal for an efficient and secure hierarchical KPS (HKPS). To extend the idea of designing deterministic KPS from the combinatorial design (see Sect. 2.4), we introduced the concept of combinatorial hierarchical design for building an HKPS. This idea of mapping can be a basic theory to design several HKPS. Hence, we propose a simple and elegant product based HKPS next. This HKPS is built from a set of basic KPS, where a KPS is chosen at each level of the hierarchy. As a result, the designer has the freedom to choose an appropriate KPS as per the requirements (e.g., number of nodes, size of the key ring, efficiency, resiliency, connectivity) at that level. Further, to ensure the security of parent nodes after a capture of several child nodes, we proposed the hash chain technique. This hash chain technique ensures resilience against compromise of any number of lower level nodes. Such a hash chain based HKPS is denoted as HC-HKPS. Further, we have discussed an instant of such HKPS by building over a very efficient KPS Sensornet. Our contribution is theoretical and starting point of such a design. Therefore, the paper does not contain any experimental and comparative results.

1.3 Organization

We have already outlined our research objectives. Rest of the paper is organized as follows. Important preliminary requirements for this work are drafted in Sect. 2. A brief survey of KPS and HKPS are presented in Sects. 2.1 and 2.2 respectively. Two important metrics resilience (R_t) and connectivity (C)for the evaluation of a KPS is defined in Sect. 2.3. Further, Sect. 2.4 presents the definition of useful combinatorial designs and the mapping to build a KPS from it.

The main contribution is presented in Sect. 3. In this section, the *hierarchical set design* is introduced which can be mapped for the construction of an HKPS. Further, an HKPS is designed from the proposed product based hierarchical design. To improve the resilience at the parent level, a hash chain technique is implemented to build a secure HKPS. Section 4 investigates instantiation of the proposed HKPS to a class of a very efficient KPS, Sensornet. Section 5 concludes the paper and states relevant research directions.

2 Preliminary

2.1 Key Predistribution Scheme: An Overview

An approach for authentication in open network [22] assume that trust on nodes is rather risky as nodes are vulnerable to several attacks. Further, mutual sharing of keys is impractical for the large networks (with hierarchy) due to storage overheads. These considerations led to the evolution of key predistribution schemes (KPS).

Ideally, any KPS should have small key rings, yet support large networks with appreciable resilience and connectivity. However, the authors in [15,16] indicate the impossibility of constructing such a 'perfect KPS' that meets all these criteria. This motivates proposals of several designs that are robust for the specific purpose(s). Next, we recall the steps executed by any KPS.

- *Offline generation and preallocation of keys:* A large (ν) collection of keys (key pool $:= \mathcal{K}; |\mathcal{K}| = \nu$) and their identifiers (ids) are generated offline. Equal sized subsets of keys (rank $:= z$) are preallocated into each sensor node at the time of their joining the network. Each key gets shared by the same number of nodes (degree $:= r$). Fixed value of z and r may ensure equal load (desirable).
- *Key establishment:* This process is one of two cases, as described below:
  - *(i) Shared key discovery* phase establishes shared key(s) among the participants. Individual users broadcast all their key ids or, node id. From each other's ids, each sensor matches them or, follows a computation to trace their mutual shared key id(s), hence common key(s).
  - *(ii) Path key establishment*: establishes an optimized path key between a given pair of nodes that do not share any common key and involves intermediate nodes.

Depending on whether the above processes are probabilistic or deterministic, such schemes are broadly classified into two types: (a) *random* and (b) *deterministic*. We present below a brief overview of individual type of schemes.

Random Key Predistribution Schemes (RKPS): First generation KPS rely on random graph theory [11]) to randomly preload (symmetric) cryptographic keys into the sensors. This leads to random formation of key rings and hence, probabilistic *key sharing* and *establishment* process followed in such KPS. Later is achieved by either broadcast of key ids or *challenge and response* as described in the first ever random distributed KPS [12, Section 2.1]). Ramkumar et al. [17] used the work [12] to propose a *random hierarchical key predistribution scheme*. The scheme [17] has been elegantly used to propose a random hierarchical KPS in identity based settings by Gennaro et al. [13]. This scheme achieves full resilience against leaf node compromise attacks, but at the expense of heavy bilinear map computations. Implementation of such maps may not be feasible in low cost IoT environments. Being a random design, connectivity of this scheme is not assured and is quite degraded like the protocols [12,17].

Deterministic Key Predistribution Schemes (DKPS): The deterministic KPS are based on combinatorial set system/design [23]. Deterministic schemes have the advantage of predictable behavior of system parameters that are probabilistic in random ones (see [15,16]). Consequently, numerous combinatorial KPS [5,8,15,18] have been proposed. Patterson and Stinson [16] presents a unified platform to study these combinatorial objects through their notion of partially balanced t–designs. Certain deterministic approaches [1,9] generically fix deficiency of particular parameters (like resilience) of prominent KPS, random or deterministic. Hash chain technique in [1] that we use in our work to achieve full resilience against leaf node compromise attacks.

2.2 Hierarchical KPS (HKPS)

Some solutions with hierarchy provided by state-of-the-art protocols like [13,17,21] relies on random graph theory [11], identity-based key agreement protocol of Sakai et al. [20] and PBIBD [19] respectively. Random solutions [17] have the inherent problem of unpredictable behavior of crucial system parameters like connectivity, resilience. Gennaro et al. [13] propose two random hierarchical KPS that involve identity based public key computations which are expensive. Moreover, such scheme has high computational and memory requirement as the schemes use public key based Diffie-Hellman key exchange at a certain stage. The scheme proposed by Sarkar [21] has lack of practicality as the difference of the number of keys between parent and child is one. However, the hash chain technique [1,2] used in [21] to enhance the resilience is too used in our proposed scheme. These facts make their deployment impractical in real life scenarios.

2.3 Evaluation Metrics

If an adversary captures a node, it can read all secret information from the node's memory. Hence, a capture of nodes leads to partial disclosure of the key pool $\mathcal{K}$ and other device's key ring. Use of the links that were secured by these keys are no longer permitted. A system's link failure probability or oppositely, the resilience against an attack that compromises t nodes is measured by a standard metrics $R(t)$ [1,2,6]. We restate the definitions next.

Definition 1. *The network resiliency $R(t)$ is defined as the fraction of uncompromised links in the original network nodes when t nodes are captured.*
Notationally, $R(t) = 1 - \frac{d_t}{L} = 1 - P(LC \mid NC_t)$ *where*

- *L is the total number of links in the network;*
- *d_t is the number of compromised links after compromise of t nodes;*
- *LC is the event that an arbitrary link is compromised;*
- *NC_t is the event that t nodes are compromised in a network.*

Two nodes can communicate them self if there is a shared key between them and able to establish a link. Not all proposed KPS in literature are fully connected. If two nodes are not having a link then they have to communicate through other nodes establishing multiple links. This way of communication becomes vulnerable to information leak and attack, slows down the performance, consumes more energy etc. Hence a good KPS must have high connectivity. The metric connectivity (C) in a KPS is defined as the probability that two nodes can establish a link in the network i.e., $C = \frac{\text{number of possible links in the network}}{\text{number of pair of nodes in the network}}$.

2.4 Combinatorial Designs and KPS

There have been several papers that have used combinatorial design technique on the basic idea presented in [12]. The use of different combinatorial designs was primarily presented in paper [15] for having deterministic KPS. After then there are several KPS based on combinatorial designs have been proposed. A survey on KPS in WSN are available by Chen and Chao [7]. Recently, Paterson and Stinson have unified the combinatorial design techniques by partially balanced t–design [16]. The same paper has listed the important schemes based on combinatorial designs with proper references.

Let $\mathcal{X}$ be a finite set. The elements of $\mathcal{X}$ are called varieties. Each subset of $\mathcal{X}$ is termed as a block. Consider $\mathcal{A}$ to be a collection of blocks of $\mathcal{X}$. Then the pair $(\mathcal{X}, \mathcal{A})$ is said to be a *set system* or, a *design.* $(\mathcal{X}, \mathcal{A})$ is regular (of degree r) if each variety is contained in r blocks. $(\mathcal{X}, \mathcal{A})$ is uniform (of rank z) if all blocks have the same size, say z.

Further, a design $(\mathcal{X}, \mathcal{A})$ is said to form a (v, b, r, z)–*design* if

- $|\mathcal{X}| = v$ and $|\mathcal{A}| = b$;
- $(\mathcal{X}, \mathcal{A})$ is regular of degree r and uniform of rank z.

A (v, b, r, z)–design can be used to construct a KPS (see [15]) by mapping:

1. the v *varieties* of $\mathcal{X}$ to the set of keys in the scheme (i.e., *key pool* $\mathcal{K}$),
2. b to the number of nodes in the system (i.e., *network size*),
3. r to the number of nodes sharing a key (i.e., *degree of the resultant KPS*)
4. z to the number of keys per node (i.e., *size of key rings*).

The elements of $\mathcal{X}$ mapped as the key identifier of the keys in $\mathcal{K}$ and the nodes are assigned the key identifiers in the mapped block and the corresponding keys of the identifiers. To shorten some statements, the KPS formed from a design $\mathcal{S} = (\mathcal{X}, \mathcal{A})$ is called as KPS $\mathcal{S}$. Target is to construct KPS with identical burden on each sensor. This leads to opting for design with uniform rank (z) and regular degree (r); so that every *key ring* is of equal size (z) and same number of nodes (r) share each key for the resultant network.

A (v, b, r, k)–design forms a (v, b, r, k)–*configuration* if any arbitrary pair of blocks intersect in *at most* one point. A (v, b, r, z)–configuration $(\mathcal{X}, \mathcal{A})$ is said to form a μ–*common intersection design (CID)* in case:
$|\{A_\alpha \in \mathcal{A} : A_i \cap A_\alpha \neq \emptyset \text{ and } A_j \cap A_\alpha \neq \emptyset\}| \geq \mu$ whenever $A_i \cap A_j = \emptyset,\ \forall\, i \neq j$.

That is, if two nodes A_i and A_j do not share any key then there are at least μ other nodes which share keys with both A_i and A_j. In this case, the nodes A_i and A_j can communicate via another node which share keys with both A_i and A_j. It is important to construct design that maximize the value of μ.

3 A Deterministic Hierarchical KPS

The design of a KPS from a combinatorial design is described in Subsect. 2.4. In this section, we will introduce a new kind of design call as hierarchical design and will propose a hierarchical KPS (HKPS) by mapping to the new design.

3.1 Hierarchical Design and HKPS

Let $\mathcal{X}$ be a finite set of varieties. Each subset of $\mathcal{X}$ is termed as a block. Let l set of blocks $\mathcal{B}^1, \mathcal{B}^2, \cdots, \mathcal{B}^l$ and $\mathcal{B}^0 = \{\mathcal{X}\}$ satisfy the following condition:

- For each $B \in \mathcal{B}^i$, there is a $A \in \mathcal{B}^{i-1}$ such that $B \subseteq A$ for $1 \leq i \leq l$.

We name the new design as a *hierarchical set system* (or, *hierarchical design*) of depth l and denote as $(\mathcal{X}, \mathcal{B}^1, \mathcal{B}^2, \cdots, \mathcal{B}^l)$. The blocks in $\mathcal{B}^i$ are too called the blocks at depth i.

With the above condition, $\mathcal{B}^i$ can have a disjoint partition such that every block in a partition of $\mathcal{B}^i$ is a subset of a block in $\mathcal{B}^{i-1}$. If a block $B \in \mathcal{B}^i$ is a subset of more than one blocks in $\mathcal{B}^{i-1}$, we put the block B in exactly one of the partitions. Hence, the subset relation in $(\mathcal{X}, \mathcal{B}^1, \mathcal{B}^2, \cdots, \mathcal{B}^l)$ can be viewed as a tree structure where the elements in a partition of $\mathcal{B}^i$ are children of an element in $\mathcal{B}^{i-1}$. The superscripted index i in $\mathcal{B}^i$ refers to the depth/level of hierarchy in the design or the height of the element in the tree. The set of blocks at depth i is $\mathcal{B}^i$ and the number of blocks in depth i is $|\mathcal{B}^i|$. The following is an example of a hierarchical design of depth 2.

Example 1. The set system $(\mathcal{X}, \mathcal{B}^1, \mathcal{B}^2)$, where
$\mathcal{X} = \{1, 2, 3, 4, 5, 6\}, \mathcal{B}^1 = \{\{1, 2, 3, 4\}, \{3, 4, 5, 6\}\}$ and
$\mathcal{B}^2 = \{\{1, 2, 3\}, \{1, 2, 4\}, \{1, 3, 4\}, \{2, 3, 4\}, \{3, 4, 5\}, \{3, 4, 6\}, \{3, 5, 6\}, \{4, 5, 6\}\}$,
is a hierarchical design of depth 2. Figure 1 presents the tree structure of the hierarchical design.

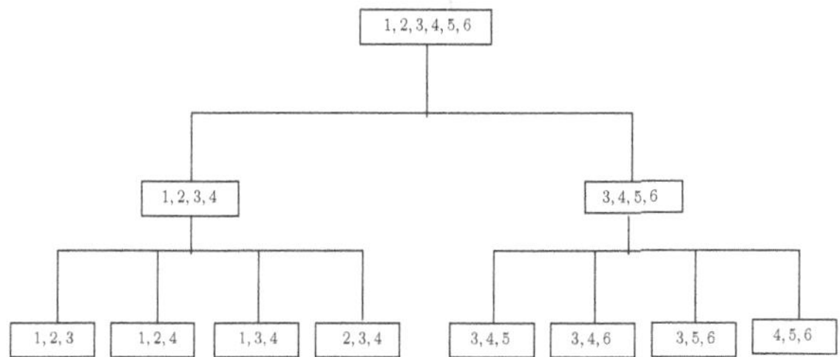

Fig. 1. Tree representation of the hierarchical design $(\mathcal{X}, \mathcal{B}^1, \mathcal{B}^2)$

A $(\mathcal{X}, \mathcal{B}^1, \mathcal{B}^2, \cdots, \mathcal{B}^l)$ hierarchical design can be used to construct an HKPS by mapping:

1. the v varieties of $\mathcal{X}$ to the set of keys in the scheme (i.e., key pool $\mathcal{K}$),
2. the blocks in $\mathcal{B}^i$ to the key ring of the nodes at depth i in HKPS.

The elements of $\mathcal{X}$ mapped as the key identifier of the keys in $\mathcal{K}$ and the nodes are assigned the key identifiers in the mapped block and the corresponding keys of the identifiers. A KPS from a hierarchical design $\mathcal{S} = (\mathcal{X}, \mathcal{B}^1, \mathcal{B}^2, \cdots, \mathcal{B}^l)$ is called as HKPS $\mathcal{S}$. This basic theory of building an HKPS by the mapping from a hierarchical design tempts to design several well suited hierarchical designs. We propose such a hierarchical design and equivalent HKPS in next.

3.2 A Product Based HKPS

We propose a simple construction of a deterministic HKPS using Cartesian product of a number of deterministic KPS. Let $\mathcal{S}_1 = (\mathcal{X}_1, \mathcal{A}_1), \mathcal{S}_2 = (\mathcal{X}_2, \mathcal{A}_2), \cdots, \mathcal{S}_l = (\mathcal{X}_l, \mathcal{A}_l)$ be the set designs of l KPS. The l designs may possibly be generated from different techniques as per the requirement of each level. Consider that each design $\mathcal{S}_i$ is a (v_i, b_i, r_i, z_i)–design with the set of blocks $\mathcal{A}_i = \{A_{i1}, A_{i2}, \cdots, A_{ib_i}\}$ for $1 \leq i \leq l$. For $1 \leq i \leq l$, this implies that

i. $|\mathcal{X}_i| = v_i$,
ii. $|\mathcal{A}_i| = b_i$,
iii. $|A_{ij}| = z_i$ for $1 \leq j \leq b_i$,
iv. each $x \in \mathcal{X}_i$ belongs to r_i blocks in $\mathcal{A}_i$.

Let denote $\mathcal{X} = \mathcal{X}_1 \times \mathcal{X}_2 \times \cdots \times \mathcal{X}_l$ (the Cartesian product of l set of varieties) and $\mathcal{X}_i^l = \mathcal{X}_i \times \mathcal{X}_{i+1} \times \cdots \times \mathcal{X}_l$. A construction of an HKPS on the set of varieties $\mathcal{X}$ is designed from the following hierarchical design.

Construction 1. *Given l designs $\mathcal{S}_1, \mathcal{S}_2, \cdots, \mathcal{S}_l$ as defined above. A hierarchical design $(\mathcal{X}, \mathcal{B}^1, \mathcal{B}^2, \cdots, \mathcal{B}^l)$ for a deterministic HKPS of depth l is constructed as follows.*

1. **Depth** 1*: The set of blocks at depth* 1 *is $\mathcal{B}^1 = \{A_{11} \times \mathcal{X}_2^l, A_{12} \times \mathcal{X}_2^l, \cdots, A_{1b_1} \times \mathcal{X}_2^l\}$. Recall that $\mathcal{A}_1 = \{A_{11}, A_{12}, \cdots, A_{1b_1}\}$ is the set of blocks in the design $\mathcal{S}_1$.*
2. **Depth** d $(1 < d \leq l)$*: For each block $A_{1i_1} \times \cdots \times A_{(d-1)i_{d-1}} \times \mathcal{X}_d^l$ in $(d-1)$-th depth, generate blocks $A_{1i_1} \times \cdots \times A_{(d-1)i_{d-1}} \times A_{di} \times \mathcal{X}_{d+1}^l$ for each $1 \leq i \leq b_d$. Recall that $\mathcal{A}_d = \{A_{d1}, A_{d2}, \cdots, A_{db_d}\}$ is the set of blocks in the design $\mathcal{S}_d$.*

Example 2. Consider two designs $\mathcal{S}_1 = \{\mathcal{X}_1, \mathcal{A}_1\}$ and $\mathcal{S}_2 = \{\mathcal{X}_2, \mathcal{A}_2\}$ where
$\mathcal{X}_1 = \{a, b, c\}, \mathcal{A}_1 = \{\{a, b\}, \{b, c\}, \{a, c\}\}$ and
$\mathcal{X}_2 = \{1, 2, 3, 4\}, \mathcal{A}_2 = \{\{1, 2, 3\}, \{1, 2, 4\}, \{1, 3, 4\}, \{2, 3, 4\}\}$.
Here, $\mathcal{S}_1$ and $\mathcal{S}_2$ are $(3, 3, 2, 2)$ and $(4, 4, 3, 3)$ designs respectively.
Then, $(\mathcal{X}, \mathcal{B}^1, \mathcal{B}^2)$ is a hierarchical design of depth 2 where $\mathcal{X} = \mathcal{X}_1 \times \mathcal{X}_2$,
$\mathcal{B}^1 = \{\{a, b\} \times \mathcal{X}_2, \{b, c\} \times \mathcal{X}_2, \{a, c\} \times \mathcal{X}_2\}$ and
$\mathcal{B}^2 = \{\{a, b\} \times \{1, 2, 3\}, \{a, b\} \times \{1, 2, 4\}, \{a, b\} \times \{1, 3, 4\}, \{a, b\} \times \{2, 3, 4\}$,
$\{b, c\} \times \{1, 2, 3\}, \{b, c\} \times \{1, 2, 4\}, \{b, c\} \times \{1, 3, 4\}, \{b, c\} \times \{2, 3, 4\}$,
$\{a, c\} \times \{1, 2, 3\}, \{a, c\} \times \{1, 2, 4\}, \{a, c\} \times \{1, 3, 4\}, \{a, c\} \times \{2, 3, 4\}\}$.
Figure 2 presents the tree structure of the hierarchical design, where the elements in the nodes of the form xi means $\{x, i\}, x \in \mathcal{X}_1, i \in \mathcal{X}_2$ in the set notation.

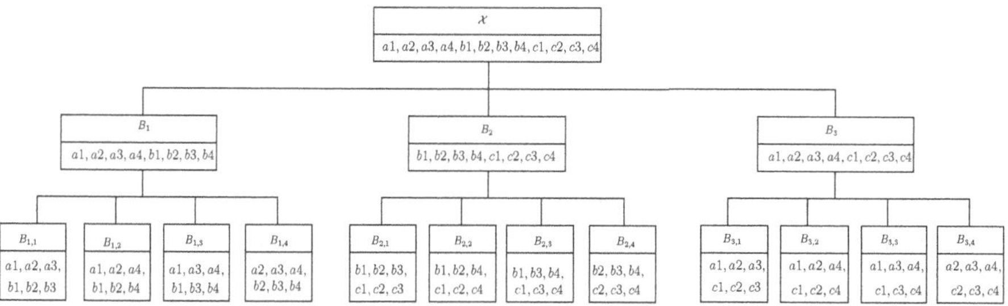

Fig. 2. Tree representation of the above product based hierarchical design $(\mathcal{X}, \mathcal{B}^1, \mathcal{B}^2)$

Notation 1. *For a fixed l, we have the following notations in the hierarchical design.*

- $B_{i_1,\cdots,i_d}$ *denotes the block* $A_{1i_1} \times \cdots \times A_{di_d} \times \mathcal{X}^l_{d+1}$ *for* $1 \leq d \leq l$ *at depth* d.
- *The set of blocks in depth d is* $\mathcal{B}^d = \{B_{\{i_1,\cdots,i_d\}} : 1 \leq i_1 \leq b_1, \cdots, 1 \leq i_d \leq b_d\}$.
- b^d, z^d *and* r^d *are defined in Theorem 1. Note that, the superscript 'd' represents the corresponding values at depth d and not to be confused with the exponential power.*
- $\alpha^d_{ij} = |A_{di} \cap A_{dj}|$ *denotes the number of common elements between the blocks* A_{di} *and* A_{dj} *in the set design* $\mathcal{S}_d$.

Theorem 1. *Given a hierarchical design as in Construction 1 and the corresponding HKPS, we have the following properties.*

1. *The number of blocks at depth d is* $b^d = |\mathcal{B}^d| = \prod_{j=1}^d b_j$.
2. *The number of elements in each block at depth d is* $z^d = \prod_{j=1}^d z_j \times \prod_{j=d+1}^l v_j$.
3. *Each element* $x \in \mathcal{X}$ *belongs to* $r^d = \prod_{j=1}^d r_j$ *blocks in* $\mathcal{B}^d$ *at depth d. Further, x belongs to* $\sum_{d=1}^l \prod_{j=1}^d r_j$ *blocks in the whole hierarchical design.*
4. (a) *The number of common elements between two blocks* $B_{i_1,i_2,\cdots,i_d}$ *and* $B_{j_1,j_2,\cdots,j_d}$ *at depth d is* $|B_{i_1,\cdots,i_d} \cap B_{j_1,\cdots,j_d}| = (\alpha^1_{i_1j_1} \times \cdots \times \alpha^d_{i_dj_d}) \times (v_{d+1} \times \cdots \times v_l)$.
   (b) *The number of common elements between two blocks* $B_{i_1,i_2,\cdots,i_d}$ *and* $B_{j_1,j_2,\cdots,j_e}$ *of depths d and e, with $e \geq d$, is* $|B_{i_1,i_2,\cdots,i_d} \cap B_{j_1,j_2,\cdots,j_e}| = (\alpha^1_{i_1j_1} \times \cdots \times \alpha^d_{i_dj_d}) \times (z_{d+1} \times \cdots \times z_e) \times (v_{e+1} \times \cdots \times v_l)$.
5. *Let $R_i(t)$ be the resilience of the KPS $\mathcal{S}_i$ after a capture of t nodes for* $1 \leq i \leq l$. *Then the resilience among the nodes in the network at depth d after a capture of t nodes at depth d is* $R^d(t) = 1 - \prod_{i=1}^d (1 - R_i(t))$.
   In particular, the resilience among the nodes in the network of leave nodes (i.e., at depth l) is $R^l(t) = 1 - \prod_{i=1}^l (1 - R_i(t))$.
6. *Let C_i be the connectivity (i.e., the probability that two nodes has a link) of the KPS $\mathcal{S}_i$ for* $1 \leq i \leq l$. *Then the connectivity in the network at depth d is* $C^d = \prod_{i=1}^d C_i$.

In particular, the connectivity in the network of leave nodes (i.e., at depth l) is $C^l = \prod_{i=1}^{l} C_i$.

Proof. 1. Since $\mathcal{B}^d = \{B_{i_1,\cdots i_d} : 1 \leq i_1 \leq b_1, \cdots, 1 \leq i_d \leq b_d\}$, $b^d = |\mathcal{B}^d| = \prod_{j=1}^{d} b_j$.
2. Each block at depth d is of the form $B_{\{i_1,\cdots,i_d\}} = A_{1i_1} \times \cdots \times A_{di_d} \times \mathcal{X}_{d+1}^l$. We have $|A_{ji_j}| = z_j$ for $1 \leq j \leq d$, $|\mathcal{X}_j| = v_j$ for $d+1 \leq j \leq l$. Hence, $z^d = \prod_{j=1}^{d} z_j \times \prod_{j=d+1}^{l} v_j$.
3. Each element $x \in \mathcal{X}$ can be viewed as $x = (x_1, x_2, \cdots, x_l)$ where $x_i \in \mathcal{X}_i$ for $1 \leq i \leq l$. As each $x_1 \in \mathcal{X}_1$ is present in r_1 blocks in $\mathcal{A}_1$, x is present in r_1 blocks at depth 1. Further, since each $x_2 \in \mathcal{X}_2$ is present in r_2 blocks in $\mathcal{A}_2$, there are r_2 blocks at depth 2 under each parent block in depth 1 containing x. Hence, x is present in r_1r_2 blocks at depth 2. Continuing like this, we inductively conclude that there are $\prod_{j=1}^{d} r_j$ blocks containing x at depth d.
4. As Item 4(a) is a special case of Item 4(b) when $e = d$, we will prove Item 4(b). As $e \geq d$, the blocks $B_{i_1,\cdots,i_d}$ and $B_{j_1,\cdots,j_e}$ can respectively, be expressed as $A_{1i_1} \times \cdots \times A_{di_d} \times \mathcal{X}_{d+1}^l = (A_{1i_1} \times \cdots \times A_{di_d}) \times (\mathcal{X}_{d+1} \times \cdots \times \mathcal{X}_e) \times \mathcal{X}_{e+1}^l$and $A_{1j_1} \times \cdots \times A_{ej_e} \times \mathcal{X}_{e+1}^l = (A_{1j_1} \times \cdots \times A_{dj_d}) \times (A_{d+1j_{d+1}} \times \cdots \times A_{ej_e}) \times \mathcal{X}_{e+1}^l$. Here, we have
   - $\alpha_{i_w j_w}^w$ common elements between the blocks A_{wi_w} and A_{wj_w} for $1 \leq w \leq d$;
   - $A_{wj_w} \subseteq \mathcal{X}_w$ and $|A_{wj_w}| = z_w$ for $d+1 \leq w \leq e$;
   - $|\mathcal{X}_w| = v_w$ for $e+1 \leq w \leq l$.

   Hence, $|B_{i_1,\cdots,i_d} \cap B_{j_1,\cdots,j_e}| = (\alpha_{i_1j_1}^1 \times \cdots \times \alpha_{i_dj_d}^d) \times (z_{d+1} \times \cdots \times z_e) \times (v_{e+1} \times \cdots \times v_l)$.
5. Consider a link L between two nodes

$$B_{i_1,\cdots,i_d} = A_{1i_1} \times \cdots \times A_{di_d} \times \mathcal{X}_{d+1}^l \text{ and}$$
$$B_{j_1,\cdots,j_e} = A_{1j_1} \times \cdots \times A_{dj_d} \times \mathcal{X}_{d+1}^l$$

   at depth d. The link L can fail if and only if all d links $l_w, 1 \leq w \leq d$ between the nodes A_{wi_w} and A_{wj_w} in the KPS $\mathcal{X}_w$ fail. On capture of t nodes at depth d, the probability of the fail of the link l_w is $F_w(t) = 1 - R_w(t)$ for each $w(1 \leq w \leq d)$. Hence the fail probability of the link L on capture of t nodes is $R^d(t) = 1 - \prod_{w=1}^{d}(1 - R_w(t))$.
6. Similar to the proof of Item 5., there is a link L between two nodes

$$B_{i_1,\cdots,i_d} = A_{1i_1} \times \cdots \times A_{di_d} \times \mathcal{X}_{d+1}^l \text{ and}$$
$$B_{j_1,\cdots,j_e} = A_{1j_1} \times \cdots \times A_{dj_d} \times \mathcal{X}_{d+1}^l$$

   at depth d if and only if there are links $l_w, 1 \leq w \leq d$ between the nodes A_{wi_w} and A_{wj_w} in the KPS $\mathcal{X}_w$. Hence, the connectivity of the network at depth d is $C^d = \prod_{w=1}^{d} C_p$.

One can verify the above theorem with Example 2. Now we summarize the effects of Theorem 1 on the HKPS designed from Construction 1.

1. Theorem 1.1 provides the maximum number of nodes can be allocated in each depth. It can be observed that the number of blocks in depth d increased by b_d times than the number of blocks in depth $d-1$. As we need a larger number blocks in higher depth, we can choose the designs of a higher number of blocks.
2. Theorem 1.2 provides the maximum size of key ring of nodes at each depth. It can be observed that the size of key ring in depth $d-1$ is $\frac{v_d}{z_d}$ times than the size of key ring in depth i. To minimize the storage space, we need to choose smaller v_d or larger z_d at lower depth nodes than the higher depth nodes. This can be achieved as in our network design goal, we have a smaller number of nodes (but more powerful) at lower depth than the number of nodes at higher depth.
3. Theorem 1.3 presents the degree of a key (i.e., the number of nodes are having a key). This value is involved to compute the connectivity and resilience of KPS.
4. Theorem 1.4 provides the number of common keys between two nodes. The common keys between two nodes are used to establish a link between them. This value is involved to compute the resilience of the KPS.
5. Theorem 1.5 presents the resilience of the network among the nodes at a particular depth. That is, the failure probability of a link in the network at depth d is computed after the capture of t nodes from the same network. The failure probability may vary if a number of nodes are captured from different depths. For example, if a node is captured at depth d, then all the nodes in the subtree with root as the captured node are exposed. Hence, all the links involving a node in the subtree fail.

   Further, capture of a node at higher depth exposes some keys in nodes at lower depth and it is possible that capturing some nodes in higher depth may completely expose a node at lower depth. Hence, this HKPS does not provide the resilience against the compromise of any number of nodes at higher depth in the hierarchy or leave nodes.
6. Theorem 1.6 presents the connectivity of the network among the nodes at a particular depth. That is, the probability that two nodes at a particular depth d can set a link between them. Further, as a parent node stores all keys of a child node under its subtree, the parent node and its child can always establish a link between them.

3.3 A Hash Chain Based HKPS (HC-HKPS)

As we discussed in the above Subsection (Item 5) that a capture of a number of nodes at higher depth can expose some keys of the nodes at a lower depth (parental level). This may allow the adversary to expose some links at nodes of lower depth. Hence, the HKPS does not provide the resilience against the compromise of any number of nodes at higher depth in the hierarchy. Now we propose hash chain technique to prevent this problem.

Bechkit et al. [1,2] presented a hash chain application on the keys in every node following a KPS to increase the resilience in the network. In [21], the hash chain idea is used to achieve the goal. We too use the same hash chain idea in the direction of depth of the hierarchy as follows.

1. Given an HKPS $(\mathcal{X}, \mathcal{B}^1, \mathcal{B}^2, \cdots, \mathcal{B}^l)$ as described in Subsect. 3.1.
2. Given a key K and a full domain cryptographic hash function $h : \mathcal{K} \mapsto \mathcal{K}$, let inductively define $h^i(K) = h(h^{i-1}(K))$ for $i \geq 1$ and $h^0(K) = K$.
3. Depth of the hierarchy is used to discriminate the initially preloaded KPS keys as described below:
   (a) instead of the original key, K, a node at depth d is preloaded with the key $h^d(K)$, for each key K to be distributed to the node in the HKPS.
   (b) thus, two nodes at depth d and e that shared the same key K in the HKPS end up possessing $h^d(K)$ and $h^e(K)$ respectively;
   (c) if $d < e$ then the node at depth d (lower depth) can compute the key at higher depth e i.e., $h^e(K) = h^{(e-d)}(h^d(K))$ and due to the preimage resistant property of the cryptographic hash function h, the node at depth e can not compute the key at lower depth d i.e., $h^d(K)$.
4. Key establishment of the nodes at depth d and e where $d \leq e$, establish the shared secret key $K_{d,e} = h^e(K)$, that can be computed at the both end where K is a shared key due to the HKPS.
5. Capture of a node at depth d exposes all its keys $h^d(K)$ to the adversary. Then, the adversary
   (a) can expose the keys of the nodes at higher or same depth if that possess a key $h^e(K)$ where $d \leq e$;
   (b) can not expose a single key of the nodes at lower depth.

So, the hash chain based HKPS (i.e., $HC-HKPS$) is *resilient* against the compromise of *any number of lower level users.* Further, the connectivity, storage overhead and communication overhead remains the same as the HKPS. On the computation point of view, the nodes at lower depth have to pay for hash function computations, which is not bothersome as nodes at lower depth are supposed to be more powerful than the nodes at a higher depth. Hence the product based hierarchical scheme $HC-HKPS$ satisfies the following criteria.

1. *decentralized hierarchy* of a fixed number of depths (l). Decentralization is necessary for large networks to distribute computational burden and security threat to lower level users by reducing the burden of the central authority.
2. *resilient* against compromise of (i) any number of lower level nodes; and (ii) a threshold number of nodes of same level in the hierarchy. This is achieved by exploiting the hash chains technique in $HC-HKPS$.
3. *non-interactive* which saves bandwidth and energy.
4. *deterministic* KPS which implies the nodes in the network have predictable behaviour of key rings.
5. *efficient* as it uses hash chains rather than any public key based key exchange or bilinear maps.
6. *free* to choose any basic KPS at any level/depth of hierarchy as per the requirement of that level.
7. *simplicity* in design as it uses the Cartesian product and hash chains over the underlying basic schemes.

4 Instantiation to a Selected KPS

Now that we have introduced and analyzed the concepts of HKPS and HC-HKPS, we instantiate these ideas to a selected KPS for a realization. We have chosen a very efficient and simple structured KPS Sensornet [10] to build the hierarchy. Sensornet is a combinatorial configuration with at most single common key. At first, we briefly recall the construction of the selected KPS and its salient parameters, especially resilience.

4.1 Sensornet [10]

Consider the finite field $\mathbb{F}_p$ with p elements where p is a prime number. Let $V_n = \mathbb{F}_p^n$ be the n−dimensional vector space over $\mathbb{F}_p$ with the zero vector $\mathbf{0}$. Consider any subspace E of the vector space V_n. Any coset of E in V_n is of the form $\alpha + E = \{\alpha + v : v \in E\}$ for $\alpha \in V_n$. The set of cosets creates a disjoint partition in V_n. Consider the element α to be a coset representative of the coset $\alpha + E$. Further, assume $n = 2m$ to be an even positive integer when dealing with the KPS class, *Sensornet*.

Definition 2 (partial spread). *A* partial spread Σ *of order* s *in* V_n *is a set of pairwise supplementary* m*−dimensional subspaces,* $E_0, E_1, \cdots, E_{s-1}$ *of* V_n*, i.e., their direct sum* $E_i \oplus E_j = \{u + v : u \in E_i, v \in E_j\} = V_n$ *and* $E_i \cap E_j = \{\mathbf{0}\}$ *for all* $0 \leq i < j < s$.

Definition 3 (net). *For a given partial spread* $\Sigma = \{E_0, E_1, \cdots, E_{s-1}\}$ *in* V_n*, let* E_i^c *be a set of representatives of the cosets of subspace* E_i *for all* i $(0 \leq i < s)$*. The set of all cosets for every subspace* $E_i, 0 \leq i < s$*, i.e.,* $\mathcal{A} = \{\alpha + E_i : \alpha \in E_i^c \text{ and } 0 \leq i < s\}$ *is called a* net *in* V_n *(for the partial spread* Σ*).*

An interested reader can refer to [10, Section 4.1] for some examples of nets. Now to construct the class of KPS, *Sensornet*, consider a *net* in V_n that comprises of the design $(\mathcal{X}, \mathcal{A})$, where $\mathcal{X} = V_n$ is set of varieties and the set of blocks is $\mathcal{A} = \{\alpha + E_i : \alpha \in E_i^c$ and $0 \leq i < s\}$. The design of the KPS class, *Sensornet* is a combination of [10, Theorem 1] with Sect. 2.4, that is restated in Result 1.

Result 1. *For a partial spread* Σ *of order* s $(1 \leq s \leq p^m + 1)$ *in* V_n*, the set design* $(\mathcal{X}, \mathcal{A})$ *is a* (p^n, sp^m, s, p^m)*−CID where* $\mu = (s-1)p^m$.

The KPS *Sensornet* is designed by assigning a sensor node N_{ij} to the j-th coset of E_i (i.e., $A_{ij} = \alpha_{ij} + E_i$) as its set of key identifiers for $0 \leq i < s, 0 \leq j < p^m$. *Sensornet*$(s, p^m)$; whereas *Sensornet* denotes the generic KPS class. Due to the affine structure of blocks in *Sensornet*, a key establishment process is exceptionally efficient and is of $O(n^3) = O\left((\log \mathcal{N})^3\right)$.

Lemma 1. *Given a KPS Sensornet which is a* (p^n, sp^m, s, p^m)*-configuration, we have,*

1. *the resilience after a capture of* t *nodes* $R(t) = (1 - p^{-m})^t$;
2. *the connectivity of the KPS is* $C = 1 - \frac{1}{s}$.

Proof. The proof for connectivity and another metric for resilience ($\mathtt{fail}(t)$) is available in [10, Corollary 1, Corollary 2] respectively. We will prove for the resilience $R(t)$.

Here, each node stores p^m keys from p^n keys. Let a node is captured by the adversary. An arbitrary link L secured by a key from the captured node is with probability $\frac{p^m}{p^n} = p^{-m}$. The link L is not affected with probability $1 - p^{-m}$. Hence, the link L is not affected by a capture of t nodes is $(1-p^{-m})^t$. Therefore, $R(t) = (1 - p^{-m})^t$.

4.2 Instantiation to Sensornet

We will use l different Sensornets to have an HKPS of depth l. Let p_i be prime, $n_i = 2 * m_i$ be even integers and $s_i (1 \leq s_i \leq p_i^{m_i} + 1)$ be integers for $1 \leq i \leq l$. Consider the Sensornets which are $(p_i^{n_i}, s_i p_i^{m_i}, s_i, p_i^{m_i})$–configuration for $1 \leq i \leq l$ to design the corresponding HKPS as described in Construction 1. Further, we denote the resultant HKPS as HKPS-Sensornet and its hash chain version as HC-HKPS-Sensornet. The following is the properties of the HC-Sensornet from Theorem 1.

Theorem 2. *Let the HKPS-Sensornet of depth l is designed from the Sensornets $(p_i^{n_i}, s_i p_i^{m_i}, s_i, p_i^{m_i})$-configuration for $1 \leq i \leq l$ where p_i be prime, $n_i = 2*m_i$ be even integers and $s_i (1 \leq s_i \leq p_i^{m_i} + 1)$ be integers for $1 \leq i \leq l$. Then, we have the following properties.*

1. *The number of blocks at depth d is $b^d = \prod_{i=1}^{d} s_i \times \prod_{i=1}^{d} p_i^{m_i}$.*
2. *The number of elements in each block at depth d is $z^d = \prod_{i=1}^{d} p_i^{m_i} \times \prod_{i=d+1}^{l} p_i^{n_i}$.*
3. *Each element $x \in \mathcal{X}$ belongs to $r^d = \prod_{i=1}^{d} s_i$ blocks in $\mathcal{B}^d$ at depth d. Further, the element x belongs to $\sum_{d=1}^{l} \prod_{i=1}^{d} s_i$ blocks in the whole hierarchical design.*
4. *(a) The number of common elements between two blocks $B_{i_1,i_2,\cdots,i_d}$ and $B_{j_1,j_2,\cdots,j_d}$ at depth d is 0 or $\prod_{i=d+1}^{l} p_i^{n_i}$.*
   (b) The number of common elements between two blocks $B_{i_1,i_2,\cdots,i_d}$ and $B_{j_1,j_2,\cdots,j_e}$ of depths d and e, with $e \geq d$, is 0 or $\prod_{i=d+1}^{e} p_i^{m_i} \prod_{i=e+1}^{l} p_i^{n_i}$.
5. *The resilience among the nodes in the network at depth d after a capture of t nodes at depth d is $R^d(t) = 1 - \prod_{i=1}^{d} (1 - (1 - p_i^{-m_i})^t)$.*
   In particular, the resilience among the nodes in the network of leave nodes is $R^l(t) = 1 - \prod_{i=1}^{l} (1 - (1 - p_i^{-m_i})^t)$.
6. *The connectivity in the network at depth d is $C^d = \prod_{i=1}^{d} (1 - \frac{1}{s_i})$.*
   In particular, the connectivity in the network of leave nodes (i.e., at depth l) is $C^l = \prod_{i=1}^{l} (1 - \frac{1}{s_i})$.

As Sensornet is not fully connected (i.e., connectivity is less than 1), HKPS-Sensornet is not fully connected. Since Sensornet is very efficient and a CID with a high value of μ, it is not troublesome to establish a link through an intermediate node. Further, the designer can choose appropriate p_i, n_i and s_i to have enough nodes and storage space to store the keys in the hierarchy. For example, the designer may choose smaller $p_i^{n_i}$ for smaller value of i to have smaller key ring. Moreover, the designer can choose larger s_i to have more number of nodes and higher connectivity at a depth.

5 Conclusion

Realizing the need of HKPS with desirable properties to address the problem of key management in low cost networks, we propose a basic theory of HKPS by introducing the hierarchical design. Then we propose an HKPS on the basis of the product of different KPS. Further, to achieve leaf-resilient in the HKPS, we propose HC-HKPS by involving hash chain. For the investigation purpose, we instantiate the HKPS on the KPS Sensornet.

Each level/depth in the hierarchy allows to use different KPS as per the requirement. This freedom in the design of product based HKPS and introduction of a basic theory certainly open the doors for future research for the design of different HKPS as per the requirements of the metrics.

References

1. Bechkit, W., Bouabdallah, A., Challal, Y.: Enhancing resilience of probabilistic key pre-distribution schemes for WSNs through hash chaining. In: Proceedings of the 17th ACM Conference on Computer and Communications Security, CCS 2010, 4–8 October 2010, Chicago, Illinois, USA, pp. 642–644 (2010)
2. Bechkit, W., Challal, Y., Bouabdallah, A.: A new class of hash-chain based key pre-distribution schemes for WSN. Comput. Commun. **36**(3), 243–255 (2013)
3. Çamtepe, S.A., Yener, B.: Combinatorial design of key distribution mechanisms for wireless sensor networks. In: Samarati, P., Ryan, P., Gollmann, D., Molva, R. (eds.) ESORICS 2004. LNCS, vol. 3193, pp. 293–308. Springer, Heidelberg (2004). https://doi.org/10.1007/978-3-540-30108-0_18
4. Chakrabarti, D., Maitra, S., Roy, B.: A key pre-distribution scheme for wireless sensor networks: merging blocks in combinatorial design. In: Zhou, J., Lopez, J., Deng, R.H., Bao, F. (eds.) ISC 2005. LNCS, vol. 3650, pp. 89–103. Springer, Heidelberg (2005). https://doi.org/10.1007/11556992_7
5. Chakrabarti, D., Seberry, J.: Combinatorial structures for design of wireless sensor networks. In: Zhou, J., Yung, M., Bao, F. (eds.) ACNS 2006. LNCS, vol. 3989, pp. 365–374. Springer, Heidelberg (2006). https://doi.org/10.1007/11767480_25
6. Chan, H., Perrig, A., Song, D.: Random key predistribution schemes for sensor networks. In: IEEE Symposium On Security and Privacy, pp. 197–213. IEEE Computer Society (2003)
7. Chen, C.Y., Chao, H.C.: A survey of key predistribution in wireless sensor networks. Secur. Commun. Netw. **7**(12), 2495–2508 (2014)
8. Dalai, D.K., Sarkar, P.: Key predistribution schemes using bent functions in distributed sensor networks. In: Chen, K., Lin, D., Yung, M. (eds.) Inscrypt 2016. LNCS, vol. 10143, pp. 367–385. Springer, Heidelberg (2016). https://doi.org/10.1007/978-3-319-54705-3_23

9. Dalai, D.K., Sarkar, P.: Enhancing resilience of KPS using bidirectional hash chains and application on sensornet. In: Yan, Z., Molva, R., Mazurczyk, W., Kantola, R. (eds.) NSS 2017. LNCS, vol. 10394, pp. 683–693. Springer, Cham (2017). https://doi.org/10.1007/978-3-319-64701-2_54
10. Dalai, D.K., Sarkar, P.: Sensornet - a key predistribution scheme for distributed sensors using nets. In: Proceedings of the 6th International Conference on Sensor Networks - SENSORNETS, pp. 49–58. INSTICC, ScitePress (2017)
11. Erdős, P., Rényi, A.: On the evolution of random graphs. In: Publication of the Mathematical Institute of the Hungarian Academy of Sciences, pp. 17–61 (1960)
12. Eschenauer, L., Gligor, V.D.: A key-management scheme for distributed sensor networks. In: ACM Conference on Computer and Communications Security, pp. 41–47 (2002)
13. Gennaro, R., Halevi, S., Krawczyk, H., Rabin, T., Reidt, S., Wolthusen, S.D.: Strongly-resilient and non-interactive hierarchical key-agreement in MANETs. In: Jajodia, S., Lopez, J. (eds.) ESORICS 2008. LNCS, vol. 5283, pp. 49–65. Springer, Heidelberg (2008). https://doi.org/10.1007/978-3-540-88313-5_4
14. Kendall, M., Martin, K.M.: Graph-theoretic design and analysis of key predistribution schemes. Des. Codes Cryptogr. **81**(1), 11–34 (2016)
15. Lee, J., Stinson, D.R.: A combinatorial approach to key predistribution for distributed sensor networks. In: IEEE Wireless Communications and Networking Conference WCNC 2005, New Orleans, USA, pp. 1200–1205 (2005)
16. Paterson, M.B., Stinson, D.R.: A unified approach to combinatorial key predistribution schemes for sensor networks. Des. Codes Cryptogr. **71**(3), 433–457 (2014)
17. Ramkumar, M., Memon, N., Simha, R.: A hierarchical key pre-distribution scheme. In: Electro/Information Technology Conference, EIT 2005. IEEE (2005)
18. Ruj, S., Roy, B.K.: Key predistribution using combinatorial designs for grid-group deployment scheme in wireless sensor networks. TOSN **6**(1), 4:1–4:28 (2009)
19. Ruj, S., Roy, B.K.: Key pre-distribution using partially balanced designs in wireless sensor networks. IJHPCN **7**(1), 19–28 (2011)
20. Sakai, R., Ohgishi, K., Kasahara, M.: Cryptosystems based on pairings. In: Proceedings of SCIS 2000 (2000)
21. Sarkar, P.: Lightweight deterministic non interactive (ni) hierarchical key agreement scheme (KAS). In: Yan, Z., Molva, R., Mazurczyk, W., Kantola, R. (eds.) NSS 2017. LNCS, vol. 10394, pp. 315–331. Springer, Cham (2017). https://doi.org/10.1007/978-3-319-64701-2_23
22. Steiner, J.G., Neuman, B.C., Schiller, J.I.: Kerberos: an authentication service for open network systems. In: USENIX Winter, pp. 191–202 (1988)
23. Stinson, D.R.: Combinatorial Designs - Constructions and Analysis. Springer, Heidelberg (2004). https://doi.org/10.1007/b97564
24. Wei, R., Wu, J.: Product construction of key distribution schemes for sensor networks. In: Handschuh, H., Hasan, M.A. (eds.) SAC 2004. LNCS, vol. 3357, pp. 280–293. Springer, Heidelberg (2004). https://doi.org/10.1007/978-3-540-30564-4_20

Adversarial Examples for Hardware-Trojan Detection at Gate-Level Netlists

Kohei Nozawa[1(✉)], Kento Hasegawa[1], Seira Hidano[2], Shinsaku Kiyomoto[2], Kazuo Hashimoto[3], and Nozomu Togawa[1]

[1] Department of Computer Science and Communications Engineering, Waseda University, Shinjuku, Japan
kohei.nozawa@togawa.cs.waseda.ac.jp
[2] KDDI Research, Inc., Fujimino, Japan
[3] Center for Research Strategy, Waseda University, Shinjuku, Japan

Abstract. Recently, due to the increase of outsourcing in integrated circuit (IC) design and manufacturing, the threat of injecting a malicious circuit, called a hardware Trojan, by third party has been increasing. Machine learning has been known to produce a powerful model to detect hardware Trojans. But it is recently reported that such a machine learning based detection is weak against adversarial examples (AEs), which cause misclassification by adding perturbation in input data. Referring to the existing studies on adversarial examples, most of which are discussed in the field of image processing, this paper first proposes a framework generating adversarial examples for hardware-Trojan detection for gate-level netlists utilizing neural networks. The proposed framework replaces hardware Trojan circuits with logically equivalent circuits, and makes it difficult to detect them. Second, we define Trojan-net concealment degree (TCD) as a possibility of misclassification, and modification evaluating value (MEV) as a measure of the amount of modifications. Third, judging from MEV, we pick up adversarial modification patterns to apply to the circuits against hardware-Trojan detection. The experimental results using benchmarks demonstrate that the proposed framework successfully decreases true positive rate (TPR) by at most 30.15 points.

Keywords: Hardware trojan · Netlist · Logic gate · Machine learning · Adversarial example

1 Introduction

Demand of integrated circuits (ICs) has recently been increased due to introduction of Internet of Things (IoT) in foundries and home. In order to effectively design and produce hardware devices at low cost, they have been become complicated. Hardware design and production level can be divided into two steps: the design step and the manufacturing step. In the design step, hardware vendors

S. Katsikas et al. (Eds.): ESORICS 2019 Workshops, LNCS 11980, pp. 341–359, 2020.
https://doi.org/10.1007/978-3-030-42048-2_22

design IC chips according to product specifications, and describe the design in hardware description language (HDL). This step is often outsourced to third-party vendors [24]. A frequently-used circuit such as a processor or communication interface is packed as modules called intellectual property (IP), and a hardware vendor often purchases it from a third-party vendor. In the manufacturing step, a circuit is manufactured at a foundry based on the information designed in the design step. As shown above, hardware design and manufacturing level steps involve several third-party vendors. At the same time, it is reported that an adversary including an untrusted third-party vendor may modify a hardware design or product with malicious intent in the design or manufacturing step [9,29]. A malicious circuit inserted into a genuine product is called a "hardware Trojan" [20]. A hardware Trojan often leaks internal information, degrades performance, and/or deactivates functionalities. IoT devices can be infected with hardware Trojans. This is an emerging threat since IoT devices are spreading to our home. Now we focus on the hardware design step. A hardware design is often described at gate level which describes how to connect circuit elements with wires (also called nets). A gate-level netlist, which is a list of nets and circuit elements, includes millions of nets, and therefore it is difficult to inspect each net in detail. How to detect a hardware Trojan from such a huge gate-level netlist is a serious concern. Ref. [23] proposes a hardware-Trojan detection method at gate-level netlist based on the structure features, and Refs. [6,12,13] develop it leveraging machine learning. In particular, a hardware-Trojan detection method leveraging neural networks is expected to detect subspecies of hardware Trojans [14].

In the field of machine learning, an attack which makes a classifier erroneously classify a given sample has been proposed [10,27]. According to [10], a test sample with a certain noise, which is called perturbation, will be classified into the different label from the original one. Such a test sample with perturbation is named an adversarial example (AE), and we call the attack utilizing it an AE attack. A number of AE attack schemes have been proposed [1], and how to solve the problems becomes a serious concern. While initial studies related to AEs started with image recognition, some of recent ones focus on different use cases. For instance, there is an attempt to generate AEs for object recognition [8]. An AE attack method against a malware detection system has also been proposed [11].

Existing hardware-Trojan detection methods leveraging neural networks have been designed with no consideration for advanced attacks such as AE attacks. Thus, they will also be exposed to the risk of AE attacks. An AE attack to hardware-Trojan detection will deceive a classifier and a hardware-Trojan circuit will be misclassified as normal. If the attack is realized, hardware-Trojan detection becomes more difficult. In order to put hardware-Trojan detection to practical use, it is necessary to clarify its potential risks against AE attacks. We can generate AEs for images just by calculating perturbation. For circuits, however, there are additional constraints of keeping logical equivalency. We can't modify circuits arbitrarily reflecting calculated perturbation. Thus, a different approach from conventional AE-attack methods is needed to generate AEs for hardware-Trojan detection.

In this paper, we propose a framework generating adversarial examples for hardware-Trojan detection for gate-level netlists utilizing neural networks. In the proposed method, we define Trojan-net concealment degree (TCD) and modification evaluating value (MEV) which can be obtained from a loss function of the neural networks utilized for hardware-Trojan detection. Utilizing TCD and MEV, we generate adversarial examples which cause misclassification in hardware-Trojan detection. The proposed method enables us to generate adversarial examples against hardware-Trojan detection without exploring all of the modification patterns of a target circuit. As far as we know, this is the first study on adversarial examples against hardware-Trojan detection and its application to the benchmark dataset.

The contributions of this paper are summarized as follows:

1. We propose a framework that generates an AE against hardware-Trojan detection.
2. In the framework above, we propose TCD and MEV to evaluate the amount of modifications, and utilizing them we can effectively pick up optimal modifications on generating an AE.
3. By applying our method, TPR is decreased by 30.15 points at most, validating modification patterns and MEV.

The rest of this paper is organized as follows: In Sect. 2, we discuss related works on hardware-Trojan detection utilizing machine learning and AE. In Sect. 3, we propose a framework generating adversarial examples for hardware-Trojan detection for gate-level netlists utilizing neural networks and TCD and MEV for evaluating modification. In Sect. 4, we perform experiments and demonstrate their results. In Sect. 5, we conclude this paper.

2 Related Works

2.1 Hardware Trojan and Its Detection Utilizing Neural Networks

A hardware Trojan is a malicious circuit embedded in ICs. A hardware Trojan often consists of two parts of circuits, a trigger circuit and a payload circuit [4]. A trigger circuit enables a payload circuit when a start-up condition such as a certain primary input or an internal state is satisfied. A payload circuit performs a malicious function such as leakage of information or performance degradation when the trigger condition is satisfied. If hardware Trojans are embedded in home appliances especially in IoT devices, they can be a familiar threat for people. Since a hardware Trojan is much small compared to a genuine circuit, how to find the features of a hardware Trojan is an important issue.

In general, a netlist, which is a list of nets, at gate level can be represented by a graph structure. Let a graph $G = (V, E)$ be a whole netlist at gate level. V is a set of vertexes, or gates. E is a set of edges, or nets. Similarly, let a graph $G_t = (V_t, E_t)$ be a Trojan circuit. V_t is a set of vertexes, or Trojan gates. E_t is a set of edges, or Trojan nets. V_t and E_t satisfy $V_t \subseteq V$ and $E_t \subseteq E$, respectively.

Table 1. Several feature values for hardware-Trojan detection utilizing neural networks [12].

#	Description
1	The number of logic-gate fanins 4-level away from the target net n
2	The number of logic-gate fanins 5-level away from the target net n
3	The number of flip-flops up to 4-level away from the input side of the target net n
4	The number of flip-flops up to 3-level away from the output side of the target net n
5	The number of flip-flops up to 4-level away from the output side of the target net n
6	The number of up to 4-level loops from the input side of the target net n
7	The number of up to 5-level loops from the output side of the target net n
8	The minimum level to the primary input from the target net n
9	The minimum level to the primary output from the target net n
10	The minimum level to any flip-flop from the output side of the target net n
11	The minimum level to any multiplexer from the output side of the target net n

Here we focus on hardware-Trojan detection utilizing machine learning. In [12], a hardware-Trojan detection method utilizing a neural network have been proposed. The method extracts feature values of each net in a gate-level netlist and identifies whether the net is a Trojan net or a normal net. At first, the learning flow, the method extracts several features shown in Table 1 from each net $e \in E$, and then obtains feature values $\boldsymbol{x}(e)$. After that, a neural network learns the extracted feature values. As for each net e, we give features $\boldsymbol{x}(e) = (x_1, x_2, \ldots, x_k)$ to the neural network as an input, and then we obtain an output $\boldsymbol{z} = (z_1, z_2)$, where z_1 shows the possibility that e is a normal net and z_2 shows the possibility that e is a Trojan net. Secondly, the classification flow, the method extracts features from an unknown netlist and classifies them with the classifier leaned at the learning flow. In the classification flow, the classifier identifies e as a Trojan net when z_2 is larger than z_1, or identifies e as a normal net when z_1 is larger than z_2. On hardware-Trojan detection utilizing a neural network, we give great importance to correctly identify Trojan nets as Trojan nets. Now let $e_{t'}$ be a net classified as a Trojan net, and $E_{t'}$ be a set of the nets classified as Trojan nets. The goal on hardware-Trojan detection is that $e_{t'}$ involves all the Trojan nets E_t. Therefore, maximizing true positive rate (TPR)[1] is the first priority in hardware-Trojan detection. In [12], the average TPR value becomes 84.8% and the maximum TPR value becomes 100%. They give good results in hardware-Trojan detection in terms of TPR.

[1] The number of Trojan nets identified as Trojan nets is called as true positive (TP). The number of Trojan nets identified as normal nets is called as false negative (FN). The true positive rate is obtained from TP / (TP + FN).

2.2 Adversarial Example

Recently, an attack scheme where a certain test sample causes misclassification to the target classifier utilizing machine learning including a neural network has been proposed [10]. This is an attack for machine learning models which causes misclassification results by adding perturbation to test data which are originally classified into their correct classes. These data which cause misclassification are called adversarial examples (AE). In this paper, we call the attack using AE an AE attack.

AEs for images are generated as follows [27]. Let $f : \mathbb{R}^n \longrightarrow \{1 \ldots k\}$ be a classifier that maps image pixel vectors to a discrete label set. We also assume that f has an associated continuous loss function that is expressed by $\text{loss}_f : \mathbb{R}^n \times \{1 \ldots k\} \longrightarrow \mathbb{R}^+$. For a given image $\boldsymbol{x} \in \mathbb{R}^n$ and target label $l \in \{1 \ldots k\}$, we aim to solve the following box-constrained optimization problem:

$$\begin{aligned} &\min_{r} ||\boldsymbol{r}||_2 \\ &\text{s.t. } f(\boldsymbol{x}+\boldsymbol{r}) = l, \boldsymbol{x}+\boldsymbol{r} \in \mathcal{X} \end{aligned} \tag{1}$$

where $|| \cdot ||_2$ is an L_2 norm and $\mathcal{X}$ is a feature space of a pixel. In this equation, $\boldsymbol{r}$ shows perturbation. Here, we express one such $\boldsymbol{x}+\boldsymbol{r}$ for an arbitrarily chosen minimizer as $D(\boldsymbol{x}, l)$. $\boldsymbol{x}+\boldsymbol{r}$ is the closest image to $\boldsymbol{x}$ classified as l by f. Then, we can derive $D(\boldsymbol{x}, f(\boldsymbol{x})) = f(\boldsymbol{x})$, and this task is non-trivial only if $f(\boldsymbol{x}) \neq l$. In most cases, the exact computation of $D(\boldsymbol{x}, l)$ is a hard problem, therefore we approximate it by using a box-constrained L-BFGS [21]. Concretely, we find an approximate of $D(\boldsymbol{x}, l)$ by performing line-search to find the minimum $c > 0$ for which the minimizer $\boldsymbol{r}$ of the following problem satisfies $f(\boldsymbol{x}+\boldsymbol{r}) = l$.

$$\begin{aligned} &\min_{r} c|\boldsymbol{r}| + \text{loss}_f(\boldsymbol{x}+\boldsymbol{r}, l) \\ &\text{s.t. } \boldsymbol{x}+\boldsymbol{r} \in \mathcal{X} \end{aligned} \tag{2}$$

Given the fact of the development in machine learning utilizing neural networks, novel attack methods have been proposed. In [10], for example, a method generating test data that cause misclassification in image recognition has been proposed. Image recognition is frequently leveraged in physical world such as self-driving and face recognition, thus both of the attack methods and defense methods are getting much attention [7,8,18]. Although we cannot distinguish adversarial examples from original ones, a classifier misclassifies them. In addition to image recognition, audio recognition [3], sentence recognition [15,16] and graph data [5,30] become new targets these days. In this paper, we propose a framework to generate AEs against hardware-Trojan detection by modifying hardware designs. In image recognition, AEs are generated with minimizing visible impacts. Likewise, in this case, we aim to generate AEs which hardly degrade circuit performance such as power consumption and path delay. The AEs cause misclassification as a Trojan net mistakenly classified as a normal net.

Now we focus on AE attacks on hardware-Trojan detection utilizing neural networks. In AE attacks against hardware-Trojan detection, an adversary aims to decrease $|E_{t'}|$. When $|E_{t'}|$ is dramatically decreased, most of the Trojan nets are mistakenly classified as normal nets. If the AE attack is realized, it becomes hard to detect hardware Trojans in a netlist. In order to learn hardware design information utilizing machine learning methods, we represent hardware circuits as graph structures as shown in Sect. 2.1. The conversion from a graph structure space into a feature space is one-way. Therefore, even if we add perturbations in feature value space, we can not specify corresponding changes in graph structure.

In case of hardware-Trojan detection, it is difficult to completely represent circuit structures as graph structures because circuit elements have several characteristics such as particular I/O ports, power consumption, and delay time. In particular, power consumption and delay time are important in hardware design. We must take account of these characteristics towards AE attacks on hardware-Trojan detection. For these reasons, we need to take a different approach from conventional AE-attack methods.

3 AE Attacks on Hardware Design

3.1 Scenario of the AE Attacks

Let us consider AE attacks in hardware-Trojan detection utilizing neural networks for logic gates. Adversaries aim to design hardware Trojans which are difficult to be detected by a hardware-Trojan detection system in order to insert malicious circuits into hardware products. In this paper, we assume the conditions below, and discuss the threat of AEs against hardware-Trojan detection.

Purposes that Adversaries Have:

P1 Adversaries insert Trojan nets to hardware design information at gate level.

P2 Adversaries make a classifier misclassify a Trojan net as a normal net.

P3 Adversaries degrade the performance of the classifier for hardware-Trojan detection with minimizing the amount of modification.

For the purposes described above, adversaries may try to attack hardware designs. We assume a white-box attack, the worst-case scenario of an AE attack to analyze an attack scheme in an initial examination of AE attacks on hardware design. This will give us the meaningful clues to further develop hardware-Trojan detection methods based on machine learning. In this paper, we assume that adversaries might know the following points.

Information that Adversaries Know:

I1 Adversaries have already known that the hardware vendor utilizes neural networks to detect hardware Trojans.

I2 Adversaries have already known the structure and parameters of the neural networks.

Based on the assumption above, adversaries slightly modify Trojan nets, which is similar to perturbation of AEs on image recognition, and let a classifier misclassify Trojan nets as normal nets. If this attack succeeds, the Trojan nets that adversaries newly design will be classified as normal nets by the hardware-Trojan detection utilizing a neural network at hardware vendors. Thus, adversaries are able to hide the hardware Trojan into hardware design information and an AE attack is realized.

AE Attacks on Hardware Design Information. On AE attacks to hardware design information, a small change to a circuit structure causes a significant change to the feature values of the nets in the circuit. In image recognition, perturbation can be theoretically obtained [22]. In contrast, generating adversarial examples for hardware-Trojan detection is quite different. Since the conversion from a graph structure space to a feature space is one-way, we cannot take the same scheme as in image recognition. Even if we can add perturbation to feature values of nets in an original circuit and obtain the modified feature values, we cannot always generate a modified circuit which has the modified feature values. In addition, the circuit with arbitrary perturbation is not guaranteed to be logically equivalent to the original one. The modified circuit whose functionality is not logically equivalent to the original one can be easily detected by an existing test process due to the lack of the original functionality. Assume that the function of trigger circuits in a hardware Trojan is destroyed and trigger conditions are satisfied in most of cases. Then the hardware Trojan frequently works. In this case, the malicious behavior of a hardware Trojan can be easily detected in a normal product test process. Such circuits are inappropriate for hardware Trojans. Therefore, an adversary must modify hardware Trojans with logically equivalent so that the modified circuit keeps the functionalities of the original circuit. Since logically equivalent circuits are dependent on a target circuit, the detail is described in Sect. 4.2.

Furthermore, on generating AEs for hardware-Trojan detection, an adversary should not significantly decrease the performance of a circuit. When we apply arbitrary modifications to hardware design, power consumption and path delay are also affected in addition to logical equivalence. These features are meaningful factors on hardware design. Thus, significant changes in such factors can be easily detected in existing test processes [2]. In particular, path delay is an complicated factor since several existing hardware-Trojan detection methods focus on it [17, 19]. We must consider the amount of modification based on the factors such as power consumption and path delay to generate an effective AE. In this paper, we target on the circuit where a hardware Trojan has already been inserted. Generally, a hardware-Trojan circuit is inserted into a non-critical path of an original circuit and thus it may not affect the entire path delay of the original circuit, even if the path delay of the hardware-Trojan circuit is slightly increased. Also, since a hardware-Trojan circuit is small enough in most cases compared to an original circuit, it may not affect the entire power consumption even if the power consumption of the hardware-Trojan circuit is slightly increased. On the other hand, if adversaries modify the original circuit, original designers can easily detect the modification because the original circuit itself is elaborately designed to satisfy the requirements such as critical path delay and power consumption. Therefore, adversaries should modify Trojan nets to achieve AE attacks.

Based on the discussion above, generating AEs against hardware-Trojan detection is summarized as follows.

Point 1 Modified circuits are logically equivalent to the original ones.
Point 2 Only Trojan nets are modified.
Point 3 AEs degrade classification performance and conceal Trojan nets with small modification.

In this paper, we propose Trojan-net concealment degree (TCD) and modification evaluating value (MEV), which indicates how likely the Trojan-nets are classified as normal. Then, we design AEs for hardware design information and examine its validity by those two evaluating values.

Based on these values, we further propose an AE generation method that enables us to degrade the performance of hardware-Trojan detection in a short time. It is impractical that we modify all the nets in a netlist because the number of modification patterns is exponentially increased. Our proposed method chooses the modification whose MEV is the best at that time. Based on the method, we realize to generate an appropriate AE against hardware-Trojan detection in a practical time.

3.2 Trojan-Net Concealment Degree and Modification Evaluating Value

An ideal adversarial example largely degrades detection performance by modifying a circuit as slightly as possible. Thus, in this section, we propose TCD, a degree which indicates the possibility of hiding a hardware Trojan, and MEV, a value evaluating the amount of modification. By evaluating modifications using TCD and MEV in advance, we select more effective modification patterns.

Definition of Trojan-Net Concealment Degree. In this paper, we aim to degrade classification performance by modifying a circuit as shown in Sect. 3.1. In order to degrade classification performance, we maximize the loss function of the neural network used in the learning flow. In this case, the loss function is a cross entropy H expressed as follows [12]:

$$H = -\sum_{i=1}^{K} p_i(\boldsymbol{x}(e)) \log q_i(\boldsymbol{x}(e)) \tag{3}$$

where K is the number of units in the output layer ($K = 2$ in the case of [12]), $p_1(\boldsymbol{x}(e))$ and $p_2(\boldsymbol{x}(e))$ are the functions to return answer labels of $\boldsymbol{x}(e)$. When e is a Trojan net, $p_1(\boldsymbol{x}(e))$ equals to 0 and $p_2(\boldsymbol{x}(e))$ equals to 1. $q_1(\boldsymbol{x}(e))$ and $q_2(\boldsymbol{x}(e))$ are the functions to return prediction by the classifier. q_1 and q_2 satisfy following equations: $q_1(\boldsymbol{x}(e)) = z_1, q_2(\boldsymbol{x}(e)) = z_2$, where z_1 shows the possibility that e is a normal net and z_2 shows the possibility that e is a Trojan net.

To adapt Eq. (3) to the whole Trojan nets, we sum up the values for each net and define the total sum as Trojan-net concealment degree (TCD):

$$\mathrm{TCD} = -\frac{1}{|E_t|} \sum_{e_t \in E_t} \left(\sum_{i=1}^{K} p_i(\boldsymbol{x}(e_t)) \log q_i(\boldsymbol{x}(e_t)) \right) \tag{4}$$

When TCD is large, the difference between the prediction and answer is large. Therefore, if the value is large enough, adversaries can easily achieve their purposes to conceal Trojan nets.

Definition of Modification Evaluating Value. A modification to the target circuit affects the whole circuit. More modifications lead to bigger impacts on the whole. To achieve the purpose P3 in Sect. 3.1, we need to modify the hardware Trojan circuit as small as possible. Therefore, we focus on the amount of modification in addition to TCD.

From the viewpoint of circuit design, there are several evaluating indicators such as (i) increment of gates; (ii) increment of power consumption; (iii) increment of path delay; Although (i) and (ii) are proportional to the increment of gates, (iii) is not necessarily proportional to the increment of gates. Therefore, it is not always true that minimizing the number of altered gates works well to generate AE. It is significantly important to consider that on modifying circuits. Generalizing these features, we define Modification Evaluating Value (MEV) as follows:

$$\begin{aligned} \mathrm{MEV} &= -\mathrm{TCD} + \sum_{j=1}^{N} \lambda_j m_j \\ &= \frac{1}{|E_t|} \sum_{e_t \in E_t} \left(\sum_{i=1}^{K} p_i(\boldsymbol{x}(e_t)) \log q_i(\boldsymbol{x}(e_t)) \right) + \sum_{j=1}^{N} \lambda_j m_j \end{aligned} \tag{5}$$

where $m_j (1 \leq j \leq N)$ is one of the N kinds of evaluation indicators, and $\lambda_j (1 \leq j \leq N)$ is corresponding coefficients. To consider hardware-Trojan detection utilizing neural networks, in this paper, we take (i) increment of gates and (iii) increment of path delay in logic levels into account as the amount of modification, i.e., $N = 2$.

3.3 Modification Method

It is impractical that we modify all the nets in a netlist because the number of modification patterns is exponentially increased. In order to effectively generate an AE, we have to approximate the evaluation of AEs. Therefore, based on MEV, we further propose an AE generation method that enables us to degrade the performance of hardware-Trojan detection in a short time. Our proposed method chooses the modification whose MEV is the best at that time. The proposed method is shown in Algorithm 1 below. Note that P is a set of possible AE patterns by which a Trojan gate is modified to a logically equivalent circuit. Examples of such patterns are provided in Sect. 4.2.

4 Experiments

In this section, we apply AE patterns shown in Sect. 4.2 to the hardware Trojan circuits and classify them with the hardware-Trojan classifier proposed in [12] under the conditions shown in Sect. 4.1. We perform the experiments in two cases: (1) we do not consider the amount of modifications and (2) we consider the amount of modifications. Then, we compare the results so that we can verify the validity of MEV. We show the results when we do not consider the amount of modifications in Sect. 4.3, and the results when we consider the amount of modifications in Sect. 4.4.

Algorithm 1. Generate AEs based on MEV

Inputs: Leaned classifier f, the circuit infected with a hardware Trojan $G = (V, E)$, AE patterns P, the number of iterations K
Output: An AE circuit

```
i ⇐ 0, best_MEV ⇐ 0
now_circuit ⇐ G
next_candidate is null
while i < K do
  for all v_t ∈ V_t in now_circuit that has not yet been modified do
    for all p ∈ P that can be applied to v_t do
      Apply p to v_t and generate the modified circuit G'
      Calculate MEV of G' w.r.t. f
      if MEV < best_MEV then
        next_candidate ⇐ G'
        best_MEV ⇐ MEV
      end if
    end for
  end for
  now_circuit ⇐ next_candidate
  i ⇐ i + 1
end while
return now_circuit
```

4.1 Experimental Setup

In this section, we perform experiments with benchmarks, and demonstrate experimental results. 15 benchmarks in Trust-HUB [25,26,28] are used in our experiments. Table 2 shows the benchmarks from Trust-HUB that we used in the experiments. We classify the nets in RS232-T1000 as a test set while all the nets in the other benchmarks are learned. We adopt over-sampling for imbalanced training data distribution between positive and negative samples. The parameters of the neural network utilized in the experiments are as follows: 51 units in input layer; 3 layers in middle layer; 200 units, 100 units and 50 units in middle layer respectively [12]. We use Sigmoid for an activation function. We use an Intel Xeon Bronze 3104 computer environment with a 93 GB memory.

In our experiments, we apply the six AE patterns described in Sect. 4.2 to the Trojan nets of RS232-T1000 shown in Fig. 1. After that, we generate AEs for hardware-Trojan detection based on the method proposed in Sect. 3.3. Note that we set the number of iterations to three in the experiments.

Table 2. List of benchmarks used in our experiments.

Benchmark [28]	# of all nets	# of Trojan nets
RS232-T1000	319	36
RS232-T1100	320	36
RS232-T1200	323	34
RS232-T1300	316	29
RS232-T1400	318	45
RS232-T1500	322	39
RS232-T1600	321	29
s15850-T100	2446	27
s35932-T100	6422	15
s35932-T200	6417	12
s35932-T300	6442	37
s38417-T100	5810	12
s38417-T200	5813	15
s38417-T300	5845	44
s38584-T100	7362	19

4.2 Six AE Patterns

Most of hardware Trojans have trigger conditions to hide their activity in normal operation. In general, trigger conditions are set based on the values of internal signals and internal states. If we modify the Trojan circuits with arbitrary conditions, trigger conditions are also altered. Therefore, modified circuits must be logically equivalent to the original hardware Trojan to satisfy the condition of Point 1 mentioned in Sect. 3.1. In addition, these modifications should be applied only to Trojan nets for condition of Point 2.

The hardware-Trojan detection method in [12] utilizes the distance from the net to a near flipflop, multiplexer and primary input/output and thus modifications with changing the distance are efficient. For instance, the number of logic levels between two gates increases by replacing a four-input-gate with multiple two-input-gates. In this way, we generate a circuit and alter feature values at the same time.

We generate six AE patterns shown in Fig. 2. The first two, $t1$ and $t2$, replace single four-input-OR with three two-input-ORs. $t3$ adds constant 0 and $t5$ adds constant 1. $t4$ injects two inverters. $t6$ replaces gates with logically equivalent gates. Note that these AE patterns clearly give the logically equivalent modifications.

Table 3 shows applicable gates of each AE pattern shown in Fig. 1. For example, the AE pattern $t1$ can be applied to the gate OR1 in Fig. 2 since OR1 is a four-input OR gate. $t1$ can be also applied to the gate OR2 in Fig. 2. Although $t4$ could be applied to every net, we just apply it to WIRE1 because modification $t4$ typically appears at a junction point to drive multiple gates.

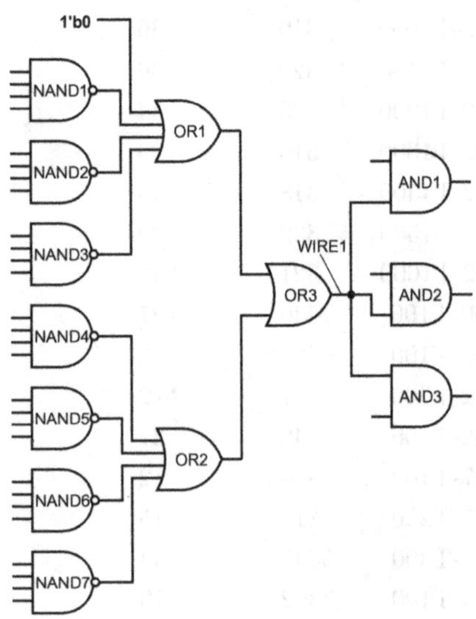

Fig. 1. Hardware Trojan (Trojan nets and Trojan gates) embedded in RS232-T1000 [28].

Table 3. Applicable gates of each AE pattern.

Pattern	Applicable gates
$t1$, $t2$	OR1, OR2
$t3$	OR3
$t4$	WIRE1
$t5$	AND1, AND2, AND3
$t6$	NAND1, NAND2, NAND3, NAND4, NAND5, NAND6, NAND7

4.3 Evaluation Without the Amount of Modifications

In this experiment, we set λ in Eq. (5) to 0. We consider only the loss function of neural networks on generating AE in this case.

Table 4 shows the results when we apply the six AE patterns to RS232-T1000. Table 4 contains TN, FP, FN, TP, TPR, TNR (True Negative Rate)[2], accuracy and MEV (Eq. (5)). From the viewpoint of MEV, the most efficient modification to induce misclassification is $t4$ (WIRE1). The MEV becomes −1.69. In fact, $t4$ (WIRE1) shows the lowest TPR. TP is decreased from 34 to 26 by 8 compared to the original circuit. Hence, TPR decreases to 68.42 % by 26.02 points. Note that the number of Trojan nets is increased by 2 due to the modification. Therefore, the denominator of TPR, the total number of Trojan nets (FN and TP), is also increased.

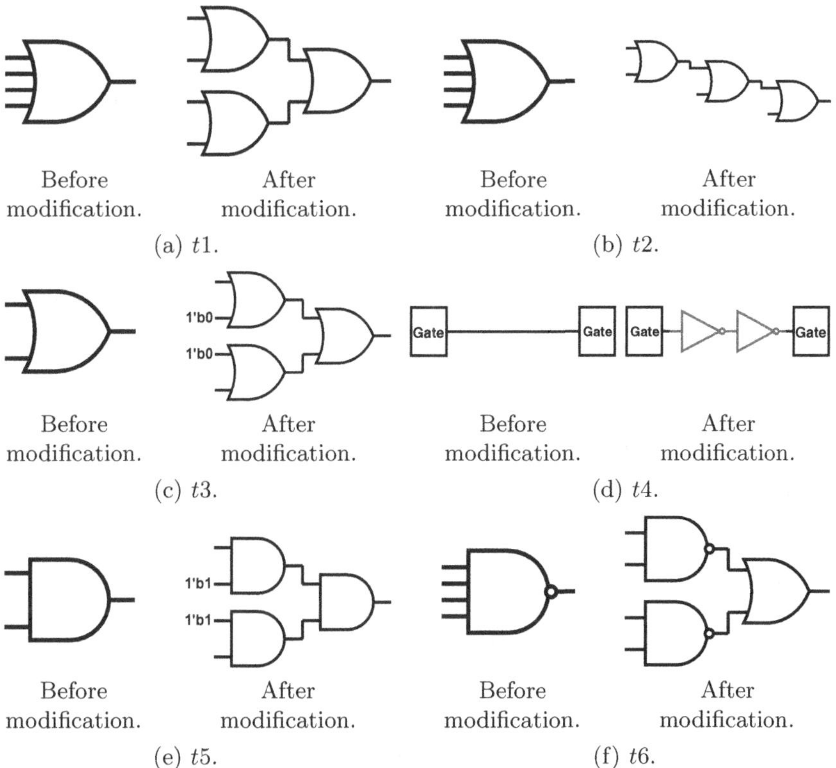

Before modification. After modification.
(a) $t1$.

Before modification. After modification.
(b) $t2$.

Before modification. After modification.
(c) $t3$.

Before modification. After modification.
(d) $t4$.

Before modification. After modification.
(e) $t5$.

Before modification. After modification.
(f) $t6$.

Fig. 2. Six AE modification patterns that we generate.

[2] The number of normal nets identified as normal nets is called as true negative (TN). The number of normal nets identified as Trojan nets is called as false positive (FP). The true negative rate is obtained from TN/(TN + FP).

Other modifications that significantly decrease TPR are $t1$ (OR2) and $t2$ (OR2). The experimental results demonstrate that how to pick up the gate we modify is an important factor to generate an AE. In this point, our proposed method effectively picks up appropriate gates to modify.

We repeatedly apply modifications to the circuit with $t4$ (WIRE1). Table 5 shows the results when we repeatedly apply modifications up to three times. In Table 5, the first row shows the result of the original circuit. The second row shows the result of the first modification where WIRE1 in the original circuit is replaced with $t4$. The third row shows the result of the second modification where OR2 in the circuit of the first modification is replaced with $t1$. The following rows show the circuit where each gate in the circuit of the second modification is replaced with an applicable pattern. We pick up the modification whose MEV is the lowest in each iteration. Finally, we pick up $t4$ (WIRE1) first, $t1$ (OR2) second and $t6$ (NAND5). From the viewpoint of MEV, the most efficient modification to induce misclassification is $t6$ (NAND5). The MEV becomes −4.46. TP is decreased from 34 to 19 by 15 compared to the circuit without modification. Hence, TPR is decreased to 45.24% by 49.20 points. This is the second lowest TPR, which means that we successfully pick up near-optimal modifications to decrease TPR by just utilizing MEV.

Table 4. Experimental results of RS232-T1000 with a single AE modification regardless of the amount of modifications.

Pattern	Gate	TN	FP	FN	TP	TPR	TNR	Accuracy	The increased number of gates	The increased number of logic levels	MEV
None	–	275	8	2	34	94.44%	97.17%	96.87%	0	0	−0.24
$t1$	OR1	275	8	4	34	89.47%	97.17%	96.26%	2	1	−0.25
$t1$	OR2	275	8	6	32	84.21%	97.17%	95.64%	2	1	−0.73
$t2$	OR1	275	8	3	35	92.11%	97.17%	96.57%	2	2	−0.31
$t2$	OR2	275	8	6	32	84.21%	97.17%	95.64%	2	2	−0.98
$t3$	OR3	277	8	5	33	86.84%	97.19%	95.98%	2	1	−0.42
$t4$	WIRE1	275	8	12	26	68.42%	97.17%	93.77%	2	2	<u>−1.69</u>
$t5$	AND1	277	8	4	34	89.47%	97.19%	96.28%	2	1	−0.28
$t5$	AND2	277	8	2	36	94.74%	97.19%	96.90%	2	1	−0.23
$t5$	AND3	277	8	3	35	92.11%	97.19%	96.59%	2	1	−0.33
$t6$	NAND1	275	8	2	36	94.74%	97.17%	96.88%	2	1	−0.23
$t6$	NAND2	275	8	5	33	86.84%	97.17%	95.95%	2	1	−0.79
$t6$	NAND3	275	8	5	33	86.84%	97.17%	95.95%	2	1	−0.39
$t6$	NAND4	275	8	3	35	92.11%	97.17%	96.57%	2	1	−0.59
$t6$	NAND5	275	8	5	33	86.84%	97.17%	95.95%	2	1	−0.94
$t6$	NAND6	275	8	4	34	89.47%	97.17%	96.26%	2	1	−0.86
$t6$	NAND7	275	8	5	33	86.84%	97.17%	95.95%	2	1	−0.67

Table 5. Experimental results of RS232-T1000 with up to three times AE modifications regardless of the amount of modifications.

Pattern	Gate	TN	FP	FN	TP	TPR	TNR	Accuracy	The increased number of gates	The increased number of logic levels	MEV
None	–	275	8	2	34	94.44%	97.17%	96.87%	0	0	−0.24
*t*4	WIRE1	275	8	12	26	68.42%	97.17%	93.77%	2	2	−1.69
*t*1	OR2	275	8	20	20	50.00%	97.17%	91.33%	4	3	−3.56
*t*1	OR1	275	8	23	19	45.24%	97.17%	90.46%	6	3	−3.93
*t*2	OR1	275	8	25	17	40.48%	97.17%	89.85%	6	4	−4.40
*t*3	OR3	277	8	12	30	71.43%	97.19%	93.88%	6	4	−1.43
*t*5	AND1	277	8	22	20	47.62%	97.19%	90.83%	6	4	−4.40
*t*5	AND2	277	8	20	22	52.38%	97.19%	91.44%	6	4	−3.39
*t*5	AND3	277	8	22	20	47.62%	97.19%	90.83%	6	4	−3.52
*t*6	NAND1	275	8	23	19	45.24%	97.17%	90.46%	6	4	−3.98
*t*6	NAND2	275	8	22	20	47.62%	97.17%	90.77%	6	4	−4.09
*t*6	NAND3	275	8	25	17	40.48%	97.17%	89.85%	6	4	−4.40
*t*6	NAND4	275	8	23	19	45.24%	97.17%	90.46%	6	4	−4.34
*t*6	NAND5	275	8	23	19	45.24%	97.17%	90.46%	6	4	<u>−4.46</u>
*t*6	NAND6	275	8	22	20	47.62%	97.17%	90.77%	6	4	−3.78
*t*6	NAND7	275	8	23	19	45.24%	97.17%	90.46%	6	4	−4.00

4.4 Evaluation with the Amount of Modifications

In this experiment, we set both λ_1 and λ_2 in Eq. (5) to 1. We consider the amount of modifications as well as the loss function of neural networks on generating AEs.

Table 6 shows the results when we apply the six AE patterns to RS232-T1000. From the viewpoint of MEV, the most efficient modification to induce misclassification is *t*6 (NAND5). The MEV becomes 2.06. TP is decreased from 34 to 33 by 1 compared to the original circuit. Hence, TPR is decreased to 86.84 % by 7.60 points.

We repeatedly apply modifications to the circuit with *t*6 (NAND5). Table 7 shows the result when we repeatedly apply modifications up to three times. In the same way as Table 6, the rows 1, 2 and 3 in Table 7 show the results of the original circuit, the first modification and the second modification, respectively. The following rows show the third modification. We pick up the modification whose MEV is the lowest in each iteration. Finally, we pick up *t*6 (NAND5) first, *t*6 (NAND6) second and *t*1 (OR2). From the viewpoint of MEV, the most efficient modification to induce misclassification is *t*1 (OR2). The MEV becomes 4.29. TP is decreased from 34 to 27 by 7 compared to the original circuit. Hence, TPR is decreased to 64.29 % by 30.15 points.

According to Table 5, applying *t*6 (NAND5) at the third iteration increases six gates and four logic levels compared to the original circuit. On the other hand, as shown in Table 7, applying *t*1 (OR2) at the third iteration increases six gates and just one logic level compared to the original circuit. *t*1 (OR2) has less amount of modification than *t*6 (NAND5). Reflecting this difference to MEV

Table 6. Experimental results of RS232-T1000 with a single AE modification considering the amount of modifications.

Pattern	Gate	TN	FP	FN	TP	TPR	TNR	Accuracy	The increased number of gates	The increased number of logic levels	MEV
None	–	275	8	2	34	94.44%	97.17%	96.87%	0	0	−0.24
*t*1	OR1	275	8	4	34	89.47%	97.17%	96.26%	2	1	2.75
*t*1	OR2	275	8	6	32	84.21%	97.17%	95.64%	2	1	2.27
*t*2	OR1	275	8	3	35	92.11%	97.17%	96.57%	2	2	3.69
*t*2	OR2	275	8	6	32	84.21%	97.17%	95.64%	2	2	3.02
*t*3	OR3	277	8	5	33	86.84%	97.19%	95.98%	2	1	2.58
*t*4	WIRE1	275	8	12	26	68.42%	97.17%	93.77%	2	2	2.31
*t*5	AND1	277	8	4	34	89.47%	97.19%	96.28%	2	1	2.72
*t*5	AND2	277	8	2	36	94.74%	97.19%	96.90%	2	1	2.77
*t*5	AND3	277	8	3	35	92.11%	97.19%	96.59%	2	1	2.67
*t*6	NAND1	275	8	2	36	94.74%	97.17%	96.88%	2	1	2.77
*t*6	NAND2	275	8	5	33	86.84%	97.17%	95.95%	2	1	2.21
*t*6	NAND3	275	8	5	33	86.84%	97.17%	95.95%	2	1	2.61
*t*6	NAND4	275	8	3	35	92.11%	97.17%	96.57%	2	1	2.41
*t*6	NAND5	275	8	5	33	86.84%	97.17%	95.95%	2	1	2.06
*t*6	NAND6	275	8	4	34	89.47%	97.17%	96.26%	2	1	2.14
*t*6	NAND7	275	8	5	33	86.84%	97.17%	95.95%	2	1	2.33

Table 7. Experimental results of RS232-T1000 with up to three times AE modifications considering the amount of modifications.

Pattern	Gate	TN	FP	FN	TP	TPR	TNR	Accuracy	The increased number of gates	The increased number of logic levels	MEV
none	–	275	8	2	34	94.44%	97.17%	96.87%	0	0	−0.24
*t*6	NAND5	275	8	5	33	86.84%	97.17%	95.95%	2	1	2.06
*t*6	NAND6	275	8	8	32	80.00%	97.17%	95.05%	4	1	3.48
*t*1	OR1	276	8	8	34	80.95%	97.18%	95.09%	6	1	5.51
*t*1	OR2	275	8	15	27	64.29%	97.17%	92.92%	6	1	4.29
*t*2	OR1	275	8	9	33	78.57%	97.17%	94.77%	6	2	6.48
*t*2	OR2	275	8	13	29	69.05%	97.17%	93.54%	6	2	5.44
*t*3	OR3	277	8	14	28	66.67%	97.19%	93.27%	6	2	5.88
*t*4	WIRE1	275	8	19	23	54.76%	97.17%	91.69%	6	3	5.76
*t*5	AND1	277	8	15	27	64.29%	97.19%	92.97%	6	2	5.90
*t*5	AND2	277	8	9	33	78.57%	97.19%	94.80%	6	2	6.47
*t*5	AND3	277	8	9	33	78.57%	97.19%	94.80%	6	2	6.46
*t*6	NAND1	275	8	8	34	80.95%	97.17%	95.08%	6	1	5.55
*t*6	NAND2	275	8	11	31	73.81%	97.17%	94.15%	6	1	5.05
*t*6	NAND3	275	8	11	31	73.81%	97.17%	94.15%	6	1	5.40
*t*6	NAND4	275	8	9	33	78.57%	97.17%	94.77%	6	1	5.19
*t*6	NAND7	275	8	11	31	73.81%	97.17%	94.15%	6	1	5.12

by setting λ_1 and λ_2 to 1, we can pick up modifications to decrease TPR with minimizing amount of modifications to the circuits. Therefore, we can achieve the purpose P3 discussed in Sect. 3.1.

From the discussion above, our proposed method effectively decreases the TPR by repeatedly modifying the hardware Trojan based on MEV. In addition, the experimental results demonstrate that our proposed method effectively picks up the effective gates to apply to AE patterns. Moreover, our proposed method effectively generates AEs for hardware-Trojan detection which decrease TPR.

5 Conclusion

In this paper, we propose a framework generating adversarial examples for hardware-Trojan detection for gate-level netlists utilizing neural networks. The experimental results demonstrate that an AE attack degrades TPR decreasing by 30.15 points at most base on MEV. We also show the validity of the attack and the evaluation values by applying the patterns to benchmarks. In the future, we will evaluate hardware Trojans with other modifications and benchmarks, and adapting our method to gray-box or black-box attacks. Furthermore, in order to defeat our AE attack, we will develop a robust hardware-Trojan detection method utilizing adversarial training techniques, for example, retraining the models with circuits containing AEs.

References

1. Akhtar, N., Mian, A.: Threat of adversarial attacks on deep learning in computer vision: a survey. IEEE Access **6**, 14410–14430 (2018)
2. Bhunia, S., Hsiao, M.S., Banga, M., Narasimhan, S.: Hardware Trojan attacks: threat analysis and countermeasures. Proc. IEEE **102**(8), 1229–1247 (2014)
3. Carlini, N., Wagner, D.: Audio adversarial examples: targeted attacks on speech-to-text. In: 2018 IEEE Security and Privacy Workshops (SPW) (2018)
4. Chakraborty, R.S., Narasimhan, S., Bhunia, S.: Hardware Trojan: threats and emerging solutions. In: Proceedings of International High-Level Design Validation and Test Workshop (HLDVT), pp. 166–171 (2009)
5. Dai, H., et al.: Adversarial attack on graph structured data. In: Proceedings of International Conference on Machine Learning (ICML) (2018)
6. Dong, C., He, G., Liu, X., Yang, Y., Guo, W.: A multi-layer hardware trojan protection framework for IoT chips. IEEE Access **7**, 23628–23639 (2019)
7. Eykholt, K., et al.: Physical adversarial examples for object detectors. CoRR (2018)
8. Eykholt, K., et al.: Robust physical-world attacks on deep learning models. CoRR (2017)
9. Francq, J., Frick, F.: Introduction to hardware Trojan detection methods. In: 2015 Design, Automation and Test in Europe Conference and Exhibition (DATE), pp. 770–775. EDAA (2015)
10. Goodfellow, I.J., Shlens, J., Szegedy, C.: Explaining and harnessing adversarial examples. In: Proceedings of 2015 International Conference on Learning Representations (ICLR) (2015)

11. Grosse, K., Papernot, N., Manoharan, P., Backes, M., McDaniel, P.: Adversarial examples for malware detection. In: Foley, S.N., Gollmann, D., Snekkenes, E. (eds.) ESORICS 2017. LNCS, vol. 10493, pp. 62–79. Springer, Cham (2017). https://doi.org/10.1007/978-3-319-66399-9_4
12. Hasegawa, K., Yanagisawa, M., Togawa, N.: Hardware Trojans classification for gate-level netlists using multi-layer neural networks. In: Proceedings of 2017 IEEE 23rd International Symposium on On-Line Testing and Robust System Design (IOLTS), pp. 227–232 (2017)
13. Inoue, T., Hasegawa, K., Yanagisawa, M., Togawa, N.: Designing hardware Trojans and their detection based on a SVM-based approach. In: Proceedings of International Conference on ASIC, pp. 811–814 (2018)
14. Inoue, T., Hasegawa, K., Yanagisawa, M., Togawa, N.: Designing subspecies of hardware Trojans and their detection using neural network approach. In: Proceedings 2018 IEEE 8th International Conference on Consumer Electronics in Berlin (ICCE-Berlin) (2018)
15. Iyyer, M., Wieting, J., Gimpel, K., Zettlemoyer, L.: Adversarial example generation with syntactically controlled paraphrase networks. In: Proceedings of the 2018 Conference of the North American Chapter of the Association for Computational Linguistics: Human Language Technologies, Volume 1 (Long Papers), pp. 1875–1885. Association for Computational Linguistics (2018)
16. Jia, R., Liang, P.: Adversarial examples for evaluating reading comprehension systems. In: Proceedings of the 2017 Conference on Empirical Methods in Natural Language Processing, pp. 2021–2031. Association for Computational Linguistics (2017)
17. Jin, Y., Makris, Y.: Hardware Trojan detection using path delay fingerprint. In: Proceedings of IEEE International Workshop on Hardware-Oriented Security and Trust (HOST), pp. 51–57 (2008)
18. Kurakin, A., Goodfellow, I.J., Bengio, S.: Adversarial examples in the physical world. In: Proceedings of 2017 International Conference on Learning Representations (ICLR) (2017)
19. Lamech, C., Plusquellic, J.: Trojan detection based on delay variations measured using a high-precision, low-overhead embedded test structure. In: 2012 IEEE International Symposium on Hardware-Oriented Security and Trust, pp. 75–82, June 2012
20. Liu, B., Qu, G.: VLSI supply chain security risks and mitigation techniques: a survey. Integr. VLSI J. **55**, 438–448 (2016)
21. Liu, D.C., Nocedal, J.: On the limited memory bfgs method for large scale optimization. Math. Program. **45**(1), 503–528 (1989)
22. Moosavi-Dezfooli, S.M., Fawzi, A., Frossard, P.: DeepFool: a simple and accurate method to fool deep neural networks. In: IEEE Conference on Computer Vision and Pattern Recognition, pp. 2574–2582 (2016)
23. Oya, M., Shi, Y., Yanagisawa, M., Togawa, N.: A score-based classification method for identifying hardware-Trojans at gate-level netlists. In: Proceedings of 2015 Design, Automation and Test in Europe Conference and Exhibition, pp. 465–470 (2015)
24. Rostami, M., Koushanfar, F., Rajendran, J., Karri, R.: Hardware security: threat models and metrics. In: Proceedings of International Conference on Computer-Aided Design (ICCAD), pp. 819–823 (2013)
25. Salmani, H., Tehranipoor, M., Karri, R.: On design vulnerability analysis and trust benchmarks development. In: 2013 IEEE 31st International Conference on Computer Design (ICCD), pp. 471–474 (2013)

26. Shakya, B., He, T., Salmani, H., Forte, D., Bhunia, S., Tehranipoor, M.: Benchmarking of hardware trojans and maliciously affected circuits. J. Hardware Syst. Secur. **1**(1), 85–102 (2017)
27. Szegedy, C., et al.: Intriguing properties of neural networks. CoRR (2013)
28. Trust-HUB. http://trust-hub.org/benchmarks/trojan
29. Xiao, K., Forte, D., Jin, Y., Karri, R., Bhunia, S., Tehranipoor, M.: Hardware trojans: lessons learned after one decade of research. ACM Trans. Design Autom. Electron. Syst. (TODAES) **22**(1), 1–23 (2016)
30. Zügner, D., Akbarnejad, A., Günnemann, S.: Adversarial attacks on neural networks for graph data. In: Proceedings of the 24th ACM SIGKDD International Conference on Knowledge Discovery and Data Mining - KDD 2018, pp. 2847–2856. ACM Press (2018)

Selective Forwarding Attack on IoT Home Security Kits

Ali Hariri, Nicolas Giannelos, and Budi Arief(✉)

School of Computing, University of Kent, Canterbury, UK
hariri.ali.93@gmail.com, nikognl@gmail.com, b.arief@kent.ac.uk

Abstract. Efforts have been made to improve the security of the Internet of Things (IoT) devices, but there remain some vulnerabilities and misimplementations. This paper describes a new threat to home security devices in which an attacker can disable all functionality of a device, but to the device's owner, everything still appears to be operational. We targeted home security devices because their security is critical as people may rely on them to protect their homes. In particular, we exploited a feature called "heartbeat", which is exchanged between the devices and the cloud in order to check that the devices are still connected. Even though network traffic was encrypted, we successfully identified the heartbeats due to their fixed size and periodic nature. Thereafter, we established a man-in-the-middle attack between the device and the cloud and selectively forwarded heartbeats while filtering out other traffic. As a result, the device appears to be still connected (because the heartbeat traffic is being allowed through), while in reality the device's functionality is disabled (because non-heartbeat traffic is being filtered out). We applied this exploit on a set of six devices, and five were found to be vulnerable. Consequently, an intruder can use this exploit to disable a home security device and break into a house without the awareness of the owner. We carried out a responsible disclosure exercise with the manufacturers of the affected devices, but the response has been limited. This shows that IoT security is still not taken completely seriously and many threats are still undiscovered. Finally, we provide some recommendations on how to detect and prevent the threats posed by insecure IoT devices, which ironically include IoT home security kits.

Keywords: IoT · Security · Attack · Off-the-shelf devices · Heartbeats · Selective forwarding · SSL/TLS · WPA2

1 Introduction

The Internet has considerably changed in the last decade. It has become more than just a platform for email exchanges, web browsing, instant messaging or media streaming. The connected devices are no longer just servers, computers and smartphones, but instead the Internet has become an Internet of Things (IoT), of connected wearables, home appliances, biomedical devices, cars, cities,

S. Katsikas et al. (Eds.): ESORICS 2019 Workshops, LNCS 11980, pp. 360–373, 2020.
https://doi.org/10.1007/978-3-030-42048-2_23

and many more. IoT is gaining more and more popularity and experts predict that it will become an Internet of Everything in the near future [1]. It is estimated that the number of connected devices will reach up to 20 billion by 2020 [2].

Despite its convenience, IoT and its applications introduce major privacy threats and critical security risks. For instance, IoT devices may be compromised to access personal information, or to gain control over industries, cities and public organisations or disrupt their services. This has been shown by several incidents like the Mirai botnet [3,4]. Mirai is a computer worm that compromised hundreds of thousands of IoT devices, which were then used to mount a Distributed Denial of Service (DDoS) attack to disrupt well-known services like Netflix and Twitter [5]. IoT also imposes personal privacy threats through smart home devices like cameras, personal assistants and home automation kits. For example, Trendnet home security and monitoring cameras were found to be vulnerable, allowing an attacker to access live video feeds of the camera without any authentication [6]. Likewise, customers of Swann home cameras reported that they were able to access recordings from cameras of other customers [7]. A very recent report of security vulnerabilities in three specialist car alarm systems further illustrates the danger of connecting your device to the Internet without proper security testing [8]. These vulnerabilities allowed attackers to steal or hijack affected vehicles through the compromised alarm system. What is ironic here is that whoever bought these vulnerable car alarm systems did so out of a desire to improve the security of their vehicle. But inadvertently, they introduced security vulnerabilities that would allow attackers to take control of their vehicle. This irony resonates with the message we aim to convey in our paper.

Evidently, the security of IoT devices is a major issue that needs to be continuously evaluated and addressed due to its impact on the physical world. This motivated us to explore new and common vulnerabilities in a selected set of consumer IoT products. Particularly, we targeted home security devices because their security is critical as people may rely on them to protect their homes.

Contribution. The main contribution of this paper is the *exploitation of a vulnerability in the heartbeat exchange of IoT devices*. By exploiting this vulnerability, an attacker can disable IoT home security devices without the awareness of their owners. Particularly, the device will appear to be online and working normally, but in fact it will be completely disabled. This was due to wrong implementations of heartbeat messages exchanged between devices and their cloud infrastructure. Our second contribution relates to a *potential misimplementation of the WPA2 four-way handshake protocol in some IoT devices*. This misimplementation allows an attacker to carry out an evil twin access point attack, which would force the device to connect to the attacker's LAN. This would allow the attacker to exploit further vulnerabilities, or eavesdrop on the communications between the device and the cloud.

The rest of this paper is organised as follows. Section 2 presents related work. Section 3 outlines our methodology, while Sect. 4 presents our findings and results. Section 5 describes the threat model to illustrate the feasibility of our attack. Section 6 dissects the risks and consequences of the discovered vulnerability. We present some insights from the responsible disclosure exercise we carried out with the affected manufacturers of the devices. We also propose some recommendations to how to fix the vulnerabilities uncovered by our research. Finally, Sect. 7 concludes the paper and provides ideas for future work.

2 Related Work

Visan et al. [9] assessed the security of Samsung Smart Things hub. They first attempted to extract credentials from the hub using various traffic sniffing methods. They also demonstrated that the hub is robust and secure. However, they discovered that a DoS attack against the hub is possible, if the attacker has access to the LAN. The attack would give an intruder an 8-minute window to break into a house before notifying the owner. Visan et al. argue that home security kits are not completely reliable.

Another good example is the work by Fernandes et al. [10], which demonstrated again that despite the effort put into security, there may remain some security issues due to the complex nature of the products. More precisely, they discovered vulnerabilities inside the architecture, in the capability model and the event subsystem of Samsung Smart Things, due to the numerous and complex functionalities exposed to the user. By exploiting them, they managed to insert backdoor pin-codes into a connected door lock, eavesdrop door lock pin-codes, cause a fake fire alarm and disable the vacation mode of the device. More importantly, those vulnerabilities were significant as they targeted the architecture of the application layer at its core, thus making them difficult to patch.

Apthrope et al. [11] proved that users' privacy can be breached without compromising devices or network communications. They showed that any party having network access – e.g. Internet Service Providers (ISPs) – can infer sensitive information just by analysing network traffic. They particularly analysed DNS requests, IP and TCP headers and packet rates to identify device types and user interaction. For instance, they were able to determine if a user is sleeping by analysing a sleep sensor's traffic, or if the user is moving inside a house by analysing a motion sensor's traffic. This work highlights that privacy is a critical challenge in IoT security, and it cannot be achieved with cryptography only.

Jerry Gamblin discovered that Google home assistant can be controlled by any device that has network access to the LAN. The device can send commands to the assistant without any authentication and it can cause to reboot and even to disconnect from Wi-Fi. This is due to an undocumented API that can be exploited by sending rogue commands [12].

Very recently, OConnor et al. [13] uncovered a design flaw in the messaging protocols of 22 IoT devices. The design flaw they uncovered is very similar to the weakness we discuss in this paper. We independently carried out our research and developed a proof-of-concept automated tool to exploit this flaw.

3 Methodology

We chose smart home IoT devices because they provide a wider attack surface due to their numerous interconnected components such as cameras, alarms, motion detectors and many other sensors. We targeted a set of home security devices including Swann Smart Home Security Kit (SWO-HUB01K), D-Link Home Security Kit (DCH-G020), D-Link camera (DCS-935L), Panasonic Home Monitoring and Control Kit (KX-HN6012EW), Telldus Smart Home Start-up Kit and Samsung SmartThings (F-H-ETH-001). We performed DoS attacks on the selected devices, mainly Wi-Fi deauthentication and blackhole attacks. We used `arpspoof` tool [14] for a blackhole attack and `aireplay-ng` tool [15] for Wi-Fi deauthentication attack. `arpspoof` tool was used to achieve a MITM position and IP forwarding was disabled to complete the blackhole attack. Moreover, we analysed network traffic thoroughly to find patterns that were then used in our selective forwarding attack. Traffic analysis was mainly conducted using `Wireshark` [16], in which several `Wireshark` filters were used to analyse and identify patterns in network traffic of each device. In addition, our selective forwarding attack requires achieving a MITM position on the Transport layer. Thus, it was necessary to run a TCP proxy and force the devices to connect to the proxy instead of connecting to their legitimate servers. DNS poisoning was the best option to force the devices to connect to the proxy. For that, we used `Wireshark` to view DNS requests and responses, and identify the domain names and the IP addresses of the servers. Then, we used `Bind9` and configured it to resolve the identified DNS requests to the IP address of the machine that is running the proxy. As a result, all devices connected to the proxy instead of connecting to their servers. The proxy was developed as a Python script, and it can be found with the Bind9 configurations on GitHub[1].

4 Results

We conducted blackhole and Wi-Fi de-authentication attacks on the selected devices to determine the required time to alert or display that the device went offline. The results showed that the devices took between 5 s and 2 min to alert the user depending on the vendor. Thereupon, we deduced that the devices must be exchanging periodic messages with the cloud to prove that they are still online. Once the cloud stops receiving those messages, it reports to the user application that the device was disconnected. Those messages are known as heartbeats and they are defined as "a periodic signal generated by hardware or software to indicate that it is still running" [17].

We realised that heartbeats will always have a fixed size during one session because the payload is always the same and it is always encrypted with the same algorithm over this session. Subsequently, we postulated that heartbeat messages can be identified in network traffic even if they were encrypted due to their periodic nature and constant payload size. Therefore, we presumed that we can

[1] https://github.com/HaririAli/IoTHeartbeatProxy.git.

exploit this pattern by selectively forwarding heartbeats and TLS handshakes, and blocking any other traffic. This will deceive the server into believing that the device is still online and sending heartbeats, when in fact its traffic is blocked. We designated this attack as the "heartbeat attack".

4.1 Heartbeats in Swann

We noticed that every 10 s, the hub sends 92 bytes of data and the server responds with 425 bytes of payload as shown in Fig. 1. Subsequently, we wrote a Python script that opens two TCP streams with the hub and the server, and selectively forwards data between them. The proxy initially forwards all data for few seconds to ensure that the TLS handshake was completed, then it only forwards 92-byte and 425-byte long data. Thus, the proxy will only forward heartbeats and block any other traffic.

27245	317.232384	192.168.137.117	35.190.18.224	TLSv1.2	158	Application Data
27247	317.413550	35.190.18.224	192.168.137.117	TLSv1.2	491	Application Data
27249	327.428000	192.168.137.117	35.190.18.224	TLSv1.2	158	Application Data
27251	327.453656	35.190.18.224	192.168.137.117	TLSv1.2	491	Application Data
27270	337.468366	192.168.137.117	35.190.18.224	TLSv1.2	158	Application Data
27271	337.493264	35.190.18.224	192.168.137.117	TLSv1.2	491	Application Data
27274	347.507892	192.168.137.117	35.190.18.224	TLSv1.2	158	Application Data
27275	347.531465	35.190.18.224	192.168.137.117	TLSv1.2	491	Application Data

Fig. 1. Wireshark capture of heartbeats in Swann's traffic

4.2 Heartbeats in D-Link Hub

Similarly, we analysed network traffic from D-Link hub looking for a periodic pattern. However, we did not find any periodic data packets exchanged between the server and the hub. We rather found that the server sends TCP keepalive packets every 5 s and the hub responds with a TCP keepalive ACK. Thus, D-Link relied on TCP keepalive packets to ensure that the hub is still online and connected. This, in fact, makes the exploit much simpler as the proxy does not have to forward any data but rather just acknowledge TCP keepalive packets once the connection is established. Thereupon, we edited the Python proxy to forward the TLS handshake and then terminate the TCP connection with the hub. Consequently, the proxy will establish a connection with the server because the TLS handshake was completed. The proxy will then acknowledge any traffic coming from the server including TCP keepalive packets. The behaviour of this exploit is illustrated in Fig. 2.

4.3 Heartbeats in D-Link Camera

We also analysed D-Link camera's traffic and observed that it sends a 314-byte long heartbeat every 55 s and the server responds with two heartbeats of 90 and 218 bytes of data. This pattern is shown in Fig. 3. Thereupon, we edited our Python script to selectively forward those 3 heartbeat messages and block everything else.

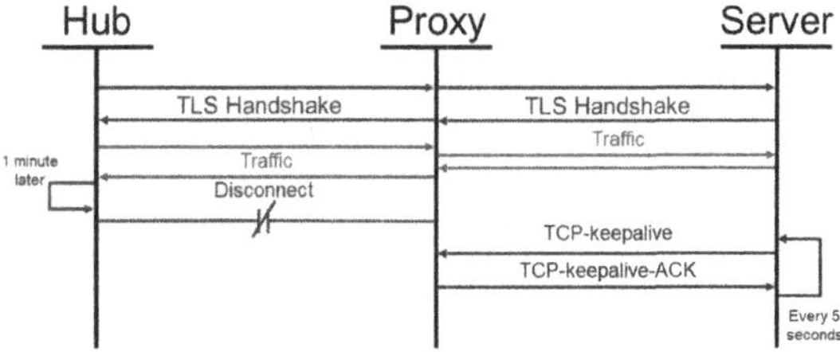

Fig. 2. Behaviour of heartbeat exploit against D-Link hub

No.	Time	Source	Destination	Protocol	Length
32276	1553.5283938…	192.168.1.100	54.194.162.25	TLSv1	380
32278	1553.5565975…	54.194.162.25	192.168.1.100	TLSv1	156
32280	1553.5766084…	54.194.162.25	192.168.1.100	TLSv1	284
32330	1608.6073990…	192.168.1.100	54.194.162.25	TLSv1	380
32331	1608.6820104…	54.194.162.25	192.168.1.100	TLSv1	156
32333	1609.1305161…	54.194.162.25	192.168.1.100	TLSv1	284
32359	1663.7695987…	192.168.1.100	54.194.162.25	TLSv1	380

Fig. 3. Wireshark capture of heartbeats in D-Link camera's traffic

4.4 Heartbeats in Panasonic

We discovered that the heartbeats are sent as 48-byte long UDP datagrams every 15 s. Since the heartbeats are sent as UDP datagrams, there was no need to run a TCP proxy and selective forwarding could be achieved using iptables only. Subsequently, we wrote iptables rules to allow only 48-byte long UDP packets and drop everything else. However, this exploit was only tested when both the hub and the smartphone are on the same LAN. Testing the exploit on WAN was not possible due to unknown technical issues in which the mobile application was not able to access the hub. The exploit succeeded on the LAN and the application displayed that the hub is online. However, the application was completely unresponsive because it could not receive anything apart from heartbeats.

4.5 Heartbeats in Telldus

Telldus TellStick was found to send its traffic in cleartext. Thus, it is possible to capture heartbeats and replay them with a custom HTTP client. This will display that the device is online without any selective forwarding and without even connecting it at all. To validate our assumption, we analysed traffic from Telldus to identify the cleartext heartbeat. Subsequently, we wrote a Python script that connects to the server and sends the same payload every two minutes.

4.6 Heartbeats in Samsung SmartThings

Visan et al. [9] proved that under a DoS attack, Samsung Smartthings provides a time-window of 8 min before notifying the user. To build on their work, we decided to apply the heartbeat exploit on the same device to check if it can provide an infinite time window. We analysed network traffic collected from the hub and noticed that both the server and the hub exchange heartbeats every 31 s; the hub sends 49 bytes and the server responds with 55 bytes of data.

Unlike the other devices, Samsung SmartThings proved that its heartbeat exchange is robust and secure. The hub disconnected immediately upon selectively forwarding its heartbeats. Subsequently, we analysed the behaviour of the device to understand how it detected the exploit. We discovered that upon blocking non-heartbeat messages, either the device or the server disconnects right after the next heartbeat. This means that the server was reporting in its heartbeat whether it received the last message or not. This allowed the device to detect that the last message was not received by the server, thus it disconnected. As such, we think that the heartbeat messages in this system have some sort of checking whether other (non-heartbeat) messages have passed through or not.

4.7 Summary

The sizes, types and periods of heartbeats of each device are summarised in Table 1. During the experiment, we developed custom proxies for each device and used them to conduct selective forwarding exploits. Once we confirmed our results, we developed a generic selective forwarding proxy (outlined in Sect. 3) that takes a set of arguments to customise its behaviour.

Table 1. Summary of heartbeat patterns in the analysed devices

Device	Heartbeat type	Size of Server heartbeat (bytes)	Size of device heartbeat (bytes)	Period (seconds)
Swann	TCP payload	425	92	10
D-Link	TCP keepalive	N/A	N/A	5
D-Link Camera	TCP payload	90; 218	314	55
Panasonic	UDP datagram	20	20	15
Telldus	TCP payload	"Ping" (cleartext message)	"Pong" (cleartext message)	120
Samsung	TCP payload	55	49	31

The results of this exploit proved that the devices can be completely disabled while their corresponding applications still display them as online and operational. This exploit can be considered as an unnoticed DoS attack, because the system was not really available, but the application displayed that it was normally working. The results of the heartbeat exploit are summarised in Table 2, where the third column states if the device can be physically disconnected during the attack (which indicates a more severe security violation), and the last column presents relevant further details for each device.

Table 2. Summary of heartbeat exploit results

Device	Heartbeat exploit	Can be physically disconnected	Notes
Swann	Succeeded	Yes	Swann has 2 heartbeats implemented on the Application layer. But the server is not checking for the one coming from the device
D-Link	Succeeded	Yes	D-Link implements heartbeat on the Transport layer with TCP keepalives sent every 5 s
D-Link camera	Succeeded	No	D-Link camera employs three heartbeats on the Application layer. The camera sends a heartbeat and the server responds with two heartbeats
Panasonic	Succeeded	No	On the LAN, both the hub and the mobile app are exchanging heartbeat messages every 15 s encapsulated in UDP
Telldus	Succeeded	Yes	Hub and cloud exchange periodically messages at the application layer in cleartext
Samsung SmartThings	Failed	No	The hub sends heartbeat messages every 31 s and the server responds. But it detects our attempt to attack the heartbeat, and on the next heartbeat, the server closes the connection

5 Threat Model

In this section, we demonstrate how an attacker can theoretically and practically exploit the vulnerability in the heartbeat exchange. We then describe an automated attack that we have successfully applied to one of the devices.

5.1 Wi-Fi Attacks

The easiest way for an attacker to exploit heartbeats is by gaining access to the LAN to which the device is connected. This is relatively straightforward for an attacker to achieve, as many users still use broken protocols like WEP and WPA; many do not even use Wi-Fi encryption at all. According to Wigle, around 4% of access points are unencrypted, 6.3% use WEP and 5.8% use WPA [18]. An attacker can also compromise Wi-Fi networks protected by WPA2 using dictionary attacks like the attack demonstrated in [19]. An attacker can compromise a Wi-Fi AP by exploiting the vulnerability of Wi-Fi Protected Setup (WPS) protocol, which allows association to an AP using an 8-digit PIN [20].

5.2 DNS Server Hijacking

An attacker can hijack a DNS server and change the records directly. This may be a primary DNS server of the IoT device's vendor or a resolver or cache server of an ISP. In all cases the attacker would be able to exploit the vulnerability in a large group of devices that are served by the compromised DNS server. This attack is infeasible in most situations, but it is still possible and there are several real-world examples, such as the DNSpionage attack, which targeted governmental and private organisations in Lebanon and the UAE. The attackers redirected email and VPN traffic to an IP address managed by them [21]. Similarly, attackers can redirect heartbeat traffic to a TCP proxy using this attack and eventually exploit the vulnerability in the heartbeat exchange.

5.3 Network Attacks

Theoretically, an attacker can gain access to one or more routers of an ISP by exploiting a vulnerability in the router's operating system. Subsequently, the attacker can use the compromised router to spoof DNS responses or to filter out traffic. This indeed is practically almost infeasible as it is very difficult to gain access to ISP's network devices. Nonetheless, there are some real-world examples that prove this kind of attacks possible in specific situations. For instance, in 2015, FireEye discovered that a group of attackers did manage to take over Cisco routers [22]. Similarly, Cisco has recently discovered and patched serious security holes that allow root access in their SD-WAN software [23]. This proves that such attacks although very difficult, are still possible and can allow attackers to eventually exploit the heartbeat vulnerability against not only one but a large group of devices.

5.4 Automated Attack Against Swann Using Evil-Twin Wi-Fi AP

For devices that support Wi-Fi connections, attackers can try Evil Twin attacks to force a device to connect to their own LAN on which they can spoof DNS records. We experimented this attack on the Swann hub and successfully managed to force it to connect to our LAN and eventually exploited its heartbeats. In WPA2, a four-way handshake needs to be completed before sending any data, but the handshake cannot be completed because the evil twin does not know the password. Surprisingly, Swann hub connected to the rogue AP anyway and sent DHCP, DNS and TCP traffic normally. After exchanging few packets, the hub then fell back to association request/responses and kept repeating the same behaviour in a loop. An illustration of this behavior is shown in Fig. 4.

The IEEE802.11i standard [24] states that an AP and a Station (STA) must exchange four EAPoL messages to complete the 4-way handshake for authentication before sending any data. Based on the IEEE802.11i standard we deduced that this is a misimplementation of the standard in the driver of the devices' wireless chipset. By analysing Swann hub's hardware, we discovered that it uses a Jorjin WG7831-D0 Wi-Fi chipset. According to its documentation, the chipset is based on the Texas Instruments WL1831MOD chipset and WiLink8 driver [25,26].

By exploiting this misimplementation, we managed to achieve a MITM between the hub and the server, and perform the heartbeat attack. The attack was then automated using bash and the Python proxy script. The whole process can be found on GitHub[2]. Consequently, our exploit can disable any Swann device located nearby our attacking machine, without its owner's awareness.

[2] https://github.com/SRJanel/SWO_exploit.

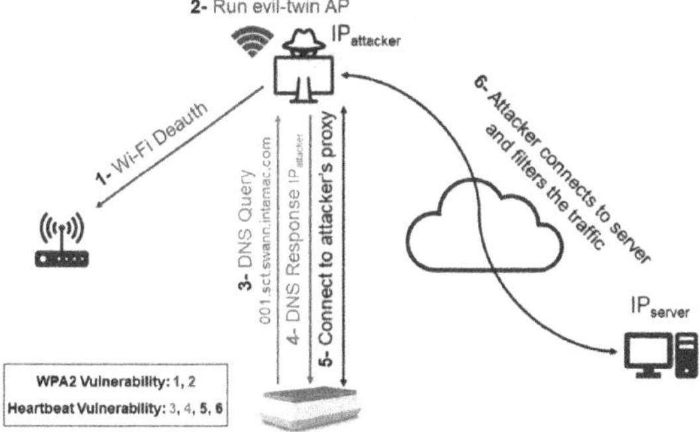

Fig. 4. Combination of the WPA2 and Heartbeat vulnerabilities in Swann.

6 Discussion

Exploiting the heartbeat pattern is not critical in all IoT applications like light bulbs for example. However, it can be remarkably critical in home security kits and in some health care applications which are used to remotely monitor patients. Furthermore, this attack can be extended to identify other patterns in encrypted traffic like sensor readings or controller commands and selectively forward and drop those patterns. For instance, attackers can block some control commands in water distribution systems to cause floods, or in electricity distribution systems to cause blackouts. Autonomous vehicles can also be affected by this attack in which attackers filter communications between the vehicles leading to deadly accidents. Therefore, detection and defence mechanisms must be studied and developed to prevent such attacks and to reach a more secure IoT. To exploit heartbeats, an attacker must redirect network traffic to a malicious proxy. Nevertheless, attackers can find many ways to gain access over the network. This was proven by Chapman [27] who compromised WLAN credentials by exploiting a vulnerability in LIFX light bulbs. Alternatively, attackers can compromise Wi-Fi credentials using social engineering techniques. Therefore, it is necessary to secure the heartbeat exchange in IoT, even though its exploit requires network access.

6.1 Recommendations and Countermeasures

Some "secure" implementations of the heartbeat pattern were proposed by different authors. For instance, IBM proposes an implementation that uses freshness and challenge-response mechanisms and provides security against spoofing and replay attacks [28]. However, this solution is not secure against our attack, because the proxy can simply detect the challenge-response pattern due to its periodic nature and selectively forward it, while blocking any other traffic. For that, we propose some recommendations and countermeasures that can make heartbeat exchanges more secure in IoT. Firstly, heartbeats must always be implemented on the application layer instead of the transport layer like TCP keepalive packets. Secondly, heartbeats must include information about the last message that was sent before the heartbeat. This would allow both endpoints to detect if any messages were filtered out. To understand this mechanism better, consider this scenario:

- Device sends an encrypted heartbeat. It contains a sequence number of the last message sent, which was a heartbeat too.
- Server confirms that the previous message was indeed a heartbeat.
- Device sends an alert that also contains previous message's sequence number.
- Attacker selectively blocks the alert.
- Device sends a heartbeat message that contains a sequence number of the alert that was blocked.
- Server understands that the alert was not delivered due to the missing sequence number.
- Finally, server notifies the user that alerts are being filtered out.

A prevention mechanism would be to always pass the last message within the heartbeat. This would allow the server to receive the blocked message and detect the attack because it did not receive the message as a stand-alone. Another prevention would be using IPSec as it prevents redirecting traffic to a proxy.

The proposed countermeasure will affect the efficiency of the IoT system especially if the devices have limited resources. This is due to the additional metadata the must be sent in heartbeats or the overhead introduced by IPSec. However, security usually comes at the cost of performance.

6.2 Responsible Disclosure Exercise

We contacted most of the manufacturers of the affected devices. Furthermore, we conducted more in-depth conversation with Swann since its device has another serious flaw. We also contacted Texas Instruments, which manufactured the Wi-Fi chipset used by the Swann device under our investigation.

D-Link confirmed our findings but decided that the occurrence of such attack is uncommon and eventually lowered the development priority of a patch. Swann also confirmed our findings and reported that they will release a security patch for their products. Panasonic stated that the discovered pattern is not a heartbeat, but rather a mechanism to establish a peer-to-peer connection between the device and the mobile application. Thus, they think that there is no need to release a patch. Texas Instruments tried to reproduce our WPA2 results in Swann. They tested several versions of their driver and all proved to be secure. They also sent us an evaluation module to test it ourselves and we do confirm their results. After thorough investigations by Swann, they confirmed that the module was installed by a company that went out of operation, so although the root cause has not been found, the vulnerability most likely stems from the specific WPA supplicant and software used in the product. This means that the company that installed the module is probably responsible for the poor implementation.

7 Conclusion

Although the security of IoT devices has substantially improved in the past few years, some vulnerabilities remain undiscovered in many IoT systems. Our paper describes a new threat to home security devices in which an attacker can disable a device while making it appear to be working normally to the user.

We demonstrated that heartbeats can be identified in network traffic even if they were encrypted. Subsequently, we proved that heartbeats can be exploited using selective forwarding attack. In particular, we redirected network traffic from the devices to a TCP proxy that only forwards heartbeats between the hub and the server and discards any other data. As a result, the user application displays that the device is online because heartbeats are passed. However, the device is in fact disabled because the rest of its traffic was blocked. This allows an intruder to disable home security devices and break into houses without the awareness of their owners.

We applied this exploit on a set of home security devices and most of them were found to be affected by this vulnerability. We disclosed our findings to the affected companies to fix the issue and release the necessary patches. To mitigate this vulnerability, we propose some recommendations to implement a robust and secure heartbeat exchange. Our results confirm the findings of OConnor et al. [13], although our research was carried out independently and on a different set of devices.

Our work proves that further research is still needed for a more secure IoT. In addition, researchers should work closely with industry to ensure that security standards are implemented correctly. To build on this work, selective forwarding exploits should be extended to cover any type of traffic patterns rather than just heartbeats. This would help researchers to develop robust frameworks that can prevent or at least detect any type of selective forwarding.

References

1. Evans, D.: How the internet of everything will change the world...for the better IOE [infographic], April 2013. https://blogs.cisco.com/digital/how-the-internet-of-everything-will-change-the-worldfor-the-better-infographic
2. Meulen, R.V.D.: Gartner says 8.4 billion connected "things" will be in use in 2017, up 31 percent from 2016', February 2017. https://www.gartner.com/en/newsroom/press-releases/2017-02-07-gartner-says-8-billion-connected-things-will-be-in-use-in-2017-up-31-percent-from-2016
3. Antonakakis, M., April, T., Bailey, M., et al.: Understanding the mirai botnet. In: 26th USENIX Security Symposium (USENIX Security 17), pp. 1093–1110. USENIX Association (2017)
4. Cetin, O., Ganán, C., Altena, L., et al.: Cleaning up the internet of evil things: real-world evidence on ISP and consumer efforts to remove Mirai. In: Network and Distributed Systems Security (NDSS) Symposium (2019)
5. Kolias, C., Kambourakis, G., Stavrou, A., Voas, J.: DDoS in the IoT: Mirai and other botnets. Computer **50**(7), 80–84 (2017). https://doi.org/10.1109/mc.2017.201

6. Zetter, K.: Flaw in home security cameras exposes live feeds to hackers, June 2012. https://www.wired.com/2012/02/home-cameras-exposed/
7. Kelion, L.: Swann's home security camera recordings could be hijacked, July 2018. https://www.bbc.co.uk/news/technology-44809152
8. Simmons, D.: Security holes found in big brand car alarms, March 2019. https://www.bbc.co.uk/news/technology-47485731
9. Visan, B., Lee, J., Yang, B., Smith, A.H., Matson, E.T.: Vulnerabilities in hub architecture IoT devices. In: 2017 14th IEEE Annual Consumer Communications Networking Conference (CCNC), pp. 83–88, January 2017
10. Fernandes, E., Jung, J., Prakash, A.: Security analysis of emerging smart home applications. In: IEEE Symposium on Security and Privacy (SP), pp. 636–654 (2016)
11. Apthorpe, N., Reisman, D., Feamster, N.: A smart home is no castle: privacy vulnerabilities of encrypted IoT traffic. CoRR, vol. abs/1705.06805 (2017). http://arxiv.org/abs/1705.06805
12. Shaun, N.: This one weird trick turns your google home hub into a doorstop, November 2018. https://www.theregister.co.uk/2018/10/31/google_home_api
13. OConnor, T., Enck, W., Reaves, B.: Blinded and confused: uncovering systemic flaws in device telemetry for smart-home internet of things. In: Proceedings of the 12th Conference on Security and Privacy in Wireless and Mobile Networks, pp. 140–150. ACM (2019)
14. Whalen, S., Engle, S., Romeo, D.: An introduction to ARP spoofing, April 2001. http://index-of.es/Misc/pdf/arpspoofing_slides.pdf
15. Aircrack-NG tool. https://www.aircrack-ng.org/doku.php?id=aireplay-ng
16. Wireshark: Wireshark Tool. https://www.wireshark.org/
17. PC Magazine Encyclopedia: Heartbeat Definition. https://www.pcmag.com/encyclopedia/term/44190/heartbeat
18. All the networks. found by everyone. https://wigle.net/
19. Nakhila, O., Attiah, A., Jin, Y., Zou, C.: Parallel active dictionary attack on WPA2-PSK wi-fi networks. In: MILCOM 2015–2015 IEEE Military Communications Conference, pp. 665–670. IEEE (2015)
20. Viehböck, S.: Brute forcing wi-fi protected setup, December 2011. https://sviehb.files.wordpress.com/2011/12/viehboeck_wps.pdf
21. Krebs, B.: A deep dive on the recent widespread DNS hijacking attacks, February 2019. https://krebsonsecurity.com/2019/02/a-deep-dive-on-the-recent-widespread-dns-hijacking-attacks/
22. Greene, T.: Attackers can take over cisco routers; other routers at risk, too, September 2015. https://www.networkworld.com/article/2984124/attackers-can-take-over-cisco-routers-other-routers-at-risk-too.html
23. Cisco Security Advisory: Cisco security threat and vulnerability intelligence, January 2019. https://tools.cisco.com/security/center/content/CiscoSecurityAdvisory/cisco-sa-20190123-sdwan-file-write
24. IEEE Computer Society LAN/MAN Standards Committee: IEEE Standard for Information technology-Telecommunications and information exchange between systems-Local and metropolitan area networks-Specific requirements Part 11: Wireless LAN Medium Access Control (MAC) and Physical Layer (PHY) Specifications. IEEE Std 802.11 (2007)

25. Jorjin: Jorjin WG7831-D0 Wi-Fi chipset. https://www.jorjin.com/product.php?id=79
26. Jorjin: WG78XX Serial Module - Support Note. https://www.jorjin.com/upload/1470892430.pdf
27. Chapman, A.: Hacking into internet connected light bulbs, July 2014. https://www.contextis.com/blog/hacking-into-internet-connected-light-bulbs
28. Identifying and Preventing Threats to Your IoT Devices. https://developer.ibm.com/articles/iot-prevent-threats-iot-devices/#heartbeat

Denial-of-Service Attacks and Countermeasures in the RPL-Based Internet of Things

Philokypros P. Ioulianou(✉) and Vassilios G. Vassilakis

Department of Computer Science, University of York, York, UK
{pi533,vv573}@york.ac.uk

Abstract. Internet of Things (IoT) is already playing a significant role in our lives, as more and more industries are adopting IoT for improving existing systems and providing novel applications. However, recent attacks caused by Mirai and Chalubo botnets show that IoT systems are vulnerable and new security mechanisms are required. In this work, we design and implement a prototype of Intrusion Detection System (IDS) for protecting IoT networks and devices from Denial-of-Service (DoS) attacks. Our focus is on detecting attacks that exploit the IPv6 Routing Protocol for Low-Power and Lossy Networks (RPL), which is a widely used protocol for packet routing in low-power IoT networks. Our considered Operating System (OS) is the popular ContikiOS and we use the Cooja simulator to study DoS attacks and test the detection algorithms. In particular, we simulated scenarios that involve both benign and malicious/compromised IoT devices. A compromised device exploits RPL control messages to cause other devices perform heavy computations and disrupt the established network routes. The obtained simulation results help us understand the characteristics of an RPL-based IoT network under its normal operation and devise effective countermeasures against malicious activity. A new threshold-based IDS is proposed and a first prototype is implemented in ContikiOS. The IDS relies on tunable parameters and involves both centralised and distributed components in order to effectively detect malicious RPL messages. Experimental results show high detection rate and low false positives in large networks.

Keywords: DoS · RPL · Intrusion detection · ContikiOS · Cooja

1 Introduction

Due to resource-constrained nature of typical Internet of Things (IoT) devices, traditional security approaches and cryptographic mechanisms are not always applicable [7]. As a consequence, many IoT devices are left with weak or no security measures [13] and become targets of cyberattacks. Such attacks have multipled over the last years [29]. A recent example is the Chalubo botnet [11] which exploited the default/weak passwords of IoT devices running Secure Socket Shell

S. Katsikas et al. (Eds.): ESORICS 2019 Workshops, LNCS 11980, pp. 374–390, 2020.
https://doi.org/10.1007/978-3-030-42048-2_24

(SSH) service. Its goal was to subvert a large number of devices and coordinate Distributed Denial of Service (DDoS) attacks to multiple targets. Chalubo is an evolution of Mirai botnet [18,35] that compromised over 100,000 IoT devices (mostly IP cameras, home routers, and digital video recorders) and used them for DDoS attacks. These and other similar incidents indicate that the security of IoT devices and networks must be re-examined and appropriate solutions should be developed to protect businesses, consumers, and critical infrastructure.

Two widely used Operating Systems (OSes) for IoT are ContikiOS [1,10] and TinyOS [2]. The behaviour of ContikiOS can be simulated using the Cooja simulator [30]. Cooja is particularly suitable for real-world experiments, since the developed applications can be directly uploaded to real hardware.

In this work, the main aim is to develop an Intrusion Detection System (IDS) to detect DoS attacks which exploit RPL control packets. In order to achieve that, we first simulate the behaviour of benign and malicious smart sensors in Cooja using the Zolertia Z1 motes [3]. The malicious nodes attempt to consume the energy of benign nodes and to disrupt their communications by launching DoS attack. In particular, these attacks exploit the features of RPL - the IPv6 Routing Protocol for Low-Power and Lossy Networks [41].

We utilise the obtained results to design and develop a lightweight IDS for RPL-based IoT networks.

Our IDS comprises both centralised and distributed components/modules. In particular, a centralised router hosts the detection module and acts as a firewall, whereas a number of spatially-distributed lightweight modules are deployed at the network edge for the purposes of traffic monitoring and local detection [25]. Distributed modules send periodic reports to the router. They also send alerts whenever certain predefined thresholds are exceeded, indicating abnormal or unexpected activity in their proximity.

One of the advantages of our approach is that no software modification of current devices/sensors is required. Furthermore, the IDS modules support both wireless and wired connectivity. The latter might be particularly useful to avoid wireless attacks.

The key contributions in the paper are as follows:

- IoT-specific DoS attack is implemented in ContikiOS and is simulated in Cooja simulator. Mean packet interval and mean number of messages were utilised to show the effects of the attack and to help us develop a method for detecting these kind of attacks.
- A lightweight IDS for RPL-based IoT networks is implemented for detecting RPL attacks.
- The IDS detection module is evaluated in Cooja simulator.

The rest of the paper is organized as follows. In Sect. 2, we provide the required background information. Subsect. 2.1 presents our considered 7-layer IoT reference model. Subsect. 2.2 briefly provides an overview of the RPL protocol. In Sect. 3, we discuss the existing DoS attacks and defenses in IoT. In Sect. 4, we describe our DoS attack implementation in Cooja. Subsects. 4.1 and 4.2 describe the considered scenarios and simulation parameters used to simulate

DoS attack, respectively. Subsect. 4.3, presents the results obtained from simulating DoS attack. In Sect. 5, we describe our proposed IDS design, including a high-level architecture and its main components. In Sect. 6, we present the evaluation of our IDS. Subsect. 6.1 describes the implemented algorithms. Subsects. 6.2 and 6.3 discuss the simulation settings and the considered scenarios used to evaluate the IDS, respectively. Subsect. 6.4 presents the experimental results from IDS evaluation. Finally, in Sect. 7, we conclude and discuss future work.

2 Background

2.1 IoT Reference Model and Attack Vectors

In the literature, a number of different reference models have been proposed for IoT [27]. Among them, CISCO's 7-layer model [9] provides sufficient level of detail and has been considered in this study. The layers of CISCO's model are the following:

1. Physical Devices & Controllers (the "things" in IoT)
2. Connectivity (communication & processing units)
3. Edge (Fog) Computing (data element analysis & transformation)
4. Data Accumulation (storage)
5. Data Abstraction (aggregation & access)
6. Application (reporting, analytics, control)
7. Collaboration & Processes (involving people & business processes)

Our current work mostly contributes in the first three layers. Below, we briefly describe each layer and review possible attack vectors against IoT devices. At Layer 1, we have the physical IoT devices such as sensors and actuators. Possible attacks are malicious modification of firmware, and DoS attacks such as battery draining and resource exhaustion [43].

Layer 2 refers to the connectivity among the devices, which send or receive generated/censored data within the same network or across different networks. Here, an adversary may sniff network packets and try to modify or contaminate the routing information by launching routing, and Man-in-the-Middle (MitM) attacks [5]. Furthermore, IoT devices can be turned into bots and used for DoS attacks against selected targets, as was the case with the infamous Mirai botnet [19]. Layer 3 operations include data analysis and transformation performed at the network edge. Some of the attacks are malicious input that cause data leaking from a device or server.

2.2 RPL Protocol: Overview

RPL [41] is a standardised lightweight routing protocol for IoT devices. It is mainly used in IPv6 over Low-Power Wireless Personal Area Networks (6LoWPAN) networks. RPL builds a Destination-Oriented Directed Acyclic Graph (DODAG) between the nodes in a 6LoWPAN network according to an Objective Function (OF). OFs optimize routing metrics such as Expected Transmission

Count (ETX) so that routes are formed in the DODAG. RPL supports both unidirectional traffic towards DODAG root and bidirectional traffic between smart devices and the root. Each node has an IPv6 address which is used as node's ID. Nodes keep a list of their DODAG neighbours and they have one or more parents, except for the root. Moreover, RPL nodes have a rank indicating their position with respect to the root, who has the lowest rank. The direction from root to other nodes is called *downward route*, while the direction from other nodes to root is called *upward route*.

RPL introduces new ICMPv6 control messages. The root begins by sending out DODAG Information Option (DIO) messages. These messages are used for keeping the DODAG and include information about the rank of the broadcasting node (which is the distance of the node from the backbone network), the OF, and the DODAG ID. As soon as a node gets a DIO message, it determines its rank (according to the rank in the received message) and the cost of getting to the node from itself. DIO messages are sent regularly from each node, triggered by trickle timer [21]. Using a timer reduces the redundant transmissions of DIO messages.

When a new node joins the network, it either waits for a DIO message or it may multicast a DODAG Information Solicitation (DIS) message to request a DIO message. Other nodes listening to the DIS message, begin sending DIO messages, and the new node can join the DODAG. Then, the new node also sends the Destination Advertisement Option (DAO) message to its parent; parent nodes may also request DAO messages by sending a DIO message to sub-DODAG. DAO messages are used for advertising information needed to create downward routes. Receivers of DAO messages update their routing table.

The RPL-specific DIS attack may be launched when a malicious RPL node creates massive amount of traffic by sending DIS messages to other RPL nodes, causing the recipient nodes to respond by sending DIO messages. As a result, congestion is created in the network and nodes are energy exhausted.

3 Related Work

IoT devices have limited computation power, different network structures, and various communication protocols. These features introduce new challenges that should be addressed by an IoT-based IDS [44]. Below we briefly describe recent works in the field of DoS attacks and the most important IDS solutions for IoT.

Islam et al. [17] discuss the security issues for IoT devices in the healthcare domain. Among the different types of DoS attacks, the authors analyse the *permanent DoS attack* in which the device's functionality is permanently affected due to the execution of specific Linux commands. BrickerBot is the name of such a bot which spreads the malicious code [12].

Regarding DDoS attacks, many works exist in the literature. Kolias et al. [19] analysed the Mirai botnet and tried to extract some attack vectors for using them in detecting vulnerabilities of IoT devices. In another work, Lyu et al. [24] evaluate the capability of eight household IoT devices to participate in reflective

DDoS attacks. Results show that devices can amplify an attack by a factor of 20 to inflict 1.2 Mbps of malicious traffic on a victim.

Several DDoS protection frameworks exist in the literature. A multi-level DDoS detection framework was proposed in [42]. Authors use traditional mechanisms in different levels including fog computing, edge computing and cloud computing to defend against DDoS attacks. Authors in [8] suggest an entropy-based DDoS detection. This approach is one of the most effective in the literature because of the low computing overhead.

Regarding password guessing attacks, it is increasingly popular for attackers to compromise IoT devices by guessing default/weak passwords. Several works such as [38–40] study password policies of various services. All highlight the huge variety of password specifications and password management that the services are implementing.

Raoof et al. [32] present a comprehensive study of RPL attacks. They classify RPL attacks into WSN-inherited and RPL-specific attacks. They also discuss and classify the latest IDS solutions for RPL-based networks. Authors report that although some IoT-based IDSes exist, RPL-specific attacks such as DIS attack have no dedicated mitigation method until today.

A recent work by Muna et al. [28] focuses on detecting malicious activities in industrial IoT. They propose an anomaly-based IDS, which learns the normal behaviour of the TCP/IP traffic and automatically detects any abnormal behaviour.

Kalis [26] is one of the first developed IoT-based IDSes that aims at protecting smart devices irrespective of the IoT protocol or application used. Kalis is a network-based, hybrid signature/anomaly-based, hybrid centralized/distributed, online IDS. Kalis attempts to prevent DoS attacks based on the current network topology, traffic analysis, and mobility information. Experimental results show that Kalis has better detection performance in IoT environments compared to the traditional IDSes. Another remarkable work in the field is the SVELTE IDS [33]. This is a signature- and anomaly-based IDS, developed to protect IoT devices from routing attacks based on RPL. Some of the considered attacks include altering information, sinkhole forwarding, and selective forwarding.

In our previous works [15,16] we implemented two variants of DoS attacks, namely DIS attack and version number modification. Results depicted that these attacks negatively impact devices' power consumption. We also provided a high-level design of signature-based IDS for protecting IoT networks from these attacks.

Despite good progress in developing IoT-based IDSes, current solutions have several limitations. Kalis, for example, requires installation of specialised detection modules for detecting each type of attack. This could create a complex network and could lead in poor detection performance. Moreover, Kalis relies on WiFi. This means that interference between the smart sensors and Kalis nodes is possible if they are in close proximity. SVELTE has also some limitations as it requires the modification of sensors' software. This, however, would be very inconvenient for networks with large numbers of sensors, which is a typical case in many IoT application domains.

All in all, a new technologically improved solution is needed to protect IoT networks from a wide range of possible attacks. The aforementioned limitations have been taken into account when designing our proposed IDS solution.

4 Implementing IoT Attacks in Cooja

In order to design an effective IDS, the first step is to implement a number of attacks and observe their impact on the individual devices and on the network as a whole. After that, by launching attacks with different configuration parameters and intensities, various detection techniques can be implemented, tested, and improved. For testing and experimentation we use the Cooja simulator [30], which is gaining popularity among IoT researchers. Cooja is particularly suitable for real-world experiments, since the developed applications can be easily tested with real hardware.

In this work, we have implemented an IoT-specific DoS attack, namely DIS attack. This attack is based on the RPL routing protocol (described in Subsect. 2.2) and affects the availability of the network. Cooja provides an implementation of RPL, called ContikiRPL [36].

4.1 Scenarios

Two main scenarios were simulated, *normal* and *malicious*. Initially, our aim is to examine the behaviour of sensors in an environment without a compromised node. Next, this behaviour will be compared to a scenario where one or more nodes are compromised. The obtained results have been used to design and implement an IDS *detector* for identifying malicious nodes and stopping the DIS attack. The application used in IoT nodes/sensors is based on the UDP client-server model. The hardware used for each node is Zolertia Z1 [3] running ContikiOS.

Table 1. Number of node types in each scenario

	Servers	Benign nodes	Malicious nodes	Detectors	Total
Normal scenario	1	2 to 8	–	1	4 to 10
Malicious scenario	1	First case: 2 to 7 Second case: 3 Third case: 4	First case: 1 Second case: 1 to 6 Third case: 1 to 6	1	First case: 5 to 10 Second case: 6 to 11 Third case: 7 to 12

In the normal scenario, each node regularly sends 1 DIS message per minute. This is the default sending rate implemented in ContikiOS and was also used by Le et al. [20]. In contrast, the malicious scenario has one or more nodes malicious/compromised and have been modified to send 10 DIS messages per second. This was implemented to demonstrate DIS attack which causes IoT nodes to perform unnecessary computations and consume energy.

Each scenario uses a variable number of nodes. Table 2 describes the different node types and the configuration used for compiling node's firmware. The number of nodes used in each scenario is depicted in Table 1. As it is indicated, malicious motes are used only in the malicious scenario, while other nodes are used in both scenarios.

Overall, we performed 7 and 6 simulations for the normal and malicious scenarios, respectively.

Table 2. Node types and configuration

Node type	Description	Radio duty cycle driver	DIS sending interval
Server	Acts as a sink node. Receives messages without doing any processing or sending replies	NullRDC	N/A
Benign node	Uses RPL to create a mesh network and sends data periodically to server	ContikiMAC or NullRDC	60 s
Malicious node	Uses RPL to broadcast DIS control messages to neighbours (DIS attack)	ContikiMAC or NullRDC	1 s
Detector	Sniffs traffic from neighbours in order to detect malicious nodes. Stores information about other nodes (messages exchanged, packet interval)	NullRDC	N/A

4.2 Simulation Parameters and Metrics

Simulations were configured using the default settings of Cooja.

An important parameter is the seed number which affects nodes' behaviour such as packet transmission times. This value is chosen to be autogenerated during the initialization phase.

Nodes' transmission range is also significant for a node. The default value is 50 m for both transmission and interference value. In our scenarios, we place nodes within the range of all other nodes. RPL is configured in storing mode, using Minimum Rank with Hysteresis Objective Function (MRHOF) [14] as OF and ETX as metric which are the defaults of ContikiOS. The duration of each simulation is 25 min and each scenario is repeated 25 times. In this way, results are cross-validated and a large sample is gathered for analysis. IDS detector sniffs packets and sends a report to IDS root every 5 s. This means that the total number of reports sent are 300 over the whole duration of each simulation.

Various metrics, shown below, were used to obtain the characteristics of a normal sensor network. These metrics show the average numbers taken from each simulation over 25 repetitions. The server is not included in the calculations because it acts as a sink. The metrics and the equations used for each one are explained below:

- *Mean packet interval:* Indicates how often a node sends a packet.
- *Mean number of DIS messages:* Indicates how many DIS messages are sent by a node.
- *Mean number of other messages:* Indicates how many other messages are sent by a node, apart from DIS messages. These could be DIO, DAO, or UDP messages.

Below we provide mathematical definitions for the aforementioned metrics. The mean packet interval, $E[I_{pkt}]$, is given by:

$$E[P_{int}] = \frac{\sum_{i=1}^{m}\left(\sum_{j=1}^{n}\frac{p_j}{n}\right)}{m \times r} \tag{1}$$

where: m is the number of detector's measurements, n is the number of neighbours, p_j is the packet interval of j-th neighbour, and r is number of repetitions of each simulation.

The mean number of DIS messages, $E[N_{dis}]$, is given by:

$$E[N_{dis}] = \frac{\sum_{k=1}^{r}(\sum_{i=1}^{m} d_i)}{r} \tag{2}$$

where: d_i is the number of DIS messages detected during i-th measurement.

The mean number of other node's messages, $E[N_{other}]$, is given by:

$$E[N_{other}] = \frac{\sum_{k=1}^{r}(\sum_{i=1}^{m} o_i)}{r} \tag{3}$$

where: o_i is the number of other messages detected during i-th measurement.

4.3 Simulation Results

This section presents our simulation results after implementing DIS attack. IDS detector was used to sniff packets, and record packet intervals and messages (DIS, DIO, DAO, UDP) exchanged by network nodes. Starting with the *mean packet interval* metric, in normal scenarios the mean interval is above 60 s while in malicious scenarios is under 4 s. The reason is that malicious nodes sends more frequently DIS packets than a normal node. Examining the *mean number of DIS messages*, several conclusions can be drawn. First of all, almost all benign nodes have an average of 1 DIS message. This number goes up to 3.5 when number of nodes is higher. Thus, in larger networks the number of DIS messages also increases. In malicious scenarios, the number of DIS messages is much higher than normal scenarios due to malicious nodes. Another metric used is *mean number of other messages* which shows the average number of DIO, DAO and UDP messages in each simulation. Based on the simulation results, the normal scenario starts with a very low number of DIO and DAO messages, while UDP messages constitute the majority. This is an expected behaviour because nodes form the network and communicate with root by sending UDP packets. On the other hand, the number of other messages, especially DIO, rises dramatically if malicious node exist. The reason is that nodes respond with DIO when malicious nodes send DIS messages. As a consequence, malicious nodes affect the network performance and the operation of benign nodes.

5 Proposed Threshold-Based IDS

5.1 IDS Architecture and Components

In this section, our proposed IDS solution is described. This is an extended design that builds on our previous work [16] and is threshold-based, as such approaches are more accurate in detecting known attacks compared to anomaly-based detection, and can be designed to avoid heavy computations [23].

Apart from typical sensor nodes, we consider two new types of devices: (i) IDS routers for running both the detection module and a firewall, and (ii) IDS detectors which are sensor-like devices that monitor and send suspicious traffic to the router. A typical small IoT network consists of one IDS router and several IDS detectors. The IDS router may also play the role of the Border Router (BR) of the network. This means that sensors requiring to communicate with a server, will send all the requests through the IDS router. Thus, BR will take the decision whether the sending node is malicious or not. Our proposed BR will be a router with larger memory and better processing capabilities. However, in the current work we simulate BR using Zolertia Z1 mote.

IDS detectors sniff network traffic to help in detecting malicious nodes. Compromised devices may exchange malicious packets internally without having to communicate with the BR or external networks. For such cases, IDS detectors will log network packets and, if a node's behaviour resembles a known attack, the related information will be forwarded to the BR for further analysis and decision making.

The detectors support both wireless and wired connection. This is needed for communicating with BR. Wired connection helps to avoid attacks such as jamming or eavesdropping via a wireless channel. In cases where a wireless channel between the BR and the detectors is preferable, appropriate secure wireless communication scheme will be in place (e.g., [6]). Any traffic exchanged between the sensors is captured by the nearest detector. Afterwards, a lightweight algorithm is executed to decide if traffic should be forwarded to the BR or not. We assume that detectors will be resource-constrained. Hence, algorithms that require heavy computations or large amounts of memory and storage, would not be suitable.

The combination of BR and detectors helps in capturing traffic from both internal and external communications. For example, some compromised devices may try to communicate with a remote server in order to download commands.

Other compromised devices may exchange traffic locally. Our design considers all types of communications so that malicious nodes can be blocked. The BR captures traffic from both WiFi and IEEE 802.15.4 interfaces and can detect attacks from Zigbee/6LoWPAN devices.

5.2 Attack Detection Methods

The proposed IDS aims at detecting and preventing a wide range of attacks. For example, DoS attacks that may occur inside IoT networks to achieve resource exhaustion of the sensor nodes. In addition to that, routing attacks are usually exploiting the RPL protocol; sinkhole attacks, selective forwarding, and clone ID are some of the widely known routing attacks [31,37].

The above mentioned attacks can be mitigated by measuring DIS message sending rate, the Received Signal Strength (RSS), packet interval, and packet data drop rate [34]. Specifically, DIS message sending rate is used in this work to detect DIS attack. The packet rate of smart devices is usually very low. A device that behaves abnormally and sends more packets than others, could be considered as a malicious one. The rate of false positives must be kept sufficiently low to avoid generating many false alerts [22].

Another promising metric is the packet interval. Each device is configured to sleep most of the time. Malicious devices could exploit this feature and wake up the device to send more requests in the network. Our IDS detects this behaviour by taking into account the sending intervals of all nodes in the network and calculating the average packet interval which will constitute the "normal" behaviour. Thus, any node exceeding the packet interval threshold will be considered as malicious. According to reports [4,13], DoS and routing attacks are the ones most commonly used and may affect the availability as well as the integrity of IoT systems. Therefore, designing and developing an efficient IDS to protect IoT networks from these attacks is currently an open problem.

As far as the scalability of the proposed IDS is concerned, even in large networks good efficiency is expected. To ensure that, IDS detectors perform certain calculations (e.g., packet sending rate and packet interval) and only if the metric of interest is above a threshold, node's traffic will be forwarded to the BR for further investigation (e.g., decision making).

5.3 Border Router

An important part of the proposed IDS is the detection module within the BR. This module is responsible for classifying a node as malicious or not. The decision is based on the individual information collected for each node. For instance, if a node sends too many packets to other nodes, or the node's signal power is above a threshold, then this node may be considered as malicious. In that case, the node may be removed from the network, its IP will be blacklisted, an appropriate firewall rule will be created, and the network administrator will be alerted.

The firewall inside the BR serves as an additional layer of protection. Nodes are blocked only if the detection module has information of malicious behaviour.

In that case, a new rule with the node's IP is created and the node cannot send or receive data from the Internet.

As far as the placement strategy of IDS modules is concerned, a hybrid approach has been adopted. The centralized node (i.e, BR) analyzes traffic, and detects attacks originating from the sensors or coming from the Internet. The decentralized nodes (i.e., IDS detectors), perform lightweight tasks such as monitoring and reporting network data to the BR. This placement strategy helps in capturing traffic and detecting attacks from all network segments.

6 IDS Evaluation

In this subsection, our aim is to evaluate the implemented IDS in terms of detection rate and scalability. Moreover, simulations will help us to find out which IDS configuration is the best for optimized performance.

6.1 Implemented Algorithms

Following the previous design considerations, an implementation of IDS was done in ContikiOS and was tested using Cooja simulator. Particularly, the IDS detector was configured to collect information from nodes and forward suspicious traffic to IDS root/BR. BR was programmed to receive reports from detectors and decide if malicious sensors exist or not in the network based on thresholds.

The algorithms for detection and information collection are given in Algorithms 1 and 2, respectively. In our experiment, the IDS detector captured each packet in the network and calculated the number of DIS packets, other messages and packet interval of each node as shown in Algorithm 2. Then, every 5 s the IDS detector processes the collected information and forwards details of possible malicious nodes to the IDS root. Algorithm 1 is executed by the IDS root every 3 s so that compromised nodes are quickly detected. The detection algorithm counts the number of reports received by different IDS detectors and if $threshold_{detectors}$ is passed then this node is seen as malicious one. In case that a node is covered by only one IDS detector, BR will consider the number of total reports sent by this detector to determine if a node is malicious.

In order to define the most suitable thresholds, results from Sect. 4.3 were utilized. Two thresholds are used in the IDS detector; packet interval and number of DIS messages. We defined $threshold_{time}$ to be 30 s and the $threshold_{DIS}$ to be 3 packets. These thresholds were defined by taking the measurements of each metric from the simulations of Sect. 4.3. The $threshold_{detectors}$ is defined to be 3 so that a node is reported by detectors at least 3 times.

6.2 Metrics and Simulation Configuration

Simulations were created using the same configurations as described in Sect. 4.2. The only difference is that each scenario is repeated 5 times for cross-validation. The metrics used for IDS evaluation are the following:

Algorithm 1. Centralised detection module

```
Monitored[NumNodes] ← array with monitored Nodes
Function CheckNodes(Monitored):
for each node in Monitored do
    node.countDetect++;
    if node.interval ≤ threshold_time or node.totalDIS ≥ threshold_DIS then
        if node.countDetect ≥ threshold_detectors then
            alarm Node compromised
        end if
    end if
end for
```

Algorithm 2. Local monitoring module: Updating metrics

```
On capturing a new packet:
for each node in Monitored do
    if packet == DIS_type then
        node.totalDIS++;
    else
        node.otherMes++;
    end if
    node.interval=clockNow-node.timestamp;
    node.timestamp=clockNow;
end for
```

- *True positive (TP) rate:* Percentage of malicious nodes that are correctly detected as malicious.
- *False positive (FP) rate:* Percentage of normal nodes that are incorrectly detected as malicious.
- *IDS warnings:* Indicates how many times the IDS generated a warning for a malicious node.
- *Messages sent to IDS root:* Indicates the number of messages sent to IDS root by IDS detectors.

Each metric is calculated after taking into account results from all the repetitions of individual scenario.

6.3 Scenarios and Topologies

Evaluating an IDS requires testing various topologies. The IDS should be able to detect compromised nodes in different environments. Therefore, scenarios were created assuming that attackers target several edge nodes. DIS attack was configured to be launched by compromised nodes after 30 s so that the network is properly formed. In other words, compromised nodes attack the network by sending 10 DIS messages every 30 s. A large network with 30 benign nodes, a variable number of IDS detectors, 6 malicious nodes and one IDS root was created. The number of malicious nodes remains fixed, whereas the number of

IDS detectors varies. Using a large number of sensors helps in evaluating the scalability of proposed IDS. Sensors were deployed throughout the network as depicted in Fig. 1. IDS detectors increase by one in each scenario. We created 10 scenarios that are repeated 5 times each for cross-validation. Each scenario is simulated for 25 min.

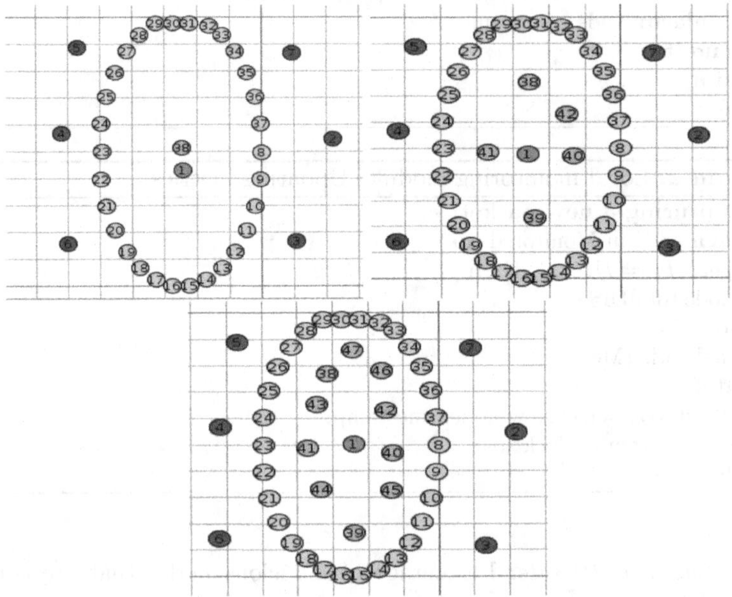

Fig. 1. Topology used in IDS simulations. Scenarios with 1, 5 and IDS detectors shown. They increase up to 10. Colours for node types: green = server, yellow = benign node, purple= malicious node, orange = detector (Color figure online)

6.4 Results

Results from 5 repetitions of each simulation are very encouraging. Figure 2(a) illustrates the TP and FP rates using different IDS detectors. As it is expected, the TP rate is 100% if 3 or more detectors are used in the network. This percentage falls to 97% and 83% when detectors are one and two respectively. However, FP rate increases if detectors are 8 or more. Therefore, this metric suggests using between 3 and 7 including IDS detectors.

Figure 2(b) shows the number of warnings generated by IDS root. These warnings are the output of the detection module algorithms. As it is depicted, the number is below 2,500 when IDS detectors are less than 3. However, this number is rocketed to over 7,000 when 3 or more detectors are deployed. The number remains at similar levels when detectors are between 5 and 8, with a small increase when 9 or more detectors exist in the network.

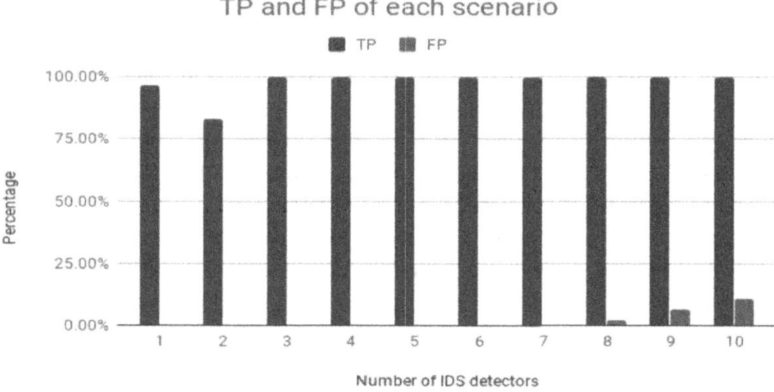

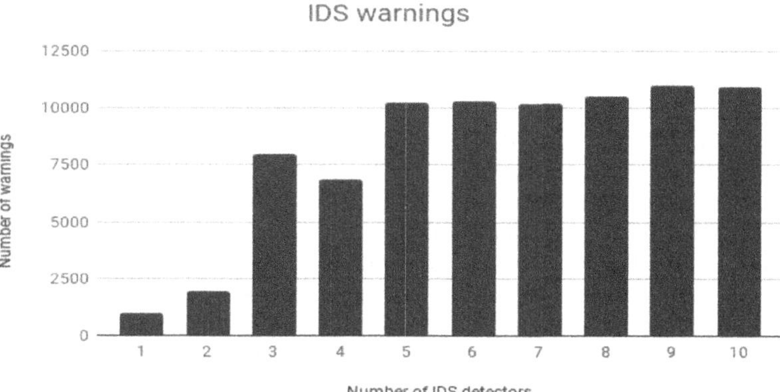

Fig. 2. (a) TP and FP rates for each scenario, (b) Number of warnings generated by IDS root

In conclusion, the IDS achieves high detection rate in almost all cases. This means that all 6 malicious nodes are detected even in large networks. Furthermore, results suggest that more than 3 and less than 8 IDS detectors should be deployed for best performance and low overhead. However, this could be different if more compromised nodes exist.

7 Conclusion and Future Work

In this work, we study the effects of IoT-specific DoS attack, called DIS attack, in RPL-based networks and evaluate a proposed lightweight IDS for protecting the IoT network and devices. Firstly, we simulated sensor nodes in Cooja which supports application development for ContikiOS. Simulations were performed for studying the characteristics of normal and malicious IoT environments. In attack scenarios, compromised nodes perform DoS attack that relies on RPL control messages. The attack introduces a large number of packets in the network that constitute some nodes unreachable and may negatively impact their power consumption. Based on these results we develop detection algorithms and implement an IDS. The proposed system involves both centralised and distributed modules for detecting intrusions originating from external networks as well as from internal compromised nodes. Experimental results showed that high detection rate can be achieved if IDS detectors are 3 or more. However, the more the detectors, the higher the overhead introduced in the network.

In our future work, we plan to minimize the introduced overhead and test the proposed architecture in a real-world IoT environment. This will be achieved by importing the IDS modules to ContikiOS devices. Also, we will implement more types of routing attacks such as selective forwarding and rank attack. Mitigation techniques will be developed to detect and prevent new attacks in IoT networks.

References

1. Contiki: The Open Source OS for the Internet of Things. http://www.contiki-os.org/. Accessed 13 Aug 2019
2. TinyOS: An OS for Embedded, Wireless Devices. https://github.com/tinyos/tinyos-main. Accessed 13 Aug 2019
3. Zolertia technical documentation (2017). https://github.com/Zolertia/Resources/wiki/Zolertia-Technical-documentation
4. McAfee Labs Threats Report, September 2018. https://www.mcafee.com/enterprise/en-us/assets/reports/rp-quarterly-threats-sep-2018.pdf
5. Alaba, F.A., Othman, M., Hashem, I.A.T., Alotaibi, F.: Internet of Things security: a survey. J. Netw. Comput. Appl. **88**, 10–28 (2017). https://doi.org/10.1016/j.jnca.2017.04.002
6. Alohali, B.A., Vassilakis, V.G., Moscholios, I.D., Logothetis, M.D.: A secure scheme for group communication of wireless IoT devices. In: Proceedings 11th IEEE/IET International Symposium on Communication Systems, Networks, and Digital Signal Processing (CSNDSP), Budapest, Hungary, pp. 1–6, July 2018. https://doi.org/10.1109/csndsp.2018.8471871
7. Ammar, M., Russello, G., Crispo, B.: Internet of things: a survey on the security of IoT frameworks. J. Inform. Secur. Appl. **38**, 8–27 (2018). https://doi.org/10.1016/j.jisa.2017.11.002
8. Bhuyan, M.H., Bhattacharyya, D., Kalita, J.K.: An empirical evaluation of information metrics for low-rate and high-rate ddos attack detection. Pattern Recogn. Lett. **51**, 1–7 (2015)
9. CISCO: The Internet of Things Reference Model (2014). http:/cdn.iotwf.com/resources/71/IoT_Reference_Model_White_Paper_June_4_2014.pdf
10. Dunkels, A., Gronvall, B., Voigt, T.: Contiki - a lightweight and flexible operating system for tiny networked sensors. In: Proceedings 29th IEEE International Conference on Local Computer Networks, Tampa, FL, USA, pp. 455–462, November 2004. https://doi.org/10.1109/lcn.2004.38
11. Easton, T.: Chalubo botnet wants to DDoS from your server or IoT device, October 2018. https://news.sophos.com/en-us/2018/10/22/chalubo-botnet-wants-to-ddos-from-your-server-or-iot-device/
12. Geenens, P.: BrickerBot - The Dark Knight of IoT (2017). https://blog.radware.com/security/2017/04/brickerbot-dark-knight-iot/

13. Gemalto: The state of IoT security (2018). http://www2.gemalto.com/iot/index.html
14. Gnawali, O., Levis, P.: The minimum rank with hysteresis objective function. Technical report (2012)
15. Ioulianou, P.P., Vassilakis, V.G., Logothetis, M.D.: Battery drain denial-of-service attacks and defenses in the internet of things. J. Telecommun. Inform. Technol. **2**, 37–45 (2019)
16. Ioulianou, P.P., Vassilakis, V.G., Moscholios, I.D., Logothetis, M.D.: A signature-based intrusion detection system for the internet of things. In: Proceedings of IEICE Information and Communication Technology Forum (ICTF), Graz, Austria, pp. 1–6, July 2018
17. Islam, S.R., Kwak, D., Kabir, M.H., Hossain, M., Kwak, K.S.: The internet of things for health care: a comprehensive survey. IEEE Access **3**, 678–708 (2015). https://doi.org/10.1109/access.2015.2437951
18. Kambourakis, G., Kolias, C., Stavrou, A.: The Mirai botnet and the IoT zombie armies. In: Military Communications Conference (MILCOM), pp. 267–272. IEEE (2017). https://doi.org/10.1109/MILCOM.2017.8170867
19. Kolias, C., Kambourakis, G., Stavrou, A., Voas, J.: DDoS in the IoT: Mirai and other botnets. Computer **50**(7), 80–84 (2017). https://doi.org/10.1109/MC.2017.201
20. Le, A., Loo, J., Chai, K.K., Aiash, M.: A specification-based IDS for detecting attacks on RPL-based network topology. Information **7**(2), 1–19 (2016). https://doi.org/10.3390/info7020025
21. Levis, P., Clausen, T., Hui, J., Gnawali, O., Ko, J.: The Trickle algorithm (2011)
22. Li, W., Meng, W., Luo, X., Kwok, L.F.: MVPSys: toward practical multi-view based false alarm reduction system in network intrusion detection. Comput. Secur. **60**, 177–192 (2016). https://doi.org/10.1016/j.cose.2016.04.007
23. Liao, H.J., et al.: Intrusion detection system: a comprehensive review. J. Netw. Comput. Appl. **36**(1), 16–24 (2013). https://doi.org/10.1016/j.jnca.2012.09.004
24. Lyu, M., Sherratt, D., Sivanathan, A., Gharakheili, H.H., Radford, A., Sivaraman, V.: Quantifying the reflective DDoS attack capability of household iot devices. In: Proceedings of the 10th ACM Conference on Security and Privacy in Wireless and Mobile Networks, pp. 46–51. ACM (2017)
25. Meng, W., Wang, Y., Li, W., Liu, Z., Li, J., Probst, C.W.: Enhancing intelligent alarm reduction for distributed intrusion detection systems via edge computing. In: Susilo, W., Yang, G. (eds.) ACISP 2018. LNCS, vol. 10946, pp. 759–767. Springer, Heidelberg (2018). https://doi.org/10.1007/978-3-319-93638-3_44
26. Midi, D., Rullo, A., Mudgerikar, A., Bertino, E.: Kalis - A system for knowledge-driven adaptable intrusion detection for the internet of things. In: Proceedings IEEE 37th International Conference on Distributed Computing Systems (ICDCS), Atlanta, GA, USA, pp. 656–666, June 2017. https://doi.org/10.1109/ICDCS.2017.104
27. Mosenia, A., Jha, N.K.: A comprehensive study of security of internet-of-things. IEEE Trans. Emerg. Top. Comput. **5**(4), 586–602 (2017). https://doi.org/10.1109/tetc.2016.2606384
28. Muna, A.H., Moustafa, N., Sitnikova, E.: Identification of malicious activities in industrial Internet of things based on deep learning models. J. Inform. Secur. Appl. **41**, 1–11 (2018). https://doi.org/10.1016/j.jisa.2018.05.002
29. Nawir, M., Amir, A., Yaakob, N., Lynn, O.B.: Internet of things (IoT): taxonomy of security attacks. In: Proc. 3rd International Conference on Electronic Design (ICED), pp. 321–326. IEEE (2016). https://doi.org/10.1109/iced.2016.7804660

30. Osterlind, F., et al.: Cross-level sensor network simulation with COOJA. In: Proceedings of 31st IEEE International Conferene on Local Computer Networks, Tampa, FL, USA, pp. 641–648, November 2006. https://doi.org/10.1109/lcn.2006.322172
31. Pongle, P., Chavan, G.: A survey: attacks on RPL and 6LoWPAN in IoT. In: Proceedings of International Conference on Pervasive Computing (ICPC), pp. 1–6. IEEE (2015). https://doi.org/10.1109/pervasive.2015.7087034
32. Raoof, A., Matrawy, A., Lung, C.H.: Routing attacks and mitigation methods for RPL-based internet of things. IEEE Commun. Surv. Tutor. **21**, 1582–1606 (2018)
33. Raza, S., Wallgren, L., Voigt, T.: SVELTE: real-time intrusion detection in the Internet of Things. Ad Hoc Netw. **11**(8), 2661–2674 (2013). https://doi.org/10.1016/j.adhoc.2013.04.014
34. Rghioui, A., Khannous, A., Bouhorma, M.: Denial-of-service attacks on 6LoWPAN-RPL networks: threats and an intrusion detection system proposition. J. Adv. Comput. Sci. Technol. **3**(2), 143–153 (2014). https://doi.org/10.14419/jacst.v3i2.3321
35. Symantec Security Response: Mirai: what you need to know about the botnet behind recent major DDoS attacks, October 2016
36. Tsiftes, N., Eriksson, J., Dunkels, A.: Low-power wireless IPv6 routing with ContikiRPL. In: Proceedings of 9th ACM/IEEE International Conference on Information Processing in Sensor Networks, pp. 406–407 (2010)
37. Wallgren, L., Raza, S., Voigt, T.: Routing attacks and countermeasures in the RPL-based Internet of things. Int. J. Distrib. Sens. Netw. **9**(8), 1–11 (2013). https://doi.org/10.1155/2013/794326
38. Wang, D., Cheng, H., Wang, P., Huang, X., Jian, G.: Zipf's law in passwords. IEEE Trans. Inf. Forensics Secur. **12**(11), 2776–2791 (2017)
39. Wang, D., Wang, P.: The emperor's new password creation policies. In: Pernul, G., Ryan, P.Y.A., Weippl, E. (eds.) ESORICS 2015. LNCS, vol. 9327, pp. 456–477. Springer, Heidelberg (2015). https://doi.org/10.1007/978-3-319-24177-7_23
40. Wang, D., Zhang, Z., Wang, P., Yan, J., Huang, X.: Targeted online password guessing: an underestimated threat. In: Proceedings of the 2016 ACM SIGSAC Conference on Computer and Communications Security, pp. 1242–1254. ACM (2016)
41. Winter, T., et al.: RPL: IPv6 routing protocol for low-power and lossy networks. RFC 6550, March 2012
42. Yan, Q., Huang, W., Luo, X., Gong, Q., Yu, F.R.: A multi-level DDoS mitigation framework for the industrial internet of things. IEEE Commun. Mag. **56**(2), 30–36 (2018)
43. Yang, Y., et al.: A survey on security and privacy issues in internet-of-things. IEEE Internet Things J. **4**(5), 1250–1258 (2017). https://doi.org/10.1109/jiot.2017.2694844
44. Zarpelão, B.B., Miani, R.S., Kawakani, C.T., de Alvarenga, S.C.: A survey of intrusion detection in internet of things. J. Netw. Comput. Appl. **84**, 25–37 (2017). https://doi.org/10.1016/j.jnca.2017.02.009

Study of DNS Rebinding Attacks on Smart Home Devices

Dennis Tatang(✉), Tim Suurland, and Thorsten Holz

Ruhr University Bochum, Bochum, Germany
{dennis.tatang,tim.suurland,thorsten.holz}@rub.de

Abstract. *DNS rebinding* is an attack technique know for more than 20 years, which is experiencing a revival caused by the ever-increasing networking of Internet of Things (IoT) devices. Thus, the potential attack surface is growing rapidly, and this paper shows that DNS rebinding attacks on many smart home devices are still successful. Nevertheless, various conditions must be fulfilled for this type of attack. This leads to the fact that such attacks rarely occur in practice since router vendors often provide DNS rebinding protection. Nevertheless, we believe that it is valuable to investigate whether individual devices are theoretically vulnerable and to create a certain awareness so that the existing countermeasures are used correctly.

As part of this paper, we conducted a study analyzing five devices, four smart home devices and one router as a smart-home gateway connected with the IoT products. Three out of four of the smart home devices are vulnerable, and the router is partially vulnerable because queries reach localhost despite activated DNS rebinding protection; thus, services on localhost are vulnerable. This indicates that the manufacturers of smart home devices rely on the countermeasures of the routers in the first place, but it might even improve the security of the devices if they already implement their own additional countermeasures.

Keywords: DNS · IoT · DNS rebinding

1 Introduction

The spread of smart appliances leads to increase networking between the devices themselves and thus to smart homes. For attackers, this development represents an increased attack surface. In particular, devices accessible via the Internet are attractive targets. Consumers may assume that if smart home devices are reachable locally only, they pose no risk to the home network. However, with DNS rebinding attacks, it is possible to communicate with only internally accessible devices. DNS rebinding allows unauthorized access to private networks.

DNS rebinding attacks are known since 1996 [5,6]. As a result, various attack methods, as well as countermeasures, were already published [4,9]. However, a recent study from 2018 demonstrates that DNS rebinding attacks are still feasible today [1]. Even the assigned CVEs (a total of 25) indicate that DNS rebinding, since 2017 (11 out of 25 CVEs), experiences a revival [3]. This observation

S. Katsikas et al. (Eds.): ESORICS 2019 Workshops, LNCS 11980, pp. 391–401, 2020.
https://doi.org/10.1007/978-3-030-42048-2_25

correlates with the increasing number of Internet of Things (IoT) devices. Worldwide, approximately half a billion devices are estimated to be vulnerable to DNS rebinding attacks in 2018 [2].

In this paper, we investigate DNS rebinding attacks on smart household appliances, a subset of the IoT. We show that sensitive data can be extracted and remote control from the Internet is possible. We analyze the execution of the attacks systematically and summarize them. In addition, we investigate which prerequisites must be fulfilled in order to carry out the attacks. In this way, we discuss how serious the risk is for smart home device owners to become victims. Finally, we analyze the top 100 Alexa web pages that communicate over HTTP to investigate whether DNS rebinding is performed unnoticed on one of these pages. It was demonstrated that protection mechanisms of dnsmasq do not detect attacks on localhost (127.0.0.1), 4 out of 5 investigated devices are vulnerable, and none of the top 100 sites performs DNS rebinding attacks.
To summarize, we make the following contributions:

- We systematically analyze DNS rebinding attacks on four smart home devices and summarize our results in an overview.
- We investigate requirements for successfully DNS rebinding attacks and discuss the risk of becoming a victim of such an attack.
- We present a brief measurement study on the execution of DNS rebinding on popular websites.

In the remainder of the paper, we first introduce basic knowledge and identify requirements for successfully DNS rebinding attacks in Sect. 2. Afterwards, we describe our conducted experiments in Sect. 3, followed by presenting the results in Sect. 4. In Sect. 5, we discuss the results and limitations. Section 6 presents some related work and we conclude our work in Sect. 7.

2 DNS Rebinding Attack

During a DNS rebinding attack, an attacker bypasses the security mechanism of the firewall in the router and communicates interactively with devices in its local network by using the browser of the victim. This is achieved by manipulating the hostname and IP address mapping, which makes the attacker's browser become a proxy into the victim's private network.

2.1 High-Level Concept

The attacker bypasses the router firewall in a DNS rebinding attack by abusing the browser within the internal network as a proxy to communicate with the devices inside the local network. Figure 1 visualizes the concept of the attack.

To establish a connection to an internal local device of the victim, the attacker must assign the DNS hostname of his web server to the internal IP address of the target device. This works by the attacker running a DNS name server next to his web server on his attack server. If the domain of his website is to be resolved into

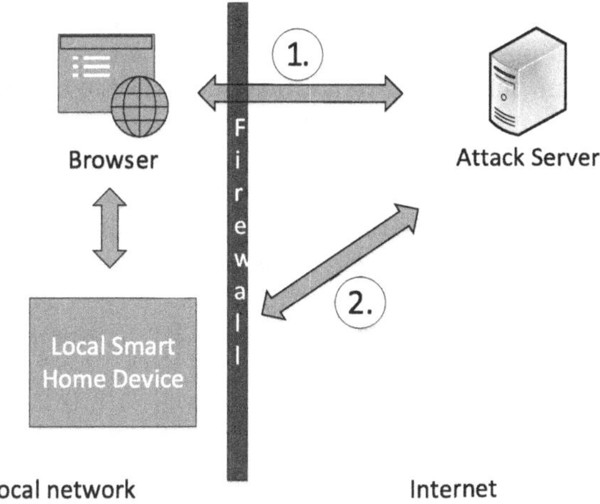

Fig. 1. High-level concept of DNS Rebinding attacks. The browser becomes by manipulating the mapping of hostnames and IP addresses to the proxy into the internal network (see ①). Direct access is blocked by the router firewall (see ②).

an IP address, he also receives the corresponding DNS request, which can then be manipulated. The browser trusts the DNS response, and thus the connection to a local network device can be established by the manipulated domain name and IP address assignment. An attacker does not have to compromise a DNS server; it is sufficient to generate valid DNS replies for requests to resolve his/her domain. Note, DNSSec is not able to prevent this attack scenario because the attacker only generates valid DNS responses to queries for his/her domain.

2.2 Attack Methods

To perform a DNS rebinding attack, different methods can be exploited. In the following, we describe two examples. First, multiple A records were historically exploited to perform DNS rebinding attacks. A second vulnerability is time-varying DNS, which can be used to perform DNS rebinding attacks. Our experiments conducted subsequently are related to the second type of DNS rebinding attack.

Multiple a Records. The mapping of a domain to an IP address is implemented using A record requests. The DNS allows mapping multiple IP addresses to one domain. These multiple A records are used to realize a load distribution in the DNS. All IP addresses are summarized as Resource Record set.

The primary attack of Princeton University is based on multiple A records [6]. They used Java applets for this. Once a victim accesses the domain of the attacker, the Java applet is loaded in the browser of the victim. The applet then requests a subdomain of the attack domain. For this request, the attacker server provides a resource record set with IP addresses. The first entry in this record set must contain the internal IP address of the target device in the local network of the victim. The second IP address is identical to the IP of the attacker server. In this way, an external attacker can use a Java applet to implement interactive access to devices in the local network of the victim. It is exploited that a connection request is allowed by the Java system as soon as the IP address from which the Java applet was loaded appears in the resource record.

However, this attack is no longer feasible as DNS pinning has been introduced and the security policies for Java applets have been changed. Nowadays, an applet can only establish connections to the IP address from which it was originally loaded (Same Origin Policy) [8].

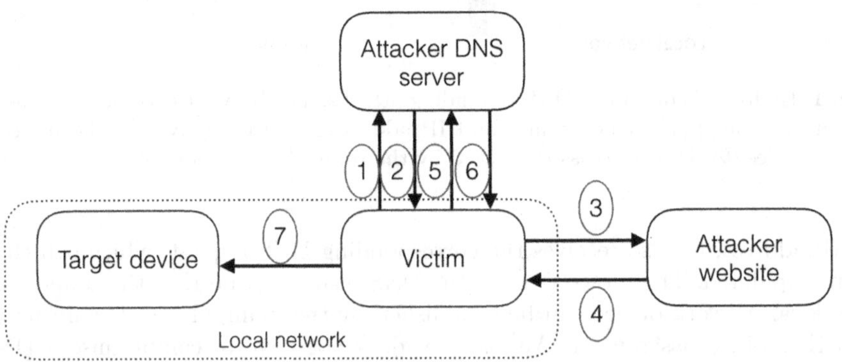

Fig. 2. Steps of a time varying DNS rebinding attack. The DNS request of the victim ① is answered by the attacker DNS server with his IP address and a short TTL ②. The victim's browser downloads malicious code from the attacker's website ③ and ④. When the malicious code is executed, the TTL has expired so that a new DNS request must be sent to the attacker's server ⑤. The response contains the IP address of the target device in the victim's local network ⑥. Thus, the request is redirected to the target device ⑦.

Time Varying DNS. In 2011 Roskind demonstrated that the Time-To-Live (TTL) of a DNS response is not trustworthy and that the mapping between a domain and IP address should be saved independently of that time (DNS Pinning). He introduced time-varying DNS rebinding attacks [14]. Figure 2 visualizes the steps during this attack.

In this attack, the DNS name server of the attacker responds to the request of the victim with a very short TTL, e.g., one second. The browser of the victim now uses this IP address to access the website of the attacker and downloads the HTML document together with malicious code. When the victim executes the malware code, an asynchronous connection request is made to a resource of the attacker server. At this time, the entry in the DNS cache of the browser with the domain and IP address of the attacker is already deleted due to the very short TTL. Thus, to resolve the domain, a new DNS request must be triggered that the DNS server of the attacker responds with the private IP address of the target device in the network of the victim. In this way, the domain of the attacker in the DNS cache of the browser is assigned to the private IP address of the device by the victim. As a result, the asynchronous connection request is not sent to the Web server of the attacker, but the local network component of the victim. Thus, the attacker succeeds in establishing an interactive session to a device in the private network of the victim. The attack detection of routers can easily detect this attack method when a private IP address is resolved according to RFC1918 [13]. DNS pinning also prevents the attack in modern browsers. As a result, this simple attack is no longer exploitable.

The simple time-varying attack described above can be blocked by DNS pinning in the browser. The most straightforward strategy to bypass DNS pinning is to make the malicious script wait with the asynchronous connection request until the DNS entry expires in the cache of the browser. This trivial approach is called anti-DNS pinning [7]. In 2013, Dai and Resig showed that it is possible to significantly speed up the waiting period by flooding the DNS cache [4].

2.3 Countermeasures

DNS rebinding attacks have been known for a long time and so there are functioning countermeasures. On the server side, every web server in the local network can have its own authentication methods. Furthermore, communication with the web server should be secured by TLS; thus, no DNS rebinding attack is possible. The firewall settings should be such that requests from external host names must not be resolved with internal IP addresses. The DNS settings should also be configured so that external hostnames cannot be resolved with internal IP addresses. This adjustment is straightforward to do by using DNS rebinding protection mechanisms on many routers, e.g., dnsmasq uses this protection in the default settings. On the client side, browser extensions such as NoScript can be used when visiting web pages.

2.4 Requirements

In order to successfully perform a DNS rebinding attack today, several requirements must be fulfilled. We identified a total of six requirements and describe them in the following.

1. No transport layer security (TLS): If TLS is used, no DNS rebinding attack can be performed. This is because a TLS certificate is issued to a full hostname or a unique IP address. When a new connection request is made to the target device to perform a DNS rebinding attack, the TLS certificate verifies that the domain of the new connection matches the information of the certificate. Since the domain of the local target device differs from the information in the TLS certificate the TLS handshake fails and the connection request is rejected.

2. No authentication: If authentication is used on the application layer based on well-selected credentials, the attacker must first break them in order to perform a DNS rebinding attack successfully.
3. Visit the website of the attacker: The victim must visit the web page of the attacker to run malicious JavaScript in the background.
4. Dwell time: In addition to the fact that the victim must surf on the attacker's website itself, the victim must also stay on the website until the attack is successful.
5. IP address and port must be known: The attack targets are local network components with an open web server. An attacker must, therefore, know the IP address of the target device in the victim's private network and the port of the web server.
6. No specific countermeasures: The countermeasures presented in Sect. 2.3 may not be used.

3 Descriptions of Experiments

In the following, we describe the experiments we conducted as part of our study. We start with the description of the Attacker Model, continue with the setup, and finally our measurement.

3.1 Attacker Model

Primarily, DNS rebinding attacks aimed at classic network components such as routers, printers, or internal servers. We look at smart home devices. We investigate whether they are vulnerable and what possibilities a potential attacker has. We assume the following scenario for the following investigation: The victim stays on the website of the attacker long enough until the attack is completed, the attacker knows the internal IP in the local network, and the API endpoints of the device to be attacked.

The attacker model is reasonably realistic, as an attacker can use interesting content to trick the victim into spending the necessary time on a website, and the internal IP address of the target device may, e.g., be discovered by misconfigured information-leaking DNS servers [17].

3.2 Experimental Setup

For the conducted experiments, we use a private network consisting of the smart home devices to be examined and the computer of the victim user. All devices use standard configurations and are connected to the Internet via a router. Figure 3 illustrates the experimental setup.

The used router is a mobile router RUT500 from Teltonika. The web interface can be reached under 192.168.1.1 from the local network. The computer of the victim has the local IP 192.168.1.181 and installed the Chrome browser version 63 for the investigations. Furthermore, there are four smart home devices to be examined in the local network. We are examining a Google Home Mini, a Sonoff Basic, a Foscam IP Camera, and a Bose Soundtouch.

The Google Home Mini is a voice-controlled speaker, i.e., a smart assistant who is representative for other voice assistants in our study, such as the Alexa speakers. The Sonoff Basic is a smart switch that can be controlled via WLAN. The switch is flashed with the Tasmota firmware [16] and therefore representative for all devices with the Tasmota firmware. The Foscam IP camera is an IP camera with the exact designation FI9900p, and the Bose Soundtouch 10 is a WLAN controllable speaker.

We used the DNS rebinding attack framework Singularity of Origin of the NCC Group for the execution of the attacks [15]. This framework performs a time-varying DNS rebinding attack as already introduced in Sect. 2.2. As part of the work, we have accelerated an attack method of the framework by applying the DNS cache flooding technique presented by Dai and Resig [4] to the method used in the framework. In this way, the duration of the attack could be reduced from 60 s to 5 s.

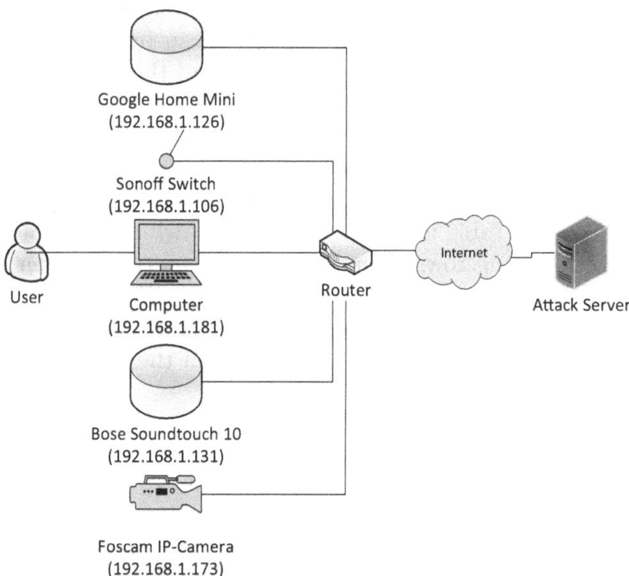

Fig. 3. Overview of experimental setup.

3.3 DNS Rebinding on Websites in the Wild

To complement our study, we examine websites and check whether they perform DNS rebinding attacks in the background. We performed this measurement by setting up a Ubuntu system and installing the DNS server dnsmasq. With DNS Rebinding Attack Protection enabled by default, dnsmasq reliably detects whether private IP addresses are contained in DNS packets. Subsequently, we implemented a script that automatically visits websites and evaluates the log file from dnsmasq to detect DNS rebinding attempts.

4 Results

In this section, we present the results of our investigations. First, we describe the results of our conducted attacks on smart home devices. Second, we present the results of our brief measurement of DNS rebinding on popular websites.

4.1 Smart Home Devices

During the conducted tests it turned out that the router RUT500 is not vulnerable to DNS rebinding attacks due to the activation of the DNS rebinding protection of dnsmasq and therefore none of the devices behind the router. The manufacturer activates the protection that all incoming DNS packets with private IP addresses are directly blocked from dnsmasq by default. However, we noticed that requests reach localhost (127.0.0.1) and therefore services running on localhost might be vulnerable.

To enable the testing of the other smart home devices, we deactivated the DNS rebinding protection in the following. We summarized the results in Table 1 and detailed descriptions of the result are in the following paragraphs. The first row (Vulnerable) of the table indicates whether the device is potentially vulnerable or not. The following rows indicate what a potential attacker can achieve with a DNS rebinding attack on the particular device. We differentiate between the control of hardware functions, the extraction of personal data, finding out the MAC, the extraction of location data, finding out the user name, and getting further Wifi information.

Table 1. Overview of the results of the conducted DNS rebinding attacks against four different smart home devices. Three out of four devices were attacked successfully.

	Google home	Sonoff basic	Bose soundtouch	Foscam
Vulnerable	✓	✓	✓	✗
Control of HW functions	✓	✓	✓	✗
Personal data	✓	✓	✓	✗
MAC	✓	✓	✓	✗
Location data	✓	✓	✓	✗
User name	✓	✗	✓	✗
Wifi information	✓	✓	✗	✗

Google Home Mini is potentially vulnerable to DNS rebinding attacks. An undocumented HTTP server was found on port 8008 and a Web API interface without authentication mechanisms. During a DNS rebinding attack, sensitive data can be extracted via the Web API. In addition, hardware functions of the device can be managed over the Internet.

Sonoff Basic with the Tasmota firmware and default configurations is also vulnerable to DNS rebinding attacks. The firmware uses a Web API interface. Therefore all Sonoff devices with the Tasmota firmware are potentially vulnerable. The active control of hardware functions is limited to toggling the relay of the switch. However, sensitive data such as usage habits and power consumption are readable.

Bose Soundtouch also has a Web API interface without authentication mechanisms and no TLS support. Thus, this device is also potentially vulnerable to DNS rebinding attacks. It provides access to hardware functions such as volume, as well as stored data such as MAC addresses of paired devices. Other Bose devices also use the same firmware. Therefore, we suspect that these devices are vulnerable as well.

Foscam FI9900p is the only tested device not potentially easily vulnerable to DNS rebinding attacks. When setting up the device, the user is forced by the vendor to set a username and password. When connecting to the web service of the camera, the user has to authenticate with his credentials. For this reason, a DNS rebinding attack is only possible if the attacker knows the credentials or is able to break the authentication.

4.2 Measuring DNS Rebinding Attempts on Popular Websites

This measurement led to the result that none of the top 100 Alexa sites that use HTTP execute DNS rebinding and is thus not surprising. However, the approach can be used to check a more significant number of websites.

5 Discussion

The results demonstrate that four out of five examined devices are vulnerable to DNS rebinding attacks. However, it should be noted that for the selection of the test devices, devices with open Web services were explicitly selected. Accordingly, this selection of test devices cannot be used to make a statement about all smart home devices. However, since the total number of smart home devices is very high, the number of potentially vulnerable devices should still be a non-negligible amount. In addition, our insights also confirm the results of Acar et al. [1] that many IoT devices are vulnerable to DNS rebinding attacks.

Furthermore, we have seen that for a successful DNS rebinding attack, many requirements have to fit, which limits it as a real-world threat. However, as soon as the attack is feasible, it can have serious consequences. For this reason, it is important to check which conditions have to be fulfilled and to evaluate the applied countermeasures. The results of the study indicate that manufacturers do not focus sufficiently on the security of their products when developing them. The potential vulnerability of smart home devices highlights the lack of security of IoT devices, which has repeatedly attracted media attention in recent years. In many cases, inadequate authentication was the cause of attacks. The well-known Mirai botnet [12], for example, targeted IoT devices that were operated with standard credentials and accessible to the public. Manufacturers of smart home devices could protect their customers by introducing mandatory authentication at the application layer. A mandatory change to the authentication credentials was implemented for the Foscam IP camera, for example, so that no unauthorized access to web services can be made.

6 Related Work

Since the attack technique is long-established, there is much work in this area. The first publication on DNS rebinding attacks was published in 1996 [5], after which further papers were presenting new variants of the attack [4,9,11]. Corresponding work with countermeasures also exists [8,10]. One of the most recent papers deals with DNS rebinding attacks on IoT devices [1]. Especially the analysis of new as well as already known attacks on IoT devices is important, as the Mirai Botnet demonstrates [12].

We follow the course of the history of work on DNS rebinding and rely in particular on the current paper in the field of IoT devices. We perform the attack on smart home devices and give a rough overview of vulnerable devices. In addition, we discuss the attack surface and conclude that due to various countermeasures, despite the vulnerability of the devices themselves to DNS rebinding attacks, it is not likely to become a victim.

7 Conclusion

We showed that DNS rebinding attacks in the world of IoT are reviving and four out of five devices tested are vulnerable (three out of four smart home devices and a router). Nevertheless, possible attack targets are limited, as many countermeasures exist and several conditions must be fulfilled and as routers often already contain DNS rebinding attack detection. The manufacturers of smart home devices, therefore, rely on the router firewalls to provide security against this attack. In many cases, this will also be the case, but ideally, the smart home devices themselves should also be protected. In summary, this work suggests that when connecting all things, one needs to keep in mind known weaknesses and issues in order not to become vulnerable to attacks that have been known for years.

Future work in the DNS rebinding attacks IoT area can extend the results of our study by testing further smart home devices and also check a more significant number of websites to see whether a DNS rebinding attack is being carried out in the wild.

Acknowledgment. We would like to thank the anonymous reviewers for their valuable feedback.

References

1. Acar, G., Huang, D.Y., Li, F., Narayanan, A., Feamster, N.: Web-based attacks to discover and control local IoT devices. In: Proceedings of the 2018 Workshop on IoT Security and Privacy (2018)
2. DNS Rebinding Exposes Half a Billion Devices in the Enterprise. https://armis.com/dns-rebinding-exposes-half-a-billion-iot-devices-in-the-enterprise/. Accessed 06 June 2019
3. CVE - Common Vulnerabilities and Exposures. https://cve.mitre.org/cgi-bin/cvekey.cgi?keyword=DNS+Rebinding. Accessed 06 June 2019
4. Dai , Y., Resig, R.: FireDrill: interactive {DNS} rebinding. In: 7th {USENIX} Workshop on Offensive Technologies (2013)
5. Dean, D., Felten, E.W., Wallach, D. S.: Java security: From HotJava to Netscape and beyond. In: IEEE Symposium on Security and Privacy (1996)
6. DNS Attack Scenario, February 1996. http://sip.cs.princeton.edu/news/dns-scenario.html. Accessed 06 June 2019
7. Grossman, J., Fogie, S., Hansen, R., Rager, A., Petkov, P.D.: XSS Attacks: Cross Site Scripting Exploits and Defense. Syngress (2007)
8. Jackson, C., Barth, A., Bortz, A., Shao, W., Boneh, D.: Protecting browsers from DNS rebinding attacks. In: ACM Conference on Computer and Communications Security (CCS) (2007)
9. Johns, M., Lekies, S., Stock, B.: Eradicating DNS rebinding with the extended same-origin policy. In: USENIX Security Symposium (2013)
10. Johns, M., Winter, J.: Protecting the intranet against "JavaScript malware" and related attacks. In: M. Hämmerli, B., Sommer, R. (eds.) DIMVA 2007. LNCS, vol. 4579, pp. 40–59. Springer, Heidelberg (2007). https://doi.org/10.1007/978-3-540-73614-1_3
11. Karlof, C., Shankar, U., Tygar, J.D., Wagner, D.: Dynamic pharming attacks and locked same-origin policies for web browsers. In: ACM Conference on Computer and Communications Security (CCS) (2007)
12. Kolias, C., Kambourakis, G., Stavrou, A., Voas, J.: DDoS in the IoT: Mirai and other botnets. Computer **50**(7), 80–84 (2017)
13. Rekhter, Y., Moskowitz, B., Karrenberg, D., de Groot, G., Lear, E.: Address allocation for private internets. RFC 1918, RFC Editor, February 1996
14. Roskind, J.: Attacks against the netscape browser. In: Talk at the RSA Conference (2001)
15. Singularity of Origin. https://github.com/nccgroup/singularity. Accessed 06 June 2019
16. Fonoff-Tasmota. https://github.com/arendst/Sonoff-Tasmota. Accessed 06 June 2019
17. Tatang, D., Schneider, C., Holz, T.: Large-scale Analysis of Infrastructure-leaking DNS Servers. In: Perdisci, R., Maurice, C., Giacinto, G., Almgren, M. (eds.) DIMVA 2019. LNCS, vol. 11543, pp. 353–373. Springer, Cham (2019). https://doi.org/10.1007/978-3-030-22038-9_17

Anomaly Detection in the HVAC System Operation by a RadViz Based Visualization-Driven Approach

Evgenia Novikova[1(✉)], Mikhail Bestuzhev[1], and Igor Kotenko[2]

[1] Department of Computer Science and Engineering, Saint Petersburg Electrotechnical University "LETI", Professora Popova Str. 5, Saint-Petersburg, Russia
evgenia.novikova123@gmail.com
[2] Laboratory of Computer Security Problems Saint Petersburg Institute for Informatics and Automation (SPIIRAS), Saint-Petersburg, Russia

Abstract. The appearance of the smart houses, buildings, and cities has defined new attack scenarios targeting industrial information systems. The paper suggests a visualization-driven approach to the analysis of the data from heating, ventilating and conditioning system (HVAC). The key element of the approach is the RadViz visualization that is used to form daily operation patterns and can detect suspicious deviations that could be the signs of fraudulent activity in the system. It is supplemented by a matrix-based representation of the HVAC parameters that is constructed in the way that allows highlighting changes in values of parameters being analyzed. The distinctive feature of the proposed visualization models is the ability to display data from different data sources. To demonstrate and evaluate the efficiency of the proposed approach we used the VAST MiniChallenge-2 2016 data set that contains logs from the HVAC system and the access control system.

1 Introduction

The IoT technology has provided a convenient platform for constructing smart houses, buildings, and cities. The application of the interconnected distributed devices with embedded data mining algorithms allows one to create the intelligent resource efficient control systems that provide conditions comfortable for the habitants' living and suitable for the equipment functioning.

The smart heating, ventilation and air conditioning (HVAC) system is an important part of the smart building, it monitors outside and inside temperature, humidity, electricity or gas consumption to fit better the needs of the buildings usage or its occupants' behavior.

However, the usage of the meters and other HVAC devices connected to the Internet for control and analytics purposes has defined new attack vectors against the industrial information systems [1].

The compromise of the HVAC system may result in failure of the temperature sensitive equipment and degradation of the life quality of the building

S. Katsikas et al. (Eds.): ESORICS 2019 Workshops, LNCS 11980, pp. 402–418, 2020.
https://doi.org/10.1007/978-3-030-42048-2_26

users (inhabitants or employees). It can be used to get access to the sensitive data by requesting the sensor readings directly or by exploiting side channels such as timing information, electromagnetic or power consumption leaks [2–4]. For instance, the authors of [3] demonstrated how the thermal channel can be used to organize covert communication. They proposed the line-encoding protocol suitable for this type of channel and implemented experiments showing the feasibility of the attack.

To enhance the security of the smart building, it is necessary to adopt best practices in information security considering the peculiarities of the building automation. Instead of relying solely on confirmatory data analysis, exploratory visualization driven analysis has proven to be extremely valuable and effective when analyzing network security incidents [5–8]. The application of the visual analytics techniques may significantly increase the efficiency of the investigation of the suspicious activity in the HVAC system. They could be used to reveal malicious scenarios, describe distinctive attack features and, therefore, consider them when designing defense techniques.

However, existing visual analytics tools designed to analyze the HVAC data are focused on assessment of the energy consumption, as it is the main factor in the building cost, and thus these tools are not applicable to investigate different incidents that could be associated with malefactor's activity. Thus, there is a need to develop novel visual analytics techniques supporting exploratory analysis of the HVAC data in order to reveal signs of the fraudulent activity in the system.

The paper presents a novel approach to the analysis of the HVAC data based on the RadViz visualization that helps to detect daily patterns of the HVAC functioning and to reveal suspicious deviations in the state of the HVAC system and is supported by a matrix-based visualization of the HVAC parameters and a set of interactive line charts. The distinctive feature of the proposed visualization models is the ability to display data from different data sources allowing an analyst to assess HVAC data, for example, in context of the data from the access control system. The latter is important for both understanding the peculiarities of the HVAC system functioning and investigating anomalies in employees' movement [9]. The approach proposed can be applied for exploratory analysis of the HVAC data when there is no prior information on typical patterns of the HVAC functioning and possible attack scenarios, the results obtained can be applied further when designing automated analysis models.

Specifically, the contribution of the paper to the field of cybercrime forensics is a visualization-driven approach to the analysis of the data generated by the smart buildings that enables establishing patterns of the buildings' life cycle and detecting possibly anomalous deviations. The rest of the paper is organized as follows. Section 2 discusses the related work on visual analytics techniques for anomaly detection in the HVAC system. In Sect. 3 we describe the proposed visualization models and interaction mechanisms with them. Section 4 presents a case study used to evaluate the approach, discusses the results and defines the directions of the future research. Conclusions sum up our contributions.

2 Related Work

Visual analytics techniques allows one to transform enormous volumes of heterogeneous and noisy security data into a valuable evidence of the fraudulent activity and cyber crime in an intuitively clear form and do not require explicit application of complex mathematical and statistical methods [10,11]. Due to the heterogeneity of the security data, many sophisticated visualization and interaction techniques supporting the analysis of security incidents have been proposed [10].

To reveal connections between security events both complicated compound visualization models requiring additional learning [12–15] and rather simple easy interpretable visualization models [16–18] are suggested. For example, in [12] the authors propose a compound visualization model consisting of several graphical elements to analyze events from IDS, firewall, operating system and other available security sensors. The linked graph displays network topology and is placed in the circle; the circle is the second graphical element and represents a ring of security events that are arranged along the ring according to their type. The sources of the events are linked to the corresponding segment of the ring. The histogram located along the inner circumference of the ring is used to display the distribution of the events of the given type in time, and the outer circumference is used to display the overall number of the events per time unit. In [16] authors propose to correlate data from different sources using standard linear graphs. The events from different sources are combined on the basis either time scale or selected nominal attribute.

Mansmann et al. [19] adopt a RadViz visualization technique to analyze the behavior of the network hosts. The distribution of the network protocols in the host network traffic determines the position of nodes on the chart. This representation allows discovering anomalies in the behavior of hosts or higher level network entities. In [20] authors apply the RadViz to analyze transactions in the mobile money transfer services and demonstrate that it is helpful to reveal different fraudulent activities including mobile botnet infection.

In [11] authors discuss and give recommendations how to choose a visualization technique appropriate to the data type being analyzed and forensics task being solved.

There is not much research devoted to the visual analytics for efficient smart building management and investigation of anomalous deviations in its functioning. The most of visual analytic techniques is focused on the problem of the energy consumption. For example, in [5] the authors present a map-based visualization technique to analyze the energy consumption, they map the energy use to the building elements (rooms, elevators) and color different building zones according to the level of the energy consumption. Palm and Ellegård [6] adopt the stacked bar chart with the time axis to display how different entities consume energy for different everyday activities such as cooking, watching TV, etc. The periods with energy consumption are shown by the colored bar, where the color encodes the type of the entity's activity. Abdelalim et al. [7] propose to visualize energy and mass flows of the HVAC system using the Sankey diagram. The sensor data are converted into estimated energy flows for each HVAC component, the color of the flows indicate whether it is normal or abnormal.

Another interesting visual analytics approach to examination of the energy consumption data and anomaly detection in the system is described in [8]. The authors investigate the applicability of three different visualization techniques supplemented with anomaly scoring system to the anomaly detection process. They assess the Recursive Pattern, the Spiral view and the line charts. The Recursive pattern is a pixel–based visualization technique that allows generating overview on large amounts of data. The pixel color encodes either the value of the attribute or its anomaly score. The Spiral View is also a pixel-based technique, but the pixels are located using spiral layout. In the approach, each round of the spiral displays one day of data. The authors propose to enforce the line charts with the indicator bar reflecting the anomaly score for each value of the parameter and, thus, facilitating efficient search of the time periods with anomalous deviations in power consumption data. The authors show that pixel-based approach is efficient for displaying temporal patterns in energy consumption.

The visualization techniques considered above are designed for presenting one attribute of the data being analyzed. Thus, establishing visually the correlation between data from different data sources is rather complicated. Meanwhile, the process of the anomaly detection in the HVAC system requires consideration of many factors such as the number of people present in the office, and weather conditions which determine the functioning mode of the HVAC system.

The specific feature of the RadViz is the ability to analyze many attributes in order to produce a graphical representation of the multidimensional data. Therefore, it can be used to analyze HVAC data in context of data from different sources. This means that the attacker needs to consider numerous factors including weather conditions to simulate normal behavior of the HVAC system. In the approach, it is used to reveal the typical life cycle of the HVAC system and detect suspicious deviations in its state. To the best of our knowledge, our work is the first to apply the RadViz visualization technique to analyze HVAC data and data from access control system.

3 Visualization-Driven Approach

3.1 RadViz Visualization of the HVAC Data

The goal of the HVAC system is to provide conditions comfortable for the habitants and suitable for the equipment. Its functioning depends on many factors both internal and external, and metaphorically its operation can be represented as balancing between different external factors and tuning internal parameters in order to achieve some equilibrium to provide conditions required. The increase of the one factor, e.g. temperature outside the building, may require increasing or decreasing the setting points of the HVAC sensors. If the balance breaks then this may be a sign of physical degradation of the sensor as well as a sign of some potentially malicious activity. Such understanding of the HVAC system led us to the idea to present the HVAC data and the data from the access control system using the RadViz visualization [21].

The RadViz is a multivariate data visualization algorithm that performs projection of the original multidimensional space into 2-dimensional space. The idea of the data projection can be easily explained by the metaphor from physics that is used to determine the position of the object. The analyzed attributes are considered as anchors or dimension nodes and are placed uniformly around the circumference of a circle. Then the objects are represented by the points inside the circle connected by imaginary n springs to the n respective anchors. The stiffness of each spring is proportional to the value of the corresponding attribute. Thus, the point is placed, where the spring forces are in equilibrium.

The usage of this metaphor defines the following specific features of the visualization technique. The objects having higher value for some attribute then for the others are set closer to the corresponding dimension node. If all n coordinates have the same value (regardless of whether they are low or high), the data point lies exactly in the center of the circle.

Figure 1 illustrates the RadViz scheme. The values of the attributes S1 and S2 for the Point1 are greater than the values of the rest attributes, at that the value of the attribute S2 is the highest. The values of all attributes of the Point2 are equal; however, their numerical values are unknown.

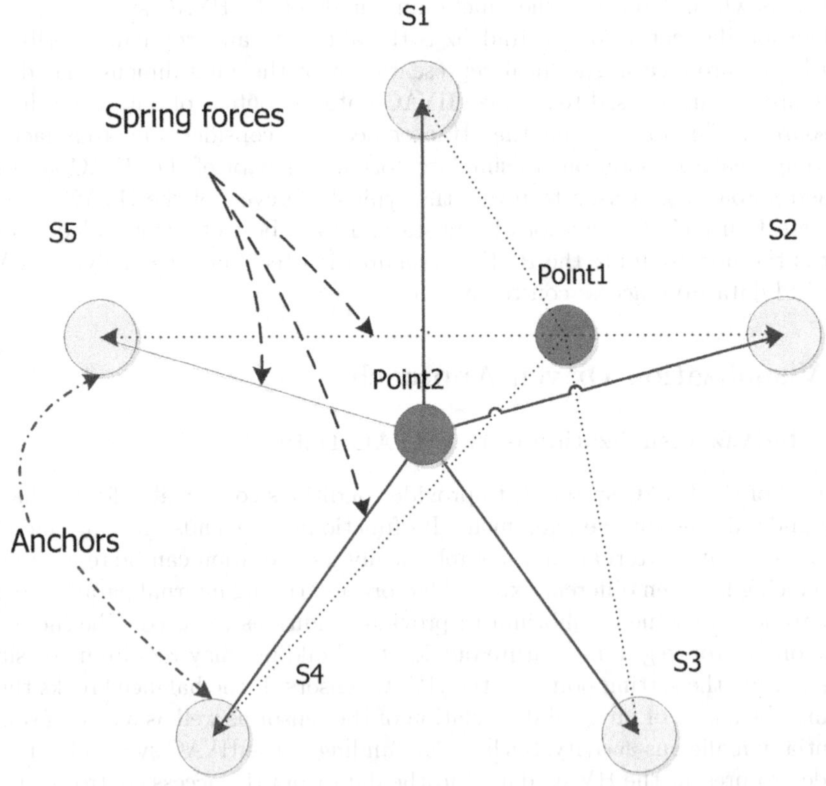

Fig. 1. Scheme of the RadViz visualization

Other important feature of the RadViz visualization is that the position of the data points in the 2-dimentional space can be easily interpreted. This distinguishes the RadViz from other techniques implementing projection of the multivariate data into spaces of the smaller dimension such as multidimensional scaling [22], some machine learning algorithms such as t-SNE [23] and self-organizing maps [24]. These techniques do not provide any explicit information about the values of the objects' attributes explaining the way they were mapped into 2- or 3- dimensional space.

The RadViz visualization allows using as many dimension anchors as can easily be located on a circumference, expanding, thus, the dimensionality of the visualization significantly. However, this feature defines a problem of the appropriate dimension nodes arrangement as for n variables there are $(n-1)!\ /\ 2$ possible RadViz projections [25].

The RadViz can be considered as clustering tool that does not require a prior knowledge about number of clusters, but the quality of the clustering depends on dimension node layout. It was shown that in order to produce meaningful visualization the dimensional anchors corresponding to similar attributes should be close on the circle [25]. In our approach, we firstly assess the similarity of the attribute pairwise and use similarity parameters to produce default layout. However, an analyst can select attributes and set their order on the circle.

In our approach, the node in the RadViz visualization corresponds to the state of the HVAC system at some moment of time.

In general case, its functioning is determined by the readings of the sensors monitoring the building's climate and defining the set points for the HVAC equipment.

Let $S = \{s_i\}_{i=1}^{n}$ be a set of HVAC sensors. Each s_i sensor generates data either regularly, for example, every 5 s, or irregular, for example, when the state of the equipment or the facility changes.

Let $v_{s_i}^t$ is a reading of the s_i sensor at the time t, then vector $\bar{v}^t = \{v_{s_1}^t, v_{s_2}^t, ... v_{s_n}^t\}$ defines the HVAC system state at the time t.

The set S of HVAC sensors form the dimension anchors, and the vector $\bar{v}^t$defines the position of the data point corresponding to the state of the system at the time moment t on the RadViz.

To support visual exploration of the data apart from manipulating the anchors layout, we propose to use following interaction techniques:

(1) filtering mechanism based on the analysis of the selected values of the attributes and
(2) interactive color encoding of the temporal attributes of the data.

It is possible to set color scheme depending on the day of week or the time intervals of the day. The latter is useful in establishing life patterns depending on time of the day or day of the week (work day or day off).

We also provide an analyst an ability to adjust the transparency of the color, than it is possible to produce image close to the heat map, the more saturated the area of the RadViz the more typical behavior HVAC system exposes.

Figure 2 shows the RadViz visualization of the HVAC data characterizing the general state of the building during 8 working days. The color scheme is set to highlight the day functioning pattern. The blue color is used for early morning and late evening hours (from 0 am till 6 am and from 9 pm till 12 pm); data points in violet color correspond to the working hours (from 9 am till 6 pm) when the majority of the employees are on their working places.

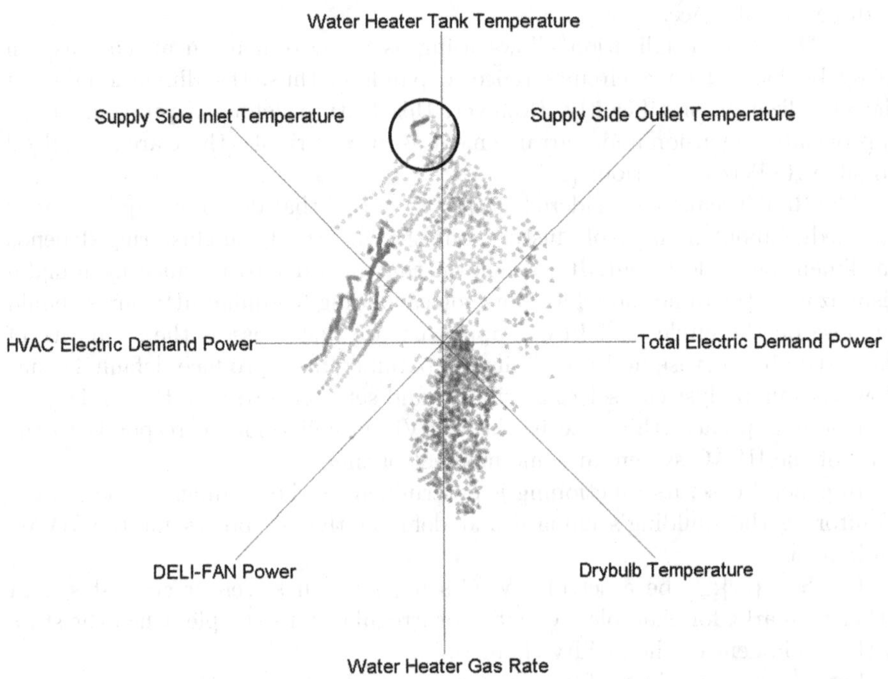

Fig. 2. The RadViz visualization of the HVAC data (Color figure online)

The points in green color characterize transitive state of the HVAC system when the employees arrive to their working place or leave it. The color of the data point has a non–zero transparency, thus the overlapping points located close to each other look darker, while scattered points look much lighter. The transitive period of the HVAC is presented by a region of points with relatively low density, it overlaps with the region of scattered points in blue. The dense cluster of the blue points near the green points highlighted by the circle in Fig. 2 looks rather atypical. The location of the points allows us to suggest that the possible problem is in the increase of the *Water Heater Tank Temperature* parameter.

The certain problem of the RadViz visualization is that it places objects with comparable values of attributes to one position. Moreover, an analyst needs to know how the parameters change, and what their values are. To solve this problem we suggest supplementing it with matrix-based presentation and line charts of the attributes values described in the next subsection.

3.2 Supplementary Visualization Models

To visualize the changes in the HVAC system over the time, we used the concept of data slices. Its key idea is to aggregate the data into data slices in the real time mode if the changes in them do not exceed some given threshold. The average values of the attributes are then displayed using selected visualization technique.

In our approach the state of the HVAC system is represented by a point in the multidimensional space. Then its functioning can be presented as a trajectory of the point. If the position of the point does not change significantly, i.e. its deviation from initial position does not exceed the given threshold during some period of time, it is possible to group all data points generated during this period of time into one data slice.

The usage of this metaphoric representation of the HVAC functioning let us to use *dbscan* algorithm to form data slices [26]. The *dbscan* algorithm is a density-based spatial clustering technique that aggregates the data points that are close to each other according to some distance metric. This algorithm is designed to analyze static data, however, in our case it is necessary to consider the time of data points generation.

The idea of the modified dbscan algorithm is described briefly as follows.

When a new data point is generated, we calculate the distances to the points included already in the current data slice. Then, if the maximum distance is not greater then threshold value ε, and the point timestamp does not start a new day, the point is included in the current data slice, otherwise a new slice is formed.

We included the condition that checks the beginning of a new day in order lately to have a possibility to group data slices by the day, this is helpful in revealing daily patters in the HVAC system functioning.

The modified *dbscan* algorithm extracts groups of data points that have two important temporal attributes - the beginning of the data slice and its duration.

Formally, the data slice is defined as follows:

$$dc = \left\{t, dur, \left\{\bar{v}^{t_j}\right\}, t_j \in [t, t + dur)\right\},$$

where t is a timestamp of the first data point that starts the data slice, dur is a duration of the data slice, and the vector $\bar{v}^{t_j}$ defines the values of the analyzed parameters at the t_j moment. The attribute t is used to sort data slices in order of their appearance.

We propose to use a matrix-based representation to visualize HVAC data slices. It is constructed in the following way. The y-axis corresponds to the analyzed parameters, while the x-axis corresponds to the time or sequence number of the data slice. In our approach each cell of the matrix represents the average value of the corresponding attribute in the data slice. The saturation of the color is used to encode the values. The higher the value, the darker the matrix cell. Figure 3 shows the scheme of matrix-based representation of the HVAC data and data from the access control system for the one day for the meeting room.

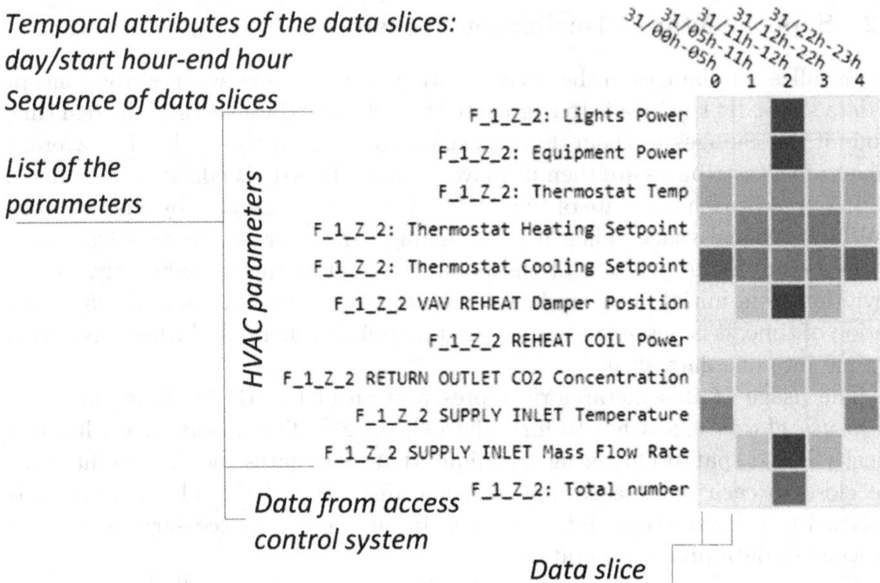

Fig. 3. The matrix-based presentation of the HVAC data

According to it, this location was visited once approximately at 11–12 am. The data from the access control system are fully conformed by the HVAC data. The lights and equipment power supply were on at the same period as well as the parameters characterizing the room ventilation increased at the same period of time. The CO2 concentration measured at the room's return air grille was also slightly increased after the visit. Note, that rather long time period from 12 am till 10 pm is represented by only one column of cells. This means that there are no significant changes in the values of the HVAC and access control system parameters during the given period of time.

It should be noted that threshold parameter ε used to group data into the data slices defines the level of changes that will be highlighted using the matrix presentation. The higher its value the coarser the aggregation of the data into data slices, the more significant changes in the HVAC data are highlighted. Thus by manipulating the parameter ε an analyst may control the data detail level.

The obvious disadvantage of the matrix-representation is the non-linear transformation of the displayed time scale, as the size of the matrix element does not depend on the duration of the data slice. On one hand, this solution highlights changes that may have very short duration and present a certain interest to an analyst; but on the other hand, it may be confusing for the analyst and requires studying the visualization model. In addition, it does not show absolute values of the attributes the analyst may be interested in. To support analysis of the absolute values and give understanding of the real time scale we supplement the matrix-based representation with a set of interactive line charts with time scale. By clicking on the attribute of the matrix representation an analyst gets its timeline, clicking on the element of the matrix highlights the corresponding time interval on the time line.

4 Case Study and Discussion

We developed a software prototype using NW.js framework and d3.js library to test our approach.

To assess the proposed approach we used a data set provided within the VAST Challenge 2016: Mini-Challenge 2 [27]. It contains HVAC data that describes the functioning of a 3 story building with multiple air handling zones per floor. The data are sampled every 5 min. The data set also contains logs from access control proximity card readers. When an employee with proximity card enters a new controlled zone, their card is detected and recorded. The dataset contains a two-week set of HVAC and access control system logs. An analyst is also provided with building layout for the offices, including the maps of the controlled zones, and HVAC zones. It should be noted that the HVAC and proximity card zones do not always match each other. One access control zone may be served by several HVAC zones. This introduces a certain level of the uncertainty. At the moment we propose depending on the primary focus of the research – employees' movement or HVAC functioning - to select either all HVAC zones servicing the given controlled zone or all proximity zones serviced by the given HVAC zone. In addition, the VAST Challenge data set has a ground proof in the form of the answers to the contest tasks that could be used to assess the efficiency of the proposed approach.

We started the analysis of the HVAC system state with analysis of its parameters for the whole building using the RadViz visualization. We colored the data points depending on the day of week, and set its transparency to non-zero in order to assess the density of the data points. We assumed that regions with high density of the points may indicate about typical behavior of the system while single outliers may indicate about some suspicious deviations in the state of the system. The image of the HVAC data for the working days produced by the RadViz is shown on Fig. 4.

It is clearly seen, that the majority of the data points is located under the axis Supply Side Inlet Temperature – DELI-FAN Power. This region is characterized by rather even density of the points. We noticed a set of interesting dense clusters of linear form located above this axis. They are marked by the oval in Fig. 4. The points belonging to such clusters are colored by one color, and only four colors were used to color them. There are also several single outliers, marked by arrows on the Figure. Their colors match the colors of the suspicious clusters. These allowed us to assume that these clusters and outliers correspond to four different days, and this assumption was proved by the detailed information available for each data point. The location of the anomalous data points indicates that they are characterized by the increased energy consumption by the HVAC data. The days with atypical energy consumption are the 7th, 8th, 10th and 13th of June.

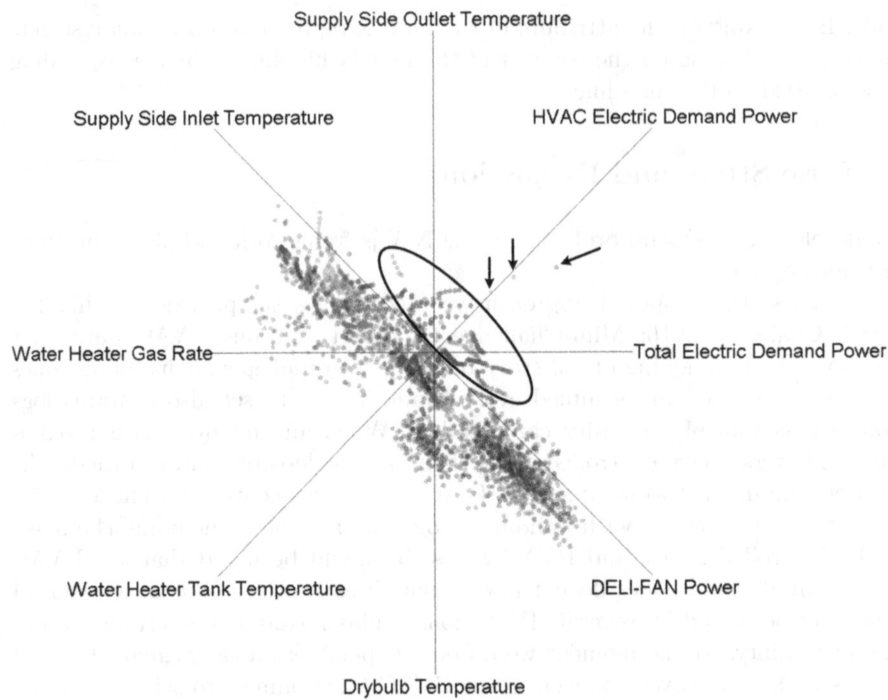

Fig. 4. The RadViz visualization of the HVAC data for 10 working days (Color figure online)

The comparison of the matrix representations of the days with and without energy anomaly give us a clue what the anomaly took place (Fig. 5). While the rest parameters look very similar, the total energy consumption and the HVAC energy consumption (*HVAC Electric Demand Power* and *Total Electric Demand Power* parameters) have a burst in the morning at 7 o'clock on the abnormal day, and then the HVAC system energy consumption falls to almost zero.

When analyzing the rest HVAC zones we kept in mind these anomalous days in order to determine typical and atypical behavior of the system and started the analysis of the zones with comparing days with and without energy anomaly. It allowed us to detect the possible cause of the anomaly:the cooling and heating set points were set to the maximum values. For example, for the room with server equipment these parameters are typically set to the 18.1 °C and 15.5 °C correspondingly, however, during the anomalous days these parameters were set to 26 °C and 29.5 °C correspondingly.

The RadViz visualization helped us to detect another interesting anomaly for this room. The color scheme used to color the data points encoded the days of week. After filtering out days with anomaly, we noticed that there are several groups of points (Fig. 6).

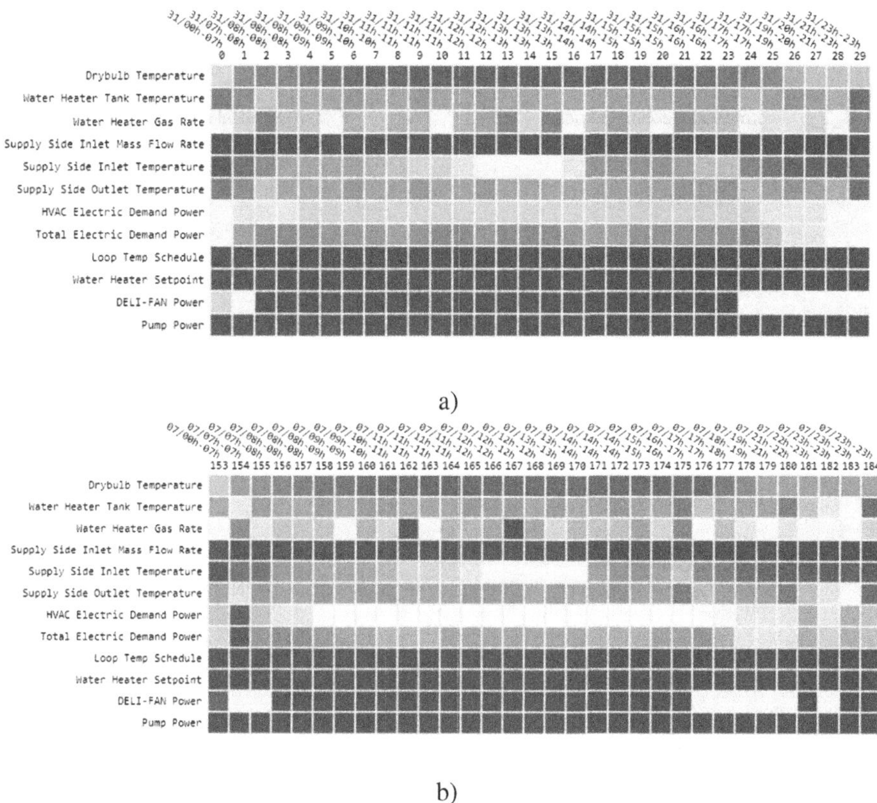

Fig. 5. The matrix-based representation of the data, characterizing functioning of the whole building: (a) a day with normal mode of functioning; (b) a day with atypically high energy consumption by the HVAC system

One numerous group of points of different colors corresponds to the periods of the typical functioning of the HVAC system and when no one is present in the room. The group B in Fig. 6 corresponds to the state of the server room when it is visited by the employees. This is indicated by the fact that points are shifted towards the anchor *F_3_Z_9: Total number* that stands for the number of employees present at the room at the given moment of time. They differ only in the number of people present in the room: one, or two. These points have different colors, thus we may conclude that it is rather typical state for these location. The points of the group A lie apart, and closer to the *F_3_Z_9 Supply Inlet Temperature*. These points belong to only one day, and this indicates that this is not normal and the problem may be in the corresponding parameter. The matrix representation proved this assumption by showing abnormal increase in three parameters simultaneously – *F_3_Z_9 Supply Inlet Temperature*, *F_3_Z_9 VAV Damper Position*, *F_3_Z_9 Return Outlet CO2 concentration* and unusual set points for *F_3_Z_9 Thermostat Heating Point* and *F_3_Z_9 Thermostat Cooling*

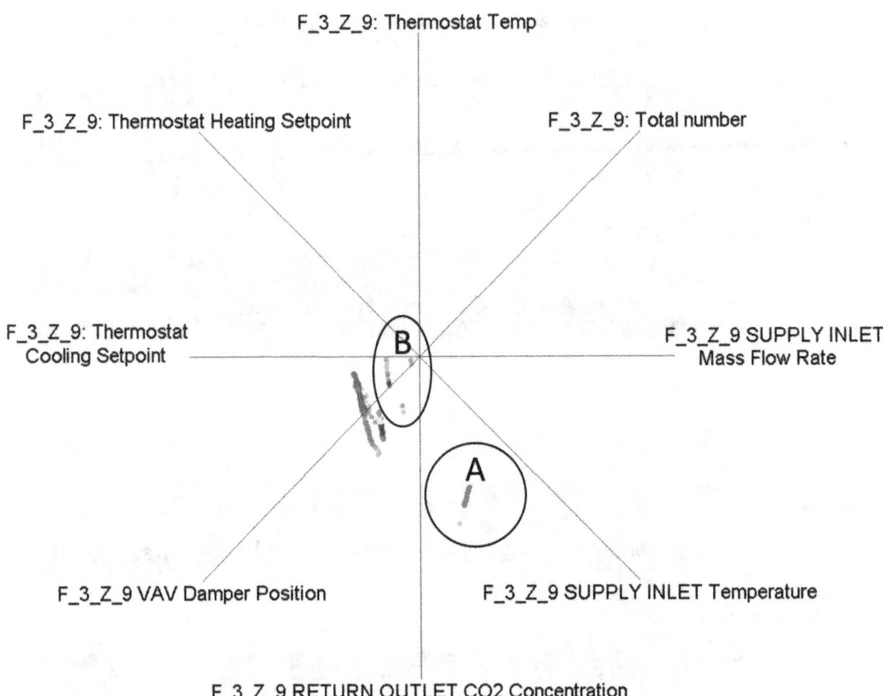

Fig. 6. The RadViz visualization of the HVAC and access control system data for the server room

Point parameters which were set to 0. This anomaly became a reason for the visit of the three employees simultaneously that took place next day.

Combining the RadViz and the matrix representation of the HVAC and the assess control system we detected all anomalous situations present in the VAST Challenge, such as increase of the temperature up to 30 °C in the HVAC zone 1 on the third floor, increase of the CO2 concentration in almost all zones due to failures in the HVAC system or wrong cooling and heating set points, the failures of the conditioning in the zone 8 on the second floor, etc.

When analyzing data with RadViz we noticed the following. The RadViz produces rather big clusters with even density for the days with normal functioning of the system. The anomalous days are characterized by a presence of several very dense clusters and/or single outliers. The visual patterns for the normal functioning of the HVAC system for the locations with specific attributes such as offices, canteen, server room, on the contrast, are characterized by compact dense clusters of the linear form, while anomalous days are characterized by large dispersion of the points. This fact could be explained that the HVAC system for the locations with specific attributes has rather strict functioning routine depending on day time or day of week; while the general parameters HVAC such as total energy consumption, water heater tank temperature, water heater rate, supply air rate, etc. depend on a set of such routines, and thus, produce "cloud" of colored points with even density. We assume that these visual patterns produced by the RadViz visualization can be used in further research to produce automatic assessment of the HVAC state.

To evaluate the efficiency of the proposed visualization models we presented our approach to the 10 specialists having both practical and research experience in the information security and intrusion detection techniques. We also invited specialist in the industrial control systems. Firstly, we presented them our approach, described the peculiarities of the RadViz visualization technique and explained how to interpret its results. We also discussed what the matrix-presentation displays and how data slices are formed and, then the participants were given a test task formed on the basis of the VAST Challenge dataset. The test tasks included the following questions: determine the typical patterns of the HVAC system functioning, i.e. the dependencies between its parameters, the character of their changes, how they depend on the presence of the employees in the controlled zone, and weather outside the building; describe the possible anomalies in the HVAC system if present, i.e. determine the parameters with atypical values, describe the character of the anomalous changes, determine the possible causes of anomalous changes. The participants were also asked to rank the visual models (from very bad to very good) and give their feedback and their suggestions to the enhancement of the visual models.

The overall assessment of the visualization models was good. Interestingly, that the specialists in information security and data analysis captured the idea of visual models quickly as they are more used to different non trivial visualization techniques, while the specialist in complex system automation firstly was skeptic, as he is more used to traditional line charts to monitor the object state. However, after studying them and doing the test he changed his mind and proposed to adopt the models to the real time data monitoring. He suggested presenting typical behavior of the system as a heat map on the RadViz visualization and mapping the current position on it to monitor the state of the HVAC system. All participants of the evaluation process marked that the matrix-representation was helpful in explaining what is wrong for the particular state of the HVAC system. They highlighted the possibility to analyze the data from the access control system in context of the HVAC, as it gives understanding on why some HVAC parameters change and, correspondingly, the changes in HVAC parameters may explain further behavior of the employees. They also liked the possibility to change the color scheme according to the values of the temporal attributes of the HVAC parameters but recommended to add a possibility to highlight data belonging to different HVAC zones, as it enables comparing HVAC zones servicing locations with similar characteristics, i.e. offices, lifts, corridors, etc. The specialists also advised to enhance the interaction techniques linking the RadViz and the matrix-based visualization to simplify the analysis process. Another interesting suggestion is connected with automation of the analysis process. The experts suggested adding possibility to mark visual patterns for typical work days and days off and use them as a baseline to assess automatically the rest graphical presentation. This feature could significantly increase the efficiency of the exploratory process.

The comments from the experts define the directions of our future work. We are planning to enhancement of the software prototype by elaborating interaction techniques connecting the RadViz and the matrix-based visualization more tightly. We also plan to develop recommendations how to organize the analysis work flow and choose the threshold for generating data slices and layout RadViz anchors. Another direction of the future research is connected to the testing of the proposed visualization technique against the streaming data in order to detect anomalous deviations in real time mode.

5 Conclusions

Application of the IoT technology to construct smart homes, buildings and cities caused the appearance of the new attacks on the industrial information systems. The compromised HVAC system may lead to the life threatening scenarios and degradation of the temperature and humidity sensitive equipment.

In the paper we proposed a visualization driven approach to the exploratory analysis of the HVAC data in order to investigate different suspicious events that could be a sign of the fraudulent activity. The key element of the approach is the RadViz visualization that is used to reveal typical life cycle of the HVAC system and detect suspicious deviations in its state. The RadViz allows one to analyze parameters from the HVAC system and other systems controlling smart building. This RadViz ability may be helpful when detecting attack scenarios that include fabricating HVAC sensors readings.

We demonstrated that it is possible to form graphical patterns for normal and abnormal functioning of the HVAC system.

To overcome some problems of the RadViz visualization we complemented it with the matrix representation of the HVAC data. It is used to display changes in the state of the system, the data points characterizing the HVAC state are aggregated in one data slice if the state of the HVAC system remains almost unchanged, thus, it is possible to both reduce the volumes of the data being analyzed and attract the analyst attention to the changes in data. However, in case of necessity the analyst can get the values of the attributes using standard line charts.

Both visual models allow one to investigate the data from different sources, and we illustrated this by applying our approach to the data set provided by the VAST Challenge 2016. It contains logs from the HVAC system and the access control system. Analyzing these data simultaneously it is possible to understand the behavior of the HVAC system better and explain the motifs of the unusual employees' moves.

In the paper we discussed the result obtained, and defined future directions of work devoted to the enhancement of the prototype and usability evaluation of the proposed visual analytical system.

References

1. Ciholas, P., Lennie, A., Sadigova, P., Such, J.M.: The security of smart buildings: a systematic literature review. https://arxiv.org/abs/1901.05837v3. Accessed 28 Jan 2019
2. Mirsky, Y., Guri, M., Elovici, Y.: HVACKer: bridging the air-gap by attacking the air conditioning system https://arxiv.org/abs/1703.10454. Accessed 9 Aug 2019
3. Mundt, P., Wickboldt, P.: Security in building automation systems-a first analysis. In: International Conference On Cyber Security And Protection of Digital Services (Cyber Security), pp. 1–8. IEEE (2016)
4. Caviglione, L., Lalande, J.-F., Mazurczyk, W., Wendzel, S.: Analysis of human awareness of security and privacy threats in smart environments. In: Tryfonas, T., Askoxylakis, I. (eds.) HAS 2015. LNCS, vol. 9190, pp. 165–177. Springer, Cham (2015). https://doi.org/10.1007/978-3-319-20376-8_15
5. Truong, H., Francisco, A., Khosrowpour, A., Taylor, J.E., Mohammadi, N.: Method for visualizing energy use in building information models. Energy Proc. **142**, 2541–2546 (2017). https://doi.org/10.1016/j.egypro.2017.12.089
6. Palm, J., Ellegård, K.: Visualizing energy consumption activities as a tool for developing effective policy. Int. J. Consum. Stud. (2011). https://doi.org/10.1111/j.1470-6431.2010.00974.x
7. Abdelalim, A., O'Brien, W., Shi, Z.: Development of sankey diagrams to visualize real HVAC performance. Energy Build. **149**, 282–297 (2017). https://doi.org/10.1016/j.enbuild.2017.05.040
8. Janetzko, H., Stoffel, F., Mittelstädt, A., Keim, D.A.: Anomaly detection for visual analytics of power consumption data. Comput. Graph. (2014). https://doi.org/10.1016/j.cag.2013.10.006
9. Novikova, E.S., Murenin, I.N., Shorov, A.V.: Visualizing anomalous activity in the movement of critical infrastructure employees. In: Proceedings of IEEE Conference of Russian Young Researchers in Electrical and Electronic Engineering (EIConRus), St. Petersburg, pp. 504–509 (2017)
10. Novikova, E., Kotenko, I.: Analytical visualization techniques for security information and event management. In: Proceedings of 21st Euromicro International Conference on Parallel, Distributed, and Network-Based Processing Belfast, Ireland, pp. 519–525 (2013)
11. Kolomeets, M., Chechulin, A., Kotenko, I., Chevalier, Y.: A visual analytics approach for the cyber forensics based on different views of the network traffic. J. Wirel. Mob. Netw. Ubiquit. Comput. Dependable Appl. **9**(2), 57–73 (2018)
12. Song, H., Muelder, C.W., Ma, K.-L.: Crucial nodes centric visual monitoring and analysis of computer networks. In: Proceedings of the 2012 International Conference on Cyber Security (CYBERSECURITY 2012). IEEE Computer Society, Washington (2012) https://doi.org/10.1109/CyberSecurity.2012.9
13. Zhao, Y., Zhou, F., Fan, X.: A real-time visualization framework for IDS alerts. In: Proceedings of the 5th International Symposium on Visual Information Communication and Interaction (VINCI 2012). ACM, New York (2012) https://doi.org/10.1145/2397696.2397698
14. Arendt, D.L., et al.: Ocelot: user-centered design of a decision support visualization for network quarantine. In: Proceedings of 2015 IEEE Symposium on Visualization for Cyber Security (VizSec), Chicago, IL (2015). https://doi.org/10.1109/VIZSEC.2015.7312763

15. Chen, S., Guo, C., Yuan, X., Merkle, F., Schaefer, H., Ertl, T.: OCEANS: online collaborative explorative analysis on network security. In: Proceedings of the Eleventh Workshop on Visualization for Cyber Security (VizSec 2014). ACM, New York (2014). https://doi.org/10.1145/2671491.267149
16. Humphries, C., Prigent, N., Bidan, C.E., Majorczyk, F.: CORGI: combination, organization and reconstruction through graphical interactions. In: Proceedings of the Eleventh Workshop on Visualization for Cyber Security (VizSec 2014). ACM, New York (2014). https://doi.org/10.1145/2671491.2671494
17. Cappers, B.C.M., van Wijk, J.: SNAPS: semantic network traffic analysis through projection and selection. In: Proceedings of the IEEE Symposium on Visualization for Cyber Security (VizSec 2015), pp. 1–8 (2015). https://doi.org/10.1109/VIZSEC.2015.7312768
18. Landstorfer, J., Herrmann, I., Stange, J., Dork, M., Wettach, R.: Weaving a carpet from log entries: a network security visualization built with cocreation. In: Proceedings of Visual Analytics Science and Technology (VAST). IEEE (2014)
19. Mansmann, F., Meier, L., Keim, D.A.: Visualization of host behavior for network security. In: Goodall, J.R., Conti, G., Ma, K.L. (eds.) VizSEC 2007. Mathematics and Visualization, pp. 187–202. Springer, Heidelberg (2008). https://doi.org/10.1007/978-3-540-78243-8_13
20. Novikova, E., Kotenko, I.: Visual analytics for detecting anomalous activity in mobile money transfer services. In: Teufel, S., Min, T.A., You, I., Weippl, E. (eds.) CD-ARES 2014. LNCS, vol. 8708, pp. 63–78. Springer, Cham (2014). https://doi.org/10.1007/978-3-319-10975-6_5
21. Ankerst, M., Berchtold, S., Keim, D.A.: Similarity clustering of dimensions for an enhanced visualization of multidimensional data. In: Proceedings 1998 IEEE Symposium on Information Visualization (INFOVIS 1998), pp. 52–60. IEEE Computer Society (1998)
22. Hout, M.C., Papesh, M.H., Goldinger, S.D.: Multidimensional scaling. WIREs Cogn. Sci. **4**, 93–103. https://doi.org/10.1002/wcs.1203
23. van der Maaten, L.J.P., Hinton, G.E.: Visualizing high-dimensional data using t-SNE. J. Mach. Learn. Res. **9**(Nov), 2579–2605 (2008)
24. Kohonen, T., Honkela, T.: Kohonen network. Scholarpedia **2**(1), 1568 (2007)
25. Di Caro, L., Frias-Martinez, V., Frias-Martinez, E.: Analyzing the role of dimension arrangement for data visualization in radviz. In: Zaki, M.J., Yu, J.X., Ravindran, B., Pudi, V. (eds.) PAKDD 2010. LNCS, vol. 6119, pp. 125–132. Springer, Heidelberg (2010). https://doi.org/10.1007/978-3-642-13672-6_13
26. Ester, M., Kriegel, H.-P., Sander, J., Xu, X.: A density-based algorithm for discovering clusters a density-based algorithm for discovering clusters in large spatial databases with noise. In: Simoudis, E., Han, J., Fayyad, U. (eds.) Proceedings of the Second International Conference on Knowledge Discovery and Data Mining (KDD 1996), pp. 226–231. AAAI Press (1996)
27. Vast Challenge Homepage. http://vacommunity.org/. Accessed 10 Aug 2019

Secure Location Verification: Why You Want Your Verifiers to Be Mobile

Matthias Schäfer[1], Carolina Nogueira[1], Jens B. Schmitt[1(✉)], and Vincent Lenders[2]

[1] DISCO Labs, TU Kaiserslautern, Kaiserslautern, Germany
{schaefer,nogueira,jschmitt}@uni-kl.de

[2] armasuisse, Thun, Switzerland
vincent.lenders@armasuisse.ch

Abstract. The integrity of location information is crucial in many applications such as access control or environmental sensing. Although there are several solutions to the problem of secure location verification, they all come with expensive requirements such as tight time synchronization, cooperative verification protocols, or dedicated hardware. Yet, meeting these requirements in practice is often not feasible which renders the existing solutions unusable in many scenarios. We therefore propose a new solution which exploits the *mobility of verifiers* to verify locations. We show that mobility can help minimize system requirements while at the same time achieves strong security. Specifically, we show that two moving verifiers are sufficient to securely verify location claims of a static prover without the need for time synchronization, active protocols, or otherwise specialized hardware. We provide formal proof that our method is secure with minimal effort if the verifiers are able to adjust their movement to the claimed location ("controlled mobility"). For scenarios in which controlled mobility is not feasible, we evaluate how more general claim-independent movement patterns of verifiers affect the security of our system. Based on extensive simulations, we propose simple movement strategies which improve the attack detection rate up to 290% with only little additional effort compared to random (uncontrolled) movements.

1 Introduction

Many real-world distributed systems require sharing of location information among network nodes. For example, in location-based access control or environmental sensing applications, the location of individual nodes is often crucial for distributed coordination, service delivery or decision making.

A common approach to sharing location information with neighboring nodes is broadcasting them periodically over a wireless link (e.g., ADS-B, AIS, RTK, WiFi, or Bluetooth). While this method has advantages in terms of simplicity and scalablity, a known weakness of this scheme is that nodes may (intentionally or not) advertise wrong location claims. In order to detect such false location information, secure location verification schemes have been proposed in the literature with the aim to securely verify whether the advertised ("claimed") location

S. Katsikas et al. (Eds.): ESORICS 2019 Workshops, LNCS 11980, pp. 419–437, 2020.
https://doi.org/10.1007/978-3-030-42048-2_27

corresponds to the real position of the sender. Since Brands and Chaum first addressed this problem in 1993 [2] and Sastry et al. later defined location (or in-region) verification in 2003 [12], many solutions and methods have been proposed in the literature to solve this problem. The existing solutions can broadly be classified into methods based on distance bounding [2,10,12,15,19,20], time-difference of arrival measurements (TDoA) [1,16,19,22], angle of arrival measurements [6,8], or hybrid methods [3,4].

All of these techniques have in common that they verify location claims by checking physical properties of the transmitted radio signals. For example, distance bounding protocols or TDoA systems exploit the fact that a radio signals cannot propagate faster than the speed of light. A location claim violating this condition must be false. While the majority of these schemes have been shown to be secure within their assumptions, the requirements to the underlying systems limit their applicability significantly. More specifically, TDoA-based methods generally require many verifiers and tight time synchronization between verifiers. This is usually achieved by additional infrastructure (e.g. wired networks) and the exchange of synchronization information between nodes. This dependency, however, significantly reduces the flexibility and increases the communication overhead, rendering the approaches unsuitable for ad hoc or mobile scenarios, especially when energy supply is limited. Distance bounding and angle of arrival measurements, on the contrary, do not require time synchronization. However, since they rely on active verification protocols and specialized hardware (see [11] for more details), we argue that their applicability is also limited. For example, they cannot be applied to systems that are already in place such as mobile phones. Upgrading the billions of smartphones in use today to meet the requirements of distance bounding seems rather impracticable.

In our prior works [13] and [14], we have shown that by adding mobility of nodes to the model, requirements of similar verification systems can be lowered significantly. More specifically, we have shown that tracks and motion of *moving provers* can be verified without any of the aforementioned limitations while at the same time strong security can be provided. However, the downside of these approaches is that they are only applicable to scenarios with *moving provers.* They are not applicable to the classic location verification problem which considers *stationary provers* at single locations or within certain areas.

In this work, we bridge this gap by bringing the benefits of mobility to the problem of verifying single locations. We present a novel method based on *mobile verifiers* which achieves strong security without limiting the attacker's knowledge (i.e., no "security by obscurity") nor does it rely on time synchronization or active verification protocols. We introduce the concept of "controlled mobility" and show that by being able to adjust the verifiers' movements to the claimed locations, provable security can be achieved with just two verifiers and two location claim transmissions. Compared to existing approaches, this is both lightweight and fast. In addition to that, we also analyze more general movement strategies for scenarios that require batch verification, i.e., the simultaneous verification of multiple location claims. We conducted extensive simulations to find claim-independent movement strategies which maximize security while at the same time minimize resources and overhead. Our results indicate that by using specific movement patterns, only three verifiers or four location claim transmissions are required to achieve a 100% detection rate.

The remainder of this paper is organized as follows. In Sect. 2, we provide a detailed problem and system description as well as a real-world example which matches this model. Section 3 then introduces our location verification protocol based on the mobility-differentiated time of arrival as well as the concept of controlled mobility. The security of this concept is then formally analyzed in Sect. 4. Afterwards, in Sect. 6, we extend our analysis by evaluating the security of our scheme in uncoordinated scenarios. Finally, we discuss and compare related methods in Sect. 7.

2 System Model and Notation

2.1 Problem Statement

In line with the definition by Sastry et al. [12], we define the problem of secure location verification as follows. A set of verifiers $\mathcal{V} = \{\mathcal{V}_1, \mathcal{V}_2, \ldots, \mathcal{V}_n\}$ wishes to check whether a prover $\mathcal{P}$ is at a location l of interest.

2.2 System Model

We assume that verifiers are moving while $\mathcal{P}$ advertises its location $m > 1$ times. This implies that each transmission is received by the verifiers from different locations. To minimize the verification overhead, we also assume that verifiers are passive receivers and there is no communication between prover and verifiers other than the prover's location advertisements. We further assume that the inter-transmission time $\Delta^{i,i+1}$ of two subsequent location advertisements is known to each verifier. This can be achieved by either using a predefined constant interval Δ, i.e., $\Delta^{(i,i+1)} = \Delta$ for all i, or by having the prover include transmission timestamps $t_{\mathcal{P}}^{(i)}$ in the location claim broadcasts, i.e., $\Delta^{i,i+1} = t_{\mathcal{P}}^{(i+1)} - t_{\mathcal{P}}^{(i)}$. It is worth noting that the first option reduces the communication overhead since less information needs to be transmitted by the prover while the second option provides much more flexibility, e.g., to support random medium access protocols such as ALOHA. Finally, we assume that each verifier knows its location at all times and has a stable but *unsynchronized* local clock.

2.3 Threat Model

We consider all information coming from the prover as untrustworthy. More specifically, we consider a malicious prover (adversary) which has full control over the reported timestamps $t_{\mathcal{P}}^{(i)}$, the real transmission intervals $\Delta_{\mathcal{A}}^{(i,j)}$, and the actual claimed location l. As l is the actual property of interest here, we assume that the adversary is located at a location different from the claimed location, i.e., $\mathcal{A} \neq l$.[1]

As we aim at strong security rather than security by obscurity, we do not limit the adversary's knowledge. In effect, our adversary has perfect knowledge of the verifiers' locations at any point in time and it can even predict the verifiers' future locations. This assumption is an important difference from the ranging-based scheme proposed by Čapkun et al. in [21], where security is based on the adversary's lack of knowledge of the "hidden" verifiers' location.

Finally, we assume that the verifiers are not compromised and they have secure means to determine their locations. Consequently, we can consider locations $\mathcal{V}_a^{(i)}$ and timestamps $t_a^{(i)}$ of the verifiers trustworthy for all $a \in \{1, \ldots, n\}$ and $i \in \{1, \ldots, m\}$.

2.4 Use Cases

A specific real-world example for a system that could (and should) be extended with our verification scheme are navigational aid systems used in aviation such as non-directional radio beacons (NDB) or VHF omnidirectional radio range (VOR) [7]. In both systems, ground stations at fixed locations transmit signals that are used by aircraft for navigation. Each transmitter is assigned a unique identifier that can be used by pilots and onboard systems to look up the station's location. Once their location is known, aircraft use them to stay on track by flying towards or in a certain angle to the ground station.

As is the case with most systems used in aviation, security has not been part of the design of NDB and VOR. As a consequence, they are highly vulnerable to spoofing attacks which can be used to mislead pilots or automatic flight control systems [17]. Although many aircraft have more accurate means of navigation (GPS), many pilots around the world still rely on these systems. Our verification scheme could be used to mitigate this threat in a scalable and light-weight manner. The ground transmitters can be considered as stationary provers while aircraft equipped with additional means of positioning (GPS) can act as moving verifiers. Onboard verification systems can then detect fake signals and inform ground personnel and other pilots.

Another use case is access control for services which should only be available to users within a certain physically restricted area. For instance, addtional premium information about a sports match could be offered in a mobile app to fans within a stadium. To prevent that people on the outside have access to that service, drones or moving cameras can be used to verify that people are in the stadium. Moreover, existing wireless technologies such as Bluetooth or WiFi could be used by the app for verification without the need for additional hardware.

[1] As for verifiers and prover, we use $\mathcal{A}$ interchangeably for the adversary's identity and location whenever the meaning is clear from the context.

3 Location Verification Protocol (MoVers)

In order to claim a location, a prover $\mathcal{P}$ broadcasts its location $m > 1$ times with pre-defined inter-transmission times $\Delta^{(i-1,i)}$ $(i = 2 \dots m)$. For the sake of simplicity, we use a constant inter-transmission time Δ, i.e., $\Delta^{(i-1,i)} = \Delta$ for all $i = 2 \dots m$ (see Sect. 2). On reception of $\mathcal{P}$'s i-th transmission $(1 < i \leq m)$, each verifier $\mathcal{V}_a$ stores its current location $\mathcal{V}_a^{(i)}$ and receiver timestamp $t_a^{(i)}$.

The verification protocol is based on the following condition: for all $i > 1$, all verifiers check whether the verification condition

$$\Delta_a^{(i-1,i)} \stackrel{?}{=} \Delta + (\delta_a^{(i)} - \delta_a^{(i-1)}) \tag{1}$$

holds. They estimate the propagation delay $\delta_a^{(i)}$ using the known positions, i.e., $\delta_a^{(i)} = dist(\mathcal{V}_a^{(i)}, \mathcal{P})/c$ with $dist(\cdot,\cdot)$ denoting the Euclidean distance between two locations and c the signal propagation speed (usually speed of light). If the equation is satisfied, the verifier remains silent. Otherwise it raises an alarm. The verification procedure terminates successfully, i.e., $\mathcal{P}$'s location is verified, after m transmissions without any alarm.

3.1 Controlled Mobility

We assume that the verifiers are changing their locations between the location claim transmissions, i.e., $\mathcal{V}_a^{(i)} \neq \mathcal{V}_a^{(i-1)}$. Verifiers can choose their next location $\mathcal{V}_a^{(i)}$ within the physical limitations using different strategies. We call this conscious choice of the next position "controlled mobility" (as opposed to "opportunistic" or "random" mobility) and distinguish between *coordinated* and *uncoordinated* controlled mobility. In coordinated controlled mobility, verifiers choose their direction of movement collaboratively to maximize security. To avoid communication overhead, we assume that verifiers coordinate their movements solely based on the claimed location and some fixed identifier. In the following security analysis, we derive such a coordinated movement pattern and prove its security. The disadvantage of this approach, however, is that the verification of multiple location claims simultaneously ("batch verification") is not possible. While this is not a requirement per se, there are scenarios with many participants (e.g., verifying people's locations in a stadium) that require a more scalable approach. We therefore extend our analysis with simulations evaluating more general uncoordinated (yet controlled) movement patterns that allow for batch verification. Based on our results, we can provide heuristics for verifier movements that maximize security while preserving a high efficiency in terms of verification time and minimum required number of verifiers.

4 Security Analysis

The two main design goals of our protocol are *security* and *efficiency*. While security as a goal is inherent to the problem, efficiency in terms of resources and verification time is crucial for the protocol's applicability in mobile scenarios. For instance, using antenna arrays for beamforming or high performance computers for complex algorithms on mobile nodes such as drones is impracticable since both weight and energy consumption must be low to maintain adequate operating times. We therefore start our security analysis by setting up the theoretical foundations and then successively increase the transmission time (in terms of number of transmissions) and number of verifiers until security is established. In this way, we obtain the fastest and most resource-efficient configuration that can provide strong security. For the sake of presentation, we conduct our analysis in two-dimensional space. Extending the results to three dimensions is straightforward.

4.1 Single Verifier

In order to let an adversary's location claims appear genuine to a verifier $\mathcal{V}_a$, Eq. (1) must be met for all $i = 2, \ldots, m$. In particular, if the adversary wants to spoof a certain location $\mathcal{P}$ from its location $\mathcal{A}$, it needs to choose its inter-transmission intervals such that

$$\Delta_{\mathcal{A}}^{(i-1,i)} + (\delta_{\mathcal{A},a}^{(i)} - \delta_{\mathcal{A},a}^{(i-1)}) = \Delta + (\delta_a^{(i)} - \delta_a^{(i-1)})$$

holds, where $\delta_{\mathcal{A},a}^{(i)} = dist(\mathcal{A}, \mathcal{V}_a)/c$ is the propagation delay of the i-th transmission from the adversary to verifier $\mathcal{V}_a$. Considering only a single verifier, this can easily be achieved by simply choosing

$$\begin{aligned} \Delta_{\mathcal{A}}^{(i-1,i)} &= \Delta + (\delta_a^{(i)} - \delta_a^{(i-1)}) - (\delta_{\mathcal{A},a}^{(i)} - \delta_{\mathcal{A},a}^{(i-1)}) \\ &= \Delta_a^{(i-1,i)} - (\delta_{\mathcal{A},a}^{(i)} - \delta_{\mathcal{A},a}^{(i-1)}) \,. \end{aligned} \tag{2}$$

In other words, the adversary can simply compensate for its unexpected propagation delays to $\mathcal{V}_a$ by choosing an inter-transmission interval equal to the difference of the expected from the actual inter-arrival time. *We conclude that a single verifier cannot provide any security since an adversary can spoof arbitrary locations.*

We point out that this result is equal to the case of a single verifier in [13]. The only difference is that in [13], a moving sender is considered whereas here we assume that the receiver moves. However, by adding another verifier in the next step of our analysis, we diverge from the analysis in [13] since we then face multiple moving nodes in our system whereas [13] always considers just a single moving node. Facing multiple mobile nodes increases the complexity of the analysis significantly.

4.2 Two Verifiers

We now consider a system with two verifiers $\mathcal{V}_a$ and $\mathcal{V}_b$. Then, Eq. (2) must be satisfied by $\Delta_{\mathcal{A}}^{(i-1,i)}$ for both verifiers, i.e.,

$$\begin{aligned} \Delta_{\mathcal{A}}^{(i-1,i)} &= \Delta_a^{(i-1,i)} + (\delta_{\mathcal{A},a}^{(i)} - \delta_{\mathcal{A},a}^{(i-1)}) \\ \Delta_{\mathcal{A}}^{(i-1,i)} &= \Delta_b^{(i-1,i)} + (\delta_{\mathcal{A},b}^{(i)} - \delta_{\mathcal{A},b}^{(i-1)}) \end{aligned}$$

must both hold for all $i = 2, \ldots, m$. By equating both constraints, re-arranging and plugging Eq. (1) into them, we can conclude that such a $\Delta_{\mathcal{A}}^{(i-1,i)}$ exists if and only if the following requirement is met:

$$\begin{aligned}(\delta_{\mathcal{A},a}^{(i)} - \delta_{\mathcal{A},a}^{(i-1)}) - (\delta_{\mathcal{A},b}^{(i)} - \delta_{\mathcal{A},b}^{(i-1)}) \\ &= \Delta_a^{(i-1,i)} - \Delta_b^{(i-1,i)} \\ &= (\delta_a^{(i)} - \delta_a^{(i-1)}) - (\delta_b^{(i)} - \delta_b^{(i-1)}) \end{aligned} \tag{3}$$

This means that the inter-transmission interval $\Delta_{\mathcal{A}}^{(i-1,i)}$ only exists if the adversary is either located at a position where the differences of distances[2] to each verifier changes between two consecutive transmissions exactly by the same amount as the differences of distances from $\mathcal{P}$ to $\mathcal{V}_a$ and $\mathcal{V}_b$. Alternatively, since the adversary is clairvoyant, it can also try to find and claim a location $\mathcal{P}$ (e.g., within an area of interest) which satisfies this constraint. From a mathematical point of view both strategies are equal since the adversary either tries to find an $\mathcal{A}$ (left-hand side of Eq. (3)) which matches a given $\mathcal{P}$ (right-hand side) or vice versa.

From the verifier perspective, however, it makes more sense to analyze whether for a given $\mathcal{P}$ there is a location $\mathcal{A} \neq \mathcal{P}$ which also satisfies Eq. (1) for all verifiers. Hence, without loss of generality, we further analyze the existence of such a location $\mathcal{A}$ given a claimed location $\mathcal{P}$. Since $\mathcal{P}$ and the verifier's locations can be considered fix in that case, the only free parameter left in Eq. (3) is $\mathcal{A}$ and we therefore summarize its right-hand side by a constant

$$k_{\mathcal{P}}^{(i)} = (\delta_a^{(i)} - \delta_a^{(i-1)}) - (\delta_b^{(i)} - \delta_b^{(i-1)})$$

which yields the requirement

$$(\delta_{\mathcal{A},a}^{(i)} - \delta_{\mathcal{A},a}^{(i-1)}) = (\delta_{\mathcal{A},b}^{(i)} - \delta_{\mathcal{A},b}^{(i-1)}) + k_{\mathcal{P}}^{(i)} \tag{4}$$

for two consecutive transmissions of a false claim. As a result, $\mathcal{P}$ can be spoofed from all locations $\mathcal{A}$ at which the distance change between two transmissions from $\mathcal{A}$ to $\mathcal{V}_a$ differs exactly by $k_{\mathcal{P}}^{(i)}$ from that to $\mathcal{V}_b$.

Figure 1 shows an example scenario with two transmissions of location claims for $\mathcal{P}$, two verifiers, and the implicit curve defined by Eq. (4) (dashed line). A possible location $\mathcal{A}$ of an adversary is also indicated by a red dot, although it could be anywhere on the dashed line. It is worth mentioning that $\mathcal{P}$ is by construction on the implicit curve. While this is natural since the legitimate $\mathcal{P}$ must satisfy the above constraint, the curve's continuity implies that there are locations within a potential area of interest (e.g., nearby $\mathcal{P}$) where an adversary could be located without being detected.

We conclude that for two verifiers, the adversary's degree of freedom is reduced to the implicit curve described by Eq. (4). In particular, MoVers is only secure for two verifiers, if this equation is satisfied by no location other than $\mathcal{P}$.

---

[2] We interpret propagation delays as direct representatives of distances.

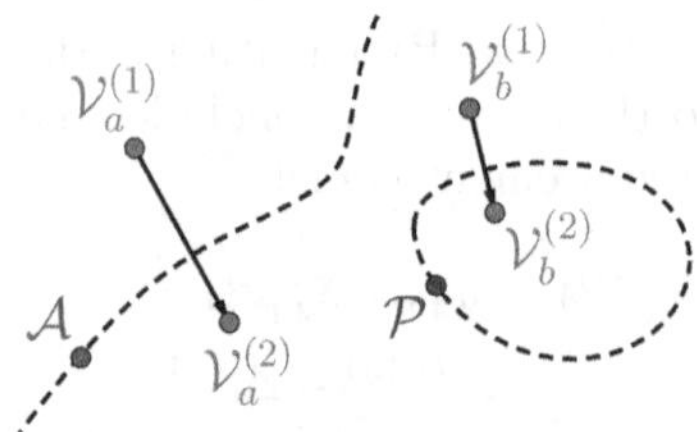

Fig. 1. Example scenario with two verifiers and the resulting restrictions (implicit curve) for the adversary's location $\mathcal{A}$. (Color figure online)

4.3 More Verifiers or More Transmissions

Analogously to the previous step, each additional verifier ($|\mathcal{V}| \geq 3$) or location claim ($m \geq 3$) further restricts the adversary since they add more equations such as Eq. (4) to the system. Similarly to the previous case, the adversary has to be positioned on several curves at the same time. In fact, the adversary is then limited to a (finite) set of unconnected points rather than a curve. In order to spoof a location, a clever adversary would compute the implicit curves beforehand and then try to find such an intersection different from $\mathcal{P}$. However, the probability that these erratic implicit curves intersect more than once becomes increasingly unlikely with each additional verifier or transmission.

Since an analytical exploration of the behavior of these intersections is extremely challenging (if not impossible), we now focus our analysis on coordinated controlled mobility and then revisit the behavior and existence of such intersections in our simulations in Sect. 6.

5 Coordinated Controlled Mobility

In scenarios where verifiers are able to adapt their movements to a claimed location, they have some degree of control over the implicit curves and thus the adversary's constraints. In the optimal case, the verifiers change their locations in a way such that the resulting implicit curves (Eq. (4)) only intersect at $\mathcal{P}$. If this is achieved, MoVers is secure since an adversary located at $\mathcal{A} \neq \mathcal{P}$ would violate the verification check Eq. (1) for at least one verifier according to our above analysis. In the following, we propose such a movement pattern and prove its security.

Theorem 1. *If one verifier moves exactly towards $\mathcal{P}$ while another one moves exactly away from $\mathcal{P}$ and not in line with the first one, then* MoVers *is secure for $m = 2$.*

Proof. Let two verifiers $\mathcal{V}_a, \mathcal{V}_b \in \mathcal{V}$ and two transmissions by a prover claiming location $\mathcal{P}$ be given. Without loss of generality, we assume that $\mathcal{V}_a$ is the verifier heading directly towards and $\mathcal{V}_b$ directly away from $\mathcal{P}$. More formally, let $\boldsymbol{v}_{a/b} =$

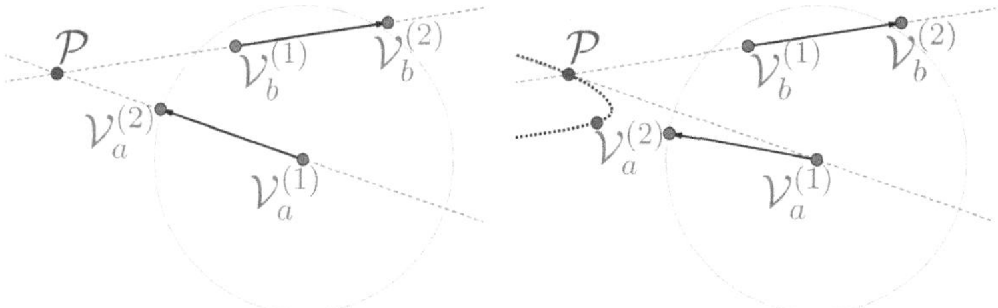

(a) Movement pattern according to Theorem 1. The implicit curve defined by Eq. (4) is reduced to $\mathcal{P}$.

(b) Deviations from the movement pattern according to Theorem 1 may result in vulerabilities to spoofing attacks.

Fig. 2. Security through coordinated controlled mobility

$(\mathcal{V}_{a/b}^{(2)} - \mathcal{V}_{a/b}^{(1)})$ be the vectors describing the position changes of the two verifiers between the two transmissions. Then there is an $s_a \in \mathbb{R}$ with $s_a > 0$ such that

$$\mathcal{P} = \mathcal{V}_a^{(1)} + \boldsymbol{v}_a \cdot s_a \ .$$

Similarly, there is an $s_b \in \mathbb{R}$ with $s_b < 0$ such that

$$\mathcal{P} = \mathcal{V}_b^{(1)} + \boldsymbol{v}_b \cdot s_b.$$

We further assume that the two verifiers are not in line with each other, i.e., there is no $s \in \mathbb{R}$ such that

$$\mathcal{V}_b^{(1)} = \mathcal{V}_a^{(1)} + \boldsymbol{v}_a \cdot s.$$

An example scenario showing such a movement is depicted in Fig. 2a. Under these circumstances, the absolute distance change between $\mathcal{P}$ and $\mathcal{V}$ is maximal and thus the estimated propagation delays from the prover to both verifiers change by the maximum possible absolute values

$$\delta_a^{(2)} = \delta_a^{(1)} - \frac{\|\boldsymbol{v}_a\|}{c} \quad \text{and} \quad \delta_b^{(2)} = \delta_b^{(1)} + \frac{\|\boldsymbol{v}_b\|}{c} \ ,$$

since both distances change exactly by the full movements' lengths by the verifiers between the transmissions, yet, in opposite directions. Additionally, $\frac{\|\boldsymbol{v}_a\|}{c} \leq \delta_a^{(2)} - \delta_a^{(1)}$ is required, meaning that $\mathcal{V}_a$ should not move beyond $\mathcal{P}$. Plugging this into Eq. 1 yields

$$\begin{aligned} \Delta_a^{(1,2)} &\stackrel{?}{=} \Delta + (\delta_a^{(2)} - \delta_a^{(1)}) \\ &= \Delta - \frac{\|\boldsymbol{v}_a\|}{c} \end{aligned}$$

and, analogously, $\Delta_b^{(1,2)} \stackrel{?}{=} \Delta + \frac{\|\boldsymbol{v}_b\|}{c}$.

Let us now consider an adversary located at $\mathcal{A} \neq \mathcal{P}$. In order to pass the verification checks of the two verifiers, it has to choose $\Delta_{\mathcal{A}}^{(1,2)}$ such that the two equations

$$\Delta_{\mathcal{A}}^{(1,2)} + (\delta_{\mathcal{A},a}^{(2)} - \delta_{\mathcal{A},a}^{(1)}) = \Delta - \frac{\|\boldsymbol{v}_a\|}{c} \tag{5}$$

$$\underbrace{\Delta_{\mathcal{A}}^{(1,2)} + (\delta_{\mathcal{A},b}^{(2)} - \delta_{\mathcal{A},b}^{(1)})}_{\text{"real" signal propagation}} = \Delta + \frac{\|\boldsymbol{v}_b\|}{c} \tag{6}$$

are satisfied. Let us now assume $\mathcal{A}$ would not be located in line with $\mathcal{V}_a$ and $\mathcal{P}$. Then

$$\delta_{\mathcal{A},a}^{(2)} - \delta_{\mathcal{A},a}^{(1)} > -\frac{\|\boldsymbol{v}_a\|}{c}$$

holds, since $\mathcal{V}_a$ does not move exactly towards $\mathcal{A}$. This means for the adversary that it has to choose $\Delta_{\mathcal{A}}^{(1,2)} < \Delta$ to compensate for the difference. Yet, then it cannot satisfy Eq. 6 since it would be required that

$$\delta_{\mathcal{A},b}^{(2)} - \delta_{\mathcal{A},b}^{(1)} > \frac{\|\boldsymbol{v}_b\|}{c}.$$

However, given the distance moved by $\mathcal{V}_b$ between the two transmissions and the associated maximum possible distance change of $\|\boldsymbol{v}_b\|$, this is impossible. Hence, $\mathcal{A}$ must be located in line with $\mathcal{V}_a$.

We can show analogously that $\mathcal{A}$ must also be in line with $\mathcal{P}$ and $\mathcal{V}_b$ in order to satisfy Eq. 5. As a consequence, $\mathcal{A}$ must be located on two lines which both cross $\mathcal{P}$. Since $\mathcal{V}_a$ and $\mathcal{V}_b$ are not in line with each other, these two lines are different. Since furthermore two different lines can only have one intersection, we can conclude that $\mathcal{P}$ is the only location from which a sender can satisfy both equations at the same time. Thus, Theorem 1 holds and MoVers is secure.

We conclude that by adapting the verifiers' movements to the claimed location ("coordinated controlled mobility"), *MoVers can provide provable security with an efficient configuration of two verifiers and two transmissions.*

Summary: The key results from this theoretical analysis are that (i) a single verifier cannot provide any security, (ii) two verifiers can provide provable security with coordinated controlled mobility (Theorem 1), and (iii) the security increases with each additional transmission or verifier as more restrictions are added for the adversary's location.

6 Uncoordinated Mobility

As explained in Sect. 3.1, coordinated controlled mobility can only be used if there is only one location to be verified at a time. For scenarios with more than one prover, a movement strategy independent from $\mathcal{P}$ is required. So far we considered only two transmissions of the location claim in the presence of two verifiers. As we know from Sect. 4, having more than two verifiers ($n > 2$) or more than two transmissions ($m > 2$), each reduces the degree of freedom for the adversary by adding more implicit curves to the constraints for $\mathcal{A}$. More specifically, since the verifiers move between each transmission, the focal points for the implicit curve defined by Eq. (4) change for every $i \in \{2, \dots, m\}$ and each pair $\mathcal{V}_a, \mathcal{V}_b \in \mathcal{V}$. As a result, $\mathcal{A}$ needs to be located at an intersection of $(m-1) \cdot \binom{n}{2}$ different implicit curves in order to remain undetected when claiming $\mathcal{P} \neq \mathcal{A}$. Moreover, this set of intersections can be assumed to be finite since the curves are not periodic. The number of such intersections can be considered a direct measure of the attacker's degree of freedom and thus the security of our scheme. Our scheme is in particular secure if there is only one intersection of all curves (which is $\mathcal{P}$ by construction) since false claims will then violate Eq. (1) for at least one verifier.

Most related problems are of a simple hyperbolic nature (e.g. [13,14,18]) and can often be analyzed algebraically. Unfortunately, having more than one mobile node makes the exact analysis hard because each moving element contributes to the equations. For example, in contrast to the analysis of intersections of a set of hyperbolas, which is common, e.g., for TDoA or ranging-based approaches, we face curves defined by intersections of intersections of hyperbolas with multiple parameters. These curves are of a higher order than hyperbolas which makes an exact analysis of the intersections extremely difficult. Although there exist methods to decrease the computational complexity when computing the intersection of hyperbolas (e.g., homogeneous coordinates [9]), we could not find any analytical method to analyze it in a general way, since the parameters that may determine the hyperbolas are unknown. We therefore continue our analysis by extending our theoretical findings with simulations analyzing the behavior of the intersections with respect to the verifiers' movements independent from $\mathcal{P}$.

In the following simulations, we differentiate between opportunistic and (uncoordinated) controlled mobility. In opportunistic (or random) mobility, nodes are not moving according to any predefined pattern. This reflects scenarios where uncontrolled nodes act as verifiers (e.g., cellphones, agricultural machines, or airplanes). In controlled mobility, verifiers follow certain patterns aiming at improving the security of the verification scheme.

6.1 Simulation Design

We implemented a simulation framework in MATLAB® which allows us to analyze the intersections for arbitrary constellations of verifiers and provers. By controlling the movement of verifiers between the reception of location claims, we show the effect of the geometry on the security of our approach and identify beneficial movement strategies for verifiers.

In accordance with our verification process, we implemented our simulations as a discrete-event simulation. The events are the transmissions of a location claim and we recorded the locations of all n verifiers at each transmission. Based on the recorded locations and $\mathcal{P}$ we then setup the nonlinear equation system consisting of all $(m-1) \cdot \binom{n}{2}$ instances of Eq. (4). Using the solver `fsolve` of MATLAB®'s optimization toolbox we then calculated all solutions to the system, i.e., the intersections of the curves, within a pre-defined area of interest.

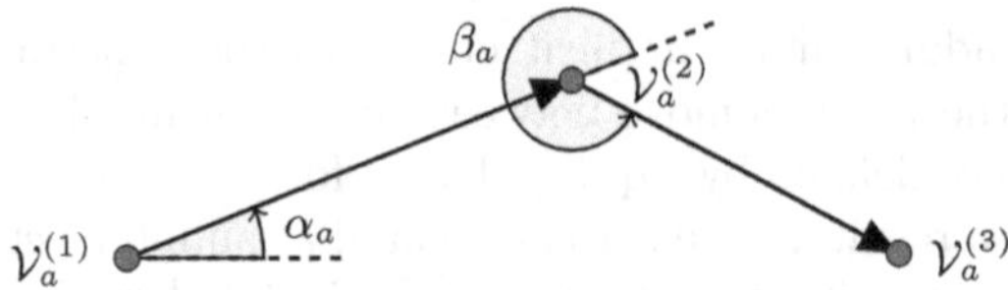

Fig. 3. Description of a verifier $\mathcal{V}_a$'s movement in our simulations. The initial direction is the counter-clockwise angle α_a relative to a horizontal axis through $\mathcal{V}_a^{(1)}$. After the initial step (i.e., for $i > 1$), we only consider the direction changes (β_a, γ_a, ...), i.e., the counter-clockwise angle between the old and the new direction.

To analyze the effect of the verifier's movement on the number of intersections within the area of interest, we define the verifiers' movements as depicted in Fig. 3. At the first ($i = 1$) reception of the prover's claim, a verifier $\mathcal{V}_a$ is located at $\mathcal{V}_a^{(1)}$ and moves into direction α_a at a certain speed. As the prover re-transmits the location claim after Δ while the verifier moves at speed v into direction α_a, we can approximate the verifier's location at reception of the second transmission ($i = 2$) by adding a vector of length $\Delta \cdot v$ and direction α_a to the initial location $\mathcal{V}_a^{(1)}$. It is worth noting that we set the verifier's location at the time of transmission equal to that of the reception time. While this is not realistic, we argue that this error is negligible in practice since the verifier's speed is extremely small compared to the signal propagation speed. For further transmissions ($i > 1$) we consider only the direction change β_a, γ_a, and so on. In summary, a verifier's movement during the verification process can be completely described by its initial location $\mathcal{V}_a^{(1)}$, its speed v, the inter-transmission interval Δ, the initial direction α_a, and the direction changes β_a, γ_a, ... between the receptions.

6.2 Parameter Selection

To keep our simulations realistic, we have chosen the simulation parameters according to the stadium use case described in Sect. 2.4. The speed of the verifiers is assumed to be in the range of off-the-shelf drones (10–30 m/s). The distance covered between two transmissions of a location claim is the product of this speed and the inter-transmission interval Δ. For simplicity, we set $\Delta = 1$ s for all our simulations. The area of interest considered in our simulations is motivated by the size of a football stadium and set to a rectangle of 209 $\times$ 255 m. All verifiers and location claims must be within this area.

As for the adversary's location, we allow it to be located outside this area but limit its distance to the verifiers in the following way. We assume that each verifier has a circular reception range with a radius sufficient to cover the largest possible distance between two locations within the area of interest. As a consequence, if all verifiers are located at the same side of the area, an attacker located outside the area could still be in their coverage. We therefore extend the area in which we search for intersections with a safety margin of the length of the diagonal of the area of interest.

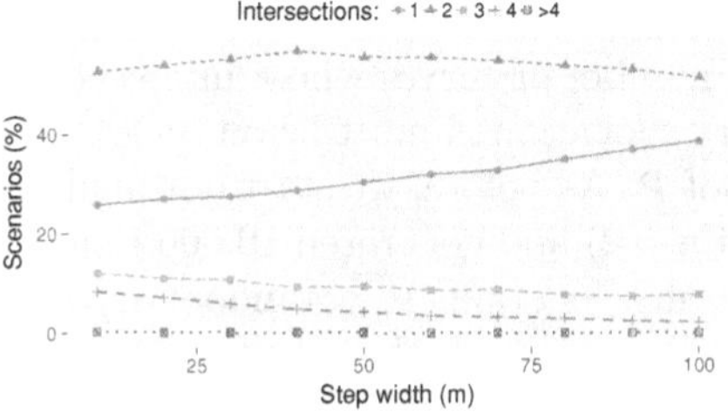

(a) Effect of step width/speed on the number of intersections. The gray solid line is the percentage of the cases in which the location was securely verified. The other lines represent the percentages where an adversary could have been located at an increasing number of locations other than $\mathcal{P}$.

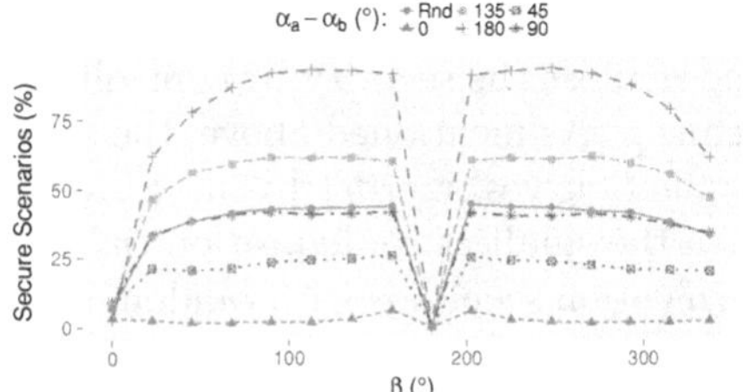

(b) Effect of relative movement ($\alpha_a - \alpha_b$) and different $\beta_a = \beta_b = \beta$ on the number of intersections. This graph only shows the percentage of the 10.000 random scenarios that were secure, i.e., the set of intersections $\mathcal{I}$ only contained $\mathcal{P}$.

Fig. 4. Simulation results (Color figure online)

An example scenario matching this parameter selection would be a location-based service which should only be available to people within the stadium. To access the service without having to pay entry, the adversary tries to spoof a location within the stadium while being located outside (but in range). Drones are hovering in the stadium and act as verifiers.

6.3 Opportunistic/Random Mobility

Effect of Speed v. The speed of the verifiers defines the distance covered by a verifier between the periodic re-transmissions of a location claim. To evaluate whether the resulting step width has an impact on the number of intersections, we randomly generated 10.000 scenarios for the "cheapest" configuration $n = 2$ and $m = 3$. Each verifier starts at a random location $\mathcal{V}_{a/b}^{(1)}$ and moves into a random direction at different speeds $10 \leq v \leq 100$ m/s. For each scenario, we recorded the number of intersections $|\mathcal{I}|$. We did not consider larger speeds since they would be unrealistic given an area of interest of 209×255 m. The results are shown in Fig. 4a. While the percentage of scenarios in which the claimed location could be securely verified (gray solid line) slightly increased with increasing step width, the percentage of $|\mathcal{I}| = 2$ was constantly over 50%. For smaller v, there were even about 20% of scenarios in which an adversary could have chosen between two (dashed blue with squares) or three (green dashed with pluses) locations different to $\mathcal{P}$ which also satisfied Eq. (1) for both verifiers. We conclude that the step width (or speed) has only a minor effect on the number of intersections. On the one hand, this means that the step width does not provide much room for improving the security. However, on the other hand, this also means that slow verifiers do not suffer big disadvantages.

Effect of Number of Transmissions m and Verifiers n. Both numbers m and n affect the security by controlling the number of curves whose intersections define $\mathcal{I}$. As mentioned above, the adversary's location $\mathcal{A}$ must lie on $(m-1)\cdot\binom{n}{2}$ implicit curves in order to successfully spoof $\mathcal{P}$. As before, we start our analysis with the smallest configuration ($m = 3$ and $n = 2$) and generated 10.000 random verification scenarios with random initial verifier locations $\mathcal{V}_{a/b}^{(1)}$, random $\alpha_{a/b}$ and $\beta_{a/b}$, and random speeds $10 \leq v \leq 100$ m/s. As expected, the results were equal to those for the average step width of 55 m shown in Fig. 4a. Only 31.65% of all tested scenarios could be securely verified with the basic configuration of $m = 3$ and $n = 2$. A large number of scenarios resulted in two intersections (54.35%). The probability for more than two intersections, however, is significantly lower (less than 10% for three intersections). We conducted another 10.000 random simulations for $m = 4$ as well as for $n = 3$ and the number of intersections dropped to 1 for all tested scenarios, indicating that *our verification scheme is secure for $m > 3$ or $n > 2$.*

We can conclude that if the verifiers move opportunistically (random) within the area of interest, 31.65% of the location verification scenarios can be securely verified with $n = 2$ verifiers and $m = 3$ transmissions. In order to securely verify the other 68.35%, at least one additional transmission ($m > 3$) or at least one additional verifier ($n > 2$) is required. That means that if, for instance, the inter-transmission interval is $\Delta = 1$ s, an adversary would be discovered after 2 s in 31.65% of the scenarios and at latest after 3 s, resulting in an average verification time of 2.6835 s. Conversely, with an additional verifier, the verification time is reduced to 2 s.

6.4 Uncoordinated Controlled Mobility

The previous results show that our scheme is secure for $m > 3$ or $n > 2$. However, depending on the use case, reducing the verification time and minimum number of verifiers might be crucial. For example, if the area of interest is larger, parts of the area might only be covered by very few verifiers. In addition, message loss due to frequency overuse might reduce the number of messages received by a sufficient number of verifiers. To further increase the efficiency of our scheme for a better robustness against such problems, we now analyze whether the security of the minimum configuration ($m = 3$ and $n = 2$) improves if the verifiers' movements are controlled. Being able to securely verify a larger fraction of locations with the minimal configuration reduces the average verification time and the required number of verifiers.

Movement Pattern (α and β). Our next set of simulations aims at shedding light on the influence of the movement directions $\alpha_{a/b}$ and $\beta_{a/b}$ on $|\mathcal{I}|$. It is worth noting that we do not analyze the effect of the initial location $\mathcal{V}_{a/b}^{(1)}$ since we assume that the adversary controls the point in time when the verification process is initiated. Hence, the verifiers can only control what happens after the first location claim was received. In addition, we do not consider movement patterns as functions of $\mathcal{P}$ since this would prevent the verification of multiple positions at the same time.

For the following simulations, we set the speed of the verifiers to that of commercial off-the-shelf drones such as DJI's Phantom 4, i.e., $v = 20$ m/s. The turns of the verifiers between the two steps are controlled by β_a and β_b. To keep our scheme light-weight, we assume that the verifiers do not communicate for coordination and assume constant pre-defined $\beta_a = \beta_b = \beta$. However, since the curves determining $|\mathcal{I}|$ do not only depend on β but also on α_a and α_b, we further analyze how the difference between the two angles, i.e., the relative direction of the verifiers to each other affects the intersections. As before, we conducted 10.000 random simulations for different combinations of β and $\alpha_a - \alpha_b$.

The results are shown in Fig. 4b. The graph shows that both the effect of β and that of $\alpha_a - \alpha_b$ on $|\mathcal{I}|$ are almost independent from each other. Regardless of the difference in direction, any β close to 0° (respectively 360°) should be avoided. For large direction differences $\alpha_a - \alpha_b$, the best choice for β is around 110° or 250°. Note that both angles represent the same absolute change in direction since 360° − 250° = 110°.

An interesting special case is $\beta = 180°$, i.e., the third location of each verifier is the same as the first one ($\mathcal{V}^{(1)} = \mathcal{V}^{(3)}$). As a result, the implicit curve generated by the first two transmissions coincides with that one of the second and third transmission. In other words, the third transmission does not impose a new constraint on the adversary and it is only limited to locations on the implicit curve (compare Sect. 4.2).

More specifically, let us assume two verifiers $\mathcal{V}_a$ and $\mathcal{V}_b$ receiving three transmissions of a location claim for $\mathcal{P}$. According to Sect. 4.2 a potential adversary's location $\mathcal{A}$ must satisfy the following system of instances of Eq. (4):

$$(\delta^{(2)}_{\mathcal{A},b} - \delta^{(1)}_{\mathcal{A},b}) = (\delta^{(2)}_{\mathcal{A},a} - \delta^{(1)}_{\mathcal{A},a}) + k^{(2)}_{\mathcal{P}}$$
$$(\delta^{(3)}_{\mathcal{A},b} - \delta^{(2)}_{\mathcal{A},b}) = (\delta^{(3)}_{\mathcal{A},a} - \delta^{(2)}_{\mathcal{A},a}) + k^{(3)}_{\mathcal{P}}$$

If $\beta = 180°$, i.e, $\mathcal{V}^{(3)}_a = \mathcal{V}^{(1)}_a$ and $\mathcal{V}^{(3)}_b = \mathcal{V}^{(1)}_b$ then

$$\begin{aligned} k^{(3)}_{\mathcal{P}} &= (\delta^{(3)}_b - \delta^{(2)}_b) - (\delta^{(3)}_a - \delta^{(2)}_a) \\ &= (\delta^{(1)}_b - \delta^{(2)}_b) - (\delta^{(1)}_a - \delta^{(2)}_a) \\ &= -k^{(2)}_{\mathcal{P}} \end{aligned}$$

and thus

$$\begin{aligned} & (\delta^{(3)}_{\mathcal{A},b} - \delta^{(2)}_{\mathcal{A},b}) = (\delta^{(3)}_{\mathcal{A},a} - \delta^{(2)}_{\mathcal{A},a}) + k^{(3)}_{\mathcal{P}} \\ \Leftrightarrow\quad & (\delta^{(1)}_{\mathcal{A},b} - \delta^{(2)}_{\mathcal{A},b}) = (\delta^{(1)}_{\mathcal{A},a} - \delta^{(2)}_{\mathcal{A},a}) - k^{(2)}_{\mathcal{P}} \\ \Leftrightarrow\quad & (\delta^{(2)}_{\mathcal{A},b} - \delta^{(1)}_{\mathcal{A},b}) = (\delta^{(2)}_{\mathcal{A},a} - \delta^{(1)}_{\mathcal{A},a}) + k^{(2)}_{\mathcal{P}} \end{aligned}$$

Consequently, the third transmission does not impose a new constraint on the adversary's location $\mathcal{A}$ if $\beta = 180°$.

Regarding the direction difference $\alpha_a - \alpha_b$, we can summarize that the closer it is to 180°, the higher the percentage of locations which could be securely verified

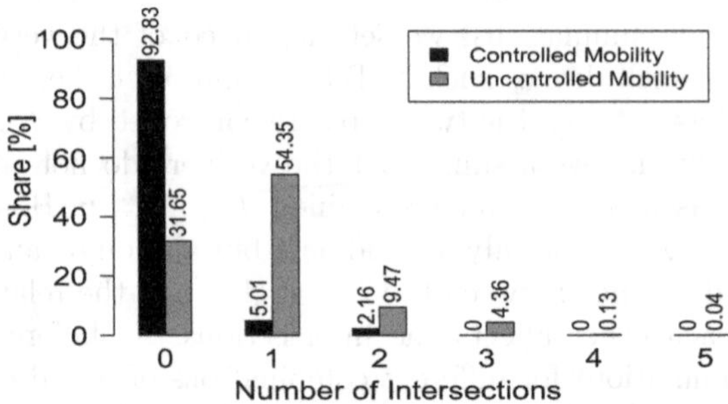

Fig. 5. Comparison of the distribution of the number of possible adversary positions for controlled and uncontrolled mobility ($n = 2$, $m = 3$). For controlled mobility we used $\alpha_a - \alpha_b = 180°$ and $\beta \approx 110°$.

after the third transmission. In fact, we also did the simulations for $\alpha_a - \alpha_b > 180°$ but the results were identical to those for $360° - (\alpha_a - \alpha_b)$.

We conclude from our simulations that with $\beta = 110°$ or $\beta = 250°$ and a direction difference of $|\alpha_a - \alpha_b| = 180°$, more than 92.5% of all scenarios could be securely verified with two verifiers and three transmissions of the location claim. This is a huge improvement compared to random movement as shown in Fig. 5.

7 Related Work

As already mentioned in the introduction, many solutions and methods have been proposed in the literature to solve the problem of secure location verification. Existing solutions can broadly be classified into methods based on distance bounding [2,12,15,19,20], time-difference of arrival measurements (TDoA) [16,19,22], angle of arrival measurements [6,8], or hybrid methods [3,4]. As mentioned in the introduction, each of these schemes comes with limiting requirements such as tight time synchronization, specialized hardware, directional antennas, or limited attacker knowledge. We therefore argue that they are not applicable to scenarios where passive and lightweight solutions are required.

Only a few works have tackled the case of mobile verifiers for secure location verification. However, these protocols differ significantly from ours. Čapkun et al. [21] proposed a location verification scheme, in which a mobile verifier initiates a challenge-response protocol from a known position and then moves to an unknown position to receive the response. The response is sent simultaneously via ultrasound and RF so that the verifier can estimate its distance to the prover based on the time-difference of arrival of the two signals due to their differing propagation speed (ranging). The security of the approach derives from the fact that although dishonest provers could modify the transmission times of the two response signals, they would need to correctly guess the verifier's new location in order to mimic the expected time-difference of arrival. This scheme, however, is cooperative and requires nodes to be equipped with two transceivers (ultrasound and RF). Moreover, we challenge the assumption 'untraceability' of the moving verifier. Even though the verifier does not actively transmit revealing signals from its new location, a more sophisticated adversary could track the verifier via reflections of signals of opportunity and passive radar techniques [5].

In [10], Perazzo et al. propose a location verification system in which a verifier drone performs distance bounding with a prover consecutively from several different locations. The locations are carefully chosen such that they form a triangle containing the prover's location. In this way an adversary claiming a false location inside the triangle needs to mimic a shorter distance to at least one of the locations chosen by the drone. As shown by Čapkun et al. in [20], this is infeasible and hence, the scheme is secure. However, their approach inherits all the aforementioned system requirements from distance bounding and is therefore not well-suited for location verification in existing systems or systems with limited resources.

Baker and Martinovic proposed a TDoA-based scheme in [1]. Their scheme relies on two verifiers, one fixed and the other one moving, to measure the TDoA of multiple location broadcasts by the prover. Since one verifier is changing location between each of the prover's transmissions, different TDoAs are expected each time. Analogously to traditional multilateration, each TDoA measurement reduces the set of possible locations of the transmitter to one arm of a hyperbola. By repeating the measurements at least three times (in 2D) and comparing the expected to the measured TDoAs, the adversary can be localized by intersecting the resulting hyperbolas. As mentioned, however, TDoA measurements require tight time synchronization and extra communication to collect all measurements at a central processing unit which our protocol does not require.

Finally, we want to highlight the difference of this work to our related works on track verification [13] and motion verification [14]. First, the underlying problem considered in this paper (verification of locations) is different to that considered in [13] (verification of sequences of locations) or [14] (verification of motion). The seemingly strong similarity is largely a result of the common theoretical foundations on which these works are based on. This work, however, diverges significantly in terms of problem statement, use cases, and security properties from our previous works. More specifically, the theoretical analysis conducted in this paper considers multiple moving nodes at the same time, whereas the analyses of [13] and [14] are only applicable to systems with one moving node. As a result, the analytical nature of the security guarantees of our scheme is not hyperbolic anymore, making them much harder to analyze.

8 Conclusion

In this paper, we presented *MoVers*, a simple yet secure location verification method which leverages the mobility of verifiers to relax system requirements. We have provided a formal security analysis which shows that our scheme MoVers achieves provable security with only two transmissions by adjusting the movements of two verifiers to the claimed location. We have furthermore shown in simulations how more general types of mobility affect the security of our scheme.

References

1. Baker, R., Martinovic, I.: Secure location verification with a mobile receiver. In: Proceedings of the 2nd ACM Workshop on Cyber-Physical Systems Security and Privacy (CPS-SPC), October 2016
2. Brands, S., Chaum, D.: Distance-bounding protocols. In: Helleseth, T. (ed.) EUROCRYPT 1993. LNCS, vol. 765, pp. 344–359. Springer, Heidelberg (1994). https://doi.org/10.1007/3-540-48285-7_30
3. Chiang, J.T., Haas, J.J., Choi, J., Hu, Y.C.: Secure location verification using simultaneous multilateration. IEEE Trans. Wirel. Commun. **11**(2), 584–591 (2012)
4. Chiang, J.T., Haas, J.J., Hu, Y.C.: Secure and precise location verification using distance bounding and simultaneous multilateration. In: Proceedings of the 2nd ACM Conference on Wireless Network Security (WiSec), March 2009
5. Howland, P.: Editorial: passive radar systems. IEE Proc. - Radar Sonar Navigat. **152**(3), 105–106 (2005). https://doi.org/10.1049/ip-rsn:20059064
6. Hu, L., Evans, D.: Using directional antennas to prevent wormhole attacks. In: Network and Distributed System Security Symposium (NDSS), February 2004
7. International Civil Aviation Organization (ICAO): International Standards and Recommended Practices, Annex 10: Aeronautical Telecommunications, 6 edn. Volume I: Radio Navigation Aids (2006)
8. Lazos, L., Poovendran, R., Čapkun, S.: ROPE: robust position estimation in wireless sensor networks. In: Proceedings of the 4th International Symposium on Information Processing in Sensor Networks (IPSN). IEEE Press, April 2005
9. Li, H., Hestenes, D., Rockwood, A.: Generalized homogeneous coordinates for computational geometry. In: Sommer, G. (ed.) Geometric Computing with Clifford Algebras, pp. 27–59. Springer, Heidelberg (2001). https://doi.org/10.1007/978-3-662-04621-0_2
10. Perazzo, P., Ariyapala, K., Conti, M., Dini, G.: The verifier bee: a path planner for drone-based secure location verification. In: Proceedings of the 16th IEEE International Symposium on A World of Wireless, Mobile and Multimedia Networks (WoWMoM), June 2015
11. Rasmussen, K.B., Čapkun, S.: Realization of RF distance bounding. In: Proceedings of the 19th USENIX Conference on Security (2010)
12. Sastry, N., Shankar, U., Wagner, D.: Secure verification of location claims. In: Proceedings of the 2nd ACM Workshop on Wireless Security (WiSe), September 2003
13. Schäfer, M., Lenders, V., Schmitt, J.B.: Secure track verification. In: IEEE Symposium on Security and Privacy, May 2015
14. Schäfer, M., Leu, P., Lenders, V., Schmitt, J.: Secure motion verification using the doppler effect. In: Proceedings of the 9th ACM Conference on Security and Privacy in Wireless and Mobile Networks (WiSec), July 2016
15. Singelee, D., Preneel, B.: Location verification using secure distance bounding protocols. In: IEEE International Conference on Mobile Adhoc and Sensor Systems Conference (MASS), November 2005
16. Strohmeier, M., Lenders, V., Martinovic, I.: Lightweight location verification in air traffic surveillance networks. In: Proceedings of the 1st ACM Workshop on Cyber-Physical System Security (CPSS) (2015)
17. Strohmeier, M., Schäfer, M., Pinheiro, R., Lenders, V., Martinovic, I.: On perception and reality in wireless air traffic communication security. IEEE Trans. Intell. Transp. Syst. **18**(6), 1338–1357 (2017)

18. Tippenhauer, N.O., Pöpper, C., Rasmussen, K.B., Capkun, S.: On the requirements for successful GPS spoofing attacks. In: Proceedings of the 18th ACM Conference on Computer and Communications Security (CCS), October 2011
19. Čapkun, S., Hubaux, J.P.: Securing position and distance verification in wireless networks. Technical report, École polytechnique fédérale de Lausanne (EPFL) (2004)
20. Čapkun, S., Hubaux, J.P.: Secure positioning of wireless devices with application to sensor networks. In: Proceedings IEEE 24th Annual Joint Conference of the IEEE Computer and Communications Societies (INFOCOM), vol. 3, March 2005
21. Čapkun, S., Rasmussen, K.B., Čagalj, M., Srivastava, M.: Secure location verification with hidden and mobile base stations. IEEE Trans. Mob. Comput. **7**(4), 470–483 (2008)
22. Čapkun, S., Čagalj, M., Srivastava, M.: Secure localization with hidden and mobile base stations. In: Proceedings of the 25th IEEE International Conference on Computer Communications (INFOCOM), April 2006

Author Index

Printed in the United States
By Bookmasters